에듀윌 토익

단기완성 700+

LC & RC

세상을 움직이려면
먼저 나 자신을 움직여야 한다.

– 소크라테스(Socrates)

머리말

토익은 역시 에듀윌입니다!

어디로 항해해야 할지 모르는 사람에게 순풍이란 없다

어떤 공부를 하든 목표가 분명해야 합니다. 자격증 공부를 한다면 올해 안에 자격증을 따겠다는 목표, 외국어 공부를 한다면 자막 없이 외국 드라마를 보거나 여행지에서 외국인과 그 나라 언어로 간단한 일상 대화 정도는 하겠다는 목표 말입니다. 분명한 목표 없이 시작하는 공부는 작은 유혹에 휘둘리기 쉽고, 대수롭지 않은 난관에 흔들리며, 결국 뜻하지 않은 긴 여정에 이를 수도 있습니다.

토익도 마찬가지입니다. 많은 기업과 각종 국가시험에서 영어 점수를 토익 점수로 대체하는 일이 많다 보니 취업을 위해 토익을 공부한다면 무엇보다 구체적인 점수를 목표로 세우는 것이 중요합니다. 그래야 흔들리지 않고 그 목표에 좀 더 일찍 다다를 수 있습니다. 직종이나 업무가 영어와 밀접하게 관련되어 있지 않은 이상 대개는 600~700점 정도를 요구하는 추세입니다. 토익은 빈출 유형들이 고정적으로 출제되고, 출제 경향이 쉽게 바뀌지 않는 시험이기 때문에 제대로 설계된 교재만 뒷받침된다면 '700점'은 어렵지 않게 정복할 수 있는 점수입니다.

단 2주 만에 700+ 점수 달성이 가능한 커리큘럼

토익 700점 달성에는 대단한 영어 지식이 필요하지 않습니다. 토익의 대화와 지문들은 기본적으로 일상적인 비즈니스 상황을 토대로 하며, 거기에 쓰이는 상당수의 어휘와 표현들은 매 시험 반복됩니다. 이 책은 여러분이 갖고 있는 영어의 기초 위에 목표 점수 달성에 꼭 필요한 '스킬'을 얹어 효율적으로 토익 문제에 접근할 수 있게 해 드립니다. 이것이 가능할 수 있는 이유는, 에듀윌 어학연구소가 최근 3개년 기출 문제를 분석한 빅 데이터를 바탕으로 700점을 얻는 데 꼭 필요한 빈출 문제들만을 뽑아냈기 때문입니다. 덕분에 이 책에는 지나친 고난도 문제나 자질구레한 설명 없이 700점 이상을 받는 데 꼭 필요한 정수만이 담겨 있습니다.

〈에듀윌 토익 단기완성 700+ LC&RC〉와 함께 단기간에 원하는 목표를 달성하길 바라며, 여러분의 앞날을 에듀윌이 응원하겠습니다.

에듀윌 어학연구소

목차

RC

이 책의 **특장점**

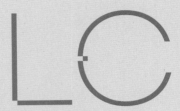

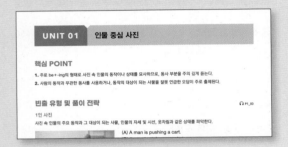

유형별 핵심 POINT 및 풀이 전략

토익 리스닝에 가장 자주 출제되는 유형들을 선별하고 각 유형에 맞는 핵심 전략을 제시하였다. 특히 PART 3, 4에서는 자주 쓰이는 단서 유형들을 함께 수록하여 지문 속에서 빠르게 답을 찾아내는 능력을 키울 수 있다.

PRACTICE

최신 토익 기출 문제를 완벽하게 분석하여 리스닝 기출 경향에 맞는 고퀄리티 문제만을 출제하였다. 앞서 학습한 내용을 문제에 바로바로 적용해보며 확실하게 익히고 실전에 완벽하게 대비할 수 있다.

700+ 뛰어넘기

입문자들이 점수를 올리기가 상대적으로 수월한 PART 1, 2에서 가장 유용한 고득점 팁을 담았다. 최단 기간에 목표 점수 700점을 달성하고 토익을 끝내고 싶다면 꼼꼼하게 학습해 두는 것이 좋다.

RC

이론 다지기

최신 출제 경향을 완벽하게 분석하여 목표 점수 700점 이상
을 달성하는 데 꼭 필요한 핵심 내용만 골라 담았다.

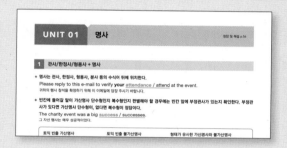

CHECK-UP & PRACTICE

앞에서 학습한 이론과 전략을 CHECK-UP으로 가볍게 점
검하고 PRACTICE에서는 최신 출제 경향을 반영한 토익
기출 변형 문제를 풀면서 실력을 다진다.

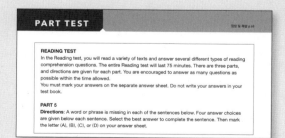

PART TEST

각 파트의 마지막을 PART TEST로 마무리하면서 실전 감
각을 익힌다.

2주 완성 학습 일정표

LC, RC 개별 학습 일정표

1주	DAY 1	DAY 2	DAY 3	DAY 4	DAY 5	DAY 6	DAY 7
LC	UNIT 01~02	UNIT 03~05	UNIT 06~08	UNIT 09~12	UNIT 13~15	UNIT 16~18	UNIT 19~20
	월 일	월 일	월 일	월 일	월 일	월 일	월 일

2주	DAY 8	DAY 9	DAY 10	DAY 11	DAY 12	DAY 13	DAY 14
RC	UNIT 01~03	UNIT 04~06	UNIT 07~08	UNIT 09~12	UNIT 13~14	UNIT 15~16	실전 모의고사
	월 일	월 일	월 일	월 일	월 일	월 일	월 일

LC, RC 동시 학습 일정표

1주	DAY 1	DAY 2	DAY 3	DAY 4	DAY 5	DAY 6	DAY 7
LC	UNIT 01	UNIT 02	UNIT 03~04	UNIT 05~06	UNIT 07	UNIT 08	UNIT 09~10
RC	UNIT 01	UNIT 02	UNIT 03	UNIT 04	UNIT 05	UNIT 06	UNIT 07
	월 일	월 일	월 일	월 일	월 일	월 일	월 일

2주	DAY 8	DAY 9	DAY 10	DAY 11	DAY 12	DAY 13	DAY 14
LC	UNIT 11~12	UNIT 13~14	UNIT 15	UNIT 16~17	UNIT 18~19	UNIT 20	실전 모의고사
RC	UNIT 08	UNIT 09~10	UNIT 11~12	UNIT 13~14	UNIT 15	UNIT 16	
	월 일	월 일	월 일	월 일	월 일	월 일	월 일

4주 완성 학습 일정표

LC, RC 개별 학습 일정표

1주	DAY 1	DAY 2	DAY 3	DAY 4	DAY 5
LC	UNIT 01~02 월 일	UNIT 03~04 월 일	UNIT 05~06 월 일	UNIT 07~08 월 일	UNIT 09~10 월 일

2주	DAY 6	DAY 7	DAY 8	DAY 9	DAY 10
LC	UNIT 11~12 월 일	UNIT 13~14 월 일	UNIT 15~16 월 일	UNIT 17~18 월 일	UNIT 19~20 월 일

3주	DAY 11	DAY 12	DAY 13	DAY 14	DAY 15
RC	UNIT 01~02 월 일	UNIT 03~04 월 일	UNIT 05~07 월 일	UNIT 08 월 일	UNIT 09~10 월 일

4주	DAY 16	DAY 17	DAY 18	DAY 19	DAY 20
RC	UNIT 11~12 월 일	UNIT 13~14 월 일	UNIT 15 월 일	UNIT 16 월 일	실전 모의고사 월 일

LC, RC 동시 학습 일정표

1주	DAY 1	DAY 2	DAY 3	DAY 4	DAY 5
LC RC	UNIT 01~02 UNIT 01 월 일	UNIT 03 UNIT 02 월 일	UNIT 04 UNIT 03 월 일	UNIT 05 UNIT 04 월 일	UNIT 06 UNIT 05 월 일

2주	DAY 6	DAY 7	DAY 8	DAY 9	DAY 10
LC RC	UNIT 07 UNIT 06 월 일	UNIT 08 UNIT 07 월 일	UNIT 09 UNIT 08 명사 월 일	UNIT 10 UNIT 08 형용사 월 일	UNIT 11 UNIT 08 부사 월 일

3주	DAY 11	DAY 12	DAY 13	DAY 14	DAY 15
LC RC	UNIT 12 UNIT 08 동사 월 일	UNIT 13 UNIT 09 월 일	UNIT 14 UNIT 10 월 일	UNIT 15 UNIT 11 월 일	UNIT 16 UNIT 12 월 일

4주	DAY 16	DAY 17	DAY 18	DAY 19	DAY 20
LC RC	UNIT 17 UNIT 13 월 일	UNIT 18 UNIT 14 월 일	UNIT 19 UNIT 15 월 일	UNIT 20 UNIT 16 월 일	실전 모의고사 월 일

TOEIC 소개

토익이란?

TOEIC은 Test of English for International Communication(국제적인 의사소통을 위한 영어 시험)의 약자로, 영어가 모국어가 아닌 사람들이 비즈니스 현장 및 일상생활에서 필요한 실용 영어 능력을 갖추었는가를 평가하는 시험이다.

시험 구성

구성	파트		문항 수	시간	배점
Listening Comprehension	Part 1	사진 묘사	6	45분	495점
	Part 2	질의 응답	25		
	Part 3	짧은 대화	39		
	Part 4	짧은 담화	30		
Reading Comprehension	Part 5	단문 빈칸 채우기	30	75분	495점
	Part 6	장문 빈칸 채우기	16		
	Part 7	독해 단일 지문	29		
		독해 이중 지문	10		
		독해 삼중 지문	15		
합계	7 Parts		200문항	120분	990점

Listening Comprehension 100문항, Reading Comprehension 100문항

출제 범위 및 주제

업무 및 일상생활에서 쓰이는 실용적인 주제들이 출제된다. 특정 문화나 특정 직업 분야에만 해당되는 주제는 출제하지 않으며, 듣기 평가의 경우 미국, 영국, 호주 등 다양한 국가의 발음이 섞여 출제된다.

일반 업무	계약, 협상, 영업, 홍보, 마케팅, 사업 계획
금융 / 재무	예산, 투자, 세금, 청구, 회계
개발	연구, 제품 개발
제조	공장 경영, 생산 조립 라인, 품질 관리
인사	채용, 승진, 퇴직, 직원 교육, 입사 지원
사무실	회의, 메모 / 전화 / 팩스 / 이메일, 사무 장비 및 가구
행사	학회, 연회, 회식, 시상식, 박람회, 제품 시연회
부동산	건축, 부동산 매매 / 임대, 기업 부지, 전기 / 수도 / 가스 설비
여행 / 여가	교통수단, 공항 / 역, 여행 일정, 호텔 및 자동차 예약 / 연기 / 취소, 영화, 전시, 공연

접수 방법

- 한국 TOEIC 위원회 사이트(www.toeic.co.kr)에서 인터넷 접수 기간을 확인하고 접수한다.
- 시험 접수 시 최근 6개월 이내에 촬영한 jpg 형식의 사진 파일이 필요하므로 미리 준비한다.
- 시험 10~12일 전부터는 특별 추가 접수 기간에 해당하여 추가 비용이 발생하므로, 접수 일정을 미리 확인하여 정기 접수 기간 내에 접수하도록 한다.

시험 당일 준비물

신분증	주민등록증, 운전면허증, 기간 만료 전 여권, 공무원증 등 규정 신분증만 인정 (중·고등학생에 한하여 학생증, 청소년증도 인정)
필기구	연필, 지우개 (볼펜, 사인펜은 사용 불가)

시험 진행

오전 시험	오후 시험	진행 내용
09:30 – 09:45	02:30 – 02:45	답안지 작성 오리엔테이션
09:45 – 09:50	02:45 – 02:50	쉬는 시간
09:50 – 10:05	02:50 – 03:05	신분증 확인
10:05 – 10:10	03:05 – 03:10	문제지 배부 및 파본 확인
10:10 – 10:55	03:10 – 03:55	듣기 평가 (LC)
10:55 – 12:10	03:55 – 05:10	독해 평가 (RC)

성적 확인

성적 발표	미리 안내된 성적 발표일에 한국 TOEIC 위원회 사이트(www.toeic.co.kr) 및 공식 애플리케이션을 통해 확인 가능하다.
성적표 수령	온라인 출력 또는 우편 수령 중에서 선택할 수 있고, 온라인 출력과 우편 수령 모두 1회 발급만 무료이며, 그 이후에는 유료로 발급된다.

파트별 문제 유형

PART 1 사진 묘사

파트 소개	제시된 사진을 보고, 4개의 문장을 들은 뒤 그중 사진을 가장 잘 묘사한 문장을 고르는 파트
문항 수	6문항
사진 유형	1인 사진, 2인 이상 사진, 사물 및 풍경 사진

문제지 형태

1.

2.

🔊

Number 1.

Look at the picture marked number 1 in your test book.

(A) He's staring at a vase.
(B) He's pouring a beverage.
(C) He's spreading out a tablecloth.
(D) He's sipping from a coffee cup.

PART 2 질의 응답

파트 소개	질문과 3개의 응답을 듣고, 질문에 가장 적절한 응답을 고르는 파트
문항 수	25문항
질문 유형	의문사 의문문, 일반 의문문, 제안·요청 의문문, 부가 의문문, 선택 의문문, 간접 의문문, 평서문

PART 2

Directions: You will hear a question or statement and three responses spoken in English. They will not be printed in your test book and will be spoken only one time. Select the best response to the question or statement and mark the letter (A), (B), or (C) on your answer sheet.

7.   Mark your answer on your answer sheet.
8.   Mark your answer on your answer sheet.
9.   Mark your answer on your answer sheet.
10. Mark your answer on your answer sheet.
11. Mark your answer on your answer sheet.
12. Mark your answer on your answer sheet.
13. Mark your answer on your answer sheet.
14. Mark your answer on your answer sheet.
15. Mark your answer on your answer sheet.
16. Mark your answer on your answer sheet.
17. Mark your answer on your answer sheet.
18. Mark your answer on your answer sheet.
19. Mark your answer on your answer sheet.

20. Mark your answer on your answer sheet.
21. Mark your answer on your answer sheet.
22. Mark your answer on your answer sheet.
23. Mark your answer on your answer sheet.
24. Mark your answer on your answer sheet.
25. Mark your answer on your answer sheet.
26. Mark your answer on your answer sheet.
27. Mark your answer on your answer sheet.
28. Mark your answer on your answer sheet.
29. Mark your answer on your answer sheet.
30. Mark your answer on your answer sheet.
31. Mark your answer on your answer sheet.

Number 7.

When will the landlord inspect the property?

(A) No, it failed the inspection.
(B) I'll e-mail him about it.
(C) Do you like the apartment?

PART 3 짧은 대화

파트 소개	두 명 또는 세 명의 대화를 듣고, 이와 관련된 3개의 문제에 대해 가장 적절한 답을 고르는 파트
문항 수	39문항 (13개 대화문×3문항)
대화 유형	2인 대화(11개)와 3인 대화(2개)로 이루어지며, 2인 대화 중 마지막 3세트(62~70번)는 시각 자료와 함께 제시된다.
문제 유형	주제·목적, 화자·장소, 세부사항, 제안·요청, 다음에 할·일어날 일, 의도 파악, 시각 자료 연계

문제지 형태

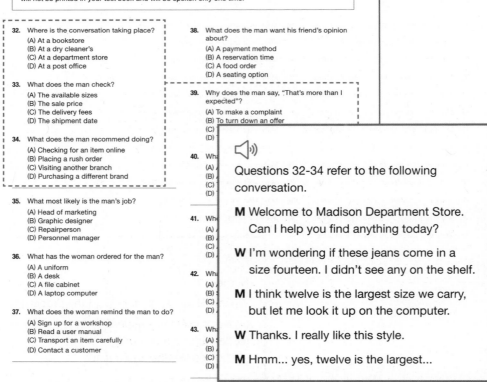

PART 3

Directions: You will hear some conversations between two or more people. You will be asked to answer three questions about what the speakers say in each conversation. Select the best response to each question and mark the letter (A), (B), (C), or (D) on your answer sheet. The conversations will not be printed in your test book and will be spoken only one time.

32. Where is the conversation taking place?
   (A) At a bookstore
   (B) At a dry cleaner's
   (C) At a department store
   (D) At a post office

33. What does the man check?
   (A) The available sizes
   (B) The sale price
   (C) The delivery fees
   (D) The shipment date

34. What does the man recommend doing?
   (A) Checking for an item online
   (B) Placing a rush order
   (C) Visiting another branch
   (D) Purchasing a different brand

35. What most likely is the man's job?
   (A) Head of marketing
   (B) Graphic designer
   (C) Repairperson
   (D) Personnel manager

36. What has the woman ordered for the man?
   (A) A uniform
   (B) A desk
   (C) A file cabinet
   (D) A laptop computer

37. What does the woman remind the man to do?
   (A) Sign up for a workshop
   (B) Read a user manual
   (C) Transport an item carefully
   (D) Contact a customer

38. What does the man want his friend's opinion about?
   (A) A payment method
   (B) A reservation time
   (C) A food order
   (D) A seating option

39. Why does the man say, "That's more than I expected"?
   (A) To make a complaint
   (B) To turn down an offer
   (C)
   (D)

40. Wha
   (A)
   (B)
   (C)
   (D)

41. Whe
   (A)
   (B)
   (C)
   (D)

42. Wha
   (A)
   (B)
   (C)
   (D)

43. Wha
   (A)
   (B)
   (C)
   (D)

Questions 32-34 refer to the following conversation.

M Welcome to Madison Department Store. Can I help you find anything today?

W I'm wondering if these jeans come in a size fourteen. I didn't see any on the shelf.

M I think twelve is the largest size we carry, but let me look it up on the computer.

W Thanks. I really like this style.

M Hmm... yes, twelve is the largest...

PART 4 짧은 담화

파트 소개	한 사람이 말하는 담화를 듣고, 이와 관련된 3개의 문제에 대해 가장 적절한 답을 고르는 파트
문항 수	30문항 (10개 담화문 × 3문항)
담화 유형	전화 메시지, 공지 · 안내, 연설 · 강연, 광고 · 방송, 관광 · 견학 등으로 이루어지며, 마지막 2세트 (95~100번)는 시각 자료와 함께 제시된다.
문제 유형	주제 · 목적, 화자 · 청자 · 장소, 세부사항, 제안 · 요청, 다음에 할 · 일어날 일, 의도 파악, 시각 자료 연계

문제지 형태

PART 4

Directions: You will hear some talks given by a single speaker. You will be asked to answer three questions about what the speaker says in each talk. Select the best response to each question and mark the letter (A), (B), (C), or (D) on your answer sheet. The talks will not be printed in your test book and will be spoken only one time.

71. How does each workshop tour end?
    (A) An employee answers questions.
    (B) An informative video is shown.
    (C) A group photo is taken.
    (D) A piece of equipment is demonstrated.

72. What does each tour participant receive?
    (A) A piece of jewelry
    (B) A voucher
    (C) A map of the site
    (D) A beverage

73. What do the listeners receive a warning about?
    (A) Which entrance to use
    (B) Where to meet
    (C) What clothing to bring
    (D) How to book in advance

74. Who most likely is giving the speech?
    (A) A factory worker
    (B) A driving instructor
    (C) A gym manager
    (D) A bank employee

75. What have the listeners been given?
    (A) A product sample
    (B) An employee directory
    (C) A daily pass
    (D) A list of classes

76. What does the speaker mean when she says, "You won't see anything like it again"?
    (A) A membership process can be confusing.
    (B) A presentation is worth watching.
    (C) The business is expected to succeed.
    (D) Listeners should take advantage of an offer.

77. What kind of business do the listeners most likely work for?
    (A) A construction company
    (B) An international delivery service
    (C) A newspaper publisher
    (D) A medical facility

78. What does the speaker say he is reassured about?
    (A) A worker's attention to detail
    (B) An investor's future plan
    (C) The responses from a customer survey
    (D) The score on an inspection

Questions 71-73 refer to the following advertisement.

Are you tired of the same old tourist sites? Try something new and tour the Lodgevile Jewelry Workshop. You'll get to see each step of the jewelry-making process. And, at the end, you'll have the chance to get your questions addressed by one of our talented jewelry makers. Each participant is given a beautiful bracelet to identify their tour group, and this gift is yours to keep...

PART 5 단문 빈칸 채우기

파트 소개	빈칸이 포함된 하나의 문장이 주어지고, 빈칸에 알맞은 단어나 구를 4개의 선택지 중에서 고르는 파트
문항 수	30문항
문제 유형	• 문법 문제 (문법의 적절한 쓰임을 묻는 문제) • 어휘 문제 (문맥에 어울리는 어휘를 묻는 문제)

문제지 형태

READING TEST

In the Reading test, you will read a variety of texts and answer several different types of reading comprehension questions. The entire Reading test will last 75 minutes. There are three parts, and directions are given for each part. You are encouraged to answer as many questions as possible within the time allowed.

You must mark your answers on the separate answer sheet. Do not write your answers in your test book.

PART 5

Directions: A word or phrase is missing in each of the sentences below. Four answer choices are given below each sentence. Select the best answer to complete the sentence. Then mark the letter (A), (B), (C), or (D) on your answer sheet.

101. Some officials ------- expressed concerns about the changes to the corporate tax structure.
(A) privacy
(B) privatize
(C) private
(D) privately

102. The new electric car from Baylor Motors is intended for ------- journeys within an urban environment.
(A) shortness
(B) short
(C) shortly
(D) shorten

103. Ames Manufacturing developed a packaging method that ------- much less cardboard.
(A) uses
(B) using
(C) to use
(D) use

104. The building's owner increased the fees ------- parking lot access.
(A) for
(B) about
(C) at
(D) among

105. Few market analysts ------- predicted the industry effects of the factory's closure.
(A) locally
(B) constantly
(C) kindly
(D) correctly

106. Customers who wish to ------- us a review on social media are encouraged to do so.
(A) explain
(B) say
(C) give
(D) have

107. Every weekend ------- the month of August, the hotel's restaurant features live musical performances.
(A) even
(B) during
(C) when
(D) while

108. Portland Insurance's employees should complete a form with ------- desired vacation days.
(A) their
(B) its
(C) themselves
(D) it

PART 6 장문 빈칸 채우기

파트 소개	4개의 빈칸이 포함된 지문이 주어지고, 각각의 빈칸에 들어갈 알맞은 단어나 구, 문장을 고르는 파트
문항 수	16문항 (4개 지문×4문항)
문제 유형	• 문법 문제 (문법의 적절한 쓰임을 묻는 문제) • 어휘 문제 (문맥에 어울리는 어휘를 묻는 문제) • 문장 삽입 문제 (문맥에 어울리는 문장을 묻는 문제)

문제지 형태

PART 6

Directions: Read the texts that follow. A word, phrase, or sentence is missing in parts of each text. Four answer choices for each question are given below the text. Select the best answer to complete the text. Then mark the letter (A), (B), (C), or (D) on your answer sheet.

Questions 131-134 refer to the following letter.

Georgina Harrison
962 Warner Street
Cape Girardeau, MO 63703

Dear Ms. Harrison,

Thank you for your interest in making a group booking at Westside Hotel. I have attached a comprehensive ------- of our amenities for your convenience. We aim to personalize the guest
131.
experience. We are prepared to meet the needs of most guests on short notice. However, if you
have ------- requests, we may need advance notice in order to fulfill them. Once your booking is
132.
made, you may be charged a fee according to our cancellation policy. -------. Before confirming your
133.
booking, please download a copy of the payment details and ------- them carefully.
134.

Warmest regards,

The Westside Hotel Team

131. (A) describe
(B) describes
(C) described
(D) description

132. (A) unusual
(B) absent
(C) plain
(D) flexible

133. (A) The front desk is open twenty-four hours a day.
(B) You should complete the form with honest feedback.
(C) We appreciate your ongoing patronage.
(D) The terms of this are included on our Web site.

134. (A) reviewing
(B) review
(C) to review
(D) reviewed

PART 7 독해

파트 소개	지문을 읽고, 지문 내용과 관련된 2~5개 문제에 대해 가장 적절한 답을 고르는 파트	
지문 / 문항 수	단일 지문	10개 (지문당 2~4문항 ; 총 29문항)	총 15개 지문 (54문항)
	이중 지문	2개 (지문당 5문항 ; 총 10문항)	
	삼중 지문	3개 (지문당 5문항 ; 총 15문항)	
지문 유형	이메일 · 편지, 광고, 공지 · 회람, 기사, 양식(웹페이지, 설문지, 청구서 등), 문자 메시지 대화문 등	
문제 유형	주제 · 목적, 세부사항, NOT/True, 추론 · 암시, 의도 파악, 동의어 찾기, 문장 삽입	

문제지 형태 (단일 지문)

PART 7

Directions: In this part, you will read a selection of texts, such as magazine and newspaper articles, e-mails, and instant messages. Each text or set of texts is followed by several questions. Select the best answer for each question and mark the letter (A), (B), (C), or (D) on your answer sheet.

Questions 147-148 refer to the following article.

New Library Program Creates "Buzz"

April 30—This summer, Syracuse Library is launching a program to help local bees. The number of local bees has sharply declined, and the library aims to help these creatures. It will have a special section with books about bees and will host lectures about how they benefit the environment. Anyone who attends a lecture will be given a free pack of seeds for flowers that will attract bees.

147. What is the purpose of the program?
(A) To support the bee population
(B) To teach people a new skill
(C) To attract new library members
(D) To raise money for a charity

148. How can participants get a free gift?
(A) By completing a survey
(B) By attending a talk
(C) By making a donation
(D) By showing a library card

Questions 186-190 refer to the following article and forms.

Oakdale (April 9)—Preparations are underway for Oakdale's 8th Annual Health and Well-Being Expo, which will take place on Sunday, June 19. The expo will feature businesses offering a variety of health-related goods and services. Additionally, local physicians and nurses will provide free screenings for blood pressure and cholesterol levels as well as a basic eye exam.

After many years at Juniper Hall, the expo has been moved to the Bayridge Convention Center this year. "Due to the growing popularity of the event, Juniper Hall could no longer contain the number of vendors interested in participating in the expo," said Ken Exley, one of the event planners. "Visitors can easily find what they're looking for, with vendors of vitamins and health supplements in the main hall, massage therapists and spa representatives in the east wing, and gym representatives and sports-related businesses in the west wing."

To register, visit www.o
get a twenty percent dis

Name: Anna Pie
Business/Compan

I was informe
Oakdale Busin
as a vendor, a
would have lik
spoke to some
has the same
future.

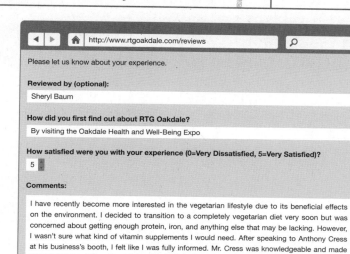

http://www.rtgoakdale.com/reviews

Please let us know about your experience.

Reviewed by (optional):

Sheryl Baum

How did you first find out about RTG Oakdale?

By visiting the Oakdale Health and Well-Being Expo

How satisfied were you with your experience (0=Very Dissatisfied, 5=Very Satisfied)?

5

Comments:

I have recently become more interested in the vegetarian lifestyle due to its beneficial effects on the environment. I decided to transition to a completely vegetarian diet very soon but was concerned about getting enough protein, iron, and anything else that may be lacking. However, I wasn't sure what kind of vitamin supplements I would need. After speaking to Anthony Cress at his business's booth, I felt like I was fully informed. Mr. Cress was knowledgeable and made great recommendations for my specific circumstances. Overall, it was a very positive experience for me.

186. According to the article, why did the event planners use a different site this year?

(A) To ensure more space
(B) To minimize traffic problems
(C) To promote a new building
(D) To reduce travel times

187. What is suggested about Ms. Pierson?

(A) She qualified for early registration.
(B) She recently started her business.
(C) She has participated in past events.
(D) She was eligible for a discount.

188. What does Ms. Pierson recommend for the next expo?

(A) Addressing some noise complaints
(B) Providing more power outlets
(C) Offering booths in various sizes
(D) Advertising the event to more people

189. What is implied about Mr. Cress?

(A) He has lived in Oakdale for a long time.
(B) He worked at a booth in the main hall.
(C) He was an event planner for the expo.
(D) He is considering hiring Ms. Baum.

190. What does Ms. Baum plan to do?

(A) Undertake further research on a topic
(B) Write another online review
(C) Change her daily eating habits
(D) Start a health-related business

PART

1

PART 1 출제 경향 및 전략

제시된 사진을 보고 4개의 문장을 들은 뒤, 그중 사진을 가장 적절하게 묘사한 보기를 고르는 파트이다. LC 전체 100개의 문항 중 총 6문항이 출제된다.

사진 유형

사진은 크게 인물이 나오는 사진, 사물이나 풍경만 나오는 사진으로 분류할 수 있다.

🎧 P1_01

1인 사진

사람이 한 명만 등장하는 사진으로, 사진 속 인물의 동작이나 상태를 주로 묘사한다.

(A) She's planting some seeds.
(B) She's using a spray bottle.
(C) She's dusting a shelf.
(D) She's painting a pot.

(A) 그녀는 씨앗을 심고 있다.
(B) 그녀는 분무기를 사용하고 있다.
(C) 그녀는 선반의 먼지를 털고 있다.
(D) 그녀는 화분을 칠하고 있다.

2인 이상 사진

여러 명의 사람들이 등장하는 사진으로, 인물들의 공통된 모습 또는 두드러지는 어떤 한 사람이나 일부의 모습을 묘사한다.

(A) One of the men is purchasing a tire.
(B) One of the men is riding to work.
(C) They're fixing a bicycle.
(D) They're opening a toolbox.

(A) 남자들 중 한 명이 타이어를 구매하고 있다.
(B) 남자들 중 한 명이 탈것을 타고 출근하고 있다.
(C) 그들은 자전거를 수리하고 있다.
(D) 그들은 공구 상자를 열고 있다.

사물 · 풍경 사진

사람이 없고 사물이나 배경만 등장하는 사진으로, 사진 속 사물의 위치나 상태 또는 전반적인 풍경을 묘사한다.

(A) Some boxes are stacked on the floor.
(B) Some art has been hung on the wall.
(C) A ladder is leaning against a desk.
(D) There's a lamp on a rug.

(A) 상자 몇 개가 바닥에 쌓여 있다.
(B) 미술품이 벽에 걸려 있다.
(C) 사다리가 책상에 기대어져 있다.
(D) 러그 위에 램프가 있다.

문제 풀이 전략

🎧 P1_02

(A) She's weighing some fruit on a scale.
(B) She's holding up some fruit. ◀
(C) She's adjusting her hat.
(D) She's chopping some vegetables.

STEP 1 │ 사진 파악하기

인물의 주요 동작 및 상태부터 눈에 띄는 사물의 위치 및 상태, 주위 배경까지 빠르게 사진을 파악한다.

동작: 손에 과일을 들고 있음
상태: 모자를 쓰고 있음

STEP 2 │ 오답 소거하며 정답 선택하기

동사 위주로 음성을 들으면서 오답을 하나씩 소거하고, 남은 보기가 사진을 적절하게 묘사하는지 확인 후 정답으로 선택한다.

(A) 그녀는 저울에 과일의 무게를 달고 있다.
  (×) 저울이 없음

(B) 그녀는 과일을 들고 있다.
  (○) 과일을 들고 있음

(C) 그녀는 모자를 바로잡고 있다.
  (×) 모자를 바로잡고 있지 않음

(D) 그녀는 채소를 썰고 있다.
  (×) 무언가를 썰고 있지 않음

핵심 POINT

1. 주로 be+-ing의 형태로 사진 속 인물의 동작이나 상태를 묘사하므로, 동사 부분을 주의 깊게 듣는다.

2. 사람의 동작과 무관한 동사를 사용하거나 동작의 대상이 되는 사물을 잘못 언급한 오답이 주로 출제된다.

빈출 유형 및 풀이 전략　　　🎧 P1_03

1인 사진

사진 속 인물의 주요 동작과 그 대상이 되는 사물, 인물의 자세 및 시선, 옷차림과 같은 상태를 파악한다.

(A) A man is pushing a cart.
(B) A man is sitting on a chair.
(C) A man is lifting some furniture.
(D) A man is putting on a hard hat.

(A) 남자가 카트를 밀고 있다.
(B) 남자가 의자에 앉아 있다.
(C) 남자가 가구를 들어 올리고 있다.
(D) 남자가 안전모를 착용하고 있다.

2인 이상 사진

인물들의 공통 동작/상태 및 특정 인물의 개별 동작/상태를 파악한다. 다수의 사람이 workers나 travelers와 같은 주어를 사용해 묘사되기도 한다.

(A) They're looking at a document.
(B) They're adjusting a computer monitor.
(C) One of the people is taking off a pair of glasses.
(D) One of the people is drinking from a glass.

(A) 그들은 문서를 보고 있다.
(B) 그들은 컴퓨터 모니터를 조절하고 있다.
(C) 사람들 중 한 명이 안경을 벗고 있다.
(D) 사람들 중 한 명이 유리잔에 든 것을 마시고 있다.

인물/사물 혼합 사진

인물 중심의 사진이라도 사물 묘사가 정답이 될 수 있으므로, 주변 사물의 상태 및 위치까지 파악해 둔다.

(A) The woman is drinking some water.
(B) Some plants have been arranged in a row.
(C) The woman is wiping a window.
(D) Some shelves are being assembled.

(A) 여자가 물을 마시고 있다.
(B) 몇몇 식물이 일렬로 정렬되어 있다.
(C) 여자가 창문을 닦고 있다.
(D) 일부 선반들이 조립되고 있다.

PRACTICE

사진을 적절하게 묘사한 보기를 고르세요.

1.

(A) (B) (C) (D)

2.

(A) (B) (C) (D)

3.

(A) (B) (C) (D)

4.

(A) (B) (C) (D)

5.

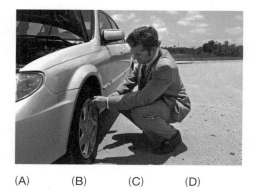

(A) (B) (C) (D)

6.

(A) (B) (C) (D)

사물 · 풍경 중심 사진

핵심 POINT

1. 사물의 위치를 나타내는 전치사(구)와 부사구를 주의 깊게 듣는다.

2. 사진에 등장하지 않는 사람이나 사물을 이용한 오답에 주의한다.

빈출 유형 및 풀이 전략

🎧 P1_05

사물 사진

주로 집이나 사무실 등의 실내에 있는 사물을 가까이에서 찍은 사진이다. 눈에 띄는 주요 사물의 위치 및 상태를 파악해야 한다.

(A) Some dishes have been spread around the table.
(B) A light fixture is hanging above a dining area.
(C) Chairs have been set up in a garden.
(D) Kitchen appliances are arranged for sale.

(A) 접시 몇 개가 식탁 주위에 흩어져 있다.
(B) 조명 기구가 식사 공간 위에 매달려 있다.
(C) 의자들이 정원에 놓여 있다.
(D) 주방용품이 판매를 위해 정리되어 있다.

풍경 사진

건물 외관이나 호수, 공원 등의 자연 환경을 넓게 찍은 풍경 중심의 사진이다. 'There is/are + 명사' 형태의 선택지가 자주 출제된다.

(A) There's a deck overlooking a lake.
(B) Some boats are tied to a pier.
(C) Waves are crashing against the rocks.
(D) A ship is stopped at a dock.

(A) 호수가 내려다보이는 갑판이 있다.
(B) 몇몇 배들이 부두에 묶여 있다.
(C) 파도가 바위에 부서지고 있다.
(D) 배가 부두에 세워져 있다.

PRACTICE

사진을 적절하게 묘사한 보기를 고르세요.

1.

(A)   (B)   (C)   (D)

2.

(A)   (B)   (C)   (D)

3.

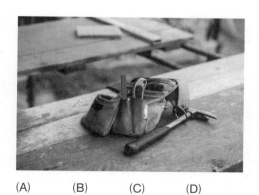

(A)   (B)   (C)   (D)

4.

(A)   (B)   (C)   (D)

5.

(A)   (B)   (C)   (D)

6.

(A)   (B)   (C)   (D)

1 동작 – 상태 혼동 동사를 이용한 오답에 주의한다.

putting on an apron (×)
앞치마를 입는 중이다 → 입는 동작

wearing an apron (○)
앞치마를 입고 있다 → 입고 있는 상태

picking up a cup (×)
컵을 집어 드는 중이다 → 드는 동작

holding a cup (○)
컵을 들고 있다 → 들고 있는 상태

2 사물 주어로 인물의 동작을 묘사할 수 있다. 이 경우에는 항상 현재진행 수동태(be+being+p.p.)로 쓰인다.

A window is being installed. 창문이 설치되고 있다.

= They're installing a window.
　그들은 창문을 설치하고 있다.

Some potted plants are being watered.
화분에 담긴 식물들에 물이 뿌려지고 있다.

= A woman is watering some potted plants.
　여자가 화분에 담긴 식물들에 물을 주고 있다.

PRACTICE

사진을 적절하게 묘사한 보기를 고르세요.

1.

(A)   (B)   (C)   (D)

2.

(A)   (B)   (C)   (D)

3.

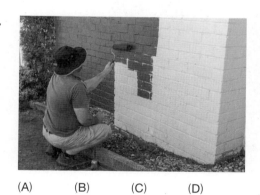

(A)   (B)   (C)   (D)

4.

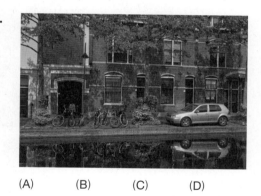

(A)   (B)   (C)   (D)

5.

(A)   (B)   (C)   (D)

6.

(A)   (B)   (C)   (D)

PART 1

LISTENING TEST

In the Listening test, you will be asked to demonstrate how well you understand spoken English. The entire Listening test will last approximately 45 minutes. There are four parts, and directions are given for each part. You must mark your answers on the separate answer sheet. Do not write your answers in your test book.

PART 1

Directions: For each question in this part, you will hear four statements about a picture in your test book. When you hear the statements, you must select the one statement that best describes what you see in the picture. Then find the number of the question on your answer sheet and mark your answer. The statements will not be printed in your test book and will be spoken only one time.

Statement (C), "He's making a phone call," is the best description of the picture, so you should select answer (C) and mark it on your answer sheet.

1.

2.

GO ON TO THE NEXT PAGE ➡

3.

4.

5.

6.

PART

2

PART 2 출제 경향 및 전략

질문과 3개의 응답을 듣고, 질문에 가장 적절한 응답을 고르는 파트이다. LC 전체 100개의 문항 중 총 25문항이 출제된다.

질문 유형

Who 의문문 Who(누구)로 시작하는 질문으로, 사람과 관련된 내용으로 답변할 수 있다.
Q Who's leading the new staff orientation? 누가 신입 직원 오리엔테이션을 진행하나요?
A Mr. Barrera always does it. 항상 바레라 씨가 합니다.

What·Which 의문문 What(무엇)이나 Which(어느 것)로 시작하는 질문으로, 의문사 뒤 세부 정보와 관련된 내용으로 답변할 수 있다.
Q What products does your company make? 당신의 회사는 무슨 제품을 만드나요?
A Office supplies. 사무용품이요.

When 의문문 When(언제)으로 시작하는 질문으로, 시간과 관련된 내용으로 응답한다.
Q When did Ms. Morgan return from her trip? 모건 씨는 언제 여행에서 돌아왔나요?
A Tuesday afternoon. 화요일 오후요.

Where 의문문 Where(어디)로 시작하는 질문으로, 주로 장소나 출처와 관련된 내용으로 응답한다.
Q Where are the presenters? 발표자들은 어디에 있나요?
A In the break room. 휴게실에요.

How 의문문 How(어떻게/얼마나)로 시작하는 질문으로, 방법이나 수단 외에도 의견, 수량 등을 묻기도 한다.
Q How should I get to the airport? 공항에 어떻게 가야 하나요?
A Just take a taxi. 택시를 타세요.

Why 의문문 Why(왜)로 시작하는 질문으로, 이유나 목적과 관련된 내용으로 응답한다.
Q Why is Mr. Stanley traveling to Atlanta? 스탠리 씨는 왜 애틀랜타로 가나요?
A To inspect the new factory. 신규 공장을 점검하기 위해서요.

일반 의문문 조동사/be동사로 시작하는 질문으로, 긍정 또는 부정을 나타내거나 부연 설명하는 내용으로 응답한다. 조동사나 be동사에 not이 붙은 질문이 나오기도 한다.
Q Did you request a transfer overseas? 당신은 해외로 전근을 요청했나요?
A No, I decided to stay here instead. 아니요, 대신 여기 있기로 결정했어요.

제안·요청 의문문 의문문 형태이지만 무언가를 권유하거나 요청하는 문장으로, 해당 사항을 수락하거나 거절하는 내용으로 응답한다.
Q Can you pick up the dry cleaning? 드라이클리닝한 세탁물을 찾아와 줄래요?
A Sure. I've got time right now. 물론이에요. 지금 시간이 있어요.

부가 의문문 평서문 뒤에 aren't you?, didn't you?와 같은 꼬리말이 붙은 질문으로, 일반 의문문과 같이 긍정 또는 부정을 나타내거나 부연 설명하는 내용으로 응답한다.

Q Class registration hasn't closed, has it? 수강 신청이 마감되지 않았죠, 그렇죠?
A No, there are two days left. 네, 이틀 남아 있어요.

선택 의문문 접속사 or(또는)를 이용해 두 가지 사항 중에 어느 것을 선택할지 묻는 질문이다.

Q Do you prefer to take the bus or the train? 버스 타길 선호하세요, 아니면 기차를 선호하세요?
A I'd rather take the bus. 저는 차라리 버스를 타겠어요.

간접 의문문 일반 의문문 안에 의문사 의문문이 포함되어 있는 형태의 질문으로, 질문 속 의문사와 관련된 내용으로 응답한다.

Q Do you know how I can turn on this machine? 이 기계를 어떻게 켜는지 아세요?
A Yes, let me show you. 네, 제가 보여드릴게요.

평서문 의문문이 아닌 서술 문장 형태로, 정해진 답변 패턴이 없기 때문에 난이도가 가장 높다.

Q I lost Ms. Lee's business card. 저는 이 씨의 명함을 잃어버렸어요.
A Her contact details are online. 그녀의 연락처는 온라인에 있어요.

문제 풀이 전략

🎧 P2_01

Who proofread the quarterly report?

STEP 1 │ 질문 파악하기
질문 속 의문사와 키워드를 듣고 묻는 내용을 파악한다.

누가 분기 보고서의 교정을 보았나요?

(A) I think Joseph did that.
(B) To inform our shareholders.
(C) Yes, before April 1st.

STEP 2 │ 오답 소거하며 정답 선택하기
음성을 들으면서 오답을 하나씩 소거하고, 남은 보기가 질문에 적절한 답변인지 확인 후 정답으로 선택한다.

(A) 조지프가 본 것 같아요.
  (○) 보고서 교정 본 사람을 묻는 Who 의문문에 사람 이름(Joseph)으로 적절하게 답변
(B) 우리 주주들에게 알리기 위해서요.
  (×) 보고서의 용도를 묻는 질문에 어울릴 만한 오답
(C) 네, 4월 1일 전에요.
  (×) 의문사 의문문에 Yes로 답변한 오답

UNIT 03 Who, What · Which 의문문

1 Who 의문문

핵심 POINT

1. 어떤 일의 담당자가 누구인지를 묻는 질문이 주로 출제된다.

2. 사람 이름이나 직책 등을 이용해 직접적으로 답하는 경우가 많다.

대표 유형 맛보기   🎧 P2_02

Who's transferring to the Marketing team? 누가 마케팅팀으로 옮기나요?

(A) Yes, I am. Thank you. 네, 접니다. 감사합니다.

(B) Great, it's like a promotion. 잘됐네요, 그건 승진인 셈이에요.

(C) I heard it will be Ms. Stanley. 스탠리 씨라고 들었어요.

빈출 질문 및 응답

사람 이름으로 답변	**Q** Who's in charge of the training program? 누가 교육 프로그램을 담당하나요? **A** Ms. Kelson is. 켈슨 씨요.
직책/부서명으로 답변	**Q** Who notified the interns of the time and venue changes? 누가 인턴 사원들에게 시간과 장소의 변경 사항을 알렸나요? **A** The director of Human Resources. 인사부장이요.
회사 이름으로 답변	**Q** Who's going to sponsor this year's fund-raiser? 올해 모금 행사는 어디에서 후원할 예정이죠? **A** A new hotel called Paradise View. 파라다이스 뷰라는 새로운 호텔에서요.
모른다고 답변	**Q** Who needs to review this order form? 누가 이 주문서를 검토해야 합니까? **A** I'm not sure. 잘 모르겠어요.

PRACTICE   🎧 P2_03 정답 및 해설 p.8

질문을 듣고 적절한 응답을 고르세요.

1.	(A)	(B)	(C)	**2.**	(A)	(B)	(C)
3.	(A)	(B)	(C)	**4.**	(A)	(B)	(C)
5.	(A)	(B)	(C)	**6.**	(A)	(B)	(C)

핵심 POINT

1. 시간/종류/의견 등 다양한 내용을 물을 수 있으므로, 의문사 What과 Which 뒤에 나오는 명사와 동사에 집중해서 듣는다.

2. Which 의문문에서는 주로 대명사 one을 포함한 답변이 정답으로 출제된다.

대표 유형 맛보기

🎧 P2_04

What is included in the rent? 집세에는 무엇이 포함됩니까?

(A) Electricity and water. 전기와 수도요.
(B) On Atlantic Avenue. 애틀랜틱 가예요.
(C) She lent me a bicycle. 그녀가 제게 자전거를 빌려주었어요.

빈출 질문 및 응답

◆ **What**

시간	**Q** What time is the band scheduled to perform? 그 밴드가 몇 시에 공연할 예정인가요? **A** The announcement said at 5. 안내방송에서 5시라고 했어요.
종류	**Q** What type of file cabinet do you need? 어떤 종류의 서류 캐비닛이 필요하신가요? **A** A metal one. 금속으로 된 것이요.
의견	**Q** What did you think of the president's speech? 사장님의 연설에 대해 어떻게 생각했어요? **A** She really inspired me. 그녀는 제게 정말 큰 영감을 주었어요.

◆ **Which**

대명사 one을 이용한 답변	**Q** Which factory produces these umbrellas? 어느 공장이 이 우산들을 생산하나요? **A** The one in Louisville. 루이스빌에 있는 거요.

PRACTICE

🎧 P2_05 정답 및 해설 p.8

질문을 듣고 적절한 응답을 고르세요.

1.	(A)	(B)	(C)	2.	(A)	(B)	(C)
3.	(A)	(B)	(C)	4.	(A)	(B)	(C)
5.	(A)	(B)	(C)	6.	(A)	(B)	(C)

UNIT 04 When, Where 의문문

1 When 의문문

핵심 POINT

1. 여러 가지 시제로 특정 시점을 묻는 문제가 출제되므로, 의문사 When 뒤에 나오는 be동사/조동사의 시제(과거, 현재, 미래)를 주의해서 듣는다.

2. 정답은 주로 전치사와 함께 구체적인 시간이 언급되거나 다양한 시간 관련 표현들이 자주 등장한다.

대표 유형 맛보기 ∩ P2_06

When's the art gallery's fund-raiser? 미술관의 모금 행사는 언제인가요?

(A) Yes, a few paintings. 네, 그림 몇 점이요.
(B) At least a thousand dollars. 최소 1,000달러입니다.
(C) Next Friday at seven. 다음 주 금요일 7시요.

빈출 질문 및 응답

시간/요일/날짜 등 특정 시점으로 답변	**Q** When can I expect the morning mail delivery? 오전 우편배달은 언제 오나요? **A** Around nine o'clock. 9시쯤이요.
구체적으로 정해지지 않은 모호한 시점으로 답변	**Q** When will construction begin? 공사가 언제 시작되나요? **A** After the budget is approved. 예산이 승인된 이후에요.
우회적 답변/제3의 답변	**Q** When will our pasta be ready? 저희 파스타는 언제 나오나요? **A1** I'll check with our chef. 주방장에게 물어볼게요. **A2** The kitchen is very busy tonight. 오늘 밤 주방이 너무 바쁘네요.

PRACTICE ∩ P2_07 정답 및 해설 p.9

질문을 듣고 적절한 응답을 고르세요.

1. (A) (B) (C) **2.** (A) (B) (C)

3. (A) (B) (C) **4.** (A) (B) (C)

5. (A) (B) (C) **6.** (A) (B) (C)

핵심 POINT

1. 장소나 위치, 출처 등을 묻는 질문이 출제된다.

2. 전치사를 포함한 장소/위치로 답하는 경우가 많지만 전치사를 이용한 오답 또한 종종 출제되므로 유의한다.

대표 유형 맛보기

🎧 P2_08

Where did you meet Ms. Taylor? 테일러 씨를 어디에서 만났어요?

(A) At 4 o'clock. 4시예요.

(B) Yes, she was there. 네, 그녀가 거기 있었어요.

(C) In the cafeteria. 카페테리아에서요.

빈출 질문 및 응답

장소/위치로 답변	**Q** Where can I store my luggage? 제 짐을 어디에 보관하면 될까요?
	A At the service desk over there. 저쪽 서비스 창구예요.
출처로 답변	**Q** Where's last year's quality control report? 작년의 품질 관리 보고서는 어디에 있나요?
	A You can find them on the company's Web site. 회사의 웹사이트에서 그것들을 찾을 수 있어요.
사람으로 답변	**Q** Where should the new filing cabinets be placed? 새로운 서류 캐비닛을 어디에 두어야 할까요?
	A Jenice has a floor plan. 제니스에게 평면도가 있어요.

PRACTICE

🎧 P2_09 정답 및 해설 p.10

질문을 듣고 적절한 응답을 고르세요.

1. (A) (B) (C)   **2.** (A) (B) (C)

3. (A) (B) (C)   **4.** (A) (B) (C)

5. (A) (B) (C)   **6.** (A) (B) (C)

UNIT 05 | How, Why 의문문

1 | How 의문문

핵심 POINT

1. How 다음에 조동사나 be동사가 나오면 '어떻게'의 의미이거나 방법, 수단, 또는 의견을 묻는 질문이다.

2. How 다음에 나오는 형용사나 부사에 따라 기간/수량/빈도/가격 등 묻는 내용이 결정되므로, 질문의 앞부분을 특히 유의해서 들어야 한다.

대표 유형 맛보기

🎧 P2_10

How can I place an order for catering? 출장연회 서비스 주문은 어떻게 하나요?

(A) Yes, you can. 네, 그러시면 됩니다.
(B) Just fill out this order form. 이 주문서를 작성하시면 돼요.
(C) About 70 to 100 people. 약 70~100명이요.

빈출 질문 및 응답

방법/수단	**Q** How do I set the security alarm? 어떻게 보안 경보를 설정하나요? **A** First, input your five-digit code. 우선, 당신의 5자리 암호를 입력하세요.
의견	**Q** How was the employee holiday party yesterday? 어제 직원 휴가 파티는 어땠어요? **A** It was great. 아주 좋았어요.
수량/가격	**Q** How many people visited the house for sale on Mill Street? 밀 가에 매물로 나온 그 집에 몇 명이 방문했나요? **A** About 25. 25명 정도요.
기간/빈도	**Q** How long will it take to get to Chicago? 시카고에 가는 데 얼마나 걸릴까요? **A** Four hours by train. 기차로 4시간이요.

PRACTICE

🎧 P2_11 정답 및 해설 p.11

질문을 듣고 적절한 응답을 고르세요.

1. (A)   (B)   (C)   **2.** (A)   (B)   (C)

3. (A)   (B)   (C)   **4.** (A)   (B)   (C)

5. (A)   (B)   (C)   **6.** (A)   (B)   (C)

핵심 POINT

1. 질문 속 'Why + 조동사/be동사' 다음에 나오는 주어와 동사를 집중해서 듣는다.

2. because/for 또는 to부정사를 이용해 답하는 경우가 많지만 이를 생략한 형태의 정답도 자주 출제된다.

대표 유형 맛보기

🎧 P2_12

Why is the library closing early tonight? 도서관이 왜 오늘 밤 문을 일찍 닫나요?

(A) Because it's a holiday. 휴일이기 때문이에요.
(B) A couple of librarians. 사서들 두어 명이요.
(C) This was the closest place. 여기가 가장 가까운 곳이었어요.

빈출 질문 및 응답

이유/원인으로 답변	**Q** Why didn't Ms. Granger's article appear in the magazine? 왜 그레인저 씨의 기사가 잡지에 실리지 않았나요? **A** They're still fact-checking it. 그들이 아직 사실 확인을 하고 있어요.
목적으로 답변	**Q** Why is Mr. Gonzalo visiting our branch? 곤살로 씨가 왜 우리 지사에 방문하나요? **A** To meet the staff. 직원들을 만나기 위해서요.
반문으로 답변	**Q** Why has the train been stopped so long at this station? 기차가 왜 이 역에 이렇게 오래 정차하나요? **A** Didn't you hear the announcement? 안내 방송 못 들었어요?

PRACTICE

🎧 P2_13 정답 및 해설 p.12

질문을 듣고 적절한 응답을 고르세요.

1. (A)	(B)	(C)		**2.** (A)	(B)	(C)
3. (A)	(B)	(C)		**4.** (A)	(B)	(C)
5. (A)	(B)	(C)		**6.** (A)	(B)	(C)

UNIT 06 일반, 제안·요청 의문문

1 일반 의문문

핵심 POINT

1. 사실, 의견, 경험, 계획 등을 묻는 내용이 주로 출제되며, be동사/조동사의 시제와 질문의 주어를 잘 들어야 한다.

2. Yes/No가 포함된 직접적인 응답이 자주 나오지만, Yes/No를 생략하고 부연 설명하거나 우회적으로 답하는 정답의 출제 비율이 높아지고 있다.

3. be동사나 조동사에 not이 붙은 부정 의문문도 나올 수 있다. 이 경우 긍정이면 Yes, 부정이면 No로 응답한다.

대표 유형 맛보기

🎧 P2_14

Do you have fresh fruits on your dessert menu? 디저트 메뉴에 신선한 과일이 있나요?

(A) Thanks, but I'm not hungry. 고맙지만, 전 배가 고프지 않아요.
(B) Yes, we have strawberries and peaches. 네, 딸기와 복숭아가 있어요.
(C) They make these locally. 그들은 이것들을 현지에서 만듭니다.

빈출 질문 및 응답

Be	Q Are you interested in taking an online Italian class? 온라인으로 이탈리아어 수업을 듣는 데 관심 있어요? A No, I'm very busy these days. 아니요, 저는 요즘 매우 바빠요.
Do / Does / Did	Q Did you hear the news about the vacation policy? 휴가 정책에 관한 소식을 들었어요? A I wasn't in the meeting. 저는 회의에 참석하지 않았어요.
Have	Q Have you seen the play at the Three Moons Theater? 쓰리 문스 극장에서 하는 연극 봤어요? A Yes, I went there last weekend. 네, 지난 주말에 그곳에 갔었어요.
Can	Q Can I place an international call from my hotel room? 제 호텔 방에서 국제전화를 할 수 있나요? A There will be an extra fee. 추가 요금이 있을 것입니다.

PRACTICE

🎧 P2_15 정답 및 해설 p.13

질문을 듣고 적절한 응답을 고르세요.

1. (A) (B) (C)   2. (A) (B) (C)

3. (A) (B) (C)   4. (A) (B) (C)

5. (A) (B) (C)   6. (A) (B) (C)

핵심 POINT

1. 권유하거나 요청하는 사항을 직접적으로 수락하거나 거절하는 답변이 주로 정답으로 출제된다.

2. 요청을 수락할 수 없는 이유나 이미 완료했다는 등의 간접 응답 출제 비율이 높아지고 있으므로 유의한다.

대표 유형 맛보기

🎧 P2_16

Could you recommend some good restaurants in this town? 이 동네의 괜찮은 식당들을 좀 추천해 주시겠어요?

(A) Sure, I know some places you'll like. 물론이죠, 당신이 좋아할 만한 장소를 몇 군데 알아요.

(B) There are several banks. 몇몇 은행들이 있어요.

(C) I recommend James for security. 보안 담당으로 제임스를 추천합니다.

빈출 질문 및 응답

◆ 제안

Why don't you/we ...?	**Q** Why don't you take next week off? 다음 주에 쉬는 게 어때요? **A** I'd rather finish my work. 일을 먼저 끝내야 해요.
Would you like ...?	**Q** Would you like some help filling out that application? 지원서 작성에 도움이 필요하신가요? **A** Yes, thank you. 네, 감사합니다.

◆ 요청

Can/Could you (please) ...?	**Q** Can you look up the restaurant's opening times online? 그 식당의 영업시간을 인터넷으로 찾아봐 주시겠어요? **A** Absolutely, I'll do that right away. 물론이죠, 제가 지금 바로 할게요.
Would you (mind) ...?	**Q** Would you take my work shifts this week? 이번 주에 저 대신 근무해 주시겠어요? **A** I'm traveling to London tomorrow. 저는 내일 런던으로 출장을 가요.

PRACTICE

🎧 P2_17 정답 및 해설 p.14

질문을 듣고 적절한 응답을 고르세요.

1. (A)　　　　(B)　　　　(C)　　　　　　**2.** (A)　　　　(B)　　　　(C)

3. (A)　　　　(B)　　　　(C)　　　　　　**4.** (A)　　　　(B)　　　　(C)

5. (A)　　　　(B)　　　　(C)　　　　　　**6.** (A)　　　　(B)　　　　(C)

UNIT 07 부가, 선택 의문문

1 부가 의문문

핵심 POINT

1. 평서문 뒤 꼬리말은 내용을 확인하는 차원에서 물어보는 것이므로 질문의 앞부분인 평서문에 집중해서 듣는다.

2. 일반 의문문과 같이 긍정 또는 부정을 나타내거나 부연 설명하는 내용으로 답하며, 꼬리말의 형태와 상관없이 묻는 내용에 대해 긍정이면 Yes, 부정이면 No로 응답한다.

대표 유형 맛보기 🎧 P2_18

You are planning to visit Dr. Schmidt today, aren't you? 오늘 슈미트 박사를 방문할 계획이죠, 그렇지 않나요?

(A) Let's sit together. 같이 앉아요.
(B) I have a rash on my arm. 팔에 발진이 생겼어요.
(C) Yes, later today. 네, 오늘 늦게요.

빈출 질문 및 응답

be	**Q** Their plane is half an hour late, <u>isn't it</u>? 그들의 비행기가 30분 연착하죠, 그렇지 않나요? **A** Yes, I just heard. 네, 방금 들었어요.
do / have / will	**Q** You transferred to this branch recently, <u>didn't you</u>? 당신은 최근에 이 지점으로 옮기셨죠, 그렇지 않나요? **A** No, I've worked here for years. 아니요, 이곳에서 몇 년 동안 일해 왔어요.
기타	**Q** This badge should be returned to the reception desk, <u>right</u>? 이 배지를 접수처에 반납해야 하죠, 맞죠? **A** Nicholas knows the procedure. 니콜라스가 절차를 알고 있어요.

PRACTICE 🎧 P2_19 정답 및 해설 p.15

질문을 듣고 적절한 응답을 고르세요.

1.	(A)	(B)	(C)	**2.**	(A)	(B)	(C)
3.	(A)	(B)	(C)	**4.**	(A)	(B)	(C)
5.	(A)	(B)	(C)	**6.**	(A)	(B)	(C)

핵심 POINT

1. 질문에 나오는 두 가지의 선택 사항을 놓치지 않고 들어야 한다.

2. 두 가지 선택 사항 중 하나를 골라 응답하는 경우가 가장 많지만, 둘 다 선택/거절하거나 제3의 선택 등 다양한 답변이 정답으로 출제될 수 있으므로 유의한다.

대표 유형 맛보기

🎧 P2_20

Do you want to practice the speech here or in my office?
연설 연습을 여기서 하고 싶으세요, 아니면 제 사무실에서 하고 싶으세요?

(A) Let's go through it here. 여기서 하죠.
(B) Yes, I saw him. 네, 그를 봤어요.
(C) He spoke about it on Tuesday. 그가 화요일에 그것에 대해 이야기했어요.

빈출 질문 및 응답

Would you (rather/like/ prefer) ... or ...?	**Q** Would you like coffee or tea? 커피로 하시겠어요, 아니면 차로 하시겠어요? **A** Just water, please. 물만 주세요.
Do you (want to) ... or ...?	**Q** Do you want to take a morning or afternoon flight to New York? 뉴욕행 오전 비행기를 타고 싶으세요, 아니면 오후 비행기를 타고 싶으세요? **A** Which one's less expensive? 어느 것이 덜 비싼가요?
Are you (going to) ... or ...? /Is it ... or ...?	**Q** Are you going to buy a laptop or a desktop computer? 노트북을 사실 건가요, 아니면 데스크톱 컴퓨터를 사실 건가요? **A** Laptops are more convenient. 노트북이 더 편리해요.

PRACTICE

🎧 P2_21 정답 및 해설 p.15

질문을 듣고 적절한 응답을 고르세요.

1.	(A)	(B)	(C)	**2.**	(A)	(B)	(C)
3.	(A)	(B)	(C)	**4.**	(A)	(B)	(C)
5.	(A)	(B)	(C)	**6.**	(A)	(B)	(C)

간접 의문문, 평서문

1 간접 의문문

핵심 POINT

1. 질문 속 의문문의 의문사, 주어, 동사를 주의해서 듣는다.

2. 질문 속 의문사에 맞게 직접적인 정보를 알려주는 정답이 자주 출제되지만, 일반 의문문에 맞게 Yes/No로 시작하거나 요청 사항에 대해 수락/거절하는 답변도 나올 수 있다.

대표 유형 맛보기   🎧 P2_22

Do you know when I can get a parking permit? 제가 언제 주차증을 받을 수 있는지 아세요?

(A) Yes, thanks. I like it, too. 네, 고마워요. 저도 좋아해요.
(B) You can pick it up tomorrow morning. 내일 아침에 받을 수 있어요.
(C) There are many shops near the park. 공원 주변에 상점들이 많이 있어요.

빈출 질문 및 응답

Do you know + **who / what / when / where /** **how / why …?**	**Q** Do you know who is going to be the keynote speaker for the conference? 누가 그 학회의 기조 연설자가 될 예정인지 아세요? **A** The same speaker as last year. 작년과 같은 연설자예요.
Can you tell me + **who / what / when / where /** **how / why …?**	**Q** Could you tell me why I was charged additional fifty dollars? 왜 제게 추가로 50달러가 청구되었는지 알려 주시겠어요? **A** That's the sales tax. 그것은 판매세예요.
Can you show me + **how to …?**	**Q** Can you show me how to operate this ticket machine? 이 승차권 발매기를 작동하는 방법을 보여 주시겠어요? **A** Yes, just a moment, please. 네, 잠깐만 기다려 주세요.

PRACTICE   🎧 P2_23 정답 및 해설 p.16

질문을 듣고 적절한 응답을 고르세요.

1. (A)   (B)   (C)   **2.** (A)   (B)   (C)

3. (A)   (B)   (C)   **4.** (A)   (B)   (C)

5. (A)   (B)   (C)   **6.** (A)   (B)   (C)

핵심 POINT

1. 문장 전체의 내용을 집중해서 듣고 무엇에 대해 말하고 있는지 파악해야 하므로 Part 2에서 난이도가 가장 높다.

2. 평서문임에도 Yes/No로 시작하는 응답이 종종 출제되므로 유의한다. 이러한 경우 뒤에 따라오는 부연 설명이 Yes/No와 일치하는지 주의해서 듣는다.

대표 유형 맛보기 🎧 P2_24

That was an amazing orchestra concert. 그것은 놀라운 오케스트라 연주회였어요.

(A) The violin soloist is talented. 그 바이올린 독주자가 재능이 있네요.
(B) Sorry, I'm working that day. 미안해요, 저는 그날 일해요.
(C) How did the audition go? 오디션은 어떻게 됐어요?

빈출 질문 및 응답

문제점 언급	Q The laundry machine isn't working properly. 세탁기가 제대로 작동하지 않아요. A Let's call a repair technician. 수리공을 부릅시다.
정보 전달/ 상황 설명	Q The staff meeting has been postponed until Thursday. 직원 회의가 목요일로 미뤄졌어요. A Why is it being moved? 왜 옮기는 거죠?
의견 제시/ 감정 표현	Q I think my employee performance review went well. 제 직원 업무 평가가 잘 나온 것 같아요. A That's good to hear. 그거 좋은 소식이네요.
제안/요청	Q We should hire one more photographer for our company. 우리 회사에 사진 작가를 한 명 더 고용해야 해요. A I'll start the search soon. 조만간 찾아보기 시작할게요.

PRACTICE 🎧 P2_25 정답 및 해설 p.17

질문을 듣고 적절한 응답을 고르세요.

1.	(A)	(B)	(C)	2.	(A)	(B)	(C)
3.	(A)	(B)	(C)	4.	(A)	(B)	(C)
5.	(A)	(B)	(C)	6.	(A)	(B)	(C)

700+ 뛰어넘기

1 빠르게 발음하면 When과 Where의 발음이 비슷하게 들릴 수 있으므로 이를 함정으로 이용한 오답에 유의한다.

Q When is the new blender going to be released? 신상 믹서기는 언제 출시되나요?

A In the kitchen cabinet. (×) 부엌 찬장 안에요.
The prototype is still being tested. (○) 시제품이 아직 테스트 중이에요.

2 Why 의문문에 because/for 또는 to부정사로 시작하는 함정 답변도 있으므로 뒤 내용까지 놓치지 않고 듣는다.

Q Why does the office look so empty this afternoon? 오늘 오후에 왜 이렇게 사무실이 비어 보이죠?

A Because your office is next to mine. (×) 당신의 사무실이 제 사무실 옆이기 때문이에요.
A lot of people left early. (○) 많은 사람들이 일찍 퇴근했어요.

3 일반, 부가 의문문에 Yes/No로 답한 후 연상 어휘나 유사 발음 어휘를 이용한 오답에 주의한다.

Q Will you go on the business trip with me? 저와 함께 출장 가시나요?

A No, it's in terminal A. (×) 아니요, A터미널에 있어요. → trip(여행)에서 연상할 수 있는 terminal(터미널)을 이용한 오답
Yes, I'd be glad to join you. (○) 네, 합류하게 되어 기뻐요.

Q This contract was reviewed by our legal team, wasn't it? 이 계약서는 법무팀에서 검토했죠, 그렇지 않나요?

A Yes, the view outside is so nice. (×) 네, 바깥 전망이 아주 좋아요. → review와 발음이 비슷한 view를 이용한 오답
Celine just approved it this afternoon. (○) 셀린이 오늘 오후에 그걸 승인했어요.

4 특정 정보를 묻는 의문사 의문문에는 Yes/No 답변이 불가하지만, How about ~?(~하는 게 어때요?)으로 시작하는 의문문에는 Yes/No로 답변이 가능하다. 또한, 정보를 전달하거나 의견을 제시하는 평서문에 동의/수락을 하기 위해 Yes나 Okay로 응답하는 답변이 정답이 될 수도 있다.

Q How about hiring an event planner to organize the holiday party?
연휴 파티를 준비할 이벤트 플래너를 고용하는 게 어때요?

A Yes, that's a good idea. 그래요, 좋은 생각이에요.

Q The storage room is very full. 창고가 아주 가득 찼어요.

A Yes, there's no more space in there. 네, 그곳에는 더 이상 공간이 없어요.

5 단순히 질문의 표면적인 의미가 아닌 질문의 의도나 대화가 벌어지고 있는 상황을 짐작하여 정답을 찾아야 하는 경우도 있다.

Q Who was in the break room last? 누가 마지막으로 휴게실에 있었나요?

A I noticed that it was messy, too. 저도 지저분하다고 느꼈어요.

Q Why are they cleaning the carpets now? 왜 그들은 지금 카펫을 청소하고 있는 거죠?

A Is the noise bothering you? 소음이 신경 쓰이나요?

🎧 P2_26 정답 및 해설 p.18

1. (A)   (B)   (C)

2. (A)   (B)   (C)

3. (A)   (B)   (C)

4. (A)   (B)   (C)

5. (A)   (B)   (C)

6. (A)   (B)   (C)

7. (A)   (B)   (C)

8. (A)   (B)   (C)

9. (A)   (B)   (C)

10. (A)   (B)   (C)

11. (A)   (B)   (C)

12. (A)   (B)   (C)

PART 2

PART 2
Directions: You will hear a question or statement and three responses spoken in English. They will not be printed in your test book and will be spoken only one time. Select the best response to the question or statement and mark the letter (A), (B), or (C) on your answer sheet.

7. Mark your answer on your answer sheet.

8. Mark your answer on your answer sheet.

9. Mark your answer on your answer sheet.

10. Mark your answer on your answer sheet.

11. Mark your answer on your answer sheet.

12. Mark your answer on your answer sheet.

13. Mark your answer on your answer sheet.

14. Mark your answer on your answer sheet.

15. Mark your answer on your answer sheet.

16. Mark your answer on your answer sheet.

17. Mark your answer on your answer sheet.

18. Mark your answer on your answer sheet.

19. Mark your answer on your answer sheet.

20. Mark your answer on your answer sheet.

21. Mark your answer on your answer sheet.

22. Mark your answer on your answer sheet.

23. Mark your answer on your answer sheet.

24. Mark your answer on your answer sheet.

25. Mark your answer on your answer sheet.

26. Mark your answer on your answer sheet.

27. Mark your answer on your answer sheet.

28. Mark your answer on your answer sheet.

29. Mark your answer on your answer sheet.

30. Mark your answer on your answer sheet.

31. Mark your answer on your answer sheet.

느리더라도 꾸준하면 경주에서 이긴다.

– 이솝(Aesop)

PART

3

PART 3 출제 경향 및 전략

두 명 또는 세 명의 대화를 듣고, 이와 관련된 3개의 문제에 알맞은 답을 고르는 파트이다. LC 전체 100문항 중에서 총 39문항 (13개 대화문×3문항)이 출제되며, 매회 3인 대화문 2개가 포함된다.

문제 유형

주제·목적
대화의 주제 또는 화자의 전화/방문 목적을 묻는 문제

화자·장소
직업/근무지 등 화자의 신분을 묻거나, 대화가 일어나는 장소를 묻는 문제

세부사항
- 특정 정보: 무엇/누구/언제/어디/어떻게/왜 등 대화에서 언급된 구체적인 정보를 묻는 문제
- 언급한 내용: 화자가 특정 대상에 대해 언급한 내용을 묻는 문제

제안·요청사항
화자가 상대방에게 제안하거나 부탁/요청하는 것을 묻는 문제

다음에 할·일어날 일
화자가 다음에 할 일 또는 미래에 일어날 일을 묻는 문제

화자의 의도 파악
화자가 한 말의 의미나 그 말을 통해 암시하는 것, 또는 그것을 말한 이유를 묻는 문제

시각 자료 연계
목록/지도/그래프 등 다양한 유형의 시각 자료가 함께 제시되는 문제

문제 풀이 전략

STEP 1 | 질문 파악하기
대화가 나오기 전, 질문을 읽고 키워드를 통해 묻는 내용을 파악하고, 정답의 단서가 어느 부분에서 나올지 예상한다.

STEP 2 | 대화 속 단서 찾기
파악한 키워드를 바탕으로 대화를 들으면서 단서가 되는 내용을 찾는다.

STEP 3 | 정답 선택하기
대화에서 들은 단서 내용을 동일하게 또는 다른 어휘로 바꾸어 적절하게 표현한 보기를 정답으로 선택한다.

🎧 P3_01

32. What is the purpose of the woman's visit?
(A) To update an address
(B) To apply for a job
(C) To book a consultation
(D) To make a complaint

33. What does the woman say about her neighbor?
(A) He recommended a business.
(B) He works as a technician.
(C) He was disappointed with a service.
(D) He has recently moved.

34. What does the man suggest the woman do?
(A) Call another branch
(B) Pay in installments
(C) Read a pamphlet
(D) Purchase some insurance

W Hello. I'm here about solar panels for a residential property. [32] I heard that you give a free consultation to potential customers, so I'd like to make an appointment for one of those. My name is Christine Arnold, and I live at 935 Roane Avenue.

M Thanks for coming. Let's see... Are you available this Saturday at 2 P.M.?

W Yes, that would be great, thanks. Actually, [33] my neighbor used your services last year, and he suggested that I get my panels from you. But I'm a little worried they'll be too expensive for me.

M If that's your concern, [34] you could make the payments in several installments to spread out the cost.

해석

32. 여자의 방문 목적은 무엇인가?
(A) 주소를 갱신하기 위해
(B) 일자리에 지원하기 위해
(C) 상담을 예약하기 위해
(D) 불만을 제기하기 위해

33. 여자는 이웃에 대해 무엇이라고 말하는가?
(A) 그가 업체를 추천했다.
(B) 그는 기술자로 일한다.
(C) 그는 서비스에 실망했다.
(D) 그는 최근에 이사했다.

34. 남자는 여자에게 무엇을 하라고 제안하는가?
(A) 다른 지점에 전화하기
(B) 분할하여 납부하기
(C) 팸플릿을 읽기
(D) 보험 상품 구매하기

여 안녕하세요. 주택용 태양 전지판 관련해서 왔어요. [32] 당신이 잠재 고객들에게 무료 상담을 해 주신다고 들었어요. 그래서 그런 상담들 중 하나를 예약하고 싶습니다. 제 이름은 크리스틴 아널드이고, 론가 935번지에 삽니다.

남 와 주셔서 감사합니다. 어디 볼게요... 이번 토요일 오후 2시에 시간 되시나요?

여 네, 그때면 좋아요, 감사합니다. 사실, [33] 제 이웃이 작년에 당신의 서비스를 이용했는데, 그가 제게 당신으로부터 전지판을 구매하라고 제안했어요. 하지만 제게는 너무 비쌀까 봐 조금 걱정이 됩니다.

남 그 점이 걱정이시면, [34] 비용이 분산되도록 여러 번 분납해서 지불하실 수 있어요.

핵심 POINT

1. 주로 대화 초반에 단서가 언급되므로, 대화 초반부를 놓치지 않고 듣는다.

2. 대화 주제가 후반부에 등장하는 경우도 종종 있으므로, 대화 초반부를 듣고서 주제가 파악되지 않는다면 나머지 2문제를 먼저 해결한 뒤 마지막에 푼다.

빈출 질문

주제 What are the speakers (mainly) discussing? 화자들은 (주로) 무엇에 관해 이야기하고 있는가?
      What is the conversation (mainly/mostly) about? 대화는 (주로) 무엇에 관한 것인가?

목적 Why is the man calling? 남자는 왜 전화하고 있는가?
      What is the purpose of the woman's visit/call? 여자의 방문/전화 목적은 무엇인가?

대표 유형 맛보기

🎧 P3_02

M Good morning, Dove Botanical Gardens.

W Hello. I recently learned that you hold weddings at your site. I've just started planning my wedding, and I'm looking for a venue... um... I'm wondering how much it would cost to hold the event there.

M Well, it depends on the duration of the event. I can e-mail you an information packet, if you'd like.

W That would be wonderful. I saw the photo gallery on your Web site, and everything looks so beautiful. And I love that it's a remote setting.

M Oh, about that... We are no longer running our shuttle service from Renwick Subway Station. So, make sure to take that into consideration.

남 안녕하세요, 도브 식물원입니다.

여 안녕하세요. 그곳에서 결혼식을 열기도 한다는 걸 최근에 알게 되었어요. 제가 막 결혼 계획을 세우기 시작했거든요, 그래서 장소를 찾고 있는데... 음... 그곳에서 행사를 열려면 비용이 얼마나 드는지 궁금합니다.

남 음, 행사의 기간에 따라 달라요. 원하시면 제가 이메일로 자료집을 보내 드릴 수 있어요.

여 그래 주시면 정말 좋겠어요. 그곳의 웹사이트에서 사진첩을 봤는데, 모든 것이 정말 아름다워 보여요. 그리고 한적한 장소라는 점이 아주 마음에 들고요.

남 아, 그거 말인데요... 저희가 더 이상 렌윅 지하철역에서 셔틀 서비스를 운행하지 않아요. 그러니, 반드시 그 점을 고려해 주세요.

Why is the woman calling?
To inquire about fees

여자는 왜 전화하고 있는가?
요금에 관해 문의하기 위해

놓치지 말아야 할 단서 표현

I'd like to book a flight from Miami to Seattle on May 17. 5월 17일에 마이애미에서 시애틀로 가는 비행편을 예약하고 싶습니다.
I'm calling to see if you have time to work on a project for my marketing firm.
제 마케팅 회사의 프로젝트를 할 시간이 있으신지 알아보려고 전화했어요.
Let's talk about your job performance this year. 올해 당신의 업무 성과에 대해 이야기해 봅시다.
Have you heard the news about our merger with Vocon Automotive? 보콘 자동차와의 합병 소식 들었어요?

대화를 들으면서 빈칸을 채운 뒤, 알맞은 답을 고르세요.

> **W** Hi, Mr. Davis. This is Christina Whitley from the Westbury Small Business Association.
>
> **M** Oh, yes. Hello, Ms. Whitley.
>
> **W** _____.
>
> **M** I see. I can probably still attend it.
>
> **W** I hope so. I'll e-mail you an updated registration packet. Also, your travel and registration fees will be covered by us.
>
> **M** Thank you. I'll double check whether or not I can participate in the event. If not, I will probably send my assistant manager in my place.

1. Why is the woman calling the man?

    (A) To request the payment of a bill

    (B) To inform him of a schedule change

    (C) To invite him to give a presentation

    (D) To share some management strategies

대화를 듣고 알맞은 답을 고르세요.

2. What are the speakers mainly discussing?

    (A) A headquarters relocation

    (B) A software upgrade

    (C) A proposed merger

    (D) A market regulation

3. What is the purpose of the woman's call?

    (A) To promote an event at a park

    (B) To introduce a cleaning service

    (C) To arrange a facility tour

    (D) To ask about volunteer opportunities

4. What is the conversation mainly about?

    (A) Organizing some merchandise

    (B) Training staff members

    (C) Changing a window display

    (D) Labeling boxes for shipping

핵심 POINT

1. 주제·목적 문제와 마찬가지로 주로 초반에 단서가 언급되므로, 대화 초반부에 나오는 직업, 장소 표현을 놓치지 않고 듣는다.

2. 화자 문제는 신분이나 직업뿐만 아니라 업종, 근무지, 부서 등을 묻는 다양한 형태로 출제될 수 있다.

빈출 질문

화자   Who (most likely) is the man? 남자는 누구인가?
        Where do the speakers (most likely) work? 화자들은 어디에서 일하는가?
        What field/industry/department do the speakers (most likely) work in? 화자들은 어떤 분야/업계/부서에서 일하는가?

장소   Where (most likely) is the man? 남자는 어디에 있는가?
        Where does the conversation (most likely) take place? 대화는 어디에서 일어나는가?

대표 유형 맛보기

🎧 P3_04

W Alex, I heard you did a great job leading the meeting with Allstar Incorporated. They really liked the new advertising campaign you proposed. You're setting up more meetings with new clients this month, right?

M Yes, but I've been thinking of doing video conferences rather than meeting face to face.

W Aren't there always problems with the video conference system?

M Well... I've just read an article about a new system that we might want to purchase. I'll send some details about it to you when I get back to my desk.

여 알렉스, 당신이 올스타 사와의 회의를 잘 이끌었다고 들었어요. 그들이 당신이 제안한 새로운 광고 캠페인을 정말 좋아했어요. 당신은 이번 달에 새로운 의뢰인들과 더 많은 회의를 준비하고 있죠, 맞죠?

남 네, 하지만 대면 회의보다는 화상 회의를 고려 중이에요.

여 화상 회의 시스템에는 항상 문제가 있지 않나요?

남 음... 제가 방금 우리가 구매하면 어떨까 하는 새로운 시스템에 관한 기사를 읽었어요. 제 자리로 돌아가면 그것에 관한 몇 가지 정보를 당신에게 보내 줄게요.

What field do the speakers most likely work in?
Advertising

화자들은 어떤 분야에서 일하는 것 같은가?
광고

놓치지 말아야 할 단서 표현

Welcome to Alpha Gym. How can I help you? 알파 헬스장에 오신 것을 환영합니다. 무엇을 도와드릴까요?

This is Jack Wilson, a freelance photographer. 저는 프리랜서 사진작가 잭 윌슨입니다.

Hi, **I'm calling from** the company Greenwood. We're interested in filming a scene for a movie in the library.
안녕하세요, 그린우드 사에서 전화드립니다. 저희는 도서관에서 영화의 한 장면을 찍는 것에 관심이 있습니다.

I'm pleased with the sales of **our brand's** cakes, pies and cookies this season.
이번 시즌 우리 브랜드의 케이크, 파이, 쿠키 판매량이 만족스러워요.

대화를 들으면서 빈칸을 채운 뒤, 알맞은 답을 고르세요.

W _____ .

Are you a member here?

M Actually, this is my first visit. I recently moved to the area.

W Well, there is no charge to become a member. You just have to show proof of address, such as a utility bill or apartment lease.

M Great. Do you offer any classes for the community?

W Absolutely. We have a wide range of classes for adults. Here is the schedule for this month. But just so you know, we're closed next week because of the holiday.

M Okay. Are there public computers as well?

W Yes, just over there. You can use them anytime.

---

1. Where is the conversation most likely taking place?

(A) At a library
(B) At a real estate agency
(C) At an electronics store
(D) At a fitness center

대화를 듣고 알맞은 답을 고르세요.

2. Who most likely is the woman?

(A) An electrician
(B) A janitor
(C) An interior decorator
(D) A property manager

3. What industry does the man work in?

(A) Publishing
(B) Food service
(C) Health care
(D) Agriculture

4. Where does the man work?

(A) At a restaurant
(B) At a television station
(C) At a business institute
(D) At a movie theater

UNIT 11 세부사항을 묻는 문제

핵심 POINT

1. What, Who, How, Why 등의 다양한 의문사로 대화 속 특정 정보 또는 화자가 언급한 내용을 묻는 문제가 출제된다.

2. 대화 속 정답 단서는 대부분 패러프레이징되어 선택지에 제시되며, 주로 문장 형태의 긴 선택지가 출제되므로 선택지를 미리 읽고 내용을 파악해 두는 것이 좋다.

빈출 질문

특정 정보	What did/does/will the man ~? 남자는 무엇을 ~했는가/~하는가/~할 것인가? Who/When/Where/How/Why did/does/will the woman ~? 여자는 누구를/언제/어디에서/어떻게/왜 ~했는가/~하는가/~할 것인가?
언급한 내용	What does the man say about ~? 남자는 ~에 대해 무엇이라고 말하는가?

대표 유형 맛보기

🎧 P3_06

W Good morning, and welcome to Sunburg Community Center. How may I help you?

M Hello. I'm interested in finding a place to play racquetball. I just moved to this town for a new job, and someone at work recommended this place.

W Great! We have four racquetball courts, but you have to be a member to use them.

M Okay. Would it be possible to see your facilities?

W Of course. I'll ask my coworker, Amy, to show you around. Wait here just a moment, please.

여 안녕하세요, 선버그 커뮤니티 센터에 오신 것을 환영합니다. 어떻게 도와드릴까요?

남 안녕하세요. 저는 라켓볼을 할 장소를 찾는 데 관심이 있습니다. 새 직장 때문에 이 동네로 막 이사 왔는데, 직장의 어떤 사람이 이곳을 추천했어요.

여 잘됐네요! 저희는 라켓볼 코트가 4개 있습니다만, 그것들을 이용하기 위해서는 회원이 되셔야 해요.

남 알겠습니다. 이곳의 시설들을 볼 수 있을까요?

여 물론이죠. 제 동료 에이미에게 당신이 둘러보시도록 안내해 드리라고 요청할게요. 잠시만 여기서 기다려 주세요.

What did the man recently do?
He moved into the area.

남자는 최근에 무엇을 했는가?
그는 이 지역으로 이사 왔다.

놓치지 말아야 할 단서 표현

질문의 키워드가 대화 속 단서 문장에서 그대로 언급되거나 다른 말로 바꾸어 표현된다.

What is some **software** being used for? 소프트웨어는 무엇에 사용되고 있는가?
I recently purchased your **software** to keep track of my warehouse inventory.
저는 창고 재고를 파악하기 위해 최근에 귀사의 소프트웨어를 구입했습니다.

Why does the woman want to **make a change**? 여자는 왜 변경하기를 원하는가?
We may need to **alter the route** so it's less difficult for our camera operators to follow the action.
우리는 카메라 감독이 움직임을 따라가기가 더 쉽도록 경로를 변경해야 할 것입니다.

대화를 들으면서 빈칸을 채운 뒤, 알맞은 답을 고르세요.

M Hello, I'm supposed to meet Anthony Shaw here for an interview. I'm from the *Worthington Herald*.

W Ah, yes. He's expecting you, so he'll be out in a moment. _____
_____.

M Yes, he's been such a big part of the local basketball scene. A lot of people will miss him when he retires at the end of the season.

W Right. He's very talented. Anyway, could I get you something to drink while you wait?

M Thanks, but I'm fine.

---

1. Who is Anthony Shaw?

(A) A maintenance worker
(B) A coach
(C) A receptionist
(D) A journalist

대화를 듣고 알맞은 답을 고르세요.

2. Why is the man disappointed?

(A) A proposal was rejected.
(B) A meeting was canceled.
(C) A board member has resigned.
(D) A presentation included some errors.

3. What problem does the woman mention?

(A) There's a misprint on the ticket.
(B) Some bus fares have increased.
(C) The weather is bad.
(D) Some repairs are needed.

4. What does the man say about a brand?

(A) It receives many positive reviews.
(B) It has an affordable price.
(C) It is currently out of stock.
(D) It uses high-quality materials.

PART 3

제안 · 요청사항을 묻는 문제

핵심 POINT

1. 주로 마지막 문제로 출제되며, 대화 후반부에서 단서가 언급된다.

2. 질문을 미리 읽고 화자의 성별을 확인한 뒤, 해당 화자의 말 속에서 무언가를 해 주겠다고 제안하거나 상대방에게 해 달라고 요청하는 표현을 놓치지 않고 듣는다.

빈출 질문

제안   What does the man suggest (doing)?   남자는 무엇을 (할 것을) 제안하는가?
         What does the man offer to do?   남자는 무엇을 해 주겠다고 제안하는가?

요청   What does the man ask/tell the woman to do?   남자는 여자에게 무엇을 해 달라고 요청하는가?
         What does the woman ask for?   여자는 무엇을 요청하는가?

대표 유형 맛보기

🎧 P3_08

W Hi, I've purchased a ticket for your special exhibit of contemporary art. I'd like to take some pictures of the paintings. Is that allowed?	**여** 안녕하세요, 제가 이곳의 현대 미술 특별전 입장권을 구매했는데요. 그림들 사진을 좀 찍고 싶어요. 그래도 되나요?
M Yes, um... but please make sure you turn off your flash first.	**남** 그렇습니다만, 음... 반드시 먼저 플래시를 끄도록 해 주세요.
W Okay, great. I'm looking forward to this exhibit.	**여** 네, 좋습니다. 전 이번 전시가 기대돼요.
M I hope you enjoy it. And here's a brochure of our future events that you might be interested in.	**남** 재미있게 보시길 바랍니다. 그리고 앞으로 있을 저희 행사에 대한 책자가 여기 있는데 관심이 있으실지도 모르겠네요.
W Thanks. I'll give that a look.	**여** 감사합니다. 한번 볼게요.
M Also, I suggest you hold onto your ticket. You can show it at the café to get a discount.	**남** 또한, 입장권을 소지하고 계시기를 추천합니다. 카페에서 보여주고 할인을 받으실 수 있습니다.

- - -

What does the man suggest doing?	**남자는 무엇을 할 것을 제안하는가?**
Keeping a ticket	입장권을 가지고 있는 것

놓치지 말아야 할 단서 표현

Why don't you send me a detailed description of the work?   그 업무에 대한 자세한 설명을 저에게 보내 주시면 어떨까요?
Maybe we should organize more workshops to draw people in.   사람들을 끌어들이기 위해 워크숍을 더 준비해야 할 것 같아요.
I can / I'd be happy to teach my system to the rest of the department.
제가 부서의 나머지 사람들에게 제 방식을 가르칠게요.
Could you bring me a sandwich from the cafeteria?   구내식당에서 샌드위치 하나만 가져다 주시겠어요?

대화를 들으면서 빈칸을 채운 뒤, 알맞은 답을 고르세요.

M Mijin, I plan to apply for the assistant manager role, but _____

_____?

W I'd be happy to. You've been doing an excellent job on the sales team, and I'm really impressed with how hard you worked after being assigned to a new territory.

M Thanks a lot. I'm actually quite proud of how I was able to exceed my sales targets by so much. It helped to boost my confidence.

---

1. What does the man ask the woman to do?

(A) Proofread a sales catalog

(B) Visit a client

(C) Give a presentation

(D) Write an evaluation

대화를 듣고 알맞은 답을 고르세요.

2. What does the woman offer to do?

(A) Work on the weekend

(B) Order some flowers

(C) Look for some materials

(D) Hold a tenants' meeting

3. What does the man suggest doing?

(A) Making promotional videos

(B) Inviting celebrities to the store

(C) Offering discount coupons

(D) Holding a decorating contest

4. What does the man ask for?

(A) A dessert recipe

(B) A promotional brochure

(C) A copy of an invitation

(D) A contact list

핵심 POINT

1. 주로 대화 후반부에서 will, be going to 등 미래나 계획을 나타내는 표현과 함께 단서 문장이 언급된다.

2. 앞으로 일어날 일을 묻는 문제의 경우 대부분 선택지가 완전한 문장으로 제시되므로, 주어까지 미리 읽고 키워드를 파악해 두는 것이 좋다.

빈출 질문

다음에 할 일
What will the man (most likely) do next? 남자는 다음에 무엇을 할 것인가?
What does the woman say she will do? 여자는 무엇을 할 것이라고 말하는가?

다음에 일어날 일
What will happen ~? ~에 무슨 일이 일어날 것인가?
What event will take place ~? ~에 무슨 행사가 개최될 것인가?

대표 유형 맛보기

🎧 P3_10

M The new billboard for our gym went up yesterday. I think it's going to be a great way to advertise our business.	남 우리 체육관을 위한 새로운 옥외 광고판이 어제 올라갔어요. 우리 업체를 광고하는 훌륭한 방법이 될 것 같아요.
W I saw it as I was driving to work this morning. It looks great.	여 오늘 아침 차로 출근하는 중에 그걸 봤어요. 아주 멋있더라고요.
M Yeah, and I'm glad it's on such a busy road.	남 네, 그리고 그렇게 통행량이 많은 도로에 있어서 다행이에요.
W Right. Many people will see it, so we'll probably get a lot of new members this month. We should make sure all employees know how to register new members.	여 맞아요. 많은 사람이 그것을 볼 테니, 아마도 우리가 이번 달에 많은 신규 회원들을 모으게 될 거예요. 반드시 모든 직원들이 신규 회원을 등록시키는 방법을 숙지하도록 해야 해요.
M That's a good point. I'll e-mail everyone now with a reminder of how to do it.	남 좋은 지적이에요. 제가 지금 모든 사람들에게 그렇게 하는 방법을 상기시키는 메모와 함께 이메일을 보낼게요.

What does the man say he will do? | 남자는 무엇을 할 것이라고 말하는가?
Send a message | 메시지 보내기

놓치지 말아야 할 단서 표현

I'll / I'm going to <u>send you links</u> to their Web site. 그들의 웹사이트 링크를 보내드리겠습니다.
I need to <u>look for the service records</u> for the lawn mower. 잔디 깎는 기계의 서비스 기록을 찾아봐야 해요.
Let me <u>show you around</u> our facility. 제가 당신에게 시설을 안내해 드리겠습니다.
There'll be a children's <u>poster competition</u> next month. 다음 달에 어린이 포스터 대회가 있을 거예요.

PRACTICE

대화를 들으면서 빈칸을 채운 뒤, 알맞은 답을 고르세요.

> **W** Hi, I tried to use the library's self-checkout machine, but there was a message saying that I owe a fine. Here is my card.
>
> **M** Let me see... Yes, it looks like one of your books was returned late. You'll have to pay a fine of $1.25 before checking out anything new.
>
> **W** Oh, that's no problem. I can pay it now. Sorry about that.
>
> **M** It happens. _____.
> We're selling used books to purchase new computers for the library.

1. What will take place next Saturday?

   (A) A writing workshop
   (B) A poetry reading
   (C) A computer class
   (D) A fund-raising event

대화를 듣고 알맞은 답을 고르세요.

2. What will the woman most likely do next?

   (A) Write down an address
   (B) Confirm a schedule
   (C) Introduce a crew member
   (D) Provide a cost estimate

3. What will happen next week?

   (A) A theater will be renovated.
   (B) A play will open.
   (C) A poster will be printed.
   (D) An acting award will be presented.

4. What does the woman say she will do?

   (A) Take some measurements
   (B) Paint a room
   (C) Sign a contract
   (D) Install some lights

핵심 POINT

1. 질문에 제시된 인용구를 미리 확인한 뒤, 대화 속 해당 문장의 앞뒤 대사에 주목한다.

2. 문장의 사전적 의미가 아니라 문맥상 알맞은 의미나 화자의 의도를 파악해야 하므로, 대화의 전체적인 흐름과 맥락을 이해해야 답을 고를 수 있다.

빈출 질문

의미/암시하는 것　What does the woman mean/imply when she says, "~"?　여자는 "~"라고 말할 때 무엇을 의미/암시하는가?

목적　　　　　　Why does the man say, "~"?　남자는 왜 "~"라고 말하는가?

대표 유형 맛보기

🎧 P3_12

M Hello, Ms. Hodge? This is Tony from Fremont Furniture. I'm calling about your order of three leather sofas for your hotel's lobby. They were supposed to be delivered today, but I'm afraid there's going to be a delay.

W We're shooting the commercial on Friday. Our site needs to look its best.

M I'm very sorry for the inconvenience. Our supplier is having some distribution issues. I'll call you tomorrow to confirm the new delivery date.

남 여보세요, 하지 씨? 저는 프레몬트 가구사의 토니입니다. 호텔 로비용으로 가죽 소파 세 개를 주문하신 건에 관해 전화드립니다. 그것들이 오늘 배달되기로 되어 있었으나, 유감스럽게도 지연이 있겠습니다.

여 저희가 금요일에 광고를 촬영해요. 저희 장소가 최상의 상태로 보여야 하는데요.

남 불편을 끼쳐 드려 대단히 죄송합니다. 저희 공급업체가 유통 문제를 좀 겪고 있어요. 내일 전화드려서 새로운 배송 날짜를 확정하겠습니다.

Why does the woman say, "We're shooting the commercial on Friday"?
To show concern

여자는 왜 "저희가 금요일에 광고를 촬영해요"라고 말하는가?

우려를 나타내기 위해

놓치지 말아야 할 단서 표현

인용 문장 앞에 상대방의 제안이나 요청이 나올 경우: 동의/승낙 또는 반대/거절의 의미일 수 있다.

W **What if we donated our reusable water bottles for the registration gift bags?**
만약 우리가 등록 선물에 재사용 가능한 물병을 기부한다면 어떨까요?

M You know, <u>our company hasn't made a profit yet</u>. 음, 우리 회사는 아직 수익을 내지 못했어요. → 제안에 반대

인용 문장 뒤에 사과나 해결책, 공감 또는 상대를 안심시키는 문장이 나올 경우: 불만, 놀라움, 걱정 등의 감정 표현 가능성이 높다.

M They want 3,000 full color brochures printed by Friday. 그들은 금요일까지 컬러 책자 3천 부가 인쇄되기를 원해요.

W <u>Four of our people are on vacation.</u> 우리 직원들 중 네 명이 휴가 중이에요. → 주문에 대해 걱정 표현

M **What about increasing the rate we pay for overtime, just for this job?**
이 건에 한해 초과 근무 수당을 인상하는 것은 어때요?

PRACTICE

대화를 들으면서 빈칸을 채운 뒤, 알맞은 답을 고르세요.

> **W** Hi, Mr. Fox. Our team of consultants has gone over your business model, and we've come up with some ideas to expand your footwear brand.
>
> **M** That's great. We've been struggling to make a name for ourselves in the market, so your insights will be helpful.
>
> **W** Alright. So, _____?
>
> **M** They usually market to an older clientele.
>
> **W** Hmm... _____.

1. Why does the man say, "They usually market to an older clientele"?

   (A) To express disappointment
   (B) To agree with a plan
   (C) To reject a suggestion
   (D) To offer assistance

대화를 듣고 알맞은 답을 고르세요.

2. What does the man mean when he says, "it's very cold today?"

   (A) He wants to change his seating request.
   (B) Taking public transportation was uncomfortable.
   (C) The heater should be turned up.
   (D) He may have to postpone a meeting.

3. Why does the man say, "That property was just posted a few days ago"?

   (A) To make an offer
   (B) To provide an excuse
   (C) To explain an error
   (D) To express surprise

4. What does the woman imply when she says, "that equipment gets used a lot"?

   (A) A high-quality product was purchased.
   (B) A problem is not surprising.
   (C) A training session is not needed.
   (D) An expense is reasonable.

핵심 POINT

1. 목록/표, 지도/평면도, 그래프, 쿠폰, 기타 그림 등의 다양한 시각 자료가 나올 수 있다. 모든 시각 자료는 대화가 나오기 전에 미리 읽고 키워드를 파악해 두어야 한다.

2. 선택지와 상응하는 네 가지 항목이 대화에서 언급되는 부분에 주목한다. 만약 대화에서 여러 개의 항목이 언급된다면, 시각 자료와 대화의 내용이 일치하는지 비교하면서 듣는다.

빈출 질문

Look at the graphic. What/Which/Who/When/Where ~? 시각 자료를 보시오. 무엇이/어떤 것이/누가/어디에서/언제 ~?

대표 유형 맛보기

🎧 P3_14

W Jason, have you had a chance to try out the new software yet? It has a lot of nice new features, but it doesn't run very fast.

M Are the other team members experiencing the same problem?

W Yeah. Many of my team members have said the same thing. We should report it to someone in charge.

M I'll call the IT department and ask them to look into this issue.

여 제이슨, 새로운 소프트웨어를 시험적으로 사용해 볼 기회가 있었어요? 좋은 새 기능이 많이 있지만, 그다지 빨리 작동하지는 않아요.

남 나머지 팀원들도 같은 문제를 겪고 있나요?

여 네. 저희 팀원들 다수가 같은 얘기를 했어요. 그것을 담당자에게 보고해야 합니다.

남 제가 IT 부서에 전화해서 이 문제를 조사해 달라고 요청할게요.

Extension	Title
567	Accounting Manager
599	IT Manager

Look at the graphic. Which extension number will the man most likely call?
599

내선 번호	직함
567	회계 부장
599	IT 부장

시각 자료를 보시오. 남자는 어느 내선 번호로 전화할 것 같은가?
599

놓치지 말아야 할 단서 표현

시간 순서	The live music will start **at the same time as** dinner.	저녁 식사와 동시에 라이브 음악이 시작될 거예요.
위치/방향	It's a corner room that's **right next to** the food court.	푸드코트 바로 옆에 있는 코너 룸입니다.
비교급/최상급	**The highest** category is worth investing in.	가장 높은 항목이 투자할 가치가 있습니다.
모양/패턴	They're the ones with the **large star in the middle** and **smaller ones around the edge**. 가운데에 큰 별과 가장자리에 작은 별들이 있는 것입니다.	

PRACTICE

대화를 들으면서 빈칸을 채운 뒤, 알맞은 답을 고르세요.

> **W** I missed the staff meeting yesterday. Is there anything I need to know about?
>
> **M** Well, the planning for the city's Environmental Awareness Day is going well. There's going to be a cleanup project at Hartford Park in the morning. We'll also be collecting recyclable items at city hall.
>
> **W** Great. Did we find any sponsors for the event?
>
> **M** Yes. Finch Landscaping is donating three hundred saplings that people can plant at home.
>
> _____ .

Trees	Heights
Alder	15 meters
Hawthorne	10 meters
Gray Willow	8 meters
Holly	6 meters

1. Look at the graphic. What kind of saplings will be donated?

  (A) Alder
  (B) Hawthorne
  (C) Gray Willow
  (D) Holly

대화를 듣고 알맞은 답을 고르세요.

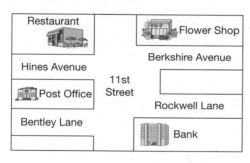

2. Look at the graphic. Which road can be closed?

  (A) Hines Avenue
  (B) Berkshire Avenue
  (C) Bentley Lane
  (D) Rockwell Lane

Flights to Berlin

Departure Time	Airline
1:35 P.M.	Kershaw Budget
3:58 P.M.	Rosco Skyteam
7:31 P.M.	Powell Airlines
8:02 P.M.	GT Airways

3. Look at the graphic. When does the woman's flight depart?

  (A) At 1:35 P.M.
  (B) At 3:58 P.M.
  (C) At 7:31 P.M.
  (D) At 8:02 P.M.

PART 3

Directions: You will hear some conversations between two or more people. You will be asked to answer three questions about what the speakers say in each conversation. Select the best response to each question and mark the letter (A), (B), (C), or (D) on your answer sheet. The conversations will not be printed in your test book and will be spoken only one time.

32. Where does the conversation most likely take place?

(A) At a hardware store
(B) At a community center
(C) At a car dealership
(D) At a shoe store

33. What does the man suggest doing?

(A) Hiring part-time workers
(B) Rearranging a display
(C) Holding a sports competition
(D) Contacting a supplier

34. What will the man do next?

(A) Speak to a supervisor
(B) Send a message
(C) Update a Web site
(D) Review some figures

35. Who most likely is the man?

(A) A landlord
(B) A facility manager
(C) A plumber
(D) An electrician

36. According to Carol, what is the problem?

(A) Some instructions were incorrect.
(B) A coworker has been absent.
(C) She is missing some components.
(D) She noticed a water leak.

37. What does the man mention about a repair?

(A) It cannot be completed right away.
(B) It may require special parts.
(C) It is not necessary at this time.
(D) Its charge has recently increased.

38. Where does the man most likely work?

(A) At a government office
(B) At a construction firm
(C) At a medical clinic
(D) At an employment agency

39. According to the man, what should applicants provide?

(A) A letter of reference
(B) A mailing address
(C) Proof of certification
(D) A copy of a photo ID

40. What is scheduled for Friday?

(A) An information session
(B) An interview
(C) A staff dinner
(D) A board meeting

41. What kind of product are the speakers discussing?

(A) A digital camera
(B) A video game system
(C) A printer
(D) A smartphone

42. What event will take place this weekend?

(A) A film screening
(B) An annual parade
(C) A musical performance
(D) A business conference

43. What does the woman ask about?

(A) How long a warranty lasts
(B) How to get an item
(C) How much a delivery fee is
(D) How to return a product

44. What did the woman need help with?

(A) Installing a window
(B) Building a garage
(C) Planting a garden
(D) Removing a tree

45. Why does the woman thank the man?

(A) He offered a discount.
(B) He provided a recommendation.
(C) He explained a procedure.
(D) He arrived quickly.

46. What will the woman most likely do next?

(A) Move her vehicle
(B) Get a power cord
(C) Make a payment
(D) Select a color

47. What kind of business is the woman calling?

(A) A hotel
(B) An insurance firm
(C) A theater
(D) A catering company

48. Why is the woman planning an event?

(A) To promote a grand opening
(B) To present some awards
(C) To celebrate a company anniversary
(D) To raise funds for a project

49. Why does the man say, "I was going to order everything today"?

(A) To thank the woman for a reminder
(B) To confirm that a request can be fulfilled
(C) To accept a change in a deadline
(D) To ask for a payment

50. Where do the speakers work?

(A) At a law firm
(B) At an employment agency
(C) At a newspaper publisher
(D) At a photography studio

51. What problem does the man mention?

(A) Some equipment is missing.
(B) Some confidential information was shared.
(C) Employees are working too much.
(D) A system is running slowly.

52. What does Stacey think the business should do?

(A) Upgrade some software
(B) Gather feedback from employees
(C) Change the hours of operation
(D) Provide annual bonuses

53. Who most likely is the man?

(A) A senior accountant
(B) A hotel manager
(C) A building cleaner
(D) A clothing shop owner

54. What does the woman want to do later this year?

(A) Move to a new city
(B) Take a trip abroad
(C) Start her own business
(D) Purchase a house

55. What does the man ask the woman about?

(A) Her career goals
(B) Her preferred start date
(C) Her availability
(D) Her expected salary

GO ON TO THE NEXT PAGE

56. Who most likely are the speakers?

(A) Environmental scientists
(B) Company investors
(C) City council members
(D) Construction workers

57. What is the city expected to approve?

(A) Holding a festival
(B) Building a pedestrian path
(C) Expanding a parking lot
(D) Renovating a stadium

58. What advantage of a project is mentioned?

(A) It will save money.
(B) It will create jobs.
(C) It will promote health.
(D) It will attract tourists.

59. What is the conversation mainly about?

(A) Publishing a cookbook
(B) Starting a podcast
(C) Presenting at a trade show
(D) Launching a household appliance

60. Why does the man say, "Everyone is familiar with that"?

(A) To reject a suggestion
(B) To confirm survey results
(C) To praise a strategy
(D) To acknowledge an accomplishment

61. What do the speakers agree to do?

(A) Contact some suppliers
(B) Visit a shop together
(C) Record a demonstration
(D) Browse a Web site

Poetry	$10
Watercolor Painting	$18
Ballet	$14
Sewing	$22

62. Look at the graphic. How much will the man most likely pay?

(A) $10
(B) $18
(C) $14
(D) $22

63. What information does the woman ask for?

(A) A credit card number
(B) An e-mail address
(C) A start date
(D) A difficulty level

64. What does the woman suggest doing?

(A) Watching a video
(B) Renting some equipment
(C) Wearing special clothing
(D) Printing a brochure

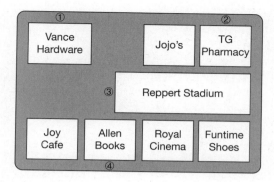

①			②
Vance Hardware	Jojo's		TG Pharmacy
③	Reppert Stadium		
Joy Cafe	Allen Books	Royal Cinema	Funtime Shoes
		④	

Philadelphia Weekly Forecast				
Monday	Tuesday	Wednesday	Thursday	Friday
Rainy	Rainy	Sunny	Cloudy	Sunny

65. Why is the woman visiting the site?

(A) To meet with investors
(B) To perform an inspection
(C) To hear a lecture
(D) To have a job interview

66. What is the woman surprised about?

(A) The transportation fee
(B) The number of attendees
(C) The travel time
(D) The size of a venue

67. Look at the graphic. Where will the woman most likely get off the bus?

(A) At stop 1
(B) At stop 2
(C) At stop 3
(D) At stop 4

68. Why does the man apologize?

(A) Some measurements must be taken again.
(B) A work estimate was not accurate.
(C) Some supplies have not arrived.
(D) An employee did not provide a bill.

69. What does the man think was a good idea?

(A) Using a different material
(B) Changing to another company
(C) Assessing a property's value
(D) Requesting a rush service

70. Look at the graphic. When will the man's team most likely come back?

(A) On Monday
(B) On Tuesday
(C) On Wednesday
(D) On Thursday

PART

4

PART 4 출제 경향 및 전략

한 사람이 말하는 짧은 담화를 듣고, 이와 관련된 3개의 문제에 알맞은 답을 고르는 파트이다. LC 전체 100문항 중에서 총 30문항(10개 담화문×3문항)이 출제된다.

담화 유형

전화 메시지 전화 건 사람이 자동 응답기에 남긴 음성 메시지, 회사나 관공서에서 미리 녹음해 둔 부재중 자동 응답 메시지

공지·안내 업무 관련 사내 공지 및 회의 발췌록, 운영 시간이나 특별 행사 등 공공장소에서 이루어지는 안내 방송

연설·강연 컨퍼런스나 개관식 같은 각종 행사에서의 기조연설이나 짧은 강연

광고·방송 제품이나 서비스, 업체 등을 홍보하기 위한 광고, 지역 뉴스나 일기 예보, 교통 안내 등의 방송 프로그램

관광·견학 유적지 같은 여행 장소나 공장 등 다양한 시설물에서 관광이나 견학을 이끄는 가이드의 안내

문제 유형

주제·목적 메시지 주제, 회의 목적 등 담화의 주제나 목적을 묻는 문제

화자·청자·장소 직업/근무지 등 화자나 청자의 신분을 묻거나, 담화가 일어나는 장소를 묻는 문제

세부사항 무엇/누구/언제 등 담화에서 언급된 구체적인 정보 또는 화자가 특정 대상에 대해 언급한 내용을 묻는 문제

제안·요청사항 화자가 청자에게 제안하거나 부탁/요청하는 것을 묻는 문제

다음에 할·일어날 일 화자나 청자가 다음에 할 일 또는 미래에 일어날 일을 묻는 문제

화자의 의도 파악 화자가 한 말의 의미나 그 말을 통해 암시하는 것, 또는 그것을 말한 이유를 묻는 문제

시각 자료 연계 목록/지도/그래프 등 다양한 유형의 시각 자료가 함께 제시되는 문제

STEP 1 | 질문 파악하기
담화가 나오기 전, 질문을 읽고 키워드를 통해 묻는 내용을 파악하고, 정답의 단서가 어느 부분에서 나올지 예상한다.

STEP 2 | 담화 속 단서 찾기
파악한 키워드를 바탕으로 담화를 들으면서 단서가 되는 내용을 찾는다.

STEP 3 | 정답 선택하기
담화에서 들은 단서 내용을 동일하게 또는 다른 어휘로 바꾸어 적절하게 표현한 보기를 정답으로 선택한다.

🎧 P4_01

71. Where does the speaker most likely work?
(A) At a bank
(B) At a pharmacy
(C) At a post office
(D) At a bookstore •

72. According to the speaker, what is a requirement of the job?
(A) Management experience •
(B) Sales training
(C) Computer skills
(D) A business network

73. What does the speaker ask the listener to do?
(A) Attend an interview •
(B) Upload a document
(C) Send a reference letter
(D) Read a contract

[71] Hi, this is Kate Edwards from Sapphire Bookstore. You recently applied for a sales clerk position with us. I'm sorry to say that we offered that job to someone else. However, we've just had an opening for a weekend supervisor. Your résumé said that [72] you have experience managing others. That's one of the main requirements of this role. I think you would be great for the job. So, [73] I'd like to invite you to an interview next week. Please call me back at 555-8763 if you're interested.

PART 4

해석

71. 화자는 어디에서 일하는 것 같은가?
(A) 은행에서
(B) 약국에서
(C) 우체국에서
(D) 서점에서

72. 화자에 따르면, 직무의 자격 요건은 무엇인가?
(A) 관리 경험
(B) 영업 교육
(C) 컴퓨터 능력
(D) 사업상의 인맥

73. 화자는 청자에게 무엇을 하라고 요청하는가?
(A) 면접에 참석하기
(B) 문서 업로드하기
(C) 추천서 보내기
(D) 계약서 읽기

[71] 안녕하세요, 저는 사파이어 서점의 케이트 에드워즈입니다. 당신은 최근 저희의 판매원 자리에 지원하셨습니다. 말씀드리기 죄송하지만 그 자리는 다른 분에게 제안을 드렸습니다. 하지만, 방금 주말 관리자 자리에 공석이 생겼습니다. 당신의 이력서에는 [72] 다른 사람들을 관리한 경험이 있다고 기재되어 있었습니다. [72] 그것이 이 역할의 주요 자격 요건들 중 하나입니다. 저는 당신이 이 직무에 아주 적합하실 거라고 생각합니다. 그래서, [73] 당신을 다음 주 면접에 모시고 싶습니다. 관심이 있으시다면 555-8763으로 제게 다시 전화 주시기 바랍니다.

핵심 POINT

1. 예약/주문 확인, 채용 제안, 업무 논의, 휴점 안내 등 정보를 전달하거나 문의사항을 남기는 메시지 내용이 주로 나오며, 인사말 및 본인 소개 → 전화 목적 및 세부사항 → 요청사항의 흐름으로 전개된다.

2. 전화 목적, 화자 정보, 요청사항을 묻는 문제가 자주 출제된다.

대표 유형 맛보기

🎧 P4_02

인사말 및 본인 소개 Hi, this message is for Hank Howard. [1] This is Tonya from the Jacobson Appliance Store.

전화 목적 및 세부사항 You stopped by yesterday and placed an order for one of our compact ovens. They're currently on sale, but [2] I believe one of our cashiers charged you incorrectly. She wasn't aware that the six-piece oven accessory set is included with all oven purchases during the promotion.

요청사항 [3] If you have time, could you please stop by our store so we can correct your receipt? If not, we can do this over the phone. Thank you for your understanding, and we apologize for the inconvenience.

안녕하세요, 이 메시지는 행크 하워드에게 전하는 것입니다. [1] 저는 제이콥슨 가전 매장의 토냐입니다.

고객님께서는 어제 매장에 들러서 저희 소형 오븐 중 하나를 주문하셨죠. 그것들이 현재 세일 중인데, [2] 저희 계산원 중 한 명이 고객님께 잘못 청구한 것 같습니다. 그녀는 판촉 기간 동안 모든 오븐 구매에 6개들이 오븐 부대용품 세트가 포함된다는 것을 모르고 있었습니다.

[3] 시간이 되시면, 저희가 영수증을 정정할 수 있도록 저희 매장에 들러 주시겠습니까? 그렇지 않으시면, 전화로 처리할 수 있습니다. 양해해 주셔서 감사드리며, 불편을 드려 죄송합니다.

1. Where does the speaker most likely work?
At a store

2. What is the purpose of the message?
To correct a mistake

3. What does the speaker ask the listener to do?
Visit the business

1. 화자는 어디에서 일하는 것 같은가?
상점에서

2. 메시지의 목적은 무엇인가?
실수를 바로잡기 위해

3. 화자는 청자에게 무엇을 해 달라고 요청하는가?
업체 방문하기

놓치지 말아야 할 단서 표현

화자 / 청자	Hi, **this is a message for** the technology department. **This is** Satomi **from** human resources. 안녕하세요, 이것은 기술부에 보내는 메시지입니다. 저는 인사부의 사토미입니다.
주제 / 목적	**I'm calling about** your novel, *Silver Fox* that came out last year. 작년에 출판된 당신의 소설 '은빛 여우'와 관련하여 전화 드립니다.
제안 / 요청사항	**Please** let us know which time of day you prefer. 어느 시간대가 좋으신지 저희에게 알려주세요.

담화를 듣고 알맞은 답을 고르세요.

1. Where does the speaker most likely work?

   (A) At a medical clinic
   (B) At a law firm
   (C) At an employment agency
   (D) At a software company

2. Why is the speaker calling?

   (A) To ask the listener for a reference
   (B) To ask the listener to give a presentation
   (C) To change an interview location
   (D) To make a job offer

3. What is the reason for a delay?

   (A) A committee must have a meeting.
   (B) A venue is fully booked.
   (C) A staff member will be unavailable.
   (D) Some supplies have not arrived.

4. What is the message mainly about?

   (A) A business trip overseas
   (B) The launch of a new product
   (C) An interview for a magazine
   (D) The relocation of a business

5. What does the speaker ask the listener to do on Thursday?

   (A) Sign a contract
   (B) Work later than usual
   (C) Bake additional items
   (D) Make a dinner reservation

6. Where will the speaker go this weekend?

   (A) To a training workshop
   (B) To a board meeting
   (C) To a music festival
   (D) To a job fair

7. What type of business is the listener calling?

   (A) An auto repair shop
   (B) A utility provider
   (C) A transportation company
   (D) An appliance store

8. What does the speaker imply when he says, "we are monitoring the situation"?

   (A) A departure schedule is uncertain.
   (B) A complaint will be filed.
   (C) Customer feedback will be assessed.
   (D) New policies have been adopted.

9. How can the listener stay updated?

   (A) By talking to a driver
   (B) By signing up for a newsletter
   (C) By sending an e-mail
   (D) By checking information online

PART 4

핵심 POINT

1. 업무나 매출/실적 또는 제도 변경과 관련된 회의 내용, 공공장소에서 특별 행사 및 영업시간이나 지연/변경을 알리는 안내 방송이 자주 나오며, 공지 주제 → 세부사항 → 요청사항/다음에 할 일의 흐름으로 전개된다.

2. 주제, 청자/장소, 요청사항 또는 다음에 할 일을 묻는 문제가 자주 출제된다.

대표 유형 맛보기

P4_04

공지 주제 To begin this meeting, I have some exciting news about Charles Kent.

세부사항 [1,2] This month, he sold 35 vehicles from our lot. [2] That's the most anyone has ever sold. The previous record was 28. Great job, Charles! This month, we're going to hold a contest to keep all of the sales staff motivated. The group that has the highest sales will win a prize.

요청사항/다음에 할 일 [3] I'll put you in your groups now, and then we can discuss the details.

찰스 켄트에 관한 흥분되는 소식으로 이번 회의를 시작하겠습니다.

[1,2] 이번 달에 그가 우리 지구에서 35대의 차량을 판매했습니다. [2] 그것은 지금까지 누군가가 판매한 수량 중 가장 많은 수치입니다. 이전 기록은 28대였습니다. 잘했어요, 찰스! 이번 달에, 모든 판매 직원들에게 동기를 부여하기 위해 대회를 열 것입니다. 판매 실적이 가장 높은 그룹이 상을 타게 될 것입니다.

[3] 제가 지금 여러분을 그룹으로 나누고, 그런 다음 자세한 이야기를 나눠보겠습니다.

1. Where do the listeners most likely work?
   At a car dealership

2. What has Charles Kent recently done?
   He set a new sales record.

3. What will the speaker do next?
   Assign the listeners to groups

1. 청자들은 어디에서 일하는 것 같은가?
   자동차 대리점에서

2. 찰스 켄트는 최근에 무엇을 했는가?
   그는 새로운 판매 기록을 세웠다.

3. 화자는 다음에 무엇을 할 것인가?
   청자들을 그룹에 배치하기

놓치지 말아야 할 단서 표현

청자/장소	**Attention** Norton Department Store shoppers.　노턴 백화점 쇼핑객 여러분께 안내 말씀 드립니다.
주제/목적	**I'm happy to announce** that our new line of home office desks is selling very well. 우리의 새로운 홈 오피스 책상이 아주 잘 팔리고 있다는 것을 알려드리게 되어 기쁩니다.
제안/요청사항	Now, **I'd like everyone to** help with a deep cleaning of the refrigerators. 자, 여러분 모두가 냉장고를 깨끗이 청소하는 것을 도와주셨으면 합니다.
다음에 할 일	**We're going to** hold a company party next Thursday evening. 다음 주 목요일 저녁에 회사 파티를 열 거예요.

PRACTICE

담화를 듣고 알맞은 답을 고르세요.

1. Where most likely are the listeners?

(A) At a clothing shop
(B) At a hardware store
(C) At an electronics store
(D) At a bookstore

2. What does the speaker say is offered to loyalty program members?

(A) A free item
(B) Discount coupons
(C) Express delivery
(D) Advance notice of sales

3. What will begin next Monday?

(A) Extended business hours
(B) Some construction
(C) An anniversary event
(D) A clearance sale

4. What will be delivered next Friday?

(A) Business cards
(B) Potted plants
(C) Light refreshments
(D) Leather sofas

5. What is mentioned about productivity?

(A) It has improved recently at the office.
(B) It can be increased through regular breaks.
(C) It directly results in higher profits.
(D) It is the focus of the new management team.

6. According to the speaker, what is available at the reception desk?

(A) A contract
(B) A survey form
(C) A catalog
(D) An updated schedule

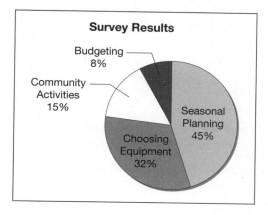

Survey Results

- Budgeting 8%
- Community Activities 15%
- Seasonal Planning 45%
- Choosing Equipment 32%

7. What kind of club are the listeners members of?

(A) Painting
(B) Sewing
(C) Cycling
(D) Gardening

8. Look at the graphic. According to the speaker, which workshop will likely be held first?

(A) Seasonal Planning
(B) Choosing Equipment
(C) Community Activities
(D) Budgeting

9. What does the speaker ask the listeners to do?

(A) Update some contact information
(B) Recommend venues for a workshop
(C) Explain their survey answers
(D) Recruit new group members

핵심 POINT

1. 각종 모임 및 행사에서 일어나는 기조연설 또는 워크숍이나 학회에서 특정 주제에 대해 설명/교육하는 내용이 주로 나오며, 인사말 및 본인 소개 → 행사/강연 주제 → 세부사항 → 요청사항/다음에 할 일 순으로 전개된다.

2. 주제, 화자/청자/장소, 요청사항 또는 다음에 할 일을 묻는 문제가 자주 출제된다.

대표 유형 맛보기   🎧 P4_06

인사말 및 본인 소개 Hello, everyone. My name is Janet, and I'll be leading this workshop.

강연 주제 [1] Today you'll learn how to use the latest project management software.

세부사항 There are numerous tasks needed [2] when developing advertising campaigns for your clients. This program will help you manage resources, create custom images, track a brand's success, and more.

요청사항/다음에 할 일 At the end, [3] I'll ask you to provide your opinions about the parts you found most helpful.

안녕하세요, 여러분. 제 이름은 재닛이고, 제가 이번 워크숍을 이끌 것입니다.

[1] 오늘 여러분은 최신 프로젝트 관리 소프트웨어를 사용하는 법을 배우게 됩니다.

[2] 여러분의 고객들을 위해서 광고 캠페인을 전개할 때 필요한 수많은 작업들이 있습니다. 이 프로그램은 여러분이 자원을 관리하고, 맞춤 이미지를 만들고, 브랜드의 성공을 추적하는 것 외에도 많은 것을 도와줄 것입니다.

끝날 때, [3] 여러분이 가장 도움이 되었다고 생각하신 부분에 대한 의견을 제공해 주실 것을 요청드리겠습니다.

---

1. What is the topic of the workshop?
   How to use some software

2. What industry do the listeners most likely work in?
   Advertising

3. What are the listeners asked to do?
   Share their feedback

1. 워크숍의 주제는 무엇인가?
   소프트웨어를 사용하는 법

2. 청자들은 어떤 업계에서 일할 것 같은가?
   광고

3. 청자들은 무엇을 하라고 요청받는가?
   그들의 의견 공유하기

놓치지 말아야 할 단서 표현

장소 / 주제	**Thanks for attending** this workshop on making candles. **Today we'll focus on** scented candles. 양초 제작 워크숍에 참석해 주셔서 감사합니다. 오늘 우리는 향초에 초점을 맞추겠습니다.
화자 / 청자	**As** a software engineer, I design computer programs that help real estate agents **like you**. 소프트웨어 엔지니어로서, 저는 여러분과 같은 부동산 중개인들을 돕는 컴퓨터 프로그램을 설계합니다.
제안 / 요청사항	**Don't forget to** check your programs for the list of topics, speakers, and locations. 행사 계획표에서 주제, 발표자, 장소 목록을 확인하는 것을 잊지 마십시오.
다음에 할 일	Before we begin the discussion, **let's** look at an aerial view of the railway in this short video. 토론을 시작하기 전에, 공중에서 내려다 본 철도 전경을 담고 있는 짧은 영상을 보시겠습니다.

PRACTICE

담화를 듣고 알맞은 답을 고르세요.

1. What event is taking place?

(A) An art festival
(B) A fund-raising event
(C) A music lesson
(D) A baking contest

2. What does the organization plan to do?

(A) Replace a roof
(B) Train some volunteers
(C) Change its opening hours
(D) Provide online services

3. What does the speaker encourage the listeners to do?

(A) Watch a presentation
(B) Purchase clothing
(C) Enjoy refreshments
(D) Come back again soon

4. Who is the speaker?

(A) A government employee
(B) A university professor
(C) A textbook editor
(D) A software specialist

5. According to the speaker, why were certain debate participants selected?

(A) They have recently published books.
(B) They come from different countries.
(C) They are considered to be experts.
(D) They have started their own business.

6. What does the speaker imply when she says, "this session will be recorded"?

(A) Questions can be answered at the end.
(B) Note-taking is not necessary.
(C) Cell phones should be put away.
(D) The audience should remain seated.

7. What is the topic of the seminar?

(A) Time-saving methods
(B) Communication skills
(C) Retirement planning
(D) Job hunting

8. Why does the speaker thank some of the listeners?

(A) They registered early.
(B) They changed seats.
(C) They set up a room.
(D) They submitted questions.

9. Why does the speaker mention the side entrance?

(A) Materials for the event can be found there.
(B) It will remain locked throughout the seminar.
(C) Beverages are available for participants there.
(D) It can be used in case of emergency.

핵심 POINT

1. 제품이나 서비스, 업체 등을 홍보하는 광고는 주의 환기 및 광고 대상 → 특징 및 장점 → 할인 혜택 등의 추가 정보 순으로, 지역 뉴스 및 라디오 방송은 프로그램 및 주제 → 주요 소식 → 다음 방송 안내 순으로 전개되는 경우가 많다.

2. 광고 대상 및 방송 주제, 관련 세부사항을 묻는 문제가 자주 출제된다.

대표 유형 맛보기

🎧 P4_08

주의 환기 및 광고 대상 Do you have customers visit your business in person? It's important to make a good impression with a modern-looking office space. ¹ That's why you should consider moving to the Doyle Business Complex.

특징 및 장점 ² We're close to Newport subway station and several bus stops, so it is easy for your employees and customers to get here, even if they don't drive.

추가 정보 We have a wide variety of unit sizes available, ³ e-mail our property manager at inquiries@ doylebusiness.com to find out more. We guarantee that we'll get back to you within two business days.

고객들이 직접 여러분의 업체를 방문하게 하시나요? 현대식 사무 공간으로 좋은 인상을 주는 것은 중요합니다. ¹ 그래서 도일 비즈니스 복합 단지로 이사하는 것을 고려해야 하는 것입니다.

² 저희는 뉴포트 지하철역 및 여러 버스 정류장과 가까워서, 운전을 하지 않더라도 직원들이나 고객들이 오기 편합니다.

저희는 다양한 크기의 세대를 보유하고 있으니, ³ 더 많이 알아보시려면 inquiries@doylebusiness. com으로 저희 건물 관리자에게 이메일을 보내세요. 영업일로 이틀 이내에 회신드릴 것을 약속합니다.

1. What is being advertised?
An office complex

2. What benefit of the site does the speaker highlight?
Access to public transportation

3. According to the speaker, how can the listeners get more information?
By sending an e-mail

1. 무엇이 광고되고 있는가?
사무 복합 단지

2. 화자는 장소의 어떤 이점을 강조하는가?
대중교통 접근성

3. 화자에 따르면, 청자들은 어떻게 더 많은 정보를 얻을 수 있는가?
이메일을 보냄으로써

놓치지 말아야 할 단서 표현

방송 주제	**On today's episode, we'll be taking** a deep dive into the topic of making a career change. 오늘 방송에서는 진로 변경이라는 주제에 대해 자세히 알아보겠습니다.
광고 대상	**Looking for** a great place to exercise? **Try** Salt Creek Fitness Center on Beach Avenue. 운동하기 좋은 장소를 찾고 계신가요? 비치 가에 있는 솔트 크릭 피트니스 센터를 이용해 보세요.
할인 혜택	**We are offering a special discount** to students who show their university identification cards. 대학교 학생증을 제시하는 학생들에게 특별 할인을 제공합니다.

담화를 듣고 알맞은 답을 고르세요.

1. What kind of business is being advertised?

(A) An employment agency
(B) A computer repair shop
(C) A health-care clinic
(D) A car rental service

2. Why is a business celebrating?

(A) It was nominated for an award.
(B) It will open a new branch.
(C) It has been in business for twenty years.
(D) It has acquired a competitor.

3. What do the listeners need to do to get a discount?

(A) Attend an in-person event
(B) Sign up for a newsletter
(C) Complete a survey
(D) Make an appointment

---

4. What is the podcast mainly about?

(A) Career changes
(B) Writing skills
(C) Medical breakthroughs
(D) Nutrition advice

5. What did Maya Dalavi recently do?

(A) She started a Web site.
(B) She taught a course.
(C) She won a competition.
(D) She published a magazine article.

6. What does the speaker say about podcast membership?

(A) It can be canceled anytime.
(B) It charges a monthly fee.
(C) It provides additional benefits.
(D) It helps hire new staff.

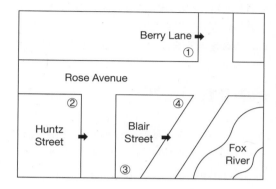

7. What is the broadcast mainly about?

(A) The repairs of a road
(B) The opening of a department store
(C) The construction of a sports facility
(D) The route of an upcoming parade

8. What has a company donated?

(A) Some paintings
(B) Some seats
(C) Some lumber
(D) Some machinery

9. Look at the graphic. Where will the bus stop be located?

(A) Location 1
(B) Location 2
(C) Location 3
(D) Location 4

PART 4

UNIT 20　관광 · 견학

핵심 POINT

1. 버스 투어나 유적지 답사 등의 관광을 이끄는 내용 또는 공장/박물관 같은 시설물에서 견학을 안내하는 가이드의 담화가 주로 나오며, 인사말 및 본인 소개 → 관광/견학 세부사항 → 당부 및 다음 일정 안내와 같은 흐름으로 전개된다.

2. 화자/장소, 제안/요청사항 또는 다음에 할 일을 묻는 문제가 자주 출제된다.

대표 유형 맛보기

🎧 P4_10

인사말 및 본인 소개 [1] Welcome to Bella Beverage Company. I'm Tina, your guide for this tour.

관광/견학 세부사항 Now, we would usually begin with a video about the company's history, but [2] I'm sorry our projector is not working. I'll send you all a link so you can watch it on our Web site later.

당부 및 다음 일정 안내 [3] And at the end of the tour, we'll stop by the gift shop. There you can buy items with our logo such as T-shirts, tote bags, and calendars as a reminder of your visit today. As we get started, please stay with the group at all times, as machinery is currently in operation.

[1] 벨라 음료 회사에 오신 것을 환영합니다. 저는 이 견학의 가이드인 티나입니다.

자, 보통은 회사의 역사에 관한 영상으로 시작하는데, [2] 죄송하지만 프로젝터가 작동하지 않습니다. 나중에 저희 웹사이트에서 보실 수 있도록 여러분 모두에게 링크를 보내드리겠습니다.

[3] 그리고 견학이 끝나면, 기념품 가게에 들를 겁니다. 그곳에서 오늘 방문을 기념하는 티셔츠, 토트백, 그리고 달력 등과 같은 저희 회사의 로고가 새겨진 물품들을 구입하실 수 있습니다. 이제 시작을 할 건데요, 현재 기계가 작동 중이므로 항상 그룹과 함께 있어 주시기 바랍니다.

1. Where is the tour taking place?
At a beverage factory

2. Why does the speaker apologize to the listeners?
Some equipment is not working.

3. What can the listeners do at the end of the tour?
Purchase some souvenirs

1. 견학은 어디에서 일어나고 있는가?
음료 공장에서

2. 화자는 왜 청자들에게 사과하는가?
일부 장비가 작동하지 않는다.

3. 청자들은 견학이 끝날 때 무엇을 할 수 있는가?
기념품 구입하기

놓치지 말아야 할 단서 표현

장소 / 화자	**Welcome to** this virtual tour of Lakeview Medical Center. **I'm** the director of the hospital, Dr. Dirk Hertz. 레이크뷰 의료 센터의 가상 투어에 오신 것을 환영합니다. 저는 병원장인 더크 헤르츠입니다.
제안 / 요청사항	**I recommend** stopping at the top of the mountain for bird watching. 산 정상에 들러 새를 관찰해 보실 것을 추천합니다.
다음에 할 일	**Next, I'll** show you the latest models of our solar panels so you understand how they work. 다음으로, 태양 전지판이 어떻게 작동하는지 여러분이 이해하실 수 있도록 그것의 최신 모델을 보여드리겠습니다.

PRACTICE

담화를 듣고 알맞은 답을 고르세요.

1. Who most likely is the speaker?

(A) A tour guide
(B) A film director
(C) A store manager
(D) An art critic

2. What will happen at three o'clock?

(A) Some singers will perform.
(B) Some food will be served.
(C) A business will close.
(D) A video will be shown.

3. What is The First Step?

(A) A club
(B) A book
(C) A podcast
(D) A play

---

4. Why is Hamilton Manor famous?

(A) It has been the filming location for movies.
(B) It was designed by a prominent architect.
(C) It is the venue for a popular festival.
(D) It has an extensive art collection.

5. According to the speaker, what do visitors like to do at Hamilton Manor?

(A) Make a wish
(B) Sample food
(C) Go swimming
(D) Collect flowers

6. What are the listeners asked to do in one hour?

(A) Take a group picture
(B) Attend a performance
(C) Get back on the bus
(D) Meet at a café

7. Where does the tour take place?

(A) At a manufacturing facility
(B) At a nature park
(C) At a concert hall
(D) At a shopping center

8. What did Annette Harvey do?

(A) She built a bridge.
(B) She filmed a commercial.
(C) She designed a building.
(D) She donated some money.

9. What does the speaker mean when she says, "that area is closed to visitors"?

(A) The tour will be shorter than usual.
(B) A partial refund will be issued.
(C) The listeners should not worry.
(D) Some signs should be followed.

PART 4

PART 4
Directions: You will hear some talks given by a single speaker. You will be asked to answer three questions about what the speaker says in each talk. Select the best response to each question and mark the letter (A), (B), (C), or (D) on your answer sheet. The talks will not be printed in your test book and will be spoken only one time.

---

71. What kind of business is being advertised?

(A) A car rental company
(B) A dance studio
(C) A sporting goods store
(D) A garden center

72. According to the advertisement, who can get a discount?

(A) Business owners
(B) Card holders
(C) Charity workers
(D) University students

73. What is the business known for?

(A) Its helpful advice
(B) Its large facility
(C) Its numerous branches
(D) Its modern Web site

74. Who is the speaker?

(A) A property manager
(B) A real estate agent
(C) A safety inspector
(D) A construction worker

75. What does the speaker imply when he says, "I'm sure it's full of furniture"?

(A) An entrance may be blocked.
(B) A storage area is probably in use.
(C) Completing a task may be difficult.
(D) Choosing a style will take time.

76. Why should the listener call the speaker back?

(A) To pay a deposit
(B) To confirm a color
(C) To provide a reference
(D) To select a convenient day

77. Who most likely are the listeners?

(A) Product reviewers
(B) Sales agents
(C) Job candidates
(D) Newspaper journalists

78. What aspect of the product is the speaker proud of?

(A) It is produced domestically.
(B) It uses very little packaging.
(C) It is available in many countries.
(D) It was developed by scientists.

79. What will the speaker give the listeners after the session?

(A) A box of samples
(B) A complimentary meal
(C) A discount coupon
(D) A certificate of completion

80. Who is Valentino Arruda?

(A) A scientist
(B) A painter
(C) An author
(D) A chef

81. According to the speaker, what inspires Mr. Arruda?

(A) Listening to music
(B) Traveling abroad
(C) Working with experts
(D) Spending time in nature

82. What does the speaker mean when he says, "he has a very busy schedule"?

(A) A cancellation could not be avoided.
(B) A talk with a guest will be brief.
(C) The interview is a rare opportunity.
(D) Mr. Arruda has started a new business.

83. Who is giving the talk?

(A) A professional athlete
(B) A financial advisor
(C) A structural engineer
(D) The city's mayor

84. According to the speaker, what have some people proposed?

(A) Using recycled materials
(B) Changing a roof design
(C) Increasing admission fees
(D) Expanding a parking structure

85. What will the listeners most likely do next?

(A) Review a schedule
(B) Watch a demonstration
(C) Share their questions
(D) Meet a new colleague

86. What is the broadcast mainly about?

(A) Designing a Web site
(B) Enhancing creativity
(C) Improving communication skills
(D) Developing healthy habits

87. What does the speaker say about Ms. Morrison's classes?

(A) They are at full capacity.
(B) They are aimed at beginners.
(C) They are available online.
(D) They are offered at no charge.

88. What does the speaker say will happen during the next show?

(A) A contest winner will be announced.
(B) A new host will be introduced.
(C) Some listeners' questions will be answered.
(D) Some event tickets will be sold.

GO ON TO THE NEXT PAGE

89. Where does the speaker most likely work?

(A) At a photography studio
(B) At an auto-repair shop
(C) At a stationery store
(D) At a furniture factory

90. Why does the speaker say, "we've had a lot of cancellations"?

(A) To explain a decision
(B) To confirm her availability
(C) To make a complaint
(D) To suggest more advertising

91. What does the speaker offer to do for the staff?

(A) Order a catered meal
(B) Provide a day off
(C) Let some people leave early
(D) Hold a training event

92. Where are the listeners?

(A) At an employee orientation
(B) At a grand opening
(C) At a health fair
(D) At a fund-raising dinner

93. According to the speaker, how does the product help the user?

(A) By tracking shipments
(B) By reducing expenses
(C) By charging quickly
(D) By sending an alert

94. What did the speaker learn from a survey?

(A) That a modern design was needed
(B) That a price was too high
(C) That users were concerned about safety
(D) That some instructions were confusing

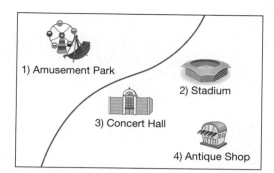

1) Amusement Park

2) Stadium

3) Concert Hall

4) Antique Shop

Product Fact Sheet		
Line 1	Cost	$800,000
Line 2	Architect	Steven Gray
Line 3	Completion Date	September 1
Line 4	Size	1,200 square meters

95. According to the speaker, what has caused a problem?

(A) Heavy traffic
(B) Severe weather
(C) A construction delay
(D) A computer error

96. Look at the graphic. Where does the speaker recommend going this afternoon?

(A) Location 1
(B) Location 2
(C) Location 3
(D) Location 4

97. What can the listeners do at dinner?

(A) Request a partial refund
(B) Express activity preferences
(C) Take an additional tour
(D) Choose meals for the next day

98. What kind of building is most likely being expanded?

(A) An art gallery
(B) A school
(C) A fitness facility
(D) A post office

99. What will the listeners do at the next meeting?

(A) Volunteer for an event
(B) View some blueprints
(C) Meet a new employee
(D) Provide budget reports

100. Look at the graphic. Which line has been changed?

(A) Line 1
(B) Line 2
(C) Line 3
(D) Line 4

PART

5

절과 문장

두 개 이상의 단어가 모이되 주어와 동사의 구조를 갖추고 있을 경우 절이라 한다. 하나의 절은 하나의 문장(단문)을 이루기도 하며, 두 개 이상의 절이 모여 복문, 중문을 이룬다.

복문(complex sentence)은 독립적으로 쓸 수 있는 주절과 독립적으로 쓸 수 없는 종속절로 이루어진다. 종속절은 시간이나 이유 등을 나타내는 부사절로 쓰이거나 주어, 보어, 목적어 구실을 하는 명사절, 명사를 수식하는 형용사절 역할을 한다. 중문(compound sentence)은 독립해서 쓸 수 있는 두 개 이상의 대등한 절로 이루어지며, and, but, so 등의 등위 접속사가 절과 절을 이어 준다.

단문

BT News advertises heavily on social media.
　　주어　　　　동사　　　　부사　　　　　전치사구

BT News는 소셜 미디어에 대대적으로 광고를 한다.

복문

Although the building is old, it is well maintained.
　　　　부사절　　　　　　　　　　주절(main clause)

그 건물은 오래되었지만 관리가 잘 되어 있다.

➡ 부사절은 시간, 조건, 이유, 양보 등을 설명한다. 여기에서는 Although가 이끄는 절이 양보를 나타내는 부사어 역할을 한다.

The red light indicates that the microphone is turned on.
　　主어　　　　　　동사　　　　　　　명사절

빨간 불은 마이크가 켜져 있다는 것을 나타낸다.

➡ 명사절은 문장에서 주어, 보어, 목적어 역할을 한다. 여기에서는 that이 이끄는 절이 목적어 역할을 한다.

Ms. Morris is replacing Mr. Khan who is retiring this month.
　　주어　　　　동사　　　　목적어　　　　　형용사절

Ms. Morris는 이번 달에 은퇴하게 될 Mr. Khan을 대신할 것이다.

➡ 형용사절은 명사를 수식하는 역할을 한다. 여기에서는 who 이하의 관계사절이 Mr. Khan이라는 명사를 수식한다.

중문

The survey was sent to 500 people, but only a few responded.
　　독립해서 쓸 수 있는 절　　　　　　독립해서 쓸 수 있는 절

그 설문지는 500명에게 발송되었는데 극소수만 응답해 줬다.

➡ 두 개의 완전한 문장이 but이라는 접속사에 의해 대등하게 연결되어 있다.

주어 + 동사

Some participants arrived late. 몇몇 참가자가 늦게 도착했다.
　　　주어　　　　　동사　부사어

➡ 주어 자리에는 명사, 대명사 및 명사 역할을 하는 어구가 온다. 부사어는 주로 동작이나 상황에 대한 추가적인 정보(시간, 장소, 방법, 정도, 빈도, 태도)를 제공하며, 필수 성분은 아니지만 부사어가 빠졌을 때 의미가 제대로 전달되지 않을 수 있다.

주어 + 동사 + 주격 보어

The data was incorrect. 그 데이터는 부정확했다.
　주어　　동사　　주격 보어

Ms. Kim became head of the finance department last year. Ms. Kim은 작년에 재무 부장이 되었다.
　주어　　동사　　　　　주격 보어　　　　　　　　부사어

➡ 보어는 주어와 동사만으로는 뜻이 완전하지 못할 때, 그 불완전한 의미를 보충해 준다. 보어 자리에는 형용사, 전치사구, 명사, 대명사, to부정사, 동명사, 명사절 등이 올 수 있다.

주어 + 동사 + 목적어

Mr. Carter will receive a replacement this afternoon. Mr. Carter는 오늘 오후에 교체품을 받을 것이다.
　주어　　　동사　　　목적어　　　　부사어

They will begin shipping internationally next month. 그들은 다음 달에 국제 배송을 시작할 것이다.
　주어　　동사　　목적어　　　부사어　　　부사어

➡ 타동사는 목적어를 취하며, 목적어 자리에는 명사, 대명사, to부정사, 동명사, 명사절 등이 올 수 있다.

주어 + 동사 + 간접목적어 + 직접목적어

LY Clothing offers new customers free delivery. LY Clothing은 신규 고객에게 무료 배송을 제공한다.
　주어　　　동사　　간목　　　직목

➡ 간접목적어는 '~에게', 직접목적어는 '~을/를'로 해석되며, give, send, tell, offer 등의 동사가 토익에 주로 쓰인다.

주어 + 동사 + 목적어 + 목적격 보어

Many critics found the movie enjoyable. 많은 비평가는 그 영화가 재미있다고 생각했다.
　주어　　　동사　　목적어　　목적격 보어

The manager asked Ms. Yi to review the report. 그 부장은 Ms. Yi에게 보고서를 검토해 달라고 요청했다.
　주어　　동사　목적어　　목적격 보어

➡ 목적격 보어는 목적어를 보완해 주며, 형용사, 분사, 명사, to부정사, 원형동사 등이 쓰인다.

PART 5 출제 경향 및 전략

PART 5는 크게 문법 문제와 어휘 문제로 나눌 수 있다. PART 5 문제는 모두 한 문장으로 되어 있는 데다 30문제밖에 되지 않기 때문에 RC 파트 중 제일 쉬운 파트라고 생각할 수 있지만 실제로는 만점 받기에 가장 어려운 파트가 바로 PART 5이다. 문법 문제의 비중이 높았던 과거와 달리 요즘에는 문법과 어휘가 거의 비슷한 비중으로 출제되고 있는 데다 어휘 문제는 소위 꼼수가 잘 통하지 않고 영어가 모국어가 아닌 입장에서는 왜 오답인지 선뜻 이해되지 않는 문제가 매회 1~2문제 정도 나오기 때문이다. 따라서 목표 점수가 700점대라면 잘 모르는 문제는 과감하게 버리고 PART 5를 늦어도 10분 내에 풀어야 PART 6와 PART 7을 푸는 시간을 확보할 수 있다.

문법 문제

PART 5 문제를 풀 때는 선택지를 먼저 훑어보는 것이 좋다. 선택지가 여러 품사나 어형으로 구성되어 있다면 문법 문제이므로 빈칸과 주변 단어들과의 관계를 파악하여 알맞은 것을 정답으로 고른다. 토익 문법 문제는 품사/어형 고르기부터 가정법, 도치 구문과 같이 다소 난이도가 높은 문제까지 광범위하게 출제되지만 어려운 고급 문법은 출제되는 일이 거의 없기 때문에 여기서는 가장 빈출되는 몇 가지 유형만 소개한다.

알맞은 품사/어형 고르기

동일한 어근을 공유하는 명사, 부사, 형용사, 동사, 분사, to부정사, 동명사 등으로 선택지가 구성된 문제이다. 알맞은 품사나 어형을 고르는 문제는 굳이 해석을 하지 않아도 정답을 고를 수 있는 경우가 많다.

Mitch Stallings set the ------- goal of increasing revenues by 40% this year.

(A) ambitiously (B) ambition
(C) most ambitiously (D) ambitious

해석 Mitch Stallings는 올해 수익을 40% 늘린다는 야심 찬 목표를 세웠다.

❶ 빈칸 앞에 정관사 the가 있고 뒤에는 명사 goal이 이어지므로 빈칸은 명사를 수식하는 자리이다.

❷ 선택지 중 형용사인 (D) ambitious가 정답이다.

최근 1~2년 사이에 품사/어형을 판단하고 난 후 어휘까지 확인해야 하는 복합 문제의 출제율이 증가했다. 이때는 별 수 없이 해석까지 해야 하지만 무난하게 풀 수 있는 수준으로 출제된다.

The north wing of the Hawkins Library houses a ------- of rare books.

(A) collect (B) collectively
(C) collector (D) collection

해석 Hawkins Library의 북관에는 희귀 서적들이 소장되어 있다.

❶ 빈칸 앞에 부정관사 a가 있고 뒤에는 전치사구가 이어지므로 빈칸은 명사 자리이다.

❷ 선택지 중 명사인 (C) collector와 (D) collection이 정답 후보인데, 문맥상 희귀 서적들이 소장되어 있다는 내용이 되는 게 자연스러우므로 '수집(품), 소장(품)'을 뜻하는 (D)가 정답이다.

-ly로 끝나지 않는 부사나 전치사, 접속사 등과 같이 생김새가 전혀 다른 품사들로 선택지가 구성되기도 한다. 이런 경우를 대비하여 -ly로 끝나지 않는 부사(➔ p.107)와 전치사 및 접속사(➔ p.108)는 별도로 암기해 두는 것이 좋다.

The Web site is ------- unavailable as it is undergoing routine maintenance.

(A) now (B) beside
(C) until (D) of

해석 그 웹사이트는 정기 점검을 하고 있기 때문에 현재 이용할 수 없다.

❶ 빈칸은 be동사 is와 형용사 unavailable 사이의 부사 자리이다.

❷ 따라서 (A) now가 정답이다.
  (A) 부사; 접속사 (B) 전치사
  (C) 접속사; 전치사 (D) 전치사

알맞은 대명사 고르기

대명사 격을 묻는 문제도 출제된다. 3초 문제라고 할 정도로 난이도가 매우 낮은 편이기 때문에 문장 내 빈칸의 역할만 빠르게 파악하여 답을 고르고 다음 문제로 넘어가야 한다.

The candidate's previous job involved customer service, so ------- has the right experience for this role.

(A) himself
(B) his
(C) him
(D) he

❶ 빈칸 앞에 접속사 so가 있고 뒤에는 동사 has가 이어지므로 빈칸에는 주어 역할을 할 수 있는 말이 들어가야 한다.

❷ 따라서 선택지 중 주격 대명사인 (D) he가 정답이다.

해석 그 지원자의 이전 직업은 고객 서비스와 관련이 있기 때문에 이 직무에 적합한 경력을 가지고 있습니다.

알맞은 동사 형태 고르기

선택지가 동사의 활용형으로 구성된 문제이다. 수 일치, 태, 그리고 시제 중에서 한 가지를 묻거나 두 가지를 복합적으로 묻는 문제가 출제된다. 복합 문제일 때는 수 일치 여부를 먼저 판단한 다음 태 또는 시제를 따지는 것이 효율적인 문제 풀이 방법이다.

Our restaurant's seating area ------- to offer outdoor dining when the weather is favorable.

(A) renovate
(B) were renovating
(C) is renovating
(D) has been renovated

❶ 주어 Our restaurant's seating area가 단수이므로 동사도 단수형으로 수 일치해야 한다.

❷ (C) is renovating과 (D) has been renovated가 정답 후보인데, 빈칸 뒤에 목적어가 없으므로 [be + 과거분사] 형태의 수동태인 (D)가 정답이다.

해석 저희 식당의 좌석 구역은 날씨가 좋을 때 야외 식사를 제공하기 위해 보수되었습니다.

어휘 문제

선택지가 품사는 같지만 각기 다른 단어로 구성되어 있다면 어휘 문제이므로 문장 전체의 맥락을 파악하여 문맥상 가장 자연스러운 것을 정답으로 고른다. 한두 번 읽어도 답이 나오지 않을 때는 과감하게 포기하고 다음 문제로 넘어간 후 PART 7까지 마치고 나서 시간이 남았을 때 다시 풀어 본다. PART 5의 성공 여부가 사실상 어휘에 달려 있다고 해도 과언이 아닐 정도로 어휘 문제의 비중이 높아졌기 때문에 단어를 많이 암기해 둬야 한다.

Mr. Feldman has been participating ------- in all of VB Auto's professional development workshops.

(A) currently
(B) actively
(C) absolutely
(D) finally

❶ 선택지가 여러 부사로 구성되어 있는 것으로 보아 어휘 문제이므로 문장 전체를 읽으며 맥락을 파악한다.

❷ 문맥상 워크숍에 적극적으로 참여했다는 내용이 되는 게 자연스러우므로 (B) actively가 정답이다.

해석 Mr. Feldman은 VB Auto의 모든 전문성 개발 워크숍에 적극적으로 참여했다.

어휘 문제는 빈칸 주변의 단어로 정답 단서를 찾을 수 있는 경우도 있다. 따라서 단어를 암기할 때는 단일 어휘보다는 콜로케이션으로 외우는 것이 도움이 된다.

The sales manager has successfully negotiated contracts with a ------- variety of corporate clients.

(A) long
(B) wide
(C) tall
(D) fast

❶ 선택지가 여러 형용사로 구성되어 있는 것으로 보아 어휘 문제이므로 문장 전체를 읽으며 맥락을 파악한다.

❷ a variety of는 wide와 어울려 쓰이는 표현이므로 (B)가 정답이다.

해석 그 판매 담당자는 다양한 분야의 기업 고객들과 성공적으로 계약을 협상해 왔다.

UNIT 01 명사

1 관사/한정사/형용사 + 명사

◆ 명사는 관사, 한정사, 형용사, 분사 등의 수식어 뒤에 위치한다.

Please reply to this e-mail to verify **your** <u>attendance</u> / attend at the event.
귀하의 행사 참석을 확정하기 위해 이 이메일에 답장 주시기 바랍니다.

◆ 빈칸에 들어갈 말이 가산명사 단수형인지 복수형인지 판별해야 할 경우에는 빈칸 앞에 부정관사가 있는지 확인한다. 부정관사가 있다면 가산명사 단수형이, 없다면 복수형이 정답이다.

The charity event was **a** big <u>success</u> / successes.
그 자선 행사는 매우 성공적이었다.

토익 빈출 가산명사	토익 빈출 불가산명사	형태가 유사한 가산명사와 불가산명사	
an opening 공석	support 지원, 지지	a permit 허가증	permission 허가
an appointment 약속, 예약	consent 동의	a process 과정	processing 처리
results 성과	access 접근 (권한)	a cause 원인	caution 주의, 조심
benefits (급여 외) 수당	manufacture 제조, 생산	an account 계좌	accounting 회계

CHECK-UP

1. Kenway Construction has begun keeping a greater <u>supply</u> / supplies of materials on hand in case additional projects become available.

2. Due to unexpected equipment issues, Retha Dentistry is not scheduling appointment / <u>appointments</u> until next week.

2 주어와 목적어 역할을 하는 명사

◆ 명사는 주어 자리나 타동사와 전치사의 목적어 자리에 위치할 수 있다. 빈칸 주변의 정보만으로 빈칸에 들어갈 말이 무엇인지 판단하기 어려울 때는 빈칸 자체가 문장에서 어떤 역할을 하는지 파악해야 한다.

<u>Access</u> / Accessible to the Web site **was** blocked.
그 웹사이트에 접근이 차단되었다.

The interior designer **provided** <u>suggestions</u> / suggest for remodeling the store.
그 인테리어 디자이너는 상점을 리모델링하는 데 몇 가지 제안을 했다.

The new branch will not be **in** <u>operation</u> / operate until September 1.
새 지점은 9월 1일이 되어야 운영될 것이다.

CHECK-UP

3. Many event planners have expressed <u>surprisingly</u> / surprise at the rental fee for the Villa Hall.

4. <u>Delivers</u> / Deliveries from Del Logistics occasionally arrive two or three days ahead of schedule.

3 사람 명사와 사물/추상 명사

◆ 빈칸이 명사 자리이고 정답 후보로 뜻이 다른 명사 두 개가 남는다면 문장 전체를 읽고서 문맥에 어울리는 명사를 골라야 한다.

사람 명사	사물/추상 명사	사람 명사	사물/추상 명사
publisher 출판인, 출판사	publication 출판(물), 발행	accountant 회계사	account 계좌; 계정; 거래처; 거래
subscriber 구독자	subscription 구독(료)	depositor 예금주	deposit 보증금
producer 생산자, 제작자	production 생산	contributor 기여자	contribution 기여
electrician 전기 기사	electricity 전기	director 임원; 감독	direction 방향; 지시
consultant 고문, 상담가	consultation 상담; 협의, 상의	instructor 강사	instructions 설명(서); 지시
applicant 지원자	application 지원(서), 신청(서)	committee 위원회	commitment 헌신, 전념; 약속

<u>Applications</u> / Applicants should be sent to hr@electronix.com by February 20.
지원서는 2월 20일까지 hr@electronix.com으로 보내 주세요.

Our records show that your <u>electricity</u> / electrician usage has increased significantly recently.
저희 기록에 귀하의 전기 사용량이 최근 상당히 증가한 것으로 나타납니다.

CHECK-UP

5. The managing <u>director</u> / direction strongly opposed the budget cuts that the company had proposed.

6. Customers have trusted Mantique Furniture for decades because of its <u>committee</u> / commitment to quality.

4 복합 명사

◆ 복합 명사는 개별 뜻이 있는 두 개의 명사가 결합하여 하나의 명사로 쓰이는 것을 말한다. 토익에서는 복합 명사의 첫 번째나 두 번째 자리에 명사를 채우는 문제로 출제된다.

tourist attraction 관광지, 관광 명소	flight attendant 승무원
security/vacation policy 보안/휴가 정책	flight arrangements 항공편 일정
cancellation fee 취소 수수료	earnings growth 수익 성장
expiration date 유효 기간, 만기일	sales figures 판매 수치
building management 건물 관리	job creation 일자리 창출
e-mail reminder (약속, 일정 등을) 상기시키기 위한 이메일	budget surplus/deficit 예산 흑자/적자
service fee[charge] 서비스 요금	safety regulation 안전 규정
baggage allowance 수하물 허용량	price reduction 가격 인하

Customers were happy about the <u>price</u> / pricey **reduction** of the popular cereal product.
고객들은 그 유명 시리얼 제품의 가격 인하를 반겼다.

CHECK-UP

7. The tax credit would result in substantial job <u>creation</u> / creativity among small businesses.

8. According to <u>selling</u> / sales figures released by Jerome's Technologies, company profits rose 3% last quarter.

UNIT 02 대명사와 한정사

1 인칭대명사

◆ 인칭대명사는 사람이나 사물을 가리키는 대명사이다. 수와 성별, 격에 따라 형태가 달라진다.

Coco Designs takes **secondhand items** and uses <u>them</u> / they to make new clothes.
Coco Designs는 중고품을 가져가서 새 옷을 만드는 데 쓴다.

◆ 재귀대명사는 주어와 목적어가 동일할 때 목적어 자리에 쓴다. 단, 주어나 목적어를 강조하기 위해 재귀대명사를 쓰기도 하는데, 이때는 부사 자리에 위치하며 재귀대명사를 생략할 수 있다.

Mr. Ronaldo described <u>himself</u> / him as an artist, inventor, and architect.
Mr. Ronaldo는 스스로를 예술가 겸 발명가 겸 건축가라고 설명했다.
→ 주어 Mr. Ronaldo와 목적어가 동일하므로 재귀대명사가 정답이다.

Ms. Watson designed the pamphlets <u>herself</u> / hers with a software program.
Ms. Watson은 소프트웨어 프로그램으로 그 팸플릿들을 직접 디자인했다.
→ 밑줄이 없어도 완전한 문장이므로 밑줄에는 생략해도 문장이 성립할 수 있는 말이 들어가야 한다. 따라서 재귀대명사가 정답이다.

CHECK-UP

1. Ms. Cailot arrived to work five minutes late because <u>she</u> / her was stuck in traffic.

2. The grocery store prides <u>itself</u> / it on using only local suppliers for its produce.

2 지시대명사와 부정대명사

◆ 지시대명사(this, these, that, those)는 특정 대상을 가리킬 때 쓰는 대명사이며, 앞에서 언급된 명사를 대신할 때 쓰기도 한다. 토익에는 those가 자주 출제되는데 주로 분사구나 전치사구, 주격 관계대명사절의 수식을 받는 구조로 나온다.

<u>Those</u> / Few **who wish to participate in the seminar** are encouraged to sign up early.
그 세미나에 참석하길 원하는 분들은 일찍 등록할 것을 권장합니다.

◆ 부정대명사(one, the other, others, another, some, any, many, none 등)는 정해지지 않은 불특정한 대상을 대신하는 대명사이다.

Mr. Li brought two microphones: **one** for the moderator, <u>the other</u> / others / another for the presenter.
Mr. Li는 마이크를 두 개 가져왔는데, 하나는 사회자 것이고 나머지 하나는 발표자 것이다.
→ the other (언급된 것을 제외한) 나머지 하나 / others (불특정한) 다른 것들[사람들] / another (언급된 것과 같은 종류의) 또 다른 하나

Mr. Kamau tried to get a ticket, but there **weren't** <u>any</u> / some left.
Mr. Kamau는 표를 구하려고 노력했지만 남은 표가 전혀 없었다.
→ some 몇몇, 약간 / any (긍정문) 모든; (부정문) 전혀; (조건문) 어떤 ~라도

CHECK-UP

3. All coupons for Zack's Diner, including <u>that / those</u> issued online, will expire on December 31.

4. Participants of the conference can join <u>any / none</u> of the events which interest them.

◆ 한정사는 명사 앞에 위치하여 명사의 의미나 수, 양을 한정하는 역할을 한다.

	관사	a(n), the
의미 한정	지시한정사	this, these, that, those
	소유한정사	my, our, your, his, her, its, their
	의문한정사	what, whatever, which, whichever, whose
수 또는 양 한정	수량한정사	every, another + 단수 명사 (a) few, many, several, both + 복수 명사 the other + 단 · 복수 명사 (a) little, much + 불가산명사 all, more, most, other + 복수 명사/불가산명사 some, any + 단 · 복수 명사/불가산명사

Harrolds Department Store has just opened <u>its / itself</u> **first overseas branch** in Sydney.
Harrolds Department Store가 이제 막 시드니에 첫 해외 지점을 열었다.

CHECK-UP

5. The secretary orders office supplies <u>every / when</u> Thursday, so please e-mail him any requests you have before then.

6. JC's Camping Supplies is offering discounts on <u>a few / any</u> merchandise that is manufactured by Flash Sailing Co.

◆ **each, every + 단수 명사 → 단수 동사**

<u>Every / Many</u> product **complies** with the brand's strict safety standards.
모든 제품은 그 브랜드의 엄격한 안전 기준을 따른다.

◆ **each of + 복수 명사 → 단수 동사**

<u>Each / Most</u> of the budgets **was** approved. 각 예산안이 승인되었다.

◆ **several, many (+ of) + 복수 명사 → 복수 동사**

<u>Several / Each</u> properties on this street **are** for sale. 이 거리의 몇몇 부지는 팔려고 내놓은 것이다.

◆ **all, more, most (+ of) + 복수 명사/불가산명사 → 복수 동사/단수 동사**

<u>All / Every</u> items **are** 30% off this week. 이번 주에 모든 제품은 30% 할인됩니다.

CHECK-UP

7. <u>Every / All</u> staff currently on business trips are exempt from the mandatory monthly meeting.

8. The committee narrowed down the candidates in the logo design competition from 358 to five, and <u>each / several</u> of the candidates was contacted for a meeting.

1. Henson Apartment's owner approved funds for the ------- of the main lobby.

(A) renovates
(B) renovated
(C) renovate
(D) renovation

2. Ian Paints lets customers take unlimited paint samples home to compare ------- with their current decor.

(A) themselves
(B) them
(C) they
(D) their

3. One of the receptionist's duties is answering ------- incoming call.

(A) few
(B) every
(C) other
(D) past

4. ------- will have access to all of Greenwich News's premium content upon remitting the initial payment.

(A) Subscriptions
(B) Subscribing
(C) Subscribers
(D) Subscribe

5. Human Resources has not yet decided ------- candidate to hire for the position.

(A) if
(B) which
(C) regarding
(D) because

6. The organizers have employed several sign language ------- for the international conference.

(A) interpreters
(B) interpreter
(C) interpreting
(D) interpret

7. A parking permit is required of ------- who wish to park in this lot.

(A) those
(B) itself
(C) theirs
(D) enough

8. A crucial ------- between the two washing machine models is that one of them has an energy-saving setting.

(A) distinction
(B) distinctively
(C) distinct
(D) distinctive

9. One occupant, Victor Guerrero, said that the construction noise was not a nuisance, but ------- reported being bothered by it.

(A) himself
(B) whoever
(C) others
(D) anyone

10. Reway Manufacturing received low customer service ratings due to confusing ------- in its manuals.

(A) instructors
(B) instruct
(C) instructions
(D) instructional

11. Ms. McGuire gives ------- team members regular breaks throughout their shifts.

(A) hers
(B) she
(C) her
(D) herself

12. The board of trustees will consider expanding the business into other ventures if ------- remain high.

(A) profited
(B) profiting
(C) profitable
(D) profits

13. The ------- working on the audit must make sure their numbers are as accurate as possible.

(A) accounted
(B) accountants
(C) accounts
(D) accountable

14. Brightwood Water refunded $80 to Mr. Gilmore because ------- had been overcharged.

(A) himself
(B) his
(C) him
(D) he

15. This apartment is within walking distance of many tourist -------, making it prime real estate.

(A) attract
(B) attractions
(C) attractiveness
(D) attractively

16. ------- documents undergo an approval process for compliance with data protection laws.

(A) Another
(B) All
(C) Each
(D) This

PART 5

1 형용사 자리

◆ **형용사는 명사 앞에 위치한다.**

Mr. Yi will step away from his duties for a <u>brief / briefness</u> **time** to deal with a health issue.
Mr. Yi는 건강 문제를 해결하기 위해 잠시 동안 일선에서 물러날 것이다.

◆ **형용사는 보어 자리에 위치하여 주어나 목적어를 보충 설명한다.**

The company **is** always <u>responsive / respond</u> to negative customer feedback.
그 회사는 부정적인 고객 피드백에 항상 즉각 대응한다.

The city launched a mobile app for its residents to **stay** <u>informed / information</u> of all municipal updates.
그 시는 주민들이 시의 모든 최신 정보를 계속 받을 수 있도록 모바일 앱을 출시했다.

We require bolder investments to **make** the business <u>profitable / profitably</u>.
그 사업을 수익성 있게 만들려면 더 과감한 투자가 필요하다.

CHECK-UP

1. Considering that Ms. Ortiz has a master's degree and five years' experience, the <u>initial / initially</u> salary offer was fairly low.

2. Following safety regulations at the construction site is <u>mandate / mandatory</u> for all visitors.

2 부사 자리

◆ **토익에 자주 출제되는 부사 자리 문제는 크게 여섯 가지 유형으로 정리할 수 있다.**

부사 + 타동사	**finally sign** the contract 마침내 계약서에 서명하다	be동사 + 부사 + 분사	**be carefully selected** 엄선하다
자동사 + 부사	**increase rapidly** 급격히 증가하다	조동사 + 부사 + 동사	**can comfortably accommodate** 무리 없이 수용할 수 있다
부사 + 형용사	**unusually high** demand (평소와 달리) 유별나게 높은 수요	have + 부사 + 과거분사	**have publicly stated** 공개적으로 언급했다

Ms. Wheeler <u>strongly / strong</u> **encouraged** her team members to attend the technology seminar.
Ms. Wheeler는 팀원들이 그 기술 세미나에 참석하도록 적극 독려했다.

◆ **부사는 문장 끝에 위치하기도 한다. 따라서 빈칸이 문장 끝에 있을 때 빈칸을 생략해도 완전한 문장이라면 빈칸을 부사 자리로 판단하면 된다.**

Your order will be processed <u>promptly / prompt</u>.
귀하의 주문은 신속히 처리될 것입니다.

CHECK-UP

3. Since graduating from university, Mr. Shaw has <u>action / actively</u> pursued a career in the film industry.

4. The filter on the air purifier should be replaced at regular intervals to ensure it is working <u>efficient / efficiently</u>.

3 주의해야 할 부사

◆ -ly로 끝나지 않는 부사에 주의한다. 이때 오답 선택지는 주로 전치사와 접속사 등으로 구성된다.

at least 최소한, 적어도 **even** 심지어 **now** 지금, 현재	**indeed** 정말로, 확실히; 사실은 **seldom** 거의 ~ 않는 **apart** (따로) 떨어져	**still** 아직, 여전히; 그래도, 그런데도; 훨씬, 더욱 **alike** 비슷하게; 둘 다, 똑같이 **soon** 곧, 머지않아

Most of our employees have been working here for <u>at least</u> / along with five years.
우리 직원 대부분은 이곳에서 최소 5년간 근무한 분들입니다.

◆ 접속부사는 앞 문장과 뒤 문장의 문맥을 연결하면서 뒤 문장을 수식하는 부사이다. 말 그대로 부사이기 때문에 절과 절을 연결하는 역할을 할 수 없다는 점에 주의한다.

however 하지만 **besides** 게다가 **moreover, furthermore** 더욱이 **instead** 대신에	**otherwise** 그렇지 않으면 **therefore, accordingly** 그러므로 **likewise** 마찬가지로 **above all** 무엇보다도	**consequently, as a result** 결과적으로 **meanwhile** 한편; 그동안 **nevertheless** 그럼에도 불구하고 **then** 그리고 나서

Al's Diner serves quality food, but <u>above all</u> / even though, it is known for its reasonable prices.
Al's Diner는 질 좋은 음식을 제공하는데, 무엇보다도 합리적인 가격으로 유명하다.

CHECK-UP

5. Some audience members were <u>until / still</u> trying to find their seats while the CEO made his opening remarks at the event.

6. Our latest marketing strategy has been largely unsuccessful and must <u>therefore / regarding</u> be reevaluated and restructured.

PART 5

4 비교 구문

◆ 비교급 비교

The new laptop is <u>lighter</u> / light **than** the previous one.
새 노트북은 예전 것보다 가볍다.

Sonora Trucking is searching for ways to deliver packages to its customers <u>much</u> / very **faster**.
Sonora Trucking은 고객에게 택배를 훨씬 더 빨리 배달할 수 있는 방법들을 모색하고 있다.
→ 비교급 앞에 much, even, still, far, a lot을 써서 '훨씬 더'의 의미를 더할 수 있다.

◆ 최상급 비교

Merose Motors is recognized as **one of the** <u>highest</u> / high quality automakers.
Merose Motors는 최고의 자동차를 만드는 회사 중 하나로 인정받고 있다.

CHECK-UP

7. The new air conditioner circulates cool air much <u>evenly / more evenly</u> than the old one.

8. Strong interpersonal skills are the <u>most important / as important as</u> qualifications for the position.

UNIT 04 전치사와 접속사

1 토익 빈출 전치사

◆ at vs. on vs. in

시간	특정 시각이나 시점 **at** 6 o'clock 6시 정각에	날짜, 요일, 특정일 **on** July 20 7월 20일에	연도, 계절, 월, 오전/오후 등 **in** 2021 2021년에
장소	특정 지점이나 위치 **at** the bus stop 버스 정류장에서	거리, 층수, 표면 위 등 **on** the second floor 2층에	넓은 지역이나 장소, 무언가의 내부 **in** the city 도시에서

◆ 다양한 토익 빈출 전치사

시점	by ~까지	until ~까지	from ~부터	since ~ 이래로
기간	during (특정 활동) 동안	for (숫자로 표현된 기간) 동안	within ~ 내에	throughout ~ 내내
장소/위치	between (둘) 사이에	among (셋 이상) 사이에	within ~ 내에	throughout ~ 전역에
이동/방향	from ~로부터, ~에서부터	through ~을 통하여	across ~을 가로질러	along ~을 따라서
도구/방법	with ~와 함께; ~을 가지고	without ~ 없이	by (방법, 수단 등)으로	
대상/주제	about, on ~에 대하여	regarding, concerning ~에 대하여		
양보	despite ~에도 불구하고	notwithstanding ~에도 불구하고		
추가/제외	besides ~ 외에도	including ~을 포함하여	excluding ~을 제외하고	
기타	following ~을 따라; ~ 후에	like/unlike ~처럼/~와 달리	as ~로서	

The supervisors must **submit** employee evaluations <u>by / until</u> the end of the month.
관리자들은 월말까지 직원 평가서를 제출해야 한다.
→ by는 특정 시점까지 행위가 '완료됨'을, until은 특정 시점까지 행위가 '지속됨'을 나타낼 때 쓴다.

CHECK-UP

1. Our success <u>on / in</u> the third quarter is the result of an aggressive marketing campaign.

2. Starting Monday, the new cafeteria will be open daily from 8 A.M. <u>by / until</u> 8 P.M.

2 토익 빈출 전치사구

이유/양보	because of, due to, owing to, on account of ~ 때문에	in spite of ~에도 불구하고
추가/제외	in addition to, on top of ~ 외에도	except (for) ~을 제외하고
	apart[aside] from ~ 외에도, ~뿐만 아니라(= in addition to); ~을 제외하고(= except (for))	
기타	in front of ~의 앞에 prior to ~ 전에	according to ~에 따르면 if not for ~가 없었다면
	instead of ~ 대신에 along with ~와 함께	rather than ~라기보다는 in light of ~을 고려하여

CHECK-UP

3. <u>In front of / Prior to / Likewise</u> working at Hosto Corp., Jane Hamilton was employed by Popka Inc.

4. More information about the project, <u>on account of / in short / along with</u> recent photos of the park, can be found on our Web site.

3 토익 빈출 접속사

◆ **등위 접속사**: 단어와 단어, 구와 구, 절과 절을 대등하게 잇는다. 단, so는 절만 연결한다.

> and 그리고   but 그러나   yet 그렇지만, 그런데도   or 또는   so 그래서

◆ **상관 접속사**: 특정 어구에 and, but, or와 같은 등위 접속사가 추가되어 한 덩어리로 쓰이는 접속사를 말한다. 등위 접속사와 마찬가지로 접속사를 중심으로 대등한 문장 성분이 연결된다.

> either A or B A 또는 B   neither A nor B A와 B 둘 다 아닌   both A and B A와 B 둘 다
> not A but B A가 아니라 B   not only A but (also) B, B as well as A A뿐만 아니라 B도

◆ **부사절 접속사**: 시간, 조건, 이유, 양보 등의 의미를 지닌 종속절을 이끌며 주어와 동사를 갖춘 완전한 절에 연결된다.

시간	until ~할 때까지	when ~할 때	while ~하는 동안; ~한 반면에	whenever ~할 때마다
조건	if, provided (that) 만약 ~라면		in case ~한 경우에 대비하여	as if 마치 ~인 것처럼
이유	since ~하기 때문에	now (that) 이제 ~이므로		
양보/대조	whereas ~한 반면에	wherever 어디로 ~하더라도		
기타	so that ~하기 위해서	given that ~을 고려할 때	whether ~이든 (아니든)	

Rex Inc. drew 30,000 appliers, <u>whereas</u> / either **only 100 people will be recruited.**
Rex Inc.에 3만 명의 지원자가 몰렸으나 100명만 채용될 것이다.

CHECK-UP

5. Human Resources keeps information about <u>not only / both</u> current and former employees.

6. <u>Above / When</u> you encounter an issue with your computer, contact Mr. Kim at extension 56.

4 전치사 vs. 부사절 접속사

◆ 전치사는 뒤에 명사(구)가 이어지고 부사절 접속사는 뒤에 절이 이어진다. 이때 의미가 유사한 전치사와 접속사에 유의한다.

뜻	전치사	부사절 접속사
~하기 전에	before, prior to	before
~한 후에	after, following	after
~하는 동안	during	while
~하자마자	(up)on -ing	as soon as, once
만약 ~가 아니라면	without	unless
~하기 때문에	because of, due to, owing to, on account of	because, as, since
비록 ~일지라도	despite, in spite of	although, even though

The parking lot on Waverly Street was closed <u>during</u> / while **the holiday.**
웨이벌리 스트리트의 주차장은 공휴일 동안 문을 닫았다.

CHECK-UP

7. <u>Owing to / Because</u> the design differed from that on the Web site, customers complained.

8. Beanie Coffee has opened another branch in Paris <u>despite / although</u> the low success of its first branch.

1. Most voters ------- believe that the city's main roads need to be better maintained.

   (A) firm
   (B) firmness
   (C) firmer
   (D) firmly

2. There are several event signs ------- the wall that should be taken down within this month.

   (A) on
   (B) as
   (C) within
   (D) in

3. Ms. Hensley created a ------- database in which comments from Globe Autos' customers can be stored.

   (A) securing
   (B) secure
   (C) secures
   (D) securely

4. The Parmona Museum offers hands-on workshops ------- short lectures.

   (A) for instance
   (B) whether
   (C) as well as
   (D) in case

5. The summer sales event will last ------- the month of July.

   (A) inside
   (B) throughout
   (C) even so
   (D) among

6. ------- Ms. Caruso rearranged the furniture in the waiting area, the space looked much larger.

   (A) After
   (B) Following
   (C) Notwithstanding
   (D) Especially

7. Bea's Beauty will ------- release its new foam cleanser on its Web site.

   (A) soon
   (B) due to
   (C) while
   (D) timely

8. The property will require extensive renovations before it is ------- to be used as an office.

   (A) suiting
   (B) suitability
   (C) suitable
   (D) suitably

9. This presentation includes ------- tips on implementing anti-fraud techniques.

(A) helpfulness
(B) help
(C) helpfully
(D) helpful

10. Board members should read the proposal prior to the meeting ------- they can be well-informed when discussing the details.

(A) given that
(B) so that
(C) with
(D) resulting

11. The director's new documentary looks ------- at the oil industry than the first one did.

(A) most closely
(B) more closely
(C) closest
(D) close

12. Martin Textiles remains ------- on the sales of cotton fibers for its profits.

(A) depends
(B) dependent
(C) depend
(D) depending

13. All confidential documents are required to be kept in locked cabinets ------- someone uses them.

(A) without
(B) otherwise
(C) even
(D) unless

14. The number of participating businesses has increased ------- since last year.

(A) signify
(B) significant
(C) significantly
(D) significance

15. We need to get consent from the city council ------- we can make plans to change this residential lot into a commercial area.

(A) rather
(B) although
(C) also
(D) before

16. ------- the employment contract, workers retain their right to form a labor union.

(A) According to
(B) Instead of
(C) Provided that
(D) Prior to

1 주어와 동사의 수 일치

◆ 선택지가 동사의 활용형으로 구성되어 있으면 주어와의 수 일치 여부를 먼저 확인한다. 주어가 단수면 단수 동사를, 복수면 복수 동사를 쓰는 것이 기본 원칙이다.

Brax Tech's new wireless headphones <u>are</u> / is on sale this month.
Brax Tech의 새 무선 헤드폰은 이번 달에 판매된다.

◆ 주어와 동사 사이에 위치한 수식어구(분사구, 관계사절, to부정사구, 전치사구)는 수 일치와 관계없는 요소이다. 따라서 동사 바로 앞에 있는 명사에 수를 일치시키지 않도록 주의해야 한다.

An appliance with these labels <u>conforms</u> / conform to all energy-efficiency regulations.
이 라벨이 붙어 있는 기기는 모든 에너지 효율 규정을 따르고 있다.
→ 주어 An appliance가 단수이므로 단수 동사 conforms로 수 일치한다.

CHECK-UP

1. Executives at Murphy Automotive <u>expect</u> / is expecting to sell at least 100 used vehicles over the next month.

2. Thornton Textiles, a producer of cotton fabrics, have supplied / <u>supplies</u> over 50 clothing factories across the country.

2 수동태

◆ 빈칸 뒤에 목적어가 없으면 수동태를, 목적어가 있으면 능동태를 쓴다.

The hand soap that <u>was produced</u> / produced last month had the wrong packaging.
지난달에 생산된 손 세정제는 포장이 잘못되어 있었다.

Hype Consultancy <u>hired</u> / has been hired **Willard Carswell** as their new vice president.
Hype Consultancy는 Willard Carswell을 새 부사장으로 고용했다.

◆ 토익에 자주 출제되는 [be p.p. + to부정사]를 숙지해 두자.

be expected to ~할 것으로 예상되다	be asked to ~하도록 요청받다	be required to ~하도록 요구받다	be encouraged to ~하도록 장려되다	be scheduled to ~하기로 예정되다
be reminded to ~하라고 (상기하는 말을) 듣다	be intended to ~하기 위한 의도이다	be prepared to ~할 준비가 되다	be allowed to ~하도록 허락되다	be advised to ~하도록 조언받다

The elevator is out of service, so visitors <u>are asked</u> / ask **to use** the stairs instead.
엘리베이터가 운행되지 않으므로 방문객은 계단을 이용하시기 바랍니다.

CHECK-UP

3. Audience members who wish to inform / <u>be informed</u> about upcoming shows should complete a form with their contact information.

4. All users <u>are required</u> / required to authenticate their account before using our cloud software.

3 시제

◆ 토익의 시제 문제는 난이도가 낮은 편이고 기본 개념을 벗어나지 않는 범위에서 출제된다. 특히 특정 표현과 어울려 출제되는 경우가 대부분이므로 각각의 시제와 함께 쓰이는 주요 표현을 함께 알아 두면 문제 풀이에 도움이 된다.

단순 시제	현재 시제: usually, generally, every week/month/year 등 과거 시제: ago, yesterday, recently, lately, last week/month/year, in + 연도 등 미래 시제: next week/month/year, tomorrow, soon, later today/this week 등
완료 시제	현재완료 시제: for ~ 동안, since ~ 이래로, already 이미, just 막, yet 아직, so far 지금까지, over ~에 걸쳐, 　　　　　　　in recent weeks 최근 몇 주간, in just one year 1년 만에 과거완료 시제: by the time + 주어 + 동사의 과거형 ~했을 무렵에는 미래완료 시제: by the time + 주어 + 동사의 현재형 ~한 무렵에는, by ~쯤에는, at/by the end of ~의 말에/말까지

The number of video streaming platforms <u>has increased</u> / increases **over the past few years**.
동영상 스트리밍 플랫폼의 수가 과거 몇 년간 증가했다.

◆ 문장 안에 시제를 유추할 수 있는 특정 표현이 없다면 등위 접속사나 주절 또는 부사절에 쓰인 동사를 바탕으로 문맥에 근거하여 알맞은 시제를 찾는다.

The work crew **repainted** the hallway walls **and then** <u>cleaned</u> / clean the carpet thoroughly.
인부들은 복도 벽에 페인트를 다시 칠한 다음에 카펫을 꼼꼼하게 청소했다.

CHECK-UP

5. Newbury National Park opened / will open for hikers and campers next month.

6. The new clothing line by Bailey Sportswear is improving / has improved significantly since July.

---

4 수 일치/태/시제 복합 문제

◆ 수 일치가 태 또는 시제와 결합된 문제를 풀 때는 수 일치를 먼저 판단한 다음 태 또는 시제를 따진다.

B&C Landscaping <u>provides</u> / provide / is provided free consultations to new customers.
B&C Landscaping은 신규 고객에게 무료 상담을 제공한다.

(1) 수 일치 판별: 주어 B&C Landscaping이 단수이므로 복수 동사인 provide는 오답으로 소거한다.
(2) 수동태/능동태 판별: 밑줄 뒤에 목적어 free consultations가 있으므로 능동태인 provides가 정답이다.

◆ 태가 시제와 결합된 문제를 풀 때는 시제를 먼저 판단한 다음에 태를 따진다. 시제를 파악할 수 있는 요소가 없으면 태를 먼저 판단하고 문맥으로 시제를 따져 본다.

The book signing event <u>will be held</u> / is holding / was held next Thursday at 2 P.M.
책 사인회는 다음 주 목요일 오후 2시에 열릴 예정입니다.

(1) 시제 판별: 미래 시제와 어울려 쓰이는 표현인 next Thursday가 있으므로 과거 시제인 was held는 오답으로 소거한다.
(2) 수동태/능동태 판별: 밑줄 뒤에 목적어가 없으므로 수동태인 will be held가 정답이다.

CHECK-UP

7. The next stage of construction at the Vivitech headquarters will begin once the permits has issued / are issued / were issuing.

8. Now under new ownership, department heads had monitored / are monitoring / will be monitored their spending more carefully than before.

UNIT 06 준동사

1 to부정사 자리

◆ to부정사는 주어, 보어, 목적어 자리에 위치하여 명사로 기능하며, 토익에서는 주로 보어나 목적어 자리에 to부정사를 채우는 문제가 출제된다.

NT&Y Technologies **is planning** <u>to merge</u> / merge with Frey in early May.
NT&Y Technologies는 5월 초에 Frey와 합병할 계획이다.

→ to부정사를 목적어로 취하는 동사: plan 계획하다, hope 희망하다, agree 동의하다, promise 약속하다, aim 목표하다, expect 기대하다, refuse 거절하다, fail ~하지 못하다, would like 원하다, wish 바라다, offer 제안하다, need ~할 필요가 있다, want 원하다, decide 결정하다, afford 여유가 있다, tend 경향이 있다

◆ to부정사는 형용사나 부사로 활용할 수도 있다. to부정사가 형용사로 기능할 때는 명사를 뒤에서 수식한다.

Atlantis Resort added a new diving pool in **an attempt** <u>to attract</u> / is attracting more visitors.
Atlantis Resort는 더 많은 방문객을 유치하려는 시도로 새로운 다이빙 수영장을 추가했다.

<u>To ensure</u> / Have ensured quality service, all product consultations are by appointment only.
양질의 서비스를 보장하기 위해 모든 제품 상담은 예약제로만 이루어진다.

→ to부정사가 부사로 쓰여 '~하기 위해서'를 뜻할 때는 in order to로도 쓸 수 있다.

CHECK-UP

1. Ms. Waite would like <u>to arrange</u> / arranging a group interview for next Friday.

2. All elevators in the building will be out of service for one hour from 10 A.M. perform / <u>to perform</u> required maintenance.

2 동명사 자리

◆ 동명사는 전치사 뒤에 위치한다.

The training session is aimed **at** <u>improving</u> / improves productivity.
그 교육은 생산성 향상을 목표로 한다.

◆ 동명사는 주어, 보어, 목적어 자리에 위치한다.

<u>Performing</u> / Performance **a thorough evaluation** is crucial before a product launch.
제품 출시 전에 철저한 평가를 수행하는 것은 중요하다.

→ 밑줄 뒤에 목적어 역할을 하는 명사구 a thorough evaluation이 있으므로 목적어를 취할 수 있는 동명사가 정답이다.

Ms. Vela will **consider** <u>approving</u> / to approve the plans to open a branch office in Tokyo.
Ms. Vela는 도쿄에 지점을 개설하는 계획을 승인하는 걸 고려할 것이다.

→ 동명사를 목적어로 취하는 동사: consider 고려하다, include 포함하다, admit 인정하다, avoid 피하다, finish 마치다, stop 멈추다, discontinue 중단하다, suggest 제안하다, recommend 추천하다, deny 부정하다, give up 포기하다, postpone 보류하다, delay 늦추다

CHECK-UP

3. The last person to leave the office must make sure the security alarm is set prior to lock / <u>locking</u> the door.

4. We suggest <u>substituting</u> / to substitute natural sweeteners for artificial ones in your favorite recipes.

◆ **[be동사 + 형용사 + to부정사] 관용 표현**

be[make] sure to 확실히 ~하다	be able to ~할 수 있다	be eligible to ~할 자격이 되다
be willing to 기꺼이 ~하다	be advisable to ~하는 것을 권하다	be eager to ~하기를 간절히 바라다
be proud to ~해서 자랑스럽다	be available to ~하는 것이 가능하다; (시간적으로) ~할 여유가 되다	

Vadica International **is eager** to enter / entering the Asian market.
Vadica International은 아시아 시장에 진출하기를 간절히 바라고 있다.

◆ **동명사 관용 표현**

look forward to -ing ~하는 것을 고대하다	have difficulty/trouble (in) -ing ~하는 데 어려움/곤란을 겪다
spend 시간/돈 (on) -ing ~하는 데 시간/돈을 쓰다	be accustomed to -ing ~하는 데 익숙하다

Customers seem to **have trouble** accessing / to access their accounts from our Web site.
고객들이 우리 웹사이트에서 계정에 접속하는 데 문제가 있는 것 같다.

CHECK-UP

5. With the backing of additional investors, the company was able increasing / to increase production.

6. We appreciate your support and look forward to be continuing / continuing to serve you.

◆ 분사는 명사를 앞이나 뒤에서 수식한다. 이때 명사와의 관계가 능동이면 현재분사를, 수동이면 과거분사를 쓴다.
Departing / Departed **passengers** must complete a security check in order to fly.
출발하는 승객들은 항공기 탑승을 위해 보안 검사를 완료해야 한다.

Weardale Ski Club is **a beautiful ski resort** located / locating near Durham.
Weardale Ski Club은 더럼 근처에 위치한 아름다운 스키 리조트입니다.

◆ 몇몇 과거분사는 그 자체가 형용사로 굳어져 쓰인다. 이때 과거분사 형태의 형용사가 반드시 수동을 의미하지는 않는다는 점에 주의해야 한다.

an **informed** decision 잘 알고 내린 결정	a **detailed** explanation 자세한 설명
an **established** company 저명한 회사	a **qualified** applicant 적격인 지원자
an **accomplished** writer 뛰어난 작가	a **distinguished** scholar 뛰어난 학자
an **experienced** employee 경력 직원	a **noted** composer 유명한 작곡가
a **dedicated** employee 헌신적인 직원	a **motivated** worker 적극적인 직원

CHECK-UP

7. Residents are mostly concerned about the rising / rise cost of public services.

8. Ms. Corbett argued that increasing the perks of the company could attract qualifying / qualified employees.

UNIT 07 관계사

1 관계대명사

◆ 관계대명사는 앞에 언급된 명사를 대신하는 대명사 역할을 하는 동시에 관계사절을 이끌어 다른 절에 연결하는 접속사 역할을 한다. 관계사절 안에서 관계대명사가 어떤 역할을 하는지에 따라 주격, 목적격, 소유격으로 나눌 수 있으며, 선행사가 사람이냐 사물/동물이냐에 따라 다르게 쓰인다.

선행사 격	주격	목적격	소유격
사람	who	who(m)	whose
사물, 동물	which	which	whose
사람, 사물, 동물	that	that	–

Mr. Brown is **a journalist** <u>who</u> / which won the Journalist of the Year Award.
Mr. Brown은 올해의 기자상을 받은 기자이다.

◆ **whom, which**가 전치사의 목적어일 때 [전치사 + whom/which]로 쓸 수 있다. 이때 관계사 이하는 완전한 절이 된다.
Private messages must only be seen by the person **whom[that]** they are sent **to**.
= Private messages must only be seen by the person <u>to whom</u> / what they are sent.
개인 메시지는 전달받은 사람만 볼 수 있다.

CHECK-UP

1. All customers <u>who</u> / which complete a survey will be offered a discount voucher.
2. Streaming Central gives a customer three warnings about late payments, after <u>whose</u> / which the account is suspended.

2 관계대명사의 생략

◆ [주격 관계대명사 + be동사]가 생략되면 선행사 뒤에 주로 분사가 이어진다. 이때 선행사와의 관계가 능동이면 현재분사를, 수동이면 과거분사를 쓴다.
The wait staff <u>working</u> / worked in the main ballroom must maintain perfect etiquette and attire.
주 연회장에서 근무하는 직원들은 완벽한 에티켓과 복장을 유지해야 한다.
→ 선행사 The wait staff는 '근무하는' 주체이기 때문에 밑줄과 능동 관계이므로 현재분사가 정답이다.

◆ 목적격 관계대명사는 단독으로 생략할 수 있다. 토익에서는 목적격 관계대명사가 생략된 관계사절의 주어 자리에 들어갈 알맞은 인칭대명사를 묻는 문제나 동사 자리를 채우는 문제가 출제된다.
The type of flooring **we** <u>were using</u> / to use / using is not available anymore.
우리가 사용하던 바닥 타입은 더 이상 사용할 수 없습니다.

CHECK-UP

3. Some information <u>containing</u> / contained in the documents is outdated.
4. The CEO does everything <u>he</u> / him can to support his employees.

◆ 관계부사는 관계사절 안에서 부사 역할을 하는 동시에 관계사절을 이끌어 다른 절에 연결하는 접속사 역할을 한다. 선행사가 시간이면 **when**, 장소면 **where**, 이유면 **why**, 방법이면 **how**로 쓴다.

Monday is **the day**. + A weekly meeting takes place **on the day**.

= Monday is **the day on which** a weekly meeting takes place.

= Monday is **the day** <u>when</u> / why a weekly meeting takes place.

월요일은 주간 회의가 열리는 날이다.

◆ 관계부사는 뒤에 문법적으로 완전한 절이 이어지고, 관계대명사는 뒤에 불완전한 절이 이어진다.

Mr. Lowe received a full-time job offer from the firm <u>where</u> / which **he did his summer internship**.

Mr. Lowe는 여름 인턴십을 했던 회사로부터 정규직 제안을 받았다.

→ 밑줄 뒤에 완전한 절이 이어지므로 부사와 접속사 역할을 겸하는 관계부사가 정답이다.

Please review the employee evaluation <u>which</u> / how **I have attached** to this message.

이 메시지에 첨부해 드린 직원 평가서를 검토해 주십시오.

→ 밑줄 뒤에 have attached의 목적어가 없는 절이 이어지므로 목적격 관계대명사가 정답이다.

> **CHECK-UP**

5. Dedicated fans of the brand are lined up in front of the store <u>what / where</u> the limited-edition sneakers will be released.

6. The cellphone is comprised of materials <u>which / how</u> resist damage from drops under five meters.

◆ 복합관계대명사는 [관계대명사 + -ever] 형태이며, 관계대명사와 마찬가지로 뒤에 불완전한 절이 이어진다.

who(m)ever	whichever	whatever
명사절: ~하는 사람은 누구든지	명사절: ~인 것은 어느 것이든지	명사절: ~인 것은 무엇이든지
부사절: 누가[누구를] ~하든지	부사절: 어느 것이[어느 것을] ~하든지	부사절: 무엇이[무엇을] ~하든지

Mr. Stevens works hard to be the best at <u>whatever</u> / any **he does**.

Mr. Stevens는 자기가 하는 일이 무엇이든 최고가 되기 위해 열심히 한다.

◆ 복합관계부사는 [관계부사 + -ever] 형태이며, 관계부사와 마찬가지로 뒤에 완전한 절이 이어진다.

whenever	wherever	however
~할 때는 언제든지; 언제 ~하더라도	~하는 곳은 어디든지; 어디에서 ~하더라도	~하는 것은 어떤 방식으로든; 아무리 ~하더라도

The manager on duty should be notified <u>whenever</u> / which **a customer makes a complaint**.

고객의 불만이 제기될 때마다 당직 관리자에게 알려야 한다.

> **CHECK-UP**

7. <u>Whoever / However</u> leaves the office last is expected to turn off the lights.

8. Pawan Tech developed a mobile application that offers users the latest traffic conditions <u>whatever / wherever</u> they go.

1. Ms. Zeller invited several candidates for an interview even though they did not have the ------- qualifications for the junior researcher position.

   (A) prefer
   (B) preferred
   (C) preferably
   (D) to prefer

2. A retirement party will be held next week for Mr. Schmidt, ------- has been working for Melon Technologies for over 30 years.

   (A) all
   (B) who
   (C) this
   (D) most

3. Mr. Farrow ------- the vehicle's engine and then report any issues.

   (A) are inspecting
   (B) having inspected
   (C) inspect
   (D) will inspect

4. Our funding comes from the support of foundations as well as readers, ------- we are grateful.

   (A) when
   (B) in order to
   (C) for which
   (D) along with

5. All employees must attend next week's workshop ------- how to operate the new machinery.

   (A) understood
   (B) is understanding
   (C) understands
   (D) to understand

6. Carsen Gym will be shut down for about two months while renovations -------.

   (A) will be completing
   (B) completing
   (C) was completed
   (D) are being completed

7. The customer service department bought ------- computers because its budget was small.

   (A) used
   (B) use
   (C) user
   (D) using

8. Later this afternoon, Ms. Bullock ------- the contract terms with one of the building materials companies.

   (A) has renegotiated
   (B) renegotiated
   (C) will be renegotiating
   (D) was renegotiating

9. You will be refunded after we receive the ------- product in the mail.

(A) to return
(B) returns
(C) returned
(D) returning

10. Mr. Grimes ------- the keynote address at the IT and security conference last Friday.

(A) will have given
(B) is giving
(C) gave
(D) was given

11. Cannon Corporation is exploring the possibility of ------- its business into Asia.

(A) extend
(B) extension
(C) extensive
(D) extending

12. Mosquito pesticide spraying operations ------- to commence before tourists come on vacation.

(A) schedule
(B) are scheduled
(C) were scheduling
(D) have scheduled

13. Customers can get a free sample of all hair-care products, ------- they prefer, in celebration of Chonie Salon's 10th anniversary.

(A) any
(B) whose
(C) indeed
(D) whichever

14. Smallville's mayor plans ------- an abandoned building into a library.

(A) to develop
(B) to be developed
(C) develop
(D) will be developed

15. The ------- product designer was awarded with the industry's top honors.

(A) accomplish
(B) accomplished
(C) accomplishing
(D) accomplishment

16. Mr. Barbour showed the electrician the light fixture ------- had been malfunctioning.

(A) that
(B) itself
(C) what
(D) whoever

PART 5

명사 빈출 어휘

excursion (짧은) 여행
go on an **excursion** to the Grand Canyon
그랜드 캐니언으로 여행을 가다

charge 요금; 책임, 담당
free of **charge** 무료로
the person in **charge** of the contract 계약 담당자

recipient 수령인, 받는 사람
announce the **recipient** of an award
수상자를 발표하다
관련어 receive 받다

obstacle 장애(물)
overcome **obstacles** 장애물을 극복하다

expertise 전문 지식, 전문성
demonstrate a wealth of **expertise**
풍부한 전문 지식을 보이다
관련어 expert 전문가; 전문적인, 전문가의

turnover 이직률; 매출액
a high **turnover** of staff 높은 직원 이직률
an annual **turnover** of $90 million
9천만 달러의 연간 매출액

alignment 정렬, 가지런함
be out of **alignment** (정렬 등이) 어긋나다
관련어 align 가지런히 하다

recommendation 추천(서); 권고
a letter of **recommendation** 추천서
on the board's **recommendation** 이사회의 권고로
관련어 recommend 추천하다; 권고하다

delegation 위임; 대표단
delegation of tasks 업무 위임
a member of a **delegation** 대표단의 일원
관련어 delegate (일, 임무 등을) 위임하다; 대표[대리인]로 선정
하다

delay 지연, 지체
cause a **delay** in shipment 배송 지연을 야기하다
apologize for a schedule **delay** 일정 지연을 사과하다

certification 증명(서)
renew one's **certification** yearly
증명서를 매년 갱신하다
관련어 certify 증명하다

estimate 견적(서); 추정(치)
examine the **estimate** carefully
견적서를 꼼꼼히 검토하다
a rough **estimate** 대략적인 추정치
관련어 estimated 견적의; 추측의

confidence 신뢰; 자신감; 비밀
have complete **confidence** 대단히 신뢰하다
in strict **confidence** 극비로

capacity 용량, 수용력; 능력; 지위, 역할
increase the **capacity** of the stadium
경기장의 수용 인원을 늘리다
operate at full **capacity** 최대치로 가동하다
in one's **capacity** as chairman of the council
의회의 의장 자격으로

defect 결함
take responsibility for **defects** 결함에 책임을 지다

request 요구, 요청(서)
process a **request** 요청을 처리하다

policy 정책, 방침
flexible work **policy** 유연한 근무 정책

critic 비평가, 평론가
draw positive reviews from **critics**
비평가들로부터 긍정적인 평가를 이끌어 내다
관련어 critique 비평, 평론
criticism 비난, 비판

clientele 고객
attract a young **clientele** 젊은 고객을 끌어들이다
동의어 customer 고객

occasion 때, 경우; 행사
for any **occasion** 어떤 경우에도
a memorable **occasion** 기억에 남을 만한 행사
관련어 occasionally 가끔, 때때로

1. The museum cannot be opened to the public until structural ------- are repaired.

   (A) definitions
   (B) defects
   (C) communications
   (D) uncertainties

2. If the dry cleaning company makes a delivery within the Philadelphia city limits, there is no extra -------.

   (A) pressure
   (B) provider
   (C) charge
   (D) area

3. Although lighter than predicted, snow caused traffic ------- all throughout rush hour.

   (A) delays
   (B) refunds
   (C) routes
   (D) suggestions

4. Should you file an auto insurance claim, we will examine the ------- within three business days.

   (A) expertise
   (B) account
   (C) registration
   (D) request

5. In addition to holding a degree from a prestigious university, Ms. Harris has several -------.

   (A) certifications
   (B) assignments
   (C) estimates
   (D) recipients

6. A small business loan helped Mr. Joslin overcome the ------- that were holding back his business.

   (A) attempts
   (B) obstacles
   (C) reactions
   (D) opposites

7. Library patrons completed the survey to share ------- for books that should be purchased.

   (A) recommendations
   (B) reimbursements
   (C) retrieval
   (D) resolutions

8. Tingley Travel has introduced ------- to Europe for students on summer break.

   (A) settlements
   (B) excursions
   (C) institutions
   (D) accomplishments

9. Although the store's refund ------- is clearly stated on its Web site, some consumers are confused about it.

   (A) policy
   (B) shelter
   (C) preference
   (D) appointment

10. The private dining hall at Verity Restaurant can be reserved for any special ------- for up to 30 people.

    (A) occasion
    (B) turnover
    (C) competence
    (D) intention

prior 사전의; 우선하는
require **prior** approval by a supervisor
관리자의 사전 승인을 필요로 하다
have a **prior** claim to the business
그 사업체에 우선권이 있다
관련어 priority 우선 사항; 우선권
　　　 prioritize 우선순위를 매기다

significant 상당한; 의미 있는, 중요한
experience **significant** growth 상당한 성장을 경험하다
statistically **significant** 통계적으로 유의미한
관련어 significantly 상당히; 의미 있게, 중요하게

frequent 잦은, 빈번한
a **frequent** customer[visitor] 단골손님
관련어 frequency 빈도

extensive 광범위한; 대규모의
have **extensive** experience 많은 경험이 있다
cause **extensive** damage 대규모 손실을 야기하다
관련어 extend 연장하다; (사업, 세력 등을) 확대하다

utmost 최고의, 최대한
make **utmost** efforts 최대한 노력하다

individual 개개의, 별개의
speak with **individual** attendees
참가자 개개인과 대화를 나누다

incremental 점차 증가하는
incremental improvements 점진적인 향상
관련어 incrementally 점차적으로

supplemental 추가의
supplemental documentation 추가 서류
동의어 extra 추가의

valid 유효한
a **valid** license 유효한 면허[자격]증

prestigious 명성 있는, 권위 있는
a highly **prestigious** award 매우 권위 있는 상
관련어 prestige 위신, 명망

substantial 상당한
a **substantial** amount of money 상당한 액수의 돈
관련어 substance 물질; 본질, 핵심

attentive 주의를 기울이는; 배려하는, 신경 쓰는
friendly and **attentive** staff 친절하고 세심한 직원들
be **attentive** to customers' needs
고객 니즈에 신경 쓰다
관련어 attend 주의를 기울이다; 참석하다
　　　 attention 주의, 주목; 관심, 배려

sizeable 꽤 큰
a **sizeable** income 꽤 많은 수입

current 현재의, 지금의
current prices 현재가
the most **current** findings 가장 최근의 조사 결과

massive 엄청나게 많은[큰]; 거대한
undergo **massive** changes 엄청난 변화를 겪다

objective 객관적인
provide **objective** information
객관적인 정보를 제공하다
관련어 object 목적, 목표; 물체

optimistic 낙관적인, 낙관하는
be cautiously **optimistic** 조심스럽게 낙관하다

exceptional (이례적으로) 뛰어난; 예외적인
an **exceptional** work of art 뛰어난 예술 작품
only in **exceptional** circumstances
예외적인 상황에서만
관련어 exception 이례, 예외

joint 공동의, 합동의
a **joint** effort 공동의 노력
finish in **joint** first place 공동 1위를 하다

dependable 믿을 만한
a **dependable** assistant 믿을 만한 보조
동의어 reliable 믿을 만한, 신뢰할 만한

1. Before the new software was installed, employees spent a ------- amount of time updating customer accounts.

(A) consecutive
(B) direct
(C) substantial
(D) visible

2. The Henley Institute's public speaking class is suitable for corporate groups and ------- students.

(A) beneficial
(B) individual
(C) deliberate
(D) distant

3. A job applicant with ------- experience in management will have a good chance of being hired.

(A) straight
(B) extensive
(C) compact
(D) attentive

4. The mayor thanked volunteers for their ------- coordinated effort to clean up the city's parks after the storm.

(A) factual
(B) massive
(C) objective
(D) original

5. The video streaming service has added a ------- number of new users in the past quarter.

(A) current
(B) defective
(C) sizeable
(D) preserved

6. Mr. Kellogg will be offered the senior accounting position if his state certification turns out to be -------.

(A) successive
(B) familiar
(C) informal
(D) valid

7. Investors were ------- about the cruise line's potential after the first trip sold out quickly.

(A) optimistic
(B) superior
(C) rare
(D) unique

8. At Rosewood Inn, guest comfort is of the ------- importance.

(A) constant
(B) diminished
(C) joint
(D) utmost

9. The new tax incentives have made a ------- difference in the number of new small businesses in town.

(A) difficult
(B) prepared
(C) significant
(D) capable

10. Following upgrades to the power plant, the city will have a more ------- supply of electricity.

(A) dependable
(B) patient
(C) enthusiastic
(D) grateful

PART 5

sincerely 진심으로
sincerely hope it will succeed
그것이 성공하기를 진심으로 바라다
관련어 sincere 진실된, 진심 어린

directly 직접, 바로
be **directly** affected by related policies
관련 정책들에 직접 영향을 받다
관련어 direct 직접적인; 직행의

newly 최근에, 새로
a **newly** hired employee 새로 채용된 직원
관련어 new 새로운

primarily 주로
be aimed **primarily** at young consumers
주로 젊은 소비자를 겨냥하다
관련어 primary 주요한

currently 현재, 지금
currently under construction 현재 공사 중인
관련어 current 현재의, 지금의

soon 곧, 머지않아
be expected to **soon** gain worldwide fame
곧 세계적인 명성을 얻을 것으로 예상되다

unexpectedly 예기치 않게, 뜻밖에
be **unexpectedly** successful 뜻밖에 성공을 거두다
관련어 unexpected 예상 밖의, 뜻밖의

thoroughly 완전히, 철저히
clean up spills **thoroughly** 쏟은 것을 제대로 닦다
thoroughly confused 몹시 혼란스러운
동의어 completely 완전히, 전적으로

diligently 부지런히, 애써
work **diligently** 부지런히 일하다
diligently complete the task
그 업무를 부지런히 완료하다

initially 처음에
be used as a theater **initially**
처음에는 극장으로 사용되다
관련어 initial 처음의, 초기의

accidentally 우연히, 뜻하지 않게; 실수로
prevent the door from opening **accidentally**
문이 저절로 열리는 걸 방지하다
accidentally delete a file 파일을 실수로 지우다
관련어 accidental 우연한, 돌발적인

comfortably 수월하게, 무리 없이; 편안[편리]하게
win **comfortably** 손쉽게 이기다
be **comfortably** furnished
(가구 등이) 편리하게 비치되어 있다
관련어 comfortable 편안한, 쾌적한

noticeably 두드러지게
noticeably higher than last quarter
지난 분기보다 눈에 띄게 높은
관련어 notice 알아채다, 인지하다, 주목하다

far 훨씬, 대단히; 멀리
fall **far** behind the competition
경쟁에서 한참 뒤처지다

unanimously 만장일치로
unanimously agree 만장일치로 동의하다
관련어 unanimous 만장일치의

temporarily 일시적으로, 임시로
temporarily out of stock 일시적으로 품절된
관련어 temporary 일시적인, 임시의

considerably 상당히
drop **considerably** in value 가치가 현저히 떨어지다
관련어 considerable (크기, 양, 정도가) 상당한

immediately 즉시, 즉각
immediately after a meeting 회의 직후에
관련어 immediate 즉각적인

recently 최근에
a **recently** launched novel 최근에 출간된 소설
관련어 recent 최근의

alike 비슷하게; 둘 다, 똑같이
try to treat all customers **alike**
모든 손님을 동등하게 대하려고 노력하다

1. Riddell Dairy Farm supplies milk ------- to local restaurants, keeping costs low.

   (A) directly
   (B) neatly
   (C) hardly
   (D) unusually

2. Our technology specialist is working ------- to restore Internet service to the office.

   (A) financially
   (B) seemingly
   (C) particularly
   (D) diligently

3. Office manager Charles Yarger ------- requested a meeting with Ms. Arlow, so she had to adjust her schedule.

   (A) commonly
   (B) indefinitely
   (C) unexpectedly
   (D) nearly

4. Founded and headquartered in Belgium, the cookware company is ------- in the process of establishing a new factory.

   (A) currently
   (B) extremely
   (C) solidly
   (D) immediately

5. The Sky Room can accommodate up to 50 guests, while the Wind Room seats between 80 and 100 people -------.

   (A) consequently
   (B) widely
   (C) comfortably
   (D) exceedingly

6. Lamora Fruit Orchard ------- confirmed that it will have a change of ownership in the upcoming quarter.

   (A) approximately
   (B) recently
   (C) heavily
   (D) randomly

7. Clotherly produces cotton T-shirts that are ------- softer than its competitors.

   (A) hurriedly
   (B) respectively
   (C) noticeably
   (D) closely

8. Waldeck's ------- released tablet features a high-resolution screen.

   (A) newly
   (B) absolutely
   (C) naturally
   (D) considerably

9. The sales department will be ------- moved to the fifth floor while the fourth floor is being renovated.

   (A) faintly
   (B) temporarily
   (C) sincerely
   (D) competitively

10. Because she was unfamiliar with the software, one of the trainees ------- printed 10 extra banners for Traylyn Inc.

    (A) mainly
    (B) vigorously
    (C) necessarily
    (D) accidentally

PART 5

ensure 보장하다, 확실히 하다
a design to **ensure** safety 안전을 보장하는 디자인
ensure the quality of a new product
신제품의 품질을 보장하다

feature 특징으로 하다, 특별히 선보이다
feature paintings by young artists
젊은 예술가들이 그린 그림을 특별히 선보이다

note 주목하다; 언급하다
Please **note** we will be closed on Monday.
우리는 월요일에 문을 열지 않는다는 점을 주의해 주십시오.
as **noted** earlier 전에 언급한 바와 같이
관련어 notice 알아채다, 인지하다, 주목하다; 공고문; 알림

prompt 촉발하다
prompt the mayor's resignation
그 시장의 사임을 촉발하다
관련어 promptly 지체 없이; 정확히 제시간에

afford (금전적, 시간적으로) 여유가 있다
cannot **afford** to buy new vehicles
새 차량을 살 형편이 안 되다
관련어 affordable (가격 등이) 알맞은

take down ~을 치우다; ~을 적다
take down an art piece from a wall
벽에 걸린 미술품을 떼다
take down the minutes 회의록을 작성하다

top 1위를 하다; (양, 기록 등이) 더 높다; ~을 얹다
top the charts for a month 한 달간 차트 1위를 하다
top the previous record 예전 기록보다 더 높다
a cake **topped** with fresh fruits
신선한 과일들을 얹은 케이크

bring together (사람들을) 한데 모으다
bring together business leaders and academics
사업가들과 교수들을 한 자리에 모으다

separate 구별하다, 분리하다
be **separated** from the land by a tall fence
높은 울타리로 그 땅과 분리되다

waive (권리, 요구 등을) 포기하다
waive a registration fee 등록비를 면제해 주다

guarantee 보장하다, 보증하다
guarantee an objective assessment
객관적인 평가를 보장하다

inquire 문의하다
inquire about the current interest rates
현재 금리에 대해 문의하다

announce 발표하다, 알리다
announce an increase in prices 가격 인상을 알리다

anticipate 예상하다; 기대하다, 고대하다
submit a list of **anticipated** expenses for a
business trip
예상 출장 비용 목록을 제출하다
anticipate pay increases 급여 인상을 기대하다

coincide with ~와 일치하다, ~와 동시에 일어나다
coincide with the conference 그 회담과 시기가 같다

compensate 보상하다
be **compensated** for any damage
어떤 피해도 보상받다

cultivate (작물을) 재배하다; (관계를) 구축하다, 쌓다
cultivate mainly wheat 주로 밀을 재배하다
cultivate good relations with competitors
경쟁사들과 좋은 관계를 구축하다

withdraw (돈을) 인출하다; 물러나다, 철회하다
withdraw money 돈을 인출하다
withdraw an offer 제안을 철회하다

implement 시행하다, 실시하다
implement decisions/recommendations
결정/권고를 시행하다
implement a recycling program
재활용 프로그램을 실시하다
동의어 carry out ~을 수행[실행]하다

obscure 모호하게 하다; (가려서) 보이지 않게 하다
obscure the main issue 주요 쟁점을 흐리다
be **obscured** by fog 안개에 가려서 보이지 않다
동의어 hide 가리다

boost 신장시키다, 북돋우다
boost productivity 생산성을 증대시키다
boost sales in Europe, its biggest market
그것의 가장 큰 시장인 유럽에서 매출을 향상시키다

1. Midco Communications and Trant Inc. have ------- a joint charity endeavor to supply Internet services to low-income households.

   (A) announced
   (B) installed
   (C) treated
   (D) calibrated

2. Please ------- that requests for time off must be approved by a supervisor one week in advance.

   (A) assess
   (B) note
   (C) secure
   (D) reschedule

3. A decrease in profits has ------- Liang Industries to increase its marketing budget.

   (A) licensed
   (B) restocked
   (C) prompted
   (D) outlined

4. The lead accountant of Kirtfield Sales reviewed the company's finances and determined that it could not ------- to renovate its building.

   (A) admit
   (B) maintain
   (C) afford
   (D) remember

5. The annual Gaming Convention ------- video game developers from across the country.

   (A) carries out
   (B) brings together
   (C) uses up
   (D) takes down

6. ------- the year's list of best-selling mystery novels is *The Door to Sandra's*.

   (A) Topping
   (B) Impressing
   (C) Generating
   (D) Seeking

7. As items often come from two or more warehouses, your order may be ------- into different packages.

   (A) mandated
   (B) separated
   (C) prioritized
   (D) demolished

8. Based on how many units were pre-ordered, the company ------- its new game console launch to be a huge success.

   (A) compiles
   (B) condenses
   (C) delegates
   (D) anticipates

9. Vance Bank reminds travelers that the bank cannot ------- the same exchange rate due to fluctuations in the currency market.

   (A) convey
   (B) guarantee
   (C) undergo
   (D) obscure

10. Reporters ------- about the stock prices and their relation to changes in executive leadership.

    (A) formulated
    (B) inquired
    (C) persuaded
    (D) occupied

PART 5

READING TEST

In the Reading test, you will read a variety of texts and answer several different types of reading comprehension questions. The entire Reading test will last 75 minutes. There are three parts, and directions are given for each part. You are encouraged to answer as many questions as possible within the time allowed.

You must mark your answers on the separate answer sheet. Do not write your answers in your test book.

PART 5

Directions: A word or phrase is missing in each of the sentences below. Four answer choices are given below each sentence. Select the best answer to complete the sentence. Then mark the letter (A), (B), (C), or (D) on your answer sheet.

---

101. Many tutors ------- their services on community forums because it is cost-effective.

(A) advertiser
(B) advertise
(C) advertisement
(D) advertising

102. The post office does not accept international packages unless ------- contents are disclosed.

(A) they
(B) their
(C) theirs
(D) them

103. The factory supervisor was pleased with how ------- Benson Manufacturing's staff repaired the broken machinery.

(A) electronically
(B) increasingly
(C) quickly
(D) highly

104. Ms. Poole and Mr. Johnson continue to exceed ------- in their managerial positions.

(A) expectant
(B) expected
(C) expect
(D) expectations

105. The lease on the two-bedroom apartment unit must be renewed ------- October 6.

(A) with
(B) by
(C) in
(D) of

106. The meeting rooms are usually closed for ------- every weekday at approximately 8 P.M.

(A) cleaning
(B) disposing
(C) speaking
(D) painting

107. Please write in all capital letters when you ------- the customs declaration form provided by the government.

(A) completed
(B) completing
(C) have completed
(D) complete

108. Ms. Delgado explained that her ------- contract with the design firm is just a short-term contract.

(A) steep
(B) current
(C) natural
(D) occasional

109. Passengers can change their seat reservations ------- 24 hours before the flight without a charge.

(A) since
(B) up to
(C) as for
(D) in case

110. A section of Greenwich Hardware's parking lot was shut down ------- after a tree fell.

(A) potentially
(B) significantly
(C) temporarily
(D) annually

111. Vensa Airways provided travel vouchers to everyone ------- was delayed because of the flight cancellation.

(A) what
(B) each
(C) who
(D) much

112. Spectators ------- to refrain from taking unnecessary personal items into the stadium.

(A) ask
(B) have asked
(C) are asked
(D) asking

113. Sunderland Insurance's policy includes emergency calls as an ------- use of personal phones at work.

(A) accepts
(B) accepting
(C) acceptable
(D) acceptably

114. All of our garments are closely inspected ------- they are sent to AJ Fashions' stores.

(A) regarding
(B) below
(C) except
(D) before

115. The news of the merger was ------- confirmed by a source within one of the organizations.

(A) reliably
(B) reliable
(C) rely
(D) reliability

116. ------- completing her master's degree, Ms. Lewis spent two years trying to launch her own catering business.

(A) That
(B) According to
(C) Prior to
(D) Moreover

117. The bus to the theater will ------- from the pharmacy's front entrance and end on Yorkshire Street.

(A) conduct
(B) extend
(C) depart
(D) withdraw

118. To reduce the start-up costs of the business, try buying ------- office equipment.

(A) use
(B) used
(C) user
(D) uses

119. Brow Supplies has plans to develop new hard hats to improve safety at work -------.

(A) notices
(B) sites
(C) goals
(D) calendars

120. For inquiries about replacing outdated equipment, ------- Mr. Arrieta in the IT department.

(A) determine
(B) apply
(C) hire
(D) contact

GO ON TO THE NEXT PAGE

121. The museum will offer free behind-the-scenes tours on Saturday mornings ------- the end of August.

(A) onto
(B) so
(C) because
(D) until

122. Visitors to Clerrick National Park should report all overnight camping plans to the ranger station, located ------- the café and the children's playground.

(A) including
(B) into
(C) throughout
(D) between

123. Arden Footwear announced that it will ------- expand its line-up of hiking boots.

(A) soon
(B) wherever
(C) most
(D) so

124. The interior designer presented several ------- before the client chose light grey and yellow as the colors for her kitchen.

(A) regions
(B) impressions
(C) functions
(D) combinations

125. Under Redding Technology's new policy, salary increases are no longer -------, so employees are compensated according to their level of experience only.

(A) negotiator
(B) negotiates
(C) negotiable
(D) negotiations

126. Due to its effect on a number of industries, media outlets have ------- publicized details of the trade deal.

(A) wide
(B) widen
(C) widely
(D) width

127. ------- an item purchased on the Strike Sports Web site arrives damaged, it can be exchanged at no cost.

(A) While
(B) If
(C) Then
(D) That

128. RadioWave Electronics' new product demonstration earned loud -------.

(A) applause
(B) applaud
(C) applauding
(D) to applaud

129. Owing to his ------- knowledge of pharmaceutical research, Max Punja will be offered the senior consultant role.

(A) amicable
(B) extensive
(C) charitable
(D) gratifying

130. Beginning immediately, all lanes of Highway 19 will be closed to non-emergency vehicles ------- severe weather conditions.

(A) so that
(B) as though
(C) rather than
(D) as a result of

네가 세상에서 보고자 하는 변화가 있다면,
네 스스로 그 변화가 되어라.

– 마하트마 간디(Mahatma Gandhi)

PART

6

PART 6 출제 경향 및 전략

PART 6는 하나의 지문에 4개의 빈칸 채우기 문제로 구성되어 있어 PART 5와 PART 7의 중간적 성격을 띤다. 한 지문에 할당된 4문제 중 3문제는 문법과 어휘 문제, 그리고 나머지 한 문제는 문맥에 맞는 문장 고르기 문제로 구성된다.

여기서 중요한 것은 PART 6의 문법과 어휘 문제는 PART 5처럼 한 문장만 읽고 풀 수 있는 문제보다는 빈칸이 있는 문장의 앞뒤 문장까지 읽어야 해결할 수 있는 문제들이 있다는 점이다. 이러한 이유로 PART 6에서는 문법 문제 중 시제 문제가 특히 자주 출제된다. 따라서 PART 6를 풀 때는 지문 맥락 파악이 중요하며, 이를 위해서는 지문을 처음부터 읽어 내려가는 것이 문제 풀이에 도움이 된다.

Questions 131-134 refer to the following instructions.   해석 및 해설 p.72

Baldrick Accessories—Creating unique accessories featuring your name or other text is easy to do through the Baldrick Accessories Web site! Simply select the item you want, input your text, and choose the font, size, and color. Be sure to examine the sample image carefully before placing your order. -------, you can use the "Back" button to make any necessary changes.
131.
-------. We cannot reuse items due to the custom nature of our products. After your order is
132.
placed, you ------- the sales receipt within a few minutes. Another e-mail will be sent when your
133.
items are -------. This may take up to five days, depending on the volume of our orders.
134.

---

131. (A) Consequently
(B) For example
(C) Conversely
(D) Additionally

132. (A) Subscribers to our newsletter can receive a discount.
(B) Please be aware that all sales are final.
(C) Don't forget to check back regularly for new merchandise.
(D) The delivery options will be presented to you.

133. (A) have been e-mailed
(B) were being e-mailed
(C) will be e-mailed
(D) were e-mailed

134. (A) ready
(B) brief
(C) similar
(D) exempt

PART 6가 하나의 글을 읽고 문제를 풀어야 하는 파트이긴 하지만 상당수의 문제들은 PART 5와 마찬가지로 빈칸이 있는 문장 만으로 답을 찾을 수 있다. 예를 들어, 품사 문제는 빈칸 문장의 문장 구조와 빈칸 앞뒤에 있는 단어들의 품사나 문장 성분만 고 려해도 답을 찾을 수 있다. 하지만 시제와 어휘 문제는 두 개 이상의 선택지가 정답 후보로 남을 경우 반드시 앞뒤 문맥을 고려해 야만 한다. 특히 문장과 문장을 연결하는 접속부사나 문맥에 맞는 문장 고르기 문제는 예외 없이 문맥을 통해 해결해야 한다.

---

131. (A) Consequently
(B) For example
(C) Conversely
(D) Additionally

접속부사
접속부사 문제를 풀 때는 빈칸이 속한 문장과 바로 앞 문장 의 논리적 연결 관계(인과, 역접, 예시 등)가 판단의 기준이 된다. additionally(덧붙여), however(그러나) 등과 같이 한 단어로 된 접속부사뿐만 아니라 in other words(달리 말하 면), as a result(결과적으로), if possible(가능하다면)과 같 이 여러 단어로 이루어진 관용 표현이 빈번하게 출제된다.

---

132. (A) Subscribers to our newsletter can receive a discount.
(B) Please be aware that all sales are final.
(C) Don't forget to check back regularly for new merchandise.
(D) The delivery options will be presented to you.

문맥에 맞는 문장 고르기
일반적으로 한 문단은 하나의 일관된 주제를 갖게 되므로 해 당 문단이 다루는 중심 내용에서 빗나가는 선택지는 소거한 다. 또한 문단의 시작 부분에 빈칸이 있는 경우를 제외하고 대부분의 빈칸은 바로 앞 문장과 얼마나 잘 연결되느냐가 우 선적인 판단의 근거가 되므로 빈칸 뒤에 오는 문장보다는 앞 에 오는 문장을 항상 먼저 확인해야 한다.

---

133. (A) have been e-mailed
(B) were being e-mailed
(C) will be e-mailed
(D) were e-mailed

시제
서로 다른 시제의 선택지가 최종 정답 후보로 남았을 경우에 는 일차적으로 빈칸이 속해 있는 문장 안의 시간 부사 또는 주절 및 종속절의 시제 등을 살펴본 뒤, 최종적으로는 앞뒤 문맥의 흐름을 통해 시제를 결정해야 한다. 또 이메일이나 기사, 공지 등은 해당 글이 작성된 날짜를 고려해 시제를 판 단해야 하는 경우도 있다.

---

134. (A) ready
(B) brief
(C) similar
(D) exempt

어휘
빈칸의 앞뒤 단어와 잘 연결되는지를 일차적으로 고려하되 두 개 이상의 어휘가 모두 답이 될 수 있을 경우에는 앞뒤 문 맥을 따져 판단해야 한다.

Questions 1-2 refer to the following Web page.

Spring Flower Arrangement Course—Now Accepting Applications

Tidwell Community College ------- a new course this spring semester for the local community.
1.
Award-winning florist Jennifer Goldsmith will show students how to build the perfect arrangement

for special occasions as well as teach students tips on how to make their creations last longer.

Classes ------- every Tuesday and Friday evening from 7 P.M. to 10 P.M.
2.

A final exhibition of their semester pieces will be shown on June 2. For tickets, visit the

community college website at www.tidwellcc.com.

1.　(A) opening
　　(B) will be opening
　　(C) had opened
　　(D) was opening

2.　(A) are held
　　(B) have been held
　　(C) were held
　　(D) being held

Questions 3-4 refer to the following announcement.

Big news, Classic Motors team!

We would like to congratulate Nathaniel Foreman on his promotion to Team Manager, effective

August 16. Mr. Foreman ------- Classic Motors as an intern through our Russel College Internship
3.
Program. He has spent the last 15 years going above and beyond for staff and making significant

contributions to the company by always looking for new and innovative solutions for our

financing team. We are certain that Mr. Foreman ------- in his new position. Please give him a big
4.
congratulations the next time you see him.

3.　(A) entering
　　(B) is entering
　　(C) will enter
　　(D) entered

4.　(A) will shine
　　(B) shone
　　(C) shines
　　(D) is shining

Questions 5-6 refer to the following advertisement.

It's Emerald Footwear's 25th anniversary!

Twenty-five years ago, Emerald Footwear opened as a small kiosk at the Plainsman Mall. Today, we have our own two-story building with a spacious display area. Our high-quality products and knowledgeable staff ------- us to become a trusted retailer. To thank our customers for their
5.
patronage over the years, we are having a special deal on September 8.

Purchase one pair of shoes and get 60% off another pair. This offer ------- to any brand, with the
6.
less expensive pair receiving the discount. Please note that the deal cannot be used with any other additional coupon.

5. (A) have helped
    (B) are helped
    (C) helping
    (D) were helping

6. (A) was applying
    (B) will have applied
    (C) had applied
    (D) applies

Questions 7-8 refer to the following customer review.

I just received my order of 100 napkins from Home Necessities, and I am thoroughly impressed! I have to order table setting supplies for my catering business. However, since the company I regularly order from was out of stock, I decided to give Home Necessities a chance. The items are better constructed, and the company ------- a wider range of colors and designs. I -------
7. **8.**
from Home Necessities exclusively from now on.

— Martin Quinn

7. (A) will have offered
    (B) offers
    (C) offering
    (D) was offering

8. (A) ordered
    (B) was ordering
    (C) will be ordering
    (D) had ordered

Question 1 refers to the following e-mail.

We would like to inform you that the Graystone Printer X302 has been discontinued, and your order has been automatically cancelled. However, many of our most recent customers have enjoyed the ------- model, the X430. Please call us at 555-2098 to place a new order or discuss
1.
refund options.

Alex's Office Supplies

---

1.   (A) accountable
      (B) comparable
      (C) amicable
      (D) applicable

Question 2 refers to the following advertisement.

Come to Auto Masters and we will service your entire vehicle in just two hours. This includes changing the oil, ------- window-washer fluid, rotating your tires, and more. Located next to the
2.
Fairhills Shopping Mall, we can do this while you spend time with your family. Call us at 555-2840 to book this service or one of our many others.

---

2.   (A) remarking
      (B) rounding
      (C) reloading
      (D) refilling

Question 3 refers to the following announcement.

September marks the beginning of the new opera season for the Toronto Opera Company. Opening night is September 12 and runs through December 31. This year, everyone is invited to sit in during one of their ------- rehearsals every Tuesday from 2:00 P.M. to 4:00 P.M. To reserve
3.
tickets for a rehearsal, please visit their Web site at www.torontooc.org.

---

3.   (A) seasonal
      (B) public
      (C) domestic
      (D) challenging

Question 4 refers to the following job posting.

> Rainbow Toys is looking for a new social marketing manager. Applicants will work on making our social media platforms more accessible and creating more ------- content for our customers. For
> **4.**
> that reason, applicants should have experience in either video creation, social media platform management, or copywriting.

4. (A) lengthy
   (B) engaging
   (C) impersonal
   (D) accelerated

Question 5 refers to the following advertisement.

> Booker is offering a special New Year's discount on our most popular reading plan! Sign up for the Deluxe reading plan and get ------- to over 500,000 books, plus 30% off purchases of this
> **5.**
> month's latest releases. And only Booker offers unlimited book rentals. You can take advantage of this deal today at www.booker.com/newyear.

5. (A) claim
   (B) control
   (C) access
   (D) entry

Questions 6-7 refer to the following customer review.

> I have been using Manaray's furniture for years and was always satisfied with my purchases. However, after visiting a Logan's Furniture showroom, I am glad I did. The quality of furniture is on another level!
>
> Their leather sofas are made using luxurious, soft leather. All of their designs can be customized to include a recliner as well. We also found the perfect dining room table set in a mahogany wood. The table and chairs feel ------- and are sure to last a lifetime.
> **6.**
> Please be aware that most items do not come -------. Professional assembly is available for a
> **7.**
> small additional fee. But that may not be necessary thanks to their easy-to-follow instructions included with everything.

6. (A) separate
   (B) stiff
   (C) simple
   (D) sturdy

7. (A) fixed
   (B) assembled
   (C) crumbled
   (D) pieced

Question 1 refers to the following letter.

To Whom It May Concern,

We here at Forever Fitness would like to invite you to become a member. We have the largest array of top-of-the-line equipment in the region in a state-of-the-art, 40-acre facility. We provide a unique feature—photo zones for those who maintain a social media presence. -------, all **1.** photography is not allowed on our regular gym floors without previous consent. Our gym offers the widest range of fitness programs of any gym, over 40 kinds. And all instructors and trainers have multiple national certifications to give you the best experience possible.

Call us at 555-2109 for a free consultation, and receive a free 1-day pass. We're sure you will come back.

Best regards,

Kelly Vasquez, Owner

1.　(A) Besides
　　(B) Otherwise
　　(C) If not
　　(D) Regardless

Question 2 refers to the following advertisement.

Get Your Business Noticed!

Do you have a great business, but nobody seems to know? We can fix that! Frankfurt Media has a team of experts ready to build the right advertising strategy for your business. We will craft the perfect TV or radio commercial and get it to your intended audience. -------, you will have more **2.** time to focus on your business.

Go to www.frankfurtmedia.com today, and have your advertisement ready in one week!

2.　(A) Nevertheless
　　(B) Even so
　　(C) Meanwhile
　　(D) Recently

Question 3 refers to the following e-mail.

To: Mark Klein <kleinm@solarnet.com>
From: Jane Lorowitz <jlorowitz@greatconstructs.com>
Date: April 20
Subject: Schedule Change

Dear Mr. Klein,

I am writing to let you know there has been a change in the construction schedule. The current schedule has us booked until June 12. However, because of the frequent rainstorms these days, we have had to stop construction on those days. ------- , we were unable to finish putting up the walls. The new estimated end date is June 20.
                                                        3.

I would be happy to chat if you would like to discuss the schedule further.

Regards,

Jane Lorowitz

3.   (A) Nonetheless
     (B) Consequently
     (C) Finally
     (D) Lastly

PART 6

Question 4 refers to the following information.

After six months of renovations, Craftsbury Library is happy to announce our reopening. Some new features include a wheelchair-accessible entrance complete with a ramp and five new classrooms to hold more of our popular after-school programs. ------- , we've established an
                                                                              4.
occupation preparation center to help Craftsbury residents look for and secure jobs. To find out all of the new features at the library, head to our Web site at www.craftsburylibrary.gov.

4.   (A) Hence
     (B) Accordingly
     (C) Therefore
     (D) Additionally

Question 1 refers to the following e-mail.

To: All Customers
From: Keritz Audio Customer Service Team
Date: December 2
Subject: End-of-Year Closure

Keritz Audio will be closed for the end-of-the-year holiday season, effective December 23.

------- . Any orders placed after this date will be shipped in the new year. Also, please remember
　　1.
that delivery dates will vary depending on your exact delivery location. To view an estimated

delivery schedule for your region, please check out the shipping section of our Web site.

We appreciate your continued support. We are looking forward to showing you the new products

we have lined up for the new year.

Sincerely,

The Keritz Audio Team

1.　(A) Please contact the courier service with your confirmation number.
　　(B) Express delivery is available for an extra $5.99.
　　(C) We are open from 9:00 A.M. to 5:00 P.M.
　　(D) The last date you can order before the end of the year is December 22.

Question 2 refers to the following announcement.

Come visit beautiful Catskills Waterpark for a day of fun and excitement for the whole family.

Not only are we the largest waterpark in the area, we are also the most eco-friendly. We are the

only waterpark in the nation to feature a completely environmentally friendly water-usage system.

------- . This is used to reduce the impact on local water supplies. The park even uses
　　2.
hydroelectricity to power all rides and tide pools. We want families to enjoy Catskills Waterpark

for generations. For tickets and information, visit us at www.catskillswaterpark.com.

2.　(A) All water is collected from natural sources, such as rainwater and natural reservoirs.
　　(B) We ask that all visitors pick up their trash when at the park.
　　(C) Please refrain from using too much water during your visit.
　　(D) All paper products are made from recycled paper.

Question 3 refers to the following notice.

We have recently been told that our current vendor, Global Produce Distributions, has decided to downsize their supply chain. This means we will be unable to export our citrus fruit to Northern Europe. -------. That is why we need to put a lot of effort into finding a new distributor.
3.

One thing we pride ourselves on is our wide array of exotic fruit. See if you can find a company that needs that area supplemented. If you find any companies, please let me know.

I would like a list of possible leads by Friday afternoon to present at the weekly managers meeting.

3. (A) None of our team has ever been to Northern Europe.
    (B) Please give us a detailed list of your citrus fruit.
    (C) We need to work on increasing our supplies.
    (D) This region was a major part of our expansion plan this year.

Question 4 refers to the following information.

Charles Hartman, owner of Hartman Landscaping, has been beautifying the region for over 20 years. His team specializes in commercial and public properties.

They are well-known for their construction of the area's most popular recreational parks and spaces. -------. This 100-acre area is home to the annual George Street Music Festival.
4.

To turn your property into a work of art, contact Hartman Landscaping today. They will help you build the perfect lawn based for your budget and size.

4. (A) Their office is located right next to the local post office.
    (B) They are responsible for the award-winning design of Campbell Park.
    (C) As a result, they prefer to use all native flowers and shrubs.
    (D) They are the biggest sponsors of the annual event.

PART 6

Directions: Read the texts that follow. A word, phrase, or sentence is missing in parts of each text. Four answer choices for each question are given below the text. Select the best answer to complete the text. Then mark the letter (A), (B), (C), or (D) on your answer sheet.

Questions 131-134 refer to the following e-mail.

To: Edward Sandoval <sandovaledward@warrenmail.com>
From: Brunswick Studios <accounts@brunswickstudios.com>
Date: February 22
Subject: Membership

Dear Mr. Sandoval,

Thank you for signing up for a one-year membership with Brunswick Studios. Our Web site is devoted to helping you reach new fans, write meaningful songs, and improve your performances. The content on our Web site ------- by musicians like you. You'll receive e-mails about special
                                          131.
deals on products you may need, such as software programs ------- projects that require editing.
                                                                132.

To ------- the content sent to your inbox, sign into your account and select your desired options.
     133.
For just $5.99 more per month, you can be upgraded to Gold Status and receive even more

content. -------. So, why not give it a try risk-free?
         134.

Warmest regards,

Tara Nelson
Brunswick Studios

---

131. (A) wrote
(B) will write
(C) is written
(D) had been written

132. (A) into
(B) for
(C) our
(D) at

133. (A) deliver
(B) personalize
(C) calculate
(D) dispute

134. (A) We are pleased to have been nominated.
(B) You can cancel anytime with no penalty.
(C) Your feedback helps us improve our services.
(D) The speed depends on your Internet service.

To: All Redhawk Towers Tenants
From: Jennifer Milligan
Date: February 20
Subject: Power outage

Dear Redhawk Towers Tenants,

An interruption to the electricity supply ------- for all buildings on Jennings Street and Pine Street
                                           135.
between 12th and 14th Avenue. Power will be shut off in order to perform essential maintenance

tasks. Work will take place on February 25 and 26 from 9 A.M. to noon.

Please plan ahead for the outage on ------- day. Computers should be shut down prior to the
                                      136.
outage. -------. Food stored in refrigerators and freezers will be fine if the doors are kept closed.
          137.
Thank you for your ------- and patience.
                     138.

Jennifer Milligan
Property Manager, Redhawk Towers

135. (A) has scheduled
    (B) schedules
    (C) is scheduled
    (D) is scheduling

136. (A) only
    (B) most
    (C) all
    (D) each

137. (A) Several apartment units are now
        available.
    (B) Those left on could be damaged by an
        unexpected shutdown.
    (C) We can confirm that safety is taken
        seriously.
    (D) The noise will no longer be a
        disturbance to everyone.

138. (A) donation
    (B) cooperation
    (C) destination
    (D) confirmation

PART 6

GO ON TO THE NEXT PAGE

Vehicles for Plumbers

If you are working as an independent plumber, it is essential that you have a vehicle. At first, you may think it's a good idea to look for the ------- option. However, it's much better to invest in a
139.
reliable vehicle from the start. -------. For example, will you have to fit into tight parking spaces
140.
or store large ------- such as power saws in it? Be sure to read the reviews for the model you are
141.
considering. -------, the vehicle you purchase will support and maybe even motivate you during
142.
your business journey.

139. (A) cheaply
(B) as cheap as
(C) cheapest
(D) cheaper than

140. (A) The fuel efficiency of the vehicle is important.
(B) Building a client base can take several months.
(C) Plumbing jobs are steadily in demand throughout the year.
(D) You should take some time to think about the size you need.

141. (A) electricians
(B) uniforms
(C) tools
(D) pipes

142. (A) Lately
(B) On the other hand
(C) Otherwise
(D) Ultimately

March 3

Dear Northwest Utilities Customers,

We would like to apologize for any confusion caused by the most recent bill for your -------. Our
                                                                                          143.
billing department experienced a software malfunction. As a result, the bills for February were

------- with the wrong information. ------- we strive to accurately reflect customers' usage, this
144.   **145.**
error sometimes happens.

-------. You can expect to receive it within the next five business days. We will also extend the
146.
deadline by two weeks because of this error. Thank you for your patience and understanding

during this process.

Northwest Utilities
4190 Woodland Terrace
Tacoma, WA 98412

143. (A) energy
(B) energize
(C) energetic
(D) energizes

144. (A) given away
(B) cashed in
(C) brought down
(D) sent out

145. (A) Despite
(B) Except
(C) Once
(D) Although

146. (A) Please ignore the bill and wait for a
new one to be issued.
(B) Some of the electricity comes from
renewable sources.
(C) The policy is clearly outlined on our
Web site.
(D) We appreciate your prompt payment
for the service.

RC

PART

7

PART 7 출제 경향 및 전략

지문 유형과 출제 경향

PART 7 지문은 영미권, 특히 미국에서 일상적으로 접할 수 있는 내용을 광범위하게 다룬다. PART 7의 난이도는 특정 지문 유형이 쉽거나 어렵다기보다는 지문의 길이와 어휘 난이도에 달려 있고, 지문의 전체 맥락을 파악해야 하는 문제의 비중도 점점 늘고 있기 때문에 지문을 정확하고 꼼꼼하게 해석하는 것이 중요해지고 있다.

이메일·편지	업무 지원 요청, 추천서, 정기 간행물 구독, 서비스 문의/불만
문자 메시지·온라인 채팅	업무 지원 요청 및 진행 상황 보고, 프로젝트에 관한 의견 교환
기사	축제/경연 대회/콘퍼런스 등의 개최 소식, 기업 소개/합병/신제품 등의 보도 자료
공지	건물/시설 보수 공사, 서비스 변경, 서비스/행사 홍보, 사내 회람
광고	상품/서비스 광고, 구인 광고
웹페이지	강좌/세미나 안내, 정책 안내, 제품/서비스 소개, 고객 후기
양식	송장, 일정표, 탑승권, 영수증

문제 유형과 출제 경향

주제·목적	처음 두세 줄을 읽고 답을 찾을 수 있는 경우가 많다. 하지만 지문의 첫 단락을 다 읽어야 하거나 마지막 단락에서 답을 찾을 수 있는 문제도 매회 1문제 이상 출제된다. · What is **the purpose** of the article? · **Why was** the e-mail **sent**?
세부 사항	PART 7에서 가장 많이 출제되는 문제 유형이며 육하원칙(Who, When, Where, What, How, Why)으로 지문의 세부 내용을 묻는다. · **When** will staff receive the message?
NOT/True	지문의 내용과 일치하거나 일치하지 않는 것을 묻는 문제 유형으로 다른 문제에 비해 풀이가 까다로운 편이다. · What is **indicated/stated** about Adnan's Auto Garage? · What is **NOT mentioned** about the offer?
추론·암시	세부 사항과 더불어 PART 7에서 가장 많이 출제된다. 지문 내용을 바탕으로 지문에 직접 언급되지 않은 내용을 유추하여 푸는 문제이다. · What is **implied/suggested** about Loretti Co.? · Who **most likely** is Ms. Fernandez?
의도 파악	문자 메시지와 온라인 채팅 지문에서 각각 1문제씩 출제된다. 문맥에 따라 의미가 달라지는 표현이 문제로 제시되기 때문에 해당 표현만 읽고서는 절대 답을 고를 수 없다. 따라서 대화의 흐름을 잘 파악하는 것이 중요하다. · At 8:59 A.M., what does Ms. Randolph most likely mean when she writes, "Not at all"?
동의어 찾기	단일 지문과 이중 지문에서 1~3문제가 출제된다. 주어진 단어의 대표 동의어가 오답 선택지로 종종 나오기 때문에 주어진 단어가 있는 문장의 문맥으로 단어의 의미를 정확하게 확인하는 것이 중요하다. · The word "sector" in paragraph 1, line 2, is closest in meaning to

문장 삽입	단일 지문에서만 2문제가 나온다. 항상 해당 지문의 마지막 문제로 나오기 때문에 앞에 있는 문제들을 먼저 풀면서 전체적인 맥락을 충분히 파악해 두어야 하며, 제시된 문장의 접속부사나 대명사, 정관사를 활용하면 문제 풀이에 도움이 된다.
	• In which of the positions marked [1], [2], [3], and [4] does the following sentence best belong?

문제 풀이 전략

모든 공부에는 왕도가 없다지만 독해만큼 요령이 잘 통하지 않는 영역은 없다. 많은 학습서나 강사가 PART 7 문제 풀이 전략을 쏟아 내지만 정작 스스로에게 신통방통하게 들어맞는 기술이나 전략이 있었는지 곰곰이 생각해 보자.
어설픈 독해 기술과 전략은 차라리 버리는 게 낫다. 물론 850점 이상의 고득점을 목표로 하는 700점 중반~800점 초반 정도의 실력자라면 기술과 전략이 통할 수 있다. 하지만 그 이하의 점수대에서는 오히려 독이 될 뿐이다. 지금 단계에서는 빠른 길이 아닌 바른 길을 찾아서 학습해도 결코 늦지 않다.

독하게 해야 하니까 독해다.
해설집이나 강의에서 설명하는 걸 백날 보기만 하면 독해력은 절대 늘지 않는다. 설명을 듣는 그 순간에는 고개를 끄덕이지만 뒤돌아서면 머리에 남는 게 없다. 배운 것을 소화해서 온전히 내 것으로 만드는 과정이 없었기 때문이다. 이 소화 과정이 다소 지루하고 힘들게 느껴질 수 있지만 독하게 해야 하니까 '독해'라고 생각하자.
PART 7 정답률이 70%가 안 되는 학습자라면 시간을 재고 문제를 푸는 연습보다는 독해를 정확하게 할 수 있는 방향으로 학습하는 것이 제일 효과적이므로 아래 두 가지 방식을 추천한다.

• 어려운 문장은 공책에 적어 두고 문장 구조를 찬찬히 뜯어보면서 이해하고 체화한다.
• PART 7의 정답 대부분은 지문에 나온 표현을 패러프레이즈(paraphrase)해서 나오므로 지문에 있는 정답 단서가 선택지에서는 어떤 식으로 표현되었는지 형광펜으로 표시하거나 따로 정리하면서 감을 익힌다.

나무를 보려 하지 말고 숲을 봐야 한다.
토익처럼 한 지문을 읽고 최소 2문제 이상 풀어야 하는 시험은 전반적인 지문 내용을 파악해야 하는 문제가 하나 이상 출제된다. 또한 최근 토익은 지문과 선택지를 하나하나 대조하면서 풀어야 하는 NOT/True 문제의 출제 비중을 늘리는 추세이기 때문에 지문의 특정 부분만 골라서 읽을 수도 없거니와 그렇게 하면 전체 맥락 파악이 어려워서 오히려 다른 문제의 정답 도출이 더 힘들어진다.
PART 7은 다른 파트에 비해 읽어야 할 양이 많아서 지문을 차근차근 읽는다는 게 다소 부담스럽게 느껴질 수 있으나 〈ETS 토익 정기시험 기출문제집 1000〉에 실린 PART 7 지문의 문장들을 하나하나 살펴보면 해석이 불가능할 정도로 어려운 건 거의 없다는 걸 알 수 있다. 오히려 쉬워 보일 수도 있다. 따라서 초급자는 정답 단서라는 나무 한 그루에 연연하지 말고 지문을 처음부터 꼼꼼하게 해석하여 전체 문맥이라는 숲을 봐야 문제 풀이가 수월해진다.

시간이 부족할 땐 다중 지문에서 쉬운 문제라도 푼다.
마킹할 시간을 제외하고 문제를 풀 수 있는 시간이 5~10분 정도 남았다면 포기하지 말고 쉬운 문제라도 푸는 것이 좋다. 대개 시간 부족으로 다중 지문 문제들을 못 푸는 경우가 많은데 다중 지문의 5문제 중 2문제 정도는 각 지문의 초반부와 후반부 3줄 정도로 해결되는 경우(주제·목적, 동의어 찾기 등)가 많기 때문에 시간이 부족하다면 이런 문제들이라도 푸는 것이 좋다.

1 지문의 구성과 흐름 파악하기

수신인 To: Bonnie Rosario <b.rosario@glendalehotel.com>
발신인 From: Philip Hawley <philip@charackconstruction.com>
날짜 Date: April 24
제목 Subject: Pool Construction

Dear Ms. Rosario,

초반부 Charack Construction has received the deposit for building an outdoor pool at your hotel. A project of this scope usually takes approximately 6–8 weeks. However, we will be able to complete the work within 3 weeks, as

중반부 you requested. We understand the importance of having the facility open before the busy summer season begins. Our team can begin the work on April 28, which will initially involve clearing and preparing the ground.

후반부 Most of the details of the project have already been finalized, but you will need to choose the tile pattern. One of my employees will drop off a box of samples later today. Please look these over and let me know at our April 30 meeting which one you prefer. I will only send you tiles that we already have in stock, so there will be no issues with distribution chain delays.

All the best,

발신인 Philip Hawley
Manager, Charack Construction

❶ 공사 소요일 안내
야외 수영장 건설은 원래 최대 8주가 걸리는 작업이지만 요청한 대로 3주 안에 마무리하겠음.

❷ 공사 시작일 안내
4월 28일에 청소와 사전 준비를 시작으로 공사를 진행하겠음.

❸ 타일 선택 요청
타일 샘플을 보낼 테니 원하는 타일 패턴을 골라서 4월 30일 회의 때 알려 줄 것을 요청함.

1. What is the purpose of the e-mail?

   (A) To suggest changes to a work plan
   (B) To request funds for a deposit
   (C) To introduce a construction business
   (D) To provide an update on a project

2. The phrase "drop off" in paragraph 2, line 3, is closest in meaning to

   (A) collect
   (B) deliver
   (C) reduce
   (D) doze

3. According to the e-mail, what should Ms. Rosario do before the April 30 meeting?

   (A) Confirm a size
   (B) Select some materials
   (C) Sign a contract
   (D) Review some sketches

1. What is the purpose of the e-mail?

> Charack Construction has received the deposit for building an outdoor pool at your hotel. A project of this scope usually takes approximately 6–8 weeks. However, we will be able to complete the work within 3 weeks, as you requested. We understand the importance of having the facility open before the busy summer season begins. Our team can begin the work on April 28, which will initially involve clearing and preparing the ground.

야외 수영장 공사를 3주 안에 끝낼 수 있다며 구체적인 공사 기간을 알리고 있다.

4월 28일에 공사를 시작할 것이라고 공사 시작 시점을 언급한 것으로 보아 야외 수영장 공사가 얼마나 걸리는지 그리고 언제 시작하는지 알리기 위해 이메일을 썼다는 걸 알 수 있으므로 (D) To provide an update on a project(프로젝트 관련 최신 정보를 전달하기 위해)가 정답이다.

동의어 찾기 문제를 풀 때는 단순히 해당 단어의 사전적 의미만 고려해서는 안 된다. 해당 단어가 포함된 문장의 문맥을 통해 단어 뜻을 파악한 다음 선택지에서 그와 가장 유사한 뜻을 가진 단어를 골라야 한다.

2. The phrase "**drop off**" in paragraph 2, line 3, is closest in meaning to

> Most of the details of the project have already been finalized, but you will need to choose the tile pattern. One of my employees will drop off a box of samples later today.

drop off가 있는 문장은 '제 직원 한 명이 오늘 늦게 샘플 한 상자를 가져다줄 것입니다.'를 의미하므로 이 문장에서 drop off는 '~을 가져다주다'라는 뜻으로 쓰였다는 걸 알 수 있다. 따라서 (B) deliver(배달하다)가 정답이다.

PART 7

3. According to the e-mail, what should Ms. Rosario do before the April 30 meeting?

> Most of the details of the project have already been finalized, but you will need to choose the tile pattern. One of my employees will drop off a box of samples later today. Please look these over and let me know at our April 30 meeting which one you prefer.

타일 패턴을 골라야 한다고 한 다음에 샘플 박스를 보낼 테니 잘 살펴보고 4월 30일 회의 때 원하는 타일을 알려 달라고 했다. 따라서 Ms. Rosario는 4월 30일 회의 전에 자신이 원하는 타일을 선택해야 한다는 걸 알 수 있으므로 (B) Select some materials(자재 선택하기)가 정답이다.

Questions 1-2 refer to the following e-mail.

To:	Ravi Singh <singhr@nayarsecurities.com>
From:	Emerald Gardening Supplies <orders@emerald-garden.com>
Date:	May 2
Subject:	Order #03795
Attachment:	RG7_manual

Dear Mr. Singh,

Thank you for your recent purchase from Emerald Gardening Supplies! For the past 10 years, we have been providing our customers with equipment and decorations to make their gardens look great. We hope that you will enjoy the RG7 solar-powered lanterns that you ordered. Please find attached the user manual, which provides tips on where to place the lanterns to maximize their sun exposure during the day.

If you have a picture of the lanterns in your garden, please share it on our social media page and you will be entered into a drawing to win a $100 voucher.

Warmest regards,

The Emerald Gardening Supplies

1. What is indicated about the lanterns?
   (A) They should not be exposed to moisture.
   (B) They can be charged by the sun.
   (C) They are available in a variety of sizes.
   (D) They come with a ten-year warranty.

2. What is Mr. Singh asked to do?
   (A) Write a review of the product
   (B) Provide an address for sending a voucher
   (C) Show the company proof of purchase
   (D) Post an image on social media

February 19

Melissa Hammond
HR Director
Eastbourne Solar
Malvern Building #203
Eastbourne, BN20 7AF

Dear Ms. Hammond,

It was a pleasure meeting you during the interview at your office, and I am honored that you have invited me to join the Eastbourne Solar team as a senior salesperson. Unfortunately, I am unable to accept the role, as I have decided to take a position at another company that does not require me to travel. I have a great deal of respect for your company, and I'm confident that it will continue to gain market share and expand its staff.

As promised, please find enclosed a list of the web-based e-signature tools that we talked about during the interview. I am not affiliated with any of the companies, but I believe the information will be useful to you. I plan to attend the Annual Solar Trade Exhibition later this year, so I hope to have a chance to see you there and to discuss the industry further.

Warmest regards,

Spencer Ingram

Spencer Ingram

Enclosure

3. What is the purpose of Mr. Ingram's letter?

(A) To inquire about job duties
(B) To introduce his company
(C) To schedule an interview
(D) To reject a job offer

4. What does Mr. Ingram indicate about Eastbourne Solar?

(A) It focuses on teamwork.
(B) It should invest more in marketing.
(C) It has a good compensation package.
(D) It will grow in the future.

5. What does Mr. Ingram send to Ms. Hammond?

(A) A signed contract
(B) A list of online tools
(C) A proposed interview schedule
(D) A Web site survey form

6. The word "attend" in paragraph 2, line 3, is closest in meaning to

(A) go to
(B) coincide with
(C) come across
(D) look after

UNIT 14 문자 메시지·온라인 채팅

1 지문의 구성과 흐름 파악하기

**용건
전달**

Gina Quan [8:25 A.M.]
Hi, Bruno. I'm having some trouble getting to the Barraza
Conference Center. I'll need to take a taxi, but I would
expect that to be covered by the company.

➊ 연락한 목적 언급
택시비를 회사에서 처리해 줄 것을 요청함.

**세부
사항**

Bruno Mota [8:28 A.M.]
That's fine. Just be sure to keep your receipt. Isn't the
Shelby Hotel running its shuttle service anymore?

➋-1 요청 승인
비용 처리 요청을 승인하며 영수증만 잘 보관해 달라고 함.

Gina Quan [8:29 A.M.]
Yes, but you have to book in advance. I guess they've
changed their policy because last time, I took the shuttle
without a reservation.

➋-2 호텔 방침 변경 언급
호텔 셔틀 서비스는 미리 예약해야 이용할 수 있음. 이용 방식이 이전과 다른 걸로 보아 방침이 바뀐 것 같다고 함.

**추가
사항
확인**

Bruno Mota [8:31 A.M.]
Do you need me to find a taxi service for you?

➌ 추가로 할 일 확인
택시 서비스를 찾아봐 줘야 할지 물어봄.

Gina Quan [8:32 A.M.]
Thanks, but I have a number I can call.

1. At 8:28 A.M., what does Mr. Mota most
likely mean when he writes, "That's fine"?

(A) He will go to a conference center in
Ms. Quan's place.
(B) He can meet Ms. Quan at a different
location.
(C) He agrees to authorize a transportation
cost.
(D) He has found the receipt for a booking.

2. What is suggested about Ms. Quan?

(A) She is Mr. Mota's supervisor.
(B) She would like help finding a contact
number.
(C) She lost her hotel reservation number.
(D) She has stayed at the Shelby Hotel
before.

1. At 8:28 A.M., what does Mr. Mota most likely mean when he writes, "**That's fine**"?

> **Gina Quan [8:25 A.M.]**
> Hi, Bruno. I'm having some trouble getting to the Barraza Conference Center. I'll need to take a taxi, but I would expect that to be covered by the company.
>
> **Bruno Mota [8:28 A.M.]**
> That's fine. Just be sure to keep your receipt. Isn't the Shelby Hotel running its shuttle service anymore?

Ms. Quan이 택시를 타야 할 것 같은데 회사에서 비용을 처리해 줬으면 좋겠다고 했다.

Mr. Mota가 괜찮다고 한 다음 영수증만 잘 챙겨 달라고 부탁한 것으로 보아 That's fine은 Ms. Quan의 요청을 수락한다는 의도로 한 말임을 알 수 있다. 따라서 (C) He agrees to authorize a transportation cost.(교통비 승인에 동의한다.)가 정답이다.

2. What is suggested about **Ms. Quan**?

> **Bruno Mota [8:28 A.M.]**
> That's fine. Just be sure to keep your receipt. Isn't the Shelby Hotel running its shuttle service anymore?
>
> **Gina Quan [8:29 A.M.]**
> Yes, but you have to book in advance. I guess they've changed their policy because last time, I took the shuttle without a reservation.

Mr. Mota가 Shelby Hotel은 셔틀 서비스를 더 이상 운영하지 않는지 물었다.

Ms. Quan이 미리 예약해야 한다고 답변하며 저번에는 예약 없이 셔틀을 탔는데 방침이 바뀐 것 같다고 한 것으로 보아 Ms. Quan은 Shelby Hotel을 이용한 적이 있다는 걸 알 수 있다. 따라서 (D) She has stayed at the Shelby Hotel before.(전에 Shelby Hotel에 묵은 적이 있다.)가 정답이다.

PRACTICE

정답 및 해설 p.81

Questions 1-2 refer to the following text-message chain.

Betsy Braun (1:46 P.M.)
Hi, Matthew. Have you or your team members been monitoring the Haven Street entrance?

Matthew Alvarado (1:48 P.M.)
In addition to the video monitoring, we had our usual hourly check in person about 20 minutes ago. Why do you ask?

Betsy Braun (1:49 P.M.)
I noticed that the door is unlocked. I thought it was supposed to remain locked at all times.

Matthew Alvarado (1:51 P.M.)
It is, except when deliveries are being made. Anchorage Supplies has just finished unloading everything. I've notified Eric.

Betsy Braun (1:53 P.M.)
Alright, that's good to know. I'm glad someone's taking care of it.

---

1. Who most likely is Mr. Alvarado?

(A) A security guard
(B) A driving instructor
(C) A video editor
(D) A receptionist

2. At 1:51 P.M., what does Mr. Alvarado mean when he writes, "I've notified Eric"?

(A) Eric will come to work early.
(B) Eric will unload a truck.
(C) Eric will lock a door.
(D) Eric will meet with Ms. Braun.

Questions 3-6 refer to the following online chat discussion.

Kathleen Arcand [10:03 A.M.]	I'm booking the train tickets today for our meeting next week with Bancroft to sign the contract.
Gordon Walters [10:04 A.M.]	We're leaving on Tuesday, right?
Kathleen Arcand [10:07 A.M.]	Actually, since the meeting isn't until Wednesday afternoon, I thought we could go that morning and then return on Thursday morning.
Gordon Walters [10:08 A.M.]	Alright. Are we bringing brochures?
Kathleen Arcand [10:10 A.M.]	Is it necessary? They've already seen our heart monitoring equipment.
Gordon Walters [10:11 A.M.]	We can introduce some of our other items for future consideration.
Kathleen Arcand [10:13 A.M.]	Okay. I'll be sure to pack some. Also, they will take us out for dinner and a show. Macy Oliver from Bancroft is wondering what kind of show we would like to see. I've got to get back to her about that.
Peter Zhang [10:16 A.M.]	That sounds like fun.
Kathleen Arcand [10:17 A.M.]	I'm not sure what's playing. Peter, can you look into that?
Peter Zhang [10:19 A.M.]	I'll do some research to see what's on at the local theaters.
Kathleen Arcand [10:20 A.M.]	Great, but the sooner the better.
Peter Zhang [10:22 A.M.]	Of course. I'll message you within the hour.

3. In what industry do the writers most likely work?

(A) Entertainment
(B) Education
(C) Publishing
(D) Health care

4. When will a contract probably be signed?

(A) On Tuesday
(B) On Wednesday
(C) On Thursday
(D) On Friday

5. What does Ms. Oliver want information about?

(A) Dietary restrictions for a meal
(B) Meeting guests' arrival time
(C) Preferences for a performance
(D) Transportation costs

6. At 10:20 A.M., what does Ms. Arcand mean when she writes, "the sooner the better"?

(A) She is concerned about missing a deadline.
(B) She thinks some train tickets will sell out.
(C) She wants to give a reply quickly.
(D) She needs to leave for a meeting shortly.

1 지문의 구성과 흐름 파악하기

| 제목 | **Library Reopening in Beaverton** |
| 주제 | (October 29)—The reopening of the Beaverton library will take place on September 25. —[1]—. Residents are excited about being able to use the library again, which was scheduled to reopen 18 months ago. |

❶ 도서관 재개관 안내
비버튼 도서관의 재개관이 9월 25일이라고 알림.

| 세부 내용 | Cowan Construction and Brock Builders were both selected to speed up the project process. —[2]—. However, this decision turned out to be a mistake as much time was wasted when both sides often worked on the same tasks without the other knowing it.

In addition, because the project had already gotten off to a bad start, there was increased scrutiny and pressure from the public. —[3]—. The time estimated to complete the project was not reasonable, especially compared to similar work.

The project was also supposed to include a small on-site café. —[4]—. The café option is likely to be revisited in future proposals. |

❷ 공사 중 발생한 문제점 기술
두 시공사를 선정했으나 서로 소통이 잘 되지 않아 많은 시간을 허비함. 그로 인해 정밀 조사와 대중의 압력이 있었고 프로젝트 일정에 차질이 생김.

❸ 미비 시설 언급
당초 구내에 갖추기로 한 작은 카페는 추후 재검토 예정.

1. What is implied about Brock Builders?

   (A) This is its first construction project.
   (B) Its staff did not communicate well with Cowan Construction.
   (C) It will soon go out of business.
   (D) It plans to merge with Cowan Construction.

2. What does the article indicate about the library site?

   (A) Its planners had to reduce the original scope of the project.
   (B) The second phase of building is scheduled for next year.
   (C) It will be partially funded by proceeds from the café.
   (D) It is the second library branch in Beaverton.

3. In which of the positions marked [1], [2], [3], and [4] does the following sentence best belong?

   "This ultimately resulted in the creation of an impossible work schedule."

   (A) [1]
   (B) [2]
   (C) [3]
   (D) [4]

1. What is implied about **Brock Builders**?

Cowan Construction and Brock Builders were both selected to speed up the project process. **However, this decision turned out to be a mistake as** much time was wasted when both sides often worked on the same tasks without the other knowing it.

Brock Builders는 도서관 공사를 위해 Cowan Construction과 함께 선정된 시공사이다.

양측이 서로 모르는 사이에 같은 작업을 하면서 시간을 허비했다고 한 것으로 보아 소통이 원활하지 않았음을 알 수 있다. 따라서 (B) Its staff did not communicate well with Cowan Construction. (직원들이 Cowan Construction과 소통이 잘 되지 않았다.)이 정답이다.

2. What does the article indicate about **the library site**?

The project was also supposed to include a small on-site café. **The café option is likely to be revisited in future proposals.**

프로젝트는 도서관 구내에 작은 카페를 포함하기로 되어 있었다고 한 것으로 보아 결과적으로는 그렇게 하지 못했음을 알 수 있다. 따라서 (A) Its planners had to reduce the original scope of the project.(기획자들은 프로젝트의 원래 범위를 줄여야만 했다.)가 정답이다.

3. In which of the positions marked [1], [2], [3], and [4] does the following sentence best belong?

"**This** ultimately resulted in the creation of an impossible work schedule."

In addition, because the project had already gotten off to a bad start, there was increased scrutiny and pressure from the public. —[3]—. The time estimated to complete the project was not reasonable, especially compared to similar work.

문장 삽입 문제를 풀 때는 주어진 문장을 미리 읽은 다음에 지문을 처음부터 읽어 내려가는 게 좋다. 주어진 문장에는 반드시 접속부사, 접속사, 정관사, 지시대명사 등과 같은 힌트가 있으므로 이를 놓치지 않도록 주의한다. 이 문제에서는 지시대명사 This와 궁극적으로 불가능한 작업 일정을 만드는 결과를 낳았다는 내용을 확인하고 지문을 읽는다.

정밀 조사와 대중의 압력이 많았다는 것이 주어진 문장의 This가 가리키는 내용이다. 이에 [3]에 주어진 문장을 넣어 보면 조사와 압력 때문에 결과적으로는 말도 안되는 작업 일정으로 일해야 했다는 내용으로 자연스럽게 연결되는 걸 알 수 있으므로 (C)가 정답이다.

PRACTICE

정답 및 해설 p.82

Questions 1-2 refer to the following job posting.

Corporate Recruitment Services

| HOME | **NEWLY ADDED** | JOBS DATABASE | SUBMIT AN APPLICATION |

Warehouse Workers Wanted

Laird Home Furnishings is currently seeking warehouse workers for its site in Wilmar. Some on-the-job training is provided, but previous experience in a warehouse environment is preferred. Responsibilities include sorting packages according to delivery routes, loading and unloading vehicles, and keeping storage areas organized. Applicants must have a dependable way to get to the warehouse on their own, as there are no bus stops or train stations nearby.

Click here to apply.

1. What information is included in the job posting?

   (A) The expected hourly wage
   (B) The number of working hours
   (C) The schedule for training sessions
   (D) The duties of the role

2. What is a requirement of the position?

   (A) A safety certificate
   (B) Excellent computer skills
   (C) Reliable transportation to a site
   (D) Previous experience in the field

Questions 3-5 refer to the following announcement.

Share a Winning Idea and Receive Spring Sensations Vouchers!

At Spring Sensations, we are proud to offer unique products that our customers love. With your help, we can make our product line even better! We're looking for ideas for new scents for our popular body lotions and hand creams. If your scent is one of three selected, you'll be sent $500 in Spring Sensations vouchers, and these never expire!

To enter the competition, visit the Spring Sensations social media page and leave a comment with your idea. The new scent can contain a combination of up to three dominant scents, and you should come up with a unique name for it as well. Be sure to check out our existing line at www.springsensations.com to make sure you don't suggest something that we already offer!

The contest will run from March 5 to April 20, and the winners will be announced on our Web site and on social media on April 25. Vouchers will be sent by e-mail on May 1.

---

3. What most likely is Spring Sensations?

(A) A marketing firm
(B) A cosmetics manufacturer
(C) An annual festival
(D) A retail clothing outlet

4. What is NOT a requirement of a submission?

(A) Using a limited number of different scents
(B) Including a name for the creation
(C) Confirming that a combination is not already in use
(D) Providing suggestions for packaging

5. When is the deadline for submitting entries?

(A) March 5
(B) April 20
(C) April 25
(D) May 1

Questions 6-8 refer to the following advertisement.

Maurita Analytical Inc.—Open Positions

Maurita Analytical Inc.(MAI) has been a trusted name in soil testing for agricultural sites and building projects ever since it opened its first branch in Plainview and quickly expanded to Lubbock. We provide employees with a supportive working environment, opportunities for professional growth within the organization, and competitive wages and paid vacation time.

Field Team Leader
Oversees a team of 4–5 soil technicians at the sites. Prepares maps for soil collection sites and assigns tasks to team members. Mainly based in Lubbock but may require work outside the area.

Soil Technician
Visits sites in and around Lubbock to collect and label soil samples. Attention to detail is a must due to the complex steps of the collection process. Technicians work in groups, and training is provided.

Senior Laboratory Technician
Leads a team of eight technicians to conduct accurate soil testing at our laboratory in Hereford. A bachelor's degree in environmental science or a similar major is required. Some occasional travel will be necessary.

6. What is indicated about Maurita Analytical Inc.?

(A) It is the only testing service in the region.
(B) It has a good reputation.
(C) It is still operated by its original founder.
(D) It has discontinued its agricultural service.

7. The word "competitive" in paragraph 1, line 4, is closest in meaning to

(A) conflicting
(B) aggressive
(C) suitable
(D) ambitious

8. What do all of the job openings have in common?

(A) They require some traveling.
(B) They are open only to university graduates.
(C) They pay annual bonuses.
(D) They include managing others.

Art Corner

By Lance Colbert

When the worlds of business and art mix, it is sometimes difficult to find a balance. But local entrepreneurs Elizabeth Sanders and Timothy Marlowe are finding a way to make it work. Their new company, Art Phase, rents original paintings for commercial premises. This is great for businesses in Asheville that want a sophisticated décor but cannot afford to invest heavily in artwork.

Ms. Sanders and Mr. Marlowe got the idea while they were operating an accounting firm together. —[1]—. "We wanted to decorate our office to make a good first impression on clients," Ms. Sanders said. "However, we were just starting out, so there were a lot of other items to purchase. —[2]—. That's because trends change frequently, so paintings can look outdated after a while."

Mr. Marlowe is an amateur artist and is active in the local art community. He and Ms. Sanders founded Art Phase as a side business, and it is expected to be popular. —[3]—. Art Phase offers a wide range of paintings for rent, most of which were created by local artists. Those interested in renting artwork can have an Art Phase consultant visit their site to make recommendations based on the colors in the room and their personal style. Once selected, the artwork is delivered to the site, and it is also picked up for free at the end of the rental period. Customers can change their artwork once per quarter, and they can even receive notes from the artist about the inspiration behind the piece.

"Art Phase is a great opportunity for artists who are not yet established," explained Neil Patterson, president of the Asheville Artists Association. "They can have their art seen by many people while also earning a percentage of the rental fee. For those who cannot afford a booth at Sunshine Street Market or those who do not have gallery space, this is an attractive option. —[4]—."

---

9. What is the purpose of the article?

(A) To introduce an investment opportunity
(B) To highlight the paintings of local artists
(C) To explain a newly available service
(D) To encourage participation in an art course

10. According to the article, what is NOT offered by Art Phase?

(A) Pick-up and delivery
(B) A free trial session
(C) In-person consultations
(D) Comments from the artist

11. What does Mr. Patterson suggest about Sunshine Street Market?

(A) It has high fees.
(B) It is decorated attractively.
(C) It is near an art gallery.
(D) It has booths of different sizes.

12. In which of the positions marked [1], [2], [3], and [4] does the following sentence best belong?

"We were also nervous about making an upfront investment in artwork."

(A) [1]
(B) [2]
(C) [3]
(D) [4]

1   지문의 구성과 흐름 파악하기

목적   Thank you for placing an order with Holly Home Goods!

Order Number: 068379
Delivery: To be shipped within 1–3 business days
Ship to: 685 Aspen Lane, Irvine, CA 92614

❶ 연락 목적 언급
고객의 주문 번호와 배송일, 배송 주소를 전달함.

세부 내용

Item	Description	Pattern	Price
H190	10.5" plates, set of 6	Forest leaves	$35.99
B836	6" bowls, set of 6	Forest leaves	$25.99
M331	Coffee cups, set of 6	Blue waves	$32.99
W275	Teapots, set of 2	Forest leaves	$49.99
		Subtotal	$144.96
참고 사항	* Code WELCOME for 10% off the total purchase for first-time customers	Code*: WELCOME	–$14.49
		Shipping	$5.99
		TOTAL	$136.46

❷ 주문 내역 상세 전달
고객이 주문한 내역과 금액을 상세하게 보여 줌.

❸ 특이 사항 전달
첫 구매 고객은 WELCOME 코드가 적용되어 10% 할인된다고 알림.

제목   **Holly Home Goods: Request a Return**

세부 내용
Customer: Howard Erickson
Order Number: 068379
Item(s) to be returned: M331
Reason for return request:
[   ] Item damaged   [✓] Other (please explain):
[   ] Wrong item sent   <u>Color not as expected</u>

❹ 반품 요청서
Holly Home Goods에서 주문한 고객이 특정 사유를 언급하며 반품 요청서를 작성함.

1. What is suggested about Holly Home Goods?

   (A) It is dedicated to environmental responsibility.
   (B) It allows customers to create a custom pattern.
   (C) It has products made from a variety of materials.
   (D) It offers a discount to new customers.

2. What kind of item is Mr. Erickson returning?

   (A) Plates
   (B) Bowls
   (C) Cups
   (D) Teapots

1. What is suggested about Holly Home Goods?

Thank you for placing an order with Holly Home Goods!

Order Number: 068379
Delivery: To be shipped within 1–3 business days
Ship to: 685 Aspen Lane, Irvine, CA 92614

* Code WELCOME for 10% off the total purchase for first-time customers	Subtotal	$144.96
	Code*: WELCOME	–$14.49
	Shipping	$5.99
	TOTAL	$136.46

> Holly Home Goods는 상품을 판매하는 업체이다.

> 마지막에 별표로 첫 주문 고객에게 WELCOME 코드를 발급하며 이는 10% 할인을 의미한다는 내용의 특이 사항을 언급하고 있다. 따라서 (D) It offers a discount to new customers.(신규 고객에게 할인을 제공한다.)가 정답이다.

2. What kind of item is Mr. Erickson returning?

Holly Home Goods: Request a Return

Customer: Howard Erickson
Order Number: 068379
Item(s) to be returned: M331
Reason for return request:
[ ] Item damaged   [✓] Other (please explain):
[ ] Wrong item sent   Color not as expected

> Mr. Erickson은 Holly Home Goods에 반품 신청을 하려는 고객이다.

> Mr. Erickson이 반품하려는 제품은 M331이다.

Item	Description	Pattern	Price
H190	10.5" plates, set of 6	Forest leaves	$35.99
B836	6" bowls, set of 6	Forest leaves	$25.99
M331	Coffee cups, set of 6	Blue waves	$32.99
W275	Teapots, set of 2	Forest leaves	$49.99
* Code WELCOME for 10% off the total purchase for first-time customers	Subtotal		$144.96
	Code*: WELCOME		–$14.49
	Shipping		$5.99
	TOTAL		$136.46

> 첫 번째 지문에서 제품이 M331인 것은 커피 컵임을 확인할 수 있다. 따라서 (C) Cups(컵)가 정답이다.

Questions 1-5 refer to the following article and online review.

CALGARY (13 July)—Rocky Apparel is a ski clothing company that offers a range of men's and women's jackets, ski pants, base layers, and more. Co-owners Noella Purcell and Travis Byler started with a small retail shop here in Calgary five years ago, and since then, the business has taken off. A second branch was opened in Edmonton, and demand for Rocky Apparel merchandise has grown significantly. The company has built a loyal customer base because it rigorously tests its clothing to make sure it can withstand extreme temperatures and rough treatment. The finished products are also colorful and fashionable.

Rocky Apparel previously only sold its goods in its retail shops, but last month it launched an online store that allowed it to reach customers around the world. Ms. Purcell and Mr. Byler now plan to open a third retail location at Lake Louise in November. The location was chosen because even though Lake Louise is a small village, it is in the heart of a popular skiing district, with numerous resorts surrounding it. The shop will only be open during the peak ski season, which runs from late November to late April. The co-owners are also looking into creating a partnership with ski instructors to offer discounts on ski lessons.

http://www.rockyapparel.ca/customer_reviews

| Home | Product Catalog | Careers | **Customer Reviews** | Contact Us |

Posted: November 30   Posted by: Daniel Blair

I visited Rocky Apparel's newest retail branch today, and I was impressed with the selection. I met one of the co-owners, Noella Purcell, who was very knowledgeable about skiing, as she used to ski professionally. It was interesting to hear how she founded the business with her partner, who handles the accounting side of the business while she focuses on fashion and customers. The atmosphere in the store was energetic, and they were showing interesting footage of skiers on the screens throughout the store. I found a few items that I loved. I will probably visit this store frequently in the winter months, as I live within walking distance of it! If you enjoy skiing, Rocky Apparel is definitely worth checking out.

1. What is stated about Rocky Apparel in the article?

   (A) It conducts significant testing on its products.
   (B) It has opened retail branches around the world.
   (C) It was nominated for a fashion award.
   (D) It manufactures its own fabrics.

2. What is indicated about Mr. Byler?

   (A) He is in charge of the business's bookkeeping.
   (B) He met Mr. Blair during his visit.
   (C) He used to be a professional skier.
   (D) He designs some of the clothing himself.

3. In the article, the phrase "taken off" in paragraph 1, line 7, is closest in meaning to

   (A) disappeared
   (B) departed
   (C) removed
   (D) succeeded

4. What is suggested about Mr. Blair?

   (A) He is an experienced skier.
   (B) He lives in Lake Louise.
   (C) He applied for a job at Rocky Apparel.
   (D) He worked with Ms. Purcell.

5. What is indicated about Rocky Apparel's newest shop?

   (A) Its size is the same as the second branch.
   (B) Its customers can book ski lessons there.
   (C) It is open throughout the year.
   (D) It has videos playing for customers.

Construction Continues on New Stadium

By Courtney Wallace

DAVENPORT (January 2)—Construction of the new sports venue in northwest Davenport, Apex Stadium, is still on track, with work on the interior beginning soon. The stadium is owned by the Sigley Group, which has many buildings in its portfolio, most of which are performance venues, and is venturing into sports venues for the first time.

One of the points of the project is to bring more tourists to Davenport through large-scale sports events. The original design is for 8,000 seats, but if it can be altered to accommodate at least 10,000 seats, it would be large enough to be eligible to host the Regional Semi-Pro Tournament.

The first game scheduled at the stadium will be between the Davenport Tigers and the Waterloo Falcons on May 2.

Baseball Fans Excited about New Stadium
By Jerry Lambert

DAVENPORT (May 3)—Apex Stadium hosted a matchup between the Davenport Tigers and the Waterloo Falcons last night. The home team brought home a 3–1 win, though the Waterloo Falcons had a great showing of fans. Stephen Wilson, the head coach of the Davenport Tigers, was proud of the team's performance. "Waterloo is a tough team to beat," said Mr. Wilson. "But thanks to the hard work of Rob Sanchez and his teammates, we were able to pull off the win."

Many attendees to the game were impressed with the new building, which was designed by architect Howard Torres. The stadium will be the hosting site of the Regional Semi-Pro Tournament later this year. To view all upcoming events, visit www.apexstadium.com/events.

6. What is indicated about the Sigley Group?

(A) It has purchased a construction firm.
(B) It has relocated to Davenport.
(C) It is under new management.
(D) It only operates one stadium.

7. In the first article, the word "points" in paragraph 2, line 1, is closest in meaning to

(A) meanings
(B) features
(C) locations
(D) aims

8. What is suggested about Apex Stadium?

(A) Its construction was funded by the city.
(B) It expanded its original seating capacity.
(C) Its grand opening was later than expected.
(D) It will host a regional tournament every year.

9. What is indicated about the Waterloo Falcons team?

(A) It has not won many games this season.
(B) It has a smaller stadium than Apex Stadium.
(C) Many of its fans traveled to attend a game.
(D) There was special seating reserved for its fans.

10. Who is Rob Sanchez?

(A) A sports reporter
(B) An architect
(C) A coach
(D) An athlete

Megalith Gym Franchise Owner Annual Meeting
Schedule for Saturday, October 21

7:15 A.M.	Tea, Coffee, and Donuts	Sparrow Room
8:00 A.M.	Welcome Speech Pranav Chetti, CEO	Eagle Room
8:30 A.M.	Promotion from National to Individual Sanhana Adwani, Marketing Director	Eagle Room
10:30 A.M.	Knowing Your Customer Priya Vadekar, Senior Researcher	Goldfinch Room
12:30 P.M.	Buffet lunch included with registration	Sparrow Room
1:30 P.M.	Franchise Owner Presentations: Dealing with Competition Group Class Management	Peacock Room Goldfinch Room
3:00 P.M.	New Equipment Demonstrations Ganesh Munshif, Purchasing Director	Peacock Room

Support for Franchise Owners

By William Lowery

Small business owners operating a Megalith Gym franchise attended the company's annual meeting in Dallas last weekend. Over three hundred people from across the U.S. attended the two-day event. Marketing Director Sanhana Adwani outlined what the parent company is doing to promote the chain of fitness centers and how branches can be promoted individually on a small budget. Several franchise owners were selected to give presentations at the event. Attendees also got a sneak peek at the Marietta, a motorized treadmill, and the Netzer, an upright rowing machine, which will be sent to the gyms later in the year.

Megalith Gym Franchise Owner Annual Meeting Feedback Form

Thank you for taking the time to share your opinions with us. Please rate the presentations you attended on a scale of 1 (poor) to 5 (excellent).

Presentations	Rating
Knowing Your Customer	5
Dealing with Competition	n/a
Group Class Management	5
Keeping Customers Motivated	5
Key Steps to Success	n/a
The Megalith Mission	5

Comments: I chose to book my overnight accommodations at the venue so I did not have an issue, but some people I spoke with said they arrived late because they were unfamiliar with the city and had to get to the site in heavy traffic. I felt very rushed between sessions, so I would suggest having each session end a bit earlier.

Name: Peggy Kearns

11. Where did attendees hear opening remarks?

   (A) In the Eagle Room
   (B) In the Goldfinch Room
   (C) In the Peacock Room
   (D) In the Sparrow Room

12. What is one purpose of the article?

   (A) To explain Ms. Adwani's new role
   (B) To provide details about upcoming courses
   (C) To encourage people to join a franchise
   (D) To highlight activities at a company meeting

13. When most likely were attendees able to see the Marietta and the Netzer?

   (A) At 8:00 A.M.
   (B) At 10:30 A.M.
   (C) At 1:30 P.M.
   (D) At 3:00 P.M.

14. What is true about Ms. Kearns?

   (A) She went to the event last year.
   (B) She attended a talk in the afternoon.
   (C) She arrived at the event late.
   (D) She lives in the city where the meeting was held.

15. What did Ms. Kearns dislike about the meeting?

   (A) The venue lacked important amenities.
   (B) There was not enough time between sessions.
   (C) It was difficult to hear the speakers.
   (D) Some sessions were held at the same time.

Chemical Engineering Conference

www.chemicalengineeringconf.com

Enjoy a weekend of informative talks and professional networking at the 5th Annual Chemical Engineering Conference beginning April 9. Our aim is to educate those working in the field about the latest trends, safety measures, and emerging technologies. For the first time, we will hold the conference at Parkview Hall, and we are pleased to have Wyatt Faber, CEO of Dalton Chemicals, as our keynote speaker.

Please see the attached brochure for the details about sponsorship.

Chemical Engineering Conference
Sponsorship Tiers

Corporate sponsorship plays an important role in the success of our conference, as it allows us to keep registration fees affordable. By becoming a sponsor, you can introduce your company to hundreds of specialists in the field, making them more familiar with your brand.

Economy—$500
• Have your company's logo featured in our printed conference program
• 10% off registration for up to 10 employees

Basic—$1,500
• Have your company's logo featured in our printed conference program and on banners in the check-in area
• 10% off registration for up to 15 employees

Premium—$2,500
• Have your company's logo featured in all areas, including on stage
• 10% off registration for all of your employees

Elite—$4,500
• Have your company's logo featured in all areas, including on stage
• 15% off registration for all of your employees
• Your employees can use our VIP lounge, which features printing and copying equipment, complimentary refreshments, phone-charging stations, and more.

E-Mail Message

To: All Holbrook Incorporated Staff <stafflist@holbrookinc.com>
From: Nancy Turner <n.turner@holbrookinc.com>
Date: March 28
Subject: Chemical Engineering Conference

Dear Staff,

The Chemical Engineering Conference is coming soon. I'm wondering who would like to attend this event, as I need to complete the registration forms. We are a sponsor for the event this year, so we are eligible for a registration discount for as many employees as we want. In addition, while you are at the event, you'll have access to the VIP lounge. Many of you will recognize this year's keynote speaker, who visited our company last year to teach a workshop on state-of-the-art chemistry tools.

Nancy Turner
Administration Director, Holbrook Incorporated

16. According to the invitation, what is indicated about the conference?

(A) It takes place annually at Parkview Hall.
(B) It lasts for two days.
(C) It is free to attend.
(D) It is being held for the first time.

17. What benefit of sponsorship is mentioned in the brochure?

(A) Sponsors can operate a booth at the conference.
(B) Sponsors can improve their brand recognition.
(C) Sponsors can get assistance with logo design.
(D) Sponsors can promote their business online.

18. What is the purpose of the e-mail?

(A) To explain the reasons for a decision
(B) To recruit volunteers to give a presentation
(C) To find out who is interested in attending an event
(D) To arrange transportation to a conference

19. What is stated about Mr. Faber?

(A) He led a training event at Holbrook Incorporated.
(B) He contacted Ms. Turner about sponsorship.
(C) He will join the Holbrook Incorporated staff.
(D) He has developed a new technology.

20. What level of sponsorship did Holbrook Incorporated get?

(A) Economy
(B) Basic
(C) Premium
(D) Elite

PART 7

Directions: In this part, you will read a selection of texts, such as magazine and newspaper articles, e-mails, and instant messages. Each text or set of texts is followed by several questions. Select the best answer for each question and mark the letter (A), (B), (C), or (D) on your answer sheet.

Questions 147-148 refer to the following instructions.

How to Set Up Your New Lanette Video Doorbell

Keep this manual for your records after installation.

1. Download the Lanette smartphone application from www.lanettetech.com and create a new account.

2. Within the app, tap "Device Setup" and select "Doorbells."

3. Scan the bar code on the back of the device. After you do so, an approval e-mail with the product number will be sent to you. Write the product ID from the e-mail here: 730950R.

4. Input your address to specify your location. Please note that this step is optional, but if you skip this step, certain features of the doorbell will not function.

5. Within the app, tap "Confirm." Your device will automatically connect to your Wi-Fi, but you will need to input the Wi-Fi password.

6. Test the device by holding down the red button on the front for three seconds. Once the green light starts flashing, your device is ready to use. Write the test date here: _____.

Should you have any questions or concerns, please contact our customer service team at 1-800-555-4950.

147. Why should the user provide a location?

(A) To determine which office will handle inquiries

(B) To be provided with a shipping estimate

(C) To be sent replacement parts

(D) To ensure that all features can work

148. What is suggested about the instructions' user?

(A) The user scanned a code.

(B) The user sent a confirmation e-mail.

(C) The user failed to receive a product number.

(D) The user conducted a test.

A Celebration of Graphic Design as an Art Form

Findlay Banquet Hall
827 Ardmore Road

Friday, July 1
7:00 P.M.–9:30 P.M.

The Findlay Society of Graphic Design (FSGD) is holding its annual banquet! We invite you to attend this exciting event, which will feature a video about the activities we've done this year, information on upcoming plans, and a keynote speech about navigating the freelance world. We'll also be presenting several awards to recognize the people who have worked so hard to make our club great this year. This is an opportunity to enjoy a delicious four-course meal while socializing with fellow FSGD participants. Live music will be provided by the Rio String Quartet during the meal. There is no cost to attend the event, as it is paid by our dues.

If you plan to attend the event, please contact Patrick Slater at pslater@fsgd.org no later than June 16. When you do so, be sure to indicate how many people are in your party.

We hope to see you there!

---

149. For whom is the invitation most likely intended?

(A) Private donors
(B) Elected officials
(C) Computer programmers
(D) Club members

150. The word "recognize" in paragraph 1, line 4, is closest in meaning to

(A) recall
(B) realize
(C) identify
(D) acknowledge

151. What is suggested about the event?

(A) Its admission fee should be paid by June 16.
(B) Its invitation recipients can bring a guest.
(C) Its venue will be finalized soon.
(D) Its activities will be filmed.

GO ON TO THE NEXT PAGE

Upgrades Approved for Valley Park

(13 February)—Mayor Christopher Wilcher has confirmed that Union City is moving forward with a project to make upgrades to Valley Park. The work is being partially funded by Union City's annual Parks and Recreation budget. The city also received a generous donation from Gary Austin, a local entrepreneur. —[1]—. Additionally, local community groups have held fundraisers to contribute to the project. For example, UC Friends hosted a used book sale.

The holes in the baseball field in the northwest section of the park will be filled in, with new grass planted where needed. —[2]—. Flower beds near the parking lot will be removed in order to make room for a covered picnic shelter that can hold up to 10 tables. Though the construction of a second parking lot was proposed, planners have decided to expand the existing lot instead. —[3]—.

Most people are looking forward to taking advantage of the improvements. —[4]—. "In my opinion, we have more pressing matters, such as the poor condition of our roads," said resident Elizabeth Arnold.

152. What is NOT mentioned as a source of funding for the upgrades?

(A) A resident's donation
(B) A bookstore
(C) An annual budget
(D) Community organizations

153. What will be a new feature of Valley Park?

(A) A sports field
(B) A picnic area
(C) A flower bed
(D) A second parking lot

154. In which of the positions marked [1], [2], [3], and [4] does the following sentence best belong?

"Nonetheless, some people think that local officials should focus on other areas."

(A) [1]
(B) [2]
(C) [3]
(D) [4]

Questions 155-158 refer to the following online chat discussion.

Naomi Rutledge [10:03 A.M.]	Good morning, team. I'd like to check in with you about the Concord Apartment Building.
Jared Padilla [10:04 A.M.]	A reporter from *Northwest Lifestyle* magazine has agreed to write an article about the upcoming grand opening, and she'd like some photographs to accompany it. Should I contact the photographer, Jonathan Webb, to arrange to take more pictures?
Naomi Rutledge [10:05 A.M.]	We already have more than enough. I'll forward you a link to our photo collection so you can choose whatever seems appropriate.
Rupert Burke [10:06 A.M.]	I'm glad we're getting additional publicity. We had aimed to get to 80% of the units reserved by this point, but we're not even at 70% yet.
Naomi Rutledge [10:07 A.M.]	The magazine article will help, and I'll keep pursuing other options.
Rupert Burke [10:09 A.M.]	We've never managed such a large building before, so it's important to get this right.
Naomi Rutledge [10:10 A.M.]	I agree. But keep in mind that there was some lost time when Katie Sullivan left the team.
Varuni Goyal [10:11 A.M.]	That's true. When Naomi stepped in, she had to get herself familiar with the work.
Naomi Rutledge [10:12 A.M.]	I feel like I'm up to speed now, so we can move forward quickly.

155. Who most likely is Ms. Rutledge?

(A) An interior designer
(B) A construction contractor
(C) A property manager
(D) A magazine journalist

156. At 10:05 A.M., what does Ms. Rutledge mean when she writes, "We already have more than enough"?

(A) She is confident that there is time to finish some work.
(B) She is considering adding storage space.
(C) She does not want more work from Mr. Webb.
(D) She thinks they can afford Mr. Webb's services.

157. What problem is mentioned in the chat?

(A) A bill has not been paid.
(B) A team goal was not reached.
(C) A building has failed an inspection.
(D) A budget was lower than expected.

158. What is suggested about Ms. Rutledge?

(A) She has not worked on the project since the beginning.
(B) She plans to hire Ms. Sullivan for additional help.
(C) She would like to visit a site soon.
(D) She is concerned about the team members' lack of experience.

GO ON TO THE NEXT PAGE

PART 7

Questions 159-163 refer to the following online article and reader comment.

http://www.theoakwoodtribune.com/mysterytrain

The Oakwood Tribune, August 15, "Mystery Train"

The train begins its journey, moving along the track with a *clickety-clack*. The passengers are in their seats, enjoying some refreshments. Suddenly, actors enter the car, and a dramatic mystery unfolds. The audience members must pick up on the clues to solve the mystery. With period costumes, intriguing characters, and a different plot to enjoy every month, Mystery Train offers exciting live performances on a unique "stage"—an old-fashioned steam train!

Mystery Train has been in operation for the past 10 years, after a local theater group was looking for a way to raise money. Adrian Urbano, who plays the lead role in the current run of performances, has been featured in most of the Mystery Train's shows from the beginning. "I love how engaged the audience members become with our performance," Mr. Urbano says. "It's fascinating to see their delight when the case is solved."

Mystery Train performances are offered every Thursday, Friday, Saturday, and Sunday evening as well as Saturday and Sunday afternoons. The shows run for two-and-a-half hours, with the exception of the Sunday afternoon show, which runs for 90 minutes, making it a popular option for families. Tickets can be purchased at www.mysterytrainboxoffice.com.

http://www.theoakwoodtribune.com/mysterytrain/comments

I attended the most recent Mystery Train performance, and it was amazing! I enjoyed watching the main character. Not only was he very talented, but I also have a personal connection to him, as we graduated from high school together. I remember that he loved drama classes even at that time. As the various scripts for the Mystery Train shows have been written by members of the Oakwood Writing Society (OWS), I'd love to see some of those people featured in a future edition. I know that you frequently do these sorts of stories, as I have subscribed to your publication for many years.

Gloria Ramirez

159. What is implied about the Mystery Train performances?

(A) Their storylines change regularly.
(B) Their audience members move around.
(C) They include well-known actors.
(D) They take place four times per week.

160. What is true about the Sunday afternoon shows?

(A) They are offered exclusively to families.
(B) They are the least expensive shows.
(C) They are the most popular performance.
(D) They are shorter than the other shows.

161. What is suggested about Mr. Urbano?

(A) He attended school with Ms. Ramirez.
(B) He plans to begin offering acting classes.
(C) He designs authentic costumes for the shows.
(D) He is the founder of a theater group.

162. What is Ms. Ramirez interested in doing?

(A) Submitting her work to the newspaper
(B) Reading an article about some writers of OWS
(C) Reviewing a show script in advance
(D) Joining a local writing group

163. What does the reader comment suggest about Ms. Ramirez?

(A) She frequently participates in local activities and events.
(B) She spent most of her childhood in Oakwood.
(C) She has attended several Mystery Train performances.
(D) She has been an *Oakwood Tribune* subscriber for a long time.

GO ON TO THE NEXT PAGE

Questions 164-168 refer to the following online message board, e-mail, and Web page.

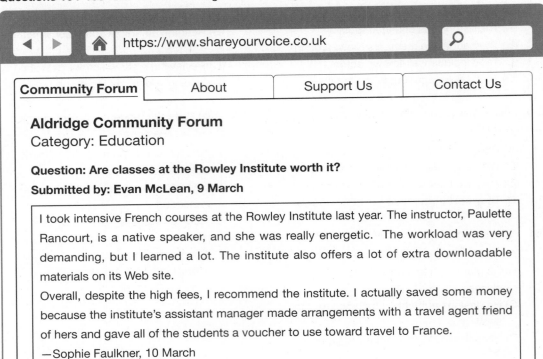

https://www.shareyourvoice.co.uk

Community Forum | About | Support Us | Contact Us

Aldridge Community Forum
Category: Education

Question: Are classes at the Rowley Institute worth it?
Submitted by: Evan McLean, 9 March

I took intensive French courses at the Rowley Institute last year. The instructor, Paulette Rancourt, is a native speaker, and she was really energetic. The workload was very demanding, but I learned a lot. The institute also offers a lot of extra downloadable materials on its Web site.

Overall, despite the high fees, I recommend the institute. I actually saved some money because the institute's assistant manager made arrangements with a travel agent friend of hers and gave all of the students a voucher to use toward travel to France.

—Sophie Faulkner, 10 March

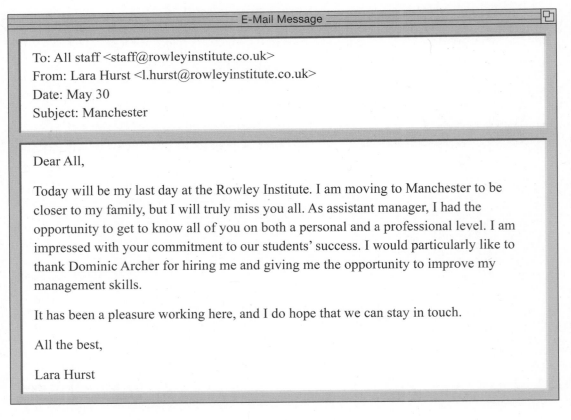

E-Mail Message

To: All staff <staff@rowleyinstitute.co.uk>
From: Lara Hurst <l.hurst@rowleyinstitute.co.uk>
Date: May 30
Subject: Manchester

Dear All,

Today will be my last day at the Rowley Institute. I am moving to Manchester to be closer to my family, but I will truly miss you all. As assistant manager, I had the opportunity to get to know all of you on both a personal and a professional level. I am impressed with your commitment to our students' success. I would particularly like to thank Dominic Archer for hiring me and giving me the opportunity to improve my management skills.

It has been a pleasure working here, and I do hope that we can stay in touch.

All the best,

Lara Hurst

Aldridge Local Business Awards
Category: Support for Local Education

Gold Award: Jack Talbot, Aldridge Community Centre

Silver Award: Dominic Archer, Rowley Institute

Bronze Award: Holly Khan, Rowley Institute

Honourable Mention: Ava Conway, Crafton Trade School

The award winners were nominated by Aldridge residents and then selected by a judging panel of city officials and small business owners. The winners will be interviewed by a reporter from *Community Cares* magazine, and their contributions will be outlined on the Aldridge government Web site. Nominations for next year will be accepted after July 10.

---

164. What does Ms. Faulkner mention about the Rowley Institute?

(A) The amount of homework is reasonable.
(B) It provides additional materials online.
(C) All of the instructors are native speakers.
(D) There is an option for remote classes.

165. What is suggested about Ms. Faulkner?

(A) Her instructor is a published author.
(B) Her classes were paid for by her company.
(C) She received a voucher from Ms. Hurst.
(D) She plans to move to France.

166. What is the purpose of the e-mail?

(A) To congratulate the staff on an achievement
(B) To say farewell to colleagues
(C) To ask for recommendations in Manchester
(D) To nominate an employee as a replacement

167. What award was given to the person who hired Ms. Hurst?

(A) Gold Award
(B) Silver Award
(C) Bronze Award
(D) Honourable Mention

168. What is suggested on the Web page?

(A) The winners can advertise for free in *Community Cares* magazine.
(B) Mr. Talbot has previously won a business award.
(C) The awards will be distributed on July 10.
(D) Mr. Archer and Ms. Khan work for the same employer.

LC+RC

실전
모의고사

실전 모의고사 **LC + RC**

LISTENING TEST

In the Listening test, you will be asked to demonstrate how well you understand spoken English. The entire Listening test will last approximately 45 minutes. There are four parts, and directions are given for each part. You must mark your answers on the separate answer sheet. Do not write your answers in your test book.

PART 1

Directions: For each question in this part, you will hear four statements about a picture in your test book. When you hear the statements, you must select the one statement that best describes what you see in the picture. Then find the number of the question on your answer sheet and mark your answer. The statements will not be printed in your test book and will be spoken only one time.

Statement (C), "He's making a phone call," is the best description of the picture, so you should select answer (C) and mark it on your answer sheet.

1.

2.

GO ON TO THE NEXT PAGE

3.

4.

5.

6.

GO ON TO THE NEXT PAGE →

PART 2

Directions: You will hear a question or statement and three responses spoken in English. They will not be printed in your test book and will be spoken only one time. Select the best response to the question or statement and mark the letter (A), (B), or (C) on your answer sheet.

7. Mark your answer on your answer sheet.

8. Mark your answer on your answer sheet.

9. Mark your answer on your answer sheet.

10. Mark your answer on your answer sheet.

11. Mark your answer on your answer sheet.

12. Mark your answer on your answer sheet.

13. Mark your answer on your answer sheet.

14. Mark your answer on your answer sheet.

15. Mark your answer on your answer sheet.

16. Mark your answer on your answer sheet.

17. Mark your answer on your answer sheet.

18. Mark your answer on your answer sheet.

19. Mark your answer on your answer sheet.

20. Mark your answer on your answer sheet.

21. Mark your answer on your answer sheet.

22. Mark your answer on your answer sheet.

23. Mark your answer on your answer sheet.

24. Mark your answer on your answer sheet.

25. Mark your answer on your answer sheet.

26. Mark your answer on your answer sheet.

27. Mark your answer on your answer sheet.

28. Mark your answer on your answer sheet.

29. Mark your answer on your answer sheet.

30. Mark your answer on your answer sheet.

31. Mark your answer on your answer sheet.

PART 3

Directions: You will hear some conversations between two or more people. You will be asked to answer three questions about what the speakers say in each conversation. Select the best response to each question and mark the letter (A), (B), (C), or (D) on your answer sheet. The conversations will not be printed in your test book and will be spoken only one time.

32. What kind of event is the man planning?
    (A) An anniversary celebration
    (B) A grand opening
    (C) A charity fund-raiser
    (D) A retirement party

33. What does the woman say is difficult to estimate?
    (A) The delivery fee
    (B) The available colors
    (C) The labor costs
    (D) The travel time

34. What will the woman send the man?
    (A) Some samples
    (B) Some photographs
    (C) An invoice
    (D) A brochure

35. Which industry do the speakers most likely work in?
    (A) Real estate
    (B) Education
    (C) Manufacturing
    (D) Healthcare

36. According to the woman, what caused a problem?
    (A) Bad weather conditions
    (B) A missed deadline
    (C) Some damaged equipment
    (D) An error in an advertisement

37. What does the man suggest doing?
    (A) Increasing a budget
    (B) Holding another event
    (C) Hiring more workers
    (D) Reading some reviews

38. What most likely is the woman's job?
    (A) Magazine reporter
    (B) Tour guide
    (C) Museum curator
    (D) Bus driver

39. Why is the man calling?
    (A) To provide a reminder
    (B) To offer a promotion
    (C) To cancel an event
    (D) To schedule an interview

40. What will the man do next?
    (A) Update a Web site
    (B) Send a timetable
    (C) Check a participant list
    (D) Explain a policy

41. Who most likely are the speakers?
    (A) Bank employees
    (B) Interior designers
    (C) Delivery drivers
    (D) Safety inspectors

42. What do the speakers have to decide?
    (A) Which software to try
    (B) Where to advertise a product
    (C) How soon to open a new branch
    (D) How to recruit new employees

43. What does the man warn the woman about?
    (A) Using outdated equipment
    (B) Completing a project late
    (C) Wasting a lot of time
    (D) Exceeding a budget

GO ON TO THE NEXT PAGE

44. Where most likely are the speakers?

    (A) At a library
    (B) At a fitness club
    (C) At a business school
    (D) At an art center

45. What does the man want to do?

    (A) Hire a presenter
    (B) Apply for a job
    (C) Give a demonstration
    (D) Negotiate a sale

46. How did the man learn about Teresa Connelly?

    (A) From searching online
    (B) From reading a newspaper article
    (C) From receiving a flyer
    (D) From talking to a coworker

47. What problem does the woman mention?

    (A) She lost the original report.
    (B) She cannot access a room.
    (C) Some products have been discontinued.
    (D) Some flooring is badly damaged.

48. Why does the man need some precise measurements?

    (A) The cost of a material is high.
    (B) A document will be inspected closely.
    (C) It will help him save time.
    (D) It is required by the city.

49. What will the woman most likely do next?

    (A) Unpack some tools
    (B) Place an express order
    (C) Contact a supervisor
    (D) Write down an estimate

50. Who most likely is the woman?

    (A) A post office employee
    (B) A financial advisor
    (C) A travel agent
    (D) A factory worker

51. Why does the woman suggest downloading a mobile application?

    (A) To get access to discounts
    (B) To check hours of operation
    (C) To promote some products
    (D) To print labels at home

52. Where does the man plan to go next?

    (A) To a mobile phone store
    (B) To a bus terminal
    (C) To a supermarket
    (D) To an outlet mall

53. Where do the speakers most likely work?

    (A) At a financial institution
    (B) At a chemistry laboratory
    (C) At a furniture manufacturer
    (D) At an art supply store

54. Why does the man say, "the Valdez Hotel is holding its grand opening at the end of the month?"

    (A) To reject a suggestion
    (B) To agree with a decision
    (C) To offer reassurance
    (D) To highlight some competition

55. What does the man say about Kyle and Ben?

    (A) They have contacted Fenton Industries.
    (B) They have a specialized skill.
    (C) They are the newest employees.
    (D) They are repairing a machine.

56. What is the purpose of the meeting?

(A) To prepare for an industry event
(B) To select job candidates
(C) To approve a budget
(D) To discuss product sales

57. What did the company do in August?

(A) It lowered its prices.
(B) It changed its management.
(C) It launched a new Web site.
(D) It expanded its color selection.

58. What do the speakers plan to do?

(A) Merge with a competitor
(B) Create some videos
(C) Hold a contest
(D) Print some brochures

59. What will most likely happen on April 3?

(A) A security system will be changed.
(B) An industry conference will be held.
(C) Some visitors will come to the business.
(D) Some award winners will be announced.

60. Why does the man say, "you've spent a lot of time in India"?

(A) To explain a delay
(B) To ask for help
(C) To make a complaint
(D) To express surprise

61. What will the woman do next?

(A) Participate in an interview
(B) Contact a travel agent
(C) Confirm her attendance
(D) Send a memo

Room 1 Sculpture	Room 3 Oil Painting
Room 2 Watercolor Painting	*Entrance* / Room 4 Photograph

62. What event are the speakers preparing for?

(A) A volunteer training
(B) An art auction
(C) A painting demonstration
(D) A film screening

63. Look at the graphic. Which room does the woman suggest using for an event?

(A) Room 1
(B) Room 2
(C) Room 3
(D) Room 4

64. According to the woman, what does the site manager want to provide?

(A) Musical entertainment
(B) Some refreshments
(C) Free parking
(D) Group photographs

GO ON TO THE NEXT PAGE

Silver Jewelry

Necklace

$120

Bracelet

$80

Earrings

$65

Ring

$40

Vacuum Model	Cordless	Removable Air Filter	Dusting Brush
Botello	✓		
Activa	✓		✓
Mammoth		✓	✓
Goodwin	✓	✓	

65. Where are the speakers?

(A) In an employee lounge
(B) In a train station
(C) In a restaurant
(D) In a conference room

66. Why will the man travel to Cleveland?

(A) To attend a ceremony
(B) To inspect a building
(C) To give a presentation
(D) To accept an award

67. Look at the graphic. How much will the man probably spend?

(A) $120
(B) $80
(C) $65
(D) $40

68. What did the woman do last month?

(A) She purchased a vacuum cleaner.
(B) She transferred to another branch.
(C) She was offered a promotion.
(D) She received a certificate.

69. Look at the graphic. Which model has the features requested by the customer?

(A) Botello
(B) Activa
(C) Mammoth
(D) Goodwin

70. What is the man pleased about?

(A) An annual bonus
(B) A staff discount
(C) A paid holiday
(D) A change in business hours

PART 4

Directions: You will hear some talks given by a single speaker. You will be asked to answer three questions about what the speaker says in each talk. Select the best response to each question and mark the letter (A), (B), (C), or (D) on your answer sheet. The talks will not be printed in your test book and will be spoken only one time.

71. Who is the speaker?

(A) A factory manager
(B) A construction worker
(C) A theater owner
(D) A computer technician

72. What is the facility famous for?

(A) Its fund-raising efforts
(B) Its knowledgeable staff
(C) Its unique architecture
(D) Its modern equipment

73. According to the speaker, how can the listeners get a coupon?

(A) By providing some feedback
(B) By downloading some software
(C) By signing up for a newsletter
(D) By e-mailing the speaker

74. What are the listeners most likely interested in?

(A) Painting
(B) Poetry
(C) Language learning
(D) Cooking

75. What did the speaker do recently?

(A) He studied abroad.
(B) He launched a Web site.
(C) He published a book.
(D) He hosted a podcast.

76. What have some listeners asked about?

(A) Getting individual advice
(B) Taking food home
(C) Reviewing class materials
(D) Purchasing supplies

77. What does the speaker say will happen on Tuesday?

(A) A crew will be announced.
(B) A parking lot will be paved.
(C) A project will be completed.
(D) A bridge will close.

78. What does the speaker remind the listener to do?

(A) Carpool to a site
(B) Display a parking pass
(C) Sign up for a training session
(D) Wear warm clothing

79. What will be provided to the listener?

(A) Safety gear
(B) A work schedule
(C) Coworkers' contact information
(D) A user manual

80. What is the speaker demonstrating?

(A) Ways to operate a salon
(B) Ways to attract new customers
(C) How to use a smartphone application
(D) How to restart a security system

81. Who most likely are the listeners?

(A) Physicians
(B) Computer programmers
(C) Pharmacists
(D) Hair stylists

82. What feature does the speaker mention?

(A) Automatic alerts
(B) Hands-free operation
(C) Easy uploading
(D) Daily reminders

GO ON TO THE NEXT PAGE

83. Where do the listeners most likely work?

(A) At a bank
(B) At a grocery store
(C) At a museum
(D) At a library

84. What are the listeners expected to do?

(A) Attend a training session
(B) Arrive to work earlier than usual
(C) Watch for people needing assistance
(D) Post some instructions near a machine

85. What does the speaker say will happen in October?

(A) A new job position will be available.
(B) A fund-raiser will be held.
(C) A building project will be completed.
(D) A report will be made public.

86. What is being advertised?

(A) An online course
(B) A real estate firm
(C) A building-inspection service
(D) A garden design service

87. Why does the speaker say, "We have a large photo gallery"?

(A) To justify a slow Web site
(B) To provide reassurance
(C) To explain a decision
(D) To criticize a competitor

88. What does the speaker say the business is proud of?

(A) Its support of local businesses
(B) Its affordable prices
(C) Its fast response times
(D) Its high customer service ratings

89. Where is the speech being given?

(A) At a training workshop
(B) At a staff dinner
(C) At a music competition
(D) At a press conference

90. What does the speaker imply when he says, "I'm sure Diana would like a few lunches out"?

(A) He can recommend a restaurant.
(B) He wants to welcome a new employee.
(C) He has a suggestion for a gift.
(D) He is looking for volunteers for a task.

91. What does the speaker say about Ahmed Sharma?

(A) He shared an innovative idea.
(B) He will be leaving the company.
(C) He has a lot of experience.
(D) He will give a talk shortly.

92. What is the focus of the talk?

(A) Improving recycling services
(B) Cleaning up a park
(C) Building an exercise trail
(D) Planting more trees

93. What does the speaker imply when she says, "we have a very long list"?

(A) Some work assignments may be changed.
(B) A deadline will need to be extended.
(C) The listeners will have a lot of support.
(D) A meeting may be longer than scheduled.

94. What will the speaker hand out?

(A) A map
(B) A business card
(C) A proposed schedule
(D) A cost estimate

Lexington Dance Troupe Show

1 → 11 May | 8:00 P.M.
2 → Seat: H35
3 → Price: $15.50
4 → Ticket Number: 2367

Igor's Quest - Setup Process

 Step 1. Unroll playing board

 Step 2. Place resource tokens on board

 Step 3. Sort cards by color

 Step 4. Choose player characters

95. Why is the performance being held?

   (A) To raise funds for a community project
   (B) To celebrate a theater's anniversary
   (C) To encourage people to join a group
   (D) To promote a national tour

96. What will happen after the show?

   (A) Some photos will be taken.
   (B) Tickets will be available for sale.
   (C) Some questions will be answered.
   (D) Posters will be signed.

97. Look at the graphic. Which line should the listeners check for the prize drawing?

   (A) Line 1
   (B) Line 2
   (C) Line 3
   (D) Line 4

98. According to the speaker, what kind of product does Dorsey make?

   (A) Sound equipment
   (B) Office furniture
   (C) Tablet computers
   (D) Software programs

99. What does the speaker like about Igor's Quest?

   (A) The characters
   (B) The instructions
   (C) The artwork
   (D) The number of players

100. Look at the graphic. Which step does the speaker think could be improved?

   (A) Step 1
   (B) Step 2
   (C) Step 3
   (D) Step 4

This is the end of the Listening test.

READING TEST

In the Reading test, you will read a variety of texts and answer several different types of reading comprehension questions. The entire Reading test will last 75 minutes. There are three parts, and directions are given for each part. You are encouraged to answer as many questions as possible within the time allowed.

You must mark your answers on the separate answer sheet. Do not write your answers in your test book.

PART 5

Directions: A word or phrase is missing in each of the sentences below. Four answer choices are given below each sentence. Select the best answer to complete the sentence. Then mark the letter (A), (B), (C), or (D) on your answer sheet.

101. The sales clerk can reprint a ------- if the customer needs it.

(A) receipt
(B) receive
(C) receivable
(D) receipts

102. Come to Fairfield Park ------- the annual community picnic this Saturday.

(A) for
(B) until
(C) unless
(D) but

103. By using the bank's smartphone application, customers can ------- check their account balances.

(A) easy
(B) easiest
(C) easily
(D) easier

104. Gym members can improve their fitness levels by following a regular exercise -------.

(A) transaction
(B) sequel
(C) response
(D) program

105. A spokesperson for Sweet-Time Bakery has confirmed that it ------- a site for a new retail branch next year.

(A) will select
(B) to select
(C) are selecting
(D) select

106. The annual dance competition includes 20 groups ------- cities across the country.

(A) from
(B) except
(C) as
(D) regarding

107. ------- check all products for manufacturing defects prior to packaging them.

(A) There
(B) Their
(C) Them
(D) They

108. Upon request, the hotel's housekeeping department can replace sheets, -------, and other bedding items.

(A) curtains
(B) carpets
(C) lighting
(D) pillowcases

109. The Chung Business Institute's spring schedule will be posted ------- 9 A.M. tomorrow on the Web site.

(A) after
(B) between
(C) recently
(D) final

110. Best-selling author George Vasquez is currently ------- in Toronto, Canada.

(A) committed
(B) written
(C) moved
(D) based

111. Successful applicants must have experience as a bookkeeper or in a related -------.

(A) occupied
(B) occupant
(C) occupation
(D) occupying

112. Carlyle Logistics is admired for achieving ------- growth without sacrificing the quality of its service.

(A) enthusiastic
(B) rapid
(C) frank
(D) native

113. The Grand Ballroom can ------- accommodate up to 300 guests.

(A) comfort
(B) comfortably
(C) comforted
(D) comfortable

114. All Tazma Co. employees should obtain ------- from the finance department before purchasing expensive equipment.

(A) approval
(B) entry
(C) regard
(D) interest

115. PJ Shopping Center hopes to boost business through ------- business hours.

(A) extension
(B) extends
(C) extended
(D) extend

116. No one should enter or exit the conference room while the job candidate ------- interviewed by the committee.

(A) is being
(B) to be
(C) to have been
(D) has been

117. The crew leader emphasized that every technical ------- of the project must be double-checked.

(A) specify
(B) specification
(C) specific
(D) specifically

118. Employees at Jacamo Incorporated should submit all vacation requests ------- to their department heads.

(A) directly
(B) entirely
(C) hardly
(D) fairly

119. The Cayla Museum maintains a relaxing atmosphere by ------- the number of visitors allowed inside at any given time.

(A) limiting
(B) limited
(C) limitation
(D) limits

120. PowerVox has found a fresh and ------- solution to the problem of waste disposal costs.

(A) loyal
(B) innovative
(C) casual
(D) appointed

GO ON TO THE NEXT PAGE

121. The committee members will tell us ------- job applicant they believe is most suitable for the role.

(A) if
(B) whenever
(C) who
(D) which

122. ------- Ericson Construction's wages are higher than average, the firm is having difficulty with recruitment.

(A) Because
(B) As if
(C) Whether
(D) Although

123. Garrison Publishing keeps ------- manuscripts on file for five years in case the market makes them desirable later.

(A) rejects
(B) rejected
(C) rejecting
(D) rejection

124. Employees who are working from home can access company documents ------- and download the files they need.

(A) remotely
(B) absolutely
(C) seriously
(D) predictably

125. The HR manager dispatched the employee handbook to new hires so they could read it a few days ------- orientation.

(A) ahead of
(B) possibly
(C) along with
(D) highly

126. ------- designing invoices themselves, many new business owners prefer to use a template.

(A) Rather than
(B) In light of
(C) Among
(D) Into

127. Customers can send their packages overseas for ------- lower rates if the items go by ship instead of by air.

(A) considers
(B) considerate
(C) considerably
(D) consideration

128. When its discount code was accidentally leaked online, orders ------- for the new tablet computer.

(A) got along
(B) carried out
(C) settled up
(D) poured in

129. Local residents are experiencing fewer traffic delays ------- the busy tourist season has ended.

(A) so that
(B) now that
(C) as though
(D) because of

130. Users will be locked out of the system after an incorrect password ------- three times.

(A) have been entered
(B) has been entered
(C) was entering
(D) are entered

PART 6

Directions: Read the texts that follow. A word, phrase, or sentence is missing in parts of each text. Four answer choices for each question are given below the text. Select the best answer to complete the text. Then mark the letter (A), (B), (C), or (D) on your answer sheet.

Questions 131-134 refer to the following advertisement.

Special deal at Romano Cinema!

Romano Cinema is helping you start the new year with a great deal on admission. From January 2 ------- January 19, tickets for all screenings are buy one, get one free. All ------- are offering this
131.   132.
deal, and you can take advantage of it as many times as you'd like. Please note that all

complimentary tickets will be for the same show as the ------- tickets. We also have a range of
133.

delicious snacks to enjoy during the film. -------.
134.

131. (A) onto
(B) toward
(C) within
(D) through

132. (A) statuses
(B) locations
(C) directors
(D) exhibits

133. (A) purchases
(B) purchased
(C) purchaser
(D) purchasing

134. (A) Award nominations will be announced soon.
(B) Contact us to apply for this role.
(C) Stop by the concession stand to purchase them.
(D) The films' running times may vary.

GO ON TO THE NEXT PAGE

Kenwyn Beach Resort has scheduled its grand opening for next month. The site ------- spacious
                                                                              135.
suites for guests, three on-site restaurants, indoor and outdoor pools, and more.

The section of the beach which is now home to the resort was left empty for decades. It was

previously owned by Capital Properties, which struggled to find funding for development. -------.
                                                                                          136.
V&G Investments procured the property to build a resort, which was named Kenwyn Beach

Resort.

Architect Oscar Strope designed the entire facility to take advantage of the beautiful setting and

-------. Based on other resorts in the area, Kenwyn Beach Resort is likely to be quite -------.
137.   **138.**

---

135. (A) will include
(B) was included
(C) being included
(D) has been included

136. (A) Other sites are still available for sale.
(B) Finally, the company decided to sell it.
(C) The tourist season runs throughout the
summer.
(D) The owner has a lot of experience in
the field.

137. (A) scenery
(B) scenic
(C) scenically
(D) scenario

138. (A) definite
(B) general
(C) heavy
(D) popular

Questions 139-142 refer to the following e-mail.

To: Marketing Staff <marketing@camdensales.com>
From: Richard Hayes <rhayes@camdensales.com>
Date: June 18
Subject: Web site
Attachment: New color scheme

Dear Marketing Staff,

Please find attached the document that ------- the options for the new color scheme for our Web
     139.
site. The updated ------- will portray a more modern image for Camden Sales. -------.
          140.   **141.**
I ask that you look over the choices carefully. By the end of Thursday, you should e-mail me your

thoughts on which color scheme would be best. -------, your opinions will not be taken into
                                              142.
consideration.

Thank you,

Richard Hayes

139. (A) outlining
(B) outline
(C) outlines
(D) had been outlined

140. (A) schedule
(B) label
(C) policy
(D) design

141. (A) In addition, it will attract a greater
number of younger customers.
(B) Most people think the software is easy
to use.
(C) Fortunately, sales improved
significantly last month.
(D) I will recommend you for future
projects that are similar.

142. (A) To that end
(B) Otherwise
(C) In contrast
(D) Similarly

GO ON TO THE NEXT PAGE

Footwear manufacturer League Footwear confirmed today that it has ------- EG Sports. "EG
143.

Sports, which is known for its trendy athletic shoes, has demonstrated ------- market success
144.

over the years, and we are proud to bring it into the League Footwear family," said Nathan Dale,

a League Footwear representative.

"We know that our customers rely ------- our high-quality materials to ensure both comfort and
145.

performance," Mr. Dale explained. "All EG Sports products sold through our company will be

held to the same high standards. ------- ."
146.

143. (A) advised
(B) acquired
(C) consented
(D) sustained

144. (A) impress
(B) impression
(C) impressive
(D) impressed

145. (A) about
(B) to
(C) on
(D) by

146. (A) So, customers can shop with
confidence.
(B) There is a range of sizes to choose
from.
(C) More information about the
competition can be found online.
(D) Therefore, each retail store will have
different hours.

PART 7

Directions: In this part, you will read a selection of texts, such as magazine and newspaper articles, e-mails, and instant messages. Each text or set of texts is followed by several questions. Select the best answer for each question and mark the letter (A), (B), (C), or (D) on your answer sheet.

Questions 147-148 refer to the following e-mail.

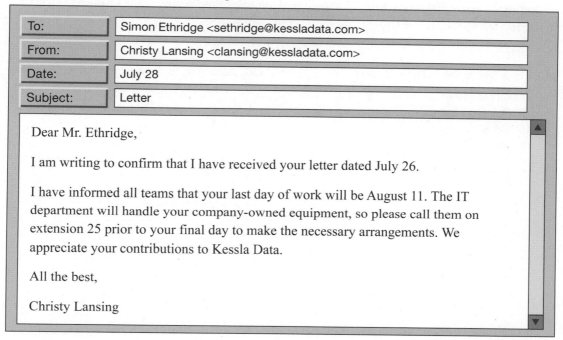

To: Simon Ethridge <sethridge@kessladata.com>

From: Christy Lansing <clansing@kessladata.com>

Date: July 28

Subject: Letter

Dear Mr. Ethridge,

I am writing to confirm that I have received your letter dated July 26.

I have informed all teams that your last day of work will be August 11. The IT department will handle your company-owned equipment, so please call them on extension 25 prior to your final day to make the necessary arrangements. We appreciate your contributions to Kessla Data.

All the best,

Christy Lansing

147. Why did Ms. Lansing send the e-mail?
(A) To confirm a business closure
(B) To update a banking record
(C) To acknowledge a resignation
(D) To offer a job promotion

148. What should Mr. Ethridge do by August 11?
(A) Complete a form
(B) Meet with Ms. Lansing
(C) Contact the IT team
(D) Remove his personal items

GO ON TO THE NEXT PAGE

NOTICE

On Tuesday, August 22, crew members from Despard Water Co. will begin replacing a sewer line in the area. Florence Street will be closed temporarily while the work is being carried out, meaning that the entrance to the parking lot here at Livonia Tower will be inaccessible during that time. Residents who plan to drive their vehicle between 8 A.M. on August 22 and 4 P.M. on August 23 should park on one of the nearby streets before the work begins. We apologize for any inconvenience this may cause.

---

149. For whom is the notice intended?

(A) City officials
(B) Building tenants
(C) Construction workers
(D) Property developers

150. According to the notice, what will happen at 4:00 P.M. on August 23?

(A) A parking lot entrance will close.
(B) A street will be paved.
(C) A road will be reopened.
(D) A crew will assess a project.

TO:	Rebekah Ingram <ringram@rivendalesales.com>
FROM:	Montoya Fashions <customerservice@montoyafashions.com>
DATE:	November 18
SUBJECT:	Return request

Dear Ms. Ingram,

We have received your returned item as listed below:

> **Description: Fieldcrest cashmere sweater, dark gray, medium**
> **Item #: 748592**
> **Purchase price: $125.00**

We are processing your refund, which will be refunded to the credit card you used for the purchase within five working days. Please note that if you earned any Montoya Fashions rewards points, these will be deducted from your account within 30 days.

Also, don't miss our new line of party dresses, now on sale for $49.99, just in time for the holiday season! Click here to browse the catalog.

Sincerely,

The Montoya Fashions Customer Service Team

151. What is one purpose of the e-mail?

(A) To promote some new products
(B) To confirm that a payment has been made
(C) To explain how to sign into an account
(D) To request credit card information

152. What is suggested about Montoya Fashions?

(A) It accepts returns within 30 days.
(B) It offers a loyalty program.
(C) It only gives store credit for returns.
(D) It sells home furnishing products.

GO ON TO THE NEXT PAGE

Questions 153-154 refer to the following text-message chain.

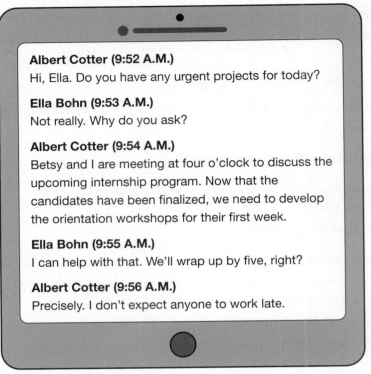

Albert Cotter (9:52 A.M.)
Hi, Ella. Do you have any urgent projects for today?

Ella Bohn (9:53 A.M.)
Not really. Why do you ask?

Albert Cotter (9:54 A.M.)
Betsy and I are meeting at four o'clock to discuss the upcoming internship program. Now that the candidates have been finalized, we need to develop the orientation workshops for their first week.

Ella Bohn (9:55 A.M.)
I can help with that. We'll wrap up by five, right?

Albert Cotter (9:56 A.M.)
Precisely. I don't expect anyone to work late.

153. Why will Mr. Cotter attend a meeting today?

(A) To review applications for an internship
(B) To create a training program
(C) To conduct group interviews
(D) To write a job description

154. At 9:56 A.M., what does Mr. Cotter most likely mean when he writes, "Precisely"?

(A) The meeting will end by 5:00 P.M.
(B) There will be five attendees at the meeting.
(C) Five documents need to be prepared.
(D) Some workers are meeting for the fifth time.

Carson's Bike Shop Still Rolling

PHILADELPHIA (October 30)—Carson's Bike Shop, a bike repair shop and retailer of bicycle parts, is celebrating its 25th anniversary. The business was founded by Carson Reese, who taught himself how to repair bicycles because cycling was his hobby. He brought in his brother, David Reese, to handle the accounting side of things, and the business steadily grew.

The business offered repair services for low prices and made most of its money through the sale of bicycle parts and cycling accessories. This approach helped the shop build up a loyal customer base over time. As demand grew, more bicycle mechanics were hired and new services were added. Five years ago, it opened a second branch in Willow Grove, and its third branch, which is in Trenton, opened last spring. Carson's Bike Shop continues to contribute to the cycling community by arranging bicycle races in Philadelphia and making donations to sports-related charities.

155. What is the article mainly about?

(A) The success of a new invention
(B) Trends in the cycling industry
(C) The relocation of a shop
(D) The history of a business

156. The word "approach" in paragraph 2, line 4, is closest in meaning to

(A) movement
(B) access
(C) arrival
(D) strategy

157. What is true about Carson's Bike Shop?

(A) It designs bicycle accessories.
(B) It organizes athletic competitions.
(C) It has recently been sold.
(D) It started in Willow Grove.

GO ON TO THE NEXT PAGE

Questions 158-160 refer to the following e-mail.

E-Mail

TO:	Shirley Amundson <s_amundson@suffolkltd.com>
FROM:	Romulus Cruise Lines <booking@romuluscruiselines.com>
DATE:	July 11
SUBJECT:	Naples Cruise

Dear Ms. Amundson,

Thank you for booking a cruise with Romulus Cruise Lines departing from Naples, Italy, on September 20 and returning on September 27.

Your luxury cabin has a flat-screen television with on-demand films, a writing desk, a king-sized bed, and a private balcony. The ship features several dining areas, lounges for musical entertainment, and a large auditorium. On the top deck, you can find a swimming pool, hot tubs, and a miniature golf course.

You can park on site at the port's lot for a fee, but please note that the lot is not affiliated with Romulus Cruise Lines. You can use our free shuttle between Naples International Airport and the port. Simply show your cruise ticket confirmation e-mail.

As you prepare for your journey, keep in mind that there are some things that you are not allowed to bring on board. To view a list of these, please visit www.romuluscruiselines.com/boarding.

Have a wonderful trip!

Michael Silva
Romulus Cruise Lines

---

158. What is one purpose of the e-mail?

(A) To request feedback from a customer
(B) To describe some on-board amenities
(C) To announce a change in a departure date
(D) To offer a cruise cabin upgrade

159. What is available to Romulus Cruise Lines passengers?

(A) Discounts on flights to Naples
(B) Free parking at the port
(C) A complimentary shuttle service
(D) Vouchers for local dining

160. According to Mr. Silva, what can Ms. Amundson find on a Web site?

(A) Coupons for future bookings
(B) Information about restricted items
(C) Photos from previous journeys
(D) Testimonials from passengers

8 May

Wendy Sanford
660 Rosewood Court
Brockport, NY 14420

Dear Ms. Sanford,

We would like to inform you that your home insurance policy will expire soon. Please see the details below. —[1]—. It is important for your property to be insured at all times. You should have a new policy in place before the expiration of your current policy. —[2]—.

Policy Type: Basic Home and Contents
Policy Number: 374109
Expiration Date: June 4

Our fees are $160 for a Basic Home Only policy, $180 for a Premium Home Only policy, $205 for a Basic Home and Contents Policy, and $225 for a Premium Home and Contents policy. These rates have not changed since the purchase of your current policy last year. —[3]—.

To renew your policy, simply visit www.trustedinsuranceinc.com/renew, input your policy number, and follow the on-screen instructions. This will take less than 10 minutes. —[4]—.

Regards,

Manuel Shapiro

Manuel Shapiro
Customer Service Agent, Trusted Insurance Inc.

---

161. Why was the letter written?

(A) To confirm the customer's contact details
(B) To check the value of a home
(C) To request an overdue payment
(D) To describe the state of a policy

162. How much did Ms. Sanford most likely pay last year?

(A) $160
(B) $180
(C) $205
(D) $225

163. In which of the following positions marked [1], [2], [3], and [4] does the following sentence best belong?

"Otherwise, your home and finances could be at risk."

(A) [1]
(B) [2]
(C) [3]
(D) [4]

GO ON TO THE NEXT PAGE

Questions 164-167 refer to the following online chat discussion.

Helen Snyder [9:24 A.M.]	Hi, Lee and Aubrey. Have the presenters for the year-end awards banquet been decided? I want to make sure the planning is on track.
Lee Roth [9:25 A.M.]	Yes, Adele Ruiz and Craig Jacobson will be the presenters this year.
Helen Snyder [9:26 A.M.]	Great! Will we have them seated near the stage for the dinner portion of the event?
Lee Roth [9:27 A.M.]	Yes, the presenters will be seated at the front. We are most likely using Glendale Hall again, but I'm just waiting for Tina Vance at Daubert Hotel to provide a quote.
Aubrey Lujan [9:29 A.M.]	There is actually one more. Bonnie Nelson will also take the stage.
Lee Roth [9:30 A.M.]	Oh, right. I had forgotten about that. Things are moving so quickly.
Helen Snyder [9:31 A.M.]	Bonnie Nelson? I thought only executive staff members were giving out the awards.
Aubrey Lujan [9:32 A.M.]	The board members have been so closely involved in choosing the winners this year, so we thought that they should be represented as well.
Helen Snyder [9:33 A.M.]	That makes sense. Lee, please contact all of the presenters to ask when they are free for a conference call.

164. Who will present some awards?

(A) Ms. Snyder
(B) Mr. Roth
(C) Mr. Jacobson
(D) Ms. Vance

165. At 9:29 A.M., what does Ms. Lujan most likely mean when she writes, "There is actually one more"?

(A) A new award category was created.
(B) An event will include a third presenter.
(C) Another venue is still available.
(D) Mr. Roth has been assigned a new task.

166. Who most likely is Ms. Nelson?

(A) An award nominee
(B) A corporate executive
(C) A board member
(D) A department head

167. What does Ms. Snyder ask Mr. Roth to do?

(A) Find out the presenters' availability
(B) Finalize a venue soon
(C) Print the list of award winners
(D) Forward a copy of an invitation

Programmers Wanted

Lynn Energy Advisors
Houston, Texas

Lynn Energy Advisors has several open positions for programmers to develop a smartphone application for tracking and reporting energy usage.

Lynn Energy Advisors has been voted the Most Trusted Advisory Firm in the industry for three consecutive years. Previous experience is not required, making this the ideal role for recent graduates. —[1]—. Candidates should be familiar with a range of software development tools and have a firm understanding of data protection procedures. The job involves creating and filing reports daily, so the ability to complete tasks while demonstrating care for even the smallest detail is a must. —[2]—. You will work on a small team of five people.

To apply, send a cover letter and résumé to hr@lynnenergyadvisors.com. —[3]—. We prefer to have the start date as soon as possible. —[4]—. For a full job description, visit www.lynnenergyadvisors.com.

168. What is suggested about Lynn Energy Advisors?

(A) It has a good reputation.
(B) It is under new ownership.
(C) It will relocate to Houston.
(D) It offers competitive wages.

169. What is indicated about the positions?

(A) They are intended for entry-level programmers.
(B) They have many opportunities for promotion.
(C) They require a background check of the applicant.
(D) They involve maintaining energy production.

170. What is stated as a requirement of the job?

(A) Managing a small team
(B) Paying attention to detail
(C) Responding to software questions
(D) Checking colleagues' reports

171. In which of the following positions marked [1], [2], [3], and [4] does the following sentence best belong?

"However, we are willing to wait for the right candidates."

(A) [1]
(B) [2]
(C) [3]
(D) [4]

GO ON TO THE NEXT PAGE

City of Orland Proposal Request

Summary

The city of Orland is accepting submissions from manufacturers for digital parking meters to be used throughout the city center. These should be supplied by August 18.

Purpose

The city's outdated coin-operated meters no longer meet the community's needs and will be replaced with digital parking meters. In addition to making the payment process more convenient, as various credit cards and phone-based payment apps are accepted, the meters will also cut costs regarding city personnel having to check and empty meters. Costs are also lower for drivers because the meters can sense when a vehicle has vacated the spot and charge only for the time used, not more. Cities that have installed digital meters have benefitted from a greater number of positive reviews from out-of-town visitors. This is due to the meters being easier to use thanks to their simple and intuitive user interface.

Specifics

The manufacturer should provide 1,800 digital parking meters suitable for outdoor use. They must be capable of round-the-clock monitoring and uploading real-time data feeds to the transportation office. The meters' touchscreens should display text clearly no matter the lighting conditions.

To submit a proposal, send your bid to Jason Bahr at j.bahr@orland.gov no later than February 3. Visit www.orland.gov/project0894 to find the list of documents needed during submission.

172. What is a purpose of the announcement?

    (A) To introduce public parking fines

    (B) To describe a city's need for parking

    (C) To explain a change in parking fees

    (D) To encourage businesses to submit bids

173. What is NOT indicated as a benefit of the parking meters?

    (A) Drivers can find parking spots more easily.

    (B) A variety of payment methods can be used.

    (C) There will be a reduction in staffing costs.

    (D) Meter users will not be overcharged.

174. What has happened in other cities that started using digital meters?

    (A) They received more favorable reviews from tourists.

    (B) They reduced traffic congestion in the city center.

    (C) They raised more money for transportation projects.

    (D) They increased the number of major manufacturers to the area.

175. What is stated about the proposed meters?

    (A) They must be the same size as the current meters.

    (B) They should have a battery backup system.

    (C) They must send information to a certain location.

    (D) They should be manufactured domestically.

GO ON TO THE NEXT PAGE

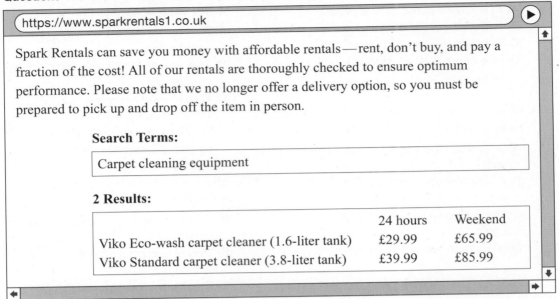

https://www.sparkrentals1.co.uk

Spark Rentals can save you money with affordable rentals—rent, don't buy, and pay a fraction of the cost! All of our rentals are thoroughly checked to ensure optimum performance. Please note that we no longer offer a delivery option, so you must be prepared to pick up and drop off the item in person.

Search Terms:

Carpet cleaning equipment

2 Results:

	24 hours	Weekend
Viko Eco-wash carpet cleaner (1.6-liter tank)	£29.99	£65.99
Viko Standard carpet cleaner (3.8-liter tank)	£39.99	£85.99

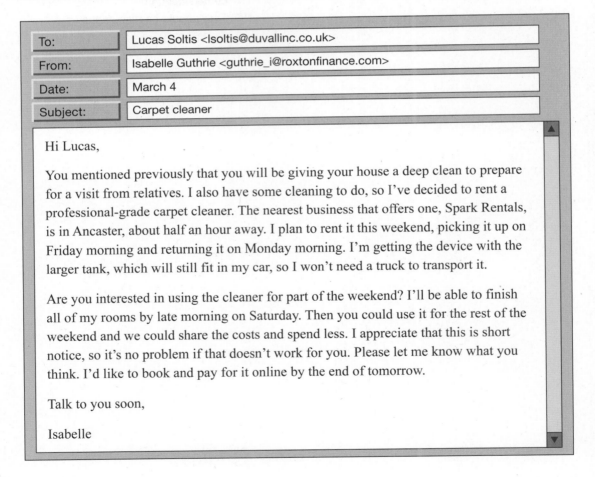

To:	Lucas Soltis <lsoltis@duvallinc.co.uk>
From:	Isabelle Guthrie <guthrie_i@roxtonfinance.com>
Date:	March 4
Subject:	Carpet cleaner

Hi Lucas,

You mentioned previously that you will be giving your house a deep clean to prepare for a visit from relatives. I also have some cleaning to do, so I've decided to rent a professional-grade carpet cleaner. The nearest business that offers one, Spark Rentals, is in Ancaster, about half an hour away. I plan to rent it this weekend, picking it up on Friday morning and returning it on Monday morning. I'm getting the device with the larger tank, which will still fit in my car, so I won't need a truck to transport it.

Are you interested in using the cleaner for part of the weekend? I'll be able to finish all of my rooms by late morning on Saturday. Then you could use it for the rest of the weekend and we could share the costs and spend less. I appreciate that this is short notice, so it's no problem if that doesn't work for you. Please let me know what you think. I'd like to book and pay for it online by the end of tomorrow.

Talk to you soon,

Isabelle

176. What does the Web page suggest about Spark Rentals?

(A) It used to deliver equipment to customers.

(B) It provides a discount to businesses.

(C) It can acquire new equipment by special request.

(D) It sells some of its equipment after use.

177. What is the purpose of Ms. Guthrie's e-mail?

(A) To change the date of a project

(B) To recommend some cleaning products

(C) To suggest a money-saving opportunity

(D) To invite Mr. Soltis for a visit

178. In the e-mail, the word "appreciate" in paragraph 2, line 3, is closest in meaning to

(A) assess

(B) understand

(C) thank

(D) enjoy

179. What is suggested about Ms. Guthrie in the e-mail?

(A) She will go to Ancaster on a weekday.

(B) She cleans her carpets annually.

(C) She owns a truck.

(D) She has used Spark Rentals before.

180. How much will Ms. Guthrie most likely pay on the Spark Rentals Web site?

(A) £29.99

(B) £39.99

(C) £65.99

(D) £85.99

GO ON TO THE NEXT PAGE

Beamont Laboratories to Expand Research and Development

BRISBANE (3 August)—Beamont Laboratories, a company that specializes in creating cosmetic products for international brands, is expanding its R&D staff to cater to clients seeking haircare products. Beamont Laboratories, headquartered in Brisbane and founded 18 years ago, has been a leader in innovation as well as environmental responsibility. This has led to steady growth, especially over the past five years. The expansion will be at the Canberra-based laboratory. There are also smaller sites in Melbourne and Newcastle.

The new team will be led by Gemma Gabriel, who has been with the business since the beginning, starting as a junior researcher and working her way up. She was in charge of the development of the popular product Ordell, a shampoo specially designed for those with sensitive skin. Ms. Gabriel will oversee the hiring process from start to finish.

Beamont Laboratories Job Opening
Title: Senior Cosmetic Scientist
Posted: 10 August
Application Deadline: 15 September

Become an integral part of our expanding R&D team.

KEY DUTIES:
• Designing product development schedules for various projects
• Developing, analyzing, and testing samples
• Keeping informed of advancements in laboratory techniques
• Sourcing all relevant equipment and materials for laboratory use
• Producing accurate cost estimates for future production

A degree in chemistry or similar is required (master's level preferred). Interviews will be held from 20 October to 1 November. The start date is 22 November.

181. What is indicated about Ms. Gabriel?

(A) She plans to relocate to Brisbane for work.

(B) She was promoted to her position five years ago.

(C) She has worked for Beamont Laboratories for 18 years.

(D) She will retire from Beamont Laboratories soon.

182. What is mentioned about Ordell?

(A) It is the company's best-seller.

(B) It is made from natural ingredients.

(C) It can be used as a skin lotion.

(D) It is a type of haircare product.

183. Where will the new senior cosmetic scientist most likely work?

(A) In Brisbane

(B) In Canberra

(C) In Newcastle

(D) In Melbourne

184. When will the successful candidate probably be selected?

(A) In August

(B) In September

(C) In October

(D) In November

185. What is one job responsibility of the position?

(A) Procuring necessary supplies

(B) Teaching techniques to team members

(C) Inspecting production facilities

(D) Meeting with prospective customers

GO ON TO THE NEXT PAGE

To:	All Community Arts Center Members
From:	Community Arts Center
Subject:	Summer Art Lecture Series
Date:	June 10
Attachment:	Summer_art_lecture_series

Dear Community Arts Center Members:

The Summer Art Lecture Series is nearly here! Please check out the attached schedule. All of our lecturers are new this year except for the one who gave a talk on the digital age of art, which we're bringing back due to high demand.

Order your tickets at www.commartscenter.org. Please note that we only accept group bookings (5 people or more) for events in our largest venues—the Rivas Room, with space for 150 people, and the Mercier Room, which accommodates 90 people.

Community Arts Center
Summer Art Lecture Series

Lecture Title	Lecturer	Date and Time	Location
Light and Watercolor	Annie Cho	June 29, 7–9 P.M.	Chester Room
Eco-Friendly Supplies	Samuel Delgado	July 2, 1–3 P.M.	Barron Room
The Digital Age of Art	Bianca Fallici	July 8, 3–5 P.M.	Rivas Room
Art in Architecture	Hugo Beckham	July 25, 3–4 P.M.	Chester Room
The Undiscovered History of Art	Hai Feng	July 31, 6–8 P.M.	Mercier Room
Mixed Media Creations	Yolanda Florez	August 4, 7–8 P.M.	Rivas Room

TO:	Gerard McCray <gerardmccray@commartscenter.org>
FROM:	Hai Feng <hfeng@hollowayinstitute.com>
DATE:	August 5
SUBJECT:	Thank you!

Dear Mr. McCray,

I wanted to thank you for inviting me to give a lecture at the Summer Art Lecture Series. I had a great experience, and I hope to participate again in the future. I was impressed with the venue for the event. Even though the room seemed rather empty, that was because it was such a large space. Actually, the number of attendees was much more than I expected, so I was very happy about that.

In addition, I was especially grateful to Tony Sheridan, who promptly responded to my request for technical assistance at the start of my talk and resolved the issue quickly. Fortunately, this meant that we only had to start 15 minutes late instead of having to cancel the talk.

Warmest regards,

Hai Feng

186. Which room can accommodate over 100 people?

(A) The Barron Room
(B) The Chester Room
(C) The Mercier Room
(D) The Rivas Room

187. Who has given a lecture at the event before?

(A) Ms. Cho
(B) Mr. Delgado
(C) Ms. Fallici
(D) Mr. Beckham

188. Who most likely is Mr. Sheridan?

(A) A technician
(B) An event planner
(C) A researcher
(D) A venue owner

189. Which lecture had a delayed start time?

(A) Eco-Friendly Supplies
(B) Art in Architecture
(C) The Undiscovered History of Art
(D) Mixed Media Creations

190. What is suggested about Mr. Feng?

(A) He used to work with Mr. McCray.
(B) He was pleased with the turnout.
(C) He wished he had a larger room.
(D) He traveled to attend the event.

GO ON TO THE NEXT PAGE

http://www.treecarefoundation.org

The Tree Care Foundation (TCF) is dedicated to ensuring the health of trees in woodland areas. Our volunteers play an essential role in identifying tree diseases and pests and determining how and where they are expanding in the area they affect. This helps us to take measures to control outbreaks and reduce the loss of trees.

About Volunteering:
• Apply by completing an application form online and have a brief phone interview
• Attend a training session to learn the skills you will need
• Commit to a minimum of 12 months of volunteer work at the TCF, conducting 2–3 survey sessions per month

TO:	Aida Ferreira, Kevin Murray, Sharad Dhibar, Ruth Bryson
FROM:	Ashley Jackson <jacksona@treecarefoundation.org>
DATE:	March 5
SUBJECT:	Training session

Dear Volunteers,

We're excited that you are joining our efforts at the Tree Care Foundation (TCF). Thanks to volunteers like you, we have been able to grow our charity considerably since Curtis Baxter founded it seven years ago.

The next step in the process is to complete an intensive training session. This is scheduled for Saturday, March 20, from 9 A.M. to 4 P.M. It will take place at the Aldredge Nature Center, and lunch will be provided. Mr. Baxter will be in charge of the session.

After the initial training, you will have one supervised survey session the following week with an experienced member, as below.

Name	Assigned Area
Aida Ferreira	Wesley Woodlands
Kevin Murray	Barnbrook Forest
Sharad Dhibar	Malham Forest
Ruth Bryson	Denton National Reserve

Please let me know if you have any questions,

Ashley Jackson

To:	Stanley Walton <s_walton@victoriamail.com>
From:	Ruth Bryson <ruth.bryson@gilbert-enterprises.com>
Date:	March 23
Subject:	Supervised survey

Dear Mr. Walton,

I'm looking forward to meeting you in person for my supervised survey session this Friday. I appreciate your adjusting your original start time to accommodate my work schedule. I plan to drive to the site, so I will meet you there at 2 P.M.

I will bring all of the gear that was distributed at the initial training session. However, I'm wondering if I have to wrap it up to protect it in some way. I'm just using a regular backpack, and I don't want to break any of the fragile components. Please let me know if there is anything special that I need to do.

Thank you,

Ruth Bryson

191. What is the main duty of TCF volunteers?

(A) Raising funds for tree projects
(B) Planting trees in woodland areas
(C) Tracking the spread of tree diseases
(D) Clearing away tree branches

192. What is suggested about the recipients of the first e-mail?

(A) They attended a group interview.
(B) They will work for TCF for at least one year.
(C) They will complete two to three surveys each week.
(D) They can choose the location where they work.

193. What is indicated about the training session on March 20?

(A) It was led by the charity's founder.
(B) It lasted for approximately three hours.
(C) It was conducted in several locations.
(D) It started in the afternoon.

194. Where will Mr. Walton most likely conduct a survey?

(A) At Wesley Woodlands
(B) At Barnbrook Forest
(C) At Malham Forest
(D) At Denton National Reserve

195. In the second e-mail, what does Ms. Bryson express concern about?

(A) Damaging some equipment
(B) Having parking difficulties
(C) Finding a remote location
(D) Purchasing the right gear

GO ON TO THE NEXT PAGE

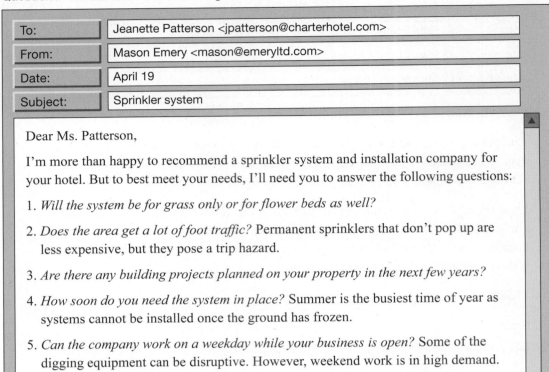

To:	Jeanette Patterson <jpatterson@charterhotel.com>
From:	Mason Emery <mason@emeryltd.com>
Date:	April 19
Subject:	Sprinkler system

Dear Ms. Patterson,

I'm more than happy to recommend a sprinkler system and installation company for your hotel. But to best meet your needs, I'll need you to answer the following questions:

1. *Will the system be for grass only or for flower beds as well?*

2. *Does the area get a lot of foot traffic?* Permanent sprinklers that don't pop up are less expensive, but they pose a trip hazard.

3. *Are there any building projects planned on your property in the next few years?*

4. *How soon do you need the system in place?* Summer is the busiest time of year as systems cannot be installed once the ground has frozen.

5. *Can the company work on a weekday while your business is open?* Some of the digging equipment can be disruptive. However, weekend work is in high demand.

Thank you in advance for providing this additional information.

Mason Emery

To:	Mason Emery <mason@emeryltd.com>
From:	Jeanette Patterson <jpatterson@charterhotel.com>
Date:	April 20
Subject:	RE: Sprinkler system

Dear Mr. Emery,

The grounds at the Bridgeview branch of Charter Hotel are completely fenced in. While we have a few raised flower beds, we want the system for our grassy area. We have a paved patio, so most guests spend their outdoor time there. Dogs often run around on the grass, but very few human guests utilize it.

The work crew can visit any day of the week, as we cannot shut down. Please note that we are willing to pay more for a high-quality system, and we want a company that has been in business for a long time.

Thank you for your assistance,

Jeanette Patterson

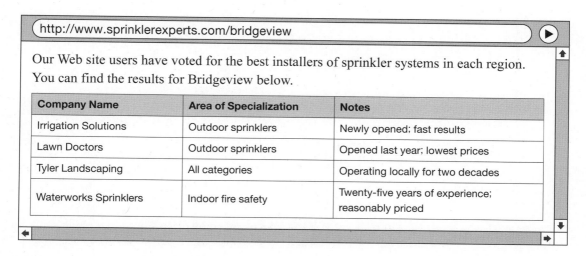

http://www.sprinklerexperts.com/bridgeview

Our Web site users have voted for the best installers of sprinkler systems in each region. You can find the results for Bridgeview below.

Company Name	Area of Specialization	Notes
Irrigation Solutions	Outdoor sprinklers	Newly opened; fast results
Lawn Doctors	Outdoor sprinklers	Opened last year; lowest prices
Tyler Landscaping	All categories	Operating locally for two decades
Waterworks Sprinklers	Indoor fire safety	Twenty-five years of experience; reasonably priced

196. Where does Mr. Emery most likely work?

(A) At a manufacturing facility
(B) At a consulting firm
(C) At a property development company
(D) At a marketing firm

197. What does Mr. Emery suggest about sprinkler systems?

(A) They should be inspected by a professional regularly.
(B) They must be installed when the ground is warm enough.
(C) They can be hooked up to the city's water supply.
(D) They will save the user money in the long run.

198. Which of Mr. Emery's questions is not addressed by Ms. Patterson?

(A) Question 1
(B) Question 2
(C) Question 3
(D) Question 5

199. According to the second e-mail, what is probably true about Charter Hotel?

(A) It has recently opened a branch in Bridgeview.
(B) It is closed for part of the year.
(C) It allows pets on site.
(D) It is located near a busy road.

200. Which company will Mr. Emery likely recommend?

(A) Irrigation Solutions
(B) Lawn Doctors
(C) Tyler Landscaping
(D) Waterworks Sprinklers

Stop! This is the end of the test. If you finish before time is called, you may go back to Parts 5, 6, and 7 and check your work.

ANSWER SHEET

ACTUAL TEST

LISTENING(Part I ~ IV)

NO.	ANSWER A B C D	NO.	ANSWER A B C D	NO.	ANSWER A B C D	NO.	ANSWER A B C D	NO.	ANSWER A B C D
1	ⓐ ⓑ ⓒ	21	ⓐ ⓑ ⓒ ⓓ	41	ⓐ ⓑ ⓒ ⓓ	61	ⓐ ⓑ ⓒ ⓓ	81	ⓐ ⓑ ⓒ ⓓ
2	ⓐ ⓑ ⓒ	22	ⓐ ⓑ ⓒ ⓓ	42	ⓐ ⓑ ⓒ ⓓ	62	ⓐ ⓑ ⓒ ⓓ	82	ⓐ ⓑ ⓒ ⓓ
3	ⓐ ⓑ ⓒ	23	ⓐ ⓑ ⓒ ⓓ	43	ⓐ ⓑ ⓒ ⓓ	63	ⓐ ⓑ ⓒ ⓓ	83	ⓐ ⓑ ⓒ ⓓ
4	ⓐ ⓑ ⓒ	24	ⓐ ⓑ ⓒ ⓓ	44	ⓐ ⓑ ⓒ ⓓ	64	ⓐ ⓑ ⓒ ⓓ	84	ⓐ ⓑ ⓒ ⓓ
5	ⓐ ⓑ ⓒ	25	ⓐ ⓑ ⓒ ⓓ	45	ⓐ ⓑ ⓒ ⓓ	65	ⓐ ⓑ ⓒ ⓓ	85	ⓐ ⓑ ⓒ ⓓ
6	ⓐ ⓑ ⓒ	26	ⓐ ⓑ ⓒ ⓓ	46	ⓐ ⓑ ⓒ ⓓ	66	ⓐ ⓑ ⓒ ⓓ	86	ⓐ ⓑ ⓒ ⓓ
7	ⓐ ⓑ ⓒ	27	ⓐ ⓑ ⓒ ⓓ	47	ⓐ ⓑ ⓒ ⓓ	67	ⓐ ⓑ ⓒ ⓓ	87	ⓐ ⓑ ⓒ ⓓ
8	ⓐ ⓑ ⓒ	28	ⓐ ⓑ ⓒ ⓓ	48	ⓐ ⓑ ⓒ ⓓ	68	ⓐ ⓑ ⓒ ⓓ	88	ⓐ ⓑ ⓒ ⓓ
9	ⓐ ⓑ ⓒ	29	ⓐ ⓑ ⓒ ⓓ	49	ⓐ ⓑ ⓒ ⓓ	69	ⓐ ⓑ ⓒ ⓓ	89	ⓐ ⓑ ⓒ ⓓ
10	ⓐ ⓑ ⓒ	30	ⓐ ⓑ ⓒ ⓓ	50	ⓐ ⓑ ⓒ ⓓ	70	ⓐ ⓑ ⓒ ⓓ	90	ⓐ ⓑ ⓒ ⓓ
11	ⓐ ⓑ ⓒ	31	ⓐ ⓑ ⓒ ⓓ	51	ⓐ ⓑ ⓒ ⓓ	71	ⓐ ⓑ ⓒ ⓓ	91	ⓐ ⓑ ⓒ ⓓ
12	ⓐ ⓑ ⓒ	32	ⓐ ⓑ ⓒ ⓓ	52	ⓐ ⓑ ⓒ ⓓ	72	ⓐ ⓑ ⓒ ⓓ	92	ⓐ ⓑ ⓒ ⓓ
13	ⓐ ⓑ ⓒ	33	ⓐ ⓑ ⓒ ⓓ	53	ⓐ ⓑ ⓒ ⓓ	73	ⓐ ⓑ ⓒ ⓓ	93	ⓐ ⓑ ⓒ ⓓ
14	ⓐ ⓑ ⓒ	34	ⓐ ⓑ ⓒ ⓓ	54	ⓐ ⓑ ⓒ ⓓ	74	ⓐ ⓑ ⓒ ⓓ	94	ⓐ ⓑ ⓒ ⓓ
15	ⓐ ⓑ ⓒ	35	ⓐ ⓑ ⓒ ⓓ	55	ⓐ ⓑ ⓒ ⓓ	75	ⓐ ⓑ ⓒ ⓓ	95	ⓐ ⓑ ⓒ ⓓ
16	ⓐ ⓑ ⓒ	36	ⓐ ⓑ ⓒ ⓓ	56	ⓐ ⓑ ⓒ ⓓ	76	ⓐ ⓑ ⓒ ⓓ	96	ⓐ ⓑ ⓒ ⓓ
17	ⓐ ⓑ ⓒ	37	ⓐ ⓑ ⓒ ⓓ	57	ⓐ ⓑ ⓒ ⓓ	77	ⓐ ⓑ ⓒ ⓓ	97	ⓐ ⓑ ⓒ ⓓ
18	ⓐ ⓑ ⓒ	38	ⓐ ⓑ ⓒ ⓓ	58	ⓐ ⓑ ⓒ ⓓ	78	ⓐ ⓑ ⓒ ⓓ	98	ⓐ ⓑ ⓒ ⓓ
19	ⓐ ⓑ ⓒ	39	ⓐ ⓑ ⓒ ⓓ	59	ⓐ ⓑ ⓒ ⓓ	79	ⓐ ⓑ ⓒ ⓓ	99	ⓐ ⓑ ⓒ ⓓ
20	ⓐ ⓑ ⓒ	40	ⓐ ⓑ ⓒ ⓓ	60	ⓐ ⓑ ⓒ ⓓ	80	ⓐ ⓑ ⓒ ⓓ	100	ⓐ ⓑ ⓒ ⓓ

READING(Part V ~ VII)

NO.	ANSWER A B C D	NO.	ANSWER A B C D	NO.	ANSWER A B C D	NO.	ANSWER A B C D	NO.	ANSWER A B C D
101	ⓐ ⓑ ⓒ ⓓ	121	ⓐ ⓑ ⓒ ⓓ	141	ⓐ ⓑ ⓒ ⓓ	161	ⓐ ⓑ ⓒ ⓓ	181	ⓐ ⓑ ⓒ ⓓ
102	ⓐ ⓑ ⓒ ⓓ	122	ⓐ ⓑ ⓒ ⓓ	142	ⓐ ⓑ ⓒ ⓓ	162	ⓐ ⓑ ⓒ ⓓ	182	ⓐ ⓑ ⓒ ⓓ
103	ⓐ ⓑ ⓒ ⓓ	123	ⓐ ⓑ ⓒ ⓓ	143	ⓐ ⓑ ⓒ ⓓ	163	ⓐ ⓑ ⓒ ⓓ	183	ⓐ ⓑ ⓒ ⓓ
104	ⓐ ⓑ ⓒ ⓓ	124	ⓐ ⓑ ⓒ ⓓ	144	ⓐ ⓑ ⓒ ⓓ	164	ⓐ ⓑ ⓒ ⓓ	184	ⓐ ⓑ ⓒ ⓓ
105	ⓐ ⓑ ⓒ ⓓ	125	ⓐ ⓑ ⓒ ⓓ	145	ⓐ ⓑ ⓒ ⓓ	165	ⓐ ⓑ ⓒ ⓓ	185	ⓐ ⓑ ⓒ ⓓ
106	ⓐ ⓑ ⓒ ⓓ	126	ⓐ ⓑ ⓒ ⓓ	146	ⓐ ⓑ ⓒ ⓓ	166	ⓐ ⓑ ⓒ ⓓ	186	ⓐ ⓑ ⓒ ⓓ
107	ⓐ ⓑ ⓒ ⓓ	127	ⓐ ⓑ ⓒ ⓓ	147	ⓐ ⓑ ⓒ ⓓ	167	ⓐ ⓑ ⓒ ⓓ	187	ⓐ ⓑ ⓒ ⓓ
108	ⓐ ⓑ ⓒ ⓓ	128	ⓐ ⓑ ⓒ ⓓ	148	ⓐ ⓑ ⓒ ⓓ	168	ⓐ ⓑ ⓒ ⓓ	188	ⓐ ⓑ ⓒ ⓓ
109	ⓐ ⓑ ⓒ ⓓ	129	ⓐ ⓑ ⓒ ⓓ	149	ⓐ ⓑ ⓒ ⓓ	169	ⓐ ⓑ ⓒ ⓓ	189	ⓐ ⓑ ⓒ ⓓ
110	ⓐ ⓑ ⓒ ⓓ	130	ⓐ ⓑ ⓒ ⓓ	150	ⓐ ⓑ ⓒ ⓓ	170	ⓐ ⓑ ⓒ ⓓ	190	ⓐ ⓑ ⓒ ⓓ
111	ⓐ ⓑ ⓒ ⓓ	131	ⓐ ⓑ ⓒ ⓓ	151	ⓐ ⓑ ⓒ ⓓ	171	ⓐ ⓑ ⓒ ⓓ	191	ⓐ ⓑ ⓒ ⓓ
112	ⓐ ⓑ ⓒ ⓓ	132	ⓐ ⓑ ⓒ ⓓ	152	ⓐ ⓑ ⓒ ⓓ	172	ⓐ ⓑ ⓒ ⓓ	192	ⓐ ⓑ ⓒ ⓓ
113	ⓐ ⓑ ⓒ ⓓ	133	ⓐ ⓑ ⓒ ⓓ	153	ⓐ ⓑ ⓒ ⓓ	173	ⓐ ⓑ ⓒ ⓓ	193	ⓐ ⓑ ⓒ ⓓ
114	ⓐ ⓑ ⓒ ⓓ	134	ⓐ ⓑ ⓒ ⓓ	154	ⓐ ⓑ ⓒ ⓓ	174	ⓐ ⓑ ⓒ ⓓ	194	ⓐ ⓑ ⓒ ⓓ
115	ⓐ ⓑ ⓒ ⓓ	135	ⓐ ⓑ ⓒ ⓓ	155	ⓐ ⓑ ⓒ ⓓ	175	ⓐ ⓑ ⓒ ⓓ	195	ⓐ ⓑ ⓒ ⓓ
116	ⓐ ⓑ ⓒ ⓓ	136	ⓐ ⓑ ⓒ ⓓ	156	ⓐ ⓑ ⓒ ⓓ	176	ⓐ ⓑ ⓒ ⓓ	196	ⓐ ⓑ ⓒ ⓓ
117	ⓐ ⓑ ⓒ ⓓ	137	ⓐ ⓑ ⓒ ⓓ	157	ⓐ ⓑ ⓒ ⓓ	177	ⓐ ⓑ ⓒ ⓓ	197	ⓐ ⓑ ⓒ ⓓ
118	ⓐ ⓑ ⓒ ⓓ	138	ⓐ ⓑ ⓒ ⓓ	158	ⓐ ⓑ ⓒ ⓓ	178	ⓐ ⓑ ⓒ ⓓ	198	ⓐ ⓑ ⓒ ⓓ
119	ⓐ ⓑ ⓒ ⓓ	139	ⓐ ⓑ ⓒ ⓓ	159	ⓐ ⓑ ⓒ ⓓ	179	ⓐ ⓑ ⓒ ⓓ	199	ⓐ ⓑ ⓒ ⓓ
120	ⓐ ⓑ ⓒ ⓓ	140	ⓐ ⓑ ⓒ ⓓ	160	ⓐ ⓑ ⓒ ⓓ	180	ⓐ ⓑ ⓒ ⓓ	200	ⓐ ⓑ ⓒ ⓓ

ANSWER SHEET
ACTUAL TEST

LISTENING(Part I ~ IV)

NO.	ANSWER (A B C D)	NO.	ANSWER (A B C D)	NO.	ANSWER (A B C D)	NO.	ANSWER (A B C D)	NO.	ANSWER (A B C D)
1	ⓐ ⓑ ⓒ ⓓ	21	ⓐ ⓑ ⓒ ⓓ	41	ⓐ ⓑ ⓒ ⓓ	61	ⓐ ⓑ ⓒ ⓓ	81	ⓐ ⓑ ⓒ ⓓ
2	ⓐ ⓑ ⓒ ⓓ	22	ⓐ ⓑ ⓒ ⓓ	42	ⓐ ⓑ ⓒ ⓓ	62	ⓐ ⓑ ⓒ ⓓ	82	ⓐ ⓑ ⓒ ⓓ
3	ⓐ ⓑ ⓒ ⓓ	23	ⓐ ⓑ ⓒ ⓓ	43	ⓐ ⓑ ⓒ ⓓ	63	ⓐ ⓑ ⓒ ⓓ	83	ⓐ ⓑ ⓒ ⓓ
4	ⓐ ⓑ ⓒ ⓓ	24	ⓐ ⓑ ⓒ ⓓ	44	ⓐ ⓑ ⓒ ⓓ	64	ⓐ ⓑ ⓒ ⓓ	84	ⓐ ⓑ ⓒ ⓓ
5	ⓐ ⓑ ⓒ ⓓ	25	ⓐ ⓑ ⓒ ⓓ	45	ⓐ ⓑ ⓒ ⓓ	65	ⓐ ⓑ ⓒ ⓓ	85	ⓐ ⓑ ⓒ ⓓ
6	ⓐ ⓑ ⓒ ⓓ	26	ⓐ ⓑ ⓒ ⓓ	46	ⓐ ⓑ ⓒ ⓓ	66	ⓐ ⓑ ⓒ ⓓ	86	ⓐ ⓑ ⓒ ⓓ
7	ⓐ ⓑ ⓒ ⓓ	27	ⓐ ⓑ ⓒ ⓓ	47	ⓐ ⓑ ⓒ ⓓ	67	ⓐ ⓑ ⓒ ⓓ	87	ⓐ ⓑ ⓒ ⓓ
8	ⓐ ⓑ ⓒ ⓓ	28	ⓐ ⓑ ⓒ ⓓ	48	ⓐ ⓑ ⓒ ⓓ	68	ⓐ ⓑ ⓒ ⓓ	88	ⓐ ⓑ ⓒ ⓓ
9	ⓐ ⓑ ⓒ ⓓ	29	ⓐ ⓑ ⓒ ⓓ	49	ⓐ ⓑ ⓒ ⓓ	69	ⓐ ⓑ ⓒ ⓓ	89	ⓐ ⓑ ⓒ ⓓ
10	ⓐ ⓑ ⓒ ⓓ	30	ⓐ ⓑ ⓒ ⓓ	50	ⓐ ⓑ ⓒ ⓓ	70	ⓐ ⓑ ⓒ ⓓ	90	ⓐ ⓑ ⓒ ⓓ
11	ⓐ ⓑ ⓒ ⓓ	31	ⓐ ⓑ ⓒ ⓓ	51	ⓐ ⓑ ⓒ ⓓ	71	ⓐ ⓑ ⓒ ⓓ	91	ⓐ ⓑ ⓒ ⓓ
12	ⓐ ⓑ ⓒ ⓓ	32	ⓐ ⓑ ⓒ ⓓ	52	ⓐ ⓑ ⓒ ⓓ	72	ⓐ ⓑ ⓒ ⓓ	92	ⓐ ⓑ ⓒ ⓓ
13	ⓐ ⓑ ⓒ ⓓ	33	ⓐ ⓑ ⓒ ⓓ	53	ⓐ ⓑ ⓒ ⓓ	73	ⓐ ⓑ ⓒ ⓓ	93	ⓐ ⓑ ⓒ ⓓ
14	ⓐ ⓑ ⓒ ⓓ	34	ⓐ ⓑ ⓒ ⓓ	54	ⓐ ⓑ ⓒ ⓓ	74	ⓐ ⓑ ⓒ ⓓ	94	ⓐ ⓑ ⓒ ⓓ
15	ⓐ ⓑ ⓒ ⓓ	35	ⓐ ⓑ ⓒ ⓓ	55	ⓐ ⓑ ⓒ ⓓ	75	ⓐ ⓑ ⓒ ⓓ	95	ⓐ ⓑ ⓒ ⓓ
16	ⓐ ⓑ ⓒ ⓓ	36	ⓐ ⓑ ⓒ ⓓ	56	ⓐ ⓑ ⓒ ⓓ	76	ⓐ ⓑ ⓒ ⓓ	96	ⓐ ⓑ ⓒ ⓓ
17	ⓐ ⓑ ⓒ ⓓ	37	ⓐ ⓑ ⓒ ⓓ	57	ⓐ ⓑ ⓒ ⓓ	77	ⓐ ⓑ ⓒ ⓓ	97	ⓐ ⓑ ⓒ ⓓ
18	ⓐ ⓑ ⓒ ⓓ	38	ⓐ ⓑ ⓒ ⓓ	58	ⓐ ⓑ ⓒ ⓓ	78	ⓐ ⓑ ⓒ ⓓ	98	ⓐ ⓑ ⓒ ⓓ
19	ⓐ ⓑ ⓒ ⓓ	39	ⓐ ⓑ ⓒ ⓓ	59	ⓐ ⓑ ⓒ ⓓ	79	ⓐ ⓑ ⓒ ⓓ	99	ⓐ ⓑ ⓒ ⓓ
20	ⓐ ⓑ ⓒ ⓓ	40	ⓐ ⓑ ⓒ ⓓ	60	ⓐ ⓑ ⓒ ⓓ	80	ⓐ ⓑ ⓒ ⓓ	100	ⓐ ⓑ ⓒ ⓓ

READING(Part V ~ VII)

NO.	ANSWER (A B C D)	NO.	ANSWER (A B C D)	NO.	ANSWER (A B C D)	NO.	ANSWER (A B C D)
101	ⓐ ⓑ ⓒ ⓓ	121	ⓐ ⓑ ⓒ ⓓ	141	ⓐ ⓑ ⓒ ⓓ	161	ⓐ ⓑ ⓒ ⓓ
102	ⓐ ⓑ ⓒ ⓓ	122	ⓐ ⓑ ⓒ ⓓ	142	ⓐ ⓑ ⓒ ⓓ	162	ⓐ ⓑ ⓒ ⓓ
103	ⓐ ⓑ ⓒ ⓓ	123	ⓐ ⓑ ⓒ ⓓ	143	ⓐ ⓑ ⓒ ⓓ	163	ⓐ ⓑ ⓒ ⓓ
104	ⓐ ⓑ ⓒ ⓓ	124	ⓐ ⓑ ⓒ ⓓ	144	ⓐ ⓑ ⓒ ⓓ	164	ⓐ ⓑ ⓒ ⓓ
105	ⓐ ⓑ ⓒ ⓓ	125	ⓐ ⓑ ⓒ ⓓ	145	ⓐ ⓑ ⓒ ⓓ	165	ⓐ ⓑ ⓒ ⓓ
106	ⓐ ⓑ ⓒ ⓓ	126	ⓐ ⓑ ⓒ ⓓ	146	ⓐ ⓑ ⓒ ⓓ	166	ⓐ ⓑ ⓒ ⓓ
107	ⓐ ⓑ ⓒ ⓓ	127	ⓐ ⓑ ⓒ ⓓ	147	ⓐ ⓑ ⓒ ⓓ	167	ⓐ ⓑ ⓒ ⓓ
108	ⓐ ⓑ ⓒ ⓓ	128	ⓐ ⓑ ⓒ ⓓ	148	ⓐ ⓑ ⓒ ⓓ	168	ⓐ ⓑ ⓒ ⓓ
109	ⓐ ⓑ ⓒ ⓓ	129	ⓐ ⓑ ⓒ ⓓ	149	ⓐ ⓑ ⓒ ⓓ	169	ⓐ ⓑ ⓒ ⓓ
110	ⓐ ⓑ ⓒ ⓓ	130	ⓐ ⓑ ⓒ ⓓ	150	ⓐ ⓑ ⓒ ⓓ	170	ⓐ ⓑ ⓒ ⓓ
111	ⓐ ⓑ ⓒ ⓓ	131	ⓐ ⓑ ⓒ ⓓ	151	ⓐ ⓑ ⓒ ⓓ	171	ⓐ ⓑ ⓒ ⓓ
112	ⓐ ⓑ ⓒ ⓓ	132	ⓐ ⓑ ⓒ ⓓ	152	ⓐ ⓑ ⓒ ⓓ	172	ⓐ ⓑ ⓒ ⓓ
113	ⓐ ⓑ ⓒ ⓓ	133	ⓐ ⓑ ⓒ ⓓ	153	ⓐ ⓑ ⓒ ⓓ	173	ⓐ ⓑ ⓒ ⓓ
114	ⓐ ⓑ ⓒ ⓓ	134	ⓐ ⓑ ⓒ ⓓ	154	ⓐ ⓑ ⓒ ⓓ	174	ⓐ ⓑ ⓒ ⓓ
115	ⓐ ⓑ ⓒ ⓓ	135	ⓐ ⓑ ⓒ ⓓ	155	ⓐ ⓑ ⓒ ⓓ	175	ⓐ ⓑ ⓒ ⓓ
116	ⓐ ⓑ ⓒ ⓓ	136	ⓐ ⓑ ⓒ ⓓ	156	ⓐ ⓑ ⓒ ⓓ	176	ⓐ ⓑ ⓒ ⓓ
117	ⓐ ⓑ ⓒ ⓓ	137	ⓐ ⓑ ⓒ ⓓ	157	ⓐ ⓑ ⓒ ⓓ	177	ⓐ ⓑ ⓒ ⓓ
118	ⓐ ⓑ ⓒ ⓓ	138	ⓐ ⓑ ⓒ ⓓ	158	ⓐ ⓑ ⓒ ⓓ	178	ⓐ ⓑ ⓒ ⓓ
119	ⓐ ⓑ ⓒ ⓓ	139	ⓐ ⓑ ⓒ ⓓ	159	ⓐ ⓑ ⓒ ⓓ	179	ⓐ ⓑ ⓒ ⓓ
120	ⓐ ⓑ ⓒ ⓓ	140	ⓐ ⓑ ⓒ ⓓ	160	ⓐ ⓑ ⓒ ⓓ	180	ⓐ ⓑ ⓒ ⓓ
						181	ⓐ ⓑ ⓒ ⓓ
						182	ⓐ ⓑ ⓒ ⓓ
						183	ⓐ ⓑ ⓒ ⓓ
						184	ⓐ ⓑ ⓒ ⓓ
						185	ⓐ ⓑ ⓒ ⓓ
						186	ⓐ ⓑ ⓒ ⓓ
						187	ⓐ ⓑ ⓒ ⓓ
						188	ⓐ ⓑ ⓒ ⓓ
						189	ⓐ ⓑ ⓒ ⓓ
						190	ⓐ ⓑ ⓒ ⓓ
						191	ⓐ ⓑ ⓒ ⓓ
						192	ⓐ ⓑ ⓒ ⓓ
						193	ⓐ ⓑ ⓒ ⓓ
						194	ⓐ ⓑ ⓒ ⓓ
						195	ⓐ ⓑ ⓒ ⓓ
						196	ⓐ ⓑ ⓒ ⓓ
						197	ⓐ ⓑ ⓒ ⓓ
						198	ⓐ ⓑ ⓒ ⓓ
						199	ⓐ ⓑ ⓒ ⓓ
						200	ⓐ ⓑ ⓒ ⓓ

삶의 순간순간이
아름다운 마무리이며
새로운 시작이어야 한다.

– 법정 스님

에듀윌 토익 단기완성 700+ LC&RC

발 행 일	2023년 5월 22일 초판
저 자	에듀윌 어학연구소
펴 낸 이	김재환
펴 낸 곳	(주)에듀윌
등록번호	제25100-2002-000052호
주 소	08378 서울특별시 구로구 디지털로34길 55
	코오롱싸이언스밸리 2차 3층

* 이 책의 무단 인용 · 전재 · 복제를 금합니다.   ISBN 979-11-360-2674-3 (13740)

www.eduwill.net

대표전화 1600-6700

여러분의 작은 소리
에듀윌은 크게 듣겠습니다.

본 교재에 대한 여러분의 목소리를 들려주세요.
공부하시면서 어려웠던 점, 궁금한 점,
칭찬하고 싶은 점, 개선할 점, 어떤 것이라도 좋습니다.

에듀윌은 여러분께서 나누어 주신 의견을
통해 끊임없이 발전하고 있습니다.

에듀윌 도서몰 book.eduwill.net
- 부가학습자료 및 정오표: 에듀윌 도서몰 → 도서자료실
- 교재 문의: 에듀윌 도서몰 → 문의하기 → 교재(내용, 출간) / 주문 및 배송

꿈을 현실로 만드는
에듀윌

공무원 교육
- 선호도 1위, 신뢰도 1위!
  브랜드만족도 1위!
- 합격자 수 2,100% 폭등시킨
  독한 커리큘럼

자격증 교육
- 7년간 아무도 깨지 못한 기록
  합격자 수 1위
- 가장 많은 합격자를 배출한
  최고의 합격 시스템

직영학원
- 직영학원 수 1위, 수강생 규모 1위!
- 표준화된 커리큘럼과 호텔급 시설
  자랑하는 전국 57개 학원

종합출판
- 4대 온라인서점 베스트셀러 1위!
- 출제위원급 전문 교수진이
  직접 집필한 합격 교재

어학 교육
- 토익 베스트셀러 1위
- 토익 동영상 강의 무료 제공
- 업계 최초 '토익 공식' 추천 AI 앱 서비스

콘텐츠 제휴 · B2B 교육
- 고객 맞춤형 위탁 교육 서비스 제공
- 기업, 기관, 대학 등 각 단체에 최적화된
  고객 맞춤형 교육 및 제휴 서비스

부동산 아카데미
- 부동산 실무 교육 1위!
- 상위 1% 고소득 창업/취업 비법
- 부동산 실전 재테크 성공 비법

공기업 · 대기업 취업 교육
- 취업 교육 1위!
- 공기업 NCS, 대기업 직무적성,
  자소서, 면접

학점은행제
- 99%의 과목이수율
- 15년 연속 교육부 평가 인정 기관 선정

대학 편입
- 편입 교육 1위!
- 업계 유일 500% 환급 상품 서비스

국비무료 교육
- '5년우수훈련기관' 선정
- K-디지털, 4차 산업 등 특화 훈련과정

에듀윌 교육서비스 **공무원 교육** 9급공무원/7급공무원/경찰공무원/소방공무원/계리직공무원/기술직공무원/군무원 **자격증 교육** 공인중개사/주택관리사/전기기사/경비지도사/검정고시/소방설비기사/소방시설관리사/사회복지사1급/건축기사/토목기사/직업상담사/전기기능사/산업안전기사/위험물산업기사/위험물기능사/도로교통사고감정사/유통관리사/물류관리사/행정사/한국사능력검정/한경TESAT/매경TEST/KBS한국어능력시험·실용글쓰기/IT자격증/국제무역사/무역영어 **어학 교육** 토익 교재/토익 동영상 강의/인공지능 토익 앱 **세무/회계** 회계사/세무사/전산세무회계/ERP정보관리사/재경관리사 **대학 편입** 편입 교재/편입 영어·수학/경찰대/의치대/편입 컨설팅·면접 **공기업·대기업 취업 교육** 공기업 NCS·전공·상식/대기업 직무적성/자소서·면접 **직영학원** 공무원학원/기술직공무원 학원/군무원학원/경찰학원/소방학원/공무원 면접전문학원/군간부학원/공인중개사 학원/주택관리사 학원/전기기사학원/세무사·회계사 학원/편입학원/취업아카데미 **종합출판** 공무원·자격증 수험교재 및 단행본/월간지(시사상식) **학점은행제** 교육부 평가인정기관 원격평생교육원(사회복지사2급/경영학/CPA)/교육부 평가인정기관 원격 사회교육원(사회복지사2급/심리학) **콘텐츠 제휴·B2B 교육** 교육 콘텐츠 제휴/기업 맞춤 자격증 교육/대학 취업역량 강화 교육 **부동산 아카데미** 부동산 창업CEO과정/실전 경매과정/디벨로퍼과정 **국비무료 교육(국비교육원)** 전기기능사/전기(산업)기사/소방설비(산업)기사/IT(빅데이터/자바프로그램/파이썬)/게임그래픽/3D프린터/실내건축디자인/웹퍼블리셔/그래픽디자인/영상편집(유튜브)디자인/온라인 쇼핑몰광고 및 제작(쿠팡, 스마트스토어)/전산세무회계/컴퓨터활용능력/ITQ/GTQ/직업상담사

교육
문의 **1600-6700** www.eduwill.net

딱 필요한 것만 하니까, 토익이 쉬워진다!

쉬운 토익 공식
에듀윌 토익

최영준   셀린   클레어   구원

YES24 22년 9월 4주

YES24 22년 5월 4주

YES24 22년 4월 4주

알라딘 22년 3월 4주

베스트셀러
1위

에듀윌 토익
선택의 이유

에듀윌 토익 단기완성 700+
LC & RC

정답 및 해설

에듀윌 토익 단기완성 700+
정답 및 해설

에듀윌 토익
단기완성 700+
LC & RC
정답 및 해설

eduwill

LC PART 1

UNIT 01 인물 중심 사진

PRACTICE
본문 p.25

1. (D) **2.** (A) **3.** (C) **4.** (B) **5.** (C) **6.** (D)

1. 🎧 미남

(A) He's leaning against a fence.
(B) He's putting away a rake.
(C) He's picking some flowers.
(D) He's holding a gardening tool.

해석
(A) 그는 울타리에 기대어 있다.
(B) 그는 갈퀴를 치우고 있다.
(C) 그는 꽃을 꺾고 있다.
(D) 그는 정원 손질용 도구를 들고 있다.

어휘 lean against ~에 기대다   put away ~을 치우다
pick (꽃을) 꺾다, (과일 등을) 따다   gardening 정원 가꾸기
tool 도구, 공구

2. 🎧 미녀

(A) Products are displayed on shelves.
(B) A large basket is being used to carry goods.
(C) Customers are entering a shop.
(D) Display racks are being assembled.

해석
(A) 제품이 선반에 진열되어 있다.
(B) 큰 바구니가 상품을 나르는 데 사용되고 있다.
(C) 고객들이 상점에 들어가고 있다.
(D) 진열용 선반이 조립되고 있다.

어휘 display 진열[전시]하다   carry 나르다   enter 들어가다
rack 선반, 받침대   assemble 조립하다

3. 🎧 미남

(A) They're pushing bicycles along a path.
(B) They're taking off their bicycle helmets.
(C) One of the people is riding a bicycle.
(D) One of the people is opening a bicycle lock.

해석
(A) 그들은 길을 따라 자전거를 밀고 있다.
(B) 그들은 자전거 헬멧을 벗고 있다.
(C) 사람들 중 한 명이 자전거를 타고 있다.
(D) 사람들 중 한 명이 자전거 자물쇠를 열고 있다.

어휘 path 길   take off (옷 등을) 벗다   lock 자물쇠; 잠그다

4. 🎧 미녀

(A) The people are walking up some stairs.
(B) The people are leaving a building.
(C) The man is repairing a walkway.
(D) The woman is turning on a machine.

해석
(A) 사람들이 계단을 올라가고 있다.
(B) 사람들이 건물을 나가고 있다.
(C) 남자가 보도를 수리하고 있다.
(D) 여자가 기계를 켜고 있다.

어휘 leave 나가다, 떠나다   repair 수리하다   walkway 보도,
통로   turn on (라디오·TV·전기·가스 따위를) 켜다

5. 🎧 호남

(A) He's driving a vehicle.
(B) He's closing a car door.
(C) He's examining a tire.
(D) He's looking for a parking spot.

해석
(A) 그는 차를 운전하고 있다.
(B) 그는 차 문을 닫고 있다.
(C) 그는 타이어를 살펴보고 있다.
(D) 그는 주차 공간을 찾고 있다.

어휘 vehicle 차량, 탈것   examine 살펴보다, 검사하다
parking spot 주차 공간

6. 🎧 영녀

(A) Some workers are carrying a ladder.
(B) Some workers are putting on hard hats.
(C) A wall is being painted.
(D) A roof is under construction.

해석
(A) 작업자 몇 명이 사다리를 들고 있다.
(B) 작업자 몇 명이 안전모를 쓰고 있다.
(C) 벽이 페인트칠되고 있다.
(D) 지붕이 공사 중이다.

어휘 ladder 사다리   put on ~을 입다, 쓰다   hard hat 안전모
roof 지붕   under construction 공사 중인

UNIT 02 사물·풍경 중심 사진

PRACTICE				본문 p.27
1. (B)	2. (C)	3. (D)	4. (A)	5. (A)	6. (C)

1. 🎧 미남

(A) Several metal jugs are lying on their sides.
(B) Some containers have been placed on a platform.
(C) Lids have been fastened to some bottles.
(D) A wooden frame is covered in flowers.

해석
(A) 금속 항아리 몇 개가 옆으로 누워 있다.
(B) 용기 몇 개가 단 위에 놓여 있다.
(C) 몇 개의 병에 뚜껑이 고정되어 있다.

(D) 나무틀이 꽃으로 덮여 있다.

어휘 metal 금속   jug 항아리, 단지   container 용기, 그릇
be placed on ~위에 놓이다   platform 단, 연단   lid 뚜껑
fasten 고정하다   wooden frame 나무틀   be covered in
~로 덮이다

2. 🎧 미녀

(A) A fence is being repaired.
(B) Some umbrellas are shading a balcony.
(C) A picnic area has been set up outdoors.
(D) Diners are seated at some tables.

해석
(A) 울타리가 수리되고 있다.
(B) 우산 몇 개가 발코니에 그늘을 만들고 있다.
(C) 야외에 피크닉 장소가 설치되어 있다.
(D) 식사하는 사람들이 테이블에 앉아 있다.

어휘 fence 울타리   shade ~에 그늘을 만들다; 그늘   set up
세우다, 설치하다   diner 식사하는 사람

3. 🎧 미남

(A) A wooden furniture is being polished.
(B) A tool belt is hanging on a hook.
(C) Some hammers are scattered across a work area.
(D) Some tools have been left on a table.

해석
(A) 목재 가구가 닦이고 있다.
(B) 공구 벨트가 고리에 걸려 있다.
(C) 망치 몇 개가 작업 구역에 흩어져 있다.
(D) 몇몇 도구들이 테이블 위에 놓여 있다.

어휘 polish 닦다, 윤을 내다   hang 걸리다, 매달리다
hammer 망치   be scattered 흩어지다

4. 🎧 미녀

(A) **Merchandise is on display at an outdoor market.**
(B) A vendor is packing goods into shopping bags.
(C) Customers are waiting in a line.
(D) Some tents are being taken down.

해석
(A) **상품이 야외 시장에 진열되어 있다.**
(B) 상인이 물건을 쇼핑백에 담고 있다.
(C) 손님들이 줄을 서서 기다리고 있다.
(D) 텐트 몇 개가 철거되고 있다.

어휘 merchandise 상품, 제품   on display 진열된, 전시 중인
outdoor 야외의   vendor 상인, 판매자   pack 담다, 싸다
wait in line 줄을 서서 기다리다   take down 치우다, 분해하다

5. 🎧 호남

(A) **There are some mountains in the distance.**
(B) People are relaxing under the trees.
(C) Some tree branches are being trimmed.
(D) A bench has been placed alongside a beach.

해석
(A) **먼 곳에 산이 있다.**
(B) 사람들이 나무 아래에서 휴식을 취하고 있다.
(C) 나뭇가지가 다듬어지고 있다.
(D) 벤치가 해변 옆에 놓여 있다.

어휘 in the distance 먼 곳에   relax 휴식을 취하다   trim 다듬다   alongside 옆에, 나란히

6. 🎧 영녀

(A) A table has been set with dishes.
(B) Light fixtures are suspended above a fireplace.

(C) **A clock is mounted on a wall between some doors.**
(D) Chairs are stacked in a corner.

해석
(A) 식탁에 접시가 놓여 있다.
(B) 조명 기구가 벽난로 위에 매달려 있다.
(C) **시계가 문들 사이의 벽에 설치되어 있다.**
(D) 의자들이 구석에 쌓여 있다.

어휘 light fixture 조명 기구   suspend 매달다
be mounted on ~에 설치되다, 고정되다   be stacked 쌓이다
in a corner 구석에

700+ 뛰어넘기 PRACTICE   본문 p.29

1. (A)   **2.** (B)   **3.** (D)   **4.** (D)   **5.** (C)   **6.** (A)

1. 🎧 미남

(A) **Some people are wearing helmets.**
(B) Some people are getting into a vehicle.
(C) Some people are putting on safety vests.
(D) Some people are printing a document.

해설
(A) **몇몇 사람들이 헬멧을 쓰고 있다.**
(B) 몇몇 사람들이 차에 타고 있다.
(C) 몇몇 사람들이 안전 조끼를 입고 있다.
(D) 몇몇 사람들이 문서를 인쇄하고 있다.

어휘 get into ~에 타다   safety vest 안전 조끼   document 문서

2. 🎧 미녀

(A) A lamp is being moved.
(B) **Artwork is hanging above a piece of furniture.**
(C) Some flowers have been planted in a garden.
(D) Some chairs are being occupied.

해석
(A) 램프가 옮겨지고 있다.

(B) 미술품이 가구 위에 걸려 있다.
(C) 꽃 몇 송이가 정원에 심어져 있다.
(D) 의자 몇 개에 사람이 앉아 있다.

어휘 artwork 미술품, 삽화 plant 심다; 식물 occupied 사용
중인, 점령된

3. 🎧 미남

(A) A man is reaching into a toolbox.
(B) A man is pulling weeds from the ground.
(C) A paintbrush is propped against a building.
(D) A brick wall is being painted.

해석
(A) 남자가 공구 상자 안에 손을 넣고 있다.
(B) 남자가 땅에서 잡초를 뽑고 있다.
(C) 페인트 붓이 건물에 기대어져 있다.
(D) 벽돌 담이 페인트칠되고 있다.

어휘 reach into ~ 안에 손을 넣다 toolbox 공구 상자 pull
뽑다, 당기다 weed 잡초 be propped against ~에 기대어져
있다 brick wall 벽돌 담

4. 🎧 미녀

(A) A tree is blocking a building.
(B) A car has stopped at a busy intersection.
(C) Items are being unloaded from a truck.
**(D) Bicycles are parked under some tree
branches.**

해석
(A) 나무 한 그루가 건물을 막고 있다.
(B) 차 한 대가 혼잡한 교차로로 멈춰 있다.
(C) 물건이 트럭에서 내려지고 있다.
(D) 자전거가 나뭇가지 아래에 주차되어 있다.

어휘 block (~의 길·출구·시야 등을) 막다 intersection 교차로
unload (짐을) 내리다 tree branch 나뭇가지

5. 🎧 호남

(A) The boat is passing under a bridge.
(B) Some people are tying a boat to a pier.
(C) Some people are taking a ride on a boat.
(D) The boat is being loaded with cargo.

해석
(A) 배가 다리 밑을 지나고 있다.
(B) 몇몇 사람들이 배를 부두에 매고 있다.
(C) 몇몇 사람들이 배를 타고 가고 있다.
(D) 배에 화물이 실리고 있다.

어휘 tie 묶다, 매다 pier 부두 take a ride (탈것 따위를) 타고
가다 load 싣다, 적재하다; 짐 cargo 화물

6. 🎧 영녀

(A) A cushion is being arranged on a sofa.
(B) Some shelves are being stocked.
(C) Some potted plants are being watered.
(D) A window is being opened.

해석
(A) 쿠션이 소파에 정리되고 있다.
(B) 선반이 채워지고 있다.
(C) 화분에 담긴 식물에 물을 주고 있다.
(D) 창문이 열리고 있다.

어휘 stock 채우다, 갖추다; 재고 potted plant 분재 water
물을 주다

PART TEST					본문 p.30
1. (D)	**2.** (C)	**3.** (B)	**4.** (A)	**5.** (C)	**6.** (A)

1. 🎧 미남

(A) He's planting some flowers.
(B) He's putting on his gloves.
(C) He's pouring himself a drink.
(D) He's lifting a watering can.

해설
(A) 그는 꽃을 심고 있다.
(B) 그는 장갑을 끼고 있다.
(C) 그는 음료를 따르고 있다.
(D) 그는 물뿌리개를 들어올리고 있다.

어휘 pour 따르다, 붓다 lift 들어올리다 watering can 물뿌리개

2. 🎧 미녀

(A) She's pushing a shopping cart.
(B) She's waiting in a checkout line.
(C) She's holding a refrigerator door open.
(D) She's chopping some vegetables.

해석
(A) 그녀는 쇼핑 카트를 밀고 있다.
(B) 그녀는 계산대 줄을 서서 기다리고 있다.
(C) 그녀는 냉장고 문을 잡아 열어 두고 있다.
(D) 그녀는 야채를 썰고 있다.

어휘 checkout 계산대 chop 썰다, 다지다

3. 🎧 영녀

(A) Some of the men are shaking hands.
(B) Some of the men are wearing ties.
(C) The men are folding a document.
(D) The men are greeting one another.

해석
(A) 남자들 중 몇 명이 악수를 하고 있다.
(B) 남자들 중 몇 명이 넥타이를 매고 있다.
(C) 남자들이 서류를 접고 있다.
(D) 남자들이 서로 인사하고 있다.

어휘 shake hands 악수하다 fold 접다 greet 인사하다, 환영하다

4. 🎧 호남

(A) Some boats are docked in a row.
(B) A ship is passing under a bridge.
(C) Some boats are filled with passengers.
(D) Some people are diving off a pier.

해석
(A) 배들이 일렬로 정박되어 있다.
(B) 배가 다리 아래로 지나가고 있다.
(C) 배들이 승객으로 가득 차 있다.
(D) 사람들이 부두에서 다이빙하고 있다.

어휘 dock 부두에 대다 in a row 일렬로 be filled with ~로 가득 차다 pier 부두

5. 🎧 미남

(A) They're cleaning off a countertop.
(B) They're fixing a coffee maker.
(C) One of the women is preparing a beverage.
(D) One of the women is arranging some baked goods.

해석
(A) 그들은 조리대를 닦고 있다.
(B) 그들은 커피 메이커를 고치고 있다.
(C) 여자들 중 한 명이 음료를 준비하고 있다.
(D) 여자들 중 한 명이 제과류를 준비하고 있다.

어휘 countertop 조리대 beverage 음료 baked goods 구운 식품, 제과류

6. 🎧 호남

(A) An outdoor area has been set up for dining.
(B) Some chairs have been arranged in a living room.

(C) A railing is being installed near some stairs.

(D) Some potted plants have been hung from a
balcony.

해석

(A) 식사를 위해 야외 공간이 설치되어 있다.

(B) 의자 몇 개가 거실에 배치되어 있다.

(C) 난간이 계단 근처에 설치되고 있다.

(D) 화분 몇 개가 발코니에 매달려 있다.

어휘 set up 세우다, 설치하다   dining 식사   railing 난간
install 설치하다   hang 매달리다, 걸리다

LC PART 2

UNIT 03 Who, What · Which 의문문

① Who 의문문

PRACTICE 본문 p.38

1. (C) **2.** (B) **3.** (B) **4.** (A) **5.** (A) **6.** (C)

1. 🎧 미남/미녀

> Who's creating the menu tomorrow?
> (A) Twenty items for the event.
> (B) Tomorrow at 3 o'clock.
> **(C) The new chef.**

해석
누가 내일 메뉴를 만드나요?
(A) 행사를 위한 20개 품목입니다.
(B) 내일 3시에요.
(C) 새로 오신 셰프님이요.

어휘 create 만들어내다, 창작하다

2. 🎧 미남/미녀

> Who needs proof of my license renewal?
> (A) No, I need to renew my membership.
> **(B) Angela does.**
> (C) You can park behind the building.

해석
누가 제 면허 갱신 증명서를 필요로 하나요?
(A) 아니요, 전 멤버십을 갱신해야 합니다.
(B) 안젤라에게 필요해요.
(C) 당신은 건물 뒤편에 주차할 수 있습니다.

어휘 proof 증명(서) license 면허, 인가 renewal 갱신, 연장

3. 🎧 미남/영녀

> Who's looking into the candidates' backgrounds?
> (A) It's an impressive example.
> **(B) We don't know yet.**
> (C) In Conference Room 1.

해석
누가 지원자들의 배경을 조사하고 있나요?
(A) 그것은 인상적인 예시네요.
(B) 아직 몰라요.
(C) 1번 회의실에서요.

어휘 look into 조사하다 candidate 지원자, 후보자
background 배경 impressive 인상적인

4. 🎧 호남/미녀

> Who's going to inspect the apartment unit before move-in?
> **(A) The property manager.**
> (B) It's a popular residential building.
> (C) Thanks, that would be great.

해석
누가 입주 전 아파트 점검을 하나요?
(A) 자산 관리자요.
(B) 그것은 인기 있는 주거용 건물입니다.
(C) 고마워요, 그러면 좋겠네요.

어휘 inspect 점검[검사]하다 property manager 자산 관리자
residential 주거의

5. 🎧 호남/영녀

> Who transported the prototypes?
> **(A) A company in Seattle.**
> (B) You should finish this report.
> (C) Yes, we built them in the lab.

해석
누가 시제품을 운송했나요?
(A) 시애틀에 있는 회사요.
(B) 당신은 이 보고서를 끝내야 합니다.
(C) 네, 우리가 실험실에서 만들었어요.

어휘 transport 수송[운송]하다 lab(= laboratory) 실험실

6. 🎧 호남/영녀

> Who's responsible for the budget report?
> (A) They reported the news.
> (B) Did you send a response?
> **(C) Andrew, I believe.**

해석
누가 예산 보고서를 담당하나요?
(A) 그들이 그 소식을 보도했어요.
(B) 회신을 보내셨어요?
(C) 제가 알기론 앤드류가요.

어휘 be responsible for ~에 책임이 있다 budget 예산
report 보고서; 보도하다 response 회신, 응답

② What · Which 의문문

PRACTICE 본문 p.39

1. (A) **2.** (C) **3.** (A) **4.** (B) **5.** (B) **6.** (C)

1. 🎧 미녀/미남

> Which post office is closest to your home?
> **(A) The one on Danvers Avenue.**

(B) Yes, that's my neighborhood.
(C) We don't open until ten.

해석

어느 우체국이 당신의 집에서 가장 가깝나요?

(A) 댄버스가에 있는 거요.
(B) 네, 거긴 우리 동네예요.
(C) 저희는 10시에 문을 엽니다.

어휘 neighborhood 동네

2. 🎧 미녀/미남

What did Gregory say about the sales pitch?
(A) A pitcher of water, please.
(B) Right, I read something about it.
(C) He said he liked it a lot.

해석

그레고리가 세일즈 프레젠테이션에 대해 뭐라고 하던가요?

(A) 물 한 병 주세요.
(B) 맞아요, 그것에 대해 읽은 게 있어요.
(C) 그는 그게 아주 좋았다고 말했어요.

어휘 sales pitch 구매를 유도하는 세일즈 프레젠테이션 pitcher 주전자

3. 🎧 미녀/호남

What flight do you prefer for our upcoming trip?
(A) The later we depart, the better.
(B) I'm excited about meeting the clients.
(C) No, it was less than one hundred dollars.

해석

다가오는 우리 여행에 어느 비행편이 좋으세요?

(A) 늦게 출발할수록 더 좋아요.
(B) 고객들을 만날 생각에 신이 나요.
(C) 아니요, 그건 100달러 미만이었어요.

어휘 prefer (더) 좋아하다, 선호하다 depart 출발하다 be excited about ~에 대해 흥분하다, 신나다 client 고객 less than ~보다 적은

4. 🎧 영녀/미남

What time does your train leave?
(A) No additional stops.
(B) At one in the afternoon.
(C) That's a popular route.

해석

당신의 기차는 몇 시에 출발하나요?

(A) 추가 정차는 없습니다.
(B) 오후 1시예요.
(C) 인기 있는 노선입니다.

어휘 additional 추가의 stop 멈춤, 정류장 route 노선, 경로

5. 🎧 영녀/호남

What kind of cell phone package do you need?
(A) That's too expensive.
(B) A standard plan.
(C) Here's my phone number.

해석

어떤 종류의 휴대폰 패키지가 필요하신가요?

(A) 그건 너무 비싸요.
(B) 기본 요금제요.
(C) 여기 제 전화번호예요.

어휘 standard 표준의, 보통의

6. 🎧 영녀/호남

Which car did Mr. Hobson drive to work?
(A) An auto mechanic.
(B) Turn off the engine, please.
(C) The black one in the first row.

해석

홉슨 씨는 어느 차를 타고 출근했나요?

(A) 자동차 정비소요.
(B) 엔진을 꺼 주세요.
(C) 첫 번째 줄에 있는 검은 차요.

어휘 auto mechanic 자동차 정비소 row 줄, 열

UNIT 04 When, Where 의문문

① When 의문문

PRACTICE   본문 p.40

1. (B) **2.** (C) **3.** (A) **4.** (C) **5.** (A) **6.** (B)

1. 🎧 미남/미녀

When do you move into your apartment downtown?
(A) Yeah, occasionally.
(B) I found a better place.
(C) That's great.

해석

시내에 있는 아파트로 언제 이사하세요?

(A) 네, 가끔요.
(B) 더 좋은 곳을 찾았어요.
(C) 잘됐네요.

어휘 downtown 시내에 occasionally 가끔

2. 🎧 미남/미녀

When will the board members meet?

(A) The board decided to hire him.
(B) Did you attend the track meet?
(C) It's scheduled for Thursday.

해석
이사진들은 언제 만나나요?
(A) 이사회는 그를 고용하기로 결정했어요.
(B) 육상 경기 대회에 참가하셨나요?
(C) 목요일로 예정되어 있습니다.

어휘 board member 이사, 임원   board 이사회, 위원회
hire 고용하다   attend 참석하다   track meet 육상 경기 대회

3. 🎧 미남/영녀

When did you visit the new office location?
(A) About two weeks ago.
(B) Yes, I've worked here a long time.
(C) They're transferring to the London branch.

해석
새로운 사무실을 언제 방문했나요?
(A) 약 2주 전에요.
(B) 네, 여기서 오래 일했어요.
(C) 그들은 런던 지점으로 전근 갈 거예요.

어휘 location 장소, 곳   transfer 전근 가다, 옮기다   branch
지점

4. 🎧 호남/미녀

When can you inform me about your days off?
(A) It was around 5:30.
(B) You should use black ink for the form.
(C) As soon as I check with my manager.

해석
당신의 쉬는 날을 언제 저에게 알려줄 수 있나요?
(A) 5시 30분쯤이었어요.
(B) 서식에는 검은색 잉크를 사용해야 합니다.
(C) 관리자에게 확인하는 대로요.

어휘 inform 알리다   form 서식, 양식

5. 🎧 호남/영녀

When can we meet to discuss the proposed cover
designs?
(A) I have a big deadline today.
(B) In the employee lounge.
(C) Fortunately, the company covers the cost.

해석
제안된 표지 디자인 논의를 위해 우리가 언제 만날 수 있을까요?
(A) 저는 오늘 중요한 마감 기한이 있어요.
(B) 직원 휴게실에서요.
(C) 다행히도, 회사가 비용을 부담합니다.

어휘 proposed 제안된   cover 표지; (비용을) 감당하다
deadline 마감 기한

6. 🎧 호남/영녀

When will the hallway carpet be installed?
(A) It's very tall.
(B) Tomorrow afternoon.
(C) We're glad you're here.

해석
복도 카펫은 언제 설치되나요?
(A) 그것은 매우 높아요.
(B) 내일 오후에요.
(C) 당신이 와서 기뻐요.

어휘 hallway 복도   install 설치하다   tall 키가 큰, 높은

② Where 의문문

PRACTICE   본문 p.41

1. (A)   **2.** (B)   **3.** (C)   **4.** (B)   **5.** (C)   **6.** (A)

1. 🎧 미녀/미남

Where did he buy that leather jacket?
(A) At a shop in the Glendale Mall.
(B) They'll add a customized lining.
(C) A range of outerwear.

해석
그는 그 가죽 재킷을 어디서 샀나요?
(A) 글렌데일 몰에 있는 가게에서요.
(B) 그들은 맞춤 안감을 더할 거예요.
(C) 다양한 겉옷이요.

어휘 customized 개개인의 요구에 맞춘   lining 안감
a range of 다양한   outerwear 겉옷, 외투

2. 🎧 미녀/미남

Where is the assistant editor's office?
(A) Yes, I have journalism experience.
**(B) There's a floor plan right next to the
   elevators.**
(C) The official release date.

해석
부편집장 사무실은 어디에 있나요?
(A) 네, 저는 언론계 경험이 있어요.
(B) 엘리베이터 바로 옆에 평면도가 있습니다.
(C) 공식 발매일이요.

어휘 journalism 신문 잡지 편집(업), 언론계   floor plan 평면도
official 공식의, 공인된   release 발간, 출시

3. 🎧 미녀/호남

> Where is Dr. Martinez?
> (A) Yes, that makes sense.
> (B) A new security badge.
> **(C) He should be in his office.**

해석

마르티네즈 선생님은 어디에 계시나요?
(A) 네, 말이 되네요.
(B) 새 보안 배지입니다.
(C) 사무실에 계실 거예요.

어휘 security 보안, 경비

4. 🎧 영녀/미남

> Where can I find the meeting agenda?
> (A) Several employees responded positively.
> **(B) Ms. McNeil still has to finalize it.**
> (C) Yes, that's what I heard.

해석

회의 안건은 어디에서 찾을 수 있나요?
(A) 몇몇 직원들은 긍정적인 반응을 보였어요.
(B) 아직 맥닐 씨가 최종 승인을 해야 해요.
(C) 네, 그렇게 들었어요.

어휘 agenda 안건 respond 반응을 보이다 positively 긍정적으로 finalize 최종 승인하다

5. 🎧 영녀/호남

> Where did these sofas come from?
> (A) The cushion colors can be changed.
> (B) Please take a seat.
> **(C) From a manufacturer in Germany.**

해석

이 소파들은 어디에서 왔나요?
(A) 쿠션 색상은 변경 가능합니다.
(B) 앉으세요.
(C) 독일의 한 제조사에서요.

어휘 take a seat 앉다 manufacturer 제조사

6. 🎧 영녀/호남

> Where should we leave our wet umbrellas?
> **(A) In the basket by the entrance.**
> (B) An easy-to-grip handle.
> (C) The weather forecast for today.

해석

젖은 우산은 어디에 두어야 할까요?
(A) 입구 옆에 있는 바구니 안에요.
(B) 잡기 쉬운 손잡이입니다.

(C) 오늘 일기 예보요.

어휘 entrance 입구 easy-to-grip 잡기 쉬운 weather forecast 일기 예보

UNIT 05 How, Why 의문문

① How 의문문

PRACTICE 본문 p.42

1. (C)   **2.** (A)   **3.** (B)   **4.** (C)   **5.** (A)   **6.** (B)

1. 🎧 미남/미녀

> How much will it cost to get express delivery?
> (A) At a reliable courier.
> (B) No, they expressed interest.
> **(C) About twenty dollars.**

해석

빠른 배송으로 받는 데 비용이 얼마나 들까요?
(A) 믿을 수 있는 택배 회사에서요.
(B) 아니요, 그들은 관심을 보였어요.
(C) 20달러 정도입니다.

어휘 express 속달편의; (감정 등을) 나타내다, 표현하다 reliable 믿을 수 있는 courier 택배 회사 interest 관심, 흥미

2. 🎧 미남/미녀

> How many lunch boxes do we need for Saturday's hike?
> **(A) I'll bring my own food.**
> (B) The national park's open all summer.
> (C) Five and a half miles.

해석

토요일 하이킹에 도시락이 몇 개 필요한가요?
(A) 저는 제 음식을 가져올게요.
(B) 국립공원은 여름 내내 개장되어 있어요.
(C) 5.5마일이요.

3. 🎧 미남/영녀

> How did you like the dance festival?
> (A) There's a music stand.
> **(B) I'm going again tomorrow.**
> (C) That's what I did.

해석

댄스 축제는 어땠어요?
(A) 악보대가 있어요.
(B) 내일 또 갈 거예요.
(C) 그건 제가 한 거예요.

어휘 music stand 악보대

4. 🎧 호남/미녀

How long will your speech be?
(A) A talk on economics.
(B) In the conference center.
(C) About ninety minutes.

해석
당신의 연설은 얼마나 걸릴까요?
(A) 경제학 강연입니다.
(B) 회의장에서요.
(C) 90분 정도요.

어휘 speech 연설 talk 강연, 회담

5. 🎧 호남/영녀

How should we advertise our specialty cakes?
(A) By using social media sites.
(B) Sorry about the error.
(C) Birthdays and anniversaries.

해석
우리의 특제 케이크를 어떻게 광고해야 할까요?
(A) 소셜 미디어 사이트를 이용해서요.
(B) 오류에 대해 사과드립니다.
(C) 생일 및 기념일이요.

어휘 advertise 광고하다 specialty 특제품, 명물
anniversary 기념일

6. 🎧 호남/영녀

How often do you visit the headquarters?
(A) Yes, I had a great time.
(B) About once a month.
(C) It has spacious offices.

해석
당신은 얼마나 자주 본사를 방문하나요?
(A) 네, 정말 즐거웠어요.
(B) 한 달에 한 번 정도요.
(C) 널찍한 사무실이 있어요.

어휘 headquarters 본사 spacious 널찍한

② Why 의문문

PRACTICE   본문 p.43

1. (A)   2. (C)   3. (C)   4. (B)   5. (A)   6. (B)

1. 🎧 미녀/미남

Why are you visiting the investors tomorrow?
(A) To demonstrate our new model.
(B) The Atlanta airport.
(C) By 5 P.M.

해석
당신은 왜 내일 투자자들을 방문하나요?
(A) 우리의 새로운 모델을 보여주기 위해서요.
(B) 애틀랜타 공항이요.
(C) 오후 5시까지요.

어휘 investor 투자자 demonstrate 보여주다, 설명하다

2. 🎧 미녀/미남

Why did the owner choose to hire a new cleaning company?
(A) Mostly vacuuming and dusting.
(B) Thanks, I worked really hard.
(C) Because we got a good rate.

해석
소유주는 왜 새로운 청소 회사를 고용하기로 결정했나요?
(A) 대부분 진공 청소나 먼지 털기요.
(B) 고마워요, 정말 열심히 일했어요.
(C) 좋은 요금으로 거래했기 때문이에요.

어휘 vacuuming 진공 청소 dusting 먼지 털기 rate 요금,
가격

3. 🎧 미녀/호남

Why is Mr. Bennett away from his desk?
(A) No, on the second floor.
(B) Yes, I'll give him the message.
(C) The IT team is away for training.

해석
베넷 씨는 왜 자리를 비웠나요?
(A) 아니요, 2층에서요.
(B) 네, 제가 그에게 전하겠습니다.
(C) IT 팀은 교육을 위해 자리를 비웠어요.

4. 🎧 영녀/미남

Why is there no furniture in this room?
(A) No, it's a much bigger space.
(B) Because it's being replaced.
(C) An interior designer.

해석
이 방에는 왜 가구가 없나요?
(A) 아니요, 훨씬 넓은 공간이에요.
(B) 교체되는 중이기 때문입니다.
(C) 인테리어 디자이너요.

어휘 furniture 가구 space 공간 replace 바꾸다, 교체하다

5. 🎧 영녀/호남

Why was the picnic canceled?
(A) Did you see the weather forecast?

(B) Please confirm your attendance.
(C) For a few days.

해석

야유회는 왜 취소되었나요?
(A) 일기 예보 보셨어요?
(B) 출석 확인 부탁드립니다.
(C) 며칠 동안요.

어휘 confirm 확인하다 attendance 출석

6. 🎧 영녀/호남

Why have the commission payments not been made?
(A) Between ten and fifteen percent.
(B) Check with our manager.
(C) Yes, they accept credit cards.

해석

왜 수수료가 지불되지 않았나요?
(A) 10퍼센트에서 15퍼센트 사이입니다.
(B) 저희 관리자에게 확인해 보세요.
(C) 네, 그들은 신용카드를 받아요.

어휘 commission 수수료 payment 지불 accept 받아 주다

UNIT O6 일반, 제안·요청 의문문

① 일반 의문문

PRACTICE 본문 p.44

1. (B) **2.** (A) **3.** (B) **4.** (C) **5.** (C) **6.** (A)

1. 🎧 미남/미녀

Are you attending the awards ceremony?
(A) It departs at seven o'clock.
(B) No, I'll be on vacation that week.
(C) Thank you so much.

해석

시상식에 참석하시나요?
(A) 7시 정각에 출발합니다.
(B) 아니요, 저는 그 주에 휴가를 갈 거예요.
(C) 감사합니다.

어휘 attend 참석하다 awards ceremony 시상식 depart 떠나다, 출발하다 be on vacation 휴가 중이다

2. 🎧 미남/미녀

Doesn't the pharmacy close at six on Saturdays?
(A) Yes, it does.
(B) Just basic medication.

(C) For this prescription, please.

해석

그 약국은 토요일에 6시에 문을 닫지 않나요?
(A) 네, 그렇습니다.
(B) 그냥 기본적인 약이에요.
(C) 이 처방전으로 주세요.

어휘 pharmacy 약국 medication 약 prescription 처방전

3. 🎧 미남/영녀

Did you send out the party invitations?
(A) A larger venue.
(B) I'm waiting for the guest list.
(C) I thought it was.

해석

파티 초대장을 보내셨나요?
(A) 더 넓은 장소요.
(B) 손님 명단을 기다리고 있어요.
(C) 그런 줄 알았어요.

어휘 invitation 초대(장) venue 장소

4. 🎧 호남/미녀

Haven't you taken any language classes?
(A) Less than $100.
(B) Was your vacation overseas?
(C) I haven't had the chance.

해석

당신은 어학 수업을 들은 적이 없나요?
(A) 100달러 미만이요.
(B) 휴가는 해외로 가셨나요?
(C) 기회가 없었어요.

어휘 overseas 해외의; 해외에

5. 🎧 호남/영녀

Have the rugs in the lobby been cleaned?
(A) Next to the front office.
(B) Two leather couches.
(C) No, not yet.

해석

로비에 있는 러그들은 청소되었나요?
(A) 프런트 옆에요.
(B) 가죽 소파 두 개요.
(C) 아니요, 아직요.

어휘 couch 소파

6. 🎧 호남/영녀

Will you join us for the team lunch?
(A) Yes, I'd be glad to come along.
(B) No, she's the newest staff member.
(C) The new Italian restaurant.

해석
팀 점심에 저희랑 같이 가실래요?
(A) 네, 기꺼이 함께 가겠습니다.
(B) 아니요, 그녀는 가장 최근에 들어온 직원이에요.
(C) 새로운 이탈리안 레스토랑이요.

어휘 come along 함께 가다[오다]

② 제안·요청 의문문

PRACTICE   본문 p.45

1. (A)   2. (B)   3. (B)   4. (C)   5. (A)   6. (C)

1. 🎧 미녀/미남

Could you please organize the supplies in the cabinet?
(A) Sure, I have time now.
(B) That surprised me, too.
(C) Our usual supplier, I think.

해석
용품을 캐비닛에 정리해 주시겠어요?
(A) 물론이죠, 지금 시간이 있어요.
(B) 저도 깜짝 놀랐어요.
(C) 제 생각엔 우리와 평소에 거래하는 공급 업체인 것 같아요.

어휘 organize 정리하다   supplies 용품, 보급품   supplier 공급자

2. 🎧 미녀/미남

Can you help me look over the candidates' résumés later today?
(A) The assistant manager position.
(B) Sorry, I won't have time until tomorrow.
(C) The salary is competitive.

해석
제가 후보자들의 이력서를 살펴보는 것을 이따가 도와줄 수 있나요?
(A) 부팀장직입니다.
(B) 죄송해요, 저는 내일까지 시간이 없을 거예요.
(C) 급여는 나쁘지 않아요.

어휘 look over 살펴보다   candidate 후보자   résumé 이력서   position 자리, 직   salary 급여   competitive 경쟁력 있는, 뒤지지 않는

3. 🎧 미녀/호남

Why don't we go to the beach this weekend?
(A) Should we go home now or later?
(B) I have some relatives visiting me.
(C) Yes, the restaurant got great reviews.

해석
우리 이번 주말에 해변에 가는 게 어때요?
(A) 지금 집에 갈까요, 아니면 나중에 갈까요?
(B) 친척 몇 명이 저를 방문할 거예요.
(C) 네, 그 식당은 좋은 평가를 받았습니다.

어휘 relative 친척

4. 🎧 영녀/미남

Would you mind turning up the heat?
(A) Benjamin turned down the offer.
(B) Yes, a coat and scarf.
(C) Not at all.

해석
온도 좀 높여 주시겠어요? (= 온도를 높이는 것을 꺼리시나요?)
(A) 벤자민은 그 제안을 거절했어요.
(B) 네, 코트와 스카프요.
(C) 물론이죠. (= 전혀요.)

어휘 mind 신경 쓰다, 꺼림칙하게 생각하다   turn up (소리·온도 등을) 높이다   heat 열, 온도   turn down 거절하다   offer 제안

5. 🎧 영녀/호남

Would you like to join me for a play on Friday?
(A) Haven't you seen the work schedule?
(B) That was an impressive performance.
(C) He plays basketball.

해석
금요일에 연극 보러 저랑 같이 가실래요?
(A) 근무 일정을 못 보셨나요?
(B) 그것은 인상적인 공연이었어요.
(C) 그는 농구를 해요.

어휘 impressive 인상적인   performance 공연

6. 🎧 영녀/호남

Can I show you our dessert menu?
(A) Fifteen dollars each.
(B) I'll show you a picture.
(C) We already ate too much.

해석
저희 디저트 메뉴를 보여드려도 될까요?
(A) 각각 15달러입니다.
(B) 제가 사진을 보여드릴게요.
(C) 저희는 이미 너무 많이 먹었어요.

UNIT 07 부가, 선택 의문문

① 부가 의문문

PRACTICE 본문 p.46

1. (A)	2. (C)	3. (B)	4. (C)	5. (A)	6. (B)

1. 🎧 미남/미녀

You have an extra phone charger, right?
(A) Of course, it's in the closet.
(B) No, I don't have enough experience.
(C) We're not in charge of recruiting.

해석
핸드폰 충전기 여분을 가지고 있죠, 맞죠?
(A) 물론이죠, 옷장 안에 있어요.
(B) 아니요, 저는 경험이 부족해요.
(C) 저희는 인원 모집을 담당하지 않습니다.

어휘 extra 추가의, 여분의 charger 충전기 in charge of ~을 담당하는

2. 🎧 미남/미녀

You used to live in a big city, didn't you?
(A) Let's use public transportation.
(B) Oh, I don't have any vacation time left.
(C) Yes, for most of my childhood.

해석
당신은 대도시에 살았었죠, 그렇지 않나요?
(A) 대중교통을 이용합시다.
(B) 아, 저는 휴가가 남아 있지 않아요.
(C) 네, 제 어린 시절의 대부분을요.

어휘 public transportation 대중교통 childhood 어린 시절

3. 🎧 미남/영녀

This tablet will have a five-year warranty, won't it?
(A) Basic office software.
(B) Definitely.
(C) Major electronics stores.

해석
이 태블릿은 5년간 품질 보증이 적용됩니다, 그렇지 않나요?
(A) 기본 사무용 소프트웨어입니다.
(B) 물론이죠.
(C) 주요 전자 기기 매장들이요.

어휘 warranty 품질 보증(서) electronics 전자 기기

4. 🎧 호남/미녀

The winner hasn't been announced, has it?
(A) Will the Web site be updated soon?

(B) Thanks, I'm honored.
(C) They're counting the votes now.

해석
당첨자가 발표되지 않았죠, 그렇죠?
(A) 웹사이트가 곧 업데이트되나요?
(B) 고마워요, 영광입니다.
(C) 지금 개표 중입니다.

어휘 announce 발표하다 honored 명예로운 count 세다 vote 표

5. 🎧 호남/영녀

The budget meeting is on the second floor, isn't it?
(A) Yes, it's in Room 205.
(B) No, I believe it starts at three.
(C) The prices have gone up.

해석
예산 회의는 2층에서 하죠, 그렇지 않나요?
(A) 네, 205호에서 해요.
(B) 아니요, 3시에 시작하는 것 같아요.
(C) 물가가 올랐어요.

어휘 budget 예산, 비용 price 가격, 물가

6. 🎧 호남/영녀

You're going to the clinic soon, aren't you?
(A) A routine checkup.
(B) My appointment was postponed.
(C) Sign the paperwork, please.

해석
곧 병원에 가실 거죠, 그렇지 않나요?
(A) 정기 검진이요.
(B) 예약이 미뤄졌어요.
(C) 서류에 서명해 주십시오.

어휘 clinic 병원 routine 일상의, 정기적인 checkup (건강) 검진 appointment 예약 postpone 연기하다, 미루다 paperwork 서류

② 선택 의문문

PRACTICE 본문 p.47

1. (B)	2. (B)	3. (A)	4. (A)	5. (C)	6. (B)

1. 🎧 미녀/미남

Do you want to walk to the theater or take a taxi?
(A) A new musical performance.
(B) Well, it's only a block away.
(C) She recommended it.

극장까지 걸어가고 싶으세요, 아니면 택시를 타고 싶으세요?

(A) 새로운 음악 공연이요.

(B) 글쎄요, 고작 한 블록 거리라서요.

(C) 그녀가 추천해 줬어요.

어휘 recommend 추천하다, 권하다

2. 🎧 미녀/미남

Would you rather discuss this over the phone or meet in person?

(A) Any time before lunch, I think.

(B) Let's do a video conference.

(C) Here's a copy of the brochure.

해석

이걸 전화로 논의하실래요, 아니면 직접 만나실래요?

(A) 제 생각에는 점심 시간 전에 언제든지요.

(B) 화상 회의를 합시다.

(C) 여기 책자가 한 부 있습니다.

어휘 discuss 논의하다 in person 직접
video conference 화상 회의 brochure 책자

3. 🎧 미녀/호남

Are you announcing your retirement before or after the meeting?

(A) Didn't you see my memo?

(B) I'll spend more time with my family.

(C) Yes, that's my final day.

해석

회의 전에 은퇴를 발표하실 건가요, 아니면 회의 후에 하실 건가요?

(A) 제 메모 못 보셨나요?

(B) 저는 가족과 더 많은 시간을 보낼 거예요.

(C) 네, 그날이 제 마지막 날이에요.

어휘 retirement 은퇴 final 마지막의

4. 🎧 영녀/미남

Would you prefer I print the manuals in color or black and white?

(A) In color is better.

(B) Only if you have to.

(C) For the orientation session.

해석

제가 설명서를 컬러로 인쇄하는 것이 좋으세요, 아니면 흑백으로 하는 게 좋으세요?

(A) 컬러가 더 좋습니다.

(B) 당신이 해야만 한다면요.

(C) 오리엔테이션 시간을 위해서요.

어휘 manual 설명서 session 시간, 기간

5. 🎧 영녀/호남

Do you store your towels in the bathroom or in another place?

(A) Let's fold the laundry now.

(B) The large one. Thanks.

(C) I put them in a closet.

해석

수건을 욕실에 보관하시나요, 아니면 다른 곳에 보관하시나요?

(A) 이제 빨래를 개킵시다.

(B) 큰 걸로요. 고마워요.

(C) 저는 그것들을 옷장에 둬요.

어휘 store 저장[보관]하다 fold 접다, 개키다

6. 🎧 영녀/호남

Is the building inspection scheduled for this week or next week?

(A) A city official.

(B) It's next Tuesday.

(C) The files are in order.

해석

건물 점검은 이번 주로 예정되어 있나요, 아니면 다음 주로 예정되어 있나요?

(A) 시 공무원이요.

(B) 다음 주 화요일입니다.

(C) 파일은 제대로 되어 있어요.

어휘 inspection 점검 official 공무원 in order 제대로 된, 알맞은

UNIT O8 간접 의문문, 평서문

① 간접 의문문

PRACTICE					본문 p.48
1. (C)	2. (A)	3. (A)	4. (B)	5. (B)	6. (C)

1. 🎧 미남/미녀

Can you show me how to open a new account?

(A) A well-respected local bank.

(B) No, at least a few days.

(C) Let me send you the link.

해석

새 계좌를 개설하는 방법을 가르쳐 주시겠어요?

(A) 높이 평가되는 지역 은행입니다.

(B) 아니요, 적어도 며칠은요.

(C) 링크를 보내드리겠습니다.

어휘 account 계좌 well-respected 높이 평가되는, 존경을 받는 at least 적어도

2. 🎧 미남/미녀

Can you tell me when the ferry departs?
(A) I can't connect to the Internet.
(B) I'll carry your suitcase.
(C) The area's largest harbor.

해석

페리가 언제 출발하는지 알려 주실 수 있나요?
(A) 인터넷에 연결이 안 돼요.
(B) 제가 여행 가방을 옮겨 드릴게요.
(C) 이 지역에서 가장 큰 항구입니다.

어휘 harbor 항구

3. 🎧 미남/영녀

Do you know who's speaking at the banquet?
(A) Each of the department managers.
(B) The flowers in the front.
(C) I can't remember how to register.

해석

연회에서 누가 연설하는지 아세요?
(A) 각 부서장들이요.
(B) 앞에 있는 꽃들이요.
(C) 어떻게 등록하는지 기억이 안 나요.

어휘 banquet 연회, 성찬 register 등록하다

4. 🎧 호남/미녀

Do you know where I can find the spices?
(A) It's five ninety-nine in total.
(B) Over there, in aisle three.
(C) At noon on Wednesday.

해석

향신료를 어디에서 찾을 수 있는지 아세요?
(A) 총 5.99달러입니다.
(B) 저쪽 3번 통로에서요.
(C) 수요일 정오에요.

어휘 spices 향신료

5. 🎧 호남/영녀

Could you tell me where the dry cleaner's is?
(A) To bring in my suit.
(B) Actually, this neighborhood doesn't have one.
(C) The floor needs cleaning.

해석

세탁소가 어디에 있는지 말씀해 주시겠어요?
(A) 제 정장을 가져오려고요.
(B) 사실 이 동네에는 없어요.

(C) 바닥을 청소해야 합니다.

어휘 suit 정장 neighborhood 동네

6. 🎧 호남/영녀

Can you show me how to reset my password?
(A) A maintenance request.
(B) Some security procedures.
(C) I'm about to leave for a training session.

해석

비밀번호를 재설정하는 방법을 보여 주시겠어요?
(A) 정비 요청입니다.
(B) 몇 가지 보안 절차요.
(C) 저는 지금 막 연수를 떠나려는 참이에요.

어휘 reset 다시 맞추다 maintenance 유지, 정비
procedure 절차 be about to 막 ~하려는 참이다

② 평서문

PRACTICE					본문 p.49
1. (B)	**2.** (C)	**3.** (B)	**4.** (A)	**5.** (A)	**6.** (C)

1. 🎧 미녀/미남

Breakfast is served at 7 A.M.
(A) Yes, dishes for vegetarians.
(B) Okay. We'll be there.
(C) The rooms are spacious.

해석

아침 식사는 오전 7시에 제공됩니다.
(A) 네, 채식주의자를 위한 요리입니다.
(B) 알겠습니다. 저희는 갈 거예요.
(C) 그 방들은 널찍해요.

어휘 serve 제공하다 vegetarian 채식주의자 spacious 널찍한

2. 🎧 미녀/미남

The customer files were lost.
(A) Yes, let's pile them here.
(B) They work in customer service.
(C) Luckily, the system makes backups.

해석

고객 파일이 유실되었습니다.
(A) 네, 여기에 쌓읍시다.
(B) 그들은 고객 서비스에서 일해요.
(C) 다행히도, 시스템상 백업 파일이 만들어져요.

어휘 lost 잃어버린, 유실된 pile 쌓다; 더미

3. 🎧 미녀/호남

This magazine cover looks perfect.
(A) No, I have a subscription.
(B) I'm glad you like it.
(C) All the latest news stories.

해석
이 잡지 표지는 완벽해 보이네요.
(A) 아니요, 저는 구독하고 있어요.
(B) 마음에 드신다니 기뻐요.
(C) 모든 최신 뉴스들이요.

어휘 subscription 구독 latest 최신의

4. 🎧 영녀/미남

I can set up the projector for you, if you'd like.
(A) Sure. That'll be helpful.
(B) It's an intense research project.
(C) His suggestions were useful.

해석
원하신다면 제가 프로젝터를 설치해 드릴 수 있습니다.
(A) 그럼요. 도움이 될 거예요.
(B) 그것은 강도 높은 연구 프로젝트입니다.
(C) 그의 제안은 유용했어요.

어휘 set up 설치하다, 준비하다 intense 치열한, 열심인
suggestion 제안 useful 유용한

5. 🎧 영녀/호남

My security badge wouldn't work this morning.
(A) How did you access the building?
(B) Sometime after lunch.
(C) Because of the high cost.

해석
제 보안 배지가 오늘 아침에 작동하지 않았어요.
(A) 건물에 어떻게 들어오셨나요?
(B) 점심 이후 언젠가요.
(C) 높은 비용 때문입니다.

어휘 access 들어가다

6. 🎧 영녀/호남

I'd like to change my mailing address.
(A) I'd rather keep the schedule the same.
(B) Thanks. It's my first home purchase.
(C) Let me transfer you to our account team.

해석
우편물 발송 주소를 바꾸고 싶어요.
(A) 일정을 그대로 유지하는 게 좋겠어요.
(B) 고마워요. 처음으로 구입한 집이에요.

(C) 고객 담당 팀으로 연결해 드리겠습니다.

어휘 purchase 구입 transfer 이동하다, 넘겨주다

700+ 뛰어넘기 **PRACTICE** 본문 p.51

| **1.** (B) | **2.** (B) | **3.** (A) | **4.** (C) | **5.** (C) | **6.** (A) |
| **7.** (B) | **8.** (A) | **9.** (A) | **10.** (C) | **11.** (C) | **12.** (B) |

1. 🎧 미남/미녀

Who can help me renew my parking pass?
(A) I'll take a bus. Thanks.
(B) It's undergoing maintenance right now.
(C) The storm will pass soon.

해설
제가 주차권을 갱신하는 걸 누가 도와줄 수 있나요?
(A) 저는 버스 탈게요. 고마워요.
(B) 그것은 지금 정비 중입니다.
(C) 폭풍우가 곧 지나갈 거예요.

어휘 renew 갱신하다 undergo 받다, 겪다 storm 폭풍(우)

2. 🎧 미남/미녀

Staff members who borrow equipment must complete this form.
(A) A larger computer monitor.
(B) Okay, that won't take long.
(C) I'm sorry. The shipment is missing a box.

해설
장비를 빌리는 직원들은 이 양식을 작성해야 합니다.
(A) 더 큰 컴퓨터 모니터요.
(B) 알겠습니다, 오래 걸리지 않을 거예요.
(C) 죄송합니다. 배송에 상자 하나가 누락되어 있습니다.

어휘 borrow 빌리다 complete a form 서식을 작성하다
shipment 배송

3. 🎧 미남/영녀

Where should we stack the empty containers?
(A) We'll need to reorganize the warehouse.
(B) It doesn't weigh very much.
(C) Early Thursday morning.

해설
빈 컨테이너를 어디에 쌓아야 할까요?
(A) 우리는 창고를 다시 정리해야 할 거예요.
(B) 그것은 무게가 많이 나가지 않습니다.
(C) 목요일 아침 일찍이요.

어휘 stack 쌓다 empty 비어 있는 reorganize 재편성하다,
개조하다 weigh 무게가 ~ 나가다

4. 🎧 호남/미녀

> Why did we hire two part-time accountants recently?
> (A) A higher quality paper.
> (B) Because it wasn't on sale.
> **(C) We took on a major client.**

해설

우리는 왜 최근에 두 명의 시간제 회계사를 고용했나요?
(A) 더 높은 품질의 종이입니다.
(B) 할인을 하지 않았기 때문이에요.
(C) 우리는 주요 고객을 맡았어요.

어휘 part-time 시간제의 accountant 회계사 quality 품질 on sale 할인 중인, 판매되는 take on 떠맡다 major 주요한 client 고객, 의뢰인

5. 🎧 호남/영녀

> Is the copy machine working?
> (A) I expect she can.
> (B) Yes, the coffee tastes delicious.
> **(C) Are you making handouts?**

해설

복사기는 작동하나요?
(A) 그녀가 할 수 있을 거라 기대해요.
(B) 네, 커피가 맛있네요.
(C) 유인물을 만들고 있나요?

어휘 taste 맛이 나다 handout 유인물

6. 🎧 호남/영녀

> Where is the cafeteria?
> **(A) We only have a vending machine.**
> (B) Later this month, I think.
> (C) She usually arrives early.

해설

구내식당이 어디에 있나요?
(A) 자동판매기밖에 없어요.
(B) 이번 달 말인 것 같아요.
(C) 그녀는 보통 일찍 도착해요.

어휘 vending machine 자동판매기

7. 🎧 미녀/미남

> How was the recent feedback from customers?
> (A) A colleague who recently left.
> **(B) We'll need further training support.**
> (C) In a few days.

해설

고객들의 최근 피드백은 어땠나요?

(A) 최근에 떠난 동료입니다.
(B) 우린 추가적인 연수 지원이 필요할 거예요.
(C) 며칠 후에요.

어휘 recent 최근의 colleague 동료 further 추가의 support 지원, 후원

8. 🎧 미녀/미남

> Who has a copy of the catalog?
> **(A) The products are listed online.**
> (B) There's plenty of space in this room.
> (C) Pamphlets and brochures.

해설

누가 카탈로그 사본을 가지고 있나요?
(A) 제품은 온라인에 목록이 올라가 있어요.
(B) 이 방에는 공간이 많아요.
(C) 팸플릿과 책자들이요.

어휘 list 목록에 올리다; 명단 plenty of 공간 brochure 책자

9. 🎧 미녀/호남

> The print shop no longer offers overnight service.
> **(A) Do you know of another option?**
> (B) My office is on the fourth floor.
> (C) A long journey.

해설

그 인쇄소는 더 이상 익일 완성 서비스를 제공하지 않습니다.
(A) 다른 방법을 알고 있나요?
(B) 제 사무실은 4층에 있습니다.
(C) 긴 여행이에요.

어휘 offer 제공하다 overnight 익일 배달의 option 선택권 journey 여행

10. 🎧 영녀/미남

> Who should I see about ordering a replacement part?
> (A) Yes, this is our newest branch.
> (B) A brand-new washing machine.
> **(C) I'd be happy to help you, ma'am.**

해설

교체 부품을 주문하려면 누구에게 문의해야 하나요?
(A) 네, 여기가 저희 새 지점입니다.
(B) 신상 세탁기요.
(C) 제가 도와드리겠습니다, 부인.

어휘 replacement 교체, 대체 part 부품 newest 최신의 brand-new 신품의, 새로운

11. 🎧 영녀/호남

There's a sale on used cars at Branson Autos.
(A) The doors open automatically.
(B) A standard loan agreement.
(C) I still don't have my license.

해설
브랜슨 자동차에서 중고차 세일을 하고 있어요.
(A) 문은 자동으로 열립니다.
(B) 표준 대출 계약이요.
(C) 전 아직 면허증이 없어요.

어휘 used 중고의 automatically 자동으로 standard 표준의 loan 대출 agreement 협정, 계약 license 면허, 인가

12. 🎧 영녀/호남

The new office chairs are comfortable, aren't they?
(A) Probably a few hundred dollars.
(B) My back feels better already.
(C) No, in three days.

해설
새 사무실 의자는 편하죠, 그렇지 않나요?
(A) 아마도 몇 백 달러요.
(B) 허리가 벌써 좋아졌어요.
(C) 아니요, 3일 후에요.

어휘 comfortable 편한 back 등, 허리

PART TEST
본문 p.52

7. (A)	8. (B)	9. (C)	10. (C)	11. (A)	12. (C)
13. (B)	14. (B)	15. (A)	16. (A)	17. (B)	18. (C)
19. (C)	20. (B)	21. (A)	22. (C)	23. (A)	24. (B)
25. (A)	26. (B)	27. (C)	28. (B)	29. (A)	30. (C)
31. (B)					

---

7. 🎧 호남/미녀

When will the next bus depart?
(A) In about twenty minutes.
(B) A round-trip ticket.
(C) The driver, I think.

해설
다음 버스는 언제 출발하나요?
(A) 약 20분 후에요.
(B) 왕복 표입니다.
(C) 운전사인 것 같아요.

어휘 depart 떠나다, 출발하다 round-trip 왕복(여행)의

8. 🎧 영녀/호남

Who is responsible for ordering company uniforms?
(A) Professional clothing.
(B) Mr. Warren is.
(C) It's reasonable.

해설
회사 유니폼 주문은 누가 책임지나요?
(A) 직업에 알맞은 옷이요.
(B) 워렌 씨가요.
(C) 합리적이네요.

어휘 be responsible for ~에 책임이 있다 professional 직업에 알맞은, 직업의 reasonable 합리적인, 적당한

9. 🎧 미녀/미남

Where did you get that magazine?
(A) Around the end of the month.
(B) Yes, I always read it.
(C) The supermarket on the corner.

해설
그 잡지 어디서 사셨어요?
(A) 월말쯤이요.
(B) 네, 항상 읽어요.
(C) 모퉁이에 있는 슈퍼마켓에서요.

10. 🎧 호남/영녀

Why has this hallway been closed off?
(A) We enjoyed the grand opening.
(B) For three days.
(C) Because it's going to be painted.

해설
이 복도는 왜 폐쇄되었나요?
(A) 우리는 개업식에서 즐거운 시간을 보냈어요.
(B) 3일 동안이요.
(C) 페인트칠될 것이기 때문이에요.

어휘 hallway 복도 grand opening 개장, 개업

11. 🎧 미녀/미남

How should we sort these résumés?
(A) By level of experience.
(B) An assistant manager.
(C) Good luck with the interview.

해설
우리가 이 이력서들을 어떻게 분류해야 할까요?
(A) 경력 수준별로요.
(B) 부팀장이요.

(C) 면접 잘 보세요.

어휘 sort 분류하다   level 수준, 정도

12. 🎧 미남/미녀

> Should the train ticket be one-way or round-trip?
> (A) For Milton Station.
> (B) A trip to meet new clients.
> **(C) I just need a one-way ticket.**

해설

기차표는 편도로 해야 할까요, 아니면 왕복으로 해야 할까요?
(A) 밀턴 역이요.
(B) 새로운 고객들을 만나기 위한 여행입니다.
(C) 편도 표만 있으면 돼요.

어휘 one-way 편도의   round-trip 왕복의

13. 🎧 호남/영녀

> Would you help to set up the projector?
> (A) An important sales presentation.
> **(B) Sure, I'm free now.**
> (C) The project was completed.

해설

프로젝터 설치를 도와주시겠어요?
(A) 중요한 영업 프레젠테이션이요.
(B) 물론이죠, 전 지금 한가해요.
(C) 그 프로젝트는 끝났어요.

어휘 presentation 발표   complete 완료하다, 끝마치다

14. 🎧 미녀/영녀

> Who has the paper forms for ordering supplies?
> (A) I don't have enough space.
> **(B) We use an online system.**
> (C) Their prices are affordable.

해설

물품 주문을 위한 서류 양식은 누가 가지고 있나요?
(A) 공간이 부족해요.
(B) 우리는 온라인 시스템을 이용해요.
(C) 그들의 가격은 적당하네요.

어휘 paper form 서류 양식   supplies 물품   affordable (가격이) 알맞은

15. 🎧 미남/영녀

> How was the workshop on designing brochures?
> **(A) I found it quite helpful.**
> (B) Yes, you should sign up.
> (C) She wants to be a fashion designer.

해설

책자 디자인 워크숍은 어땠어요?
(A) 꽤 유용했어요.
(B) 네, 등록하셔야 합니다.
(C) 그녀는 패션 디자이너가 되고 싶어 해요.

어휘 sign up 등록하다, 가입하다

16. 🎧 미녀/호남

> Where can I find the fresh herbs?
> **(A) I can show you that section.**
> (B) That's a fresh approach.
> (C) Planting a variety of seeds.

해설

신선한 허브는 어디에 있나요?
(A) 제가 그곳을 보여드릴게요.
(B) 신선한 접근이네요.
(C) 여러 가지 씨앗을 심는 것입니다.

어휘 approach 접근   a variety of 여러 가지의   seed 씨앗, 종자

17. 🎧 영녀/미남

> There are no empty seats on the main floor.
> (A) Yes, I'll fill them.
> **(B) The balcony is fine.**
> (C) I work on the third floor.

해설

메인 층에는 빈자리가 없어요.
(A) 네, 제가 채워드릴게요.
(B) 발코니는 괜찮아요.
(C) 저는 3층에서 일해요.

어휘 empty 비어 있는   fill 채우다

18. 🎧 영녀/호남

> Was Ms. Jackson pleased with the sales presentation?
> (A) All right, I'll send her in.
> (B) The head of the department.
> **(C) Everyone there loved it.**

해설

잭슨 씨는 영업 프레젠테이션에 만족했나요?
(A) 알겠어요, 제가 그녀를 들여보낼게요.
(B) 부서장이요.
(C) 그곳에 있는 모두가 좋아했어요.

어휘 be pleased with ~이 마음에 들다, 만족하다

19. 🎧 미남/미녀

> You're headed to the airport this afternoon, right?

(A) Sorry, your bag is too heavy.
(B) Five days in total.
(C) Yes, around three o'clock.

해석
오늘 오후에 공항으로 가시는 거죠, 맞죠?
(A) 죄송해요, 당신 가방은 너무 무거워요.
(B) 총 5일입니다.
(C) 네, 3시쯤이요.

어휘 be headed to ~로 향하다, 가다

20. 🎧 호남/미녀

Haven't you received your security badge yet?
(A) The receipt for the meal.
(B) No, they're still processing it.
(C) I'll keep them confidential.

해설
아직 보안 배지를 받지 못했나요?
(A) 식사 영수증이요.
(B) 네, 아직 처리 중이에요.
(C) 그것들을 비밀로 할게요.

어휘 receive 받다   receipt 영수증   process 처리하다
confidential 비밀의

21. 🎧 영녀/미남

Do you want to set up the picnic in a sunny or shady spot?
(A) I love the sunshine.
(B) It is a beautiful park.
(C) Approximately twenty people.

해설
소풍 장소를 햇살이 내리쬐는 곳으로 정하고 싶으세요, 아니면 그늘
진 곳으로 정하고 싶으세요?
(A) 햇빛이 정말 좋아요.
(B) 아름다운 공원이네요.
(C) 대략 20명 정도입니다.

어휘 shady 그늘진   spot 장소, 지점   approximately 대략,
거의

22. 🎧 미녀/미남

How much fabric should I order for the curtains?
(A) In alphabetical order.
(B) No later than 5 P.M., please.
(C) Well, we're covering ten windows.

해설
커튼을 위해 원단을 얼마나 주문해야 하나요?
(A) 알파벳 순서로요.
(B) 늦어도 오후 5시까지는 부탁합니다.

(C) 음, 우리는 창문 10개를 가릴 거예요.

어휘 fabric 직물, 원단   alphabetical order 알파벳 순서
no later than 늦어도 ~까지는

23. 🎧 호남/영녀

Do we have a few staff members willing to work overtime?
(A) Yes, six people have already volunteered.
(B) The time on the clock was incorrect.
(C) I'm sorry you were overcharged.

해설
초과근무를 할 의사가 있는 직원들이 좀 있나요?
(A) 네, 벌써 6명이 자원했습니다.
(B) 시계의 시간이 정확하지 않았어요.
(C) 금액이 너무 많이 청구되어 죄송합니다.

어휘 be willing to ~할 용의가 있다   work overtime 초과근무
를 하다   volunteer 자원하다   incorrect 부정확한
overcharge (금액을 너무) 많이 청구하다, 바가지를 씌우다

24. 🎧 미남/미녀

I need to change the address for my newspaper subscription.
(A) Maybe we should keep the same color.
(B) Please hold while I transfer your call.
(C) Thank you for the advice.

해설
제 신문 구독 주소를 변경하려고요.
(A) 아마 같은 색을 유지해야 할 거예요.
(B) 전화를 돌려드릴 테니 잠시만 기다려 주세요.
(C) 조언 감사합니다.

어휘 subscription 구독   hold (전화를) 끊지 않고 기다리다
transfer 넘겨주다

25. 🎧 영녀/호남

Doesn't Victor need to enroll in the Spanish class?
(A) He grew up in Spain.
(B) I applied for a leadership role.
(C) A one-week vacation.

해설
빅터는 스페인어 수업에 등록할 필요가 없나요?
(A) 그는 스페인에서 자랐어요.
(B) 저는 지도자 역할에 지원했어요.
(C) 일주일간의 휴가입니다.

어휘 enroll in ~에 등록하다   apply for ~에 지원하다
leadership 지도자의 지위   role 역할

26. 🎧 호남/미녀

> How can I get a library card?
> (A) What kind of books do you like?
> **(B) You'll need proof of residency.**
> (C) Until the parking lot is full.

해설

도서관 카드는 어떻게 받나요?
(A) 어떤 종류의 책을 좋아하세요?
(B) 거주 증명서가 필요할 거예요.
(C) 주차장이 꽉 찰 때까지요.

어휘 proof 증명(서)　residency 거주

27. 🎧 미남/영녀

> This entrance is designated for deliveries only.
> (A) Because we eliminated shipping costs.
> (B) Sure, you can borrow my key.
> **(C) Oh, I have some packages.**

해설

이 입구는 배달 전용으로 지정되어 있습니다.
(A) 저희가 배송비를 없앴기 때문입니다.
(B) 물론이죠, 제 열쇠를 빌리셔도 돼요.
(C) 아, 제게 소포가 몇 개 있어요.

어휘 designate 지정하다　eliminate 없애다　package 소포

28. 🎧 영녀/미남

> When are you free to mentor the interns?
> (A) To explain our company policies.
> **(B) I have several tight deadlines.**
> (C) They'll learn a lot about the industry.

해설

인턴들을 지도하기 위해 언제 시간이 되세요?
(A) 우리 회사 정책을 설명하기 위해서요.
(B) 저는 빠듯한 마감 기한이 몇 개 있어요.
(C) 그들은 이 업계에 대해 많이 배울 거예요.

어휘 mentor 조언[지도]하다　policy 정책　tight 빠듯한
industry 산업

29. 🎧 미녀/호남

> Do you have experience with investments?
> **(A) Ranjit has a degree in finance.**
> (B) It's a good investment.
> (C) We need to weigh it first.

해설

당신은 투자 경험이 있나요?
(A) 란짓이 재무학 학위가 있어요.
(B) 좋은 투자네요.

(C) 먼저 무게를 재야 해요.

어휘 investment 투자　degree 학위　finance 재무, 재정(학)
weigh 무게를 달다

30. 🎧 미남/영녀

> This is the address we should deliver the order to, isn't it?
> (A) The business is doing well.
> (B) An urgent staff meeting.
> **(C) Oh, that company moved recently.**

해설

이것이 우리가 주문을 배달해야 하는 주소죠, 그렇지 않나요?
(A) 사업이 잘 되고 있어요.
(B) 긴급 직원 회의입니다.
(C) 아, 그 회사는 최근에 이사했어요.

어휘 urgent 긴급한

31. 🎧 호남/미녀

> We should replace the carpet in the break room.
> (A) I think I've misplaced them.
> **(B) It still looks very new.**
> (C) The third door on the right.

해설

우리는 휴게실의 카펫을 교체해야 해요.
(A) 제가 그것들을 잃어버린 것 같아요.
(B) 여전히 아주 새것처럼 보이는데요.
(C) 오른쪽 세 번째 문입니다.

어휘 replace 바꾸다, 교체하다　misplace 잘못 두다, 둔 곳을 잊다

LC PART 3

UNIT 09 주제·목적을 묻는 문제

PRACTICE
본문 p.59

1. (B)   **2.** (C)   **3.** (D)   **4.** (A)

1. 🎧 미녀/미남

Question 1 refers to the following conversation.

> **W** Hi, Mr. Davis. This is Christina Whitley from the Westbury Small Business Association.
>
> **M** Oh, yes. Hello, Ms. Whitley.
>
> **W** I'm calling to let you know that the Digital Marketing Conference has been postponed until June 18.
>
> **M** I see. I can probably still attend it.
>
> **W** I hope so. I'll e-mail you an updated registration packet. Also, your travel and registration fees will be covered by us.
>
> **M** Thank you. I'll double check whether or not I can participate in the event. If not, I will probably send my assistant manager in my place.

해석

1번은 다음 대화에 관한 문제입니다.

여 안녕하세요, 데이비스 씨. 웨스트베리 중소기업협회의 크리스티나 휘틀리입니다.

남 아, 네. 안녕하세요, 휘틀리 씨.

여 **디지털 마케팅 학회가 6월 18일로 연기되었다는 것을 알려드리고자 전화드렸습니다.**

남 그렇군요. 그래도 저는 아마 참석할 수 있을 거예요.

여 그랬으면 좋겠네요. 업데이트된 등록 안내집을 이메일로 보내드리겠습니다. 또한, 당신의 여행비와 등록비는 저희가 부담할 것입니다.

남 감사합니다. 제가 그 행사에 참여할 수 있는지 다시 한번 확인해 볼게요. 그렇지 않다면, 아마 저 대신 부팀장을 보내게 될 것입니다.

어휘 Small Business Association 중소기업협회 postpone 연기하다 attend 참석하다 registration 등록 participate 참여하다 in one's place ~대신에

1. 여자는 왜 남자에게 전화하고 있는가?
(A) 청구서 지급을 요청하기 위해
(B) 그에게 일정 변경을 알리기 위해
(C) 그에게 발표해달라고 요청하기 위해
(D) 몇 가지 운영 전략을 공유하기 위해

어휘 inform 알리다 invite 요청하다 strategy 전략

2. 🎧 영녀/미남

Question 2 refers to the following conversation.

> **W** Have you heard about the negotiations with the Duluth Software representatives?
>
> **M** You mean the possible merger with that company? I think it'd give us a strong market position.
>
> **W** True, but I wonder what that means for our job security. I'm afraid they will downsize some departments.
>
> **M** Well, you can bring up that concern at the staff meeting on Friday. I know our executives are doing everything they can to protect our jobs. And there may be bonuses given to employees who stay with the company.
>
> **W** Well, I wonder how much they will be.
>
> **M** Hopefully enough to retain the best staff members.

해석

2번은 다음 대화에 관한 문제입니다.

여 **덜루스 소프트웨어 대표자들과의 협상에 대해 들으셨어요?**

남 그 회사와의 합병 가능성을 말씀하시는 거죠? 그것이 우리에게 강력한 시장 지위를 줄 거라 생각해요.

여 맞아요, 하지만 그게 우리 고용 안정에는 어떤 의미가 있는지 궁금해요. 저는 그들이 일부 부서를 축소할까 봐 걱정돼요.

남 음, 당신이 금요일 직원 회의에서 그러한 우려를 제기해도 될 것 같아요. 저는 임원들이 우리 일자리를 보호하기 위해 할 수 있는 모든 것을 하고 있다는 걸 알고 있어요. 그리고 회사에 남는 직원들에게 주어지는 보너스가 있을 거고요.

여 글쎄요, 보너스가 얼마나 될지 궁금하네요.

남 최고의 직원들을 유지할 수 있을 만큼 충분하기를 바라요.

어휘 negotiation 협상 representative 대표(자) merger 합병 market position 시장 지위 job security 고용 안정[보장] downsize 축소하다 bring up (화제를) 꺼내다 concern 우려, 걱정 executive 임원, 경영진 retain 유지하다

2. 화자들은 주로 무엇에 관해 이야기하고 있는가?
(A) 본사 이전
(B) 소프트웨어 업그레이드
(C) 합병안
(D) 시장 규제

어휘 headquarters 본사 relocation 이전 proposed 제안된 regulation 규제

3. 🎧 호남/미녀

Question 3 refers to the following conversation.

> **M** Thanks for calling the Burlington Parks and Recreation Department. What can I help you with?

W Hi, my name is Rosa Garcia. I'd like to volunteer a few hours during the week, and I heard your department runs a volunteer program.

M Yes, we do. We have several groups that assist with cleaning up our public parks. Unfortunately, though, you've just missed our recruitment event.

W Oh, I was hoping to get to work quickly.

M Well, I can take your contact information and let you know when we're recruiting new people. What's your number?

해석

3번은 다음 대화에 관한 문제입니다.

남 벌링턴 공원 및 휴양 부서에 전화해 주셔서 감사합니다. 무엇을 도와 드릴까요?

여 안녕하세요, 제 이름은 로사 가르시아입니다. **저는 주중에 자원봉사를 몇 시간 하고 싶은데, 이 부서에서 자원봉사 프로그램을 운영한다고 들었어요.**

남 네, 있습니다. 저희는 우리의 공원을 청소하는 것을 돕는 몇 개의 그룹이 있어요. 그런데 안타깝지만, 모집 행사를 이제 막 놓치셨어요.

여 아, 빨리 일을 시작하고 싶었는데요.

남 음, 제가 당신의 연락처를 받아서 새로운 인원을 모집할 때 알려 줄 수 있어요. 전화번호가 어떻게 되세요?

어휘 recreation 휴양 assist with ~을 돕다 recruitment 모집, 채용

3. 여자의 전화 목적은 무엇인가?
(A) 공원 이벤트를 홍보하기 위해
(B) 청소 서비스를 소개하기 위해
(C) 시설 투어를 계획하기 위해
(D) 자원봉사 기회에 대해 문의하기 위해

어휘 promote 홍보하다 arrange 계획하다, 준비하다

4. 🎧 호남/영녀
Question 4 refers to the following conversation.

M So, we've been tasked with unpacking these boxes of sweaters that will go on sale tomorrow. We need to sort them by size and color.

W That's a lot of boxes. Will it be just the two of us?

M Unfortunately, yes. The rest of the staff members are working at the cash registers or assisting customers.

W Well, we'll probably have to work all day on this.

M I don't know. Let's get started and see how it goes. We can give Ms. Mallory an update closer to lunch.

해석

4번은 다음 대화에 관한 문제입니다.

남 자, 우리는 내일 판매될 이 스웨터 상자들을 푸는 일을 맡았어요. 우리는 그것들을 사이즈와 색상에 따라 분류해야 합니다.

여 상자가 많네요. 우리 둘만 하나요?

남 유감스럽게도 그래요. 나머지 직원들은 계산대에서 일하거나 고객을 응대하고 있어요.

여 음, 우리는 아마 하루 종일 이 일을 해야 할 거예요.

남 잘 모르겠어요. 일단 시작해서 어떻게 진행되는지 봅시다. 점심 시간쯤에 맬러리 씨에게 진행 상황을 알리면 돼요.

어휘 task 일을 시키다; 업무 unpack (짐을) 풀다 sort 분류하다

4. 대화는 (주로) 무엇에 관한 것인가?
(A) 상품을 정리하는 것
(B) 직원들을 교육하는 것
(C) 쇼윈도 진열을 변경하는 것
(D) 배송용 상자에 라벨을 붙이는 것

어휘 merchandise 상품 display 진열, 전시

패러프레이징 unpacking these boxes of sweaters that will go on sale → Organizing some merchandise

UNIT 10 화자·장소를 묻는 문제

PRACTICE   본문 p.61

1. (A) **2.** (D) **3.** (C) **4.** (B)

1. 🎧 미녀/미남
Question 1 refers to the following conversation.

W <u>Welcome to the Camden Library</u>. Are you a member here?

M Actually, this is my first visit. I recently moved to the area.

W Well, there is no charge to become a member. You just have to show proof of address, such as a utility bill or apartment lease.

M Great. Do you offer any classes for the community?

W Absolutely. We have a wide range of classes for adults. Here is the schedule for this month. But just so you know, we're closed next week because of the holiday.

M Okay. Are there public computers as well?

W Yes, just over there. You can use them anytime.

해석

1번은 다음 대화에 관한 문제입니다.

여 **캠든 도서관에 오신 것을 환영합니다.** 이곳 회원이신가요?

남 사실, 오늘이 첫 방문이에요. 저는 최근에 이 지역으로 이사했어요.

여 음, 회원이 되는 데에는 요금이 부과되지 않아요. 공과금 청구서나 아파트 임대차 계약서 같은 주소 증명을 보여주시기만 하면 됩니다.

남 좋아요. 주민들을 위한 수업도 제공하나요?

여 물론이죠. 저희는 성인을 위한 다양한 수업이 있습니다. 여기 이번 달 일정표가 있습니다. 하지만 아시다시피, 다음 주는 연휴로 인해 문을 닫습니다.

남 알겠습니다. 공용 컴퓨터도 있나요?

여 네, 바로 저곳입니다. 언제든지 사용하실 수 있습니다.

어휘 charge 요금 proof 증명(서) utility bill 공과금 lease 임대차 계약(서)

1. 대화는 어디에서 일어나는 것 같은가?

(A) 도서관에서

(B) 부동산 중개소에서

(C) 전자제품점에서

(D) 헬스장에서

2. 🎧 영녀/미남

Question 2 refers to the following conversation.

W Good morning. What brings you into our leasing office today?

M Hi. My name is Todd Morrison, and I'm in unit 310. My lease will expire in March, but I'm thinking about moving to a larger unit within the building.

W Let me check what we have available. Hmm... it looks like apartment 501 will be available at that time. It's a three-bedroom unit for twelve hundred a month.

M That sounds perfect. I don't mind spending more in order to have more space.

W Great. I'll find out when you can have a look around the place.

해석

2번은 다음 대화에 관한 문제입니다.

여 **안녕하세요. 오늘 저희 임대 사무실에 무슨 일로 오셨나요?**

남 안녕하세요. 제 이름은 토드 모리슨이고, 310호에 살고 있습니다. 임대차 계약이 3월에 만료되는데, 건물 내에 있는 더 큰 호실로 옮길까 생각 중이에요.

여 구할 수 있는 게 뭐가 있는지 확인해 볼게요. 흠... 그 시기에 아

파트 501호가 나올 것 같네요. 한 달에 1,200달러인 침실 3개짜리 호실입니다.

남 완벽하게 들리는데요. 저는 더 큰 공간을 갖기 위해 돈을 더 쓰는 건 상관없어요.

여 좋습니다. 당신이 언제 그곳을 둘러볼 수 있는지 알아볼게요.

어휘 leasing office 임대 사무실 expire 만료되다 available 구할 수 있는

2. 여자는 누구인 것 같은가?

(A) 전기 기사

(B) 청소부

(C) 실내 장식가

(D) 부동산 관리인

3. 🎧 미녀/호남

Question 3 refers to the following conversation.

W Hello, Mr. Elliot. You said you wanted to look into getting a loan for your business?

M That's right. I own a company that sells medical supplies to hospitals and clinics.

W Okay, I've looked over the paperwork regarding your business model. It seems you are doing well.

M Yes, and we expect further growth. But we need to upgrade our Web site to help us attract more clients.

W I understand. I can look over your financial records in more detail to find out how much funding would be available to you.

M Thanks. I have all the documents right here.

해석

3번은 다음 대화에 관한 문제입니다.

여 안녕하세요, 엘리엇 씨. 사업을 위해 대출 받는 걸 알아보고 싶다고 하셨죠?

남 맞습니다. **저는 병원과 의원에 의료 용품을 판매하는 회사를 소유하고 있습니다.**

여 알겠습니다, 당신의 사업 모델에 관한 서류를 검토해 봤어요. 사업이 번창하고 있는 것 같아요.

남 네, 그리고 우리는 더 큰 성장을 기대합니다. 하지만 더 많은 고객 유치를 돕기 위해 웹사이트를 업그레이드해야 합니다.

여 이해합니다. 제가 당신의 재정 기록을 더 자세히 검토해서 당신에게 자금이 얼마나 가능할 수 있는지 알아볼 수 있습니다.

남 감사합니다. 모든 서류를 여기에 가지고 있어요.

어휘 look into 알아보다 get a loan 대출을 받다 medical supplies 의료 용품 paperwork 서류 growth 성장 attract 끌어들이다 in more detail 더 자세히 funding 자금

3. 남자는 어떤 업계에서 일하는가?

(A) 출판

(B) 외식 산업

(C) 의료

(D) 농업

4. 🎧 호남/영녀

Question 4 refers to the following conversation.

> M I enjoyed your presentation on vegetarian cooking. I really learned a lot. I'm a producer at the Channel 5 TV Station.
>
> W Oh, really? I love your morning show.
>
> M Thanks! Actually, this kind of topic would be popular with our viewers. Would you be interested in being on the show?
>
> W Well, I've never done anything like that before, but it sounds like it would be interesting. Perhaps you could tell me more about it.
>
> M Of course. How can I reach you?

해석

4번은 다음 대화에 관한 문제입니다.

남 채식 요리에 대한 당신의 발표 잘 들었습니다. 정말 많이 배웠어요. **저는 채널 5 TV 방송국의 프로듀서입니다.**

여 아, 정말요? 당신의 아침 프로그램을 정말 좋아해요.

남 감사합니다! 사실, 이런 주제는 저희 시청자에게 인기가 많을 것 같아요. 프로그램에 출연하는 것에 관심이 있으신가요?

여 글쎄요, 전에 그런 일을 해 본 적은 없지만, 흥미로운 일처럼 들리네요. 가능하시다면 그것에 관해 제게 더 말해 주세요.

남 물론이죠. 어떻게 연락드리면 되나요?

어휘 perhaps 가능하시다면, 혹시 가능하면

4. 남자는 어디에서 일하는가?

(A) 식당에서

(B) TV 방송국에서

(C) 기업 연구소에서

(D) 영화관에서

UNIT 11 세부사항을 묻는 문제

PRACTICE
본문 p.63

1. (B)   **2.** (A)   **3.** (C)   **4.** (D)

1. 🎧 미남/미녀

Question 1 refers to the following conversation.

> M Hello, I'm supposed to meet Anthony Shaw here for an interview. I'm from the *Worthington Herald*.
>
> W Ah, yes. He's expecting you, so he'll be out in a moment. I know he's looking forward to telling your readers more about his coaching career.
>
> M Yes, he's been such a big part of the local basketball scene. A lot of people will miss him when he retires at the end of the season.
>
> W Right. He's very talented. Anyway, could I get you something to drink while you wait?
>
> M Thanks, but I'm fine.

해석

1번은 다음 대화에 관한 문제입니다.

남 안녕하세요, 이곳에서 앤서니 쇼를 만나기로 되어 있어요. 저는 '워딩턴 헤럴드'에서 왔습니다.

여 아, 네. 그가 당신을 기다리고 있어요, 곧 나올 거예요. **그가 당신의 독자들에게 자신의 코치 경력에 대한 더 많은 이야기를 하는 것을 고대하고 있다는 것을 알고 있습니다.**

남 네, 그는 지역 농구 분야에서 아주 큰 비중을 차지하고 있어요. 그가 시즌 말에 은퇴하면 많은 사람들이 그를 그리워할 겁니다.

여 맞아요. 그는 아주 재능이 있어요. 어쨌든, 기다리시는 동안 마실 것 좀 갖다 드릴까요?

남 감사하지만, 괜찮아요.

어휘 be supposed to ~하기로 되어 있다   look forward to ~을 고대하다   career 경력   retire 은퇴하다   talented 재능이 있는

1. 앤서니 쇼는 누구인가?

(A) 정비사

(B) 코치

(C) 접수원

(D) 기자

2. 🎧 미남/영녀

Question 2 refers to the following conversation.

> M Sumiyo, I didn't get a chance to talk to you after yesterday's meeting. What did you think of the result?
>
> W You mean about the proposal to acquire Anaheim Logistics? I was strongly in favor of it.
>
> M Yes, I thought it would be good for our company. I'm disappointed that the board didn't approve it.
>
> W Me, too. I feel like we missed an opportunity for future growth. I'm a bit worried we won't be able to keep up with our competition.
>
> M Hmm... I think there are other options that we can explore.

해석

2번은 다음 대화에 관한 문제입니다.

남 스미요, 어제 회의 후에 당신과 얘기할 기회가 없었네요. 결과에

대해 어떻게 생각하셨어요?

여 **애너하임 물류 인수 제안**에 대해 말씀하시는 건가요? 저는 그것에 강력히 찬성했어요.

남 네, 저도 우리 회사에 좋을 거라 생각했어요. **이사회가 그것을 승인하지 않은 것에 실망했어요.**

여 저도요. 우리가 미래의 성장을 위한 기회를 놓친 것 같아요. 우리가 경쟁사를 따라가지 못할까 봐 조금 걱정돼요.

남 흠... 우리가 찾아낼 수 있는 다른 선택지가 있을 거라 생각해요.

어휘 acquire 취득하다 in favor of ~에 찬성하여 approve 승인하다 keep up with ~에 뒤지지 않다 competition 경쟁(자) explore 찾아내다

2. 남자는 왜 실망했는가?
(A) 제안이 거절되었다.
(B) 회의가 취소되었다.
(C) 이사회 임원이 사임했다.
(D) 발표에 몇 가지 오류가 있었다.

어휘 reject 거절하다 resign 사임하다

패러프레이징 didn't approve → was rejected

3. 🎧 호남/미녀
Question 3 refers to the following conversation.

> **M** Excuse me, do you know why they're not boarding the bus to Cambridge? It's supposed to depart at 3 o'clock.
>
> **W** Yes, the Department of Transportation has closed several highways due to the severe storm.
>
> **M** I see. Are all bus trips canceled for today?
>
> **W** It's possible they can start clearing the roads soon, so another announcement will be made in about an hour.
>
> **M** Okay. I guess I'll get a coffee while I wait.
>
> **W** There's a nice café near the west entrance.

해석
3번은 다음 대화에 관한 문제입니다.
남 실례합니다, 캠브리지로 가는 버스에 탑승을 왜 안하는지 아세요? 3시 정각에 출발하기로 되어 있어요.
여 네, **교통부는 심한 폭풍 때문에 몇 고속도로를 폐쇄했어요.**
남 그렇군요. 오늘은 모든 버스 여행이 취소되는 건가요?
여 그들이 곧 도로 청소를 시작할 가능성이 있기 때문에, 약 한 시간 후에 다른 안내가 있을 거예요.
남 알겠습니다. 기다리는 동안 커피 한 잔 마셔야겠어요.
여 서쪽 입구 근처에 괜찮은 카페가 있어요.

어휘 board 탑승하다 depart 출발하다 highway 고속도로 severe 극심한 storm 폭풍

3. 여자는 어떤 문제를 언급하는가?
(A) 표에 오탈자가 있다.
(B) 일부 버스 요금이 인상되었다.
(C) 날씨가 좋지 않다.
(D) 약간의 수리가 필요하다.

어휘 misprint 오탈자

4. 🎧 호남/영녀
Question 4 refers to the following conversation.

> **M** Welcome to TC Hardware Store. How can I help you?
>
> **W** Hi, I'm doing some renovations in my bathroom. My coworker recommended your business for buying paint.
>
> **M** Oh, we always appreciate recommendations. Was there a particular brand that you had in mind?
>
> **W** Sweeny Interiors.
>
> **M** That's a good brand. Its paint is made for materials that last long and do not crack easily. Some other brands use cheaper materials, so the wall coverage isn't very good. Everything's in aisle 2.
>
> **W** Thank you.
>
> **M** And if you haven't signed up for our loyalty program yet, here's a brochure with all the details.

해석
4번은 다음 대화에 관한 문제입니다.
남 TC 철물점에 오신 것을 환영합니다. 무엇을 도와드릴까요?
여 안녕하세요, 제가 화장실에 몇 가지 보수를 하고 있는데요. 동료가 페인트 구매에 이 업체를 추천했어요.
남 아, 저희는 추천을 항상 감사하게 생각해요. 특별히 생각하고 계신 브랜드가 있었나요?
여 스위니 인테리어요.
남 괜찮은 브랜드예요. **그곳 페인트는 오래 지속되고 쉽게 갈라지지 않는 원료로 만들어졌어요.** 몇몇 다른 브랜드들은 더 저렴한 원료를 사용하기 때문에, 벽의 커버력이 별로 좋지 않습니다. 모든 것이 2번 통로에 있어요.
여 감사합니다.
남 그리고 아직 저희의 고객 보상 프로그램에 가입하지 않으셨다면, 여기 모든 세부사항이 적힌 책자가 있습니다.

어휘 hardware store 철물점 renovation 수리, 보수 appreciate 고맙게 생각하다 particular 특별한, 특정한 have ~ in mind ~에 관해 생각하고 있다 material 원료, 재료 last 지속되다 crack 갈라지다 aisle 통로 sign up 가입하다

4. 남자는 브랜드에 대해 무엇이라고 말하는가?

(A) 그것은 긍정적인 평가를 많이 받는다.

(B) 그것은 가격이 적당하다.

(C) 그것은 현재 재고가 떨어졌다.

(D) 그것은 고급 원료를 사용한다.

어휘 positive 긍정적인 affordable (가격이) 적당한
currently 현재 out of stock 재고가 떨어진 high-quality
고급의

패러프레이징 made for materials that last long and do
not crack easily → uses high-quality materials

UNIT 12 제안·요청사항을 묻는 문제

PRACTICE
본문 p.65

1. (D) **2.** (C) **3.** (A) **4.** (A)

1. 🎧 미남/미녀

Question 1 refers to the following conversation.

M Mijin, I plan to apply for the assistant manager
role, but I need a letter of evaluation for the
application. Could you please write one?

W I'd be happy to. You've been doing an
excellent job on the sales team, and I'm really
impressed with how hard you worked after
being assigned to a new territory.

M Thanks a lot. I'm actually quite proud of how I
was able to exceed my sales targets by so
much. It helped to boost my confidence.

해석

1번은 다음 대화에 관한 문제입니다.

남 미진, 저는 부팀장 직책에 지원할 계획인데, **지원을 위해서는 평
가서가 필요합니다. 하나 써주실 수 있나요?**

여 기꺼이요. 영업팀에서 일을 아주 잘 해오셨는데, 새로운 지역을
배정 받고 얼마나 열심히 일하셨는지 아주 인상 깊어요.

남 정말 감사합니다. 저는 사실 제가 어떻게 매출 목표를 그렇게 많
이 초과 달성할 수 있었는지에 대해 꽤 자랑스러워요. 그것은 제
자신감을 높이는 데 도움이 되었어요.

어휘 apply for ~에 지원하다 evaluation 평가 assign 배정
하다 territory 지역, 영토 exceed 초과하다 target 목표
boost 끌어올리다, 증대시키다 confidence 자신, 확신

1. 남자는 여자에게 무엇을 해 달라고 요청하는가?

(A) 판매 카탈로그 교정 보기

(B) 고객 방문하기

(C) 발표하기

(D) 평가 작성하기

어휘 proofread 교정을 보다

2. 🎧 영녀/미남

Question 2 refers to the following conversation.

W I just got a phone call from the building owner.
She'd like us to add a flower bed to the shared
outdoor area, by the fence on the east side.
She thinks it will create a more relaxing
atmosphere for tenants.

M Okay. Let's go take some measurements now.
Also, I think we have some gardening materials
left over from our last project.

W That's right. There is some potting soil and a
few tools. I'll check what's there after we figure
out the size of the flower bed we need.

해석

2번은 다음 대화에 관한 문제입니다.

여 방금 건물주한테서 전화를 받았어요. 그녀는 우리가 동쪽 울타리
옆에 있는 공용 야외 공간에 화단을 추가하기를 원해요. 그녀는
이것이 세입자들에게 더 편안한 분위기를 만들어 줄 것이라고 생
각해요.

남 알겠어요. 지금 치수를 재러 갑시다. 또한, 지난번 프로젝트에서
남은 **원예용 재료가 좀 있는 것 같아요.**

여 맞아요. 약간의 화분용 흙과 몇 가지 도구들이 있어요. 우리가 필
요한 화단의 크기를 알아낸 뒤에 **제가 무엇이 있는지 확인해 볼게
요.**

어휘 flower bed 화단 relaxing 편한 atmosphere 분위기
tenant 세입자 take measurements 치수를 재다
gardening 원예 left over 남은 figure out 알아내다

2. 여자는 무엇을 해 주겠다고 제안하는가?

(A) 주말에 일하기

(B) 꽃 주문하기

(C) 재료 찾아 보기

(D) 세입자 회의 열기

패러프레이징 check → Look for

3. 🎧 호남/미녀

Question 3 refers to the following conversation.

M Have you seen the sales figures for the latest
quarter? Online sales of our home furnishings
have now surpassed in-person sales at the
store.

W Yes, I noticed that trend, and it's probably
going to continue. We need to find a way to
help online customers find new products
naturally, like they would if they were browsing
the shelves in the store.

M Why don't we create some videos to showcase
our best home accessories?

W I like that idea. Actually, I have a friend who's

an interior designer. She could collaborate with us to give decorating tips using our products. I'll give her a call this afternoon.

해석

3번은 다음 대화에 관한 문제입니다.

남 최근 분기의 매출액 봤어요? 우리 가정용 가구의 온라인 판매가 이제 매장의 현장 판매를 넘어섰어요.

여 네, 추세를 인지했어요, 그리고 아마 계속되겠죠. 우리는 온라인 고객들이 매장의 진열대를 둘러볼 때처럼 자연스럽게 신제품을 찾을 수 있도록 도울 방법을 찾아야 해요.

남 **우리의 가장 좋은 가정용 액세서리를 소개할 영상을 만들어 보는 건 어떨까요?**

여 그 아이디어가 마음에 드네요. 사실, 제게 인테리어 디자이너 친구가 있어요. 그녀는 우리와 협업해서 우리 제품을 사용해 장식 팁을 줄 수 있을 거예요. 제가 오늘 오후에 그녀에게 전화할게요.

어휘 sales figures 매출액 quarter 1분기 surpass 뛰어넘다 browse 둘러보다 showcase 소개하다 collaborate 협력하다 decorating 장식

3. 남자는 무엇을 할 것을 제안하는가?

(A) 홍보 영상을 만드는 것
(B) 매장에 유명 인사를 초대하는 것
(C) 할인 쿠폰을 제공하는 것
(D) 장식 대회를 개최하는 것

어휘 promotional 홍보의 celebrity 유명 인사

패러프레이징 create → Making

4. 🎧 호남/영녀

Question 4 refers to the following conversation.

M Thanks again for all of your planning for the company picnic, Wendy. I've heard a lot of positive comments about it.

W Oh, I'm glad that people had a good time.

M Yeah, everyone loved the activities and the food. Speaking of food, the cherry pie that you made was amazing. Would you mind sharing its recipe?

W It's not my own, just one I found on a Web site. I can e-mail you the link. It was pretty easy to make, so you should definitely give it a try.

M Thanks, I will.

해석

4번은 다음 대화에 관한 문제입니다.

남 웬디, 회사 야유회를 위해 당신이 세운 모든 계획에 다시 한번 고마워요. 그것에 대해 긍정적인 의견을 많이 들었어요.

여 아, 사람들이 좋은 시간을 보냈다니 기쁘네요.

남 네, 모든 사람들이 활동과 음식을 아주 좋아했어요. 음식 얘기가 나와서 말인데요, 당신이 만든 **체리 파이**는 굉장했어요. **그것의**

레시피를 공유해 주실 수 있나요?

여 그건 제 레시피가 아니라, 그냥 웹사이트에서 찾은 거예요. 당신에게 링크를 이메일로 보내드릴게요. 그것은 만들기가 꽤 쉬웠으니, 꼭 한번 시도해 보세요.

남 고마워요, 그럴게요.

어휘 speaking of ~에 관해서 말한다면 give it a try 시도하다

4. 남자는 무엇을 요청하는가?

(A) 디저트 레시피
(B) 홍보 책자
(C) 초대장 사본
(D) 연락처 목록

UNIT 13 다음에 할·일어날 일을 묻는 문제

PRACTICE 본문 p.67

1. (D)   **2.** (B)   **3.** (B)   **4.** (A)

1. 🎧 미녀/미남

Question 1 refers to the following conversation.

W Hi, I tried to use the library's self-checkout machine, but there was a message saying that I owe a fine. Here is my card.

M Let me see... Yes, it looks like one of your books was returned late. You'll have to pay a fine of $1.25 before checking out anything new.

W Oh, that's no problem. I can pay it now. Sorry about that.

M It happens. And just a reminder that we'll be holding a fund-raiser next Saturday. We're selling used books to purchase new computers for the library.

해석

1번은 다음 대화에 관한 문제입니다.

여 안녕하세요, 도서관 셀프 체크아웃 기계를 사용하려고 했는데, 벌금을 내야 한다는 메시지가 떴어요. 여기 제 카드입니다.

남 한번 볼게요... 네, 당신의 책 중 하나가 늦게 반납된 것 같습니다. 새로운 책을 체크아웃하시기 전에 1달러 25센트의 벌금을 내셔야 할 거예요.

여 아, 그건 문제 없어요. 지금 낼게요. 죄송합니다.

남 그럴 수도 있죠. **그리고 다음 주 토요일에 저희가 기금 모금 행사를 연다는 것만 다시 한번 알려드려요.** 저희는 도서관의 새 컴퓨터 구입을 위해 헌 책들을 팔 것입니다.

어휘 owe 빚지다 fine 벌금

1. 다음 주 토요일에 무엇이 열릴 것인가?
(A) 글쓰기 워크숍
(B) 시 낭송회
(C) 컴퓨터 강의
(D) 기금 모금 행사

2. 🎧 미남/영녀

Question 2 refers to the following conversation.

> **M** Thanks for meeting, Ms. Jackson. As I said on the phone, I'm relocating my jewelry shop to a building on Donovan Street. Because so much of our stock is delicate, the moving company needs to handle everything carefully.
>
> **W** I understand. I can assure you that our crew members take great care when it comes to fragile items. So, why did you decide to relocate?
>
> **M** Well, we've been growing rapidly, so we need a bigger space.
>
> **W** That's great. And what's your target move day?
>
> **M** July 12. Can you help on that day?
>
> **W** Let me open the calendar app on my phone.

해석

2번은 다음 대화에 관한 문제입니다.

남 만나주셔서 감사합니다, 잭슨 씨. 전화로 말씀드렸듯이, 제 보석 가게를 도노반 거리에 있는 건물로 이전할 것입니다. 재고의 많은 부분이 깨지기 쉽기 때문에, 이삿짐 회사는 모든 것을 조심스럽게 다뤄야 합니다.

여 알겠습니다. 저희 작업자들은 깨지기 쉬운 물건에 대해 세심한 주의를 기울임을 장담할 수 있습니다. 그런데, 왜 이전하기로 결정하셨나요?

남 음, 저희는 빠르게 성장해 왔기 때문에, 더 큰 공간이 필요합니다.

여 그거 잘됐네요. 그러면 원하시는 이사일은 언제인가요?

남 7월 12일입니다. **그날 도와주실 수 있나요?**

여 **핸드폰으로 달력 앱을 열어 볼게요.**

어휘 relocate 이전하다   stock 재고   delicate 연약한, 깨지기 쉬운   assure 보증하다, 장담하다   fragile 깨지기 쉬운   target 목표

2. 여자는 다음에 무엇을 할 것 같은가?
(A) 주소 적기
(B) 일정 확인하기
(C) 작업자 소개하기
(D) 비용 견적 제공하기

어휘 confirm 확인하다   cost estimate 비용 견적

3. 🎧 호남/미녀

Question 3 refers to the following conversation.

> **M** Rhonda, I'm glad I caught you after today's rehearsal. I wanted to talk to you about an issue that some of the actors mentioned, about the curtains being opened and closed between acts.
>
> **W** What seems to be the problem?
>
> **M** They're moving smoothly enough, but they're really squeaky. I think even audience members sitting far from the stage could be distracted by that noise. Do you know what might be causing it?
>
> **W** It's probably easy to fix. I'll try to oil the curtain track to see if that helps.
>
> **M** Thank you. Since opening night is next week, we need to make sure everything is perfect. I think this will be our best show yet.

해석

3번은 다음 대화에 관한 문제입니다.

남 론다, 오늘 리허설이 끝나고 당신을 만나서 기뻐요. 저는 몇몇 배우들이 언급한 문제에 대해 당신과 이야기하고 싶었습니다. 연극의 막 사이에 커튼이 열리고 닫히는 것에 대해서요.

여 뭐가 문제인 것 같나요?

남 커튼의 움직임은 꽤 원활한데, 삐걱거리는 소리가 엄청나요. 무대에서 멀리 떨어진 곳에 앉아 있는 관객들조차도 그 소음에 정신이 산만해질 수 있을 것 같아요. 원인이 무엇일지 아시나요?

여 아마 고치기 쉬울 거예요. 커튼 레일에 기름칠을 해 보고 그게 도움이 되는지 볼게요.

남 감사합니다. **개막일이 다음 주이기 때문에,** 우리는 모든 것이 완벽한지 확인해야 해요. 이번이 지금까지 공연 중 최고가 될 것 같아요.

어휘 smoothly 부드럽게   squeaky 삐걱거리는   distracted (정신이) 산만해진   oil 기름을 칠하다

3. 다음 주에 무슨 일이 일어날 것인가?
(A) 극장이 개조될 것이다.
(B) 연극이 시작될 것이다.
(C) 포스터가 인쇄될 것이다.
(D) 연기상이 수여될 것이다.

어휘 renovate 개조하다   present 주다, 수여하다

4. 🎧 호남/영녀/미남

Question 4 refers to the following conversation with three speakers.

> **M1** Thanks for stopping by in person to talk about the designs for our new dental clinic. Our grand opening will be September 3.

W My pleasure. I can see that this space has a lot of natural light. That's great. The waiting area is small, though.

M2 Yes, but we hope you can find a way to make the best use of the space.

M1 That's right. And we'd like to make sure the area has a calming atmosphere.

W I have a few ideas to make that happen. I'll start out by measuring each room so I know what I have to work with.

해석

4번은 다음 세 명의 대화에 관한 문제입니다.

남1 저희가 새로 여는 치과 설계에 대해 이야기하기 위해 직접 방문해 주셔서 감사해요. 저희 개원일은 9월 3일입니다.

여 천만에요. 이 공간이 많은 자연광을 가지고 있다는 게 보이네요. 잘됐어요. 하지만 대기 공간이 작아요.

남2 네, 하지만 저희는 당신이 그 공간을 최대한 활용할 수 있는 방법을 찾을 수 있기를 바라요.

남1 맞습니다. 그리고 저희는 반드시 그 공간이 차분한 분위기를 가졌으면 좋겠어요.

여 그렇게 할 수 있는 몇 가지 아이디어가 있습니다. 제가 무엇을 해야 하는지 알 수 있도록 **각 방의 치수를 재는 것부터 시작하겠습니다.**

어휘 make the best use of 최대한 활용하다 calming 진정시키는 atmosphere 분위기 measure 측정하다, 치수를 재다

4. 여자는 무엇을 할 것이라고 말하는가?

(A) 치수 재기
(B) 방에 페인트칠하기
(C) 계약서에 서명하기
(D) 조명 설치하기

어휘 install 설치하다

패러프레이징 measuring each room → Take some measurements

UNIT 14 화자의 의도를 묻는 문제

PRACTICE   본문 p.69

1. (C)   **2.** (A)   **3.** (D)   **4.** (B)

1. 🎧 미녀/미남

Question 1 refers to the following conversation.

W Hi, Mr. Fox. Our team of consultants has gone over your business model, and we've come up with some ideas to expand your footwear brand.

M That's great. We've been struggling to make a

name for ourselves in the market, so your insights will be helpful.

W Alright. So, what do you think about displaying your footwear in hardware stores?

M They usually market to an older clientele.

W Hmm... Let me see what you think of some of our other ideas.

해석

1번은 다음 대화에 관한 문제입니다.

여 안녕하세요, 폭스 씨. 저희 컨설턴트 팀이 귀사의 사업 모델을 검토했고, 신발 브랜드를 확장하기 위한 몇 가지 아이디어를 생각해 냈어요.

남 잘됐네요. 우리는 시장에서 이름을 알리기 위해 고군분투해 왔기 때문에 여러분의 통찰력이 도움이 될 것입니다.

여 알겠습니다. 그렇다면, **철물점에 귀사의 신발을 진열하는 것에 대해 어떻게 생각하시나요?**

남 그들은 보통 나이가 더 많은 고객들과 거래를 해요.

여 흠... **저희의 다른 아이디어들에 대해서는 어떻게 생각하실지 봅시다.**

어휘 consultant 자문 위원, 컨설턴트 expand 확장하다 footwear 신발 struggle 분투하다, 애쓰다 insight 통찰력 hardware store 철물점 market 거래하다; 시장 clientele 고객

1. 남자는 왜 "그들은 보통 나이가 더 많은 고객들과 거래를 해요"라고 말하는가?

(A) 실망을 나타내기 위해
(B) 계획에 동의하기 위해
(C) 제안을 거절하기 위해
(D) 도움을 주기 위해

2. 🎧 미남/영녀

Question 2 refers to the following conversation.

M Hello. I have a reservation for six people at 12:30. My name is Lawrence Scott.

W Oh, yes. We have your reservation right here, Mr. Scott.

M When I called a few days ago, I had asked to sit at a table on the rooftop. However, it's very cold today.

W Hmm... I can move your group to table 8 in the indoor dining area.

M Thank you. Also, I took public transportation here, but some of the others in our group are driving. There didn't seem to be much room in the parking lot.

W We have more spots behind the building, and customers can park there for free.

M Oh, thanks. I'll let them know.

해석

2번은 다음 대화에 관한 문제입니다.

남 안녕하세요. 12시 30분에 6명 예약했어요. 제 이름은 로렌스 스콧입니다.

여 아, 네. 여기 예약이 있네요, 스콧 씨.

남 며칠 전에 전화했을 때, **옥상에 있는 테이블에 앉겠다고 요청했어요.** 그런데, **오늘 날이 아주 춥네요.**

여 흠... **손님 일행을 실내 식사 구역에 있는 8번 테이블로 옮겨드릴 수 있어요.**

남 감사합니다. 그리고, 저는 이곳에 대중교통을 타고 왔는데, 일행 중에 운전해서 오시는 분들이 있어요. 주차장에 공간이 별로 없는 것 같았는데요.

여 건물 뒤에 자리가 더 많이 있고, 손님분들은 거기에 무료로 주차하실 수 있습니다.

남 오, 감사합니다. 그들에게 말할게요.

어휘 rooftop 옥상   take public transportation 대중교통을 이용하다   spot 자리, 지점

2. 남자는 "오늘 날이 아주 춥네요"라고 말할 때 무엇을 의미하는가?

(A) 그는 좌석 요청사항을 변경하고 싶어 한다.
(B) 대중교통을 타는 것은 불편했다.
(C) 히터의 온도를 높여야 한다.
(D) 그는 회의를 연기해야 할지도 모른다.

어휘 uncomfortable 불편한

3. 🎧 미녀/호남

Question 3 refers to the following conversation.

W Hi, Rahul. Are you busy? I've created a one-year lease agreement that I'd like you to check. I want to make sure I didn't miss anything.

M Okay. I need to show an apartment in the Clifton Building to prospective tenants at eleven, but I've got some time right now. Which property is the lease for?

W The three-bedroom unit in the Meadowview neighborhood. I showed it to a couple this morning, and they loved it.

M That property was just posted a few days ago.

W I guess Meadowview neighborhood is becoming more popular.

해석

3번은 다음 대화에 관한 문제입니다.

여 안녕하세요, 라훌. 바쁘신가요? 1년짜리 임대 계약서를 만들었는데 당신이 확인해 주셨으면 해요. 제가 아무것도 놓치지 않았는지 확실히 하고 싶어요.

남 알겠어요. 11시에 클리프턴 빌딩에 있는 아파트를 예비 세입자들

에게 보여줘야 하는데, 지금은 시간이 좀 있어요. 어떤 부동산에 대한 임대인가요?

여 메도우뷰 지역에 있는 침실 3개짜리 아파트예요. **오늘 아침에 어떤 커플에게 보여줬는데, 그들이 그곳을 아주 좋아했어요.**

남 그 부동산은 게시된지 며칠 되지 않았잖아요.

여 **메도우뷰 지역이 점점 더 인기를 얻고 있는 것 같아요.**

어휘 lease agreement 임대 계약   prospective 장래의, 기대되는   tenant 세입자   property 부동산, 건물

3. 남자는 왜 "그 부동산은 게시된지 며칠 되지 않았잖아요"라고 말하는가?

(A) 제안을 하기 위해
(B) 변명을 하기 위해
(C) 오류를 설명하기 위해
(D) 놀라움을 표현하기 위해

어휘 excuse 변명, 이유

4. 🎧 영녀/호남

Question 4 refers to the following conversation.

W Hi, Ron. I just spoke to Ms. Murphy, and she said that your crew didn't finish the landscaping work at her property today. What's going on?

M The wood chipping machine stopped working. I thought it was checked for maintenance issues a few weeks ago.

W Well, that equipment gets used a lot.

M You're right. I'm planning to borrow one from the other crew and go back tomorrow. That way, we won't have to wait for any repairs.

해석

4번은 다음 대화에 관한 문제입니다.

여 론, 안녕하세요. 방금 머피 씨와 통화했는데요, 당신의 작업 팀이 오늘 자신의 소유지에서 조경 공사를 끝내지 못했다고 하더군요. 무슨 일인가요?

남 **나무 깎는 기계가 작동을 멈췄어요. 몇 주 전에 유지보수 문제로 점검이 된 줄 알았는데요.**

여 음, 그 장비는 많이 쓰이잖아요.

남 당신 말이 맞네요. 저는 다른 작업 팀에게 장비를 빌려서 내일 다시 갈 계획이에요. 그렇게 하면 수리를 기다릴 필요가 없을 거예요.

어휘 landscaping 조경   chip 깎다, 자르다

4. 여자는 "그 장비는 많이 쓰이잖아요"라고 말할 때 무엇을 암시하는가?

(A) 품질이 좋은 제품이 구매되었다.
(B) 그 문제는 놀랍지 않다.
(C) 교육 세션이 필요하지 않다.
(D) 비용이 적당하다.

어휘 purchase 구매하다　expense 비용　reasonable 적당한

UNIT 15 시각 자료 연계 문제

PRACTICE
본문 p.71

1. (A)　**2.** (B)　**3.** (C)　**4.** (D)

1. 🎧 미녀/미남
Question 1 refers to the following conversation and list.

> **W** I missed the staff meeting yesterday. Is there anything I need to know about?
>
> **M** Well, the planning for the city's Environmental Awareness Day is going well. There's going to be a cleanup project at Hartford Park in the morning. We'll also be collecting recyclable items at city hall.
>
> **W** Great. Did we find any sponsors for the event?
>
> **M** Yes. Finch Landscaping is donating three hundred saplings that people can plant at home. We've chosen the tallest of these four varieties because it's the easiest to take care of.

해석
1번은 다음 대화와 목록에 관한 문제입니다.

여 제가 어제 직원 회의에 참석하지 못했어요. 제가 알아야 할 것이 있나요?

남 음, 우리 시의 '환경 인식의 날'을 위한 계획은 잘 진행되고 있어요. 오전에 하트포드 공원에서 대청소 작업이 있을 거예요. 시청에서 재활용품도 수거할 예정입니다.

여 좋네요. 행사를 위해 후원자는 찾았나요?

남 네. 핀치 조경 회사에서 사람들이 집에 심을 수 있는 300그루의 묘목을 기증할 겁니다. **우리는 이 네 가지 품종 중에서 가장 키가 큰 것을 선택했는데, 그게 관리하기가 가장 쉽기 때문이에요.**

어휘 recyclable 재활용할 수 있는　sponsor 후원자
sapling 묘목　variety 품종

나무	높이
오리나무	**15미터**
산사나무	10미터
큰산버들	8미터
호랑가시나무	6미터

1. 시각 자료를 보시오. 어떤 종류의 묘목이 기증될 것인가?
(A) 오리나무
(B) 산사나무
(C) 큰산버들

(D) 호랑가시나무

2. 🎧 미남/영녀
Question 2 refers to the following conversation and map.

> **M** Have you seen the map for shooting next week's commercial?
>
> **W** I'll check it now. Let's see. In the scene, the driver will be heading north on 11th Street. Hmm...
>
> **M** Is something wrong?
>
> **W** I think we'll have to adjust our original plan to make the filming easier.
>
> **M** What did you have in mind?
>
> **W** Originally, the driver was supposed to turn left on Hines Avenue. Instead, we should have her turn right and then stop in front of the flower shop.
>
> **M** Okay. We can get that road closed temporarily on the filming day. I'll make the necessary arrangements.

해석
2번은 다음 대화와 지도에 관한 문제입니다.

남 다음 주 광고 촬영을 위한 지도 보셨나요?

여 지금 확인해 볼게요. 어디 봅시다. 현장에서 운전자는 11번가에서 북쪽으로 갈 겁니다. 흠...

남 뭐가 잘못됐나요?

여 촬영을 더 쉽게 하기 위해 원래 계획을 조정해야 할 것 같아요.

남 무엇을 생각하고 계시나요?

여 **원래는 운전자가 하인즈 가에서 좌회전하기로 되어 있었어요. 그것 대신에 우리는 그녀가 우회전을 하고 나서 꽃집 앞에 세우도록 해야 해요.**

남 알겠습니다. **우리는 촬영 당일에 그 도로를 임시로 폐쇄할 수 있어요.** 제가 필요한 준비를 하겠습니다.

어휘 shoot 촬영하다　commercial 광고　scene 현장
adjust 조정하다　temporarily 임시로
make arrangements 준비하다

2. 시각 자료를 보시오. 어느 도로가 폐쇄될 것인가?
(A) 하인즈 가
(B) 버크셔 가

(C) 벤틀리 로
(D) 로크웰 로

3. 🎧 호남/영녀

Question 3 refers to the following conversation and flight schedule.

> M Hi, Bethany. I thought I might run into you here. You're headed to Berlin for the manufacturing trade fair, right?
>
> W That's right. Custer Manufacturing isn't hosting a booth this year, so I'm just going as an attendee. Are you still working at Goodwin Production?
>
> M Yes, I am. I've recently been promoted to team leader, so I've been pretty busy.
>
> W Congratulations! I'm sure you'll do a great job in that role.
>
> M Thanks! Say, it looks like my flight is boarding soon. Are you also taking the Powell Airlines flight?
>
> W No, I'm flying with GT Airways. Have a good trip. I'll see you tomorrow at the event.

해석
3번은 다음 대화와 비행 일정표에 관한 문제입니다.
남 베서니, 안녕하세요. 여기서 당신을 우연히 만날 것 같았어요. 제조업 무역 박람회 때문에 베를린으로 가시는 거죠?
여 맞아요. 커스터 제조사는 올해 부스를 열지 않아서, 그냥 참석자로 가는 거예요. 당신은 아직 굿윈 제조사에서 일하고 있나요?
남 네, 그렇습니다. 최근에 팀장으로 승진해서 꽤 바빴어요.
여 축하해요! 저는 당신이 그 역할을 잘 해낼 거라고 확신해요.
남 고마워요! 저기, 제 비행기가 곧 탑승을 할 것 같아요. 당신도 파월 항공 비행기를 타나요?
여 아니요, **저는 GT 항공 비행기를 탈 거예요.** 즐거운 여행 되세요. 내일 행사에서 뵙겠습니다.

어휘 run into ~와 우연히 만나다   trade fair 무역 박람회
attendee 참석자   promote 승진시키다

베를린행 항공편	
출발 시각	항공사
오후 1시 35분	커쇼 버짓
오후 3시 58분	로스코 스카이팀
오후 7시 31분	파월 항공
오후 8시 2분	**GT 항공**

3. 시각 자료를 보시오. 여자의 항공편은 언제 출발하는가?
(A) 오후 1시 35분에
(B) 오후 3시 58분에

(C) 오후 7시 31분에
(D) 오후 8시 2분에

32. (D)	**33.** (C)	**34.** (B)	**35.** (B)	**36.** (D)
37. (A)	**38.** (B)	**39.** (C)	**40.** (A)	**41.** (A)
42. (C)	**43.** (B)	**44.** (C)	**45.** (D)	**46.** (A)
47. (D)	**48.** (C)	**49.** (B)	**50.** (A)	**51.** (D)
52. (A)	**53.** (B)	**54.** (D)	**55.** (C)	**56.** (A)
57. (B)	**58.** (C)	**59.** (C)	**60.** (A)	**61.** (B)
62. (C)	**63.** (D)	**64.** (A)	**65.** (C)	**66.** (B)
67. (B)	**68.** (A)	**69.** (A)	**70.** (C)	

32-34. 🎧 호남/미녀

Questions 32-34 refer to the following conversation.

> M Victoria, sales of [32] our athletic shoes have declined. [33] How about we hold a 3-on-3 basketball tournament to bring more attention to our store?
>
> W Good idea! We could fence off an area of the parking lot and hold it there.
>
> M Yes, and spectators would come, too, so we could get a pretty big crowd.
>
> W We've never done anything like it. It'll take a lot of planning.
>
> M That's true. [34] I'll e-mail the staff now to see who's interested in helping.

32-34번은 다음 대화에 관한 문제입니다.
남 빅토리아, [32]**우리 운동화** 판매량이 줄었어요. [33]**우리 매장에 더 많은 관심을 끌기 위해 3대3 농구 대회를 여는 건 어떨까요?**
여 좋은 생각이에요! 우리는 주차장의 한 구역을 울타리로 막아 그곳에서 대회를 열 수 있어요.
남 네, 그리고 관중들도 올 거니까, 우리는 꽤 많은 사람들을 모을 수 있을 거예요.
여 우리는 그런 걸 해 본 적이 없잖아요. 많은 계획이 필요할 거예요.
남 맞아요. [34]**지금 직원들에게 이메일을 보내서 누가 도울 의향이 있는지 알아보겠습니다.**

어휘 athletic shoes 운동화   decline 줄어들다
bring attention to ~에 관심을 가져오다   fence off ~을 울타리로 구분하다   spectator 관중   crowd 사람들, 무리

32. 대화는 어디에서 일어나는 것 같은가?
(A) 철물점에서
(B) 주민센터에서
(C) 자동차 대리점에서
(D) 신발가게에서

PART 3

33. 남자는 무엇을 할 것을 제안하는가?
(A) 시간제 근로자들을 채용하는 것
(B) 진열을 재배치하는 것
(C) 스포츠 대회를 여는 것
(D) 공급업체에 연락하는 것

어휘 rearrange 재배치하다, 바꾸다 competition 대회
패러프레이징 3-on-3 basketball tournament → sports competition

34. 남자는 다음에 무엇을 할 것인가?
(A) 관리자와 이야기하기
(B) 메시지 보내기
(C) 웹사이트 업데이트하기
(D) 수치 검토하기

어휘 supervisor 관리자 review 검토하다 figures 수치
패러프레이징 e-mail the staff → Send a message

35-37. 🎧 미남/미녀/영녀
Questions 35-37 refer to the following conversation with three speakers.

M Hi, I'm Ronald. ³⁵ The landlord called me this morning and said you were having some issues with your ceiling.

W1 Yes, the problem is over here in my coworker's office. Hey, Carol. ³⁵ The facility manager's here.

W2 Oh, thanks for coming. During last week's heavy rain, ³⁶ I noticed water running down the wall. Look, you can see the damp patch there.

M Hmm... We often have these problems after a major storm. In this case, the floor above needs to be examined first. Anyway, ³⁷ it will take some time to figure out the exact cause and get it repaired. Is that alright?

35-37번은 다음 세 명의 대화에 관한 문제입니다.
남 안녕하세요, 저는 로널드입니다. ³⁵**임대인이 오늘 아침에 제게 전화해서 당신의 천장에 문제가 좀 있다고 했는데요.**
여1 네, 문제는 여기 제 동료 사무실에 있어요. 저기, 캐롤. ³⁵**시설 관리자가 왔어요.**
여2 와 주셔서 감사해요. 지난 주 폭우 때, ³⁶**저는 물이 벽을 타고 흘러내리는 것을 봤어요.** 보세요, 저기 얼룩진 부분이 보이네요.
남 흠... 큰 폭풍 후에 종종 이런 문제들을 겪어요. 이러한 경우에는, 먼저 윗층을 조사할 필요가 있습니다. 어쨌든 ³⁷**정확한 원인을 파악해서 수리를 받으시려면 시간이 좀 걸릴 거예요.** 괜찮으신가요?

어휘 landlord 집주인, 건물 소유주 ceiling 천장 facility 시설 damp 얼룩 patch 부분 major 중대한, 큰 examine 조사하다

35. 남자는 누구인 것 같은가?
(A) 임대인
(B) 시설 관리자
(C) 배관공
(D) 전기 기사

36. 캐롤에 따르면, 무엇이 문제인가?
(A) 몇 가지 설명이 잘못됐다.
(B) 동료가 결석했다.
(C) 그녀는 부품 몇 개를 잃어버렸다.
(D) 그녀는 물이 새는 것을 발견했다.

어휘 instruction 설명 component 부품 leak 새는 곳

37. 남자는 수리에 관해 무엇이라고 말하는가?
(A) 바로 완료될 수 없다.
(B) 특수 부품을 필요로 할 수 있다.
(C) 현재 필요하지 않다.
(D) 요금이 최근에 인상되었다.

어휘 complete 완료하다 charge 요금
패러프레이징 it will take some time → It cannot be completed right away

38-40. 🎧 영녀/미남
Questions 38-40 refer to the following conversation.

W Good morning. I saw your advertisement about open positions at your company.

M Yes, ³⁸ we're taking on more and more building projects, so we need more people to assist with that.

W Is there any previous experience required?

M No, but ³⁹ you must have completed an occupational safety certification course for the general industry. If you don't have a certificate, it's easy to obtain one.

W Can I get information about where I can take those courses?

M Actually, ⁴⁰ we're going to hold an online information session this Friday, where all your questions can be answered. Would you like me to sign you up for that?

38-40번은 다음 대화에 관한 문제입니다.
여 안녕하세요. 저는 귀사의 공석에 대한 광고를 보았습니다.
남 네, ³⁸**저희는 점점 더 많은 건설 프로젝트를 맡고 있기 때문에, 그것을 도와줄 더 많은 사람들이 필요합니다.**
여 필요한 이전 경력이 있나요?
남 아니요, 하지만 ³⁹**일반 산업을 위한 직업 안전 인증 과정을 수료하셨어야 합니다.** 증명서가 없으시다면, 쉽게 받으실 수 있습니다.
여 그 과정을 어디서 들을 수 있는지 정보를 얻을 수 있을까요?
남 사실, ⁴⁰**저희가 이번 주 금요일에 온라인 설명회를 열 예정인데,** 거기서 당신의 모든 질문에 답변을 드릴 수 있어요. 설명회에 등

록해 드릴까요?

어휘 open position 공석   assist with ~을 돕다   previous 이전의   occupational 직업의   certification 증명, 인증   certificate 증명서   obtain 획득하다

38. 남자는 어디에서 일하는 것 같은가?
(A) 관공서에서
(B) 건설 회사에서
(C) 병원에서
(D) 채용 대행사에서

39. 남자에 따르면, 지원자들은 무엇을 제공해야 하는가?
(A) 추천서
(B) 우편물 수령 주소
(C) 인증 증명서
(D) 신분증 사본

40. 금요일에 무엇이 예정되어 있는가?
(A) 설명회
(B) 면접
(C) 직원 회식
(D) 이사 회의

41-43. 🎧 미녀/호남
Questions 41-43 refer to the following conversation.

> **W** Hi, I'm interested in buying ⁴¹ the Damaro digital camera, but I'm having trouble finding it. I'm wondering if your store has any in stock.
>
> **M** It's a really popular item, so, unfortunately, we've just sold the last one.
>
> **W** That's too bad. ⁴² I'm taking pictures at an outdoor concert this weekend, and I wanted to use a new camera for that event. ⁴³ Do you know how I can get one?
>
> **M** Hmm... our system is showing that there's one left in stock at our Springdale branch. I can call them and ask them to hold it for you, if you can pick it up today.

41-43번은 다음 대화에 관한 문제입니다.
여 안녕하세요, 저는 ⁴¹ **다마로 디지털 카메라**를 사고 싶은데요, 그걸 찾기가 어렵네요. 당신의 매장에 재고가 있는지 궁금합니다.
남 그건 정말 인기 있는 상품이라서, 유감스럽게도 마지막 상품을 방금 막 팔았어요.
여 유감이네요. ⁴² **이번 주말에 야외 콘서트에서 사진을 찍을 건데,** 그 행사에 새 카메라를 사용하고 싶었어요. ⁴³ **어떻게 하면 구할 수 있는지 아시나요?**
남 흠... 저희 시스템에 스프링데일 지점에 재고가 하나 남아 있다고 나오네요. 오늘 가지러 가실 수 있으면, 제가 그곳에 전화해서 하나 남겨 달라고 요청해 드릴 수 있어요.

어휘 have trouble -ing ~하는 데 어려움이 있다   have in stock 재고가 있다

41. 화자들은 어떤 종류의 제품에 대해 이야기하고 있는가?
(A) 디지털 카메라
(B) 비디오 게임 시스템
(C) 프린터
(D) 스마트폰

42. 이번 주말에 무슨 행사가 개최될 것인가?
(A) 영화 상영회
(B) 연례 퍼레이드
(C) 음악 공연
(D) 사업 회의

패러프레이징 concert → musical performance

43. 여자는 무엇에 대해 물어보는가?
(A) 보증 기간이 얼마나 되는지
(B) 제품을 어떻게 구하는지
(C) 배송비가 얼마인지
(D) 상품을 어떻게 반품하는지

어휘 warranty 보증   return 반납하다

44-46. 🎧 미남/미녀
Questions 44-46 refer to the following conversation.

> **M** Good afternoon, Ms. Cooper. ⁴⁴ I'm here to plant the flowers and bushes that you ordered for your front garden.
>
> **W** ⁴⁵ Thanks for coming so quickly. I want to get this project started as soon as possible. I plan to put my house on the market, and I want it to look its best.
>
> **M** I understand. We'll make sure that it makes a good first impression. Now, is it alright if I leave my truck parked on the street?
>
> **W** Actually, street parking is only for residents. But ⁴⁶ I'll pull my car into the garage so you can use the driveway.
>
> **M** That's perfect. Thank you.

44-46번은 다음 대화에 관한 문제입니다.
남 안녕하세요, 쿠퍼 씨. ⁴⁴ **앞뜰을 위해 주문하신 꽃과 덤불을 심으러 왔습니다.**
여 ⁴⁵ **이렇게 빨리 와주셔서 감사해요.** 저는 이 작업을 가능한 한 빨리 시작하고 싶어요. 저는 부동산 시장에 집을 내놓을 계획이고, 집이 최상의 상태로 보이기를 원하거든요.
남 이해합니다. 저희는 반드시 이 집이 좋은 첫인상을 줄 수 있도록 할 것입니다. 이제, 제 트럭을 길에 세워 놓아도 괜찮을까요?
여 사실, 길거리 주차는 주민들만 가능해요. 하지만 당신이 진입로를 이용할 수 있도록 ⁴⁶ **제 차를 차고에 넣을게요.**
남 완벽하네요. 감사합니다.

어휘 bush 덤불   first impression 첫인상   resident 거주자   garage 차고   driveway 진입로

44. 여자는 무엇에 도움이 필요했는가?

(A) 창을 설치하는 것
(B) 차고를 짓는 것
(C) 뜰에 식물을 심는 것
(D) 나무를 베어내는 것

45. 여자는 왜 남자에게 고마워하는가?

(A) 그가 할인을 제공했다.
(B) 그가 추천을 해 주었다.
(C) 그가 절차를 설명했다.
(D) 그가 빨리 도착했다.

어휘 procedure 절차

46. 여자는 다음에 무엇을 할 것 같은가?

(A) 자신의 차를 옮기기
(B) 전원 코드 가져오기
(C) 결제하기
(D) 색상 선택하기

패러프레이징 pull my car into the garage → Move her vehicle

47-49. 🎧 호남/영녀

Questions 47-49 refer to the following conversation.

> M Thanks for calling Augusta's. How may I help you?
>
> W Hi. This is Lauren Rodriguez. ⁴⁷ You're making dinner for our office on Friday.
>
> M Oh, yes. Holt Insurance Services, right?
>
> W Yes, that's right. ⁴⁸ I'm arranging an anniversary party to commemorate twenty-five years in business.
>
> M That's wonderful. ⁴⁷ You're booked in for a delivery at 6:30 P.M. Do you need any changes?
>
> W Actually, I just found out that three of our employees are vegetarians. ⁴⁹ Would it be possible to change three of the entrees to meat-free dishes?
>
> M I was going to order everything today, so you're in luck.

47-49번은 다음 대화에 관한 문제입니다.
남 오거스타에 전화 주셔서 감사합니다. 무엇을 도와드릴까요?
여 안녕하세요. 저는 로렌 로드리게스입니다. **⁴⁷그곳에서 금요일에 저희 사무실을 위해 저녁 식사를 준비해 주실 예정이에요.**
남 아, 네. 홀트 보험사이시죠?
여 네, 맞아요. **⁴⁸창업 25주년을 기념하기 위해 제가 기념일 파티를 준비하고 있어요.**
남 정말 멋지네요. **⁴⁷오후 6시 30분에 배달이 예약되어 있습니다.** 변경이 필요하신가요?
여 사실, 저희 직원들 중 세 명이 채식주의자라는 걸 방금 알았어요.

⁴⁹3개의 메인 요리를 고기가 들어가지 않는 요리로 변경할 수 있을까요?
남 오늘 다 주문할 참이었는데요, 운이 좋으시네요.

어휘 insurance 보험(업)   commemorate 기념하다
book in 예약하다

47. 여자는 어떤 종류의 업체에 전화하고 있는가?

(A) 호텔
(B) 보험 회사
(C) 극장
(D) 출장 연회 회사

48. 여자는 왜 행사를 기획하고 있는가?

(A) 개업을 홍보하기 위해
(B) 상을 수여하기 위해
(C) 회사 기념일을 축하하기 위해
(D) 프로젝트를 위한 자금을 모으기 위해

어휘 promote 홍보하다   present 수여하다   raise funds 기금을 모으다

패러프레이징 commemorate twenty-five years in business → celebrate a company anniversary

49. 남자는 왜 "오늘 다 주문할 참이었는데요"라고 말하는가?

(A) 상기시켜준 것에 대해 여자에게 감사를 표하기 위해
(B) 요청이 이행될 수 있음을 확인해 주기 위해
(C) 마감일 변경을 수락하기 위해
(D) 지불을 요청하기 위해

어휘 reminder 상기시키는 것   fulfill 이행하다

50-52. 🎧 미남/영녀/미녀

Questions 50-52 refer to the following conversation with three speakers.

> M Joanne and Stacey, we're continually trying to make improvements to the working conditions ⁵⁰ here at our law firm. I'd like your help, since you're part of the IT team.
>
> W1 Is there anything specific you have in mind?
>
> M Well, ⁵¹ a lot of people have been complaining about the sign-in system for logging their working hours. It takes a long time to load each page. Employees say that it's frustrating.
>
> W2 I've noticed that, too. If there's room in the budget, ⁵² the company should upgrade the existing software program. That would help a lot.
>
> M Thanks, Stacey. I'll see what I can do.

50-52번은 다음 세 명의 대화에 관한 문제입니다.
남 조앤, 스테이시, 저희는 ⁵⁰**이곳 우리 법률 사무소에서** 근무 조건을 개선하려고 끊임없이 노력하고 있어요. 두 분이 IT 팀의 일원이니 여러분의 도움이 필요해요.
여1 특별히 생각하고 계신 것이 있나요?

남 음, ⁵¹많은 사람들이 근무 시간 기록을 위한 로그인 시스템에 대해 불평하고 있어요. 각 페이지를 로딩하는 데 시간이 오래 걸립니다. 직원들은 그것이 답답하다고 말해요.

여2 저도 그것을 알고 있었어요. 예산에 여유가 있다면, ⁵²회사는 기존 소프트웨어 프로그램을 업그레이드해야 합니다. 그게 도움이 많이 될 거예요.

남 고마워요, 스테이시. 제가 뭘 할 수 있는지 알아볼게요.

어휘 continually 끊임없이   make improvements 개선하다 working condition 근무 조건   log 일지에 기록하다 frustrating 답답하게 하는   existing 기존의

50. 화자들은 어디에서 일하는가?
(A) 법률 회사에서
(B) 채용 대행사에서
(C) 신문사에서
(D) 사진관에서

51. 남자는 무슨 문제를 언급하는가?
(A) 일부 장비가 누락되었다.
(B) 일부 기밀 정보가 공유되었다.
(C) 직원들이 일을 너무 많이 하고 있다.
(D) 시스템이 느리게 실행되고 있다.

어휘 confidential 기밀의

패러프레이징 It takes a long time to load each page → A system is running slowly

52. 스테이시는 회사가 무엇을 해야 한다고 생각하는가?
(A) 소프트웨어 업그레이드하기
(B) 직원들의 의견 모으기
(C) 운영 시간 변경하기
(D) 연간 보너스 제공하기

어휘 the hours of operation 운영 시간

53-55. 🎧 호남/영녀
Questions 53-55 refer to the following conversation.

> **M** Hi, Kimberly. ⁵³Thank you for your interest in working here at Lafayette. According to your résumé, you have a lot of experience cleaning guest rooms.
>
> **W** That's right. I'm currently on the housekeeping staff at the Maloy Inn. ⁵⁴I'm hoping to buy a house later this year, so I'm taking on a second job so I can save up.
>
> **M** Well, ⁵⁵the shift for this job is 7 A.M. to noon on weekdays. Can you work then? I hope it doesn't conflict with your current work schedule.
>
> **W** Not at all. I only work afternoons at the Maloy Inn.
>
> **M** That's perfect.

53-55번은 다음 대화에 관한 문제입니다.

남 안녕하세요, 킴벌리. ⁵³이곳 라파예트에서 일하는 것에 관심을 가져주셔서 감사합니다. 당신의 이력서에 따르면, 객실 청소 경험이 많으시네요.

여 맞습니다. 저는 현재 말로이 인에서 시설 관리 직원으로 일하고 있습니다. ⁵⁴저는 올해 말에 집을 사고 싶어서, 돈을 모을 수 있게 두 번째 일을 하려고 해요.

남 음, ⁵⁵이 일의 교대 근무 시간은 평일 오전 7시부터 정오까지입니다. 그때 일하실 수 있나요? 당신의 현재 업무 일정과 충돌하지 않기를 바라요.

여 전혀요. 저는 말로이 인에서 오후에만 일해요.

남 완벽하네요.

어휘 housekeeping 시설 관리과   save up (돈을) 모으다 shift 교대 근무 (시간)   conflict 충돌하다

53. 남자는 누구인 것 같은가?
(A) 선임 회계사
(B) 호텔 지배인
(C) 건물 청소부
(D) 옷가게 주인

54. 여자는 올해 말에 무엇을 하고 싶어 하는가?
(A) 새로운 도시로 이사 가기
(B) 해외여행 가기
(C) 사업 시작하기
(D) 집 구매하기

패러프레이징 buy → Purchase

55. 남자는 여자에게 무엇에 대해 물어보는가?
(A) 그녀의 직업 목표
(B) 그녀가 선호하는 시작 날짜
(C) 그녀의 시간 가능성
(D) 그녀의 예상 급여

56-58. 🎧 미녀/호남
Questions 56-58 refer to the following conversation.

> **W** ⁵⁶Have we finished all of the testing for the project along the Aimes River? I need to send the completed report by May 7.
>
> **M** ⁵⁶Yes, we've checked the environmental impact, and it seems that there will be very little disruption to wildlife in the area.
>
> **W** That's great. Unless something unexpected happens, ⁵⁷the city will approve this project by next month. Residents will be happy to finally get a walking and jogging trail.
>
> **M** I'm excited about it. ⁵⁸It'll be good for encouraging people to work out and take better care of their health.

56-58번은 다음 대화에 관한 문제입니다.

여 ⁵⁶아이메스 강을 따라 진행하는 프로젝트에 대한 모든 테스트를

마쳤나요? 저는 5월 7일까지 완성된 보고서를 보내야 합니다.

남 ⁵⁶네, 환경에 미치는 영향을 확인했는데, 그 지역의 야생 생물에게 환경이 파괴될 일은 거의 없을 거예요.

여 잘됐네요. 어떤 예기치 못한 일이 발생하지 않는 한, ⁵⁷시는 다음 달까지 이 프로젝트를 승인할 거예요. 주민들은 드디어 산책로와 조깅 코스를 갖추게 되어 기쁠 겁니다.

남 기대되네요. ⁵⁸그것은 사람들이 운동을 하고 건강을 더 잘 돌보도록 장려하는 데 좋을 거예요.

어휘 completed 완료된   environmental impact 환경에 미치는 영향   disruption 환경 파괴, 지장   wildlife 야생 생물   unexpected 예기치 못한 일   approve 승인하다   work out 운동하다

56. 화자들은 누구인 것 같은가?
(A) 환경공학자
(B) 기업 투자자
(C) 시의회 의원
(D) 건설 노동자

57. 시는 무엇을 승인할 것으로 기대되는가?
(A) 축제를 개최하는 것
(B) 보행로를 건설하는 것
(C) 주차장을 확장하는 것
(D) 경기장을 개조하는 것

어휘 pedestrian 보행자   path 길

패러프레이징 get a walking and jogging trail → Building a pedestrian path

58. 프로젝트의 어떤 이점이 언급되는가?
(A) 그것은 돈을 절약해 줄 것이다.
(B) 그것은 일자리를 창출할 것이다.
(C) 그것은 건강을 증진시킬 것이다.
(D) 그것은 관광객을 끌어들일 것이다.

어휘 promote 증진하다

59-61. 🎧 미남/영녀
Questions 59-61 refer to the following conversation.

> M ⁵⁹Sandra, our application to be one of the presenters at the Home Appliance Trade Show has been approved!
>
> W That's great news!
>
> M It really is. We were among only eight companies selected. For the event, we need to choose a recipe to demonstrate our blender.
>
> W ⁶⁰We could make a fresh fruit smoothie.
>
> M Well, everyone is familiar with that.
>
> W ⁶⁰Hmm... you're right. We should think of something new and exciting.
>
> M ⁶¹How about we go to the grocery store? Seeing the options for ingredients might inspire us.

> W ⁶¹Good idea. I have time to do that with you today after work.

59-61번은 다음 대화에 관한 문제입니다.

남 ⁵⁹산드라, 가전제품 무역 박람회의 발표자 중 한 명이 되기 위한 우리의 지원서가 승인되었어요!

여 그거 좋은 소식이네요!

남 정말 그래요. 우리는 선발된 단 8개 회사 중 하나였어요. 그 행사에서, 우리 믹서기를 시연할 레시피를 하나 선택해야 합니다.

여 ⁶⁰신선한 과일 스무디를 만들 수 있을 거예요.

남 음, 그건 모두에게 익숙해요.

여 ⁶⁰흠... 당신 말이 맞아요. 우리는 새롭고 흥미로운 무언가를 생각해야 해요.

남 ⁶¹식료품점에 가 보는 게 어때요? 재료로 선택할 수 있는 것들을 보는 게 우리에게 영감을 줄 수도 있어요.

여 ⁶¹좋은 생각이에요. 오늘 퇴근 후에 함께 그것을 할 시간이 있어요.

어휘 application 지원서   demonstrate 시연하다   ingredient 재료, 성분   inspire 영감을 주다

59. 대화는 주로 무엇에 관한 것인가?
(A) 요리책을 출간하는 것
(B) 팟캐스트를 시작하는 것
(C) 무역 박람회에서 발표하는 것
(D) 가전제품을 출시하는 것

어휘 launch 출시하다   household appliance 가전제품

60. 남자는 왜 "그건 모두에게 익숙해요"라고 말하는가?
(A) 제안을 거절하기 위해
(B) 설문조사 결과를 확인하기 위해
(C) 전략을 칭찬하기 위해
(D) 성과를 인정하기 위해

어휘 praise 칭찬하다   acknowledge 인정하다   accomplishment 성과, 업적

61. 화자들은 무엇을 하는 것에 동의하는가?
(A) 공급업체에 연락하기
(B) 함께 가게 방문하기
(C) 시연 녹화하기
(D) 웹사이트 둘러보기

어휘 browse 둘러보다

패러프레이징 go to the grocery store → Visit a shop

62-64. 🎧 호남/영녀
Questions 62-64 refer to the following conversation and list.

> M Hello. ⁶²I'm wondering if the community center offers ballet classes. My daughter is interested in joining one.
>
> W Yes, we do. You can take a look at this list of classes to see the fees.

M Alright. What day is the class?

W That depends. ⁶³Is your daughter at the beginner, intermediate, or advanced level?

M She's never done dancing before.

W Okay. Then I'd recommend the Saturday morning class. This is the registration form. ⁶⁴And, if you'd like to see some footage of past shows, there's a brief video on our Web site.

M I'll check that out.

62-64번은 다음 대화와 목록에 관한 문제입니다.

남 안녕하세요. ⁶²커뮤니티 센터에서 발레 수업을 제공하는지 궁금합니다. 제 딸이 그것에 등록하는 데 관심이 있거든요.

여 네, 합니다. 수강료를 보시려면 이 강좌 목록을 보시면 됩니다.

남 알겠습니다. 수업이 무슨 요일인가요?

여 상황에 따라 다릅니다. ⁶³따님은 초급인가요, 중급인가요, 고급인가요?

남 제 딸은 전에 무용을 해 본 적이 없어요.

여 알겠습니다. 그럼 토요일 오전 수업을 추천해 드릴게요. 이것이 신청서입니다. ⁶⁴그리고 지난 공연들의 장면을 보고 싶으시다면, 저희 웹사이트에 짧은 영상이 있습니다.

남 확인해 보겠습니다.

어휘 fee 요금, 수업료 beginner 초보자 intermediate 중급의 advanced 고급의 footage 장면

시	10달러
수채화	18달러
⁶²발레	14달러
재봉	22달러

62. 시각 자료를 보시오. 남자는 얼마를 지불할 것 같은가?
(A) 10달러
(B) 18달러
(C) 14달러
(D) 22달러

63. 여자는 어떤 정보를 요청하는가?
(A) 신용카드 번호
(B) 이메일 주소
(C) 시작일
(D) 난이도

64. 여자는 무엇을 할 것을 제안하는가?
(A) 영상을 시청하는 것
(B) 장비를 대여하는 것
(C) 특별한 옷을 입는 것
(D) 책자를 인쇄하는 것

65-67. 🎧 미녀/호남

Questions 65-67 refer to the following conversation and map.

W Hello, ⁶⁵I'm here for the lecture on economics.

M That's in the main auditorium, just to your right. The auditorium is nearly full, so I'd recommend heading straight in.

W ⁶⁶Oh, I didn't realize that so many people would be here. Could I ask you one more question?

M Of course.

W I took a taxi here, but can I get a public bus back to the Ramsey Hotel?

M Let's see... according to the map, you can take bus 47. ⁶⁷The nearest stop to your hotel is TG Pharmacy.

65-67번은 다음 대화와 지도에 관한 문제입니다.

여 안녕하세요, ⁶⁵경제학 강의를 들으러 왔습니다.

남 그건 메인 강당에서 해요, 바로 오른쪽이에요. 강당이 거의 다 찼으니, 곧장 들어가시는 것을 추천합니다.

여 ⁶⁶아, 이렇게 많은 사람들이 올 줄은 몰랐어요. 한 가지만 더 여쭤봐도 될까요?

남 물론이죠.

여 이곳에 택시를 타고 왔는데, 램지 호텔로 돌아갈 때 시내버스를 탈 수 있을까요?

남 어디 봅시다... 지도에 따르면, 47번 버스를 타실 수 있어요. ⁶⁷호텔에서 가장 가까운 정류장은 **TG 약국**입니다.

어휘 auditorium 강당

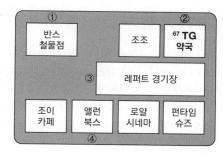

65. 여자는 왜 이 장소를 방문하고 있는가?
(A) 투자자들을 만나기 위해
(B) 점검을 하기 위해
(C) 강의를 듣기 위해
(D) 구직 면접을 보기 위해

어휘 site 장소 inspection 검사, 점검

66. 여자는 무엇에 대해 놀랐는가?
(A) 교통비
(B) 참석자 수
(C) 이동 시간
(D) 행사장 크기

어휘 transportation 교통 기관   attendee 참석자

67. 시각 자료를 보시오. 여자는 어디에서 버스를 내릴 것 같은가?

(A) 1번 정류장에서

(B) 2번 정류장에서

(C) 3번 정류장에서

(D) 4번 정류장에서

68-70. 🎧 미남/영녀

Questions 68-70 refer to the following conversation and weather forecast.

> M Hi, Ms. Chilton. [68] I'm sorry to have to bother you today. My colleague measured the property lines for your fence inaccurately, so it has to be done again.
>
> W No problem.
>
> M Thanks for understanding. [69] And it's great that you've decided to have metal instead of wood.
>
> W Yes, I think it will last longer in any kind of weather.
>
> M Speaking of the weather, my team needs a dry day to do the fence installation. [70] It's rainy now, but we'll return on the first sunny day this week.

68-70번은 다음 대화와 일기예보에 관한 문제입니다.

남 안녕하세요, 칠튼 씨. **68오늘 귀찮게 해드려서 죄송해요. 제 동료가 당신의 울타리 경계선을 잘못 측정했기 때문에 다시 해야 합니다.**

여 문제 없어요.

남 이해해 주셔서 감사해요. **69그리고 나무 대신 금속으로 하기로 결정하신 것은 잘된 일입니다.**

여 네, 어떤 날씨에도 더 오래 갈 것 같아요.

남 날씨 얘기가 나와서 말인데요, 저희 팀은 울타리 설치를 하기 위해 건조한 날이 필요합니다. **70지금은 비가 오지만, 이번 주 날이 개는 가장 빠른 날에 다시 오겠습니다.**

어휘 bother 귀찮게 하다   measure 측정하다   property line 경계선   inaccurately 부정확하게, 틀려서   last 견디다, 상하지 않다   installation 설치

	필라델피아 주간 일기예보			
월요일	화요일	**70 수요일**	목요일	금요일
비	비	**맑음**	흐림	맑음

68. 남자는 왜 사과하는가?

(A) 일부 측정을 다시 해야 한다.

(B) 작업 견적이 정확하지 않았다.

(C) 몇 가지 물품이 도착하지 않았다.

(D) 직원이 청구서를 주지 않았다.

어휘 measurement 측정   estimate 견적   bill 청구서

69. 남자는 무엇이 좋은 아이디어였다고 생각하는가?

(A) 다른 자재를 사용하는 것

(B) 다른 회사로 바꾸는 것

(C) 부동산의 가치를 평가하는 것

(D) 긴급 서비스를 요청하는 것

어휘 assess 평가하다   value 가치

70. 시각 자료를 보시오. 남자의 팀은 언제 다시 올 것 같은가?

(A) 월요일에

(B) 화요일에

(C) 수요일에

(D) 목요일에

UNIT 16 전화 메시지

PRACTICE
본문 p.81

| 1. (A) | 2. (D) | 3. (C) | 4. (C) | 5. (B) | 6. (D) |
| 7. (C) | 8. (A) | 9. (D) | | | |

1-3. 🎧 미남

Questions 1-3 refer to the following telephone message.

> **M** Hi, Sandra. I'm sorry I didn't call you back sooner. I was in Boston last week attending a medical association convention. Regarding your interview, everyone on our hiring panel was very impressed with your career history. [1,2] I would like to offer the position of healthcare assistant at our practice. Now, I realize that our job posting said the start date would be August 25. [3] However, Amar, our training coordinator, will be out of town at that time. So, that's been moved to September 1.

1-3번은 다음 전화 메시지에 관한 문제입니다.

남 샌드라, 안녕하세요. 더 일찍 전화 드리지 못해서 죄송합니다. 제가 지난주에 의사협회 총회에 참석하느라 보스턴에 있었습니다. 당신의 면접과 관련하여, 저희 채용 위원회 모두가 당신의 경력에 깊은 인상을 받았습니다. [1,2] **저희 병원의 의료 보조원 자리를 제안하고 싶습니다.** 그런데, 저희 채용 공고가 시작 날짜를 8월 25일이라고 기재했던 것을 알게 되었는데요. [3] **하지만 저희 교육 훈련 진행자인 아마르가 그때 출장을 갈 것입니다. 그래서 그것은 9월 1일로 옮겨졌습니다.**

어휘 panel 위원단 practice 개업 장소 coordinator 진행자

1. 화자는 어디에서 일하는 것 같은가?
(A) 병원에서
(B) 법률 회사에서
(C) 채용 대행사에서
(D) 소프트웨어 회사에서

2. 화자는 왜 전화하고 있는가?
(A) 청자에게 신원 보증인을 요청하기 위해
(B) 청자에게 발표를 해 달라고 요청하기 위해
(C) 면접 장소를 변경하기 위해
(D) 일자리 제안을 하기 위해

어휘 reference 신원 보증인

패러프레이징 offer the position of healthcare assistant → make a job offer

3. 지연의 이유는 무엇인가?
(A) 위원회는 회의를 해야 한다.
(B) 장소가 예약이 꽉 찼다.
(C) 직원이 부재중일 것이다.
(D) 일부 물품이 도착하지 않았다.

어휘 venue 장소

패러프레이징 out of town → unavailable

4-6. 🎧 미녀

Questions 4-6 refer to the following telephone message.

> **W** Hi, Vijay. I have some exciting news. [4] *Country Living* magazine would like to feature our bakery in the July issue. A reporter will be visiting us on Friday to interview our staff and learn more about our unique baked goods. Since you're the executive pastry chef, [5] I'll need you to stay late on Thursday to make sure everything is well organized so we can make a good impression. Unfortunately, I'm too busy to help much, as [6] I'm still planning to attend the Rockford Career Fair this weekend. Thanks.

4-6번은 다음 전화 메시지에 관한 문제입니다.

여 비제이, 안녕하세요. 신나는 소식이 있어요. [4] **'컨트리 리빙' 잡지에서 7월호에 우리 빵집을 특집으로 실으려고 합니다. 기자가 직원들을 인터뷰하고 우리의 독특한 제과류에 대해 더 알아보기 위해 금요일에 방문할 것입니다.** 당신이 총괄 제빵사니까, [5] **목요일에 늦게까지 남아서 모든 것이 잘 정리되어 좋은 인상을 줄 수 있도록 확인해 주셨으면 해요.** 안타깝게도, 저는 너무 바빠서 많은 것을 도울 수가 없어요. [6] **저는 여전히 이번 주말에 록퍼드 직업 박람회에 참석할 계획이라서요.** 감사해요.

어휘 feature (신문 따위가) ~을 특집으로 하다 issue (출판물의) 판, 호 executive 경영 간부 pastry chef 제빵사 organized 정리된 make a good impression 좋은 인상을 주다

4. 메시지는 주로 무엇에 관한 것인가?
(A) 해외 출장
(B) 신제품 출시
(C) 잡지 인터뷰
(D) 사업체 이전

어휘 launch 출시 relocation 이전

5. 화자는 청자에게 목요일에 무엇을 해 달라고 요청하는가?
(A) 계약서 서명하기
(B) 평소보다 늦게까지 일하기
(C) 추가 제품 굽기
(D) 저녁 식사 예약하기

패러프레이징 stay late → Work later than usual

6. 화자는 이번 주말에 어디에 갈 것인가?

(A) 교육 워크숍에

(B) 이사 회의에

(C) 음악 축제에

(D) 취업 박람회에

패러프레이징 Career Fair → job fair

7-9. 🎧 호남

Questions 7-9 refer to the following recorded message.

> M ⁷Thank you for calling Westlake Bus Services. Due to the severe storm in the area, several of our journeys have been delayed. We are very sorry for any inconvenience this may cause. ⁸We will confirm the new schedule for the departure times as soon as we can. However, at this time, we are monitoring the situation. ⁹For the most updated details about our services, we ask that you visit our Web site.

7-9번은 다음 녹음 메시지에 관한 문제입니다.

남 ⁷웨스트레이크 버스 회사에 전화해 주셔서 감사합니다. 지역 내 심한 폭풍 때문에, 몇몇 버스편이 지연되었습니다. 이로 인한 불편에 대단히 죄송합니다. ⁸저희는 가능한 한 빨리 출발 시각에 대한 새로운 일정표를 확정할 것입니다. 하지만 현재로서는, 상황을 주시하고 있습니다. ⁹당사 서비스에 대한 최신 정보를 보시려면, 저희 웹사이트를 방문하실 것을 요청 드립니다.

어휘 severe 심한 journey 여정, 이동 inconvenience 불편 monitor 감시하다

7. 청자는 어떤 종류의 업체에 전화하고 있는가?

(A) 자동차 수리점

(B) 전력 공급 업체

(C) 운수 회사

(D) 가전제품점

패러프레이징 Bus Services → A transportation company

8. 화자는 "상황을 주시하고 있습니다"라고 말할 때 무엇을 암시하는가?

(A) 출발 일정이 불확실하다.

(B) 불만이 제기될 것이다.

(C) 고객 피드백이 평가될 것이다.

(D) 새로운 정책이 채택되었다.

어휘 uncertain 불확실한 file 제기하다 assess 평가하다, 재다 adopt 채택하다

9. 청자는 어떻게 최신 정보를 얻을 수 있는가?

(A) 운전사와 이야기함으로써

(B) 소식지 수신을 신청함으로써

(C) 이메일을 보냄으로써

(D) 온라인으로 정보를 확인함으로써

UNIT 17 공지·안내

PRACTICE 본문 p.83

1. (A)	**2.** (A)	**3.** (B)	**4.** (D)	**5.** (B)	**6.** (C)
7. (D)	**8.** (B)	**9.** (A)			

1-3. 🎧 미녀

Questions 1-3 refer to the following announcement.

> W Attention, customers. ¹Thank you for shopping at Highland Apparel. Today's special is 20% off all leather jackets. And don't forget to register for our new loyalty rewards program. ²Each month, we offer one accessory at no charge to members of the program. So, don't miss out. Also, ³please be aware that we're going to carry out some building work at the rear of the store to expand our display space. We'll be starting that project next Monday.

1-3번은 다음 공지에 관한 문제입니다.

여 고객 여러분, 주목해 주세요. ¹하이랜드 어패럴에서 쇼핑해 주셔서 감사합니다. 오늘의 특가로 모든 가죽 재킷을 20% 할인해 드립니다. 저희의 새로운 고객 보상 프로그램에 등록하는 것도 잊지 마십시오. ²매달, 저희는 프로그램 회원들에게 무료로 액세서리를 하나씩 제공합니다. 그러니 놓치지 마세요. 또한, ³진열 공간을 확장하기 위해 매장 뒤쪽에서 일부 건물 공사를 진행할 예정이니 유의하시기 바랍니다. 저희는 다음 주 월요일에 그 작업을 시작할 것입니다.

어휘 at no charge 무료로 carry out 수행하다 rear 뒤쪽

1. 청자들은 어디에 있는 것 같은가?

(A) 옷가게에

(B) 철물점에

(C) 전자제품점에

(D) 서점에

2. 화자는 고객 보상 프로그램 회원들에게 무엇이 제공된다고 말하는가?

(A) 무료 품목

(B) 할인 쿠폰

(C) 빠른 배송

(D) 세일 사전 안내

어휘 advance 사전의

패러프레이징 one accessory at no charge → A free item

3. 다음 주 월요일에 무엇이 시작될 것인가?

(A) 영업 시간 연장

(B) 일부 공사

(C) 기념일 행사

(D) 재고 정리 세일

어휘 extended 연장된

4-6. 🎧 미남

Questions 4-6 refer to the following excerpt from a meeting.

> **M** ⁴Next Friday, Dixon Furniture will deliver three leather sofas that we will place in our employee lounge. ⁵Research has shown that taking breaks regularly can improve productivity significantly. So, we are doing our best to provide a relaxing space for our staff. We'll also be replacing everyone's office chair. If you'd like to see the options that are available, ⁶please take a look at the product catalog at the reception desk. The ones that are within our budget will be marked with a star.

4-6번은 다음 회의 발췌록에 관한 문제입니다.

남 ⁴다음 주 금요일에, 딕슨 가구사에서 우리 직원 휴게실에 비치할 가죽 소파 세 개를 배달할 예정입니다. ⁵정기적으로 휴식을 취하는 것이 생산성을 크게 향상시킬 수 있다는 연구 결과가 나왔습니다. 그래서 우리는 직원들에게 휴식 공간을 제공하기 위해 최선을 다하고 있습니다. 우리는 사무용 의자도 전부 교체할 예정입니다. 선택할 수 있는 옵션을 보려면, ⁶접수처에서 제품 카탈로그를 확인하세요. 예산 내에 있는 것들은 별 표시가 되어 있을 겁니다.

어휘 place 놓다, 두다   productivity 생산성   significantly 상당히   take a look at ~을 보다   mark 표시하다

4. 다음 주 금요일에 무엇이 배달될 것인가?
(A) 명함
(B) 화분
(C) 가벼운 다과
(D) 가죽 소파

5. 생산성에 대해 무엇이 언급되는가?
(A) 최근에 사무실에서 개선되었다.
(B) 규칙적인 휴식을 통해 증가할 수 있다.
(C) 더 높은 수익을 낳는다.
(D) 새로운 경영진의 주안점이다.

어휘 result in ~을 낳다   profits 이익, 수익

6. 화자에 따르면, 접수처에서 무엇을 이용할 수 있는가?
(A) 계약서
(B) 설문지 양식
(C) 카탈로그
(D) 업데이트된 일정

7-9. 🎧 영녀

Questions 7-9 refer to the following excerpt from a meeting and pie chart.

> **W** Good afternoon, everyone. ⁷Welcome to our monthly gardening club meeting. Last time, I gave you a list of topics related to gardening and asked you to select which ones you would like to learn more about. You can see the results here. I'm still working on finding a speaker for a workshop on the most requested topic, Seasonal Planning. ⁸So, in the meantime, we'll hold a workshop on the second most requested topic. That'll take place on August 10. I'll send some information about that later this week, so ⁹please be sure to update the e-mail address and phone number we have for you.

7-9번은 다음 회의 발췌록과 원그래프에 관한 문제입니다.

여 여러분 안녕하세요. ⁷원예 클럽 월간 모임에 오신 것을 환영합니다. 지난번에, 제가 여러분에게 정원 가꾸기와 관련된 주제들 목록을 드리고 여러분이 어떤 것에 대해 더 배우고 싶은지 선택해 달라고 요청드렸죠. 여기서 그 결과를 확인하실 수 있습니다. 저는 가장 많이 요청 받은 주제인 계절별 계획에 대한 워크숍의 발표자를 아직 구하는 중입니다. ⁸그래서, 우선은 두 번째로 요청이 많았던 주제로 워크숍을 진행하도록 하겠습니다. 그것은 8월 10일에 열릴 것입니다. 제가 이번 주 후반에 그것에 대한 정보를 보내드릴 테니, ⁹저희가 가지고 있는 여러분의 이메일 주소와 전화번호를 꼭 업데이트해 주세요.

어휘 requested 요청된

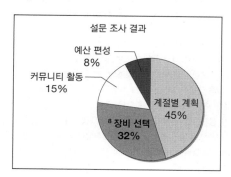

7. 청자들은 어떤 종류의 클럽 회원인가?
(A) 그림 그리기
(B) 바느질
(C) 자전거 타기
(D) 원예

8. 시각 자료를 보시오. 화자에 따르면, 어떤 워크숍이 가장 먼저 열릴 것 같은가?
(A) 계절별 계획
(B) 장비 선택
(C) 커뮤니티 활동
(D) 예산 편성

9. 화자는 청자들에게 무엇을 해 달라고 요청하는가?
(A) 연락처 정보 업데이트하기
(B) 워크숍 장소 추천하기
(C) 설문 조사 답변에 대해 설명하기
(D) 신규 회원 모집하기

어휘 recruit 모집하다

패러프레이징 the e-mail address and phone number → some contact information

UNIT 18 연설·강연

PRACTICE 본문 p.85

1. (B) **2.** (A) **3.** (B) **4.** (A) **5.** (C) **6.** (B)
7. (C) **8.** (D) **9.** (A)

1-3. 🎧 미남

Questions 1-3 refer to the following speech.

M ¹Before the benefit concert begins, I want to thank everyone for the support you have given to the Stonebrooke Community Center. ²I'm sure you're all aware that our building has been in need of a new roof for a long time. We've raised about half the money we need for the replacement, but there's still more to be done. After the show, ³I want to encourage you to purchase our community center T-shirts and sweatshirts. Profits from those sales will go toward the project. Thank you!

1-3번은 다음 연설에 관한 문제입니다.
남 ¹자선 콘서트가 시작되기 전에, 스톤브룩 커뮤니티 센터에 여러분이 보내주신 지원에 대해 모든 분들께 감사드리고 싶습니다. ²저희 건물은 오랫동안 새 지붕이 필요했다는 것을 여러분 모두 알고 계실 것이라 확신합니다. 저희는 교체에 필요한 자금의 절반 정도를 마련했지만, 아직 더 필요합니다. 공연이 끝난 후에, ³저희 커뮤니티 센터 티셔츠와 맨투맨을 구매하는 것을 권해 드리고 싶습니다. 판매 수익은 이 프로젝트에 쓰일 것입니다. 감사합니다!

어휘 benefit 자선 공연 support 지지, 도움 aware 알고 있는 in need of ~을 필요로 하는 replacement 교체 go toward ~에 도움되다

1. 무슨 행사가 일어나고 있는가?
(A) 예술제
(B) 자선 모금 행사
(C) 음악 수업
(D) 제빵 대회

패러프레이징 the benefit concert → A fund-raising event

2. 이 단체에서는 무엇을 할 계획인가?
(A) 지붕 교체하기
(B) 자원봉사자 교육하기
(C) 영업 시간 변경하기
(D) 온라인 서비스 제공하기

3. 화자는 청자들에게 무엇을 하라고 권하는가?
(A) 발표 시청하기
(B) 의류 구매하기
(C) 다과 즐기기
(D) 곧 다시 오기

패러프레이징 T-shirts and sweatshirts → clothing

4-6. 🎧 미녀

Questions 4-6 refer to the following talk.

W Hello, and welcome to today's panel discussion. My name is Esther Yang, and ⁴I'm a senior associate here at the Ministry of Education. I'm delighted to be moderating this debate on the use of technology to track performance. ⁵We're excited about hearing from our four debate participants. We chose them because they are well known as specialists in their field. I'm sure you'll find their insights to be fascinating. Now, before we begin, ⁶I see that some of you have pens and paper out. Just so you know, this session will be recorded.

4-6번은 다음 담화에 관한 문제입니다.
여 안녕하세요. 오늘 공개 토론회에 오신 것을 환영합니다. 제 이름은 양에스더이고, ⁴저는 이곳 교육부의 수석 부관입니다. 저는 성과를 추적하기 위한 기술의 사용에 대한 이 토론의 사회를 보게 되어 기쁩니다. ⁵우리는 네 명의 토론 참가자들로부터 발언을 듣는 것이 기대됩니다. 그들이 자신의 분야에서 전문가로 잘 알려져 있기 때문에 우리는 그들을 선발했습니다. 저는 여러분이 그들의 통찰력이 대단히 흥미롭다는 것을 알게 될 것이라 확신합니다. 자, 시작하기 전에, ⁶여러분 중 몇 분이 펜과 종이를 꺼내 놓으신 게 보이는데요. 참고로 말씀드리자면, 이 세션은 녹화될 것입니다.

어휘 panel discussion 공개 토론회 moderate 조정하다, 사회를 보다 track 추적하다 insight 통찰력 fascinating 대단히 흥미로운, 매력적인

4. 화자는 누구인가?
(A) 공무원
(B) 대학 교수
(C) 교과서 편집자
(D) 소프트웨어 전문가

패러프레이징 a senior associate here at the Ministry of Education → A government employee

5. 화자에 따르면, 특정한 토론 참가자들이 왜 선발되었는가?
(A) 그들은 최근에 책을 출판했다.
(B) 그들은 다른 나라에서 왔다.
(C) 그들은 전문가로 여겨진다.
(D) 그들은 사업을 시작했다.

패러프레이징 they are well known as specialists in their field → They are considered to be experts

6. 화자는 "이 세션은 녹화될 것입니다"라고 말할 때 무엇을 암시하는가?
(A) 질문은 마지막에 답변될 것이다.
(B) 필기할 필요가 없다.
(C) 휴대폰은 치워 두어야 한다.
(D) 청중들은 자리에 앉아 있어야 한다.

7-9. 🎧 영녀
Questions 7-9 refer to the following speech.

> **W** Good morning. I'm your instructor, Abigail Lambert, and I've been a financial planner for the past fifteen years. ⁷Today, I'll share my tips and tricks to help you prepare for your retirement and ensure that you are financially secure. ⁸I'd like to thank those participants who wrote down their questions and submitted them to me before the workshop. I'll address as many of them as possible. Now, before we get started, ⁹I want to make sure that all of you have the seminar handouts. If you haven't picked them up yet, they're on the table near the side entrance.

7-9번은 다음 연설에 관한 문제입니다.
여 안녕하세요. 저는 여러분의 강사 애비게일 램버트이고, 지난 15년간 재무설계사로 일해왔습니다. ⁷오늘, 저는 여러분이 은퇴를 준비하고 경제적으로 안정될 수 있도록 보장하는 데 도움이 될 조언과 요령을 공유하겠습니다. ⁸워크숍 전에 질문을 적어 저에게 제출해 주신 참가자분들께 감사드리고 싶습니다. 저는 그 질문들을 가능한 한 많이 다룰 것입니다. 자, 시작하기 전에 ⁹여러분 모두 세미나 유인물을 가지고 계시는지 확인하고 싶습니다. 아직 안 가져오셨다면, 옆문 근처 테이블 위에 있습니다.

어휘 financial planner 재무설계사   trick 요령   ensure 보장하다   secure 안정된   address 다루다, 처리하다

7. 세미나의 주제는 무엇인가?
(A) 시간 절약 방법
(B) 의사소통 기술
(C) 은퇴 계획
(D) 구직 활동

8. 화자는 왜 일부 청자들에게 고마워하는가?
(A) 그들은 등록을 일찍 했다.
(B) 그들은 자리를 바꿨다.
(C) 그들은 방을 준비했다.
(D) 그들은 질문을 제출했다.

어휘 register 등록하다

9. 화자는 왜 옆문을 언급하는가?
(A) 행사 자료를 그곳에서 찾을 수 있다.
(B) 그것은 세미나 내내 잠겨 있을 것이다.
(C) 참가자들은 그곳에서 음료를 이용할 수 있다.
(D) 그것은 비상시에 사용할 수 있다.

어휘 in case of emergency 비상시에

UNIT 19 광고·방송

PRACTICE 본문 p.87

1. (B)	**2.** (A)	**3.** (D)	**4.** (D)	**5.** (A)	**6.** (C)
7. (C)	**8.** (B)	**9.** (B)			

1-3. 🎧 미남
Questions 1-3 refer to the following advertisement.

> **M** At Sure-Tech Assistants, we're proud to serve the Omaha community. ¹We offer fast and affordable computer upgrades and repairs. Our technicians have a lot of experience, and they carefully listen to customers to fully understand their needs. ²For the third consecutive year, the Omaha Business Bureau has nominated us for the Best Customer Service Award. And to celebrate, we're offering 15% off all automated data backup packages, our newest service. ³To get this deal, you must schedule an appointment either by phone or online. Call us today at 555-2899 for more information.

1-3번은 다음 광고에 관한 문제입니다.
남 우리 슈어테크 어시스턴스는 오마하 지역 사회에 서비스를 제공하는 것을 자랑스럽게 생각합니다. ¹우리는 빠르고 저렴한 컴퓨터 업그레이드 및 수리를 제공합니다. 우리 기술자들은 경험이 풍부하고, 고객의 요구를 완전히 이해하기 위해 고객의 말을 경청합니다. ²오마하 상업 협회에서는 3년 연속으로 우리를 최고의 고객 서비스 상 후보에 올렸습니다. 그래서 이를 축하하기 위해, 우리의 신규 서비스인 모든 자동화 데이터 백업 패키지를 15% 할인된 가격으로 제공합니다. ³이 혜택을 받으시려면, 전화나 온라인으로 예약 일정을 잡으셔야 합니다. 더 알아보시려면 오늘 555-2899로 전화 주십시오.

어휘 serve (서비스를) 제공하다   affordable 가격이 적당한   consecutive 연이은   nominate (후보자로) 지명하다   automated 자동화된, 자동의

1. 어떤 종류의 사업체가 광고되고 있는가?
(A) 채용 대행사
(B) 컴퓨터 수리점
(C) 건강 관리 클리닉
(D) 렌터카 업체

2. 사업체는 왜 축하하고 있는가?
(A) 그곳은 수상 후보에 올랐다.
(B) 그곳은 새로운 지점을 열 것이다.
(C) 그곳은 20년 동안 영업을 해왔다.
(D) 그곳은 경쟁사를 인수했다.

어휘 acquire 취득하다, 매입하다

3. 청자들은 할인을 받으려면 무엇을 해야 하는가?
(A) 대면 행사에 참석하기
(B) 소식지 수신 신청하기
(C) 설문 조사 완료하기
(D) 예약하기

4-6. 🎧 미녀
Questions 4-6 refer to the following podcast.

> **W** Welcome to this week's episode of my podcast, *Taking Control*, ⁴where you'll get your weekly inspiration on preparing the right food for your nutritional needs. Today, I'll interview Maya Dalavi. ⁵Ms. Dalavi is a registered nurse who has just launched her own Web site with special meal plans to help individuals reach certain goals. We'll discuss her methods and the research behind them. Also, ⁶if you haven't signed up as a member of my podcast yet, please consider doing so. You'll receive exclusive content every week.

4-6번은 다음 팟캐스트에 관한 문제입니다.

여 저의 팟캐스트 '테이킹 컨트롤'의 이번 주 에피소드에 오신 것을 환영합니다. ⁴여기서 여러분은 매주 여러분의 영양 요구에 맞는 음식 준비에 대한 영감을 얻을 것입니다. 오늘은 마야 달라비를 인터뷰하겠습니다. ⁵달라비 씨는 공인 간호사로, 개인이 특정 목표를 달성하도록 돕는 특별한 식단을 소재로 자신의 웹사이트를 개설했습니다. 우리는 그 뒤에 숨겨진 그녀의 방식과 연구에 대해 이야기할 것입니다. 또한, ⁶여러분이 아직 제 팟캐스트에 회원가입을 하지 않으셨다면, 가입을 고려해보시기 바랍니다. 여러분은 매주 독점 콘텐츠를 받으실 수 있습니다.

어휘 inspiration 영감 nutritional 영양상의 need 필요, 요구 registered 공인된 individual 개인 exclusive 독점적인

4. 팟캐스트는 주로 무엇에 관한 것인가?
(A) 직업 변경
(B) 글쓰기 기술
(C) 의학적 발견
(D) 영양 조언

어휘 breakthrough 발전, 발견 nutrition 영양

5. 마야 달라비는 최근에 무엇을 했는가?
(A) 그녀는 웹사이트를 개설했다.
(B) 그녀는 수업을 했다.
(C) 그녀는 대회에서 우승했다.
(D) 그녀는 잡지 기사를 냈다.

패러프레이징 launched → started

6. 화자는 팟캐스트 멤버십에 대해 무엇이라고 말하는가?
(A) 그것은 언제든지 취소할 수 있다.
(B) 그것은 매달 요금이 부과된다.
(C) 그것은 추가 혜택을 제공한다.
(D) 그것은 신규 직원 채용에 도움이 된다.

7-9. 🎧 호남
Questions 7-9 refer to the following broadcast and map.

> **M** ⁷In local news, the city broke ground on the new Kembery Sports Arena yesterday. The designs show that the structure will have space for two cafés, a souvenir shop, and administrative offices. There will also be a seating capacity of eight thousand spectators, more than the original plan of six thousand. ⁸This is thanks to a generous donation of two thousand padded seats from Braun Manufacturing. Although on-site parking will be available at the arena, a new bus stop will be added to encourage the use of public transportation. ⁹It will be at the intersection of Rose Avenue and Huntz Street. A map of the area can be found online.

7-9번은 다음 방송과 지도에 관한 문제입니다.

남 ⁷지역 뉴스입니다. 시에서 어제 새로운 켐베리 스포츠 경기장 공사를 시작했습니다. 설계상 이 구조물에는 카페 두 개, 기념품점, 그리고 행정 사무실을 위한 공간이 들어서게 됩니다. 또한 원래 계획했던 6천 명보다 많은 8천 명의 관중을 수용할 수 있을 것입니다. ⁸이는 브라운 제조사로부터 2천 개의 패딩 시트에 대한 후한 기증이 이루어진 덕입니다. 경기장에는 현장 주차가 가능할 것이지만, 대중교통 이용을 장려하기 위해 버스 정류장이 새로이 추가될 예정입니다. ⁹그것은 로즈 가와 헌츠 가의 교차로에 생길 것입니다. 그 지역의 지도는 온라인에서 찾을 수 있습니다.

어휘 break ground 공사를 시작하다 structure 구조물 seating capacity 수용 능력 generous 후한, 관대한 on-site 현장의 intersection 교차로

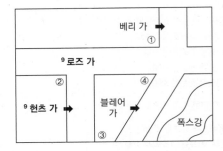

7. 방송은 주로 무엇에 관한 것인가?
(A) 도로 보수
(B) 백화점 개점

(C) 스포츠 시설 공사

(D) 다가오는 퍼레이드 경로

어휘 route 경로, 노선

8. 한 회사에서 무엇을 기증했는가?

(A) 그림

(B) 시트

(C) 목재

(D) 기계

9. 시각 자료를 보시오. 버스 정류장은 어디에 위치할 것인가?

(A) 1번 장소

(B) 2번 장소

(C) 3번 장소

(D) 4번 장소

UNIT 20 관광·견학

PRACTICE
본문 p.89

1. (A)	**2.** (D)	**3.** (B)	**4.** (D)	**5.** (A)	**6.** (C)
7. (B)	**8.** (D)	**9.** (C)			

1-3. 🎧 미녀

Questions 1-3 refer to the following talk.

> **W** ¹Thanks again for joining me on today's tour of the Darcy Ceramics Studio. I hope you enjoyed learning more about the process of making ceramics by hand. This concludes the main part of the tour, but you are welcome to explore the site on your own, especially our gift shop. ²And don't forget that we will be screening a short documentary about ancient pottery at three o'clock in our lecture hall. It is free to attend. One of our employees, Ashley Mendoza, will answer questions afterward. She is very knowledgeable, as ³she just published her second book about the topic, entitled *The First Step*.

1-3번은 다음 담화에 관한 문제입니다.

여 ¹오늘 달시 도자기 스튜디오 투어에 저와 함께해 주셔서 다시 한 번 감사드립니다. 손으로 도자기를 만드는 과정에 대해 더 많이 배우는 것이 즐거우셨기를 바랍니다. 이것으로 투어의 주요 부분을 마치지만, 여러분이 직접 현장, 특히 저희 기념품점을 둘러보시는 것을 환영합니다. ²그리고 저희가 3시에 강의실에서 고대 도자기에 관한 짧은 다큐멘터리를 상영한다는 것을 잊지 마세요. 참석은 무료입니다. 그 후에 저희 직원 중 한 명인 애슐리 멘도자가 질문에 답할 것입니다. 그녀는 매우 박식한데요, ³그 주제에 대한 두 번째 책인 '첫걸음'이라는 제목의 책을 이제 막 출판했습니다.

어휘 ceramics 도자기류   conclude 끝내다   explore 답사하

다   screen 상영하다   pottery 도자기   knowledgeable 아는 것이 많은   entitled ~라는 제목의

1. 화자는 누구인 것 같은가?

(A) 투어 가이드

(B) 영화감독

(C) 매장 관리자

(D) 미술 평론가

2. 3시에 무슨 일이 일어날 것인가?

(A) 가수들이 공연을 할 것이다.

(B) 약간의 음식이 제공될 것이다.

(C) 가게가 문을 닫을 것이다.

(D) 영상이 상영될 것이다.

패러프레이징 we will be screening a short documentary → A video will be shown

3. '첫걸음'은 무엇인가?

(A) 동호회

(B) 책

(C) 팟캐스트

(D) 연극

4-6. 🎧 미남

Questions 4-6 refer to the following tour information.

> **M** Welcome to Hamilton Manor. This is one of the most popular tourist attractions in the area. ⁴Hamilton Manor is best known for having the country's largest private collection of watercolor paintings, most of which you can see on display today. ⁵Like many visitors before you, I'm sure you'll want to make a wish at the stone fountain by tossing in a coin. You can find the fountain in the East Garden. ⁶We'll stop here for about an hour, after which time you should return to the bus. That way, we can leave on time for our next stop.

4-6번은 다음 관광 정보에 관한 문제입니다.

남 해밀턴 저택에 오신 것을 환영합니다. 이곳은 지역에서 가장 인기 있는 관광 명소 중 하나입니다. ⁴해밀턴 저택에는 국내에서 가장 많은 개인 소장 수채화가 있는 것으로 제일 잘 알려져 있는데요, 그중 대부분은 오늘 여러분이 전시품으로 관람하실 수 있습니다. ⁵이전의 많은 방문객들처럼, 분명히 여러분도 동전을 던지며 석조 분수에서 소원을 빌고 싶으실텐데요. 분수는 동쪽 정원에서 찾을 수 있습니다. ⁶우리는 여기서 한 시간 정도 정차할 것이고, 그 시간 후에 여러분은 버스로 돌아가셔야 합니다. 그렇게 해야 우리는 다음 목적지로 늦지 않게 출발할 수 있어요.

어휘 attraction 관광 명소   watercolor painting 수채화   on display 전시된   make a wish 소원을 빌다   fountain 분수   toss 던지다

4. 해밀턴 저택은 왜 유명한가?

(A) 그곳은 영화 촬영지였다.

(B) 그곳은 저명한 건축가에 의해 설계되었다.

(C) 그곳은 인기 있는 축제의 장소이다.

(D) 그곳에는 광범위한 미술품이 소장되어 있다.

어휘 filming location 영화 촬영지 prominent 저명한
extensive 광범위한

패러프레이징 the country's largest private collection of
watercolor paintings → an extensive art collection

5. 화자에 따르면, 방문객들은 해밀턴 저택에서 무엇을 하기를 좋아하는가?

(A) 소원 빌기

(B) 음식 먹어보기

(C) 수영하기

(D) 꽃 따기

6. 청자들은 한 시간 후에 무엇을 하라고 요청 받는가?

(A) 단체 사진 찍기

(B) 공연 참석하기

(C) 버스에 다시 타기

(D) 카페에서 만나기

패러프레이징 return to the bus → Get back on the bus

7-9. 🎧 영녀

Questions 7-9 refer to the following tour information.

> **W** ⁷Welcome to Vista Nature Park. It's my
> pleasure to lead you through the region's most
> diverse collection of plants and wildlife. We've
> made significant improvements to the hiking
> trails in the park, ⁸a project that was funded by
> local business owner Annette Harvey. She
> loves being in nature and wanted to make sure
> everyone could enjoy this beautiful site for
> many years to come. ⁹I know that some of you
> were worried about the recent mudslides due
> to the heavy rains. It's true that these can pose
> a risk, but that area is closed to visitors. If
> everyone's ready, let's get started.

7-9번은 다음 관광 정보에 관한 문제입니다.

여 ⁷**비스타 자연공원에 오신 것을 환영합니다.** 이 지역에서 가장 다양한 식물 및 야생 생물의 집합체를 안내하게 되어 기쁩니다. 저희는 ⁸**지역 사업주인 아네트 하비가 자금을 지원한 프로젝트로서** 공원 내 등산로를 크게 개선했습니다. 그녀는 자연 속에 있는 것을 아주 좋아하며 앞으로 수년 동안 모두가 이 아름다운 장소를 즐길 수 있도록 하고 싶어 했습니다. ⁹**여러분 중 몇 분이 폭우로 인한 최근의 산사태에 대해 걱정하셨다는 것을 알고 있습니다.** 이것이 위험을 초래할 수 있는 것은 사실이지만, 그 지역은 방문객들에게 폐쇄되어 있습니다. 다들 준비되셨으면, 시작해 봅시다.

어휘 diverse 다양한 wildlife 야생 생물 hiking trail 등산로

fund 자금을 대다 mudslide 산사태 pose 불러일으키다
risk 위험

7. 관광은 어디에서 일어나는가?

(A) 제조 시설에서

(B) 자연공원에서

(C) 공연장에서

(D) 쇼핑센터에서

8. 아네트 하비는 무엇을 했는가?

(A) 그녀는 다리를 건설했다.

(B) 그녀는 광고를 촬영했다.

(C) 그녀는 건물을 설계했다.

(D) 그녀는 돈을 기부했다.

어휘 commercial 광고

9. 화자는 "그 지역은 방문객들에게 폐쇄되어 있습니다"라고 말할 때 무엇을 의미하는가?

(A) 관광이 평소보다 짧을 것이다.

(B) 부분 환불이 될 것이다.

(C) 청자들은 걱정하지 않아도 된다.

(D) 표지판을 따라야 한다.

어휘 partial 부분적인 issue 발부[지급]하다

PART TEST				본문 p.90
71. (C)	**72.** (B)	**73.** (A)	**74.** (A)	**75.** (C)
76. (D)	**77.** (A)	**78.** (B)	**79.** (C)	**80.** (D)
81. (B)	**82.** (C)	**83.** (C)	**84.** (B)	**85.** (A)
86. (B)	**87.** (A)	**88.** (A)	**89.** (D)	**90.** (A)
91. (C)	**92.** (C)	**93.** (D)	**94.** (D)	**95.** (C)
96. (D)	**97.** (B)	**98.** (A)	**99.** (C)	**100.** (D)

71-73. 🎧 영녀

Questions 71-73 refer to the following advertisement.

> **W** Do you love playing sports and keeping
> active? ⁷¹Parker Sporting Goods has a great
> selection of equipment for athletes. We're
> conveniently located in the Finwood Mall, with
> an outdoor entrance on Snyder Street. Our
> prices can't be beat, and ⁷²we even offer a ten
> percent discount to anyone with a Parker Gold
> Card, as we appreciate their continued
> patronage. Our staff is highly knowledgeable.
> That's why ⁷³we're famous for offering useful
> guidance about the right equipment to buy.
> Stop by today. We're open daily from 9 A.M.
> to 9 P.M.

71-73번은 다음 광고에 관한 문제입니다.

여 스포츠를 하고 활동적으로 지내는 것을 좋아하시나요? ⁷¹**파커 스포츠 용품점은** 운동하는 사람들을 위한 다양한 장비를 갖추고

있습니다. 저희는 스나이더 가로 나가는 야외 출입구가 있는 핀우드 몰에 위치해 있어 편리합니다. 저희의 가격은 견줄 데가 없고, 지속적인 애용에 대한 감사의 표시로 ⁷²파커 골드 카드를 가지고 계신 분들께는 10% 할인까지 제공합니다. 저희 직원들은 지식이 아주 풍부합니다. 그렇기 때문에 ⁷³저희는 적합한 장비를 구매하는 데 유용한 안내를 제공하는 것으로 유명합니다. 오늘 들러 보세요. 매일 오전 9시부터 오후 9시까지 영업합니다.

어휘 athlete 운동선수   appreciate 고맙게 여기다
continued 지속적인   patronage 애용, 후원   guidance 안내, 지침

71. 어떤 종류의 업체가 광고되고 있는가?
(A) 렌터카 회사
(B) 댄스 스튜디오
(C) 스포츠 용품점
(D) 원예 용품점

72. 광고에 따르면, 누가 할인을 받을 수 있는가?
(A) 사업주
(B) 카드 소지자
(C) 자선 사업가
(D) 대학생

73. 이 사업체는 무엇으로 알려져 있는가?
(A) 도움이 되는 조언
(B) 넓은 시설
(C) 많은 지점
(D) 현대적인 웹사이트

어휘 numerous 많은

패러프레이징 useful guidance → helpful advice

74-76. 🎧 미남
Questions 74-76 refer to the following telephone message.

> M Hi, Ms. Evans. ⁷⁴This is Leon from the Melville Tower property management office. As you requested, I've arranged for a crew to replace the carpet in your bedroom. ⁷⁵The thing is, you'll have to remove everything from the room before their visit. <mark>I'm sure it's full of furniture</mark>, so I hope you understand. The crew may be able to assist with large items. ⁷⁶Please call me back at 555-4982 to let me know which day this week would work best for you. Thanks.

74-76번은 다음 전화 메시지에 관한 문제입니다.
남 안녕하세요, 에반스 씨. ⁷⁴멜빌 타워 건물 관리사무소의 레온입니다. 요청하셨던 대로, 당신의 침실에 있는 카펫을 교체할 작업자들을 배치했습니다. ⁷⁵문제는, 그들이 방문하기 전에 방에서 모든 것을 치워 놓아야 한다는 것입니다. <mark>분명히 가구로 가득 차 있을 텐데,</mark> 이해해 주시길 바랍니다. 큰 물건은 작업자들이 도와줄 수 있을지도 모릅니다. ⁷⁶555-4982로 다시 전화하셔서 이번 주 중 어떤 요일이 가장 좋으실지 알려 주시기 바랍니다. 감사

합니다.

어휘 management office 관리사무소   assist with ~을 돕다

74. 화자는 누구인가?
(A) 건물 관리자
(B) 부동산 중개인
(C) 안전 검사관
(D) 건설 노동자

75. 화자는 "분명히 가구로 가득 차 있을 텐데"라고 말할 때 무엇을 암시하는가?
(A) 입구가 차단될 수도 있다.
(B) 보관 공간은 아마 사용 중일 것이다.
(C) 작업을 완료하는 것이 어려울 수 있다.
(D) 스타일을 선택하는 데 시간이 걸릴 것이다.

어휘 block 막다   storage 보관, 저장

76. 청자는 왜 화자에게 다시 전화해야 하는가?
(A) 보증금을 지불하기 위해
(B) 색상을 확정하기 위해
(C) 증명서를 주기 위해
(D) 편리한 날짜를 선택하기 위해

어휘 deposit 보증금   reference 증명서, 보증서
convenient 편리한

77-79. 🎧 호남
Questions 77-79 refer to the following talk.

> M Good morning, and welcome to Hana Beverages. ⁷⁷We've asked you here today to try our new line of herbal teas. There are some feedback forms that you can use to review our products, and we ask that you be as detailed as possible in your comments. Of course, we're excited about the delicious taste of our tea. ⁷⁸We're also proud of how we use significantly less packaging than other brands, hardly any at all. We'll begin in just a few minutes. ⁷⁹And when the session is over, don't forget to pick up your coupon for sixty percent off your next purchase of our products.

77-79번은 다음 담화에 관한 문제입니다.
남 안녕하세요, 하나 음료에 오신 것을 환영합니다. ⁷⁷저희가 새로 출시한 허브차를 드셔보시라고 여러분을 이곳에 초청했습니다. 제품 평가를 위해 사용하실 수 있는 피드백 양식이 몇 가지 있으며, 의견을 가능한 한 상세하게 기재해 주시기를 부탁드립니다. 물론, 저희는 매우 뛰어난 맛을 지닌 우리 차에 기대를 걸고 있습니다. ⁷⁸저희는 또한 다른 브랜드에 비해 포장재를 거의 안 썼다고 할 정도로 훨씬 적게 사용하는 것에 대해 자랑스럽게 생각합니다. 곧 시작하겠습니다. ⁷⁹그리고 이 세션이 끝나면, 다음 번 저희 제품을 구매하실 때 60% 할인 받으실 수 있는 쿠폰을 수령하는 것을 잊지 마십시오.

어휘 detailed 상세한   comment 의견   hardly any 거의 없는   at all 전혀, 조금도

77. 청자들은 누구인 것 같은가?
(A) 제품 평가자
(B) 판매원
(C) 입사 지원자
(D) 신문기자

78. 화자는 제품의 어떤 측면에 대해 자랑스러워 하는가?
(A) 그것은 국내에서 생산된다.
(B) 그것은 포장을 거의 사용하지 않는다.
(C) 그것은 많은 나라에서 구할 수 있다.
(D) 그것은 과학자들에 의해 개발되었다.

어휘 domestically 국내에서

79. 화자는 세션이 끝나고 청자들에게 무엇을 줄 것인가?
(A) 샘플 한 상자
(B) 무료 식사
(C) 할인 쿠폰
(D) 수료 증명서

어휘 complimentary 무료의   certificate 증명서   completion 수료

80-82. 🎧 미남
Questions 80-82 refer to the following broadcast.

> M You're listening to *City Seekers*, the radio show that explores all of the exciting things going on in our city. My guest today is [80]Valentino Arruda, who works at Olivia Bistro. He's been creating delicious dishes there for the past decade. Mr. Arruda loves to try new and exotic flavors, and [81] he gets his inspiration from the many trips overseas that he takes throughout the year. [82]Our team has been chasing him for an interview for months, as he has a very busy schedule. [82]You're in for a treat. We hope you all enjoy hearing more about Mr. Arruda's fascinating career history and working process. Stay tuned.

80-82번은 다음 방송에 관한 문제입니다.
남 지금 여러분은 우리 시에서 일어나고 있는 모든 흥미로운 일들을 탐구하는 라디오 쇼, '도시 관찰자들'을 듣고 계십니다. 오늘 초대 손님은 [80]올리비아 비스트로에서 일하는 발렌티노 아루다입니다. 그는 지난 **10년 동안 그곳에서 맛있는 요리를 만들어 왔습니다.** 아루다 씨는 새롭고 이국적인 맛을 시도하는 것을 아주 좋아하고, [81]**연중 그가 하는 수많은 해외여행에서 영감을 얻습니다.** 그는 일정이 매우 바쁘기 때문에, [82]**우리 팀은 인터뷰를 위해 몇 달 전부터 그를 따라다니고 있습니다.** 기대하셔도 좋습니다. 여러분 모두가 아루다 씨의 흥미로운 경력과 일하는 과정에 대해 더 많이 듣는 걸 즐기시기를 바랍니다. 채널을 고정해 주세요.

어휘 decade 10년   exotic 이국적인   flavor 맛, 풍미

inspiration 영감

80. 발렌티노 아루다는 누구인가?
(A) 과학자
(B) 화가
(C) 작가
(D) 요리사

81. 화자에 따르면, 무엇이 아루다 씨에게 영감을 주는가?
(A) 음악을 듣는 것
(B) 해외여행을 하는 것
(C) 전문가들과 함께 일하는 것
(D) 자연에서 시간을 보내는 것

82. 화자는 "그는 일정이 매우 바쁘기 때문에"라고 말할 때 무엇을 의미하는가?
(A) 취소가 불가피했다.
(B) 게스트와의 대화는 짧을 것이다.
(C) 인터뷰는 드문 기회이다.
(D) 아루다 씨가 새로운 사업을 시작했다.

어휘 cancellation 취소

83-85. 🎧 미녀
Questions 83-85 refer to the following talk.

> W Thank you all for being here for this planning meeting. [83] As the structural engineer for the Webster Stadium project, I've been asked to review a proposed change. [84] In the original plan, the roof only partially covered the field and seating areas. Some people on this committee want a full roof for the structure. I've assessed the plans, and I can confirm that making this change is still possible at this point. Additional support beams will need to be added. [85] I've prepared a new schedule to account for the added work. Please take a look now so we can have a discussion about it.

83-85번은 다음 담화에 관한 문제입니다.
여 기획 회의를 위해 이곳에 와 주신 모든 분들께 감사드립니다. 웹스터 경기장 프로젝트의 [83]**구조 공학자로서, 저는 제안된 변경 사항을 검토해 달라는 요청을 받았습니다.** [84]**원래 계획에서, 지붕은 경기장과 좌석 구역을 일부만 덮었습니다. 이 위원회의 몇 몇 분들은 구조물을 다 덮는 지붕을 원하고 계십니다.** 저는 계획을 평가했고, 현 시점에서 이 변경이 여전히 가능하다는 것을 확인해 드릴 수 있습니다. 추가 지지대를 덧붙여야 할 필요는 있을 겁니다. [85]**저는 추가된 작업을 처리하기 위한 새로운 일정표를 준비했습니다.** 그것에 관해 논의할 수 있도록 지금 봐 주십시오.

어휘 structural engineer 구조 공학자   proposed 제안된   partially 부분적으로   field 경기장   assess 평가하다   account for 처리하다

83. 누가 담화를 이끌고 있는가?

(A) 프로 운동선수

(B) 재정 고문

(C) 구조 공학자

(D) 시장

84. 화자에 따르면, 몇몇 사람들이 무엇을 제안했는가?

(A) 재활용 자재를 사용하는 것

(B) 지붕 설계를 변경하는 것

(C) 입장료를 인상하는 것

(D) 주차장을 확장하는 것

어휘 recycled 재활용된   admission fee 입장료

85. 청자들은 다음에 무엇을 할 것 같은가?

(A) 일정표 검토하기

(B) 시연 보기

(C) 질문 공유하기

(D) 새로운 동료 만나기

86-88. 🎧 영녀

Questions 86-88 refer to the following broadcast.

> W Are you looking for a way to take your writing to the next level? Our guest today can help you! **86** Brittany Morrison will be sharing her top tips for thinking more creatively in your writing projects. This is perfect for poets, screenwriters, or anyone writing for fun. Ms. Morrison teaches classes at the McKinney Institute. **87** They're so popular that they're fully booked for the next three terms. We'll talk to Ms. Morrison in a moment. **88** And be sure to tune in to our next show, as I'll be revealing the winner of our annual contest.

86-88번은 다음 방송에 관한 문제입니다.

여 당신의 글을 한 단계 더 발전시킬 방법을 찾고 있나요? 오늘의 게스트가 도와드릴 수 있습니다! **86** 브리타니 모리슨은 여러분의 글쓰기 프로젝트에서 더 창의적으로 사고하기에 대한 그녀의 가장 중요한 조언들을 공유할 것입니다. 이것은 시인, 시나리오 작가, 또는 재미로 글을 쓰는 모든 사람에게 완벽합니다. 모리슨 씨는 맥키니 학원에서 수업을 하는데요. **87** 그것은 인기가 너무 많아서 다음 세 학기 예약이 꽉 찼습니다. 잠시 후에 모리슨 씨와 이야기해 보겠습니다. **88** 그리고 다음 방송도 꼭 청취해 주세요. 연례 대회의 우승자를 발표할 예정이니까요.

어휘 screenwriter 시나리오 작가   term 학기   reveal 밝히다

86. 방송은 주로 무엇에 관한 것인가?

(A) 웹사이트를 설계하는 것

(B) 창의성을 높이는 것

(C) 의사소통 능력을 향상시키는 것

(D) 건강한 습관을 기르는 것

어휘 enhance 높이다, 향상시키다

87. 화자는 모리슨 씨의 수업에 대해 무엇이라고 말하는가?

(A) 그것은 정원이 다 찼다.

(B) 그것은 초보자들을 대상으로 한다.

(C) 그것은 온라인으로 이용할 수 있다.

(D) 그것은 무료로 제공된다.

어휘 be at full capacity 정원이 다 차다   aimed at ~을 목표로 한, 겨냥한

패러프레이징 fully booked → at full capacity

88. 화자는 다음 방송 동안 무슨 일이 일어날 것이라고 말하는가?

(A) 대회 우승자가 발표될 것이다.

(B) 새로운 진행자가 소개될 것이다.

(C) 청취자들의 질문에 답할 것이다.

(D) 행사 표가 판매될 것이다.

패러프레이징 I'll be revealing the winner of our annual contest → A contest winner will be announced

89-91. 🎧 미녀

Questions 89-91 refer to the following telephone message.

> W Hi, Gary. **89** I wanted to update you on the wooden chairs we're making for Stewart Insurance. The designs have been finalized, and we need to have them shipped by February 6. **90** You said that you were concerned that I had accepted such a small order for customized goods. Well, I know that we don't usually do this, but we've had a lot of cancellations. In fact, **91** I'm going to let some employees go home early today and tomorrow because we don't have enough work for them to do. Fortunately, our busy season will be starting soon, so I'm not too worried.

89-91번은 다음 전화 메시지에 관한 문제입니다.

여 안녕하세요, 게리. **89** 저희가 스튜어트 보험사를 위해 만들고 있는 나무 의자에 대한 최신 정보를 알려드리려고요. 디자인은 확정되었고, 2월 6일까지 배송해야 합니다. **90** 당신은 제가 주문 제작 상품에 대해 그렇게 소량의 주문을 수락한 것에 대해 걱정된다고 말씀하셨죠. 음, 우리가 평소에 이런 일을 하지 않는다는 것은 알지만, 우리에게는 취소가 많았어요. 사실, 오늘과 내일은 할 일이 충분하지 않아서 **91** 직원 몇 명을 집에 일찍 보내려고 합니다. 다행히도, 우리의 바쁜 시즌이 곧 시작될 것이기 때문에 저는 크게 걱정하지 않아요.

어휘 finalize 확정하다   customized 주문 제작의

89. 화자는 어디에서 일하는 것 같은가?

(A) 사진관에서

(B) 자동차 수리점에서

(C) 문구점에서

(D) 가구 공장에서

90. 화자는 왜 "우리에게는 취소가 많았어요"라고 말하는가?

(A) 결정에 대해 설명하기 위해

(B) 자신이 시간을 낼 수 있음을 확인해 주기 위해

(C) 불만을 제기하기 위해

(D) 더 많은 광고를 제안하기 위해

91. 화자는 직원을 위해 무엇을 해 주겠다고 제안하는가?

(A) 출장 요리 업체의 식사 주문하기

(B) 휴가 제공하기

(C) 하루 몇몇 사람들을 일찍 퇴근시키기

(D) 교육 이벤트 개최하기

92-94. 🎧 호남

Questions 92-94 refer to the following speech.

M Welcome, everyone. I'd like to thank the event planners for inviting me to give a talk ⁹² here at the Melbourne Health Fair. Today I'm going to tell you more about the new blood pressure tracker from Dominick Enterprises. This compact device records information throughout the day. In addition, ⁹³ if your blood pressure gets out of the desired range, it sends a message to your phone to alert you to the issue. ⁹⁴ A recent survey of our customers showed that the instructions for our previous model were hard to understand. So, we've made changes to address this issue.

92-94번은 다음 연설에 관한 문제입니다.

남 모두 환영합니다. ⁹² 이곳 멜버른 건강 박람회에서 강연을 할 수 있게 초청해 주신 행사 기획자 분들께 감사드립니다. 오늘 저는 도미닉 산업의 새로운 혈압 측정기에 대해 더 말씀드리겠습니다. 이 소형 장치는 하루 종일 정보를 기록합니다. 또한, ⁹³ **혈압이 적정 범위를 벗어나면, 여러분의 핸드폰으로 메시지를 보내 문제를 알립니다.** ⁹⁴ **고객들을 대상으로 한 최근 설문 조사에서 저희의 이전 모델에 대한 설명서가 이해하기 어려웠다는 것이 나타났습니다.** 그래서, 저희는 이 문제를 해결하기 위해 변화를 주었습니다.

어휘 desired 바라는, 희망하는   range 범위   alert 알리다 instructions 지시, 안내   address 처리하다, 다루다

92. 청자들은 어디에 있는가?

(A) 직원 오리엔테이션에

(B) 개업식에

(C) 건강 박람회에

(D) 자선 모금 만찬에

93. 화자에 따르면, 제품은 어떻게 사용자를 돕는가?

(A) 발송을 추적함으로써

(B) 비용을 절감함으로써

(C) 빠르게 충전됨으로써

(D) 알림을 전송함으로써

94. 화자는 설문 조사에서 무엇을 알게 되었는가?

(A) 현대적인 디자인이 필요했다는 것

(B) 가격이 너무 비쌌다는 것

(C) 사용자가 안전에 대해 우려하고 있었다는 것

(D) 설명서가 혼동을 주었다는 것

패러프레이징 hard to understand → confusing

95-97. 🎧 미녀

Questions 95-97 refer to the following tour information and map.

W I'd like to let you know about a change to our itinerary. Unfortunately, the grand opening event at the Clifton Concert Hall has been postponed. ⁹⁵ Construction was supposed to be completed by now, but it is a few days behind schedule. Therefore, you'll have some free time between 1 and 3 P.M. this afternoon. ⁹⁶ I suggest browsing Henderson's Antique Shop. We'll have an additional activity during tomorrow's scheduled free time to make up for this change. So, ⁹⁷ at dinner tonight, I'll give you a list of options, and you can tell me which you prefer. We'll do the most popular one.

95-97번은 다음 관광 정보와 지도에 관한 문제입니다.

여 저희 여행 일정표의 변경사항에 대해 알려드리고자 합니다. 안타깝게도, 클리프턴 공연장의 오픈 행사가 연기되었습니다. ⁹⁵ **지금쯤 공사가 완료될 예정이었지만, 예정보다 며칠 늦어지고 있습니다.** 그러므로, 오늘 오후 1시에서 3시 사이에 여러분은 자유 시간을 가질 것입니다. ⁹⁶ **저는 헨더슨 골동품 가게를 둘러보는 것을 추천합니다.** 우리는 이 변경에 대해 보상하기 위해 내일 예정된 자유 시간 동안 추가 활동을 진행할 예정입니다. 그래서 ⁹⁷ **오늘 저녁 식사 때, 제가 여러분에게 선택 가능한 것들의 목록을 드릴 테니, 어느 것이 더 좋은지 제게 말씀해 주세요.** 가장 인기 있는 걸로 하겠습니다.

어휘 itinerary 여행 일정표   behind schedule 예정보다 늦은 browse 둘러보다   make up for 보상하다

1) 놀이공원
2) 경기장
3) 공연장
⁹⁶ 4) 골동품 가게

95. 화자에 따르면, 무엇이 문제를 야기했는가?

(A) 심한 교통체증

(B) 악천후

(C) 공사 지연

(D) 컴퓨터 오류

96. 시각 자료를 보시오. 화자는 오늘 오후에 어디로 갈 것을 추천하는가?

(A) 1번 장소
(B) 2번 장소
(C) 3번 장소
(D) 4번 장소

97. 청자들은 저녁 식사에서 무엇을 할 수 있는가?
(A) 부분 환불 요청하기
(B) 선호하는 활동 표현하기
(C) 추가 관광하기
(D) 다음 날 식사 선택하기

어휘 preference 선호, 기호도

98-100. 🎧 미남

Questions 98-100 refer to the following excerpt from a meeting and fact sheet.

> **M** Next, I'd like to discuss the building expansion project. [98] The new wing will allow us to host larger exhibitions or have separate spaces for two different artists. [99] Now, we've hired a new marketing manager to help with promoting these larger-scale events. She'll be at next week's meeting, so you'll have the chance to find out more about her then. About the project itself, [100] the original plan included twelve hundred square meters of new space. However, because we decided to remove two trees from the property, [100] it'll be fifteen hundred instead. So, I've changed that on the fact sheets I gave you.

98-100번은 다음 회의 발췌록과 자료표에 관한 문제입니다.
남 다음으로, 건물 확장 프로젝트에 대해 논의하고 싶습니다. [98] 새로운 건물은 우리가 더 큰 전시회를 주최하거나 두 명의 서로 다른 예술가들을 위한 분리된 공간을 가질 수 있게 해줄 것입니다. [99] 자, 우리는 이러한 대규모 행사 홍보를 도울 새로운 마케팅 관리자를 고용했습니다. 그녀는 다음 주 회의에 참석할 것이기 때문에, 여러분은 그때 그녀에 대해 더 알아볼 기회가 있을 겁니다. 프로젝트에 관해 말하자면, [100] 원래 계획에는 1,200 평방 미터의 새로운 공간이 포함되어 있었습니다. 하지만, 우리가 그 부지에서 나무 두 그루를 제거하기로 했기 때문에, [100] 그 대신에 1,500 미터가 될 것입니다. 그래서, 제가 드린 자료표에서 그것을 변경했습니다.

어휘 expansion 확장 separate 분리된 larger-scale 대규모의

결과물 자료표		
1행	비용	800,000달러
2행	건축가	스티븐 그레이
3행	완료일	9월 1일
[100] 4행	면적	**1,200 평방 미터**

98. 어떤 종류의 건물이 확장될 것 같은가?
(A) 미술관
(B) 학교
(C) 운동 시설
(D) 우체국

99. 청자들은 다음 회의에서 무엇을 할 것인가?
(A) 행사에 자원하기
(B) 설계도 보기
(C) 신규 직원 만나기
(D) 예산 보고서 제공하기

어휘 blueprint 청사진, 설계도

100. 시각 자료를 보시오. 몇 행이 변경되었는가?
(A) 1행
(B) 2행
(C) 3행
(D) 4행

RC PART 5

UNIT O1 명사

CHECK-UP
본문 p.100

1. supply
2. appointments
3. surprise
4. Deliveries
5. director
6. commitment
7. creation
8. sales

1.

해설 밑줄 앞에 부정관사가 있으므로 단수형인 supply가 정답이다.

해석 Kenway Construction은 추가 프로젝트가 가능할 경우를 대비하여 더 많은 자재를 확보하기 시작했다.

어휘 on hand (도움 등을) 구할 수 있는, 가까이에 있는 in case ~한 경우에 대비하여 available ~할 시간이 있는; 이용할 수 있는

2.

해설 appointment가 '약속, 예약'을 뜻할 때는 가산명사이기 때문에 단수형으로 쓰려면 부정관사와 함께 써야 한다. 이 문장에서는 밑줄 앞에 부정관사가 없으므로 복수형인 appointments가 정답이다.

해석 예상치 못한 장비 문제로 인해 Retha Dentistry는 다음 주쯤에나 예약을 잡아 드릴 겁니다.

어휘 unexpected 예상 밖의, 뜻밖의

3.

해설 밑줄에는 동사 have expressed의 목적어 역할을 할 수 있는 말이 들어가야 한다. 따라서 명사인 surprise가 정답이다.

해석 많은 행사 기획자가 Villa Hall의 대여료에 놀라움을 표했다.

어휘 express 표현하다 rental fee 대여료, 임대료

4.

해설 밑줄 뒤에 전치사구가 있고 그 뒤에 동사 arrive가 이어지므로 밑줄은 주어 역할을 하는 명사 자리이다. 따라서 Deliveries가 정답이다.

해석 Del Logistics의 배달물은 가끔 예정보다 이삼일 일찍 도착한다.

어휘 occasionally 가끔 ahead of schedule 예정보다 일찍

5.

해설 문맥상 예산 삭감에 반대하는 주체는 사람이 되는 게 자연스러우므로 '임원'을 뜻하는 director가 정답이다.

해석 그 전무는 회사가 제안한 예산 삭감에 강하게 반대했다.

어휘 strongly 강하게, 거세게 oppose 반대하다 propose 제안하다, 제의하다

6.

해설 문맥상 품질에 대한 고집 때문에 고객들이 신뢰했다는 내용이 되는 게 자연스러우므로 '헌신, 전념; 약속'을 뜻하는 commitment가 정답이다.

해석 Mantique Furniture의 품질에 대한 고집 때문에 고객들은 수십 년간 이 업체를 신뢰해 왔다.

7.

해설 밑줄 앞의 job과 어울려 '일자리 창출'을 의미하는 게 문맥상 자연스러우므로 creation이 정답이다.

해석 세액 공제는 소기업에서 상당한 일자리를 창출하는 결과를 가져올 것이다.

어휘 result in 결과적으로 ~가 되다 substantial 상당한

8.

해설 밑줄 뒤의 figures와 어울려 '판매 수치'를 의미하는 게 문맥상 자연스러우므로 sales가 정답이다.

해석 Jerome's Technologies에서 발표한 판매 수치에 따르면 그 회사의 수익은 지난 분기에 3%가 증가했다.

어휘 release 공개하다, 발표하다; 출시 profit 수익, 이익

UNIT O2 대명사와 한정사

CHECK-UP
본문 p.102

1. she
2. itself
3. those
4. any
5. every
6. any
7. All
8. each

1.

해설 밑줄 앞에 접속사가 있고 뒤에는 동사가 이어지므로 밑줄에는 주어 역할을 할 수 있는 말이 들어가야 한다. 따라서 주격 인칭대명사인 she가 정답이다.

해석 Ms. Cailot은 교통 체증 때문에 출근이 5분 늦었다.

어휘 stuck 움직일 수 없는, 갇힌

2.

해설 밑줄은 동사 prides의 목적어 자리이며, 문맥상 밑줄에 들어갈 말이 주어 The grocery store와 동일한 대상이므로 재귀대명사인 itself가 정답이다.

해석 그 식료품점은 농산물에 대해서는 지역의 공급업체들만 이용한다는 점에 자부심을 갖고 있다.

어휘 produce 농작물; 생산하다

3.

해설 밑줄에는 과거분사구의 수식을 받아 전치사의 목적어 역할을 하는 동시에 앞에 나온 복수 명사 coupons를 대신할 수 있는 말이 들어가야 하므로 지시대명사 복수형인 those가 정답이다.

해석 온라인으로 발급된 것들을 포함해 Zack's Diner의 모든 쿠

폰은 12월 31일에 만료될 것이다.

어휘 including ~을 포함하여   issue 발급하다, 발행하다
expire 만료되다

4.

해설 문맥상 어느 이벤트든 참여할 수 있다는 내용이 되는 게 자연스러우므로 긍정문에서 '모든'을 뜻하는 any가 정답이다.

해석 콘퍼런스 참가자는 그들의 관심을 끄는 이벤트는 무엇이든 참여할 수 있습니다.

어휘 interest 관심[흥미]을 끌다

5.

해설 밑줄 앞에 주어와 동사를 갖춘 완전한 절이 있고 뒤에는 명사가 이어지므로 밑줄에는 명사를 수식하는 말이 들어가야 한다. 따라서 한정사인 every가 정답이다.

해석 비서가 매주 목요일에 사무용품을 주문하니 요청 사항이 있으면 그 전에 그에게 이메일을 보내세요.

어휘 secretary 비서   office supplies 사무용품

6.

해설 밑줄 뒤에 불가산명사가 있으므로 any가 정답이다. a few는 복수 명사를 수식하기 때문에 답이 될 수 없다.

해석 JC's Camping Supplies는 Flash Sailing Co.가 제조하는 모든 상품에 할인을 제공하고 있다.

어휘 merchandise 물품, 상품   manufacture 제조하다

7.

해설 밑줄 뒤에 명사 staff가 있고 그 뒤에 복수 동사 are가 이어지므로 All이 정답이다. staff는 그 자체로 단수 또는 복수 명사로 쓸 수 있기 때문에 이러한 유형의 문제를 풀 때는 반드시 뒤에 이어지는 동사가 단수형인지 복수형인지 파악해야 한다.

해석 현재 출장 중인 모든 직원은 의무적으로 참석해야 하는 월간 회의에서 면제된다.

어휘 business trip 출장   be exempt from ~에서 면제되다
mandatory 의무적인

8.

해설 밑줄 뒤에 [of + 복수 명사]가 있고 그 뒤에 단수 동사 was가 이어지므로 each가 정답이다.

해석 위원회는 로고 디자인 경연 대회의 후보를 358명에서 5명으로 좁혔고 후보 각각은 만나자는 연락을 받았다.

어휘 narrow down (선택의 폭을) 좁히다, 줄이다
candidate 후보, 지원자   contact 연락하다; 접촉하다

PRACTICE UNIT 01~02
본문 p.104

1. (D)	2. (B)	3. (B)	4. (C)	5. (B)	6. (A)
7. (A)	8. (A)	9. (C)	10. (C)	11. (C)	12. (D)
13. (B)	14. (D)	15. (B)	16. (B)		

---

1. 명사 자리 [관사 뒤]

해설 빈칸 앞에 관사가 있고 뒤에는 전치사구가 이어지므로 빈칸은 명사 자리이다. 따라서 (D) renovation이 정답이다.

해석 Henson Apartment의 소유주가 메인 로비 보수를 위한 자금을 승인했다.

어휘 approve 승인하다; ~을 좋게 생각하다(~ of)   renovation 개조, 리모델링

2. 인칭대명사 [목적격]

해설 빈칸은 to부정사인 to compare의 목적어 자리이다. 선택지 중 목적어 자리에 쓸 수 있는 것은 (A) themselves와 (B) them인데, 문맥상 지칭하는 대상이 unlimited paint samples이므로 (B)가 정답이다.

해석 Ian Paints는 고객들이 페인트 샘플을 얼마든지 집에 가져가서 그들의 현재 장식과 비교할 수 있게 해 준다.

어휘 unlimited 제한 없는, 무한한   compare 비교하다

3. 한정사 every

해설 빈칸 뒤에 단수 명사가 있으므로 빈칸에는 단수 명사를 수식할 수 있는 말이 들어가야 한다. 따라서 (B) every가 정답이다. (A) few는 복수 명사를 수식하고 (C) other는 복수 명사나 불가산명사를 수식하기 때문에 답이 될 수 없다.

해석 접수원의 업무 중 하나는 걸려 오는 전화를 모두 받는 것이다.

어휘 receptionist 접수원

4. 사람 명사 vs. 사물/추상 명사

해설 빈칸 뒤에 동사 will have가 있으므로 빈칸은 주어 역할을 하는 명사 자리이다. (A) Subscriptions와 (C) Subscribers가 정답 후보인데, 문맥상 콘텐츠를 이용할 수 있는 주체는 사람이 되는 게 자연스러우므로 '구독자'를 뜻하는 (C)가 정답이다.

해석 구독자는 최초 결제 시 Greenwich News의 모든 프리미엄 콘텐츠를 이용할 수 있을 것이다.

어휘 have access to ~을 이용할 수 있다, ~에 접근할 수 있다

5. 한정사 자리

해설 빈칸 앞에 동사가 있고 뒤에는 목적어 역할을 하는 명사가 이어지므로 빈칸에는 명사를 수식하는 말이 들어가야 한다. 따라서 한정사인 (B) which가 정답이다.

해석 인사 팀은 그 직책에 어떤 후보를 채용할지 아직 결정하지 못했다.

6. 가산명사 단수형 vs. 복수형

해설 빈칸에는 sign language와 결합하여 동사 have employed의 목적어 역할을 할 수 있는 말이 들어가야 한다. 선택지 중 명사인 (A) interpreters와 (B) interpreter가 정답 후보인데, 빈칸 앞에 한정사 several이 있으므로 가산명사 복수형인 (A)가 정답이다.

해석 주최자들은 그 국제회의를 위해 수화 통역사 몇 명을 채용했다.

어휘 sign language 수화

7. 지시대명사 those

해설 빈칸은 주격 관계대명사절 who wish to park in this lot 의 수식을 받는 자리이다. 따라서 선택지 중 관계대명사절의 수식을 받을 수 있는 (A) those가 정답이다.

해석 이 주차장에 주차하려면 주차 허가증이 필요합니다.

어휘 permit 허가(증)

8. 명사 자리 [형용사 뒤]

해설 빈칸 앞에 형용사가 있고 뒤에는 전치사구가 이어지므로 빈칸은 명사 자리이다. 따라서 (A) distinction이 정답이다.

해석 두 세탁기 모델의 결정적인 차이점은 그 중 한 대에 에너지 절약 설정이 있다는 것이다.

어휘 crucial 중요한, 결정적인

9. 부정대명사 others

해설 빈칸 앞에 접속사가 있고 뒤에는 동사가 이어지므로 빈칸에는 주어 역할을 할 수 있는 말이 들어가야 한다. 선택지 중 (C) others 와 (D) anyone이 정답 후보인데, 문맥상 한 사람은 소음이 거슬리지 않았지만 다른 사람들은 신경 쓰였다고 말했다는 내용이 되는 게 자연스러우므로 '일부 다른 사람들'을 뜻하는 (C)가 정답이다. (B) whoever는 복합관계대명사로 주어 역할을 할 수 있으나 접속사 뒤에 whoever가 이끄는 절만 단독으로 쓸 수 없기 때문에 답이 될 수 없다.

해석 거주자 중 한 명인 Victor Guerrero는 공사 소음이 거슬리지 않는다고 말했지만 다른 사람들은 소음이 신경 쓰였다고 했다.

어휘 occupant 입주자, 사용자 nuisance 성가신 것, 골칫거리 report 보고하다, 알리다 bother 괴롭히다, 신경 쓰이게 하다

10. 사람 명사 vs. 사물/추상 명사

해설 빈칸 앞에 형용사가 있고 뒤에는 전치사구가 이어지므로 빈칸은 명사 자리이다. 선택지 중 (A) instructors와 (C) instructions 가 정답 후보인데, 문맥상 매뉴얼에 나와 있는 설명이 혼란스러워서 낮은 고객 서비스 평점을 받았다고 하는 게 자연스러우므로 '설명 (서)'를 뜻하는 (C)가 정답이다.

해석 Reway Manufacturing은 매뉴얼의 혼란스러운 설명 때문에 낮은 고객 서비스 평점을 받았다.

11. 소유한정사 자리

해설 빈칸 앞에 동사가 있고 뒤에는 명사구가 이어지므로 빈칸에는 명사구를 수식하는 말이 들어가야 한다. 따라서 소유한정사인 (C) her가 정답이다.

해석 Ms. McGuire는 교대 근무 내내 팀원들에게 정기적인 휴식 시간을 준다.

어휘 break 휴가, 휴식 shift 교대 근무

12. 명사의 역할 [주어]

해설 빈칸 앞에 접속사가 있고 뒤에는 동사가 이어지므로 빈칸은 주어 역할을 하는 명사 자리이다. 따라서 (D) profits가 정답이다.

해석 계속 높은 수익이 유지된다면 이사회는 그 사업을 다른 모험적인 사업으로 확장하는 걸 고려할 것이다.

어휘 board of trustees 이사회 consider 고려하다; 여기다, 간주하다 venture (다소 위험이 따르는) 새로운 사업 profit 수익, 이익 remain 계속 ~이다, 남아 있다

13. 사람 명사 vs. 사물/추상 명사

해설 빈칸 앞에 관사가 있고 뒤에는 동사 must make sure가 이어지므로 빈칸은 현재분사구 working on the audit의 수식을 받는 명사 자리이다. (B) accountants와 (C) accounts가 정답 후보인데, 문맥상 회계 감사 작업을 하는 주체는 사람이 되는 게 자연스러우므로 '회계사'를 뜻하는 (B)가 정답이다.

해석 회계 감사 작업을 하는 회계사들은 반드시 수치들이 가능한 한 정확하도록 해야 한다.

어휘 audit 회계 감사 make sure (that) 확실히 ~하다

14. 인칭대명사 [주격]

해설 빈칸 앞에 접속사가 있고 뒤에는 동사가 이어지므로 빈칸에는 주어 역할을 할 수 있는 말이 들어가야 한다. 따라서 (D) he가 정답이다.

해석 Brightwood Water는 Mr. Gilmore에게 요금이 과다 청구되었기 때문에 80달러를 환불해 줬다.

어휘 overcharge 과다 청구하다

15. 복합 명사

해설 빈칸 앞의 tourist와 어울려 '관광지, 관광 명소'를 의미하는 게 문맥상 자연스러우므로 (B) attractions가 정답이다.

해석 이 아파트는 많은 관광지에 도보로 갈 수 있는 거리에 있어서 최상급 주택이다.

어휘 within walking distance 걸어서 갈 수 있는 거리 내에 prime 최상의 real estate 부동산

16. 한정사 all

해설 빈칸 뒤에 복수 명사가 있으므로 빈칸에는 복수 명사를 수식할 수 있는 말이 들어가야 한다. 따라서 (B) All이 정답이다. 나머지 선택지는 모두 단수 명사를 수식하기 때문에 답이 될 수 없다.

해석 모든 서류는 데이터 보호법 준수를 위한 승인 절차를 밟는다.

어휘 document 서류 undergo (변화, 안 좋은 일 등을) 겪다, 받다 approval 승인 process 과정, 절차

UNIT 03 형용사와 부사

1. initial	2. mandatory
3. actively	4. efficiently
5. still	6. therefore
7. more evenly	8. most important

1.

해설 밑줄 앞에 관사가 있고 뒤에는 명사구가 이어지므로 밑줄에는 명사구를 수식하는 말이 들어가야 한다. 따라서 형용사인 initial이

정답이다.

해설 Ms. Ortiz가 석사 학위와 5년 경력이 있다는 걸 고려하면 초기 연봉 제의는 상당히 낮았다.

어휘 considering (that) ~라는 걸 고려[감안]하면 fairly 꽤, 상당히; 공정하게

2.

해설 밑줄은 be동사 is 뒤의 주격 보어 자리로 주어인 Following safety regulations를 구체적으로 설명할 수 있는 말이 들어가야 한다. 따라서 형용사인 mandatory가 정답이다.

해설 건설 현장에서 안전 규정을 따르는 것은 모든 방문객에게 의무적이다.

어휘 follow 따르다, 준수하다 safety 안전 regulations 규정 construction 건설, 공사 site 현장, 장소 mandate 명령; 권한; (공식적으로) 명령하다; 권한을 주다

3.

해설 밑줄은 조동사 has와 과거분사 pursued 사이의 부사 자리이므로 actively가 정답이다.

해설 대학 졸업 이후 Mr. Shaw는 영화 산업에서 적극적으로 경력을 쌓았다.

어휘 pursue 추구하다, 밀고 나가다

4.

해설 밑줄은 동사 is working을 수식하는 자리이므로 부사인 efficiently가 정답이다.

해설 공기 청정기 필터는 효율적으로 작동할 수 있도록 정기적으로 교체해야 합니다.

어휘 air purifier 공기 청정기 replace 대체하다, 교체하다 at regular intervals 정기적으로, 일정한 간격으로 ensure 보장하다, 확실히 하다

5.

해설 밑줄은 be동사 were와 현재분사 trying 사이의 부사 자리이므로 still이 정답이다.

해석 대표 이사가 행사에서 개회사를 하는 동안 일부 관객은 여전히 자리를 찾으려 하고 있었다.

어휘 opening remarks 개회사

6.

해설 밑줄은 조동사 must와 동사 be 사이의 부사 자리이므로 therefore가 정답이다.

해석 우리의 최근 마케팅 전략은 대부분 성공적이지 못했기 때문에 재평가해서 개편해야 합니다.

어휘 strategy 전략, 계획 largely 대체로, 주로 reevaluate 재평가하다 restructure 개편하다, 개혁하다

7.

해설 밑줄 앞에 비교급 강조 부사 much가 있고 뒤에는 비교 대상을 나타내는 전치사 than이 있으므로 밑줄은 비교급 자리이다. 따

라서 more evenly가 정답이다.

해석 새 에어컨은 예전 에어컨보다 시원한 공기를 훨씬 더 고르게 순환시킨다.

어휘 circulate 순환시키다

8.

해설 문맥상 '가장 중요한 자질'이라고 하는 게 자연스러우며, 이때 최상급 표현을 위해 정관사와 함께 쓸 수 있어야 하므로 most important가 정답이다.

해석 뛰어난 대인 관계 기술은 그 직책에서 가장 중요한 자질이다.

어휘 interpersonal skills 대인 관계 능력 qualification 자격

UNIT 04 전치사와 접속사

1. in	2. until
3. Prior to	4. along with
5. both	6. When
7. Because	8. despite

1.

해설 밑줄 뒤에 구체적이고 넓은 범위의 기간을 나타내는 말인 the third quarter가 있으므로 in이 정답이다. on은 in보다 좁은 범위의 시간 개념을 이를 때 쓰는데 뒤에 날짜, 요일, 특정일을 나타내는 말이 이어진다.

해석 3/4분기의 성공은 공격적인 마케팅 캠페인의 결과이다.

어휘 quarter 사분기; 4분의 1 result 결과; (~의) 결과로 발생하다 aggressive 공격적인

2.

해설 문맥상 특정 시점까지 '계속' 문을 열 거라는 내용이 되어야 한다. 따라서 '지속'의 의미가 있는 until이 정답이다. by는 특정 시점까지 행위나 동작이 '완료'되는 것을 강조하는 전치사이므로 이 문장에는 적절하지 않다.

해석 월요일부터 새 구내식당이 매일 오전 8시부터 오후 8시까지 운영될 것이다.

어휘 daily 매일; 매일의

3.

해설 밑줄 뒤에 동명사구가 있으므로 밑줄은 전치사 자리이다. In front of와 Prior to가 정답 후보인데, 문맥상 Jane Hamilton은 Hosto Corp.에 근무하기 전에 Popka Inc.에 고용되어 있었다는 내용이 되는 게 자연스러우므로 '(시간상) ~ 전에'를 뜻하는 Prior to가 정답이다.

해석 Jane Hamilton은 Hosto Corp.에 근무하기 전에 Popka Inc.에 고용되어 있었다.

어휘 employ 고용하다

4.

해설 밑줄 뒤에 명사구가 있으므로 밑줄은 전치사 자리이다. on account of와 along with가 정답 후보인데, 문맥상 최근 공원 사진과 더불어 더 많은 정보는 웹사이트에서 찾을 수 있다는 내용이 되는 게 자연스러우므로 '~와 함께'를 뜻하는 along with가 정답이다. In short는 '요컨대, 요약하면'을 뜻하는 접속부사이므로 오답이다.

해석 최근 공원 사진과 더불어 이 프로젝트에 대한 더 많은 정보는 저희 웹사이트에서 찾을 수 있습니다.

5.

해설 밑줄 뒤에 and로 current (employees)와 former employees가 연결되어 있으므로 밑줄에는 and와 짝을 이루는 상관 접속사가 들어가야 한다. 따라서 both가 정답이다.

해석 인사 팀은 현 직원과 예전 직원 모두에 대한 정보를 보관한다.

어휘 current 현재의, 지금의   former 예전의; 전자의

6.

해설 밑줄 뒤에 주어와 동사를 갖춘 완전한 절이 있고, 콤마로 새로운 절이 연결되어 있으므로 밑줄은 접속사 자리이다. 따라서 When이 정답이다. Above는 형용사, 부사, 전치사로 쓰인다. 형용사로 쓸 때는 '위의, 앞에서 말한'을 뜻하고, 부사로는 '위에, 위로; (특정 숫자나 기준) 이상으로', 전치사로는 '~ 위에; ~을 넘는'을 뜻한다.

해석 컴퓨터에 문제가 생기면 내선 번호 56으로 Mr. Kim에게 연락하세요.

어휘 encounter 맞닥뜨리다, 마주치다   contact 연락하다; 접촉하다   extension 내선 번호

7.

해설 밑줄 뒤에 주어와 동사를 갖춘 완전한 절이 있고, 콤마로 새로운 절이 연결되어 있으므로 밑줄은 접속사 자리이다. 따라서 Because가 정답이다.

해석 그 디자인은 웹사이트에 있는 것과 달랐기 때문에 고객들이 불평을 했다.

8.

해설 밑줄 뒤에 명사구가 있으므로 밑줄은 전치사 자리이다. 따라서 despite가 정답이다.

해석 첫 번째 지점의 저조한 성과에도 불구하고 Beanie Coffee는 파리에 또 다른 지점을 열었다.

어휘 branch 지점, 지사   success 성공, 성과

PRACTICE UNIT 03~04   본문 p.110

1. (D)	2. (A)	3. (B)	4. (C)	5. (B)	6. (A)
7. (A)	8. (C)	9. (D)	10. (B)	11. (B)	12. (B)
13. (D)	14. (C)	15. (D)	16. (A)		

1. 부사 자리 [타동사 앞]

해설 빈칸은 동사 believe를 수식하는 부사 자리이므로 (D)

firmly가 정답이다.

해석 유권자 대부분은 도시의 주요 도로가 더 잘 유지되어야 한다는 생각이 확고하다.

어휘 firmly 단호하게, 확고하게   maintain (관계, 상태, 수준 등을) 유지하다

2. 장소를 나타내는 전치사 [on vs. in]

해설 무언가의 표면 위에 있다는 걸 나타낼 때는 on을 쓴다. 따라서 (A)가 정답이다.

해석 이번 달 내에 철거되어야 하는 행사 간판 몇 개가 벽에 있다.

어휘 take down ~을 치우다; ~을 적다   as ~로(서)

3. 형용사 자리 [명사 앞]

해설 빈칸 앞에 관사가 있고 뒤에는 명사가 이어지므로 빈칸에는 명사를 수식하는 말이 들어가야 한다. 따라서 선택지 중 형용사인 (B) secure가 정답이다.

해석 Ms. Hensley는 Globe Autos 고객들의 의견을 저장할 수 있는 안전한 데이터베이스를 만들었다.

어휘 secure 안전한, 안심하는   store 저장하다, 보관하다

4. 상관 접속사 as well as

해설 빈칸 앞뒤로 명사구 hands-on workshops와 short lectures가 대등하게 연결되어 있으므로 상관 접속사인 (C) as well as가 정답이다. (A) for instance는 '예를 들어'를 뜻하는 접속부사이므로 오답이다.

해석 Parmona Museum은 짧은 강연뿐만 아니라 직접 해 보는 워크숍도 제공한다.

어휘 hands-on 직접 해 보는

5. 기간을 나타내는 전치사 throughout

해설 문맥상 할인 행사가 7월 내내 계속될 거라는 내용이 되는 게 자연스러우므로 '~ 내내'를 뜻하는 (B) throughout이 정답이다. (C) even so는 '그렇기는 하지만'을 뜻하는 접속부사이므로 오답이다.

해석 여름철 할인 행사는 7월 내내 계속될 것이다.

어휘 last 계속되다, 지속되다   inside ~의 내부에

6. 전치사 vs. 부사절 접속사

해설 빈칸 뒤에 주어와 동사를 갖춘 완전한 절이 있고, 콤마로 새로운 절이 연결되어 있으므로 빈칸은 접속사 자리이다. 따라서 (A) After가 정답이다. (D) Especially는 '특히'를 뜻하는 부사이므로 오답이다.

해석 Ms. Caruso가 대기실의 가구를 재배치한 이후에 그 공간은 훨씬 더 넓어 보였다.

어휘 rearrange 재배치하다   waiting area 대기실

7. 부사 자리 [조동사와 동사 사이]

해설 빈칸은 조동사 will과 동사 release 사이의 부사 자리이므로 (A) soon이 정답이다. (D) timely는 '시기적절한, 때맞춘'을 뜻하는 형용사이므로 오답이다.

해석 Bea's Beauty는 웹사이트에 새로운 폼 클렌저를 곧 출시할 것이다.

8. 형용사의 역할 [보어]

해설 빈칸은 be동사 is 뒤의 주격 보어 자리로 주어인 it을 구체적으로 설명할 수 있는 말이 들어가야 한다. 따라서 선택지 중 형용사인 (C) suitable이 정답이다. 명사인 (B) suitability는 주어와 동격 관계일 때만 주격 보어 자리에 위치할 수 있기 때문에 오답이다.

해석 그 건물은 사무실로 사용하기에 적합해지기 전에 광범위한 리모델링이 필요할 것이다.

어휘 property 건물; 부동산; 재산, 소유물 extensive 광범위한; 대규모의 renovation 개조, 리모델링

9. 형용사 자리 [명사 앞]

해설 빈칸 앞에 동사가 있고 뒤에는 명사가 이어지므로 빈칸에는 명사를 수식하는 말이 들어가야 한다. 따라서 선택지 중 형용사인 (D) helpful이 정답이다.

해석 이 발표에는 사기 행위 방지 기법을 실행하는 것에 관해 도움이 되는 팁이 포함되어 있다.

어휘 implement 시행하다, 실시하다 anti-fraud 사기 행위를 방지하는

10. 부사절 접속사 so that

해설 빈칸 앞뒤에 완전한 절이 있으므로 빈칸은 접속사 자리이다. (A) given that과 (B) so that이 정답 후보인데, 문맥상 세부적인 내용을 논의할 때 무슨 내용인지 잘 알 수 있도록 제안서를 읽어야 한다는 내용이 되는 게 자연스러우므로 '~하기 위해서'를 뜻하는 (B)가 정답이다.

해석 이사회 구성원은 세부 사항을 논의할 때 잘 알 수 있도록 회의에 앞서 제안서를 읽어야 한다.

어휘 well-informed 잘 아는 detail 세부 사항

11. 부사 자리 + 비교급 비교

해설 빈칸은 동사 looks를 수식하는 부사 자리이며 빈칸 뒤에 비교 대상을 나타내는 전치사 than이 있으므로 부사의 비교급이 들어가야 한다. 따라서 (B) more closely가 정답이다.

해석 그 감독의 새 다큐멘터리는 첫 번째 다큐멘터리보다 석유 산업을 더 자세히 다룬다.

어휘 look at ~을 보다

12. 형용사의 역할 [보어]

해설 빈칸은 자동사 remains 뒤의 주격 보어 자리로 주어인 Martin Textiles를 구체적으로 설명할 수 있는 말이 들어가야 한다. 따라서 선택지 중 형용사인 (B) dependent가 정답이다.

해석 Martin Textiles는 수익 면에서 여전히 면섬유 판매에 의존하고 있다.

어휘 remain 계속 ~이다, 남아 있다 dependent 의존[의지]하는; 좌우되는 cotton fibers 면섬유 profit 수익, 이익

13. 전치사 vs. 부사절 접속사

해설 빈칸 앞뒤에 완전한 절이 있으므로 빈칸은 접속사 자리이다. 따라서 (D) unless가 정답이다.

해석 모든 기밀문서는 누군가가 사용하지 않는 경우에는 잠금 장치가 된 캐비닛에 두어야 한다.

어휘 confidential 기밀의

14. 부사 자리 [자동사 뒤]

해설 빈칸은 동사 has increased를 수식하는 부사 자리이므로 (C) significantly가 정답이다.

해석 지난해 이래로 참가하는 업체들의 수가 상당히 늘었다.

어휘 participating 참가하는 significantly 상당히; 의미 있게, 중요하게

15. 부사절 접속사 before

해설 빈칸 앞뒤에 완전한 절이 있으므로 빈칸은 접속사 자리이다. (B) although와 (D) before가 정답 후보인데, 문맥상 계획을 세우기 전에 동의를 받아야 한다는 내용이 되는 게 자연스러우므로 '~하기 전에'를 뜻하는 (D)가 정답이다. (A) rather(꽤, 차라리)와 (C) also(또한)는 부사이므로 오답이다.

해석 우리는 이 주택 지구를 상업 지역으로 변경하는 계획을 세우기 전에 시 의회의 동의를 받아야 한다.

어휘 get consent 동의를 받다 residential 거주용의 commercial 상업의

16. 전치사구 according to

해설 문맥상 고용 계약서에 의거하여 노동조합을 설립할 권리가 있다는 내용이 되는 게 자연스러우므로 '~에 따르면'을 뜻하는 (A) According to가 정답이다.

해석 고용 계약서에 따르면 직원들은 노동조합을 설립할 권리가 있다.

어휘 employment contract 고용 계약서 retain 보유하다 form 구성하다, 형성하다 labor union 노동조합

UNIT 05 동사

CHECK-UP

본문 p.112

1. expect	2. supplies
3. be informed	4. are required
5. will open	6. has improved
7. are issued	8. are monitoring

1.

해설 주어 Executives가 복수이므로 동사도 복수형으로 수 일치해야 한다. 따라서 expect가 정답이다.

해석 Murphy Automotive의 경영진은 다음 달에 최소 100대의 중고차를 판매할 것으로 예상하고 있다.

어휘 at least 최소한

2.

해설 주어 Thornton Textiles가 단수이므로 동사도 단수형으로 수 일치해야 한다. 따라서 supplies가 정답이다. 회사명은 -s가 붙어도 단수 취급한다는 점에 유의한다.

해석 면직물 생산업체인 Thornton Textiles는 전국 50개 이상의 의류 공장에 제품을 공급한다.

어휘 producer 생산자, 제작자 supply 공급하다

3.

해설 밑줄 뒤에 목적어가 없고 선행사 Audience members는 행위를 받는 대상이므로 밑줄에는 [be + 과거분사] 형태의 수동태가 적절하다. 따라서 be informed가 정답이다.

해석 다가오는 공연에 대한 정보를 받길 원하는 관객은 연락처 정보가 있는 양식을 작성해야 합니다.

어휘 inform 알리다, 통지하다 upcoming 다가오는, 곧 있을 complete (서식 등을) 빠짐없이 작성하다; 완료하다, 완성하다

4.

해설 밑줄 뒤에 to부정사가 있는 것으로 보아 밑줄에는 뒤에 to부정사를 취할 수 있는 require의 활용형이 들어가야 한다. 따라서 [be + 과거분사] 형태의 수동태인 are required가 정답이다.

해석 모든 사용자는 우리의 클라우드 소프트웨어를 사용하기 전에 자신의 계정을 인증해야 합니다.

어휘 authenticate (진짜임을) 증명하다 account 계정; 계좌

5.

해설 밑줄 뒤에 미래 시제와 어울려 쓰이는 표현인 next month가 있으므로 will open이 정답이다.

해석 뉴베리 국립 공원은 다음 달에 등산객과 야영객에게 개방될 것이다.

6.

해설 밑줄 뒤에 현재완료 시제와 어울려 쓰이는 표현인 since July가 있으므로 has improved가 정답이다.

해석 Bailey Sportswear의 새로운 의류 라인은 7월 이래로 크게 개선되었다.

어휘 significantly 상당히; 의미 있게, 중요하게

7.

해설 주어 the permits가 복수이므로 동사도 복수형으로 수 일치해야 한다. are issued와 were issuing이 정답 후보인데, 밑줄 뒤에 목적어가 없고 주어 the permits는 행위를 받는 대상이므로 밑줄에는 [be + 과거분사] 형태의 수동태가 적절하다. 따라서 are issued가 정답이다.

해석 허가가 나면 Vivitech 본사의 다음 단계 공사가 시작될 것이다.

어휘 permit 허가(증) issue 발급하다, 발행하다

8.

해설 밑줄 뒤에 목적어가 있고 주어 department heads는 행위를 하는 주체이므로 밑줄에는 능동태가 들어가야 한다. had

monitored와 are monitoring이 정답 후보인데, 문맥상 이제 오너가 바뀌었기 때문에 지출을 전보다 더 주의 깊게 관리한다는 내용이 되는 게 자연스러우므로 현재진행 시제인 are monitoring이 정답이다. 과거완료 시제는 과거의 특정 시점보다 앞선 때에 발생한 일을 나타낼 때 쓰기 때문에 이 문장에는 적절하지 않다.

해석 이제 새로운 소유주의 체제 아래에서 부서장들은 지출을 전보다 더 주의 깊게 관리하고 있다.

어휘 ownership 소유(권) monitor (주기적으로) 확인하다, 보다

UNIT 06 준동사

CHECK-UP   본문 p.114

1. to arrange   2. to perform
3. locking   4. substituting
5. to increase   6. continuing
7. rising   8. qualified

1.

해설 밑줄 앞에 would like가 있고 뒤에는 명사구 a group interview가 이어지므로 밑줄에는 would like의 목적어 역할을 하는 동시에 명사구를 목적어로 취할 수 있는 말이 들어가야 한다. 따라서 to부정사인 to arrange가 정답이다.

해석 Ms. Waite는 다음 주 금요일에 그룹 인터뷰를 하고 싶어 한다.

어휘 arrange 마련하다, 준비하다

2.

해설 밑줄 앞이 완전한 절이므로 밑줄 이하는 부사 역할을 해야 한다. 따라서 to부정사인 to perform이 정답이다.

해석 건물 내 모든 엘리베이터는 필요한 정비를 위해 오전 10시부터 1시간 동안 운행을 중단할 예정입니다.

어휘 out of service 이용할 수 없는 required 요구되는, 필수의 maintenance (건물, 기계 등의) 유지

3.

해설 밑줄 앞에 전치사구가 있고 뒤에는 명사가 이어지므로 밑줄에는 전치사구의 목적어 역할을 하는 동시에 명사를 목적어로 취할 수 있는 말이 들어가야 한다. 따라서 동명사인 locking이 정답이다.

해석 마지막으로 퇴근하는 사람은 문을 잠그기 전에 보안 경보 장치가 설정되어 있는지 확인해야 한다.

어휘 security alarm 보안 경보 장치

4.

해설 밑줄은 동사 suggest의 목적어 자리이며, suggest는 동명사를 목적어로 취하므로 substituting이 정답이다.

해석 우리는 여러분이 좋아하는 요리법에서 인공 감미료를 천연 감미료로 대체할 것을 제안합니다.

어휘 substitute A for B B를 A로 대체하다 natural 천연의, 자연의 sweetener 감미료 artificial 인공적인

5.

해설 be able 뒤에는 to부정사가 이어져야 하므로 to increase 가 정답이다.

해석 추가 투자자들의 지원으로 그 회사는 생산을 늘릴 수 있었다.

어휘 with the backing of ~의 지원[후원]으로 production 생산

6.

해설 look forward to 뒤에는 동명사가 이어져야 하므로 continuing이 정답이다.

해석 귀하의 지지에 감사드리며 앞으로도 저희 서비스[업체]를 이용해 주시기 바랍니다.

어휘 appreciate 고마워하다; 인정하다; 감상하다

7.

해설 밑줄 앞에 관사가 있고 뒤에는 명사가 이어지므로 밑줄에는 명사를 수식하는 말이 들어가야 한다. 따라서 현재분사인 rising이 정답이다.

해석 주민들은 공공 서비스 비용 상승에 대해 주로 우려하고 있다.

어휘 be concerned about ~에 대해 우려하다

8.

해설 문맥상 자격을 갖춘 지원자들을 끌어들일 수 있을 거라는 내용이 되는 게 자연스러우므로 '자격이 있는, 적임의'를 뜻하는 qualified 가 정답이다.

해석 Ms. Corbett은 회사의 복지 혜택을 늘리면 자격을 갖춘 직원들을 끌어들일 수 있다고 주장했다.

어휘 argue 주장하다, 논쟁하다 perk 복지 혜택, 특전 attract 끌어들이다, 유인하다

UNIT O7 관계사

CHECK-UP 본문 p.116

1. who
2. which
3. contained
4. he
5. where
6. which
7. Whoever
8. wherever

1.

해설 밑줄 앞에 사람을 나타내는 명사가 있으므로 who가 정답이다.

해석 설문 조사를 완료한 모든 고객에게는 할인권이 제공됩니다.

어휘 complete (서식 등을) 빠짐없이 작성하다; 완료하다, 완성하다 voucher 상품권, 쿠폰

2.

해설 밑줄 앞에 전치사 after가 있으므로 밑줄에는 전치사의 목적어 역할을 할 수 있는 말이 들어가야 한다. 따라서 목적격 관계대명사인 which가 정답이다. 원래는 'which the account is

suspended after'였으나 관계대명사절 끝에 남은 전치사가 관계대명사 앞으로 이동한 것이다.

해석 Streaming Central은 연체에 대해 고객에게 세 번 경고를 주는데, 그 후에는 계정이 정지된다.

어휘 warning 경고 account 계정; 계좌 suspend 정지하다, 유예하다

3.

해설 수식 대상인 Some information이 행위자에 의해 '포함되는' 것이기 때문에 밑줄과 수동 관계이므로 과거분사인 contained 가 정답이다. 참고로 이 문장은 contained in the documents 가 Some information을 수식하는 구조로 contained 앞에 [주격 관계대명사 + be동사]가 생략되어 있다.

해석 그 문서들에 포함된 일부 정보는 오래되었다.

어휘 outdated 구식의, 예전의

4.

해설 밑줄 앞에 완전한 절이 있으므로 '------- can'은 everything을 수식하는 관계대명사절이다. 따라서 밑줄에는 동사 can (do)의 주어 역할을 할 수 있는 말이 들어가야 하므로 주격 인칭대명사인 he가 정답이다. 참고로 이 문장은 everything과 he 사이에 목적격 관계대명사가 생략된 구조이다.

해석 그 대표 이사는 직원들을 지원하기 위해 그가 할 수 있는 모든 것을 한다.

5.

해설 밑줄 앞뒤에 완전한 절이 있으므로 밑줄에는 부사와 접속사 역할을 겸하는 관계부사가 들어가야 한다. 따라서 where가 정답이다. what은 선행사를 포함하는 관계대명사이다. 따라서 관계대명사 what 앞에는 선행사가 올 수 없고 [what + 불완전한 절]이 주어, 보어, 목적어 자리에 위치하여 명사 역할을 한다.

해석 그 브랜드의 열성 팬들은 한정판 스니커즈가 출시될 매장 앞에 줄지어 서 있다.

어휘 dedicated 헌신적인 be lined up 줄을 서다 release 공개하다, 발표하다; 출시

6.

해설 밑줄 뒤에 주어가 없는 절이 이어지므로 밑줄은 주격 관계대명사 자리이다. 따라서 which가 정답이다.

해석 그 휴대 전화는 5미터 이하 추락에서 발생할 수 있는 손상을 잘 견디는 물질로 만들어졌다.

어휘 be comprised of ~로 구성되다 resist (손상 등에) 잘 견디다

7.

해설 '------- leaves the office last'가 주어 역할을 하고 있으므로 밑줄에는 명사절을 이끌 수 있는 말이 들어가야 한다. 따라서 주어가 없는 불완전한 절을 이끄는 복합관계대명사인 Whoever가 정답이다.

해석 사무실을 마지막으로 나가는 사람은 누구든지 불을 끄고 가야

한다.

어휘 be expected to do 마땅히 ~을 해야 하다; ~하기로 되어 있다, ~할 예정이다

8.

해설 밑줄 앞뒤에 완전한 절이 있으므로 밑줄에는 절을 연결할 수 있는 말이 들어가야 한다. 따라서 복합관계부사인 wherever가 정답이다.

해석 Pawan Tech는 사용자가 어디를 가든 가장 최신 교통 상황을 제공하는 모바일 애플리케이션을 개발했다.

어휘 develop 개발하다

PRACTICE UNIT 05~07 본문 p.118

1. (B)	2. (B)	3. (D)	4. (C)	5. (D)	6. (D)
7. (A)	8. (C)	9. (C)	10. (C)	11. (D)	12. (B)
13. (D)	14. (A)	15. (B)	16. (A)		

1. 분사 자리 [명사 앞]

해설 빈칸 앞에 관사가 있고 뒤에는 명사가 이어지므로 빈칸에는 명사를 수식하는 말이 들어가야 한다. 선택지 중에서 명사를 수식할 수 있는 것은 과거분사인 (B) preferred뿐이다.

해석 Ms. Zeller는 몇몇 지원자가 주임 연구원직에 우대되는 자격을 갖추지 못했음에도 불구하고 그들을 면접에 불렀다.

어휘 preferred 우대되는 qualification 자격

2. 주격 관계대명사 자리

해설 빈칸 앞에 [주어(A retirement party) + 동사(will be held) + 부사구(next week) + 전치사구(for Mr. Schmidt)] 구조의 완전한 절이 있고 뒤에는 주어가 없는 불완전한 절이 이어져 있다. 따라서 빈칸에는 두 개의 절을 하나로 연결하는 접속사 역할을 하는 동시에 불완전한 절의 주어 역할을 할 수 있는 말이 들어가야 하므로 선택지 중 주격 관계대명사인 (B) who가 정답이다.

해석 Mr. Schmidt를 위한 은퇴 파티가 다음 주에 열릴 예정인데, 그는 Melon Technologies에서 30년 넘게 일했습니다.

3. 주어와 동사의 수 일치

해설 주어 Mr. Farrow가 단수이므로 동사도 단수형으로 수 일치해야 한다. 선택지 중 (A) are inspecting과 (C) inspect는 동사 복수형이므로 오답이고 (B) having inspected는 동사 자리에 들어갈 수 없기 때문에 답이 될 수 없다. 따라서 (D) will inspect가 정답이다.

해석 Mr. Farrow가 차량 엔진을 점검한 후 문제가 있으면 보고할 겁니다.

어휘 inspect 검사하다, 점검하다 report 보고하다, 알리다 issue 문제, 사안; 주제, 안건; 쟁점

4. 전치사 + 관계대명사

해설 빈칸 앞뒤에 완전한 절이 있으므로 관계부사인 (A) when과 [전치사 + 관계대명사]인 (C) for which가 정답 후보이다. 빈칸 앞

에 특정 시간을 나타내는 선행사가 없고 빈칸 이하에 있는 형용사 grateful은 전치사 for와 어울려 쓰이므로 (C)가 정답이다.

해석 우리는 독자뿐만 아니라 여러 재단에서 자금 지원을 받고 있으며, 그에 대해 감사하고 있습니다.

어휘 foundation 재단 B as well as A A뿐만 아니라 B도 grateful 감사하는

5. to부정사

해설 빈칸 앞이 완전한 절이므로 빈칸 이하는 부사 역할을 해야 한다. 선택지에서 부사 역할을 할 수 있는 것은 to부정사인 (D) to understand뿐이다.

해석 모든 직원은 다음 주 워크숍에 참석하여 새 기계의 작동 방법을 익혀야 합니다.

어휘 machinery 기계류

6. 수 일치와 태 복합

해설 주어 renovations가 복수이므로 동사도 복수형으로 수 일치해야 한다. (A) will be completing과 (D) are being completed가 정답 후보인데, 빈칸 뒤에 목적어가 없으므로 [be + 과거분사] 형태의 수동태인 (D)가 정답이다.

해석 Carsen Gym은 수리가 완료될 동안 약 두 달 정도 문을 닫을 예정이다.

어휘 be shut down 닫다, 폐쇄되다

7. 현재분사 vs. 과거분사

해설 빈칸 앞에 동사가 있고 뒤에는 명사가 이어지므로 빈칸에는 명사를 수식하는 말이 들어가야 한다. 선택지 중 명사를 수식할 수 있는 것은 과거분사 (A) used와 현재분사 (D) using인데, 수식 대상인 computers는 행위자에 의해 '사용된' 대상이기 때문에 빈칸과 수동 관계이므로 (A)가 정답이다.

해석 고객 서비스 부서는 예산이 적어서 중고 컴퓨터를 구입했다.

어휘 budget 예산

8. 미래진행 시제

해설 빈칸 앞에 미래 시제와 어울려 쓰이는 표현인 Later this afternoon이 있으므로 (C) will be renegotiating이 정답이다.

해석 오늘 오후 늦게 Ms. Bullock은 건축 자재 회사 중 한 곳과 계약 조건을 재협상할 것이다.

어휘 renegotiate 재협상하다 terms 조건

9. 현재분사 vs. 과거분사

해설 빈칸 앞에 관사가 있고 뒤에는 명사가 이어지므로 빈칸에는 명사를 수식하는 말이 들어가야 한다. 선택지 중 명사를 수식할 수 있는 것은 과거분사 (C) returned와 현재분사 (D) returning인데, 수식 대상인 product는 행위자에 의해 '반납되는' 대상이기 때문에 빈칸과 수동 관계이므로 (C)가 정답이다.

해석 저희가 우편으로 반품된 물건을 받고 난 후에 환불해 드릴 겁니다.

10. 태와 시제 복합

해설 빈칸 뒤에 과거 시제와 어울려 쓰이는 표현인 last Friday가 있으므로 빈칸에는 동사의 과거형이 들어가야 한다. (C) gave와 (D) was given이 정답 후보인데, 빈칸 뒤에 목적어가 있고 주어 Mr. Grimes는 행위를 하는 주체이므로 빈칸에는 능동태가 적절하다. 따라서 (C)가 정답이다.

해석 Mr. Grimes는 지난 금요일에 정보 기술과 보안 학회에서 기조연설을 했다.

어휘 address 연설; 주소

11. 동명사 자리 [전치사 뒤]

해설 빈칸 앞에 전치사 of가 있고 뒤에는 명사구 its business가 이어지므로 빈칸에는 전치사의 목적어 역할을 하는 동시에 명사구를 목적어로 취할 수 있는 말이 들어가야 한다. 따라서 선택지 중 동명사인 (D) extending이 정답이다.

해석 Cannon Corporation은 아시아로 사업을 확대할 수 있는 가능성을 모색하고 있다.

어휘 explore 탐구하다, 탐색하다   possibility 가능성
extend (사업, 세력 등을) 확대하다; 연장하다

12. 수동태 vs. 능동태

해설 빈칸 뒤에 목적어가 없고 주어 Mosquito pesticide spraying operations는 행위를 받는 대상이므로 빈칸에는 [be + 과거분사] 형태의 수동태가 적절하다. 따라서 (B) are scheduled가 정답이다.

해석 모기 살충제 살포 작업은 휴가차 관광객들이 오기 전에 시작할 예정입니다.

어휘 pesticide 살충제   spray 뿌리다   on vacation 휴가차

13. 복합관계대명사 자리

해설 '------- they prefer'가 앞에 있는 절을 수식하는 부사 역할을 하고 있으므로 빈칸에는 부사절을 이끌 수 있는 말이 들어가야 한다. 따라서 선택지 중 복합관계대명사인 (D) whichever가 정답이다.

해석 Chonie Salon의 10주년을 기념하여 고객들은 모든 헤어 케어 제품의 무료 샘플을 그들이 원하는 것으로 받을 수 있다.

어휘 in celebration of ~을 맞이하여, ~을 축하하여

14. to부정사의 태

해설 빈칸 앞에 동사 plans가 있으므로 빈칸에는 동사의 목적어 역할을 할 수 있는 말이 들어가야 한다. 선택지 중 to부정사인 (A) to develop와 (B) to be developed가 정답 후보인데, 빈칸 뒤에 목적어 an abandoned building이 있으므로 빈칸에는 능동태가 적절하다. 따라서 (A)가 정답이다.

해석 스몰빌의 시장은 폐건물을 도서관으로 개발할 계획이다.

어휘 abandoned 버려진, 방치된

15. 현재분사 vs. 과거분사

해설 빈칸 앞에 관사가 있고 뒤에는 명사구가 이어지므로 빈칸에는 명사구를 수식하는 말이 들어가야 한다. 선택지 중 명사를 수식할 수 있는 것은 과거분사 (B) accomplished와 현재분사 (C)

accomplishing인데, 문맥상 뛰어난 제품 디자이너가 상을 받았다는 내용이 되는 게 자연스러우므로 '뛰어난, 걸출한'을 뜻하는 (B)가 정답이다.

해석 그 뛰어난 제품 디자이너는 업계에서 가장 큰 상을 수상했다.

어휘 be awarded with ~을 수상하다, ~을 받다   top honors 대상, 최우수상

16. 주격 관계대명사 자리

해설 빈칸 앞에 [주어(Mr. Barbour) + 동사(showed) + 간접목적어(the electrician) + 직접목적어(the light fixture)] 구조의 완전한 절이 있고 뒤에는 주어가 없는 불완전한 절이 이어져 있다. 따라서 빈칸에는 두 개의 절을 하나로 연결하는 접속사 역할을 하는 동시에 불완전한 절의 주어 역할을 할 수 있는 말이 들어가야 하므로 선택지 중 주격 관계대명사인 (A) that이 정답이다.

해석 Mr. Barbour는 전기 기술자에게 제대로 작동하지 않는 조명을 보여 줬다.

어휘 light fixture 천장이나 벽 등에 고정된 조명   malfunction 오작동하다

UNIT 08 어휘

CHECK-UP 명사
본문 p.121

1. (B)	2. (C)	3. (A)	4. (D)	5. (A)
6. (B)	7. (A)	8. (B)	9. (A)	10. (A)

1.

해석 그 박물관은 구조적 결함이 수리될 때까지 대중에게 개방될 수 없습니다.

어휘 public 대중; 대중의, 공공의   structural 구조적인
defect 결함   definition 정의, 의미   communication 의사소통   uncertainty 불확실성

2.

해석 드라이클리닝 업체가 필라델피아 시 경계 내에서 배송을 할 경우 추가 요금이 발생하지 않습니다.

어휘 make a delivery 배달하다   charge 요금; 책임, 담당
pressure 압력, 압박   provider 제공자, 제공 기관   area 지역; 구역

3.

해석 눈이 예상보다 적게 내리긴 했지만 출근 시간 내내 교통 체증을 빚었다.

어휘 predict 예측하다, 예견하다   delay 지연, 지체   refund 환불   route 길, 노선   suggestion 제안, 제의

4.

해석 자동차 보험금을 청구하면 영업일 기준 3일 이내에 요청서를 검토할 겁니다.

어휘 file a claim (보상금 등을) 청구하다, 청구서를 제출하다

examine 조사하다, 살펴보다   request 요구, 요청(서)
expertise 전문 지식, 전문성   account 계정; 계좌
registration 등록

5.
해석 Ms. Harris는 명문 대학에서 학위를 받은 것 외에도 자격증이 몇 개 있다.

어휘 in addition to ~ 외에도, ~뿐만 아니라   prestigious 명성 있는, 권위 있는   certification 증명(서)   assignment 과제, 업무   estimate 견적(서); 추정(치)   recipient 수령인, 받는 사람

6.
해석 Mr. Joslin은 중소기업 대출을 통해 사업을 발목 잡던 어려움을 극복할 수 있었다.

어휘 overcome 극복하다, 이겨 내다   obstacle 장애(물)   hold back ~을 저지[제지]하다   attempt 시도   reaction 반응   opposite 반대(되는 것)

7.
해석 도서관 이용객들은 구매해야 할 책 추천을 공유하는 설문 조사를 완료했다.

어휘 share 공유하다   recommendation 추천(서); 권고   reimbursement 상환, 환급, 배상   retrieval 회수   resolution 결의안; 해결

8.
해석 Tingley Travel은 여름 방학을 맞은 학생들을 위한 유럽 여행을 소개했다.

어휘 excursion (짧은) 여행   settlement 합의; 해결; 지불, 상환   institution 기관   accomplishment 성취, 업적

9.
해석 홈페이지에 매장의 환불 방침이 명확하게 명시되어 있음에도 일부 소비자는 이에 대해 혼란스러워한다.

어휘 policy 정책, 방침   clearly 분명히, 명확히   state 명시하다   shelter 주거지; 피신(처), 대피(처)   preference 선호(도), 선호하는 것   appointment 약속, 예약

10.
해석 Verity Restaurant의 프라이빗 연회장은 30명까지 특별한 행사를 위해 예약할 수 있습니다.

어휘 private 사유의, 전용의   reserve 예약하다; (자리 등을) 따로 잡아 두다   occasion 행사; 때, 경우   turnover 이직률; 매출액   competence 능숙함, 능숙도   intention 의도

CHECK-UP 형용사   본문 p.123

| 1. (C) | 2. (B) | 3. (B) | 4. (B) | 5. (C) |
| 6. (D) | 7. (A) | 8. (D) | 9. (C) | 10. (A) |

1.
해석 새 소프트웨어가 설치되기 전에 직원들은 고객 계정을 업데이트하는 데 상당한 시간을 소비했다.

어휘 install 설치하다   substantial 상당한   consecutive 연속의   direct 직접적인; 직행의   visible 눈에 보이는

2.
해석 Henley Institute의 연설 수업은 직장인 단체와 학생 개개인에게도 적합하다.

어휘 public speaking 연설   be suitable for ~에 적합하다   corporate 기업의   individual 개개의, 별개의   beneficial 유익한   deliberate 고의의, 의도적인   distant (거리가) 먼

3.
해석 관리 경험이 풍부한 입사 지원자는 채용될 가능성이 높다.

어휘 applicant 지원자   extensive 광범위한; 대규모의   management 경영(진), 운영, 관리   straight 곧은, 똑바른   compact 소형의, 간편한   attentive 주의를 기울이는; 배려하는, 신경 쓰는

4.
해석 그 시장은 폭풍이 지나간 후에 도시의 공원들을 청소하기 위한 협력적인 대규모 노력에 대해 자원봉사자들에게 감사를 표했다.

어휘 massive 엄청나게 많은[큰]; 거대한   coordinate 조직하다, 조정하다   factual 사실에 입각한   objective 객관적인   original 원래[본래]의; 독창적인

5.
해석 그 비디오 스트리밍 서비스는 지난 분기에 상당한 수의 신규 사용자를 추가했다.

어휘 sizeable 꽤 큰   current 현재의, 지금의   defective 결함이 있는   preserved 보존된

6.
해석 Mr. Kellogg는 국가 공인 자격증이 유효한 것으로 판명되면 고위 회계직을 제안받을 것이다.

어휘 turn out 밝혀지다, 드러나다   valid 유효한   successive 연속적인, 연이은   familiar 익숙한, 친숙한   informal 격식에 얽매이지 않는, 편안한

7.
해석 투자자들은 첫 여행이 빠르게 매진된 후 크루즈 라인의 가능성에 대해 낙관적이었다.

어휘 optimistic 낙관적인, 낙관하는   potential 잠재력, 가능성   sell out 다 팔리다   superior 우수한, 우월한   rare 희귀한, 드문   unique 독특한, 고유한

8.
해석 Rosewood Inn에서는 손님들의 편안함이 가장 중요하다.

어휘 comfort 안락, 편안; 위안   utmost 최고의, 최대한

constant 끊임없는, 거듭되는   diminished 줄어든, 약해진
joint 공동의, 합동의

9.

해석 새로운 세금 우대 조치는 지역의 신생 소기업 수에 상당한 변화를 불러왔다.

어휘 incentive 우대 조치, 장려책   significant 상당한; 의미 있는, 중요한   difficult 어려운   prepared 준비가 된   capable 유능한

10.

해석 발전소가 업그레이드되고 나면 그 도시에는 더 안정적으로 전기가 공급될 것이다.

어휘 following ~ 후에; ~을 따라   power plant 발전소
dependable 믿을 만한   supply 공급   patient 참을성 있는
enthusiastic 열광적인, 열렬한   grateful 감사하는

CHECK-UP 부사
본문 p.125

1. (A)	2. (D)	3. (C)	4. (A)	5. (C)
6. (B)	7. (C)	8. (A)	9. (B)	10. (D)

1.

해석 Riddell Dairy Farm은 지역 레스토랑에 직접 우유를 공급하여 비용을 낮게 유지한다.

어휘 supply 공급하다   directly 직접, 바로   neatly 깔끔하게
hardly 거의 ~ 않는   unusually 대단히, 몹시; 평소와 달리

2.

해석 우리의 기술 전문가는 사무실에 인터넷 서비스를 복원하기 위해 부지런히 노력하고 있습니다.

어휘 diligently 부지런히, 애써   restore 복원하다, 회복시키다
financially 재정적으로   seemingly 겉보기에는; 보아하니
particularly 특히

3.

해석 사무장 Charles Yarger가 Ms. Arlow에게 갑작스레 회의를 요청해서 그녀는 일정을 조정해야 했다.

어휘 unexpectedly 예기치 않게, 뜻밖에   request 요구하다, 신청하다   adjust 조정하다   commonly 흔히, 보통
indefinitely 무기한으로   nearly 거의

4.

해석 벨기에에 본사를 두고 설립된 이 조리용품 회사는 현재 새 공장을 세우는 과정에 있다.

어휘 found 설립하다   headquartered (특정 장소에) 본사가 있는   currently 현재, 지금   extremely 극도로, 매우   solidly
튼튼[확고]하게   immediately 즉시, 즉각

5.

해석 Sky Room은 손님을 50명까지 수용할 수 있는 반면에 Wind Room은 80명에서 100명을 무리 없이 수용할 수 있다.

어휘 accommodate 수용하다   seat (특정한 수의) 좌석이 있다
comfortably 수월하게, 무리 없이; 편안[편리]하게
consequently 그 결과, 따라서   widely 널리, 폭넓게; 대단히, 크게   exceedingly 극도로, 대단히

6.

해석 Lamora Fruit Orchard는 다음 분기에 소유권 변경이 있을 것임을 최근 확인해 주었다.

어휘 recently 최근에   ownership 소유(권)   approximately
대략, 약   heavily 매우, 심하게   randomly 무작위로

7.

해석 Clotherly는 경쟁사들보다 현저히 더 부드러운 면 티셔츠를 생산한다.

어휘 noticeably 두드러지게   competitor 경쟁자, 경쟁사
hurriedly 급하게   respectively 각자, 각각   closely 면밀히;
밀접하게

8.

해석 Waldeck에서 새로 출시된 태블릿은 고해상도 화면이 주요 특징이다.

어휘 newly 최근에, 새로   feature 특징으로 하다, 특별히 선보이다
high-resolution 고해상도   absolutely 절대적으로
naturally 당연히, 자연스럽게   considerably 상당히

9.

해석 4층에서 내부 수리가 진행되는 동안 영업 부서는 임시로 5층으로 옮겨질 것이다.

어휘 temporarily 일시적으로, 임시로   renovate 개조하다, 보수하다; 혁신하다   faintly 희미하게   sincerely 진심으로
competitively 경쟁적으로, 경쟁력 있게

10.

해석 교육생 중 한 명은 그 소프트웨어에 익숙하지 않아서 Traylyn Inc.의 배너를 실수로 열 개나 더 인쇄하고 말았다.

어휘 unfamiliar 익숙하지 않은   accidentally 실수로, 우연히,
뜻하지 않게   extra 추가의, 여분의   mainly 주로, 대개
vigorously 발랄하게, 힘차게   necessarily 어쩔 수 없이, 필연적으로

CHECK-UP 동사
본문 p.127

1. (A)	2. (B)	3. (C)	4. (C)	5. (B)
6. (A)	7. (B)	8. (D)	9. (B)	10. (B)

1.

해석 Midco Communications와 Trant Inc.는 저소득 가정

에 인터넷 서비스를 제공하기 위해 함께 자선 활동을 하겠다고 발표했다.

어휘 announce 발표하다, 알리다　joint 공동의, 합동의 charity 자선 (단체)　endeavor 노력, 시도　household 가구, 가정　install 설치하다　treat (특정한 태도로) 대하다, 취급하다 calibrate 눈금을 매기다

2.
해석 휴가 요청은 일주일 전에 상사의 승인을 받아야 합니다.

어휘 note 주목하다; 언급하다　request 요구, 요청(서)　time off 휴가, 휴식　approve 승인하다; ~을 좋게 생각하다(~ of) assess 평가하다　secure 고정하다　reschedule 일정을 다시 잡다

3.
해석 수익 감소로 Liang Industries는 마케팅 예산을 늘렸다.

어휘 prompt 촉발하다　license 허가하다　restock (사용하거나 팔린 물건들 자리에 새로운 것들을) 다시 채우다, 보충하다 outline (간략히) 설명하다

4.
해석 Kirtfield Sales의 수석 회계사는 회사의 재정 상태를 검토해서 건물을 개조할 여유가 없다는 판단을 내렸다.

어휘 determine 결정하다, 확정하다; (구체적 증거로) 판단하다, 알아내다　afford (금전적, 시간적) 여유가 있다　admit 인정하다; 입장[가입]을 허락하다　maintain (관계, 상태, 수준 등을) 유지하다　remember 기억하다

5.
해석 매년 열리는 Gaming Convention에는 전국의 비디오 게임 개발자들이 모인다.

어휘 bring together (사람들을) 한데 모으다　carry out ~을 수행[실행]하다　use up ~을 다 써 버리다　take down ~을 치우다; ~을 적다

6.
해석 올해 가장 많이 팔린 추리 소설 1위는 〈Sandra에게로 가는 문〉이다.

어휘 top 1위를 하다; (양, 기록 등이) 더 높다; ~을 얹다　impress 인상을 주다, 감명을 주다　generate 생성하다, 발생시키다　seek 찾다, 구하다

7.
해석 제품이 두 개 이상의 창고에서 오는 경우가 많기 때문에 귀하의 주문이 다른 상자에 나뉘어 담길 수도 있습니다.

어휘 separate 구별하다, 분리하다　mandate (공식적으로) 명령하다; 권한을 주다　prioritize 우선순위를 매기다　demolish (건물을) 철거하다

8.
해석 예약 판매 대수가 얼마나 많은지에 근거하여 이 회사는 새로운

게임기 출시가 큰 성공을 거둘 것을 예상한다.

어휘 unit 한 개; 구성단위; (건물의) 한 공간　anticipate 예상하다; 기대하다, 고대하다　compile 편집하다, 엮다　condense (글 등을) 줄이다; 응축하다　delegate (일, 임무 등을) 위임하다; 대표[대리인]로 선정하다

9.
해석 Vance Bank는 여행객들에게 외환 시장의 변동 때문에 같은 환율을 보장할 수 없다는 점을 상기시킨다.

어휘 remind 상기시키다　guarantee 보장하다, 보증하다 exchange rate 환율　fluctuation 끊임없는 변화, 변동 currency market 외환 시장　convey (생각, 감정 등을) 전달하다; 나르다　undergo 겪다, 경험하다　obscure 모호하게 하다; (가려서) 보이지 않게 하다

10.
해석 기자들은 주가가 경영진의 변화와 어떤 관련이 있는지 물었다.

어휘 inquire 문의하다　executive 경영의, 행정의 formulate (다른 것들을 합쳐서 새로운 것을) 만들어 내다 persuade 설득하다　occupy 차지하다; 점유하다

PART TEST
본문 p.128

101. (B)	102. (B)	103. (C)	104. (D)	105. (B)
106. (A)	107. (D)	108. (B)	109. (B)	110. (C)
111. (D)	112. (C)	113. (C)	114. (D)	115. (A)
116. (C)	117. (C)	118. (B)	119. (B)	120. (D)
121. (D)	122. (D)	123. (A)	124. (D)	125. (C)
126. (C)	127. (B)	128. (A)	129. (B)	130. (D)

101. 동사 자리
해설 빈칸은 Many tutors를 주어로 하고 their services를 목적어로 하는 동사 자리이다. 따라서 (B) advertise가 정답이다.

해석 비용이 효율적이기 때문에 많은 강사가 커뮤니티 포럼에 자신들의 서비스를 광고한다.

어휘 tutor 개인 교사; 대학 강사　advertise 광고하다 cost-effective 비용 효율이 좋은

102. 소유한정사 자리
해설 빈칸 앞에 접속사가 있고 뒤에는 명사가 이어지므로 빈칸에는 명사를 수식하는 말이 들어가야 한다. 따라서 선택지 중 소유한정사인 (B) their가 정답이다.

해석 우체국은 택배 내용물이 공개되지 않으면 국제 택배를 받지 않는다.

어휘 unless 만약 ~가 아니라면　disclose 밝히다, 공개하다

103. 부사 어휘 quickly
해석 공장 관리자는 Benson Manufacturing 직원들이 고장 난 기계를 빨리 수리해서 기뻐했다.

어휘 supervisor 관리자, 감독관　be pleased with ~에 만족하다, ~에 기뻐하다　quickly 빠르게　machinery 기계류　electronically 전자로, 컴퓨터로　increasingly 점점, 더욱 더　highly 매우, 많이

104. 명사의 역할 [목적어]

해설 빈칸은 to부정사인 to exceed의 목적어 자리이다. 선택지 중 목적어 자리에 쓸 수 있는 것은 명사이므로 (D) expectations가 정답이다.

해석 Ms. Poole과 Mr. Johnson은 관리직에서 계속 기대 이상의 모습을 보이고 있다.

어휘 exceed 초과하다　expectation 예상, 기대　managerial 경영[관리]의　expectant 기대하는

105. 전치사 어휘 by

해석 방 두 개짜리 아파트의 임대 계약은 10월 6일까지 갱신되어야 한다.

어휘 lease 임대　renew 갱신하다, 연장하다　by ~까지　with ~와 함께; ~을 가지고　in ~(안)에　of ~의

106. 동사 어휘 clean

해석 평일 오후 8시경에는 청소를 위해 대개 회의실 문을 닫는다.

어휘 clean 깨끗이 하다, 청소하다　approximately 대략, 약　dispose 없애다, 처리하다　speak 이야기하다　paint 페인트를 칠하다

107. 현재 시제

해설 주절이 현재 시제이고 문맥상 세관 신고서를 작성할 때 해야 하는 일반적인 사실을 나타내는 내용이므로 빈칸에는 현재 시제가 가장 적절하다. 따라서 (D) complete가 정답이다.

해석 정부에서 제공하는 세관 신고서를 작성할 때는 모두 대문자로 써 주세요.

어휘 capital letter 대문자　customs declaration form 세관 신고서

108. 형용사 어휘 current

해석 Ms. Delgado는 현재 디자인 회사와의 계약은 단기 계약에 불과하다고 설명했다.

어휘 current 현재의, 지금의　steep 가파른　natural 천연의, 자연의　occasional 가끔의

109. 전치사 어휘 up to

해설 빈칸 앞에 주어와 동사를 갖춘 완전한 절이 있고 뒤에는 명사가 이어지므로 빈칸은 전치사 자리이다. 따라서 부사절 접속사인 (D) in case는 오답이다.

해석 승객들은 비행 24시간 전까지 무료로 좌석 예약을 변경할 수 있습니다.

어휘 up to ~까지　charge 요금; 책임, 담당　since ~ 이래로　as for ~에 관해서는　in case ~한 경우에 대비하여

110. 부사 어휘 temporarily

해석 Greenwich Hardware 주차장의 한 구역은 나무가 넘어지면서 일시적으로 폐쇄되었다.

어휘 be shut down 닫다, 폐쇄되다　temporarily 일시적으로, 임시로　potentially 잠재적으로　significantly 상당히; 의미 있게, 중요하게　annually 매년

111. 주격 관계대명사 자리

해설 빈칸 앞에 [주어(Vensa Airways) + 동사(provided) + 목적어(travel vouchers) + 전치사구(to everyone)] 구조의 완전한 절이 있고 뒤에는 주어가 없는 불완전한 절이 이어져 있다. 따라서 빈칸에는 두 개의 절을 하나로 연결하는 접속사 역할을 하는 동시에 불완전한 절의 주어 역할을 할 수 있는 말이 들어가야 하므로 선택지 중 주격 관계대명사인 (C) who가 정답이다.

해석 Vensa Airways는 비행기 결항으로 인해 지연된 모든 사람에게 여행 상품권을 제공했다.

어휘 voucher 상품권, 쿠폰　cancellation 취소

112. 수동태 vs. 능동태

해설 주어 Spectators는 동사 ask의 행위를 받는 대상이므로 빈칸에는 [be + 과거분사] 형태의 수동태가 적절하다. 따라서 (C) are asked가 정답이다.

해석 관중들은 불필요한 개인 물품을 경기장에 반입하는 것을 삼가 주시기 바랍니다.

어휘 spectator 관중　be asked to do ~하도록 요청받다　refrain from ~을 삼가다　unnecessary 불필요한

113. 형용사 자리

해설 빈칸 앞에 관사가 있고 뒤에는 명사가 이어지므로 빈칸에는 명사를 수식하는 말이 들어가야 한다. 따라서 선택지 중 형용사인 (C) acceptable이 정답이다.

해석 Sunderland Insurance의 정책에는 직장에서 허용 가능한 개인 전화의 사용으로 긴급 통화가 포함되어 있다.

어휘 emergency 응급의, 비상의

114. 부사절 접속사 자리 + 어휘

해설 빈칸 앞뒤에 완전한 절이 있으므로 빈칸은 접속사 자리이다. (C) except와 (D) before가 정답 후보인데, 문맥상 매장에 입고되기 전에 꼼꼼하게 검수된다는 내용이 되는 게 자연스러우므로 '~하기 전에'를 뜻하는 (D)가 정답이다.

해석 우리의 모든 의류는 AJ Fashions 매장에 입고되기 전에 꼼꼼하게 검수됩니다.

어휘 garment 의복, 옷　closely 면밀히; 밀접하게　inspect 검사하다, 점검하다　except ~라는 점만 제외하면

115. 부사 자리

해설 빈칸은 be동사 was와 과거분사 confirmed 사이의 부사 자리이므로 (A) reliably가 정답이다.

해석 합병 소식은 한 조직 내 소식통에 의해 확실하게 확인되었다.

어휘 merger 합병　reliably 믿음직하게, 제대로　confirm 확

인하다; 확정하다 **source** 소식통, 정보원; 원천, 근원 **organization** 기구, 조직, 단체 **reliable** 믿을 만한, 신뢰할 만한 **reliability** 신뢰도, 믿음직함

116. 전치사 자리 + 어휘
해설 빈칸 뒤에 동명사구가 있으므로 빈칸에는 동명사구를 목적어로 취하는 말이 들어가야 한다. 선택지 중 전치사인 (B) According to와 (C) Prior to가 정답 후보인데, 문맥상 석사 학위를 마치기 전에 사업을 시작하기 위해 시간을 보냈다는 내용이 되는 게 자연스러우므로 '~ 전에'를 뜻하는 (C)가 정답이다.
해석 석사 학위를 마치기 전에 Ms. Lewis는 출장 뷔페 사업을 시작하기 위해 2년을 보냈다.
어휘 **launch** 출시하다; 출시 **catering** 출장 뷔페 **according to** ~에 따르면

117. 동사 어휘 depart
해석 극장으로 가는 버스는 약국 정문에서 출발하여 요크셔 스트리트까지 갑니다.
어휘 **depart** 출발하다 **conduct** (특정 활동을) 수행하다; 지휘하다 **extend** 연장하다; (사업, 세력 등을) 확대하다 **withdraw** (돈을) 인출하다; 물러나다, 철회하다

118. 분사 자리
해설 빈칸 앞에 동명사가 있고 뒤에는 명사구가 이어지므로 빈칸은 명사구를 수식하는 자리이다. 선택지 중 명사를 수식할 수 있는 것은 과거분사이므로 (B) used가 정답이다.
해석 창업 비용을 줄이기 위해 중고 사무용품을 구입해 보세요.
어휘 **start-up costs** 착수 비용

119. 명사 어휘 site
해석 Brow Supplies는 작업 현장의 안전을 개선하기 위해 새로운 안전모들을 개발할 계획이다.
어휘 **hard hat** 안전모 **site** 현장, 장소; 부지 **notice** 공고문, 안내문; 알림, 통지 **goal** 목적, 목표 **calendar** 달력, 일정표

120. 동사 어휘 contact
해석 오래된 장비 교체에 대해 문의하려면 IT 부서의 Mr. Arrieta에게 연락하세요.
어휘 **inquiry** 문의, 질문 **replace** 대체하다, 교체하다 **outdated** 구식의, 예전의 **contact** 연락하다; 접촉하다 **determine** 결정하다, 확정하다 **apply** 신청하다, 지원하다; 적용하다 **hire** 채용하다, 고용하다

121. 전치사 자리 + 어휘
해설 빈칸 앞에 주어와 동사를 갖춘 완전한 절이 있고 뒤에는 명사구가 이어지므로 빈칸에는 명사구를 목적어로 취하는 말이 들어가야 한다. 선택지 중 전치사인 (A) onto와 (D) until이 정답 후보인데, 문맥상 8월 말까지 무료 투어를 제공할 거라는 내용이 되는 게 자연스러우므로 '~까지'를 뜻하는 (D)가 정답이다.
해석 박물관은 8월 말까지 토요일 오전에 무료로 전시 비하인드 투어를 제공할 것이다.

어휘 **behind-the-scenes** 이면의, 대중에게 공개되지 않은 **onto** ~로, ~의 위로

122. 전치사 어휘 between
해석 클레릭 국립 공원 방문객은 카페와 어린이 놀이터 사이에 위치한 관리소에 하룻밤 캠핑 계획을 모두 신고해야 한다.
어휘 **report** 보고하다, 알리다 **overnight** 하룻밤의 **ranger station** (특히 산림) 관리소 **locate** 위치시키다, (특정 위치에) 두다 **between A and B** A와 B 사이에 **including** ~을 포함하여 **into** ~ 안으로 **throughout** ~ 내내; ~ 전역에

123. 부사 어휘 soon
해석 Arden Footwear는 곧 등산화 제품을 확대할 것이라고 발표했다.
어휘 **soon** 곧, 머지않아, 이내, 빨리 **expand** 확대하다, 확장하다 **wherever** ~하는 곳은 어디든지; 어디에서 ~하더라도 **most** 가장; 매우, 대단히 **so** 너무; 매우, 대단히

124. 명사 어휘 combination
해석 인테리어 디자이너는 고객이 주방의 색상으로 밝은 회색과 노란색을 선택하기 전에 몇 가지 조합을 제시했다.
어휘 **present** 나타내다, 보여 주다 **combination** 조합, 결합 **region** 지역 **impression** 인상, 느낌 **function** 기능

125. 형용사 자리
해설 빈칸은 be동사 are 뒤의 주격 보어 자리로 주어인 salary increases를 구체적으로 설명할 수 있는 말이 들어가야 한다. 따라서 선택지 중 형용사인 (C) negotiable이 정답이다.
해석 Redding Technology의 새로운 방침에 따라 급여 인상은 더 이상 협상이 불가능하므로 직원들은 경력 수준에 따라서만 보상을 받는다.
어휘 **under one's policy** ~의 정책[방침]에 따라 **no longer** 더 이상 ~ 않는 **compensate** 보상하다

126. 부사 자리
해설 빈칸은 조동사 have와 과거분사 publicized 사이의 부사 자리이므로 (C) widely가 정답이다.
해석 여러 산업에 미치는 영향 때문에 언론 매체들은 무역 거래에 대한 세부 사항을 널리 보도했다.
어휘 **media outlet** 언론 매체, 언론사 **publicize** 알리다

127. 부사절 접속사 자리 + 어휘
해설 빈칸 뒤에 주어와 동사를 갖춘 완전한 절이 있고, 콤마로 새로운 절이 연결되어 있으므로 빈칸은 부사절 접속사 자리이다. (A) While과 (B) If가 정답 후보인데, 문맥상 상품이 손상되어 도착하면 무료로 교환할 수 있다는 내용이 되는 게 자연스러우므로 '만약 ~라면'을 뜻하는 (B)가 정답이다.
해석 Strike Sports 웹사이트에서 구매한 상품이 파손되어 도착하면 무료로 교환할 수 있습니다.
어휘 **at no cost** 무료로 **while** ~하는 동안; ~한 반면에

128. 명사 자리

해설 빈칸 앞에 형용사가 있으므로 빈칸은 명사 자리이다. 따라서 (A) applause가 정답이다.

해석 RadioWave Electronics의 신제품 시연회는 큰 찬사를 받았다.

어휘 demonstration 시범, 시연; 설명

129. 형용사 어휘 extensive

해석 제약 연구에 대한 풍부한 지식으로 인해 Max Punja는 수석 고문직을 제안받을 것이다.

어휘 owing to ~ 때문에　extensive 광범위한; 대규모의 knowledge 지식; 이해　pharmaceutical 약학의, 제약의 consultant 자문 위원, 상담가　amicable 우호적인, 원만한 charitable 자선의, 자선을 베푸는　gratifying 흐뭇한, 기쁜

130. 전치사 자리 + 어휘

해설 빈칸 앞에 주어와 동사를 갖춘 완전한 절이 있고 뒤에는 명사구가 이어지므로 빈칸에는 명사구를 목적어로 취하는 말이 들어가야 한다. 선택지 중 전치사구인 (C) rather than과 (D) as a result of가 정답 후보인데, 문맥상 악천후로 인해 비응급 차량은 고속 도로 통행이 제한될 거라는 내용이 되는 게 자연스러우므로 '~의 결과로'를 뜻하는 (D)가 정답이다.

해석 이 시간부로 악천후로 인해 19번 고속 도로의 모든 차선이 비응급 차량들에게 폐쇄될 것이다.

어휘 immediately 즉시, 즉각　non-emergency 비응급의, 긴급하지 않은　severe weather condition 악천후　so that ~하기 위해서　as though 마치 ~인 것처럼　rather than ~라기보다는

RC PART 6

출제 경향 및 전략

131-134. 설명서

> Baldrick Accessories—Baldrick Accessories 웹사이트를 통해 이름이나 다른 글자가 있는 특별한 액세서리를 쉽게 만들 수 있습니다! 원하는 제품을 선택하고 글자를 입력한 다음에 글꼴과 크기, 색상을 고르기만 하면 됩니다. 주문하기 전에 샘플 이미지를 반드시 꼼꼼하게 검토해 주세요. **131 또한** 수정이 필요하다면 '뒤로' 버튼을 사용하시면 됩니다. **132 판매 후 교환 및 반품은 불가하다는 점을 알아 두시기 바랍니다.** 주문 제작 제품 특성상 재사용할 수가 없습니다. 주문이 완료되면 몇 분 내에 영수증을 **133 이메일로 받게 되실 겁니다.** 제품이 **134 준비되면** 또 다른 이메일이 발송될 것입니다. 주문량에 따라 최대 5일이 소요될 수 있습니다.

어휘 unique 독특한, 고유한 · simply 그저, 단순히 · input 입력하다 · examine 조사하다, 살펴보다 · place an order 주문하다 · make a change 변경하다, 수정하다 · necessary 필수적인, 필요한 · custom 주문 제작의 · up to ~까지 · depend on ~에 달려 있다; ~에 의존[의지]하다 · volume 용량; 음량

131. 접속부사 어휘 additionally
(A) Consequently 그 결과, 따라서
(B) For example 예를 들어
(C) Conversely 반대로
(D) Additionally 또한, 게다가

132. 문맥에 맞는 문장 고르기
(A) 소식지를 구독하는 분들은 할인을 받을 수 있습니다.
(B) 판매 후 교환 및 반품은 불가하다는 점을 알아 두시기 바랍니다.
(C) 새 상품을 정기적으로 다시 확인하는 것을 잊지 마세요.
(D) 배송 옵션이 표시될 겁니다.

어휘 subscriber 구독자 · receive a discount 할인을 받다 · be aware that ~라는 것을 자각[인지]하다 · all sales are final 판매 후 교환 및 반품은 불가하다 · merchandise 물품, 상품 · present 나타내다, 보여 주다; 제시하다, 제출하다

133. 미래 시제
해설 뒤에 이어지는 문장에서 제품이 준비되면 또 다른 이메일이 발송될 거라고 한 것으로 보아 빈칸이 있는 문장은 주문을 완료하고 난 다음에 일어날 일에 대해 설명하는 내용임을 알 수 있다. 따라서 미래 시제인 (C) will be e-mailed가 정답이다.

134. 형용사 어휘 ready
(A) ready 준비가 된
(B) brief 간단한; (시간이) 짧은
(C) similar 비슷한
(D) exempt 면제된, 제외된

UNIT 09 시제

> **1.** (B) **2.** (A) **3.** (D) **4.** (A) **5.** (A) **6.** (D)
> **7.** (B) **8.** (C)

1-2. 웹페이지

> 꽃꽂이 봄 강좌—지금 접수를 받고 있습니다.
> Tidwell 전문 대학이 올 봄 학기에 지역 사회를 위해 새로운 과정을 **1 개설할 예정입니다.** 수상 경력이 있는 플로리스트 Jennifer Goldsmith가 학생들에게 그들이 만든 것을 더 오래 지속시키는 방법에 대한 팁을 전수할 뿐만 아니라 특별한 날을 위한 완벽한 꽃꽂이 방법을 보여 줄 겁니다. 매주 화요일과 금요일 저녁 7시부터 10시까지 수업이 **2 진행됩니다.**
> 학기 중 만든 작품의 최종 전시회는 6월 2일에 열릴 것입니다. 표를 구하시려면 전문 대학 웹사이트 www.tidwellcc.com을 방문하세요.

어휘 flower arrangement 꽃꽂이 · occasion 때, 경우; 행사 · B as well as A A뿐만 아니라 B도 · creation 창조(물) · last 계속되다, 지속되다 · piece (작품) 한 점

1. 미래진행 시제
해설 올 봄 학기에 새로운 강좌를 개설할 예정이며 그 수업을 플로리스트 Jennifer Goldsmith가 진행하게 될 거라고 하는 흐름이 자연스럽다. 따라서 미래진행 시제인 (B) will be opening이 정답이다.

2. 현재 시제
해설 앞 문장에서 구체적인 수업 내용을 언급한 것으로 보아 빈칸이 있는 문장은 언제 수업을 하는지 알려 주는 내용임을 알 수 있다. 따라서 현재 시제인 (A) are held가 정답이다. 이미 확정된 가까운 미래의 일은 현재 시제로 나타내기도 한다.

3-4. 공고

> Classic Motors 팀에게 중대한 소식입니다!
> Nathaniel Foreman이 8월 16일부로 팀장으로 승진한 것을 축하합니다. Mr. Foreman은 러셀 대학교 인턴십 프로그램을 통해 Classic Motors에 인턴으로 **3 입사했습니다.** 그는 지난 15년간 직원들을 위해 기대치 이상으로 일을 하며 항상 우리 재무 팀을 위한 새롭고 혁신적인 해결책을 찾음으로써 회사에 상당한 기여를 했습니다. 우리는 Mr. Foreman이 새로운 위치에서 **4 빼어난 모습을 보일 거라고** 확신합니다. 다음에 그를 만나면 뜨거운 축하를 전해 주세요.

어휘 congratulate A on B B에 대해 A를 축하하다 · effective (~부로) 시행되는, 발효되는; 효과적인 · go above and beyond 기대 이상으로 잘 해내다 · make a contribution 기여하다 · look for ~을 찾다 · innovative 혁신적인, 획기적인 · certain 확실한, 틀림없는

3. 과거 시제
해설 뒤 문장에서 15년간 성실히 근무하고 있다고 한 것으로 보아

빈칸이 있는 문장은 인턴으로 회사 생활을 시작했다는 과거 내용임을 알 수 있다. 따라서 과거 시제인 (D) entered가 정답이다.

4. 미래 시제

해설 앞 문장에서 15년간 성실히 근무하며 회사에 크게 기여했다고 한 것으로 보아 빈칸이 있는 문장은 Mr. Foreman이 팀장이라는 새로운 위치에서 맡은 바 직무를 잘 해낼 거라고 기대하는 내용임을 알 수 있다. 따라서 미래 시제인 (A) will shine이 정답이다.

어휘 shine (능력이) 빼어나다; 빛나다

5-6. 광고

Emerald Footwear가 25주년을 맞았습니다!

25년 전에 Emerald Footwear는 Plainsman Mall에서 작은 매장으로 문을 열었습니다. 오늘날 우리는 넓은 전시 공간이 있는 우리만의 2층 건물을 가지고 있습니다. 우리의 고품질 제품과 지식이 풍부한 직원들이 우리가 신뢰할 수 있는 소매업체가 되는 걸 **5도왔습니다.** 지난 수년간 보내 준 고객들의 성원에 감사하기 위해 9월 8일에 특별 세일을 할 것입니다.

신발 한 켤레를 구매하고 다른 한 켤레를 60% 할인받으세요. 이 할인은 모든 브랜드에 **6적용되며** 더 저렴한 상품이 할인을 받습니다. 세일 상품에는 다른 추가 쿠폰을 사용할 수 없다는 점을 알아 두시기 바랍니다.

어휘 kiosk (신문이나 음료 등을 파는) 작은 상점 story (건물의) 층 spacious 넓은, 널찍한 knowledgeable 많이 아는 trusted 신뢰받는 patronage 애용 offer 할인; 제안 note 주목하다; 언급하다 additional 추가의

5. 태와 시제 복합

해설 빈칸 뒤에 목적어가 있고 주어 Our high-quality products and knowledgeable staffs는 행위를 하는 주체이므로 빈칸에는 능동태가 들어가야 한다. (A) have helped와 (D) were helping이 정답 후보인데, 문맥상 오늘날 Emerald Footwear가 2층 건물까지 갖게 될 수 있었던 것은 고품질 제품과 지식이 풍부한 직원들이 과거부터 현재까지 도와준 덕분이라는 내용이 되는 게 자연스러우므로 현재완료 시제인 (A)가 정답이다.

6. 현재 시제

해설 앞 문장에서 특별 세일이 무엇인지 안내하고 있으며 빈칸이 있는 문장에서는 어떤 품목에 할인이 적용되는지 언급하고 있으므로 현재 시제인 (D) applies가 정답이다.

7-8. 고객 후기

방금 Home Necessities에서 주문한 냅킨 100개를 받았는데, 정말 인상적이었습니다! 저는 출장 뷔페 사업을 위해 테이블 세팅 용품을 주문해야 합니다. 하지만 제가 정기적으로 주문하는 회사에는 재고가 없었기 때문에 Home Necessities에 주문을 한번 해 봐야겠다고 생각했어요. 제품들이 더 잘 구성되어 있고, 더 다양한 색상과 디자인을 **7제공하더라고요.** 이제부터는 Home Necessities에서만 **8주문할 겁니다.**
—Martin Quinn

어휘 order 주문(품); 주문하다 thoroughly 완전히, 철저히 impress 인상을 주다, 감명을 주다 supplies 비품 out of stock 재고가 없는 give ~ a chance ~에게 기회를 주다 construct 구성하다; 건설하다 a wide range of 다양한 exclusively 독점적으로, 오로지 from now on 이제부터

7. 현재 시제

해설 콤마 앞에서 제품들이 더 잘 구성되어 있다고 한 것으로 보아 콤마 뒤의 빈칸 절은 또 다른 좋은 점을 추가적으로 설명하는 내용임을 알 수 있다. 따라서 현재 시제인 (B) offers가 정답이다.

8. 미래진행 시제

해설 앞 문장에서 제품 구성이 더 좋고 색상과 디자인도 더 다양하다고 한 것으로 보아 빈칸이 있는 문장은 앞으로 Home Necessities에서만 주문하겠다고 결심하는 내용임을 알 수 있다. 또한 빈칸 뒤에 있는 from now on은 주로 미래 시제와 어울려 쓰이는 표현이므로 미래진행 시제인 (C) will be ordering이 정답이다.

UNIT 10 어휘

본문 p.138

1. (B)	**2.** (D)	**3.** (B)	**4.** (B)	**5.** (C)	**6.** (D)
7. (B)					

1. 이메일

Graystone 프린터 X302가 단종되어 귀하의 주문이 자동으로 취소되었음을 알려 드립니다. 그러나 가장 최근 고객 대다수는 **1비슷한** 모델인 X430을 선호했습니다. 555-2098로 전화를 걸어 새로 주문을 하거나 환불 옵션에 대해 논의해 주십시오.

Alex's Office Supplies

어휘 inform 알리다, 통지하다 discontinue 단종하다 automatically 자동으로 place an order 주문하다 refund 환불

(A) accountable (해명할) 책임이 있는
(B) comparable 비슷한, 비교할 만한
(C) amicable 우호적인, 원만한
(D) applicable 해당[적용]되는

2. 광고

Auto Masters로 오시면 2시간 만에 차량을 전체적으로 점검해 드립니다. 여기에는 오일 교환, 창문 세정액 **2보충,** 타이어 위치 교체 등이 포함되어 있습니다. Fairhills Shopping Mall 옆에 위치해 있어 여러분이 가족과 시간을 보내는 동안 이 작업을 해 드릴 수 있습니다. 555-2840으로 전화를 걸어 이 서비스나 다른 여러 서비스를 예약하세요.

어휘 service 차량을 점검[정비]하다; 서비스(업), 체제 washer fluid 세정액 rotate (차량의 앞바퀴와 뒷바퀴 위치를) 교체하다, 바꾸다; 회전하다 locate 위치시키다, (특정 위치에) 두다; (위치를) 알아내다 book 예약하다

(A) remarking (사실, 의견 등을) 말하기
(B) rounding 둥글게 하기; (모퉁이 등을) 돌기
(C) reloading 다시 싣기
(D) refilling 다시 채우기

3. 공고

9월은 토론토 오페라단의 새로운 오페라 시즌이 시작되는 달입니다. 첫 공연은 9월 12일 저녁이고 12월 31일까지 공연이 계속됩니다. 올해에는 모든 분이 매주 화요일 오후 2시부터 4시까지 하는 ³공개 리허설을 볼 수 있도록 초대됩니다. 리허설 표를 예약하려면 웹사이트 www.torontooc.org를 방문해 주세요.

어휘 mark (어떤 일이 일어날 것임을) 보여 주다; 기념하다   run (연극, 영화 등이) 상영되다   sit in 방청하다, 참석하다   reserve 예약하다; (자리 등을) 따로 잡아 두다

(A) seasonal 계절의, 계절에 따른
(B) public 공개되는; 대중의, 공공의
(C) domestic 국내의; 가정의
(D) challenging (어렵지만) 도전적인, 도전 의식을 불러일으키는

4. 채용 공고

Rainbow Toys는 새로운 소셜 마케팅 매니저를 찾고 있습니다. 지원자는 우리의 소셜 미디어 플랫폼을 더 쉽게 접근할 수 있도록 만들고 고객들을 위해 더 ⁴매력적인 콘텐츠를 제작하는 일을 하게 될 겁니다. 그러한 이유로 지원자는 비디오 제작이나 소셜 미디어 플랫폼 관리 또는 광고 문구 작성에 경험이 있어야 합니다.

어휘 look for ~을 찾다   applicant 지원자   work on ~에 착수하다, ~에 노력을 들이다   accessible 접근할 수 있는

(A) lengthy 장황한, 지루한
(B) engaging 매력적인, 호감이 가는
(C) impersonal 인간미 없는
(D) accelerated 가속화된

5. 광고

Booker가 가장 인기 있는 독서 요금제에 새해 특별 할인을 해 드립니다! 디럭스 독서 요금제에 가입하면 50만 권 이상의 책을 ⁵이용할 수 있으며, 이번 달에 출간된 최신작을 30% 할인받아 구입할 수도 있습니다. 그리고 오직 Booker만 무제한으로 도서를 대여해 드립니다. 오늘 www.booker.com/newyear 에서 이 혜택을 누려 보세요.

어휘 sign up 신청하다, 등록하다   release 출시; 공개하다, 발표하다   unlimited 제한 없는, 무한한   take advantage of ~을 이용하다

(A) claim 주장; 권리; (보상금 등의) 청구
(B) control 통제; 지배
(C) access 접근; 접속
(D) entry 출입; 가입; 참가; 출품작

6-7. 고객 후기

저는 수년간 Manaray의 가구를 사용해 왔고 항상 구매에 만족했습니다. 하지만 Logan's Furniture의 전시장을 방문한 후에 저는 그곳에 가 보길 잘했다고 생각했습니다. 가구의 질이 차원이 달랐거든요!

가죽 소파는 고급스럽고 부드러운 가죽을 사용하여 만들어졌어요. 리클라이너를 포함하여 모든 디자인을 맞춤 제작할 수도 있습니다. 우리는 마호가니 나무로 만든 완벽한 식탁 세트도 발견했어요. 식탁과 의자는 ⁶튼튼해서 평생 쓰고도 남을 정도예요.

제품은 대부분 ⁷조립되지 않은 상태로 온다는 걸 알아 두세요. 전문적인 조립은 약간의 추가 비용만 내면 가능합니다. 하지만 모든 제품에 동봉된 쉽게 따라할 수 있는 설명서 덕분에 그건 굳이 필요하지 않을 수도 있습니다.

어휘 purchase 구매[구입]한 것; 구매, 구입   customize 맞춤 제작하다   as well 또한   be sure to do 확실히 ~하다   last 계속되다, 지속되다   be aware that ~라는 것을 자각[인지]하다   assembly 조립   available 이용할 수 있는; ~할 시간이 있는   additional 추가의   necessary 필수적인, 필요한   instructions 설명서; 지시

6.
(A) separate 분리된; 별개의, 다른
(B) stiff 뻣뻣한
(C) simple 간단한
(D) sturdy 튼튼한, 견고한

7.
(A) fixed 고정된
(B) assembled 조립된
(C) crumbled 잘게 부순, 바스러진
(D) pieced (조각조각을) 짜 맞춘

UNIT 11 접속부사
본문 p.140

1. (B)   **2.** (C)   **3.** (B)   **4.** (D)

1. 편지

관계자께,

저희 Forever Fitness에서 귀하를 회원으로 모시고자 합니다. 저희는 40에이커의 최첨단 시설에 이 지역 최고급 장비를 다수 보유하고 있습니다. 저희 시설에만 있는 포토 존도 마련되어 있습니다. 소셜 미디어를 활용하는 분들을 위한 곳입니다. ¹그 외에는 사전 동의 없이 저희의 일반 시설에서 사진 촬영을 하는 것은 일절 허용되지 않습니다. 저희는 40가지 이상의 가장 다양한 피트니스 프로그램을 제공합니다. 그리고 모든 강사와 트레이너는 여러분에게 가능한 한 최고의 경험을 선사하기 위해 국가 자격증을 여러 개 갖고 있습니다.

555-2109로 전화하셔서 무료 상담을 받고 1일 무료 이용권을 받으세요. 저희는 귀하가 다시 이곳을 찾을 거라고 확신합니다.

대표 Kelly Vasquez

어휘 an array of 다수의 top-of-the-line 최고급의 state-of-the-art 최신의 feature 기능, 특징 maintain (관계, 상태, 수준 등을) 유지하다 presence 존재; 풍채 consent 동의 a wide range of 다양한 national certification 국가 자격증 consultation 상담

(A) Besides 게다가
(B) Otherwise 그 외에는; 그렇지 않으면
(C) If not 그렇지 않으면
(D) Regardless 상관없이

2. 광고

여러분의 비즈니스를 알리세요!

훌륭한 사업을 하고 있지만 아무도 모르는 것 같습니까? 저희가 해결해 드리겠습니다! Frankfurt Media는 여러분의 사업에 적합한 광고 전략을 수립할 준비가 된 전문가 팀을 보유하고 있습니다. 저희가 완벽한 TV나 라디오 광고를 만들어 목표 대상에게 전달하겠습니다. ²**그동안에** 여러분은 사업에 집중할 시간을 더 갖게 될 겁니다.

오늘 www.frankfurtmedia.com에 접속해서 일주일 만에 광고를 준비해 보세요!

어휘 notice 알아채다, 인지하다, 주목하다 strategy 전략, 계획 craft (능숙하게) 만들어 내다; 기술, 기교 commercial 광고; 상업의 intended 대상으로 하는, 의도된

(A) Nevertheless 그럼에도 불구하고
(B) Even so 그렇기는 하지만
(C) Meanwhile 그동안에; 한편
(D) Recently 최근에

3. 이메일

수신인: Mark Klein
발신인: Jane Lorowitz
날짜: 4월 20일
제목: 일정 변경

Mr. Klein께,

공사 일정에 변경 사항이 있어 연락드립니다. 현재 일정은 6월 12일까지로 잡혀 있습니다. 하지만 최근의 잦은 폭풍우로 인해 그 날들에는 공사를 중단해야만 했습니다. ³**그 결과** 벽을 쌓는 작업을 끝낼 수 없었고요. 새 예상 종료일은 6월 20일입니다.

일정에 대해 더 논의하고 싶다면 언제든 이야기 나누시죠.

Jane Lorowitz

어휘 construction 건설, 공사 be unable to do ~할 수 없다 put up ~을 세우다; ~을 (벽 등에) 걸다 estimated 추측의; 견적의 end date 종료일

(A) Nonetheless 그렇기는 하지만, 그렇더라도
(B) Consequently 그 결과, 따라서

(C) Finally 마침내; 마지막으로
(D) Lastly 마지막으로, 끝으로

4. 정보문

6개월의 보수 공사 끝에 크래프트베리 도서관은 재개관을 발표하게 되어 기쁩니다. 몇몇 새로운 특징으로는 경사로가 완비되어 휠체어로 접근할 수 있는 입구와 인기 있는 방과 후 프로그램을 더 많이 진행할 수 있는 다섯 개의 새로운 교실이 있습니다. ⁴**추가적으로** 크래프트베리 주민들이 일자리를 찾고 취직할 수 있도록 취업 준비 센터를 세웠습니다. 도서관의 모든 새로운 특징을 알아보려면 웹사이트 www.craftsburylibrary.gov를 방문하세요.

어휘 renovation 개조, 리모델링 feature 기능, 특징 accessible 접근할 수 있는; 접속 가능한 ramp 경사로 establish 설립하다, 수립하다; (제도 등을) 확립하다 occupation 직업 preparation 준비, 대비 look for ~을 찾다 secure 확보하다, 획득하다; 고정하다 head to ~로 향하다

(A) Hence 그러므로
(B) Accordingly 따라서
(C) Therefore 그러므로
(D) Additionally 추가적으로

PART 6

UNIT 12 문맥에 맞는 문장 고르기   본문 p.142

1. (D)   **2.** (A)   **3.** (D)   **4.** (B)

1. 이메일

수신인: 모든 고객
발신인: Keritz Audio 고객 서비스 팀
날짜: 12월 2일
제목: 연말 업무 종료

Keritz Audio는 12월 23일부터 연말 연휴 기간 동안 휴무입니다. ¹**연말 전에 주문할 수 있는 마지막 날짜는 12월 22일입니다.** 이 날짜 이후의 주문은 새해에 발송됩니다. 또한 배송 날짜는 정확한 배송 지역에 따라 달라질 수 있습니다. 해당 지역의 예상 배송 일정을 보려면 저희 웹사이트의 배송 항목을 확인해 주세요.

여러분의 지속적인 성원에 감사드립니다. 새해를 맞아 저희가 준비한 새 제품들을 보여 드릴 수 있기를 고대합니다.

Keritz Audio 팀

어휘 closure 폐쇄 effective (~부로) 시행되는, 발효되는; 효과적인 place an order 주문하다 ship (상품을) 배송하다 vary 달라지다; 다양하다 depend on ~에 달려 있다; ~에 의존[의지]하다 estimated 추측의; 견적의 look forward to ~하는 것을 고대하다 line up ~을 준비하다; ~을 줄 세우다

(A) 승인 번호를 가지고 택배 회사에 연락하세요.

(B) 특송은 5.99달러에 이용하실 수 있습니다.
(C) 오전 9시부터 오후 5시까지 영업합니다.
(D) 연말 전에 주문할 수 있는 마지막 날짜는 12월 22일입니다.

어휘 courier 택배 회사   confirmation number 승인[확인] 번호   express delivery 특송   available 이용할 수 있는; ~할 시간이 있는

2. 공고

온 가족의 즐겁고 신나는 하루를 위해 아름다운 Catskills Waterpark를 방문하세요. 우리는 이 지역에서 가장 큰 워터파크일 뿐만 아니라 가장 친환경적입니다. 우리는 완전히 환경 친화적인 물 사용 시스템을 갖춘 국내 유일의 워터파크입니다. **²모든 물은 빗물과 천연 저수지와 같은 자연적인 것에서 수집됩니다.** 이것은 지역 물 공급에 미치는 영향을 줄이기 위해 사용됩니다. 우리 워터파크는 나아가 수력 전기를 사용해서 모든 놀이 기구와 파도 풀에 전력을 공급합니다. 우리는 가족들이 몇 세대에 걸쳐 Catskills Waterpark를 즐기기를 원합니다. 표와 정보를 원하시면 www.catskillswaterpark.com을 방문해 주세요.

어휘 not only A (but) also B A뿐만 아니라 B도   feature 특징으로 하다, 특별히 선보이다   completely 완전히, 전적으로   environmentally friendly 환경 친화적인   be used to do ~하기 위해 사용되다 (cf. be used to (doing) something ~에 익숙하다)   hydroelectricity 수력 전기   power 동력을 공급하다   for generations 몇 세대에 걸쳐

(A) 모든 물은 빗물과 천연 저수지와 같은 자연적인 것에서 수집됩니다.
(B) 모든 방문객은 워터파크에 있을 때 쓰레기를 주워 갈 것을 부탁드립니다.
(C) 워터파크에 있는 동안에는 물을 너무 많이 사용하는 것을 삼가 주십시오.
(D) 모든 종이 제품은 재활용된 종이로 만들어집니다.

어휘 collect 모으다, 수집하다   source 원천, 근원; 소식통, 정보원   reservoir 저수지, 급수지   pick up ~을 줍다   refrain from ~을 삼가다   recycled paper 재활용 종이

3. 공지

최근 우리의 현재 판매업체인 Global Produce Distributions가 공급망을 축소하기로 결정했다는 소식을 들었습니다. 이것은 우리가 감귤류 과일을 북유럽으로 수출할 수 없다는 것을 의미합니다. **³이 지역은 올해 확장 계획의 주요 부분이었습니다.** 그렇기 때문에 우리는 새로운 유통업체를 찾는 데 많은 노력을 기울여야 합니다.

우리가 자랑하는 한 가지는 매우 다양한 이국적인 과일입니다. 그 부분에 보완이 필요한 회사를 찾을 수 있는지 알아보세요. 그런 회사를 찾으면 저에게 알려 주십시오.

금요일 오후까지 주간 관리자 회의에 제출할 가능성 있는 업체 목록을 원합니다.

어휘 vendor 판매업체   downsize (인원을) 축소하다, 줄이다   supply chain 공급망   be unable to do ~할 수 없다   export 수출하다   put effort into ~에 노력을 기울이다   distributor 유통업자   an array of 다수의   exotic 이국적인, 외래의   supplement 보충하다, 추가하다   a list of leads 예비 고객 명단   present 제시하다, 제출하다; 현재의; 참석한

(A) 우리 팀 사람들은 아무도 북유럽에 가 본 적이 없습니다.
(B) 당신의 자세한 감귤류 과일 목록을 우리에게 주세요.
(C) 우리는 공급량을 늘릴 필요가 있습니다.
(D) 이 지역은 올해 확장 계획의 주요 부분이었습니다.

어휘 work on ~에 착수하다, ~에 노력을 들이다   expansion 확장

4. 정보문

Hartman Landscaping의 소유주인 Charles Hartman은 20년 넘게 이 지역을 아름답게 가꾸어 왔습니다. 그의 팀은 상업지와 공유지를 전문으로 합니다.

그들은 이 지역에서 가장 인기 있는 휴양 공원과 공간을 만든 것으로 잘 알려져 있습니다. **⁴그들이 바로 Campbell Park의 디자인상 수상의 주역입니다.** 이 100에이커에 달하는 공간은 매년 열리는 George Street Music Festival 장소입니다.

여러분의 공간을 예술 작품으로 바꾸려면 오늘 Hartman Landscaping에 연락하세요. 그들은 여러분의 예산과 크기에 따라 완벽한 잔디밭을 만들도록 도와줄 것입니다.

어휘 beautify 아름답게 하다   specialize in ~을 전문적으로 하다   commercial 상업의; 광고   public 대중의, 공공의; 공개되는   property 부동산; 건물; 재산, 소유물   construction 건설, 공사

(A) 그들의 사무실은 지역 우체국 바로 옆에 있습니다.
(B) 그들이 바로 Campbell Park의 디자인상 수상의 주역입니다.
(C) 결과적으로 그들은 모든 토종 꽃과 관목을 사용하는 걸 선호합니다.
(D) 그들은 연례행사의 가장 큰 후원자들입니다.

어휘 be responsible for ~에 책임이 있다   native 토착의   shrub 관목

PART TEST 본문 p.144

131. (C)	**132.** (B)	**133.** (B)	**134.** (B)	**135.** (C)
136. (D)	**137.** (B)	**138.** (B)	**139.** (C)	**140.** (D)
141. (C)	**142.** (D)	**143.** (A)	**144.** (D)	**145.** (D)
146. (A)				

131-134. 이메일

수신인: Edward Sandoval
발신인: Brunswick Studios
날짜: 2월 22일
제목: 멤버십

Mr. Sandoval께,

Brunswick Studios에 1년 멤버십 등록을 해 주셔서 감사합

니다. 저희 웹사이트는 귀하가 새로운 팬들에게 다가가고, 의미 있는 곡을 쓰고, 귀하의 공연을 향상시키는 것을 돕기 위해 헌신하고 있습니다. 저희 웹사이트의 콘텐츠는 귀하와 같은 음악가들에 의해 **131 작성되었습니다.** 편집을 요하는 프로젝트**132를 위한** 소프트웨어 프로그램을 비롯해서 귀하가 필요로 할 만한 제품의 특별 판매에 대한 이메일을 받으실 겁니다.

받은 편지함에 발송된 콘텐츠를 **133 귀하의 필요에 맞추시려면** 계정에 로그인하여 원하는 옵션들을 선택하십시오. 월 5.99달러만 더 내면 골드 등급으로 업그레이드할 수 있고 훨씬 더 많은 콘텐츠를 받을 수 있습니다. **134 위약금 없이 언제든지 취소할 수 있습니다.** 그러니 부담 없이 한번 신청해 보는 건 어떠세요?

Tara Nelson
Brunswick Studios

어휘 sign up 신청하다, 등록하다   be devoted to ~에 전념[헌신]하다   require 필요하다, 요구하다   desired 원하는, 바라는   give it a try 한번 해 보다

131. 태와 시제 복합
해설 빈칸 뒤에 [by + 행위 주체]인 by musicians가 있으므로 빈칸에는 [be + 과거분사] 형태의 수동태가 들어가야 한다. (C) is written과 (D) had been written이 정답 후보인데, 앞 문장에서 Brunswick Studios의 웹사이트를 소개하고 있으며 빈칸이 있는 문장에서는 웹사이트에 있는 콘텐츠를 언급하고 있으므로 현재 시제인 (C)가 정답이다.

132. 전치사 어휘 for
(A) into ~ 안으로
(B) for ~을 위해
(C) our 우리의
(D) at ~에서

해설 빈칸 앞뒤에 명사가 있으므로 빈칸은 전치사 자리이다. 따라서 소유한정사인 (C) our는 오답이다.

133. 동사 어휘 personalize
(A) deliver 배달하다
(B) personalize 개인 맞춤화하다
(C) calculate 계산하다
(D) dispute 논쟁하다

134. 문맥에 맞는 문장 고르기
(A) 후보로 지명되어 기쁩니다.
(B) 위약금 없이 언제든지 취소할 수 있습니다.
(C) 귀하의 의견은 서비스 개선에 도움이 됩니다.
(D) 속도는 인터넷 서비스에 따라 다릅니다.

어휘 nominate 후보로 지명하다   depend on ~에 달려 있다; ~에 의존[의지]하다

135-138. 이메일

수신인: 모든 Redhawk Towers 세입자
발신인: Jennifer Milligan
날짜: 2월 20일
제목: 정전

Redhawk Towers 세입자 여러분께,

12번가와 14번가 사이의 제닝스 스트리트와 파인 스트리트에 있는 모든 건물에 전기 공급 중단이 **135 예정되어 있습니다.** 필수 유지 보수 작업을 수행하기 위해 전기가 차단될 것입니다. 작업은 2월 25일과 26일 오전 9시부터 정오까지 진행될 것입니다.

136 각각의 날짜에 정전에 대비하여 미리 계획을 세워 주십시오. 컴퓨터는 정전 전에 꺼야 합니다. **137 전원이 켜진 상태로 두면 예상하지 못한 중단으로 인해 손상될 수 있습니다.** 냉장고와 냉동고에 보관된 음식은 문만 닫아 두면 괜찮을 겁니다. 여러분의 **138 협조**와 인내에 감사드립니다.

Jennifer Milligan
Redhawk Towers 부동산 관리자

어휘 tenant 세입자   power outage 정전   interruption 중단   shut off (전원 등을) 끄다   essential 필수적인   maintenance (건물, 기계 등의) 유지   take place 열리다, 일어나다   prior to ~ 전에

135. 수동태 vs. 능동태
해설 빈칸 뒤에 목적어가 없고 주어 An interruption은 행위를 받는 대상이므로 빈칸에는 [be + 과거분사] 형태의 수동태가 적절하다. 따라서 (C) is scheduled가 정답이다.

136. 한정사 each
해설 빈칸 뒤에 단수 명사 day가 있으므로 빈칸에는 단수 명사를 수식할 수 있는 말이 들어가야 한다. 따라서 (D) each가 정답이다. (B) most와 (C) all은 복수 명사나 불가산명사를 수식하기 때문에 답이 될 수 없다.

137. 문맥에 맞는 문장 고르기
(A) 현재 아파트 몇 군데는 이용 가능합니다.
(B) 전원이 켜진 상태로 두면 예상치 못한 중단으로 인해 손상될 수 있습니다.
(C) 우리는 안전이 중요시된다는 것을 확인할 수 있습니다.
(D) 더 이상 소음이 여러분을 괴롭히지 않을 겁니다.

어휘 unit (건물의) 한 공간; 구성단위; 한 개   available 이용할 수 있는; ~할 시간이 있는   unexpected 예상 밖의, 뜻밖의   shutdown (운영, 가동 등의) 중단, 폐쇄   confirm 확인하다; 확정하다   take ~ seriously ~을 진지[심각]하게 여기다   no longer 더 이상 ~ 않는   disturbance 방해; 소란

138. 명사 어휘 cooperation
(A) donation 기부
(B) cooperation 협조
(C) destination 목적지
(D) confirmation 확인

139-142. 블로그 발췌문

배관공을 위한 차량

여러분이 독자적인 배관공으로 일하고 있다면 차량 소유는 필수입니다. 처음에는 **139 가장 저렴한** 선택지를 찾는 게 좋은 생각이라고 여길 수도 있습니다. 하지만 처음부터 믿을 만한 차량에 투

자하는 것이 훨씬 낫습니다. **140 시간을 두고 여러분에게 필요한 사이즈에 대해서 생각해 보시는 게 좋습니다.** 예를 들어 좁은 주차 공간에 맞춰야 합니까 아니면 차에 전기톱과 같은 큰 **141 도구**를 보관해야 합니까? 고려하고 있는 모델에 대한 리뷰를 반드시 읽어 보십시오. **142 궁극적으로** 여러분이 구매한 차량이 일을 하는 동안 여러분을 지원하고 심지어 동기 부여도 할 것입니다.

어휘 plumber 배관공   independent 독립된, 독립적인   essential 필수적인   look for ~을 찾다   reliable 믿을 만한, 신뢰할 만한   power saw 전기톱   motivate 동기를 부여하다

139. 최상급 비교
해설 빈칸 앞에 관사가 있고 뒤에는 명사 option이 있으므로 빈칸은 명사를 수식하는 형용사 자리이다. 문맥상 '가장 저렴한 선택지'가 되는 게 자연스러우며, 이때 최상급 표현을 위해 정관사 the와 함께 쓸 수 있어야 하므로 (C) cheapest가 정답이다.

140. 문맥에 맞는 문장 고르기
(A) 차량의 연비 효율성이 중요합니다.
(B) 고객 기반을 구축하는 데 몇 달이 걸릴 수 있습니다.
(C) 배관 작업은 일 년 내내 꾸준히 수요가 있습니다.
(D) 시간을 두고 여러분에게 필요한 사이즈에 대해서 생각해 보시는 게 좋습니다.

어휘 efficiency 효율성   steadily 점차, 꾸준히   in demand 수요가 많은

141. 명사 어휘 tool
(A) electricians 전기 기사
(B) uniforms 유니폼
(C) tools 도구
(D) pipes 파이프

142. 접속부사 어휘 ultimately
(A) Lately 최근에
(B) On the other hand 반면에
(C) Otherwise 그 외에는; 그렇지 않으면
(D) Ultimately 궁극적으로

143-146. 편지

3월 3일

Northwest Utilities 고객님께,

가장 최근의 **143 에너지** 청구서로 인해 발생한 혼란에 대해 사과 드립니다. 청구 부서에서 소프트웨어 오작동이 발생했습니다. 결과적으로 2월 청구서는 잘못된 정보로 **144 발송되었습니다.** 고객의 사용량을 정확하게 반영하기 위해 노력**145 하고 있지만** 이러한 오류는 가끔 발생합니다.

146 그 청구서는 무시하고 새 청구서가 발행될 때까지 기다려 주세요. 다음 영업일 기준 5일 이내에 받으실 수 있습니다. 또한 이 오류 때문에 납부 마감일을 2주 연장할 것입니다. 이 과정 동안 기다려 주시고 이해해 주셔서 감사합니다.

Northwest Utilities
4190 우드랜드 테라스
타코마, 워싱턴주 98412

어휘 confusion 혼란, 혼동   malfunction 오작동; 오작동하다   strive to do ~하기 위해 노력하다   usage 사용(량)   extend 연장하다; (사업, 세력 등을) 확대하다

143. 명사 자리
해설 빈칸 앞에 소유한정사 your가 있으므로 빈칸은 명사 자리이다. 따라서 (A) energy가 정답이다.

144. 구동사 어휘 send out
(A) given away (비밀 등이) 발설된; 거저 주어진
(B) cashed in (보험 증서 등이) 현금화된
(C) brought down (수준, 양 등이) 낮춰진
(D) sent out 발송된

145. 부사절 접속사 어휘 although
(A) Despite ~에도 불구하고
(B) Except ~라는 점만 제외하면
(C) Once 일단 ~하면; ~하자마자
(D) Although 비록 ~일지라도

해설 빈칸 뒤에 주어와 동사를 갖춘 완전한 절이 있고, 콤마로 새로운 절이 연결되어 있으므로 빈칸에는 부사절 접속사가 들어가야 한다. 따라서 전치사인 (A) Despite는 오답이다.

146. 문맥에 맞는 문장 고르기
(A) 그 청구서는 무시하고 새 청구서가 발행될 때까지 기다려 주세요.
(B) 일부 전기는 재생 가능한 자원에서 나옵니다.
(C) 그 정책은 저희 웹사이트에 명확하게 설명되어 있습니다.
(D) 귀하의 신속한 서비스 비용 지불에 감사드립니다.

어휘 ignore 무시하다   issue 발급하다, 발행하다   electricity 전기   renewable 재생 가능한   outline (간략히) 설명하다   prompt 즉각적인

UNIT 13 이메일·편지 본문 p.152

지문의 구성과 흐름 파악하기

수신인: Bonnie Rosario
발신인: Philip Hawley
날짜: 4월 24일
제목: 수영장 공사

Ms. Rosario께,

Charack Construction은 귀하의 호텔에 야외 수영장을 건설하기 위한 보증금을 받았습니다. 이 정도 규모의 프로젝트는 일반적으로 약 6~8주가 소요됩니다. 하지만 귀하가 요청한 대로 3주 안에 작업을 완료할 수 있을 것입니다. 여름 성수기가 시작되기 전에 그 시설을 개방하는 것의 중요성을 잘 알고 있습니다. 우리 팀은 4월 28일에 작업을 시작할 수 있는데, 이 작업에는 청소와 사전 준비를 하는 것이 처음에 포함될 것입니다.

프로젝트의 세부 사항은 대부분 이미 확정되었지만 타일 패턴을 선택하셔야 합니다. 제 직원 한 명이 오늘 늦게 샘플 한 상자를 가져다줄 것입니다. 샘플들을 훑어보시고 4월 30일 회의에서 어떤 것을 원하는지 알려 주십시오. 재고가 있는 타일만 보내 드릴 테니 유통망 지연 문제는 없을 겁니다.

Philip Hawley
Charack Construction 관리자

어휘 deposit 보증금, 착수금 approximately 대략, 약 request 요구하다, 신청하다; 요구, 요청(서) initially 처음에 finalize 결론짓다 drop off ~을 갖다 놓다 look over ~을 (대강) 살펴보다 distribution chain 유통망

1. 이메일의 목적은 무엇인가?
(A) 작업 계획 변경을 제안하기 위해
(B) 보증금을 위한 자금을 요청하기 위해
(C) 건설 사업을 소개하기 위해
(D) 프로젝트 관련 최신 정보를 전달하기 위해

2. 두 번째 단락 세 번째 줄의 'drop off'와 의미상 가장 가까운 것은?
(A) 모으다
(B) 배달하다
(C) 줄이다
(D) 깜빡 잠이 들다

3. 이메일에 따르면 Ms. Rosario는 4월 30일 회의 전에 무엇을 해야 하는가?
(A) 크기 확인하기
(B) 자재 선택하기
(C) 계약서에 서명하기
(D) 스케치 검토하기

1. (B) **2.** (D) **3.** (D) **4.** (D) **5.** (B) **6.** (A)

1-2. 이메일

수신인: Ravi Singh
발신인: Emerald Gardening Supplies
날짜: 5월 2일
제목: 주문 번호 03795
첨부 파일: RG7_설명서

Mr. Singh께,

최근에 Emerald Gardening Supplies에서 구매해 주셔서 감사합니다! 지난 10년 동안 저희는 고객 여러분께 정원을 멋지게 보이도록 하기 위한 장비와 장식을 제공해 왔습니다. 귀하가 주문한 **¹RG7 태양광 랜턴**을 잘 사용하시길 바랍니다. 첨부된 사용 설명서를 참조하십시오. **¹사용 설명서에는 낮 동안 햇빛에 최대한 노출시키기 위해 랜턴을 어디에 배치해야 하는지에 대한 팁이 있습니다.**

²정원에 랜턴이 있는 사진을 가지고 계시다면 우리의 소셜 미디어 페이지에 공유해 주세요. 추첨을 통해 100달러 상품권을 받으실 수 있습니다.

Emerald Gardening Supplies

어휘 provide A with B A에게 B를 제공하다 solar-powered 태양 에너지를 이용한, 태양광을 동력으로 한 maximize 최대로 하다 exposure 노출 drawing 추첨 voucher 상품권, 쿠폰

1. 랜턴에 대해 명시된 것은 무엇인가?
(A) 습기에 노출되어서는 안 된다.
(B) 햇빛으로 충전될 수 있다.
(C) 다양한 크기로 이용할 수 있다.
(D) 10년 품질 보증서가 딸려 온다.

해설 **NOT/True**
Mr. Singh이 태양광 랜턴을 주문했고, 사용 설명서에 낮 동안 랜턴을 햇빛에 노출시킨다는 내용이 있는 것으로 보아 랜턴은 햇빛으로 충전된다는 걸 알 수 있다. 따라서 (B)가 정답이다.

어휘 be exposed to ~에 노출되다 charge 충전하다; (요금 등을) 부과하다 a variety of 다양한 warranty 품질 보증(서)

2. Mr. Singh은 무엇을 하라고 요청받는가?
(A) 제품 후기 작성하기
(B) 상품권 발송을 위한 주소 제공하기
(C) 회사에 구매 증명서 보여 주기
(D) 소셜 미디어에 이미지 게시하기

해설 **세부 사항**
정원에 랜턴이 있는 사진이 있다면 소셜 미디어 페이지에 공유해 달라고 했으므로 (D)가 정답이다.

어휘 proof of purchase 구매 증명(서) post 게시하다

3-6. 편지

2월 19일

Melissa Hammond
인사부장
Eastbourne Solar
Malvern Building 203호
이스트본, BN20 7AF

Ms. Hammond께,

귀하의 사무실에서 인터뷰하는 동안 귀하를 뵙게 되어 기뻤고 제게 Eastbourne Solar 팀의 선임 영업 사원으로 입사할 것을 제안해 주셔서 영광입니다. **³안타깝게도 저는 출장을 가지 않아도 되는 다른 회사에서 일하기로 결정했기 때문에 그 자리를 받아들일 수 없습니다.** 저는 귀사를 매우 존경하며 **⁴귀사가 앞으로도 시장 점유율을 확대하여 직원을 늘릴 거라고 확신합니다.**

⁵약속한 대로 인터뷰 중에 말씀드렸던 웹 기반 전자 서명 도구 목록을 동봉하여 보냅니다. 저는 그 어떤 회사와도 관련 없지만 그 정보가 귀하에게 유용할 것이라고 믿습니다. 저는 올해 말에 열리는 Annual Solar Trade Exhibition에 **⁶참석할 계획입니다.** 그곳에서 귀하를 뵙고 이 산업에 대해 더 논의할 기회가 있기를 바랍니다.

Spencer Ingram

동봉

어휘 unfortunately 안타깝게도, 유감스럽게도 be unable to do ~할 수 없다 require 필요하다, 요구하다 a great deal of 많은 expand 확대하다, 확장하다 be affiliated with ~와 제휴하다

3. Mr. Ingram이 보낸 편지의 목적은 무엇인가?
(A) 직무에 대해 문의하기 위해
(B) 자신의 회사를 소개하기 위해
(C) 인터뷰 날짜를 잡기 위해
(D) 채용 제안을 거절하기 위해

해설 **주제/목적**
출장을 가지 않아도 되는 다른 회사에서 일하기로 결정했기 때문에 그 자리를 받아들일 수 없다고 했으므로 (D)가 정답이다.

어휘 inquire 문의하다 schedule 일정을 잡다

4. Mr. Ingram이 Eastbourne Solar에 대해 명시한 것은 무엇인가?
(A) 팀워크에 중점을 둔다.
(B) 마케팅에 더 많은 투자를 해야 한다.
(C) 급여 및 복지 혜택이 좋다.
(D) 미래에 성장할 것이다.

해설 **NOT/True**
Eastbourne Solar가 앞으로도 시장 점유율을 확대하여 직원을 늘릴 거라고 했으므로 (D)가 정답이다.

패러프레이징 it will continue to gain market share and expand its staff ➡ It will grow in the future.

어휘 compensation package (복지 혜택을 포함한) 보수

5. Mr. Ingram이 Ms. Hammond에게 보낸 것은 무엇인가?
(A) 서명된 계약서
(B) 온라인 도구 목록

(C) 제안된 면접 일정
(D) 웹사이트 설문 조사 양식

해설 **세부 사항**
웹 기반 전자 서명 도구 목록을 동봉했다고 했으므로 (B)가 정답이다.

6. 두 번째 단락 세 번째 줄의 'attend'와 의미상 가장 가까운 것은?
(A) ~에 가다
(B) ~와 일치하다, ~와 동시에 일어나다
(C) ~을 우연히 마주치다
(D) ~을 돌보다; ~에 책임이 있다

해설 **동의어 찾기**
attend가 있는 I plan to attend the Annual Solar Trade Exhibition은 '저는 Annual Solar Trade Exhibition에 참석할 계획입니다'라는 의미이며, 여기서 attend는 '참석하다'라는 뜻으로 쓰였다. 따라서 (A)가 정답이다.

UNIT 14 문자 메시지·온라인 채팅   본문 p.156

지문의 구성과 흐름 파악하기

> Gina Quan [오전 8시 25분] 안녕하세요, Bruno. Barraza Conference Center에 가는 데 문제가 좀 있어요. 택시를 타야 할 것 같은데 회사 경비로 처리되었으면 해요.
>
> Bruno Mota [오전 8시 28분] 괜찮아요. 영수증만 꼭 보관해 주세요. Shelby Hotel은 셔틀 서비스를 더 이상 운영하지 않나요?
>
> Gina Quan [오전 8시 29분] 운영하지만 미리 예약해야 해요. 저번에는 예약 없이 셔틀을 탔는데 방침이 바뀐 것 같아요.
>
> Bruno Mota [오전 8시 31분] 제가 택시 서비스를 찾아볼까요?
>
> Gina Quan [오전 8시 32분] 고맙지만 제게도 번호가 있어요.

어휘 cover 비용을 대다; 다루다, 포함시키다 run 운영하다
in advance 사전에, 미리

1. 오전 8시 28분에 Mr. Mota가 '괜찮아요'라고 쓴 의도는 무엇인가?
(A) Ms. Quan 대신에 콘퍼런스 센터에 갈 것이다.
(B) 다른 장소에서 Ms. Quan을 만날 수 있다.
(C) 교통비 승인에 동의한다.
(D) 예약 영수증을 찾았다.

어휘 in one's place ~ 대신에 authorize 인가[재가]하다

2. Ms. Quan에 대해 암시된 것은 무엇인가?
(A) Mr. Mota의 상사이다.
(B) 연락처를 찾는 것을 돕고 싶어 한다.
(C) 호텔 예약 번호를 잃어버렸다.
(D) 전에 Shelby Hotel에 묵은 적이 있다.

1-2. 문자 메시지

Betsy Braun (오후 1시 46분) 안녕하세요, Matthew. **¹당신이나 당신의 팀원들은 헤이븐 스트리트 입구를 계속 확인하고 있나요?**

Matthew Alvarado (오후 1시 48분) **¹비디오 모니터링 외에도 매 시간 직접 확인하는 작업을 약 20분 전에 했습니다.** 그건 왜 물으시는 건가요?

Betsy Braun (오후 1시 49분) **²문이 잠겨 있지 않은 걸 봐서요.** 문은 항상 잠겨 있어야 한다고 생각했거든요.

Matthew Alvarado (오후 1시 51분) **²배달을 하고 있는 경우를 제외하고는 그렇습니다. Anchorage Supplies가 방금 하차 작업을 다 끝냈어요.** 제가 Eric에게 알렸습니다.

Betsy Braun (오후 1시 53분) 그렇군요. 다행이네요. 누군가가 신경 쓰고 있다니 마음이 놓여요.

어휘 monitor (주기적으로) 확인하다, 보다   in addition to ~ 외에도, ~뿐만 아니라   usual 평상시의, 기존의   in person 직접   notice 알아채다, 인지하다, 주목하다   unlock (잠긴 문을) 열다   be supposed to do ~하기로 되어 있다   at all times 항상   except ~을 제외하고   unload (트럭, 배 등에서) 짐을 내리다   notify 알리다, 통지하다   take care of ~을 처리[수습]하다; ~을 돌보다

1. Mr. Alvarado는 누구이겠는가?
(A) 경비원
(B) 운전 강사
(C) 비디오 편집자
(D) 접수원

해설 **추론/암시**
오후 1시 46분에 Ms. Braun이 헤이븐 스트리트 입구를 계속 확인하고 있는지 묻자 Mr. Alvarado가 비디오 모니터링 외에도 직접 확인하는 작업을 했다고 한 것으로 보아 Mr. Alvarado는 경비 업무를 하는 사람임을 알 수 있다. 따라서 (A)가 정답이다.

2. 오후 1시 51분에 Mr. Alvarado가 '제가 Eric에게 알렸습니다' 라고 쓴 의도는 무엇인가?
(A) Eric이 일찍 출근할 것이다.
(B) Eric이 트럭에서 짐을 내릴 것이다.
(C) Eric이 문을 잠글 것이다.
(D) Eric이 Ms. Braun을 만날 것이다.

해설 **의도 파악**
오후 1시 49분에 Ms. Braun이 문이 잠겨 있지 않은 점을 지적하자 Mr. Alvarado가 배달 물건을 내리고 있는 경우에만 그렇다고 말하며, 하차 작업이 다 끝났으니 Eric에게 알렸다고 했다. 따라서 문을 잠그라는 의도로 Eric에게 말한 것이므로 (C)가 정답이다.

3-6. 온라인 채팅

Kathleen Arcand [오전 10시 03분] 다음 주 **⁴Bancroft와의 계약 체결**을 위해 오늘 기차표를 예매하려고 해요.

Gordon Walters [오전 10시 04분] 화요일에 출발하는 거 맞죠?

Kathleen Arcand [오전 10시 07분] **⁴사실 회의는 수요일 오후나 되어야 있을 거라서** 그날 아침에 갔다가 목요일 아침에 돌아와도 될 것 같아요.

Gordon Walters [오전 10시 08분] 알겠습니다. 안내 책자를 가지고 가나요?

Kathleen Arcand [오전 10시 10분] 꼭 필요할까요? 그쪽에서 이미 **³우리의 심장 모니터링 장비**를 봤잖아요.

Gordon Walters [오전 10시 11분] 나중에 고려해 보도록 우리의 다른 제품들을 소개할 수도 있죠.

Kathleen Arcand [오전 10시 13분] 그래요. 제가 잊지 않고 몇 개 챙길게요. 그리고 그분들이 저녁 식사와 공연을 위해 우리를 데리고 나갈 겁니다. **⁵Bancroft의 Macy Oliver가 우리가 어떤 공연을 보고 싶은지 궁금해하고 있어요. ⁶그에 대해 제가 그녀에게 회신해야 해요.**

Peter Zhang [오전 10시 16분] 재미있겠네요.

Kathleen Arcand [오전 10시 17분] 무슨 공연이 있는지 저는 잘 모르겠어요. **⁶Peter, 좀 알아봐 줄 수 있나요?**

Peter Zhang [오전 10시 19분] **⁶그 지역 극장에서 무슨 공연을 하는지 찾아볼게요.**

Kathleen Arcand [오전 10시 20분] 알겠어요, 하지만 빠를수록 좋아요.

Peter Zhang [오전 10시 22분] 물론이죠. 한 시간 안에 메시지를 드리겠습니다.

어휘 book 예약하다   necessary 필수적인, 필요한   be sure to do 확실히 ~하다   pack 챙겨 넣다   wonder 궁금해하다   would like to do ~하고 싶다   have got to do ~해야 하다   get back to ~에게 나중에 다시 연락하다   look into ~을 들여다보다, ~을 조사하다

3. 작성자들은 어떤 산업에 종사하겠는가?
(A) 엔터테인먼트
(B) 교육
(C) 출판
(D) 건강 관리

해설 **추론/암시**
오전 10시 10분에 Ms. Arcand가 우리의 심장 모니터링 장비라고 언급한 것으로 보아 작성자들은 의료 기구 관련 산업에 종사한다는 걸 알 수 있다. 따라서 (D)가 정답이다.

4. 계약이 언제 체결되겠는가?
(A) 화요일에
(B) 수요일에
(C) 목요일에
(D) 금요일에

오전 10시 3분에 Ms. Arcand가 Bancroft와의 계약 체결을 위해 기차표를 예매한다고 한 다음 10시 7분에 회의는 수요일 오후에 있다고 했으므로 (B)가 정답이다.

5. Ms. Oliver는 무엇에 대한 정보를 원하는가?
(A) 식사 시 음식 제약
(B) 회의 손님의 도착 시간
(C) 공연에 대한 선호
(D) 교통비

해설 **세부 사항**
오전 10시 13분에 Ms. Arcand가 Macy Oliver를 언급하며 어떤 공연을 보고 싶은지 궁금해하고 있다고 했으므로 (C)가 정답이다.

어휘 **dietary** 식단의, 음식의 **restriction** 제한, 제약
preference 선호(도), 선호하는 것

6. 오전 10시 20분에 Ms. Arcand가 '빠를수록 좋아요'라고 쓴 의도는 무엇인가?
(A) 마감일을 넘길까 봐 걱정한다.
(B) 기차표가 매진될 거라고 생각한다.
(C) 답장을 빨리 하고 싶어 한다.
(D) 곧 회의를 위해 떠나야 한다.

해설 **의도 파악**
Ms. Arcand가 오전 10시 17분에 Peter에게 공연을 알아봐 줄 수 있는지 묻자 Peter가 그 지역 극장에서 하는 공연을 찾아보겠다고 했다. 이에 대해 빠를수록 좋다고 한 것으로 보아 Ms. Oliver에게 빨리 답변하려는 의도로 한 말임을 알 수 있으므로 (C)가 정답이다.

어휘 **sell out** 다 팔리다 **shortly** 얼마 안 되어, 곧

UNIT 15 기사·공지·광고   본문 p.160

지문의 구성과 흐름 파악하기

비버튼의 도서관 재개관

(10월 29일)—비버튼 도서관의 재개관은 9월 25일에 있을 것이다. —[1]—. 주민들은 도서관을 다시 이용할 수 있게 된 것에 대해 기대하고 있다. 도서관의 재개관은 18개월 전으로 예정되어 있었다.

프로젝트 진행 속도를 높이기 위해 Cowan Construction과 Brock Builders가 모두 선정되었다. —[2]—. 하지만 양측이 서로 모르는 사이에 같은 작업을 자주 하면서 많은 시간을 허비했기 때문에 이 결정은 오판이 되어 버렸다.

게다가 그 프로젝트는 이미 출발이 좋지 않았기 때문에 정밀 조사와 대중의 압력이 많아졌다. —[3]—. 프로젝트 완료에 예상되는 시간은 특히나 비슷한 작업과 비교하면 합리적이지 않았다.

이 프로젝트는 또한 작은 구내 카페를 포함하기로 되어 있었다. —[4]—. 카페 옵션은 향후 제안에서 재검토될 것으로 보인다.

어휘 **take place** 열리다, 일어나다 **turn out** 밝혀지다, 드러나다 **get off to a bad start** 시작이 좋지 않다 **scrutiny** 정밀한

조사 **pressure** 압력, 압박 **estimated** 추측의; 견적의
complete 완료하다, 완성하다 **reasonable** 합리적인, 타당한
be supposed to do ~하기로 되어 있다 **be likely to do** ~할 가능성이 있다 **revisit** 다시 논의하다; 재방문하다

1. Brock Builders에 대해 암시된 것은 무엇인가?
(A) 이번이 그 회사의 첫 건설 프로젝트이다.
(B) 직원들이 Cowan Construction과 소통이 잘 되지 않았다.
(C) 곧 폐업할 것이다.
(D) Cowan Construction과 합병할 계획이다.

어휘 **go out of business** 폐업하다 **merge** 합병하다

2. 기사가 도서관 부지에 대해 명시한 것은 무엇인가?
(A) 기획자들은 프로젝트의 원래 범위를 줄여야만 했다.
(B) 2번째 건설 단계는 내년으로 예정되어 있다.
(C) 카페 수익금을 일부 지원받을 것이다.
(D) 비버튼의 두 번째 도서관 분관이다.

어휘 **partially** 부분적으로 **fund** 자금을 대다 **proceeds** 수익금

3. [1], [2], [3], [4]로 표시된 곳 중에서 다음 문장이 들어가기에 가장 적절한 곳은 어디인가?
"이것은 궁극적으로 불가능한 작업 일정을 만드는 결과를 낳았다."

어휘 **ultimately** 궁극적으로 **result in** 결과적으로 ~가 되다
creation 창조(물)

PRACTICE   본문 p.162

1. (D)	**2.** (C)	**3.** (B)	**4.** (D)	**5.** (B)	**6.** (B)
7. (C)	**8.** (A)	**9.** (C)	**10.** (B)	**11.** (A)	**12.** (B)

1-2. 채용 공고

기업 채용 서비스

창고 직원 채용

Laird Home Furnishings는 현재 윌마에 위치한 곳에서 근무할 창고 직원을 구하고 있습니다. 일부 현장 교육이 제공되지만 창고 환경에서 일한 경험을 우대합니다. [1]업무에는 배달 경로에 따라 상품을 분류하고 차량에서 하역하는 일과 보관 장소를 정리하는 것이 포함되어 있습니다. [2]인근에 버스 정류장이나 기차역이 없기 때문에 지원자는 혼자서 창고로 갈 수 있는 확실한 방법이 있어야 합니다.

지원하려면 여기를 클릭하십시오.

어휘 **seek** 찾다, 구하다 **on-the-job training** 직장 내 현장 훈련, 현장 연수 **previous experience** 경력 **sort** 분류하다 **according to** ~에 따라서 **applicant** 지원자 **dependable** 믿을 만한 **on one's own** 혼자서 **apply** 신청하다, 지원하다; 적용하다

1. 채용 공고에는 어떤 정보가 포함되어 있는가?
(A) 예상 시급
(B) 근무 시간
(C) 연수 일정

(D) 업무 내용

해설 **세부 사항**
지원자가 하게 될 업무로 상품 분류와 하역, 보관 장소 정리를 언급했으므로 (D)가 정답이다.

어휘 hourly wage 시급   duties 업무

2. 이 자리의 지원 요건은 무엇인가?
(A) 안전 자격증
(B) 뛰어난 컴퓨터 기술
(C) 직장으로 가는 안정적인 교통수단
(D) 해당 분야의 경력

해설 **세부 사항**
인근에 버스 정류장이나 기차역이 없기 때문에 혼자서 창고로 갈 수 있는 확실한 방법이 있어야 한다(must have)고 했으므로 (C)가 정답이다. 창고 환경에서 일한 경험은 우대 사항(preferred)일 뿐이고 반드시 갖춰야 하는 지원 요건은 아니기 때문에 (D)는 오답이다. 이와 같이 토익의 채용 관련 지문에서는 requirements(지원 자격) 또는 required(반드시 갖춰야 하는)와 preferred(우대하는)의 차이를 활용한 문제가 자주 출제되므로 꼭 기억해 두어야 한다.

어휘 certificate 자격증, 증명서   reliable 믿을 만한, 신뢰할 만한

3-5. 공고

톡톡 튀는 아이디어를 공유하고
Spring Sensations 상품권을 받으세요!

우리 Spring Sensations는 고객 여러분이 사랑하는 특별한 제품을 제공하게 되어 자랑스럽습니다. 여러분의 도움으로 우리는 제품 라인을 훨씬 더 좋게 만들 수 있습니다! **³우리의 인기 있는 보디로션과 핸드크림에 쓸 새로운 향에 대한 아이디어를 찾고 있습니다.** 만약 여러분의 향기가 세 명 안에 든다면 여러분은 500달러의 Spring Sensations 상품권을 받게 되며, 이 상품권은 유효 기간이 없습니다!

공모전에 참가하려면 Spring Sensations 소셜 미디어 페이지를 방문하여 여러분의 아이디어를 댓글로 남겨 주세요. **⁴ᴬ 새로운 향은 최대 세 가지까지 대표적인 향을 조합할 수 있으며, ⁴ᴮ 그것만의 고유한 이름도 여러분이 제안해 주셔야 합니다.** **⁴ᶜ www.springsensations.com에 있는 기존 제품 라인을 확인하여 우리가 이미 제공하는 것은 제안하지 않도록 하십시오!**

⁵공모전은 3월 5일부터 4월 20일까지 진행되며, 수상자는 4월 25일에 우리의 웹사이트와 소셜 미디어를 통해 발표될 예정입니다. 상품권은 5월 1일에 이메일로 발송될 것입니다.

어휘 winning (사람의) 마음을 끄는, 매력 있는; 우승한   look for ~을 찾다   expire 만료되다   contain 포함하다, 들어 있다   up to ~까지   dominant 지배적인, 우세한   come up with ~을 생각해 내다   as well 또한   check out ~을 확인하다   existing 기존의   run (특정 기간 동안) 계속되다

3. Spring Sensations는 무엇이겠는가?
(A) 마케팅 회사
(B) 화장품 제조업체
(C) 매년 열리는 축제

(D) 소매 의류 판매점

해설 **추론/암시**
우리의 인기 있는 보디로션과 핸드크림에 쓸 새로운 향에 대한 아이디어를 찾고 있다고 한 것으로 보아 화장품과 관련 있는 업종임을 알 수 있으므로 (B)가 정답이다.

어휘 retail 소매의

4. 제출 요건이 아닌 것은 무엇인가?
(A) 다른 향을 제한된 수로 사용하는 것
(B) 창작물에 이름을 포함하는 것
(C) 조합이 이미 사용 중이 아니란 걸 확인하는 것
(D) 포장에 대해 제안하는 것

해설 **NOT/True**
포장에 대해 제안하라는 내용은 없으므로 (D)가 정답이다.

패러프레이징 (B) should come up with a unique name for it → Including a name for the creation

어휘 submission 제출, 접수

5. 응모작 제출 마감일은 언제인가?
(A) 3월 5일
(B) 4월 20일
(C) 4월 25일
(D) 5월 1일

해설 **세부 사항**
공모전은 3월 5일부터 4월 20일까지 진행된다고 한 것으로 보아 마감일은 4월 20일이라는 걸 알 수 있다. 따라서 (B)가 정답이다.

어휘 entry 출품작; 출입; 가입; 참가

6-8. 광고

Maurita Analytical Inc. ─ 구인 공고

Maurita Analytical Inc.(MAI)는 플레인뷰에 첫 지점을 열고 빠르게 러벅으로 확장한 이래로 **⁶농업 현장 및 건축 프로젝트의 토양 테스트에서 신뢰받는 이름이 되었습니다.** 우리는 직원들에게 지원을 아끼지 않는 근무 환경과 조직 내에서 전문적인 성장을 할 기회를 제공하고, **⁷ 경쟁력 있는 임금과 유급 휴가를** 드립니다.

현장 팀장
현장에서 4~5명의 토양 기술자로 구성된 팀을 감독합니다. 토양 채취 장소에 대한 지도를 준비하고 팀 구성원에게 작업을 할당합니다. 주로 러벅에 기반을 두고 있지만 **⁸그 지역 밖에서 하는 작업이 필요할 수도 있습니다.**

토양 기술자
⁸ 러벅과 그 주변의 현장을 방문하여 토양 샘플을 수집하고 라벨을 붙여 분류합니다. 수집 과정의 복잡한 절차 때문에 꼼꼼한 성격은 필수입니다. 기술자들은 그룹으로 일하며 교육이 제공됩니다.

선임 연구소 기술자
헤리퍼드에 있는 연구소에서 8명의 기술자로 구성된 팀을 이끌고 정확한 토양 테스트를 수행합니다. 환경 과학이나 이와 유사한 전공의 학사 학위가 필요합니다. **⁸ 가끔 출장이 필요할 것입니다.**

어휘 open position 공석   trusted 신뢰받는   agricultural 농업의   expand 확대하다, 확장하다   provide A with B A에게 B를 제공하다   supportive 지원하는, 힘이 되는   competitive 경쟁력 있는; 경쟁을 하는   oversee 감독하다   assign 맡기다, 배정하다   based in (장소)에 기반을 둔   label 라벨을 붙이다   attention to detail 세심함, 세부적인 것에 주의를 기울임   conduct 실시하다, 수행하다   occasional 가끔의

6. Maurita Analytical Inc.에 대해 명시된 것은 무엇인가?
(A) 이 지역에서 유일한 테스트 회사이다.
(B) 평판이 좋다.
(C) 여전히 원래 창업자에 의해 운영된다.
(D) 농업 서비스를 중단했다.

해설 **NOT/True**
농업 현장 및 건축 프로젝트의 토양 테스트에서 신뢰받는 이름이 되었다고 했으므로 해당 분야에서 평판이 좋다는 걸 알 수 있다. 따라서 (B)가 정답이다.

패러프레이징 has been a trusted name → has a good reputation

어휘 have a good reputation 평판이 좋다   operate 운영하다   founder 설립자, 창업자   discontinue 중단하다

7. 첫 번째 단락 네 번째 줄의 'competitive'와 의미상 가장 가까운 것은?
(A) 모순되는, 상충되는
(B) 공격적인
(C) 적합한, 알맞은
(D) 야심 있는, 야심 찬

해설 **동의어 찾기**
competitive가 있는 competitive wages는 '경쟁력 있는 임금'이라는 의미이며, 여기서 competitive는 '경쟁력 있는'이라는 뜻으로 쓰였다. 즉, 다른 회사와 비교했을 때 결코 '적지 않은' 임금을 준다는 의미이므로 선택지 중에서는 '적합한, 알맞은'을 뜻하는 suitable이 competitive와 의미상 가장 가깝다. 따라서 (C)가 정답이다.

8. 모든 채용 공고 대상 자리의 공통점은 무엇인가?
(A) 출장을 필요로 한다.
(B) 대학 졸업생에게만 열려 있다.
(C) 매년 보너스를 지급한다.
(D) 다른 사람들을 관리하는 것을 포함한다.

해설 **세부 사항**
현장 팀장은 러벅 밖에서 하는 작업이 필요할 수도 있고, 토양 기술자는 러벅과 그 인근 현장을 방문해야 하며, 선임 연구소 기술자는 가끔 출장이 필요할 것이라고 했으므로 (A)가 정답이다.

9-12. 기사

예술 코너

Lance Colbert 작성

비즈니스와 예술의 세계가 섞이면 균형을 찾는 게 때로는 어렵다. 그러나 지역 사업가인 Elizabeth Sanders와 Timothy Marlowe는 균형을 잡을 수 있는 방법을 찾고 있다. **⁹그들의**

새로운 회사인 **Art Phase**는 상업적인 장소를 위해 원본 그림을 임대한다. 이것은 세련된 장식을 원하지만 예술 작품에 큰 투자를 할 여유가 없는 애슈빌의 사업체들에게 매우 적합하다.

Ms. Sanders와 Mr. Marlowe는 함께 회계 회사를 운영하면서 아이디어를 얻었다. "우리는 고객들에게 좋은 첫인상을 남기기 위해 사무실을 꾸미고 싶었습니다." Ms. Sanders가 말했다. "¹²하지만 이제 막 사업을 시작했기 때문에 구매할 다른 물건들이 많았어요. 미술품에 선투자를 하는 게 염려되기도 했고요. 유행이 자주 바뀌니까 시간이 지나면 그림이 촌스러워 보일 수 있잖아요."

Mr. Marlowe는 아마추어 예술가로 지역 예술 커뮤니티에서 활동하고 있다. 그와 Ms. Sanders는 부업으로 Art Phase를 설립했는데 인기를 끌 것으로 예상된다. Art Phase는 대여할 수 있는 다양한 그림을 제공한다. 그림 대부분은 지역 예술가들이 그린 것이다. ¹⁰ᶜ 그림 대여에 관심 있는 사람들은 **Art Phase 컨설턴트가 현장을 방문하여 방의 색상과 개인적인 스타일에 맞춰 추천하도록** 할 수 있다. ¹⁰ᴬ 그림을 고르고 나면 현장에 그림이 전달되고 대여 기간이 끝나면 무료로 수거되기도 한다. 고객들은 그림을 분기마다 한 번씩 바꿀 수 있고 ¹⁰ᴰ 작품에 담긴 영감에 대해 작가로부터 메모를 받을 수도 있다.

"Art Phase는 아직 자리를 잡지 못한 예술가들에게 좋은 기회입니다." 애슈빌 예술가 협회장인 Neil Patterson이 설명했다. "그들은 대여료의 일정 부분을 받으면서 한편으로는 많은 이에게 그들의 그림을 보여 줄 수 있죠. ¹¹Sunshine Street Market에 부스를 마련할 여유가 없거나 갤러리 공간이 없는 이들에게 이것은 매력적인 선택지입니다."

어휘 entrepreneur 사업가, 기업가   commercial 상업의; 광고   premises 부지, 구내   sophisticated 세련된, 정교한   afford to do ~할 여유가 있다, ~할 형편이 되다   heavily 매우, 심하게   operate 운영하다   first impression 첫인상   outdated 구식의, 예전의   after a while 얼마 후에, 나중에   found 설립하다   a wide range of 다양한   recommendation 추천(서); 권고   inspiration 영감   established 인정받는, 확실히 자리를 잡은

9. 기사의 목적은 무엇인가?
(A) 투자 기회를 소개하기 위해
(B) 지역 예술가들의 그림을 집중적으로 다루기 위해
(C) 새로 제공되는 서비스를 설명하기 위해
(D) 예술 수업 참여를 장려하기 위해

해설 **주제/목적**
Ms. Sanders와 Mr. Marlowe가 세운 새로운 회사인 Art Phase를 소개하고 있으므로 (C)가 정답이다. 지역 예술가들이 그린 그림을 소개하지는 않았으므로 (B)는 오답이다.

어휘 highlight 강조하다   newly 최근에, 새로   available 이용할 수 있는; ~할 시간이 있는   encourage 권장하다, 장려하다   participation 참석

10. 기사에 따르면 Art Phase에서 제공하지 않는 것은 무엇인가?
(A) 수거 및 배송
(B) 무료 시용 기간
(C) 대면 상담

(D) 아티스트의 코멘트

해설 **NOT/True**

무료로 시범 사용할 수 있는 기간에 대한 언급은 없으므로 (B)가 정답이다.

어휘 trial 시험, 사용   in-person 직접의

11. Mr. Patterson이 Sunshine Street Market에 대해 암시한 것은 무엇인가?

(A) 비용이 비싸다.

(B) 매력적으로 장식되어 있다.

(C) 미술관 근처에 있다.

(D) 부스의 크기가 다양하다.

해설 **추론/암시**

Sunshine Street Market에 부스를 마련할 여유가 없는 이들에게 매력적인 선택지라고 한 것으로 보아 자리를 잡지 못해서 형편이 어려운 예술가들에게 Sunshine Street Market은 비용 면에서 부담이 된다는 걸 추론할 수 있으므로 (A)가 정답이다.

12. [1], [2], [3], [4]로 표시된 곳 중에서 다음 문장이 들어가기에 가장 적절한 곳은 어디인가?

"미술품에 선투자를 하는 게 염려되기도 했고요."

해설 **문장 삽입**

주어진 문장에 also(또한)가 있으므로 표시된 곳의 앞 문장이 주어진 문장과 맥락상 유사해야 한다. 주어진 문장은 미술품에 선투자를 하는 게 염려되기도 했다는 내용인데, [2] 앞에서 Ms. Sanders가 이제 막 사업을 시작했기 때문에 구매할 다른 물건들이 많았다고 어려운 점을 언급했으므로 주어진 문장은 [2]에 들어가는 게 가장 적절하다. 따라서 (B)가 정답이다.

어휘 upfront 선불의, 선납의; 솔직한

UNIT 16 다중 지문

본문 p.166

지문의 구성과 흐름 파악하기

Holly Home Goods를 이용해 주셔서 감사합니다!

주문 번호: 068379

배송: 영업일 기준 1~3일 이내 배송

배송지: 685 애스펀 레인, 어바인, 캘리포니아주 92614

제품	명세	패턴	가격
H190	10.5인치 접시, 6개 세트	나뭇잎	35.99달러
B836	6인치 그릇, 6개 세트	나뭇잎	25.99달러
M331	커피 컵, 6개 세트	파란 물결	32.99달러
W275	찻주전자, 2개 세트	나뭇잎	49.99달러

	소계	144.96달러
* 첫 구매 고객은 WELCOME 코드로 전체 금액에서 10% 할인됩니다.	코드*: WELCOME	-14.49달러
	배송비	5.99달러
	합계	136.46달러

Holly Home Goods: 반품 요청

고객: Howard Erickson

주문 번호: 068379

반품하는 제품: M331

반품 요청 사유:

[ ] 제품 손상   [✓] 기타 (자세히 써 주세요):

[ ] 다른 제품 배송   예상한 색깔이 아닙니다.

어휘 damage 손상을 주다

1. Holly Home Goods에 대해 암시된 것은 무엇인가?

(A) 환경적 책임에 전념하고 있다.

(B) 고객이 주문 제작으로 패턴을 만들 수 있게 해 준다.

(C) 다양한 재료로 만들어진 제품들이 있다.

(D) 신규 고객에게 할인을 제공한다.

어휘 be dedicated to ~에 헌신하다, ~에 전념하다   custom 주문 제작의

2. Mr. Erickson은 어떤 제품을 반품하는가?

(A) 접시

(B) 그릇

(C) 컵

(D) 찻주전자

PRACTICE   본문 p.168

1. (A)   **2.** (A)   **3.** (D)   **4.** (B)   **5.** (D)   **6.** (D)
7. (D)   **8.** (B)   **9.** (C)   **10.** (D)   **11.** (A)   **12.** (D)
13. (D)   **14.** (B)   **15.** (B)   **16.** (B)   **17.** (B)   **18.** (C)
19. (A)   **20.** (D)

1-5. 기사&온라인 리뷰

캘거리 (7월 13일)—Rocky Apparel은 다양한 남녀 재킷, 스키 바지, 베이스 레이어 등을 제공하는 스키 의류 회사이다. **[2]공동 소유주인 Noella Purcell과 Travis Byler**는 5년 전 이곳 캘거리에서 작은 소매점으로 시작했고 그 이후로 사업이 **[3]빠르게 번창했다.** 에드먼턴에 두 번째 지점이 열렸고 Rocky Apparel 상품에 대한 수요가 크게 증가했다. 이 회사는 **[1]옷이 극한 온도를 견디고 거칠게 다루어도 튼튼한지 확실히 하기 위해 엄격한 테스트를 거치기 때문에** 단골 고객층을 구축했다. 완성된 제품들은 색상이 다채롭고 세련되기도 했다.

Rocky Apparel은 이전에는 자사 소매점에서만 상품을 판매했지만 지난달에는 전 세계 고객들에게 다가가도록 온라인 상점

을 시작했다. **⁴Ms. Purcell과 Mr. Byler는 이제 11월에 레이크 루이스에 세 번째 소매점을 열 계획이다.** 레이크 루이스는 작은 마을이지만 많은 리조트가 주변에 있어 인기 있는 스키 지역의 중심에 있기 때문에 그곳이 선정되었다. 그 가게는 스키 성수기에만 문을 열게 되는데, 11월 말부터 4월 말까지 이어진다. 공동 소유주들은 스키 강습에 할인을 제공하기 위해 스키 강사들과 파트너십을 맺는 것도 고려하고 있다.

어휘 **base layer** 베이스 레이어, 보온을 위해 안에 껴입는 옷 **merchandise** 물품, 상품 **significantly** 상당히; 의미 있게, 중요하게 **loyal customer** 단골 고객 **rigorously** 엄격하게 **make sure (that)** 확실히 ~하다 **withstand** 견디다 **extreme** 극도의 **rough** 거친 **treatment** 대우; 치료, 처치 **reach** 도달하다, 이르다 **district** 구역, 지역 **surround** 둘러싸다 **run** (특정 기간 동안) 계속되다 **look into** ~을 들여다보다, ~을 조사하다

---

⁴**게시일: 11월 30일**　　　　⁴**게시자: Daniel Blair**

⁴**오늘 Rocky Apparel이 가장 최근 연 소매점을 방문했는데** 상품 구성에 감명을 받았습니다. 공동 소유주 중 한 명인 Noella Purcell을 만났는데, 그녀는 스키를 전문적으로 탔기 때문에 스키에 대해 매우 잘 알고 있었습니다. ²**파트너와 어떻게 사업을 시작했는지 듣는 것은 흥미로웠어요.** 그녀가 패션과 고객에 집중하는 반면 ²**그분은 사업의 회계를 담당하고 있다고 합니다.** 매장 분위기는 활기가 넘쳤고 ⁵**매장 곳곳의 스크린에는 스키어들의 흥미로운 모습이 담겨 있었어요.** 제가 좋아하는 제품을 몇 가지 발견했습니다. ⁴**저는 매장에 걸어서 갈 수 있는 거리에 살고 있기 때문에 겨울에 자주 방문할 것 같아요!** 스키를 즐긴다면 Rocky Apparel은 확실히 가 볼 가치가 있습니다.

어휘 **selection** 선발, 선택(된 것들) **knowledgeable** 많이 아는 **used to do** ~하곤 했다 **found** 설립하다 **handle** 다루다, 처리하다 **footage** 장면, 화면 **within walking distance** 걸어서 갈 수 있는 거리 내에 **definitely** 분명히, 확실히 **worth** ~의 가치가 있는 **check out** 확인하다

1. 기사에서 Rocky Apparel에 대해 언급된 것은 무엇인가?
(A) 자사 제품에 상당한 테스트를 수행한다.
(B) 전 세계에 소매점을 열었다.
(C) 패션상 후보에 올랐다.
(D) 자체적으로 직물을 제작한다.

해설 **NOT/True**
옷이 극한 온도를 견디고 거칠게 다루어도 튼튼한지 확실히 하기 위해 엄격한 테스트를 거친다고 했으므로 (A)가 정답이다.

어휘 **conduct** 실시하다, 수행하다 **nominate** 후보로 지명하다 **manufacture** 제조하다

2. Mr. Byler에 대해 명시된 것은 무엇인가?
(A) 사업의 회계를 담당하고 있다.
(B) 방문 중에 Mr. Blair를 만났다.
(C) 프로 스키 선수였다.
(D) 일부 의류를 직접 디자인한다.

해설 **두 지문 연계_NOT/True**
첫 번째 지문에 Ms. Purcell과 Mr. Byler는 Rocky Apparel의 공동 소유주라는 내용이 있다. 이어서 두 번째 지문을 보면 Mr. Blair가 Ms. Purcell을 만나 그녀가 파트너와 어떻게 사업을 시작했는지 듣는 것은 흥미로웠다고 언급하며 그녀의 파트너, 즉 Mr. Byler는 사업의 회계를 담당하고 있다고 했으므로 (A)가 정답이다.

패러프레이징 handles the accounting side of the business → is in charge of the business's bookkeeping

어휘 **be in charge of** ~을 담당하다 **bookkeeping** 부기, 회계 장부 정리

3. 기사에서 첫 번째 단락 일곱 번째 줄의 'taken off'와 의미상 가장 가까운 것은?
(A) 사라졌다
(B) 출발했다
(C) 제거했다
(D) 성공했다

해설 **동의어 찾기**
taken off가 있는 the business has taken off는 '사업이 빠르게 번창했다'라는 의미이며, 여기서 taken off는 '빠르게 성공했다'라는 뜻으로 쓰였다. 따라서 (D)가 정답이다.

4. Mr. Blair에 대해 암시된 것은 무엇인가?
(A) 스키를 잘 탄다.
(B) 레이크 루이스에 산다.
(C) Rocky Apparel에 지원했다.
(D) Ms. Purcell과 일했다.

해설 **두 지문 연계_추론/암시**
Mr. Blair가 11월 30일에 작성한 리뷰인 두 번째 지문에서 Rocky Apparel이 가장 최근 연 소매점을 방문했다고 언급하며 그 매장에 걸어서 갈 수 있는 거리에 산다고 했다. 첫 번째 지문에서는 Ms. Purcell과 Mr. Byler가 11월에 레이크 루이스에 세 번째 소매점을 열 계획이라는 언급이 있다. 이로 미루어 보아 Mr. Blair는 레이크 루이스에 있는 매장을 방문했으며 그곳에 걸어서 갈 수 있는 정도라면 레이크 루이스에 거주한다고 추론할 수 있으므로 (B)가 정답이다.

어휘 **experienced** 숙련된, 경험이 풍부한 **apply for** ~에 지원하다

5. Rocky Apparel이 가장 최근에 연 매장에 대해 명시된 것은 무엇인가?
(A) 규모가 두 번째 지점과 같다.
(B) 고객들은 그곳에서 스키 강습을 예약할 수 있다.
(C) 연중무휴이다.
(D) 고객을 위해 재생되는 비디오가 있다.

해설 **NOT/True**
두 번째 지문에서 매장 곳곳의 스크린에 스키어들의 흥미로운 모습이 담겨 있다고 했으므로 (D)가 정답이다.

패러프레이징 they were showing interesting footage of skiers on the screens → It has videos playing for customers.

어휘 **book** 예약하다

새 경기장 건설이 계속되다

Courtney Wallace 작성

대븐포트 (1월 2일)—대븐포트 북서쪽에서 새로운 스포츠 경기장인 Apex Stadium의 건설이 순조로이 진행 중이며 곧 내부 작업이 시작된다. 이 경기장은 Sigley Group이 소유하고 있는데, Sigley Group은 자산으로 많은 건물을 보유하고 있다. 대부분은 공연장이고 **⁶처음으로 스포츠 경기장에 발을 들인 것이다.**

대규모 스포츠 행사를 통해 대븐포트로 더 많은 관광객을 끌어모으는 것이 이 프로젝트의 ⁷목표 중 하나다. **⁸당초 설계는 8,000석 규모지만 최소 1만 석을 수용하도록 변경될 수 있다면 지역 세미프로 토너먼트 개최 자격을 갖출 만큼 규모가 클 것으로 보인다.**

이 경기장에서 예정된 첫 경기는 5월 2일 Davenport Tigers와 Waterloo Falcons의 경기가 될 것이다.

어휘 venue 장소 be on track 제대로 진행 중이다, 착착 진행되다 venture into ~에 발을 들여놓다 alter 바꾸다, 변경하다 accommodate 수용하다 be eligible to do ~할 자격이 되다 host 주최하다

야구팬들, 새 경기장에 들뜨다

Jerry Lambert 작성

대븐포트 (5월 3일) — 어젯밤 Davenport Tigers와 Waterloo Falcons의 경기가 Apex Stadium에서 열렸다. **⁹Waterloo Falcons의 팬들이 많이 찾아왔음에도 불구하고** 홈 팀이 3대 1로 승리를 거두었다. Davenport Tigers의 감독인 Stephen Wilson은 팀의 경기력에 자부심을 느꼈다. "Waterloo는 이기기 힘든 팀입니다." Mr. Wilson이 말했다. "하지만 **¹⁰Rob Sanchez와 그의 팀 동료들의 노력 덕분에 승리를 거둘 수 있었습니다.**"

경기장을 찾은 많은 관중은 새 건물에 깊은 인상을 받았다. 그 건물은 건축가 Howard Torres가 설계한 것이다. **⁸이 경기장은 올해 말 지역 세미프로 토너먼트의 개최지가 될 것이다.** 다가오는 모든 행사를 보려면 www.apexstadium.com/events 를 방문하면 된다.

어휘 matchup 경기 thanks to ~ 덕분에 pull off (특히 어려운 일을) 해내다 attendee 참석자 upcoming 다가오는, 곧 있을

6. Sigley Group에 대해 명시된 것은 무엇인가?
(A) 건설 회사를 인수했다.
(B) 대븐포트로 이전했다.
(C) 새 경영진 체제 하에 있다.
(D) 경기장은 하나만 운영한다.

해설 **NOT/True**
첫 번째 지문에서 Sigley Group이 처음으로 스포츠 경기장에 발을 들인 것이라고 한 것으로 보아 Sigley Group은 경기장이 Apex Stadium 하나뿐이라는 걸 알 수 있다. 따라서 (D)가 정답이다.

어휘 relocate 이전하다 management 경영(진), 운영, 관리 operate 운영하다

7. 첫 번째 기사에서 두 번째 단락 첫 번째 줄의 'points'와 의미상 가장 가까운 것은?
(A) 의미들
(B) 특징들
(C) 지점들
(D) 목표들

해설 **동의어 찾기**
points가 있는 One of the points of the project is to bring more tourists to Davenport는 '대븐포트로 더 많은 관광객을 끌어모으는 것이 이 프로젝트의 목표 중 하나다'라는 의미이며, 여기서 points는 '목표들'이라는 뜻으로 쓰였다. 따라서 (D)가 정답이다.

8. Apex Stadium에 대해 암시된 것은 무엇인가?
(A) 건설은 시의 자금 지원을 받았다.
(B) 원래의 좌석 수를 확장했다.
(C) 개관은 예상보다 늦었다.
(D) 매년 지역 토너먼트를 개최할 것이다.

해설 **두 지문 연계_추론/암시**
첫 번째 지문에서 당초 Apex Stadium은 8,000석 규모지만 최소 1만 석을 수용하도록 변경될 수 있다면 지역 세미프로 토너먼트 개최 자격을 갖출 수 있을 거라고 했는데, 두 번째 지문에서 Apex Stadium이 올해 말 지역 세미프로 토너먼트의 개최지가 될 거라고 했다. 이로 미루어 보아 Apex Stadium은 좌석 수를 최소 1만 석으로 늘렸다는 걸 알 수 있으므로 (B)가 정답이다.

어휘 fund 자금을 대다 expand 확대하다, 확장하다 capacity 용량, 수용력; 능력

9. Waterloo Falcons 팀에 대해 명시된 것은 무엇인가?
(A) 이번 시즌에 경기에서 많이 이기지 못했다.
(B) Apex Stadium보다 작은 경기장을 가지고 있다.
(C) 많은 팬이 경기를 보기 위해 찾아왔다.
(D) 팬들을 위해 마련된 특별 좌석이 있었다.

해설 **NOT/True**
두 번째 지문에 Waterloo Falcons의 팬들이 많이 찾아왔다는 내용이 있으므로 (C)가 정답이다.

패러프레이징 the Waterloo Falcons had a great showing of fans → Many of its fans traveled to attend a game.

어휘 reserve (자리 등을) 따로 잡아 두다; 예약하다

10. Rob Sanchez는 누구인가?
(A) 스포츠 기자
(B) 건축가
(C) 코치
(D) 운동선수

해설 **세부 사항**
두 번째 지문에서 Davenport Tigers의 감독이 Rob Sanchez와 그의 팀 동료들의 노력 덕분에 승리를 거둘 수 있었다고 인터뷰한 것으로 보아 Rob Sanchez는 경기를 뛴 선수임을 알 수 있다. 따라서 (D)가 정답이다.

Megalith Gym 가맹점주 연례 회의
10월 21일 토요일 일정

오전 7시 15분	차, 커피, 도넛	Sparrow Room
오전 8시	**11 환영사** 대표 이사 Pranav Chetti	**11 Eagle Room**
오전 8시 30분	나라와 개인을 아우르는 홍보 마케팅 부장 Sanhana Adwani	Eagle Room
오전 10시 30분	고객 파악하기 선임 연구원 Priya Vadekar	Goldfinch Room
오후 12시 30분	등록에 포함된 뷔페 점심	Sparrow Room
14 오후 1시 30분	가맹점주 발표: 경쟁에 대처하기 **14 그룹 클래스 관리**	Peacock Room Goldfinch Room
13 오후 3시	**13 새 장비 시연** 구매 부장 Ganesh Munshif	Peacock Room

어휘 promotion 홍보, 판촉; 승진, 진급   deal with ~을 처리하다, ~을 다루다   demonstration 시범, 시연; 설명

가맹점주를 위한 지원

William Lowery 작성
Megalith Gym 가맹점을 운영하는 점주들이 지난 주말에 댈러스에서 열린 회사 연례 회의에 참석했다. 미국 전역에서 온 300명 이상의 사람들이 이틀간 행사에 참석했다. **12 마케팅 부장 Sanhana Adwani는** 모회사가 피트니스 센터 체인을 홍보하기 위해 무엇을 하고 있는지 그리고 적은 예산으로 어떻게 지점을 개별적으로 홍보할 수 있는지 개략적으로 설명했다. **12 몇몇 가맹점주가 그 행사에서 발표를 하기 위해 선정되었다.** **12 13 참석자들은 전동 트레드밀 Marietta와 직립식 로잉 머신인 Netzer를 살짝 엿보기도 했다.** 그것들은 올해 말에 가맹점들로 보내질 것이다.

어휘 operate 운영하다   outline (간략히) 설명하다   parent company 모회사   individually 개인적으로, 개별적으로   get a sneak peek (정식 공개되지 않은 것을) 맛보기로 보다   motorized 모터가 달린, 전동식의   upright (자세가) 똑바른, 꼿꼿한, 수직으로 선

Megalith Gym 가맹점주 연례 회의 피드백 양식

시간을 내어 의견을 공유해 주셔서 감사합니다. **14 참석하신 발표를 1(나쁨)에서 5(우수) 등급으로 평가해 주십시오.**

발표	점수
고객 파악하기	5
경쟁에 대처하기	해당 없음
14 그룹 클래스 관리	**14 5**
고객의 동기 부여 유지하기	5
성공을 위한 핵심 단계	해당 없음
Megalith 미션	5

의견: 저는 행사장에서 하룻밤 묵는 숙소를 예약했기 때문에 문제가 없었지만 제가 대화를 나눈 일부 사람들은 그 도시에 익숙하지 않은 데다 심한 교통 체증을 뚫고 와야 했기 때문에 늦게 도착했다고 말했습니다. **15 세션의 시간 간격이 너무 빠듯해서 각 세션을 조금 더 일찍 끝내는 것을 제안하고 싶습니다.**

이름: **14 15 Peggy Kearns**

어휘 overnight 하룻밤의   accommodation 숙소, 숙박 시설   rushed 서두르는

11. 참석자들은 어디에서 개회사를 들었는가?
(A) Eagle Room에서
(B) Goldfinch Room에서
(C) Peacock Room에서
(D) Sparrow Room에서

해설 세부 사항
첫 번째 지문에 Eagle Room에서 환영사를 한다는 내용이 있으므로 (A)가 정답이다.

12. 기사의 목적 중 하나는 무엇인가?
(A) Ms. Adwani의 새 역할을 설명하기 위해
(B) 앞으로 있을 과정들에 대한 세부 정보를 제공하기 위해
(C) 사람들이 가맹점에 가입하도록 권장하기 위해
(D) 회사 회의에서 한 활동들을 집중적으로 다루기 위해

해설 주제/목적
댈러스에서 열린 회사 연례 회의에서 했던 활동들을 설명하고 있으므로 (D)가 정답이다.

어휘 upcoming 다가오는, 곧 있을   encourage 권장하다, 장려하다   highlight 강조하다

13. 참석자들은 Marietta와 Netzer를 언제 볼 수 있었겠는가?
(A) 오전 8시에
(B) 오전 10시 30분에
(C) 오후 1시 30분에
(D) 오후 3시에

해설 두 지문 연계_추론/암시
Marietta와 Netzer는 두 번째 지문에서 확인할 수 있다. 각각 전동 트레드밀과 직립식 로잉 머신을 이르는 말로 연례 회의 참석자들이 이 장비들을 살짝 엿보았다고 했다. 첫 번째 지문에 있는 발표 중 이와 관련 있는 것은 '새 장비 시연'이며 오후 3시에 진행되었으므로 (D)가 정답이다.

14. Ms. Kearns에 대해 사실인 것은 무엇인가?
(A) 작년에 그 행사에 갔다.
(B) 오후에 강연에 참석했다.

(C) 행사에 늦게 도착했다.
(D) 회의가 열렸던 도시에 산다.

해설 두 지문 연계_NOT/True
Ms. Kearns는 세 번째 지문인 피드백 양식 작성자이다. Ms. Kearns가 '그룹 클래스 관리'에 5점을 준 것으로 보아 해당 발표에 참석했다는 걸 알 수 있는데 첫 번째 지문을 보면 '그룹 클래스 관리'는 오후 1시 30분에 진행되었으므로 (B)가 정답이다.

15. Ms. Kearns가 회의에서 마음에 들지 않았던 것은 무엇인가?
(A) 그 장소에 중요한 편의 시설이 부족했다.
(B) 세션 사이에 시간이 충분하지 않았다.
(C) 발표자들의 소리가 잘 들리지 않았다.
(D) 몇몇 세션은 동시에 열렸다.

해설 세부 사항
세 번째 지문에서 Ms. Kearns가 작성한 의견 중 세션의 시간 간격이 너무 빠듯해서 각 세션을 조금 더 일찍 끝내는 것을 제안하고 싶다는 내용이 있으므로 (B)가 정답이다.

어휘 lack ~가 없다, ~가 부족하다 **amenities** 편의 시설

16-20. 초대장&안내 책자&이메일

> 화학 공학 콘퍼런스
>
> [16]4월 9일부터 시작되는 제5회 연례 화학 공학 콘퍼런스에서 유익한 대화를 나누고 전문가 인맥을 만들며 즐거운 주말을 보내세요. 우리의 목표는 이 분야에서 활동하는 분들에게 최신 동향과 안전책, 그리고 신흥 기술에 대해 교육하는 것입니다. 처음으로 Parkview Hall에서 콘퍼런스를 개최하게 되었으며 Dalton Chemicals의 CEO인 [19]**Wyatt Faber**를 기조 연설자로 모시게 되어 기쁘게 생각합니다.
>
> 후원에 대한 자세한 내용은 첨부된 안내 책자를 참조하십시오.

어휘 informative (도움이 되는) 정보를 주는 **networking** 인맥 형성 **emerging** 신흥의, 떠오르는 **attach** 첨부하다; 붙이다

> 화학 공학 콘퍼런스
> 후원 등급
>
> 기업 후원은 우리가 등록비를 저렴하게 유지할 수 있도록 해 주기 때문에 우리 콘퍼런스의 성공에 중요한 역할을 합니다. [17]후원자가 됨으로써 여러분의 회사를 이 분야의 전문가 수백 명에게 소개할 수 있고, 그들이 여러분의 브랜드에 더 친숙하게 만들 수 있습니다.
>
> 이코노미—500달러
> • 인쇄된 콘퍼런스 프로그램에 귀사의 로고가 표시됩니다.
> • 최대 10명의 직원까지 등록비가 10% 할인됩니다.
>
> 베이직—1,500달러
> • 인쇄된 콘퍼런스 프로그램과 등록 구역에 있는 배너에 귀사의 로고가 표시됩니다.
> • 최대 15명의 직원까지 등록비가 10% 할인됩니다.
>
> 프리미엄—2,500달러
> • 무대를 포함한 모든 구역에 귀사의 로고가 표시됩니다.
> • 모든 직원의 등록비가 10% 할인됩니다.

> [20]**엘리트**—4,500달러
> • 무대를 포함한 모든 구역에 귀사의 로고가 표시됩니다.
> • [20]모든 직원의 등록비가 15% 할인됩니다.
> • [20]직원들이 VIP 라운지를 이용할 수 있습니다. 그곳은 인쇄 및 복사 장비와 무료 다과, 그리고 휴대 전화 충전기 등이 갖춰져 있습니다.

어휘 tier (조직, 시스템 등의) 단계 **corporate** 기업의 **play an important role** 중요한 역할을 하다 **affordable** 가격이 알맞은 **feature** 특징으로 하다, 특별히 선보이다 **complimentary** 무료의 **refreshments** 다과

> 수신인: 모든 Holbrook Incorporated 직원
> 발신인: Nancy Turner
> 날짜: 3월 28일
> 제목: 화학 공학 콘퍼런스
>
> 친애하는 직원 여러분,
>
> 화학 공학 콘퍼런스가 곧 다가옵니다. [18]제가 등록 양식을 작성해야 하기 때문에 이 행사에 누가 참석하고 싶은지 알아야 합니다. 우리는 [20]올해 행사를 후원하기 때문에 원하는 만큼 많은 직원이 등록비 할인을 받을 수 있습니다. 또한 행사에 참석하는 동안 [20]VIP 라운지를 이용하실 수 있습니다. [19]많은 분이 올해 기조 연설자를 알아볼 것 같은데요, 작년에 최신 화학 도구에 대한 워크숍을 진행하기 위해 우리 회사를 방문했던 분입니다.
>
> Nancy Turner
> Holbrook Incorporated 관리 부장

어휘 wonder 궁금해하다 **be eligible for** ~에 자격이 되다 **state-of-the-art** 최신의

16. 초대장에 따르면 콘퍼런스에 대해 명시된 것은 무엇인가?
(A) 매년 Parkview Hall에서 열린다.
(B) 이틀 동안 지속된다.
(C) 무료로 참석할 수 있다.
(D) 처음으로 열리는 것이다.

해설 NOT/True
4월 9일부터 시작되는 콘퍼런스에서 즐거운 주말을 보내라고 한 것으로 보아 콘퍼런스는 주말 내내 진행된다는 걸 알 수 있으므로 (B)가 정답이다.

어휘 take place 열리다, 일어나다 **last** 계속되다, 지속되다

17. 안내 책자에서 후원 혜택에 대해 언급된 것은 무엇인가?
(A) 후원자들은 콘퍼런스에서 부스를 운영할 수 있다.
(B) 후원자들은 브랜드 인지도를 향상시킬 수 있다.
(C) 후원자들은 로고 디자인에 도움을 받을 수 있다.
(D) 후원자들은 회사를 온라인으로 홍보할 수 있다.

해설 NOT/True
후원자가 됨으로써 회사를 전문가 수백 명에게 소개할 수 있고, 브랜드에 더 친숙하게 만들 수 있다고 했으므로 (B)가 정답이다.

어휘 operate 운영하다 **recognition** 인식; 인정 **assistance** 도움, 지원 **promote** 홍보하다; 승진시키다

18. 이메일의 목적은 무엇인가?
(A) 결정에 대한 이유를 설명하기 위해
(B) 발표에 자원할 사람을 모집하기 위해
(C) 누가 행사 참여에 관심이 있는지 알아보기 위해
(D) 콘퍼런스로 가는 교통편을 마련하기 위해

해설 주제/목적
이메일 작성자가 콘퍼런스 등록 양식을 작성해야 하기 때문에 누가 행사에 참석하고 싶은지 알아야 한다고 했으므로 (C)가 정답이다.

어휘 recruit 모집하다 **arrange transportation** 교통편을 마련하다

19. Mr. Faber에 대해 언급된 것은 무엇인가?
(A) Holbrook Incorporated에서 교육 행사를 이끌었다.
(B) 후원에 대해 Ms. Turner에게 연락했다.
(C) Holbrook Incorporated 직원으로 합류할 것이다.
(D) 새로운 기술을 개발했다.

해설 두 지문 연계_NOT/True
Mr. Faber는 첫 번째 지문인 초대장에 등장하는 이름으로 콘퍼런스의 기조 연설자가 되었다는 내용을 확인할 수 있다. 세 번째 지문에서는 올해의 기조 연설자를 언급하며 작년에 최신 화학 도구에 대한 워크숍을 진행하기 위해 Holbrook Incorporated를 방문한 적이 있다고 했으므로 (A)가 정답이다.

패러프레이징 teach a workshop → led a training event

20. Holbrook Incorporated는 어느 후원 등급을 받았는가?
(A) 이코노미
(B) 베이식
(C) 프리미엄
(D) 엘리트

해설 두 지문 연계_세부 사항
세 번째 지문에서 Holbrook Incorporated는 올해 행사를 후원했기 때문에 원하는 만큼 많은 직원이 등록비 할인을 받을 수 있고 VIP 라운지를 이용할 수 있다고 했다. 두 번째 지문의 엘리트 단계를 보면 모든 직원의 등록비가 15% 할인되고 VIP 라운지를 이용할 수 있다는 내용을 확인할 수 있으므로 (D)가 정답이다.

PART TEST				본문 p.176
147. (D)	**148.** (A)	**149.** (D)	**150.** (D)	**151.** (B)
152. (B)	**153.** (B)	**154.** (B)	**155.** (C)	**156.** (C)
157. (D)	**158.** (A)	**159.** (A)	**160.** (D)	**161.** (A)
162. (B)	**163.** (D)	**164.** (B)	**165.** (C)	**166.** (B)
167. (B)	**168.** (D)			

147-148. 설명서

새로운 Lanette 비디오 초인종 설정 방법

설치 후 보관용으로 이 설명서를 갖고 계십시오.

1. www.lanettetech.com에서 Lanette 스마트폰 애플리케이션을 다운로드하여 새 계정을 만듭니다.
2. 앱 내에서 '장치 설정'을 누르고 '초인종'을 선택합니다.

3. **148**장치 뒷면의 바코드를 스캔합니다. 이렇게 하면 제품 번호가 포함된 승인 메일이 전송됩니다. 이메일에 있는 제품 ID를 이곳에 적습니다: **730950R.**

4. **147**위치를 구체적으로 지정하기 위해 주소를 입력합니다. 이 단계는 선택 사항이지만 **147** 이 단계를 건너뛰면 초인종의 특정 기능들이 작동하지 않을 것입니다.

5. 앱에서 '확인'을 누릅니다. 장치가 자동으로 와이파이에 연결되지만 와이파이 암호를 입력해야 합니다.

6. 전면의 빨간색 버튼을 3초간 눌러 장치를 테스트합니다. 녹색 표시등이 깜박이기 시작하면 장치를 사용할 준비가 된 것입니다. 테스트 날짜를 이곳에 적습니다: _____.

문의 사항이나 우려 사항이 있으면 1-800-555-4950으로 고객 서비스 팀에 문의하십시오.

어휘 set up ~을 설치하다 **installation** 설치 **account** 계정; 계좌 **approval** 승인; 인정, 찬성 **input** 입력하다 **specify** (구체적으로) 명시하다 **optional** 선택적인 **feature** 기능, 특징 **function** 작동하다 **flash** 반짝이다, 빛나다

147. 사용자는 왜 위치를 제공해야 하는가?
(A) 어느 사무실에서 문의 사항을 처리할지 결정하기 위해서
(B) 배송 견적을 제공받기 위해서
(C) 교체 부품을 받기 위해서
(D) 모든 기능이 작동할 수 있도록 하기 위해서

해설 세부 사항
위치를 구체적으로 지정하기 위해 주소를 입력하라고 했는데, 이 단계를 건너뛰면 초인종의 특정 기능들이 작동하지 않을 거라고 했으므로 (D)가 정답이다.

어휘 determine 결정하다, 확정하다 **handle** 다루다, 처리하다 **inquiry** 문의, 질문 **estimate** 견적(서); 추정(치) **replacement** 교체(품) **ensure** 보장하다, 확실히 하다

148. 설명서 사용자에 대해 암시된 것은 무엇인가?
(A) 코드를 스캔했다.
(B) 확인 이메일을 보냈다.
(C) 제품 번호를 받지 못했다.
(D) 테스트를 수행했다.

해설 추론/암시
제품 ID를 적는 칸에 제품 번호가 있는 것으로 보아 사용자가 장치 뒷면에 있는 바코드를 스캔하여 이메일로 제품 ID를 받았다는 걸 추론할 수 있으므로 (A)가 정답이다. 사용자가 테스트를 수행하지 않았기 때문에 장치를 테스트한 날짜가 공란인 것이므로 (D)는 오답이다.

149-151. 초대장

예술의 한 형태로서의 그래픽 디자인 기념회
Findlay 연회장
827 아드모어 로드

7월 1일 금요일
오후 7시~오후 9시 30분

Findlay Society of Graphic Design(FSGD)에서 연례 연회를 개최합니다! 이 멋진 행사에 여러분을 초대합니다. 행사

에는 올해 우리가 한 활동에 대한 비디오와 향후 계획에 대한 정보, 그리고 프리랜서 세계 탐색에 대한 기조연설이 포함될 것입니다. 또한 **149올해 우리 클럽을 빛내기 위해 열심히 노력한 분들의 150공로를 인정하여 여러 상을 수여할 것입니다.** 이 기회를 통해 **149동료 FSGD 참석자들과 친목을 다지면서** 맛있는 4가지 코스 요리를 즐겨 보십시오. 식사 중에는 Rio 현악 4중주단이 라이브 연주를 할 것입니다. 우리 회비로 지불되기 때문에 행사 참석에는 비용이 들지 않습니다.

행사에 참석하실 계획이 있다면 늦어도 6월 16일까지 Patrick Slater에게 pslater@fsgd.org로 연락해 주십시오. **151연락하실 때는 일행이 몇 명인지 표시해 주셔야 합니다.**

그곳에서 만나 뵙기를 바랍니다!

어휘 celebration 기념행사 feature 특징으로 하다, 특별히 선보이다 keynote speech 기조연설 navigate 길을 찾다 socialize 사람들과 어울리다, 친목을 다지다 fellow 동료 dues 회비 no later than 늦어도 ~까지 indicate 명시하다, 나타내다 party (함께 행동하는) 단체

149. 초대장은 누구를 대상으로 하겠는가?
(A) 개인 기부자
(B) 선출직 공무원
(C) 컴퓨터 프로그래머
(D) 클럽 회원

해설 추론/암시
클럽을 빛내기 위해 노력한 사람들에게 상을 주고 동료 FSGD 참석자들과 친목을 다지라고 한 것으로 보아 초대장은 클럽 회원들에게 발송된 것임을 알 수 있다. 따라서 (D)가 정답이다.

150. 첫 번째 단락 네 번째 줄의 'recognize'와 의미상 가장 가까운 것은?
(A) 회상하다
(B) 깨닫다
(C) 확인하다, 알아보다
(D) 인정하다; (공식적으로) 감사를 표하다

해설 동의어 찾기
recognize가 있는 be presenting several awards to recognize the people who have worked so hard는 '열심히 노력한 분들의 공로를 인정하여 여러 상을 수여할 것이다'라는 의미이며, 여기서 recognize는 '인정하다, 알아주다'라는 뜻으로 쓰였다. 따라서 (D)가 정답이다.

151. 행사에 대해 암시된 것은 무엇인가?
(A) 입장료는 6월 16일까지 지불되어야 한다.
(B) 초대장 수신인은 손님을 데려올 수 있다.
(C) 장소는 곧 최종 결정될 것이다.
(D) 활동들은 촬영될 것이다.

해설 추론/암시
초대장 말미에 연락할 때는 일행이 몇 명인지 표시해 달라고 한 것으로 보아 초대장을 받은 사람은 손님을 데려갈 수 있다는 걸 추론할 수 있다. 따라서 (B)가 정답이다.

어휘 admission fee 입장료 recipient 수령인, 받는 사람 finalize 결론짓다

152-154. 기사

Valley Park 업그레이드가 승인되다

(2월 13일)—Christopher Wilcher 시장은 유니언시가 Valley Park를 업그레이드하기 위해 프로젝트를 진행하고 있다고 확인해 주었다. 이 작업은 **152C유니언시의 공원 및 휴양 시설 연간 예산을 부분적으로 지원받고 있다.** **152A유니언시는 지역 기업가인 Gary Austin으로부터 상당한 기부도 받았다.** 또한 **152D지역 사회 단체들이 이 프로젝트에 기여하기 위해 모금 행사를 개최했다.** 예를 들어 UC Friends는 중고 책 판매를 주최했다.

공원 북쪽에 있는 야구장의 구멍들은 필요한 곳에 새로운 잔디를 심어서 채울 것이다. 최대 10개의 테이블을 수용할 수 있는 **153지붕이 있는 야외 쉼터를 위한 공간을 만들기 위해 주차장 근처의 화단은 제거될 것이다.** 제2주차장 건설이 제안됐지만 기획자들은 대신 기존 부지를 확대하기로 했다.

154사람들 대부분은 개선된 점을 이용하기를 기대하고 있다. 그럼에도 불구하고 일부는 지역 공무원들이 다른 분야에 집중해야 한다고 생각한다. **154"제 생각에 우리에겐 열악한 도로 상태와 같은 더 긴급한 문제들이 있어요."** 주민 Elizabeth Arnold가 말했다.

어휘 approve 승인하다; ~을 좋게 생각하다(~ of) confirm 확인하다; 확정하다 partially 부분적으로 fund 자금을 대다 generous 후한, 관대한 entrepreneur 기업가 fundraiser 모금 행사 contribute to ~에 기여하다 flower bed 화단 propose 제안하다, 제의하다 expand 확대하다, 확장하다 look forward to ~하는 것을 고대하다 take advantage of ~을 이용하다 improvement 개선, 향상 pressing 긴급한

152. 업그레이드 자금 출처로 언급되지 않은 것은 무엇인가?
(A) 주민 기부금
(B) 서점
(C) 연간 예산
(D) 지역 사회 단체

해설 NOT/True
서점에서 자금 지원을 받았다는 내용은 없으므로 (B)가 정답이다.

153. Valley Park의 새로운 특징은 무엇인가?
(A) 운동장
(B) 피크닉 장소
(C) 화단
(D) 두 번째 주차장

해설 세부 사항
화단을 제거하여 야외 쉼터를 위한 공간을 만들 거라고 했으므로 (B)가 정답이다.

154. [1], [2], [3], [4]로 표시된 곳 중에서 다음 문장이 들어가기에 가장 적절한 곳은 어디인가?
"그럼에도 불구하고 일부는 지역 공무원들이 다른 분야에 집중해야 한다고 생각한다."

해설 문장 삽입
주어진 문장에 Nonetheless(그럼에도 불구하고)가 있으므로 표

시된 곳의 앞 문장이 주어진 문장과 맥락상 반대되는 내용이어야 한다. 주어진 문장은 일부 사람들은 지역 공무원이 다른 분야에 집중해야 한다고 생각한다는 내용인데, [4] 앞에서 사람들 대부분은 그러한 개선점을 이용할 수 있기를 기대하고 있다고 언급했으므로 주어진 문장은 [4]에 들어가는 게 가장 적절하다. 또한 [4] 뒤에서는 다른 분야가 구체적으로 무엇인지 주민의 말을 인용하고 있으므로 뒤 문장과의 연결도 자연스럽다. 따라서 (D)가 정답이다.

어휘 focus on ~에 집중하다

155-158. 온라인 채팅

> Naomi Rutledge [오전 10시 03분] 좋은 아침이에요, 팀원 여러분. **155Concord 아파트**에 대해 여러분에게 확인하고 싶은 게 있어요.
>
> Jared Padilla [오전 10시 04분] 〈Northwest Lifestyle〉 잡지의 기자가 곧 있을 준공식에 대한 기사를 쓰는 데 동의했고, 기사에 사진 몇 장을 첨부하길 원하더라고요. **156Jonathan Webb 작가에게 연락해서 사진을 더 많이 찍도록 준비해야 할까요?**
>
> Naomi Rutledge [오전 10시 05분] 사진은 이미 충분해요. 우리의 사진 모음 링크를 전달해 드릴 테니 적절한 걸 골라 보세요.
>
> Rupert Burke [오전 10시 06분] 추가적인 홍보를 받게 되다니 기쁘네요. **157이 시점에서 분양된 세대가 80%가 되는 걸 목표로 했는데 아직 70%도 못 미치네요.**
>
> Naomi Rutledge [오전 10시 07분] 잡지 기사가 도움이 될 거예요. 다른 선택지도 계속 알아볼 거고요.
>
> Rupert Burke [오전 10시 09분] **155이렇게 큰 건물은 다뤄 본 적이 없으니까** 이번에 제대로 하는 게 중요해요.
>
> Naomi Rutledge [오전 10시 10분] 동의합니다. 하지만 **158Katie Sullivan이 팀을 떠나면서** 시간이 지체된 걸 염두에 뒤야죠.
>
> Varuni Goyal [오전 10시 11분] 맞아요. **158Naomi는 투입되고서 혼자 알아서 일에 적응해야 했잖아요.**
>
> Naomi Rutledge [오전 10시 12분] 저는 이제 제법 속도를 낼 수 있을 것 같으니 빠르게 진행할 수 있어요.

어휘 check in with (주로 새로운 정보를 얻기 위해) ~에게 물어보다 accompany 동반하다, 추가로 딸리다 arrange 마련하다, 준비하다 forward 보내다 appropriate 적절한 publicity 홍보 reserve 예약하다; (자리 등을) 따로 잡아 두다 pursue 추구하다, 밀고 나가다 get ~ right ~을 제대로 하다 step in (어려운 상황에) 투입되다 up to speed 최대치로 속도를 내는; 최신 정보를 갖춘

155. Ms. Rutledge는 누구이겠는가?
(A) 인테리어 디자이너
(B) 건설업자
(C) 부동산 관리자
(D) 잡지 기자

해설 **추론/암시**
채팅의 주된 내용이 Concord 아파트 분양을 위한 홍보성 기사 작성과 관련된 것이고, 이 정도 규모의 일은 처음이니 잘해 보자는 언

급이 있는 것으로 보아 Ms. Rutledge는 부동산을 임대하고 관리하는 사람이라는 걸 추론할 수 있다. 따라서 (C)가 정답이다.

156. 오전 10시 5분에 Ms. Rutledge가 '사진은 이미 충분해요' 라고 쓴 의도는 무엇인가?
(A) 일을 끝낼 시간이 있다고 확신한다.
(B) 저장 공간을 늘리는 걸 고려하고 있다.
(C) Mr. Webb으로부터 더 많은 일을 원하지 않는다.
(D) 그들이 Mr. Webb의 서비스를 감당할 수 있다고 생각한다.

해설 **의도 파악**
오전 10시 4분에 Jared Padilla가 Jonathan Webb 작가에게 연락해서 사진을 더 많이 찍도록 준비해야 할지 묻자 Ms. Rutledge가 사진은 이미 충분하니 사진 모음 링크에 들어가서 적절한 걸 골라 보라고 했다. 따라서 Mr. Webb에게 작업을 요청할 필요가 없다는 의도로 한 말이므로 (C)가 정답이다.

어휘 confident 자신하는, 확신하는 afford 여유가 있다, 형편이 되다

157. 채팅에서 어떤 문제점이 언급되었는가?
(A) 청구서가 지불되지 않았다.
(B) 팀 목표에 도달하지 못했다.
(C) 건물이 검사에 불합격했다.
(D) 예산이 예상보다 적었다.

해설 **NOT/True**
오전 10시 6분에 Rupert Burke가 분양률 80%를 목표로 했는데 아직 70%도 못 미친다고 했으므로 목표를 달성하지 못했다는 걸 알 수 있다. 따라서 (B)가 정답이다.

158. Ms. Rutledge에 대해 암시된 것은 무엇인가?
(A) 이 프로젝트를 처음부터 하지는 않았다.
(B) 추가적인 도움을 위해 Ms. Sullivan을 고용할 계획이다.
(C) 곧 현장을 방문하고 싶어 한다.
(D) 팀원들의 경험 부족을 걱정한다.

해설 **추론/암시**
오전 10시 10분에 Ms. Rutledge가 Ms. Sullivan이 팀을 떠났다는 언급을 했고 이어서 Varuni Goyal이 Ms. Rutledge는 업무에 투입되고 혼자 알아서 일에 적응해야 했다고 한 것으로 보아 Ms. Rutledge가 프로젝트를 처음부터 함께한 것은 아니란 걸 추측할 수 있다. 따라서 (A)가 정답이다.

어휘 work on ~에 착수하다, ~에 노력을 들이다 be concerned about ~에 대해 우려하다

159-163. 온라인 기사&독자 의견

> 〈Oakwood Tribune〉, 8월 15일, '미스터리 트레인'
> 기차가 덜컹덜컹 소리를 내며 선로를 따라 여행을 시작한다. 승객들이 자리에 앉아 다과를 즐기고 있다. 갑자기 배우들이 차 안으로 들어가고 극적인 미스터리가 펼쳐진다. 관객들은 미스터리를 풀기 위해 단서를 찾아야 한다. 시대 의상과 흥미로운 캐릭터, 그리고 **159매달 즐길 수 있는 다른 줄거리로** '미스터리 트레인'은 옛날 증기 기관차라는 독특한 무대에서 흥미로운 라이브 공연을 제공한다!
> '미스터리 트레인'은 한 지역 극단이 돈을 모을 방법을 찾다가 지

난 10년 동안 운영해 왔다. **161 최근 상연한 공연에서 주연을 맡은 Adrian Urbano**는 처음부터 '미스터리 트레인'의 공연 대부분에 출연했다. "관객들이 우리 공연에 참여하는 게 정말 좋아요." Mr. Urbano가 말했다. "사건이 해결되었을 때 관객들이 기뻐하는 걸 보는 기분은 정말 짜릿하죠."

'미스터리 트레인' 공연은 토요일과 일요일 오후뿐만 아니라 매주 목요일과 금요일, 토요일, 그리고 일요일 저녁에도 진행된다. **160 이 공연은 일요일 오후 공연을 제외하고는 2시간 30분 동안 상연되는데, 일요일 오후 공연은 90분 동안 진행되어 가족들에게 인기 있는 선택지가 되었다.** 티켓은 www.mysterytrain boxoffice.com에서 구입할 수 있다.

어휘 clickety-clack 덜컹덜컹(하는 소리)   refreshments 다과
unfold 펼쳐지다, 밝혀지다   pick up on ~을 알아차리다
intriguing (낯설거나 미스터리해서) 아주 흥미로운   plot 구성, 줄거리   old-fashioned 옛날식의, 구식의   in operation 운영 중인, 가동 중인   look for ~을 찾다   raise money 모금하다, 돈을 마련하다   run 상영, 공연; (연극, 영화 등이) 상영되다   feature 특징으로 하다, 특별히 선보이다   case 사건   with the exception of ~을 제외하고

가장 최근 '미스터리 트레인' 공연을 봤는데 정말 놀라웠습니다! **161 주인공을 보는 게 재밌었어요.** 그는 재능이 뛰어날 뿐만 아니라 저랑 같은 고등학교를 나와서 개인적으로도 알거든요. 그는 그 당시에도 드라마 수업을 좋아했던 걸로 기억해요. **162 '미스터리 트레인' 공연의 다양한 대본이 오크우드 글쓰기 협회(OWS) 회원들에 의해 집필되니까 다음 호에서는 그들 중 일부를 다룬 특집 기사를 보고 싶어요. 163 저는 귀사의 출판물을 수년간 구독해 왔기 때문에** 귀사가 이런 종류의 기사를 자주 다룬다는 걸 알고 있거든요.

Gloria Ramirez

어휘 not only A but also B A뿐만 아니라 B도   personal 개인의, 개인적인   connection 관련(성); 연결, 접속   at that time 그때, 그 당시에   edition 판, 호   frequently 자주   subscribe 구독하다   publication 출판(물), 발행

159. '미스터리 트레인' 공연에 대해 암시된 것은 무엇인가?
(A) 줄거리가 주기적으로 바뀐다.
(B) 관객들이 돌아다닌다.
(C) 잘 알려진 배우들이 나온다.
(D) 일주일에 4번 공연한다.

해설 **추론/암시**
첫 번째 지문에서 매달 다른 줄거리를 즐길 수 있다고 한 것으로 보아 줄거리가 주기적으로 바뀐다는 걸 추론할 수 있으므로 (A)가 정답이다. 공연은 목요일부터 일요일까지 일주일에 4간간 하고, 횟수로 따지면 목요일/금요일/토요일/일요일 저녁 공연과 토요일/일요일 오후 공연을 합쳐서 총 6번이므로 (D)는 오답이다.

패러프레이징 a different plot to enjoy every month → Their storylines change regularly.

어휘 storyline 줄거리   take place 열리다, 일어나다

160. 일요일 오후 공연에 대해 사실인 것은 무엇인가?
(A) 가족 관객에게만 제공된다.
(B) 가장 저렴한 공연이다.
(C) 가장 인기 있는 공연이다.
(D) 다른 공연들보다 공연 시간이 짧다.

해설 **NOT/True**
첫 번째 지문에서 일요일 오후 공연은 90분 동안 진행되고 나머지 공연들은 2시간 30분 동안 진행된다고 했으므로 (D)가 정답이다.

어휘 exclusively 독점적으로, 오로지

161. Mr. Urbano에 대해 암시된 것은 무엇인가?
(A) Ms. Ramirez와 학교를 다녔다.
(B) 연기 수업을 시작할 계획이다.
(C) 공연을 위해 의상을 고증하여 디자인한다.
(D) 극단 창립자이다.

해설 **두 지문 연계_추론/암시**
첫 번째 지문에 Mr. Urbano는 최근 상연한 공연에서 주연을 맡은 배우라는 내용이 있다. 두 번째 지문은 Ms. Ramirez가 작성한 독자 의견인데 주인공을 보는 게 재미있었다고 언급하며 그와 같은 고등학교를 다녔다고 했으므로 (A)가 정답이다.

어휘 authentic 진짜와 꼭 같게 만든, 모사한   founder 설립자, 창업자

162. Ms. Ramirez는 무엇을 하는 것에 관심이 있는가?
(A) 신문에 작품 기고하기
(B) OWS 작가들에 관한 기사 읽기
(C) 공연 대본을 미리 검토하기
(D) 지역 글쓰기 단체에 가입하기

해설 **세부 사항**
두 번째 지문에서 다음에는 OWS 회원들을 다룬 특집 기사를 보고 싶다고 했으므로 (B)가 정답이다.

어휘 in advance 사전에, 미리

163. 독자 의견이 Ms. Ramirez에 대해 암시한 것은 무엇인가?
(A) 지역 활동과 행사에 자주 참여한다.
(B) 어린 시절의 대부분을 오크우드에서 보냈다.
(C) '미스터리 트레인' 공연을 여러 차례 관람했다.
(D) 〈Oakwood Tribune〉의 장기 구독자이다.

해설 **추론/암시**
두 번째 지문에서 Ms. Ramirez가 Oakwood Tribune의 출판물을 수년간 구독해 왔다고 했으므로 (D)가 정답이다.

어휘 participate in ~에 참여하다   subscriber 구독자

164-168. 온라인 게시판&이메일&웹페이지

Aldridge Community Forum
분류: 교육

질문: Rowley Institute의 수업은 들을 만한가요?
게시: Evan McLean, 3월 9일

저는 작년에 Rowley Institute에서 프랑스어 특강을 들었습니다. 강사인 Paulette Rancourt는 원어민인데 정말 활기찬 분이었어요. 수업이 무척이나 벅찼지만 많은 걸 배웠습

니다. ¹⁶⁴그 학원은 다운로드할 수 있는 추가 자료를 웹사이트에 많이 제공하기도 해요.

전반적으로 수강료가 비싸긴 하지만 추천하고 싶어요. ¹⁶⁵학원의 부팀장이 자신의 여행사 친구와 제휴하여 모든 학생에게 프랑스 여행에 사용할 수 있는 상품권을 줬기 때문에 실제로는 돈을 아낀 셈이죠.

—Sophie Faulkner, 3월 10일

어휘 intensive 집중적인   make arrangements with ~와 협정을 맺다

수신인: 전 직원
¹⁶⁵발신인: Lara Hurst
날짜: 5월 30일
제목: 맨체스터

직원 여러분께,

오늘이 ¹⁶⁵ ¹⁶⁶제게는 Rowley Institute에서의 마지막 날이 될 거예요. 가족들과 더 가까이 있기 위해 맨체스터로 이사를 가는데 ¹⁶⁶여러분 모두가 정말 그리울 거예요. ¹⁶⁵부팀장으로서 저는 개인적으로 그리고 업무적으로 여러분 모두를 알 수 있는 기회를 가졌습니다. 우리 학생들의 성공에 여러분이 헌신한 점에 깊은 감명을 받았어요. 특히 ¹⁶⁷저를 고용해 제게 운영 능력을 향상시킬 수 있는 기회를 준 Dominic Archer에게 감사의 말을 전하고 싶습니다.

여기서 일하게 되어 기뻤고 계속 연락하고 지내기를 바랍니다.

Lara Hurst

어휘 close 가까운   personal 개인의, 개인적인
commitment 헌신, 전념; 약속   particularly 특히

올드릿지 지역 사업상
분류: 지역 교육 지원

금상: Jack Talbot, Aldridge Community Centre
¹⁶⁷은상: ¹⁶⁸Dominic Archer, Rowley Institute
동상: ¹⁶⁸Holly Khan, Rowley Institute
장려상: Ava Conway, Crafton Trade School

수상자들은 올드릿지 주민들에 의해 후보로 추천된 후 시 공무원과 소상공인으로 구성된 심사위원단에 의해 선정되었다. 수상자들은 〈Community Cares〉 잡지의 기자와 인터뷰할 것이며, 그들의 인터뷰 내용은 올드릿지 정부 웹사이트에 간략하게 소개될 것이다. 내년 후보 지명은 7월 10일 이후에 받을 것이다.

어휘 trade school 직업 훈련 학교   nominate 후보로 지명하다
panel 패널, 전문가 집단   contribution (신문, 잡지 등의) 기고문
outline (간략히) 설명하다

164. Ms. Faulkner가 Rowley Institute에 대해 언급한 것은
무엇인가?
(A) 숙제 양이 적당하다.
(B) 온라인으로 추가 자료를 제공한다.
(C) 모든 강사는 원어민이다.

(D) 원격 수업 선택권이 있다.

해설 **NOT/True**
Ms. Faulkner는 첫 번째 지문인 온라인 게시판에 답변을 쓴 사람인데 Rowley Institute가 다운로드할 수 있는 추가 자료를 웹사이트에 많이 제공한다고 했으므로 (B)가 정답이다. Ms. Faulkner의 담당 강사였던 Paulette Rancourt가 원어민이라는 언급은 있으나 Rowley Institute의 모든 강사가 원어민이라는 건 확인할 수 없으므로 (C)는 오답이다.

패러프레이징 offers a lot of extra downloadable materials on its Web site → It provides additional materials online.

어휘 reasonable 합리적인, 타당한   additional 추가의
option 선택(권)   remote 원격의; 먼

165. Ms. Faulkner에 대해 암시된 것은 무엇인가?
(A) 담당 강사는 책을 낸 작가이다.
(B) 회사에서 수업료를 지불해 줬다.
(C) Ms. Hurst로부터 상품권을 받았다.
(D) 프랑스로 이사할 계획이다.

해설 두 지문 연계_추론/암시
첫 번째 지문에서 Ms. Faulkner가 학원의 부팀장이 자신의 여행사 친구와 제휴하여 모든 학생에게 프랑스 여행에 사용할 수 있는 상품권을 줬다고 했다. 두 번째 지문을 보면 이메일 작성자인 Lara Hurst는 Rowley Institute 소속임을 알 수 있는데 스스로를 부팀장이라고 언급한 것으로 보아 Ms. Faulkner에게 상품권을 준 사람은 Ms. Hurst임을 추론할 수 있으므로 (C)가 정답이다.

166. 이메일의 목적은 무엇인가?
(A) 직원들의 성과를 축하하기 위해
(B) 동료들에게 작별 인사를 하기 위해
(C) 맨체스터에서 추천을 요청하기 위해
(D) 직원을 후임자로 지명하기 위해

해설 주제/목적
Rowley Institute에서의 마지막 날에 전 직원에게 이메일을 보내며 모두가 그리울 거라는 말을 했으므로 (B)가 정답이다.

어휘 congratulate A on B B에 대해 A를 축하하다   say
farewell 작별 인사를 하다   recommendation 추천(서); 권고
replacement 후임자; 교체(품)

167. Ms. Hurst를 채용한 사람에게 무슨 상이 수여되었는가?
(A) 금상
(B) 은상
(C) 동상
(D) 장려상

해설 두 지문 연계_세부 사항
두 번째 지문에 Ms. Hurst를 채용한 사람이 Dominic Archer라는 언급이 있다. 세 번째 지문의 수상자 명단을 보면 Dominic Archer가 은상을 받았다는 걸 알 수 있으므로 (B)가 정답이다.

168. 웹페이지에서 암시된 것은 무엇인가?
(A) 수상자들은 〈Community Cares〉 잡지에 무료로 광고할 수
있다.
(B) Mr. Talbot은 이전에 사업상을 수상한 적이 있다.

(C) 이 상은 7월 10일에 수여될 것이다.

(D) Mr. Archer와 Ms. Khan은 같은 고용주를 위해 일한다.

해설 **추론/암시**

수상자 이름 옆에 소속이 병기되었는데 Mr. Archer가 Rowley Institute 소속이고 Ms. Khan 역시 Rowley Institute 소속인 것으로 보아 두 사람은 같은 회사에 근무한다는 걸 추론할 수 있다. 따라서 (D)가 정답이다.

어휘 advertise 광고하다 previously 이전에, 앞서 distribute 나누어 주다, 배부하다; (상품을) 유통시키다

LISTENING TEST

1. (D)	2. (B)	3. (A)	4. (D)	5. (C)
6. (B)	7. (A)	8. (B)	9. (C)	10. (B)
11. (A)	12. (C)	13. (B)	14. (A)	15. (B)
16. (C)	17. (A)	18. (B)	19. (C)	20. (A)
21. (B)	22. (A)	23. (C)	24. (B)	25. (C)
26. (A)	27. (B)	28. (C)	29. (A)	30. (B)
31. (A)	32. (D)	33. (D)	34. (C)	35. (A)
36. (D)	37. (B)	38. (B)	39. (A)	40. (C)
41. (B)	42. (D)	43. (C)	44. (C)	45. (A)
46. (D)	47. (B)	48. (A)	49. (C)	50. (A)
51. (D)	52. (C)	53. (C)	54. (A)	55. (B)
56. (D)	57. (A)	58. (B)	59. (C)	60. (B)
61. (A)	62. (D)	63. (C)	64. (B)	65. (D)
66. (A)	67. (B)	68. (C)	69. (D)	70. (D)
71. (C)	72. (C)	73. (A)	74. (D)	75. (C)
76. (B)	77. (D)	78. (A)	79. (A)	80. (B)
81. (D)	82. (A)	83. (D)	84. (C)	85. (C)
86. (D)	87. (B)	88. (A)	89. (C)	90. (D)
91. (A)	92. (B)	93. (C)	94. (D)	95. (A)
96. (D)	97. (B)	98. (A)	99. (D)	100. (B)

READING TEST

101. (A)	102. (A)	103. (C)	104. (D)	105. (A)
106. (A)	107. (D)	108. (D)	109. (A)	110. (D)
111. (C)	112. (B)	113. (B)	114. (A)	115. (C)
116. (A)	117. (B)	118. (A)	119. (A)	120. (B)
121. (D)	122. (D)	123. (B)	124. (D)	125. (A)
126. (A)	127. (C)	128. (D)	129. (B)	130. (B)
131. (D)	132. (B)	133. (B)	134. (C)	135. (A)
136. (B)	137. (A)	138. (D)	139. (C)	140. (D)
141. (A)	142. (B)	143. (B)	144. (C)	145. (C)
146. (A)	147. (C)	148. (C)	149. (C)	150. (C)
151. (C)	152. (B)	153. (B)	154. (C)	155. (D)
156. (D)	157. (B)	158. (B)	159. (C)	160. (B)
161. (D)	162. (C)	163. (B)	164. (C)	165. (B)
166. (C)	167. (A)	168. (A)	169. (A)	170. (B)
171. (D)	172. (D)	173. (A)	174. (A)	175. (C)
176. (A)	177. (C)	178. (B)	179. (A)	180. (D)
181. (C)	182. (D)	183. (B)	184. (D)	185. (A)
186. (D)	187. (C)	188. (A)	189. (C)	190. (B)
191. (C)	192. (B)	193. (A)	194. (D)	195. (A)
196. (B)	197. (B)	198. (C)	199. (C)	200. (C)

1. 🎧 호남

(A) A bucket is being filled with soil.
(B) A pole is being positioned in a hole.
(C) A person is putting away some tools.
(D) A person is working in a field.

해석
(A) 양동이가 흙으로 가득 채워지고 있다.
(B) 막대기가 구멍 안에 놓이고 있다.
(C) 한 사람이 연장을 치우고 있다.
(D) 한 사람이 밭에서 일하고 있다.

어휘 bucket 양동이   be filled with ~로 가득 차다   pole 막대기   hole 구멍   position 놓다, 위치를 정하다   field 들판, 밭

2. 🎧 영녀

(A) They're walking through a construction site.
(B) They're resting against a railing.
(C) They're inspecting some safety helmets.
(D) They're painting items on a balcony.

해석
(A) 그들은 공사 현장을 거닐고 있다.
(B) 그들은 난간에 기대어 있다.
(C) 그들은 안전모를 점검하고 있다.
(D) 그들은 발코니에서 물건에 페인트칠을 하고 있다.

어휘 construction site 공사 현장   rest against ~에 기대다   railing 난간   inspect 점검하다   safety helmet 안전모

3. 🎧 미녀

(A) The man is holding a tray.
(B) The man is moving a table.
(C) The man is standing near an entrance.
(D) The man is paying for some food.

해석
(A) 남자가 쟁반을 들고 있다.
(B) 남자가 테이블을 옮기고 있다.
(C) 남자가 입구 근처에 서 있다.
(D) 남자가 음식값을 지불하고 있다.

어휘 tray 쟁반   entrance 입구

4. 🎧 미남

(A) Some cups are being stored in a cupboard.
(B) Water is flowing from a faucet.
(C) Some wall tiles are lined up for sale.
(D) Eating utensils have been placed in a rack.

해석
(A) 컵이 찬장에 보관되고 있다.
(B) 수도꼭지에서 물이 흐르고 있다.

(C) 벽 타일이 판매를 위해 준비되어 있다.
(D) 식기가 받침대에 놓여 있다.

어휘 store 저장[보관]하다   cupboard 찬장   flow 흐르다
faucet 수도꼭지   line up 준비하다, 마련하다, 일렬로 세우다
eating utensil 식기   rack 받침대, 선반

5. 🎧 미녀

(A) He's reaching for a pair of gloves.
(B) He's jogging along a walkway.
(C) Leaves are scattered on the ground.
(D) A broom is leaning against a tree.

해석
(A) 그는 장갑을 잡으려고 손을 뻗고 있다.
(B) 그는 산책로를 따라 조깅하고 있다.
(C) 나뭇잎이 땅에 흩어져 있다.
(D) 빗자루가 나무에 기대어 있다.

어휘 reach for ~을 잡으려고 손을 뻗다   walkway 보도, 산책길
scatter (흩)뿌리다   broom 빗자루   lean against ~에 기대다

6. 🎧 미남

(A) Some cushions are being stacked near a container.
(B) Some sofas have been arranged in a display area.
(C) Some furniture is piled onto a truck.
(D) Some light fixtures are hanging above a dining room.

해석
(A) 쿠션이 컨테이너 근처에 쌓이고 있다.
(B) 소파가 전시 구역에 배치되어 있다.
(C) 가구가 트럭 위에 쌓여 있다.
(D) 조명 기구가 식당 위에 걸려 있다.

어휘 stack 쌓다   furniture 가구   pile 쌓다   dining room
식당

7. 🎧 호남/영녀

Where is the nearest dry cleaner's?
(A) On Cardinal Avenue.
(B) I'm nearly finished.
(C) It's for all clothing.

해석
가장 가까운 세탁소가 어디에 있나요?
(A) 카디널 가예요.
(B) 거의 다 했어요.
(C) 모든 옷이 다 돼요.

어휘 nearest 가장 가까운   nearly 거의

8. 🎧 미녀/호남

Should we send the package today or tomorrow?
(A) Five pounds.
(B) Today is better.
(C) An international address.

해석
소포를 오늘 보내야 할까요, 아니면 내일 보내야 할까요?
(A) 5파운드입니다.
(B) 오늘이 더 좋아요.
(C) 국제 주소입니다.

어휘 international 국제의

9. 🎧 호남/영녀

Does the printer need a new ink cartridge?
(A) A double set of prints, please.
(B) Jamie has the posters.
(C) No, I just replaced it.

해석
프린터에 새 잉크 카트리지가 필요한가요?
(A) 인쇄물을 두 세트 주세요.
(B) 제이미가 포스터를 가지고 있어요.
(C) 아니요, 제가 막 교체했어요.

어휘 replace 바꾸다, 교체하다

10. 🎧 미남/미녀

Who set up this display?
(A) The new winter boots.
(B) Jessica did.
(C) Mostly on the weekend.

해석
누가 이 진열을 준비했나요?
(A) 새 겨울 부츠요.
(B) 제시카가 했어요.
(C) 주로 주말예요.

어휘 display 전시, 진열

11. 🎧 영녀/미남

The company retreat is in the summer, right?
(A) Right. It's scheduled for July.
(B) She's a repeat customer.
(C) The venue is modern.

해석
회사 수련회는 여름에 있죠, 맞죠?
(A) 맞아요. 7월로 예정되어 있습니다.
(B) 그녀는 단골손님입니다.
(C) 장소가 현대적이네요.

어휘 retreat 수련회 repeat customer 단골손님 venue 장소 modern 현대적인

12. 🎧 미녀/미남

> Can I try on these dresses?
> (A) I can take your shift.
> (B) Our dress code has changed.
> **(C) The shop is closing soon.**

해석
이 드레스를 입어 봐도 될까요?
(A) 제가 교대해 드릴게요.
(B) 복장 규정이 바뀌었어요.
(C) 가게가 곧 문을 닫아요.

어휘 try on 입어 보다 take a shift 교대하다 dress code 복장 규정

13. 🎧 호남/영녀

> Is there a secure place to leave my luggage?
> (A) A new credit card.
> **(B) Sure, behind the front desk.**
> (C) At the maximum weight.

해석
제 짐을 맡길 수 있는 안전한 장소가 있나요?
(A) 새 신용카드입니다.
(B) 물론이죠, 프런트 뒤에요.
(C) 최대 무게로요.

어휘 secure 안전한, 확실한 luggage 짐, 수하물 maximum 최대의 weight 무게

14. 🎧 미녀/호남

> Are you attending the trade fair on Friday or on Saturday?
> **(A) My ticket is for Saturday.**
> (B) The Valentine Hotel.
> (C) Yes, I was impressed.

해석
무역 박람회에 금요일에 참석하시나요, 아니면 토요일에 참석하시나요?
(A) 제 표는 토요일 거예요.
(B) 발렌타인 호텔이요.
(C) 네, 감명 받았어요.

어휘 attend 참석하다 trade fair 무역 박람회 impressed 감명[감동]을 받은

15. 🎧 미남/미녀

> Why don't you reserve your table through the app?
> (A) Once a month.
> **(B) Can you show me how?**
> (C) She went out for lunch.

해석
앱을 통해 테이블을 예약하는 게 어때요?
(A) 한 달에 한 번이요.
(B) 어떻게 하는지 보여 주시겠어요?
(C) 그녀는 점심 먹으러 나갔어요.

어휘 reserve 예약하다

16. 🎧 영녀/호남

> When do I need to make a payment?
> (A) More than five hundred dollars.
> (B) For a magazine subscription.
> **(C) By the end of the week.**

해석
납부는 언제 해야 하나요?
(A) 500달러 이상이요.
(B) 잡지 구독을 위해서요.
(C) 주말까지요.

어휘 make a payment 지불하다, 납부하다

17. 🎧 영녀/미남

> Which taxi service do you usually use?
> **(A) I prefer to take the bus.**
> (B) No, these are brand-new.
> (C) It takes about twenty minutes.

해석
주로 어떤 택시 서비스를 이용하시나요?
(A) 저는 버스 타는 걸 선호해요.
(B) 아니요, 이것들은 새 거예요.
(C) 20분 정도 걸립니다.

18. 🎧 미녀/호남

> Could you work on preparing the orientation?
> (A) Five new employees.
> **(B) Certainly, I'd be happy to.**
> (C) I sat near the front.

해석
오리엔테이션 준비 작업을 해 주실 수 있나요?
(A) 신입사원 5명이요.
(B) 물론이죠, 기꺼이 할게요.
(C) 저는 앞쪽에 앉았어요.

19. 🎧 미녀/미남

> I ordered the banners two days ago.
> (A) The shop's grand opening.
> (B) Yes, she's a graphic designer.
> **(C) Custom orders take a week.**

해석

제가 이틀 전에 배너를 주문했어요.
(A) 가게 개장이요.
(B) 네, 그녀는 그래픽 디자이너입니다.
(C) 맞춤 주문은 일주일 걸립니다.

어휘 grand opening 개장, 개점   custom 맞춤의

20. 🎧 미남/영녀

> Where are the watermelons in your store?
> **(A) Those are only seasonal.**
> (B) I'll stop by the store.
> (C) Forty-five cents per pound.

해석

이 가게에 수박은 어디에 있나요?
(A) 수박은 제철에만 나와요.
(B) 제가 가게에 들를게요.
(C) 파운드당 45센트입니다.

어휘 seasonal 계절의, 계절마다의   stop by 잠시 들르다

21. 🎧 호남/미녀

> Is this a good price for a tennis racket?
> (A) The court in the corner.
> **(B) Not really. I've seen lower prices.**
> (C) Here is the lesson schedule.

해석

이것은 테니스 라켓에 괜찮은 가격인가요?
(A) 구석에 있는 코트요.
(B) 별로요. 더 낮은 가격을 봤어요.
(C) 여기 강습 일정표가 있습니다.

어휘 court 코트, 경기장

22. 🎧 영녀/호남

> How was the conference call this morning?
> **(A) The committee had to reschedule.**
> (B) The main conference room.
> (C) I'll check our inventory.

해석

오늘 아침 전화 회의는 어땠어요?
(A) 위원회는 일정을 변경해야 했어요.
(B) 주 회의실이요.
(C) 재고를 확인해 볼게요.

어휘 committee 위원회   reschedule 일정을 변경하다
inventory 재고, 물품 목록

23. 🎧 호남/미녀

> Doesn't the ferry leave at 2?
> (A) I prefer to stand.
> (B) That's too heavy.
> **(C) I believe so.**

해석

페리는 2시에 출발하지 않나요?
(A) 저는 서 있는 게 더 좋아요.
(B) 그건 너무 무겁네요.
(C) 그런 것 같아요.

어휘 stand 서다

24. 🎧 영녀/미남

> We're replacing this machine, aren't we?
> (A) Yes, he changed menu options.
> **(B) The budget isn't large enough.**
> (C) Around fifteen minutes.

해석

우리 이 기계 교체하는 거죠, 그렇지 않나요?
(A) 네, 그가 메뉴를 바꿨어요.
(B) 예산이 충분하지 않아요.
(C) 15분 정도요.

25. 🎧 호남/영녀

> Do you think you can organize a party for Sumin's
> last day?
> (A) Who gave them a gift?
> (B) The updated organization chart.
> **(C) Of course, I'm confident I can.**

해석

수민의 마지막 날을 위해 파티를 준비하실 수 있을 것 같나요?
(A) 누가 그들에게 선물을 주었나요?
(B) 업데이트된 조직 차트입니다.
(C) 물론이죠, 할 자신이 있어요.

어휘 organize 준비하다   organization 조직, 구조
confident 확신하는, 자신이 있는

26. 🎧 미남/미녀

> Why isn't the keypad at the laboratory entrance
> working?
> **(A) The manager sent an e-mail this afternoon.**
> (B) Down the hall on the right.
> (C) No, after 7:00 P.M.

해석

왜 실험실 입구에 있는 키패드가 작동하지 않는 거죠?

(A) 관리자가 오늘 오후에 이메일을 보냈어요.

(B) 복도를 따라 가서 오른쪽이요.

(C) 아니요, 오후 7시 이후예요.

어휘 laboratory 실험실 hall 복도

27. 🎧 미녀/미남

We have just launched a new loyalty program.

(A) I'm busy at lunchtime.

(B) Great, I'll check it out.

(C) She studied computer programming.

해석

저희는 새로운 고객 보상 프로그램을 출시했습니다.

(A) 점심시간에는 바빠요.

(B) 좋네요, 확인해 볼게요.

(C) 그녀는 컴퓨터 프로그래밍을 공부했어요.

어휘 launch 출시하다, 시작하다

28. 🎧 미남/영녀

Would you rather go to a concert or watch a movie?

(A) Oh, is that your new watch?

(B) Probably sometime this weekend.

(C) I love live performances.

해석

콘서트에 가시겠어요, 아니면 영화를 보시겠어요?

(A) 아, 저게 당신의 새 시계인가요?

(B) 이번 주말 언젠가일 거예요.

(C) 저는 라이브 공연을 좋아해요.

29. 🎧 영녀/미남

Is the company's Internet service working?

(A) I couldn't get connected.

(B) No, we store them upstairs.

(C) My username and password.

해석

회사의 인터넷 서비스가 작동하고 있나요?

(A) 연결이 안 됐어요.

(B) 아니요, 저희는 그것들을 위층에 보관해요.

(C) 제 사용자명과 암호입니다.

어휘 username 사용자명

30. 🎧 호남/미녀

Who should we choose to take over as assistant manager?

(A) Some clear production goals.

(B) The current one may not retire yet.

(C) Thank you for your assistance.

해석

부팀장을 인계받을 사람으로 누구를 선택해야 할까요?

(A) 몇 가지 명확한 생산 목표입니다.

(B) 현재 부팀장은 아직 은퇴하지 않을 거예요.

(C) 도와주셔서 감사합니다.

어휘 take over ~을 인계받다 production 생산(량)

current 현재의 retire 은퇴하다 assistance 도움, 지원

31. 🎧 미녀/호남

When can I expect my laptop to be repaired?

(A) We're waiting for some new components.

(B) At least two hundred dollars.

(C) They're usually sold as a pair.

해석

제 노트북 수리는 언제쯤으로 예상할 수 있을까요?

(A) 저희는 몇 가지 새 부품을 기다리고 있어요.

(B) 적어도 200달러요.

(C) 그것들은 보통 한 쌍으로 판매됩니다.

어휘 component 부품, 요소 pair 한 쌍, 한 벌

32-34. 🎧 영녀/미남

Questions 32-34 refer to the following conversation.

W Hi, this is Samantha from Daisy Flower Shop. ³²You left a message about the retirement party you're having on June 8.

M Yes, I wanted to confirm the delivery time. The event is scheduled to start at 7 P.M. So, could you deliver the flowers at 5:30?

W All right. ³³It's hard to estimate how long the driving time will be at that time of day. If our driver arrives early, will there be someone there to accept the delivery?

M Yes, I'll be there from four o'clock.

W Okay, ³⁴I'll send you the invoice for the flowers later today.

32-34번은 다음 대화에 관한 문제입니다.

여 안녕하세요, 저는 데이지 꽃집의 사만다입니다. ³²당신은 6월 8일에 열리는 은퇴 기념 파티에 대해 메시지를 남기셨더군요.

남 네, 배송 시간을 확인하고 싶어서요. 행사가 오후 7시에 시작될 예정입니다. 그럼 5시 30분에 꽃을 배달해 주실 수 있나요?

여 알겠습니다. ³³그 시간에 운전 시간이 얼마나 걸릴지 추정하기가 **어려워요.** 저희 기사님이 일찍 도착하면, 거기에 배달을 받아줄 사람이 있을까요?

남 네, 제가 4시부터 있을 거예요.

여 알겠습니다, 오늘 중으로 ³⁴꽃에 대한 청구서를 보내드릴게요.

어휘 estimate 추정하다   invoice 송장, 청구서

32. 남자는 어떤 종류의 행사를 계획하고 있는가?
(A) 기념일 축하 행사
(B) 개업식
(C) 자선 기금 모금 행사
(D) 은퇴 기념 파티

33. 여자는 무엇이 추정하기 어렵다고 말하는가?
(A) 배송비
(B) 사용 가능한 색상
(C) 인건비
(D) 이동 시간

패러프레이징 the driving time → The travel time

34. 여자는 남자에게 무엇을 보낼 것인가?
(A) 견본
(B) 사진
(C) 청구서
(D) 책자

35-37. 🎧 호남/미녀
Questions 35-37 refer to the following conversation.

> M ³⁵The turnout for the open house at the Emerson Street property was so low. Only two potential buyers stopped by.
>
> W I know. ³⁶Unfortunately, the wrong address was printed in our ad for the event. This made it difficult for people to find the site.
>
> M Well, the owner wants to sell this property as quickly as possible. ³⁷We'd better hold another open house this weekend. I know that none of us were planning to work this weekend, but we need to make up for our mistake.

35-37번은 다음 대화에 관한 문제입니다.

남 ³⁵에머슨 가 매물에서 오픈 하우스의 참가자 수가 너무 적었어요. 잠재적인 구매자가 두 명밖에 안 들렀어요.

여 그러니까요. ³⁶유감스럽게도, 그 행사의 광고에 잘못된 주소가 인쇄되었어요. 이것 때문에 사람들이 장소를 찾는 것이 어려워졌죠.

남 음, 소유주는 이 부동산을 가능한 한 빨리 팔고 싶어 해요. ³⁷우리는 이번 주말에 또 한번 오픈 하우스를 여는 것이 좋겠어요. 우리 중 아무도 이번 주말에 일할 계획이 없었다는 것을 알지만, 우리는 실수를 만회해야 합니다.

어휘 turnout 참가자의 수   potential 잠재적인   make up for ~을 만회하다

35. 화자들은 어떤 업계에서 일하는 것 같은가?
(A) 부동산
(B) 교육
(C) 제조
(D) 의료

36. 여자에 따르면, 무엇이 문제를 야기했는가?
(A) 악천후
(B) 놓친 마감 기한
(C) 손상된 장비
(D) 광고의 오류

37. 남자는 무엇을 할 것을 제안하는가?
(A) 예산을 늘리는 것
(B) 또 다른 행사를 여는 것
(C) 작업자를 더 고용하는 것
(D) 후기를 읽는 것

패러프레이징 open house → event

38-40. 🎧 호남/영녀
Questions 38-40 refer to the following conversation.

> M Hi, Allison. It's Jake. ³⁸I wanted to talk to you about the tour of the Harrisburg historical district that you're leading tomorrow.
>
> W I've just been reviewing my notes. It departs from the Waldeck Building at 9 A.M., right?
>
> M Yes, that's right. ³⁹But I wanted to remind you about the new policy. You have to be at the departure point forty-five minutes before the scheduled start time, not twenty minutes.
>
> W I'll be sure to do that. Do you know if it's a large group?
>
> M ⁴⁰I can see how many people have signed up. Just a moment, please.

38-40번은 다음 대화에 관한 문제입니다.

남 앨리슨, 안녕하세요. 저 제이크예요. ³⁸내일 당신이 이끄는 해리스버그 역사 지구 투어에 대해 얘기하고 싶어서요.

여 방금 메모 내용을 살펴보고 있었어요. 오전 9시에 발데크 빌딩에서 출발하는 거 맞죠?

남 네, 맞아요. ³⁹그런데 당신에게 새로운 정책에 대해 상기시켜주고 싶었어요. 당신은 출발 예정 시각의 20분이 아니라 45분 전에 출발 지점에 있어야 합니다.

여 반드시 그렇게 할게요. 그 그룹의 사람 수가 많은지 혹시 아시나요?

남 ⁴⁰얼마나 많은 사람들이 등록했는지 볼 수 있어요. 잠깐만 기다려 주세요.

어휘 historical district 역사 지구   lead 안내하다, 이끌다   departure point 출발지   scheduled 예정된   sign up 등록하다

38. 여자의 직업은 무엇인 것 같은가?

(A) 잡지 기자

(B) 투어 가이드

(C) 박물관 큐레이터

(D) 버스 운전사

39. 남자는 왜 전화하고 있는가?

(A) 상기시켜주기 위해

(B) 승진을 제안하기 위해

(C) 행사를 취소하기 위해

(D) 면접 일정을 잡기 위해

어휘 promotion 승진

40. 남자는 다음에 무엇을 할 것인가?

(A) 웹사이트 업데이트하기

(B) 시간표 보내기

(C) 참가자 목록 확인하기

(D) 정책 설명하기

어휘 timetable 시간표, 일정표 participant 참가자

41-43. 🎧 미녀/미남

Questions 41-43 refer to the following conversation.

> **W** Marco, **41** I've found a new supplier for the wallpaper and floor coverings we use in our designs.
>
> **M** That's great. We're getting busier and busier these days. **42** Now we have to make a decision about the best way to find new staff members.
>
> **W** Well, we could post job openings online and see how much interest we get.
>
> **M** Hmm... **43** Let's be careful not to spend too much time waiting for people to respond to online posts. Hiring a recruitment firm would be more expensive but a lot more efficient.

41-43번은 다음 대화에 관한 문제입니다.

여 마르코, **41** 우리 설계에 사용할 벽지와 바닥재의 새로운 공급 업체를 찾았어요.

남 잘됐네요. 요즘 우리는 점점 더 바빠지고 있어요. **42** 이제 우리는 새로운 직원을 찾을 수 있는 가장 좋은 방법에 대해 결정을 내려야 합니다.

여 음, 우리는 온라인에 구인 공고를 내고 우리가 얼마나 많은 관심을 받는지 볼 수 있어요.

남 흠... **43** 사람들이 온라인 게시물에 반응을 보이기를 기다리는 데 너무 많은 시간을 보내지 않도록 주의합시다. 채용 회사를 고용하는 것이 비용은 더 들지만 훨씬 효율적일 거예요.

어휘 supplier 공급 업체 make a decision 결정하다 post 게시하다 respond 반응을 보이다 recruitment firm 채용 회사

41. 화자들은 누구인 것 같은가?

(A) 은행원

(B) 실내 장식가

(C) 배송 기사

(D) 안전 감독관

42. 화자들은 무엇을 결정해야 하는가?

(A) 어떤 소프트웨어를 써볼지

(B) 제품을 어디에 광고할지

(C) 새 지점을 얼마나 빨리 열지

(D) 신입 직원들을 어떻게 채용할지

어휘 recruit 모집하다, 뽑다

패러프레이징 the best way to find new staff members → How to recruit new employees

43. 남자는 여자에게 무엇에 대해 주의하라고 말하는가?

(A) 구식 장비를 사용하는 것

(B) 프로젝트를 늦게 완료하는 것

(C) 많은 시간을 낭비하는 것

(D) 예산을 초과하는 것

어휘 outdated 구식의 waste 낭비하다 exceed 초과하다

패러프레이징 spend too much time → Wasting a lot of time

44-46. 🎧 미녀/호남/영녀

Questions 44-46 refer to the following conversation with three speakers.

> **W1** **44** Welcome to Benson Institute of Corporate Training. How may I help you?
>
> **M** **45** I'm arranging a workshop for my team on May 8, and I need someone to give a presentation.
>
> **W1** Jillian is one of our staff and can tell you more about it.
>
> **W2** Hi, it just depends on the instructor's schedule. Is there a particular instructor you had in mind?
>
> **M** Yes, Teresa Connelly.
>
> **W2** Alright. I can check with her.
>
> **W1** Someone will call you about it later today.
>
> **M** Thank you. **46** One of my coworkers took Ms. Connelly's class and highly recommended her.

44-46번은 다음 세 명의 대화에 관한 문제입니다.

여1 **44** 벤슨 기업 교육 기관에 오신 것을 환영합니다. 무엇을 도와드릴까요?

남 **45** 5월 8일에 저희 팀을 위한 워크숍을 준비하고 있는데, 발표할 사람이 필요합니다.

여1 저희 직원 중 한 명인 질리안이 그것에 대해 자세히 알려드릴 수 있습니다.

여2 안녕하세요, 그건 강사님 스케줄에 달려 있어요. 생각하고 계신 특정 강사가 있나요?

남 네, 테레사 코넬리요.

여2 알겠습니다. 그녀에게 확인해 볼게요.

여1 오늘 중으로 누군가 그것에 대해 전화드릴 거예요.

남 감사합니다. **⁴⁶제 동료 중 한 명이 코넬리 씨의 강의를 듣고 그녀를 강력하게 추천했어요.**

어휘 instructor 강사

44. 화자들은 어디에 있는 것 같은가?
(A) 도서관에
(B) 헬스장에
(C) 비즈니스 스쿨에
(D) 예술관에

패러프레이징 Institute of Corporate Training → business school

45. 남자는 무엇을 하고 싶어 하는가?
(A) 발표자 고용하기
(B) 입사 지원하기
(C) 시연하기
(D) 판매 협상하기

어휘 negotiate 협상하다

46. 남자는 테레사 코넬리에 대해 어떻게 알게 되었는가?
(A) 온라인 검색에서
(B) 신문 기사를 읽는 것에서
(C) 전단지를 받는 것에서
(D) 동료와 이야기하는 것에서

어휘 flyer 전단지

47-49. 🎧 영녀/미남
Questions 47-49 refer to the following conversation.

W Mr. Abrams, **⁴⁷I've measured all of the rooms in the building except Conference Room B, which is locked.** To save time, I can just provide a size estimate so you can order your floor tiles.

M **⁴⁸Actually, we need to know the exact measurements of the room. Because we'll be using a very expensive tile, we cannot afford to buy more than we have to.** My colleague has the keys to that room, and he'll be back in twenty minutes. Can you wait for him?

W Well... **⁴⁹I'll need to call my manager to see if it's okay for me to stay here longer.** I'm supposed to leave for another job.

M Okay. Please let me know.

47-49번은 다음 대화에 관한 문제입니다.

여 에이브람스 씨, **⁴⁷제가 건물 안에 있는 모든 방의 치수를 쟀는데요, 잠겨 있는 B 회의실만 빼고요.** 시간을 절약하기 위해서, 당신이 바닥 타일을 주문하실 수 있게 사이즈 견적만 제공해 드릴

수도 있습니다.

남 **⁴⁸사실, 저희는 그 방의 정확한 치수를 알아야 해요. 매우 비싼 타일을 사용할 것이기 때문에, 필요한 것보다 더 많이 살 여유가 없습니다.** 제 동료가 그 방 열쇠를 가지고 있고, 20분 안에 돌아올 거예요. 그를 기다려 주실 수 있나요?

여 음... **⁴⁹관리자에게 전화해서 제가 여기 더 있어도 되는지 확인해야 할 거예요.** 저는 또 다른 작업을 위해 나가봐야 해서요.

남 알겠어요. 제게 알려주세요.

어휘 lock 잠그다   afford 여유가 되다   be supposed to ~하기로 되어 있다, ~해야 하다

47. 여자는 어떤 문제를 언급하는가?
(A) 그녀는 보고서 원본을 잃어버렸다.
(B) 그녀는 방에 들어갈 수 없다.
(C) 일부 제품이 단종되었다.
(D) 일부 바닥재가 심하게 손상되었다.

어휘 access 들어가다   discontinue (생산을) 중단하다

48. 남자는 왜 정확한 치수를 필요로 하는가?
(A) 자재의 가격이 비싸다.
(B) 문서가 면밀히 검열될 것이다.
(C) 그것은 그가 시간을 절약하는 데 도움이 될 것이다.
(D) 그것은 시에서 요구한다.

패러프레이징 we'll be using a very expensive tile → The cost of a material is high

49. 여자는 다음에 무엇을 할 것 같은가?
(A) 몇 가지 도구 꺼내기
(B) 속달 주문 넣기
(C) 관리자에게 연락하기
(D) 견적서 작성하기

어휘 unpack 꺼내다

패러프레이징 call my manager → Contact a supervisor

50-52. 🎧 호남/미녀
Questions 50-52 refer to the following conversation.

M **⁵⁰Hello, I have quite a few packages to send today. I've started my own business making handmade leather bags.**

W **⁵⁰I can help you with those.** But do you plan to come to the post office often?

M Yes, as I need to send items regularly.

W **⁵¹You know, you can print your own postage labels at home if you download our smartphone application.** Then just use one of the drop-off points around town.

M Oh, right. **⁵²I saw one at my local supermarket. I'm headed there after this. That would have saved me a lot of time.**

50-52번은 다음 대화에 관한 문제입니다.

남 ⁵⁰안녕하세요, 오늘 보낼 소포가 꽤 많아요. 저는 수제 가죽 가방을 만드는 사업을 시작했어요.

여 ⁵⁰제가 도와드릴게요. 그런데 당신은 우체국에 자주 오실 계획인가요?

남 네, 정기적으로 물건을 보내야 해서요.

여 ⁵¹있잖아요, 저희 스마트폰 앱을 다운로드하면 집에서 직접 우편 요금 라벨을 인쇄하실 수 있어요. 그런 다음 시내의 배달품 전달 장소 중 하나를 이용하시면 됩니다.

남 아, 맞아요. ⁵²동네 슈퍼마켓에서 하나 봤어요. 저는 이 일이 끝나고 거기로 갈 거예요. 그러면 시간을 많이 절약할 수 있었겠네요.

어휘 package 소포   regularly 정기적으로   postage 우편 요금   drop-off point 배달품 전달 장소

50. 여자는 누구인 것 같은가?
(A) 우체국 직원
(B) 재정 고문
(C) 여행사 직원
(D) 공장 직원

51. 여자는 왜 모바일 앱을 다운로드할 것을 제안하는가?
(A) 할인 혜택을 이용하기 위해
(B) 운영 시간을 확인하기 위해
(C) 제품을 홍보하기 위해
(D) 집에서 라벨을 인쇄하기 위해

53. 남자는 다음에 어디로 갈 계획인가?
(A) 휴대폰 판매점으로
(B) 버스 터미널로
(C) 슈퍼마켓으로
(D) 아웃렛 몰로

53-55. 🎧 미남/미녀
Questions 53-55 refer to the following conversation.

M Let's take a look at our upcoming orders to make sure we're on track.

W ⁵³I've just received a request from Fenton Industries for us to make three hundred office chairs, which they need by June 10. Since the current Valdez Hotel order is so large, ⁵⁴I'm wondering if we could push back their delivery date.

M Well, the Valdez Hotel is holding its grand opening at the end of the month.

W ⁵⁴Oh, so they can't be flexible.

M Right. ⁵⁵We could add extra shifts, depending on Kyle's and Ben's availability, as they're the only ones who can operate the fabric-stretching machine.

53-55번은 다음 대화에 관한 문제입니다.

남 일이 제대로 진행되고 있는지 확인하기 위해 다음 주문 내역들을 살펴봅시다.

여 ⁵³방금 펜턴 산업으로부터 사무용 의자 300개를 만들어 달라는 요청을 받았는데, 6월 10일까지 필요해요. 현재 밸디즈 호텔의 주문량이 너무 많아서, ⁵⁴그들의 납품일을 미룰 수 있을지 궁금합니다.

남 음, 밸디즈 호텔은 이달 말에 개업식을 할 거예요.

여 ⁵⁴아, 그럼 일정을 바꿀 수 없겠네요.

남 맞아요. ⁵⁵카일과 벤이 직물 스트레치 기계를 작동할 수 있는 유일한 사람들이기 때문에, 그들의 가능 여부에 따라 교대조를 더 추가할 수도 있어요.

어휘 upcoming 다가오는, 곧 있을   on track 제대로 진행되고 있는   push back 미루다   delivery date 납품일   flexible 마음대로 바꿀 수 있는, 유연한   operate 작동하다

53. 화자들은 어디에서 일하는 것 같은가?
(A) 금융기관에서
(B) 화학 실험실에서
(C) 가구 제조사에서
(D) 미술용품점에서

54. 남자는 왜 "밸디즈 호텔은 이달 말에 개업식을 할 거예요"라고 말하는가?
(A) 제안을 거절하기 위해
(B) 결정에 동의하기 위해
(C) 안심시키기 위해
(D) 경쟁을 강조하기 위해

어휘 reassurance 안심시키는 말[행동]   highlight 강조하다

55. 남자는 카일과 벤에 대해 무엇이라고 말하는가?
(A) 그들은 펜턴 산업에 연락했다.
(B) 그들은 전문적인 기술을 가지고 있다.
(C) 그들은 신입 사원들이다.
(D) 그들은 기계를 수리하고 있다.

어휘 specialized 전문적인

56-58. 🎧 영녀/미남/호남
Questions 56-58 refer to the following conversation with three speakers.

W Alright, ⁵⁶we're here to discuss our online sales of cake-decorating equipment. Daniel?

M1 Well, we sold about the same number of units last month as in the previous months.

M2 That's surprising. ⁵⁷Since we lowered the price of the sets in August, I would have expected more sales.

M1 We need a way to make customers engage with our product.

M2 ⁵⁸How about recording short video clips of different decorating techniques? Then we could post those on our Web site to inspire people.

W ⁵⁸Good idea, Takuya. Do you know of any cake decorators who could do that?

56-58번은 다음 세 명의 대화에 관한 문제입니다.

여 좋아요, ⁵⁶우리는 케이크 장식 용품의 온라인 판매에 대해 논의하러 모였어요. 다니엘?

남1 음, 지난달에는 이전 달과 거의 같은 수량을 팔았어요.

남2 그거 놀랍군요. ⁵⁷우리가 8월에 세트 가격을 낮췄기 때문에, 저는 더 많은 판매를 기대했어요.

남1 고객들이 우리 제품에 관심을 갖게 할 방법이 필요합니다.

남2 다양한 장식 기법을 담은 ⁵⁸짧은 비디오 클립을 녹화하는 것은 어떨까요? 그리고 나서 그것들을 우리 웹사이트에 올려 사람들의 관심을 일으킬 수 있을 거예요.

여 ⁵⁸좋은 생각이에요, 타쿠야. 그것을 할 수 있는 케이크 장식가 중 알고 있는 사람이 있나요?

어휘 previous 이전의 lower 낮추다 technique 기법, 기술 inspire 영감을 주다

56. 회의의 목적은 무엇인가?
(A) 업계 행사를 준비하기 위해
(B) 입사 지원자를 선발하기 위해
(C) 예산을 승인하기 위해
(D) 제품 판매에 대해 논의하기 위해

패러프레이징 discuss our online sales of cake-decorating equipment → discuss product sales

57. 회사는 8월에 무엇을 했는가?
(A) 가격을 내렸다.
(B) 경영진을 바꿨다.
(C) 새로운 웹사이트를 출시했다.
(D) 색상 선택의 폭을 넓혔다.

어휘 management 경영진

58. 화자들은 무엇을 할 계획인가?
(A) 경쟁업체와 합병하기
(B) 영상 만들기
(C) 대회 개최하기
(D) 책자 인쇄하기

어휘 merge 합병하다

패러프레이징 recording short video clips → Create some videos

59-61. 🎧 미남/영녀
Questions 59-61 refer to the following conversation.

M Hi, Vanessa. ⁵⁹I'm sure you've heard that representatives from the Mumbai branch will be coming to our office for a visit. They've just confirmed that it will be on April 3.

W Oh, you're in charge of hosting them, right? That must be a lot of work.

M Yes, there are a lot of things to plan. ⁶⁰And I want to make sure I'm respectful of their culture. I know you've spent a lot of time in India.

W Unfortunately, I have to go right now. ⁶¹A reporter from the *Westbury Times* is about to call to interview me about our environmental initiatives. How about this afternoon? I'd be happy to share some tips.

59-61번은 다음 대화에 관한 문제입니다.

남 바네사, 안녕하세요. ⁵⁹뭄바이 지사의 대표들이 우리 사무실을 방문한다는 소식을 들으셨을 겁니다. 방문은 4월 3일에 있을 거라고 그들이 방금 확인해 주었어요.

여 아, 당신이 그들 접대를 맡고 있죠? 수고가 많겠군요.

남 네, 계획해야 할 것들이 많아요. ⁶⁰그리고 제가 그들의 문화를 존중하고 있는지 확인하고 싶은데요. 당신이 인도에서 많은 시간을 보냈다는 것을 알아요.

여 안타깝게도 저는 지금 가야 합니다. ⁶¹'웨스트베리 타임즈'에서 온 기자가 우리의 환경 계획에 대해 전화 인터뷰를 하려는 참이에요. 오늘 오후는 어때요? 몇 가지 팁을 기꺼이 공유해 드릴게요.

어휘 representative 대표 in charge of ~을 맡아서 host 접대하다 respectful 존중하는, 정중한 initiative 계획

59. 4월 3일에 무슨 일이 일어날 것 같은가?
(A) 보안 시스템이 변경될 것이다.
(B) 산업 학회가 열릴 것이다.
(C) 몇몇 방문객들이 회사에 올 것이다.
(D) 몇몇 수상자들이 발표될 것이다.

60. 남자는 왜 "당신이 인도에서 많은 시간을 보냈다는 것을 알아요"라고 말하는가?
(A) 지연을 설명하기 위해
(B) 도움을 요청하기 위해
(C) 불만을 제기하기 위해
(D) 놀라움을 나타내기 위해

61. 여자는 다음에 무엇을 할 것인가?
(A) 인터뷰 참여하기
(B) 여행사에 연락하기
(C) 참석 확정하기
(D) 회람 보내기

어휘 participate in ~에 참여하다 attendance 참석, 출석

62-64. 🎧 호남/미녀
Questions 62-64 refer to the following conversation and floor layout.

M ⁶²Caroline, next weekend we will be showing the latest documentary about art trends by director Victor Barbosa. **Which room do you think would be best for the event?**

W Well, ⁶³I think we should set up chairs in the room with the oil paintings. The sound quality will be best in there.

M Good point. And it doesn't have big displays like the Sculpture Room does.

W Exactly. Oh, and ⁶⁴I spoke to the site manager yesterday. He said he wants to serve complimentary snacks and drinks as people arrive.

62-64번은 다음 대화와 층 배치도에 관한 문제입니다.

남 **⁶²캐롤라인, 다음 주말에 우리는 예술 동향에 관해 빅터 바르보사 감독이 만든 최신 다큐멘터리를 상영할 거예요.** 어떤 전시실이 행사에 가장 적합할 것 같아요?

여 음, ⁶³유화가 있는 전시실에 의자를 준비해야 할 것 같아요. 그곳에서 음향이 가장 좋을 거예요.

남 좋은 지적이네요. 그리고 그곳은 조각품실처럼 대형 전시품을 가지고 있지 않고요.

여 맞아요. 아, 그리고 **⁶⁴제가 어제 현장 관리자와 통화했는데요. 그는 사람들이 도착하면 무료 간식과 음료를 제공하고 싶다고 했어요.**

어휘 display 전시(품)　complimentary 무료의

1번 전시실 조각품	**⁶³ 3번 전시실 유화**
2번 전시실 수채화　수묵화	4번 전시실 사진

62. 화자들은 어떤 행사를 준비하고 있는가?
(A) 자원봉사자 교육
(B) 미술품 경매
(C) 회화 시연
(D) 영화 상영

어휘 auction 경매

63. 시각 자료를 보시오. 여자는 행사를 위해 어느 전시실을 사용할 것을 제안하는가?
(A) 1번 전시실
(B) 2번 전시실
(C) 3번 전시실
(D) 4번 전시실

64. 여자에 따르면, 현장 관리자는 무엇을 제공하고 싶어 하는가?
(A) 음악 연주
(B) 다과
(C) 무료 주차

(D) 단체 사진

패러프레이징 snacks and drinks → Some refreshments

65-67. 🎧 영녀/호남

Questions 65-67 refer to the following conversation and product catalog.

W Hi, Curtis. ⁶⁵I didn't think anyone would be in the conference room. The employee lounge is full, so I thought I'd have my lunch in here. Do you mind if I sit with you?

M Go right ahead. I was just browsing this catalog.

W Oh, are you buying something as a gift?

M Yes. ⁶⁶My sister is receiving an award in Cleveland at the end of the month. I'm going to the ceremony in person **and wanted to give her something to congratulate her.**

W Oh, that'll be a nice trip.

M She already has a lot of necklaces, so ⁶⁷I think this bracelet would be perfect.

W It looks lovely.

65-67번은 다음 대화와 상품 카탈로그에 관한 문제입니다.

여 안녕하세요, 커티스. **⁶⁵회의실에 아무도 없을 거라고 생각했어요. 직원 휴게실이 꽉 차서 여기서 점심을 먹으려고 했거든요. 같이 앉아도 될까요?**

남 어서 앉으세요. 전 그냥 이 카탈로그를 훑어보고 있었어요.

여 아, 선물로 뭘 사시려고요?

남 네. **⁶⁶제 여동생이 이달 말에 클리블랜드에서 상을 받거든요. 제가 직접 시상식에 가는데** 축하 선물을 주고 싶었어요.

여 오, 멋진 여행이 되겠네요.

남 그녀는 이미 목걸이를 많이 가지고 있어서, **⁶⁷이 팔찌가 완벽할 것 같아요.**

여 멋져 보이네요.

어휘 in person 직접　necklace 목걸이　bracelet 팔찌

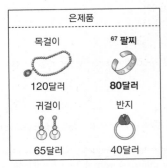

은제품

목걸이	**⁶⁷ 팔찌**
120달러	**80달러**
귀걸이	반지
65달러	40달러

65. 화자들은 어디에 있는가?
(A) 직원 휴게실에
(B) 기차역에

(C) 식당에

(D) 회의실에

66. 남자는 왜 클리블랜드로 여행할 것인가?

(A) 시상식에 참석하기 위해

(B) 건물을 점검하기 위해

(C) 발표를 하기 위해

(D) 상을 받기 위해

어휘 inspect 점검하다

67. 시각 자료를 보시오. 남자는 돈을 얼마나 쓸 것 같은가?

(A) 120달러

(B) 80달러

(C) 65달러

(D) 40달러

68-70. 🎧 미남/미녀

Questions 68-70 refer to the following conversation and chart.

> M Hi, Marta. [68] How are you settling into the new work environment since you transferred to our branch last month?
>
> W Well, this shop has a much larger selection, so I'm still learning about some of the merchandise. For example, earlier today, [69] a customer was looking for a cordless vacuum with a removable air filter. I wasn't sure which model would be best.
>
> M You can check the product chart to view the features quickly. See?
>
> W Oh, that's really helpful. Thanks.
>
> M Sure, anytime. By the way, [70] did you hear that the store is going to extend its business hours from next week? We can pick up extra shifts and earn extra money before the holidays. So, I was happy to hear that.

진공 청소기 모델	[69] 무선	[69] 분리 가능한 공기 필터	먼지털이솔
보텔로	✓		
액티바	✓		✓
맘모스		✓	✓
[69] 굿윈	✓	✓	

68. 여자는 지난달에 무엇을 했는가?

(A) 그녀는 진공 청소기를 구매했다.

(B) 그녀는 다른 지점으로 전근을 왔다.

(C) 그녀는 승진 제의를 받았다.

(D) 그녀는 증명서를 받았다.

69. 시각 자료를 보시오. 고객이 요청한 기능을 갖추고 있는 모델은 어떤 것인가?

(A) 보텔로

(B) 액티바

(C) 맘모스

(D) 굿윈

70. 남자는 무엇에 대해 기뻐하는가?

(A) 연간 보너스

(B) 직원 할인

(C) 유급 휴가

(D) 영업 시간 변경

71-73. 🎧 영녀

Questions 71-73 refer to the following tour information.

> W [71] Welcome to this virtual tour of Irvine Theater. I am the owner, Lucy Gibbs. It's my pleasure to show you our beautiful site. Since its construction in 1910, this theater has been providing a wide variety of live performances. And [72] we're well known for the unique architectural features of the building, some of which I'll be showing you today. At the end of the tour, [73] please answer a few questions to share your opinions. We'll e-mail you a 20 percent discount coupon as a thank-you.

71-73번은 다음 관광 정보에 관한 문제입니다.

여 **[71] 어바인 극장의 가상 투어에 오신 것을 환영합니다. 저는 소유주인 루시 깁스입니다.** 여러분에게 우리의 아름다운 장소를 보여드리게 되어 기쁩니다. 1910년에 지어진 이래로, 이 극장은 매우 다양한 라이브 공연을 해오고 있습니다. 그리고 **[72] 우리는 건물의 독특한 건축학적 특징으로 잘 알려져 있는데요,** 그 중 일부는 제가 오늘 보여드릴 것입니다. 투어가 끝나면, **[73] 몇 가지 질문에 답변하여 의견을 공유해 주십시오. 감사의 표시로 20% 할인 쿠폰을 이메일로 보내드리겠습니다.**

어휘 a wide variety of 매우 다양한   architectural features 건축학적 특징

68-70번은 다음 대화와 차트에 관한 문제입니다.

남 마르타, 안녕하세요. **[68] 지난달에 저희 지점으로 전근 오신 이후로 새로운 업무 환경에 어떻게 적응하고 계신가요?**

여 음, 이 매장은 상품이 훨씬 더 다양해서 저는 아직도 몇몇 상품에 대해 배우고 있습니다. 예를 들어, 오늘 오전에 **[69] 고객 한 분이 분리 가능한 공기 필터가 있는 무선 진공 청소기를 찾고 계셨어요.** 저는 어떤 모델이 가장 좋을지 확신할 수 없었고요.

남 제품 차트를 확인하면 기능을 빠르게 볼 수 있어요. 보이시죠?

여 아, 정말 도움이 되네요. 감사해요.

남 그럼요, 언제든지요. 그나저나 **[70] 매장이 다음 주부터 영업 시간을 연장한다는 소식 들었어요?** 우리는 휴일 전에 추가 근무를 하고 돈을 더 벌 수 있어요. 그래서 저는 그 말을 듣고 기뻤어요.

어휘 settle into 자리잡다   transfer 전근 가다   removable 제거할 수 있는   feature 특징

71. 화자는 누구인가?

(A) 공장 관리자

(B) 건설 노동자

(C) 극장 소유주

(D) 컴퓨터 기술자

72. 시설은 무엇으로 유명한가?

(A) 기금 모금 활동

(B) 박식한 직원

(C) 독특한 건축 양식

(D) 현대적인 장비

어휘 architecture 건축 양식

73. 화자에 따르면, 청자들은 어떻게 쿠폰을 얻을 수 있는가?

(A) 피드백을 제공함으로써

(B) 소프트웨어를 다운로드함으로써

(C) 소식지 수신을 신청함으로써

(D) 화자에게 이메일을 보냄으로써

패러프레이징 answer a few questions to share your opinions → providing some feedback

74-76. 🎧 미남

Questions 74-76 refer to the following talk.

> **M** Thanks for joining the first session of World Tastes, our newly offered four-week course. Each week, ⁷⁴ we'll cover how to create delicious dishes from around the world. You'll learn to make several easy one-pan meals. Some of these recipes come from ⁷⁵ my book, *Henry at Home*. It was published just last week. Now, ⁷⁶ some of you have asked whether you can take any leftover dishes with you at the end of the class. Yes, I have some containers here.

74-76번은 다음 담화에 관한 문제입니다.

남 새로 개설된 4주 코스인 세계인의 입맛 첫 번째 시간에 참여해 주셔서 감사합니다. 매주, ⁷⁴ 우리는 전 세계의 맛있는 요리를 만드는 방법을 다룰 것입니다. 여러분은 냄비 하나로 몇 가지 간단한 식사를 만드는 법을 배울 것입니다. 이 조리법들 중 일부는 ⁷⁵ 저의 책 '헨리 앳 홈'에서 나온 것입니다. ⁷⁵ 그것은 바로 지난주에 출간되었습니다. 자, ⁷⁶ 여러분 중 몇 분이 수업이 끝날 때 남은 음식을 가지고 갈 수 있는지 물어보셨는데요. 네, 여기 용기가 몇 개 있습니다.

어휘 recipe 조리법   leftover 남은 음식   container 그릇, 용기

74. 청자들은 무엇에 관심이 있는 것 같은가?

(A) 그림 그리기

(B) 시

(C) 언어 학습

(D) 요리

75. 화자는 최근에 무엇을 했는가?

(A) 그는 해외에서 공부했다.

(B) 그는 웹사이트를 개설했다.

(C) 그는 책을 출간했다.

(D) 그는 팟캐스트를 진행했다.

어휘 host 진행하다

76. 일부 청자들은 무엇에 대해 물어보았는가?

(A) 개별 조언을 받는 것

(B) 집에 음식을 가져가는 것

(C) 수업 자료를 검토하는 것

(D) 용품을 구입하는 것

어휘 individual 개인의

77-79. 🎧 미녀

Questions 77-79 refer to the following telephone message.

> **W** Hi, Adam. It's Isabelle. I'm calling about the work on Mercer Bridge, which your crew has been assigned to. ⁷⁷ The bridge closure is scheduled for Tuesday, so that is the official start of the project. ⁷⁸ Remember that you'll need to meet at the Coleman Building at 6 A.M. and ride to the site together with your coworkers. That's because parking at the site is very limited. ⁷⁹ There are several additional pieces of safety equipment needed for this project. I'll give those to you on Monday when you arrive. See you then.

77-79번은 다음 전화 메시지에 관한 문제입니다.

여 안녕하세요, 아담. 이자벨이에요. 당신 작업반이 배정받은 머서 다리에 대한 일로 전화드려요. ⁷⁷ 화요일에 다리 폐쇄가 예정되어 있으니, 그것이 프로젝트의 공식적인 시작입니다. ⁷⁸ 당신은 오전 6시에 콜맨 빌딩에서 만나서 동료들과 함께 차를 타고 현장으로 가야 한다는 것을 기억하세요. 현장에 주차 공간이 매우 한정적이기 때문입니다. ⁷⁹ 이 프로젝트에 필요한 몇 가지 추가 안전 장비가 있습니다. 월요일에 도착하면 그것들을 드리겠습니다. 그때 뵐게요.

어휘 assign 배정하다   closure 폐쇄   safety equipment 안전 장비

77. 화자는 화요일에 무슨 일이 일어날 것이라 말하는가?

(A) 작업반이 발표될 것이다.

(B) 주차장이 포장될 것이다.

(C) 프로젝트가 완료될 것이다.

(D) 다리가 폐쇄될 것이다.

어휘 pave (길을) 포장하다

78. 화자는 청자에게 무엇을 할 것을 상기시키는가?

(A) 차를 함께 타고 현장 가기

(B) 주차권 보여 주기

(C) 교육 세션에 등록하기

(D) 따뜻한 옷 입기

어휘 display 드러내다, 보이다

패러프레이징 ride to the site together with your coworkers → Carpool to a site

79. 청자에게 무엇이 제공될 것인가?
(A) 안전 장비
(B) 작업 일정표
(C) 동료들의 연락처 정보
(D) 사용 설명서

패러프레이징 safety equipment → Safety gear

80-82. 🎧 미녀
Questions 80-82 refer to the following talk.

> **W** [80] Today I'll show you how to use the features of the new application for making customer appointments. You no longer need to be in the salon to make a booking for someone. [81] This may be helpful when you meet a potential new customer in need of a haircut or other styling services. You can help them make an appointment right from your smartphone. Also, [82] one feature that's nice is that this program automatically sends an alert to your phone one hour before you need to see a customer. That'll help you make sure you're here when you need to be.

80-82번은 다음 담화에 관한 문제입니다.
여 [80] 오늘 저는 여러분에게 새로운 애플리케이션의 기능을 사용하여 고객 예약을 하는 방법을 보여드리겠습니다. 여러분은 더 이상 누군가에게 예약을 해 주기 위해 미용실에 있을 필요가 없습니다. [81] 이것은 여러분이 커트나 다른 스타일링 서비스를 필요로 하는 잠재적인 새로운 고객을 만났을 때 도움이 될 것입니다. 여러분은 스마트폰에서 바로 그들의 예약을 잡아줄 수 있습니다. 또한, [82] 한 가지 좋은 기능은 이 프로그램이 고객을 만나기 한 시간 전에 자동으로 전화기에 알림을 전송한다는 것입니다. 이는 여러분이 필요한 순간에 이곳에 있도록 하는 데 도움이 될 것입니다.

어휘 feature 특징, 기능   potential 잠재적인   in need of ~을 필요로 하는   alert 알림

80. 화자는 무엇을 보여줄 것인가?
(A) 미용실을 운영하는 방법
(B) 신규 고객을 유치하는 방법
(C) 스마트폰 애플리케이션을 사용하는 방법
(D) 보안 시스템을 다시 시작하는 방법

81. 청자들은 누구인 것 같은가?
(A) 의사
(B) 컴퓨터 프로그래머
(C) 약사
(D) 미용사

82. 화자는 어떤 기능을 언급하는가?
(A) 자동 알림
(B) 핸즈프리 작동
(C) 쉬운 업로드
(D) 일별 메모

83-85. 🎧 영녀
Questions 83-85 refer to the following excerpt from a meeting.

> **W** I'd like to start off [83] our monthly library staff meeting with some good news. A member of the community has donated funds so that we can purchase self-checkout machines. The machines are easy to operate. However, [84] we expect you to pay attention to patrons using them in case they need your help. They'll be positioned near the circulation desk for now. [85] After the building expansion project is finished in October, we may move them to another area.

83-85번은 다음 회의 발췌록에 관한 문제입니다.
여 몇 가지 좋은 소식과 함께 [83] 우리의 도서관 직원 월간 회의를 시작하겠습니다. 지역 사회의 주민 한 분이 우리가 셀프 체크아웃 기계를 구입할 수 있도록 자금을 기부했습니다. 기계는 작동하기가 쉽습니다. 하지만, [84] 기계를 사용하는 고객들이 여러분의 도움을 필요로 할 때를 대비하여 그들에게 주의를 기울이기를 바랍니다. 기계가 일단은 대출 데스크 근처에 배치될 거예요. [85] 10월에 건물 확장 공사가 끝나면, 다른 구역으로 옮길 수도 있습니다.

어휘 donate 기부하다   fund 돈, 자금   operate 작동하다 pay attention 주의를 기울이다   patron 고객   circulation desk 대출 데스크   expansion 확장

83. 청자들은 어디에서 일하는 것 같은가?
(A) 은행에서
(B) 식료품점에서
(C) 박물관에서
(D) 도서관에서

84. 청자들은 무엇을 할 것이 요구되는가?
(A) 교육 세션에 참석하기
(B) 평소보다 일찍 출근하기
(C) 도움이 필요한 사람들을 살펴보기
(D) 기계 근처에 안내 붙이기

어휘 assistance 도움, 지원

패러프레이징 pay attention to patrons → Watch for people

85. 화자는 10월에 무슨 일이 일어날 것이라고 말하는가?
(A) 새로운 일자리 공석이 날 것이다.
(B) 자선 모금 행사가 열릴 것이다.
(C) 건물 공사가 완료될 것이다.
(D) 보고서가 공개될 것이다.

어휘 make public 공표하다

패러프레이징 the building expansion project is finished → A building project will be completed

86-88. 🎧 미남

Questions 86-88 refer to the following advertisement.

> M Looking to create a beautiful and relaxing outdoor space at home? Norcross Solutions can help you achieve the look you want. ⁸⁶Our experienced designers can create the garden of your dreams. And they'll take into account your lifestyle when it comes to the level of maintenance needed. ⁸⁷Have no idea where to start? We have a large photo gallery. Check it out at www.norcrosssolutions.com. ⁸⁷We're sure you'll find some inspiration there. Then book your free consultation. Norcross Solutions has been a trusted business for over twenty years, and ⁸⁸we are proud to support businesses in the area, purchasing supplies from them whenever possible.

86-88번은 다음 광고에 관한 문제입니다.

남 집에 아름답고 편안한 야외 공간을 만들 예정이신가요? 노크로스 솔루션에서 당신이 원하는 외관을 구현하는 데 도움을 드릴 수 있습니다. ⁸⁶저희의 경험 많은 디자이너들이 당신이 꿈꾸는 정원을 만들어 낼 수 있습니다. 그리고 그들은 당신의 라이프스타일을 고려하여 필요한 보수 관리 수준을 정할 것입니다. ⁸⁷어디서부터 시작해야 할지 모르시겠나요? 저희는 방대한 포토 갤러리를 보유하고 있습니다. www.norcrosssolutions.com에서 확인하세요. ⁸⁷그곳에서 영감을 찾으시리라 확신합니다. 그러고 나서 무료 상담을 예약하세요. 노크로스 솔루션은 20년 이상 신뢰할 수 있는 기업으로 자리잡았고, ⁸⁸저희는 가능하면 항상 지역 사업체들로부터 용품을 구매함으로써 그들을 지원하는 것에 대해 자랑스럽게 생각합니다.

어휘 achieve 얻다, 획득하다   take into account ~을 고려하다   maintenance 보수 관리, 정비   consultation 상담   trust 신뢰하다

86. 무엇이 광고되고 있는가?
(A) 온라인 과정
(B) 부동산 회사
(C) 건물 점검 서비스
(D) 정원 설계 서비스

87. 화자는 왜 "저희는 방대한 포토 갤러리를 보유하고 있습니다"라고 말하는가?
(A) 느린 웹사이트를 정당화하기 위해
(B) 안심시키기 위해
(C) 결정에 대해 설명하기 위해
(D) 경쟁사를 비판하기 위해

어휘 criticize 비판[비난]하다

88. 화자는 사업체가 무엇을 자랑스럽게 생각한다고 말하는가?
(A) 지역 사업체들에 대한 지원
(B) 적당한 가격
(C) 빠른 응답 시간
(D) 높은 고객 서비스 등급

어휘 rating 등급, 순위

89-91. 🎧 호남

Questions 89-91 refer to the following speech.

> M ⁸⁹Good evening, everyone, and thanks for attending our quarterly staff dinner. Before we begin, I'd like to make an announcement. ⁹⁰At the moment, our receptionist, Diana Dawson, always has lunch on site so she can answer phones while everyone is away. Well, I'm sure Diana would like a few lunches out. ⁹⁰If you have some time, please let me know. And one last thing. You've all made great contributions to the company so far this year, and I'd particularly like to recognize ⁹¹Ahmed Sharma, who came up with a creative solution to our problem with limited storage space.

89-91번은 다음 연설에 관한 문제입니다.

남 ⁸⁹모두 안녕하십니까, 분기별 직원 만찬에 참석해 주셔서 감사합니다. 시작하기 전에, 한 가지 발표를 하겠습니다. ⁹⁰지금은 우리의 접수원인 다이애나 도슨이 항상 현장에서 점심을 먹기 때문에 모두가 자리를 비운 사이에 전화를 받을 수 있습니다. 그런데, 분명히 다이애나도 가끔은 점심을 나가서 먹고 싶어 할 거예요. ⁹⁰시간이 되시는 분은, 저에게 알려주세요. 그리고 마지막으로 한 가지 더요. 여러분 모두 올해 지금까지 회사에 큰 기여를 해주셨으며, 특히 ⁹¹제한된 수납 공간이라는 문제에 창의적인 해결책을 생각해 낸 아흐메드 샤르마의 공로를 인정하고 싶습니다.

어휘 quarterly 분기별의   make a contribution 공을 세우다   recognize 인정하다   storage space 수납 공간

89. 연설은 어디에서 이루어지고 있는가?
(A) 교육 워크숍에서
(B) 직원 만찬에서
(C) 음악 경연에서
(D) 기자회견에서

90. 화자는 "다이애나도 가끔은 점심을 나가서 먹고 싶어 할 거예요"라고 말할 때 무엇을 암시하는가?
(A) 그는 식당을 추천해 줄 수 있다.
(B) 그는 새로운 직원을 환영하고 싶다.
(C) 그는 선물에 대해 제안이 있다.
(D) 그는 어떤 일에 자원할 사람을 찾고 있다.

91. 화자는 아흐메드 샤르마에 대해 무엇이라고 말하는가?
(A) 그는 획기적인 아이디어를 공유했다.
(B) 그는 회사를 떠날 것이다.
(C) 그는 경험이 많다.

(D) 그는 곧 연설을 할 것이다.

어휘 innovative 획기적인, 혁신적인

패러프레이징 came up with a creative solution →
shared an innovative idea

92-94. 🎧 영녀
Questions 92-94 refer to the following talk.

> **W** Since everyone is here, let's get this committee meeting started. **92** The next upcoming project for our department is the cleanup efforts at Grove Park. This site was badly hit by the recent storm, so there are a lot of tree branches, leaves, and trash all over the ground. **93** I know our group is very small, but we've already started gathering the names of potential volunteers, and we have a very long list. Fortunately, it will be fairly inexpensive to carry out this work. **94** I've calculated the approximate expenses on this report, and I'll distribute copies in a moment.

92-94번은 다음 담화에 관한 문제입니다.

여 모두 모이셨으니, 위원회 회의를 시작합시다. **92** 우리 부서의 다음 프로젝트는 그로브 공원의 청소 작업입니다. 이 장소는 최근 폭풍으로 심하게 타격을 입어서, 땅 곳곳에 나뭇가지, 나뭇잎, 쓰레기가 많습니다. **93** 우리 그룹이 매우 작다는 것은 알지만, 우리는 이미 자원봉사 가능성이 있는 사람들의 이름을 모으기 시작했고, 매우 긴 명단을 가지고 있습니다. 다행히도, 이 작업을 수행하는 데 드는 비용은 꽤 저렴할 것입니다. **94** 제가 이 보고서에서 대략적인 비용을 계산했고, 잠시 후에 사본을 나눠드리겠습니다.

어휘 fairly 상당히, 꽤 carry out 수행하다, 완수하다
calculate 계산하다 approximate 대략의 distribute 나누어 주다

92. 담화의 주제는 무엇인가?
(A) 재활용 서비스를 개선하는 것
(B) 공원을 청소하는 것
(C) 운동 공간을 짓는 것
(D) 더 많은 나무를 심는 것

93. 화자는 "매우 긴 명단을 가지고 있습니다"라고 말할 때 무엇을 암시하는가?
(A) 작업 배정이 변경될 수 있다.
(B) 마감일을 연장해야 할 것이다.
(C) 청자들에게 많은 지원이 있을 것이다.
(D) 회의가 예정보다 길어질 수 있다.

어휘 assignment 배정, 배치 extend 연장하다

94. 화자는 무엇을 나눠줄 것인가?
(A) 지도
(B) 명함
(C) 제안된 일정표
(D) 비용 견적서

어휘 proposed 제안된 estimate 견적서

95-97. 🎧 호남
Questions 95-97 refer to the following speech and ticket.

> **M** Good evening everyone. Welcome to this performance by the Lexington Dance Troupe. **95** All proceeds from this event will go toward replacing the roof of the outdoor stage at Carrick Park. **96** After the performance, be sure to visit the lobby, where some of the dancers will be signing posters. Now, we've got the winning number for tonight's prize drawing. Let's see... **97** the person sitting in seat H35 has won a $50 gift certificate! Stop by the box office at intermission to collect your prize.

95-97번은 다음 연설과 티켓에 관한 문제입니다.

남 모두 안녕하십니까. 이곳 렉싱턴 댄스팀 공연에 오신 것을 환영합니다. **95** 이 행사의 모든 수익금은 캐릭 공원의 야외 무대 지붕을 교체하는 데 쓰일 것입니다. **96** 공연이 끝난 후, 로비를 꼭 방문해 주세요. 그곳에서 댄서들 몇 명이 포스터에 사인을 해 드릴 것입니다. 자, 오늘 밤 경품 추첨의 당첨 번호가 있습니다. 어디 봅시다... **97** H35 좌석에 앉으신 분이 50달러 상품권에 당첨되셨습니다! 중간 휴식 시간에 매표소에 들러 상품을 받으십시오.

어휘 proceeds 수익금 prize drawing 경품 추첨
intermission 중간 휴식 시간

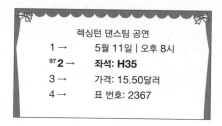

렉싱턴 댄스팀 공연	
1 →	5월 11일	오후 8시
97 **2 →**	**좌석: H35**
3 →	가격: 15.50달러
4 →	표 번호: 2367

95. 공연이 왜 개최되고 있는가?
(A) 지역사회 프로젝트를 위한 자금을 모으기 위해
(B) 극장의 기념일을 축하하기 위해
(C) 사람들이 팀에 가입하도록 장려하기 위해
(D) 전국 투어를 홍보하기 위해

96. 공연 이후에 무슨 일이 일어날 것인가?
(A) 사진을 촬영할 것이다.
(B) 티켓을 구입할 수 있을 것이다.
(C) 질문에 답변할 것이다.
(D) 포스터에 서명을 할 것이다.

97. 시각 자료를 보시오. 청자들은 경품 추첨을 위해 몇 행을 확인해야 하는가?
(A) 1행
(B) 2행
(C) 3행
(D) 4행

Questions 98-100 refer to the following podcast and instructions.

> **M** Welcome to the Gamer's World podcast. Our sponsor today is Dorsey. Enhance your gaming experience online with ⁹⁸ Dorsey's microphones, speakers, and headphones. Visit www.dorseyproducts.com to find out more. Today, I'll be reviewing the board game Igor's Quest. ⁹⁹ This game can be played by two to eight people. It's wonderful to have such a wide range like that. Though the artwork is a bit simplistic, this is a great strategy game. The setup process is easy to understand. However, ¹⁰⁰ placing the resource tokens on the board takes a long time. I think the game designers could have organized that better.

98-100번은 다음 팟캐스트와 설명서에 관한 문제입니다.

남 '게이머 월드' 팟캐스트에 오신 것을 환영합니다. 오늘 우리의 스폰서는 도시입니다. ⁹⁸ **도시의 마이크, 스피커, 헤드폰으로** 온라인 게임 환경을 개선하십시오. 더 자세히 알아보시려면 www.dorseyproducts.com을 방문하세요. 오늘 저는 보드게임 '이고르의 퀘스트'를 살펴보겠습니다. ⁹⁹ **이 게임은 2명에서 8명까지 할 수 있습니다.** 범위가 그렇게 넓은 것은 아주 멋지네요. 비록 일러스트는 다소 과하게 단순하지만, 이것은 훌륭한 전략 게임입니다. 설정 과정은 이해하기 쉽습니다. 하지만, ¹⁰⁰ **자산 토큰을 보드에 배치하는 데 시간이 오래 걸립니다.** 게임 설계자들이 그것을 더 잘 구성할 수 있었을 것 같은데요.

어휘 enhance 향상시키다 artwork 삽화 simplistic 지나치게 단순화한 organize 구성하다

> 이고르의 퀘스트 – 설정 과정
>
> 🎞 1단계. 플레이 보드 펼치기
> 🪙 ¹⁰⁰ **2단계. 보드에 자산 토큰 배치하기**
> ❓ 3단계. 카드를 색상별로 정렬하기
> 👤 4단계. 참가자 캐릭터 선택하기

98. 화자에 따르면, 도시는 어떤 종류의 제품을 만드는가?
(A) 음향 장비
(B) 사무용 가구
(C) 태블릿 컴퓨터
(D) 소프트웨어 프로그램

99. 화자는 '이고르의 퀘스트'의 어떤 점을 마음에 들어 하는가?
(A) 캐릭터
(B) 설명서
(C) 삽화
(D) 게임 참가자 수

100. 시각 자료를 보시오. 화자는 어느 단계가 개선될 수 있었다고 생각하는가?
(A) 1단계
(B) 2단계
(C) 3단계
(D) 4단계

101. 명사 자리 + 수 일치
해설 빈칸 앞에 관사가 있고 뒤에는 접속사가 이끄는 절이 이어지므로 빈칸은 명사 자리이다. 선택지 중 (A) receipt와 (D) receipts가 정답 후보인데, 빈칸 앞에 부정관사가 있으므로 빈칸에는 가산명사 단수형이 들어가야 한다. 따라서 (A)가 정답이다.

해석 판매원은 고객이 필요로 하는 경우 영수증을 다시 출력해 줄 수 있다.

102. 전치사 자리 + 어휘
해설 빈칸 앞뒤에 명사구가 있으므로 빈칸은 전치사 자리이다. 선택지 중 (A) for와 (B) until이 정답 후보인데, 문맥상 연례 지역 주민 행사에 오라는 내용이 되는 게 자연스러우므로 '~을 위해서'를 뜻하는 (A)가 정답이다.

해석 이번 주 토요일에 Fairfield Park에서 열리는 연례 지역 주민 행사에 오세요.

어휘 annual 연례의 community 주민, 지역 사회 until ~까지

103. 부사 자리
해설 빈칸은 조동사 can과 동사 check 사이의 부사 자리이므로 (C) easily가 정답이다.

해석 은행의 스마트폰 애플리케이션을 이용하여 고객들은 계좌 잔고를 쉽게 확인할 수 있다.

어휘 balance 잔고; 지불 잔액; 균형, 조화

104. 명사 어휘 program
해석 헬스장 회원들은 규칙적인 운동 프로그램을 따름으로써 체력 수준을 향상시킬 수 있다.

어휘 fitness (신체적인) 건강 program 프로그램
transaction 거래 sequel 속편 response 대답; 반응

105. 주어와 동사의 수 일치
해설 주어 it이 단수이므로 동사도 단수형으로 수 일치해야 한다. 선택지 중 (C) are selecting과 (D) select는 동사 복수형이므로 오답이고 (B) to select는 동사 자리에 들어갈 수 없기 때문에 답이 될 수 없다. 따라서 (A) will select가 정답이다.

해석 Sweet-Time Bakery 대변인은 내년에 새 소매점을 열 부지를 선정할 예정임을 확인해 주었다.

어휘 spokesperson 대변인 confirm 확인하다; 확정하다
site 부지; 현장, 장소 retail 소매의 branch 지점, 지사

106. 전치사 어휘 from
해석 연례 댄스 경연 대회에는 전국의 도시에서 온 20개 단체가 출전한다.

어휘 competition 대회; 경쟁(자) include 포함하다 from ~부터 except ~을 제외하고 as ~처럼; ~로서 regarding ~에 관하여

107. 인칭대명사 [주격]

해설 빈칸 뒤에 동사가 이어지므로 빈칸에는 주어 역할을 할 수 있는 말이 들어가야 한다. 따라서 주격 인칭대명사인 (D) They가 정답이다.

해석 그들은 제품을 포장하기 전에 제조상의 결함을 찾기 위해 모든 제품을 확인한다.

어휘 product 제품 manufacturing defect 제조상의 결함 prior to ~ 전에 package 포장하다

108. 명사 어휘 pillowcase

해석 요청을 하면 호텔의 객실 관리 부서에서 침대 시트와 베개 커버, 그리고 기타 침구류를 교체해 드릴 수 있습니다.

어휘 upon request 요청을 하면 housekeeping 객실 관리 replace 대체하다, 교체하다 pillowcase 베개 커버 bedding 침구 curtain 커튼 carpet 카펫 lighting 조명

109. 전치사 자리 + 어휘

해설 빈칸 앞에 주어와 동사를 갖춘 완전한 절이 있고 뒤에는 명사가 이어지므로 빈칸은 전치사 자리이다. 선택지 중 (A) after와 (B) between이 정답 후보인데, 문맥상 봄 학기 일정이 내일 오전 9시 이후에 게시될 거라는 내용이 되는 게 자연스러우므로 '~ 후에'를 뜻하는 (A)가 정답이다.

해석 Chung Business Institute의 봄 학기 일정은 내일 오전 9시 이후에 웹사이트에 게시될 예정입니다.

어휘 post 게시하다 between (둘) 사이에

110. 형용사 어휘 based

해석 베스트셀러 작가인 George Vasquez는 현재 캐나다의 토론토에 기반을 두고 있다.

어휘 currently 현재, 지금 based 기반을 둔; 근거로 하는 committed 헌신적인, 전념하는 written 작성된 moved 감동받은

111. 명사 자리 + 어휘

해설 빈칸 앞에 형용사가 있으므로 빈칸은 명사 자리이다. 선택지 중 (B) occupant와 (C) occupation이 정답 후보인데, 문맥상 관련 직종에 경력이 있어야 한다는 내용이 되는 게 자연스러우므로 '직업'을 뜻하는 (C)가 정답이다.

해석 회계 장부 일을 했거나 관련 직종에 경험이 있어야 지원 가능합니다.

어휘 successful applicant 합격자 bookkeeper 회계 장부 담당자 related 관련된 occupant 입주자, 사용자

112. 형용사 어휘 rapid

해석 Carlyle Logistics는 서비스의 질을 포기하지 않고도 빠른 성장을 이루어 낸 것으로 높은 평가를 받는다.

어휘 admire 존경하다, 칭찬하다 achieve 달성하다, 성취하다 rapid 빠른 sacrifice 희생하다 enthusiastic 열광적인, 열렬한 frank 솔직한 native 토착의

113. 부사 자리

해설 빈칸은 조동사 can과 동사 accommodate 사이의 부사 자리이므로 (B) comfortably가 정답이다.

해석 Grand Ballroom은 최대 300명의 손님을 거뜬히 수용할 수 있다.

어휘 accommodate 수용하다

114. 명사 어휘 approval

해석 모든 Tazma Co. 직원은 고가의 장비를 구입하기 전에 재무팀의 승인을 받아야 한다.

어휘 approval 승인; 인정, 찬성 finance 재정, 재무 purchase 구매[구입]하다 equipment 도구, 장비 entry 출입; 가입; 참가; 출품작 regard 고려 interest 관심

115. 분사 자리

해설 빈칸 앞에 전치사가 있고 뒤에는 명사구가 이어지므로 빈칸에는 명사를 수식하는 말이 들어가야 한다. 선택지 중에서 명사를 수식할 수 있는 것은 과거분사인 (C) extended뿐이다.

해석 PJ Shopping Center는 영업시간 연장으로 매출이 오를 것을 기대하고 있다.

어휘 boost 신장시키다, 북돋우다 business 사업 (실적) extend 연장하다; (사업, 세력 등을) 확대하다 business hours 영업시간

116. 동사 자리 + 시제

해설 빈칸은 부사절 접속사 while이 이끄는 절의 동사 자리이다. (A) is being과 (D) has been이 정답 후보인데, 문맥상 면접이 진행 중일 때는 회의실에 출입하지 말라는 내용이 되는 게 자연스러우므로 현재진행 시제인 (A)가 정답이다.

해석 위원회가 입사 지원자를 면접하는 동안에는 누구도 회의실에 출입해서는 안 된다.

어휘 enter 입장하다, 들어가다; 입력하다 job candidate 입사 지원자

117. 명사 자리

해설 빈칸 앞에 형용사가 있고 뒤에는 전치사구가 이어지므로 빈칸은 명사 자리이다. 따라서 (B) specification이 정답이다.

해석 팀장은 프로젝트의 모든 기술 사양을 재확인해야 한다는 점을 강조했다.

어휘 crew (특별한 기술을 가지고 공동으로 작업하는) 팀, 조 emphasize 강조하다 technical 기술적인; 전문적인 specification 사양, 명세 double-check 재확인하다

118. 부사 어휘 directly

해석 Jacamo Incorporated의 직원들은 모든 휴가 신청서를 소속 부서장에게 직접 제출해야 한다.

어휘 request 요구, 요청(서) directly 직접, 바로 entirely 전적으로, 완전히 hardly 거의 ~ 않는 fairly 꽤, 상당히; 공정하게

119. 동명사 자리
해설 빈칸 앞에 전치사가 있고 뒤에는 명사구가 이어지므로 빈칸에는 전치사의 목적어 역할을 하는 동시에 명사구를 목적어로 취할 수 있는 말이 들어가야 한다. 따라서 선택지 중 동명사인 (A) limiting이 정답이다.

해석 Cayla Museum은 언제든 입장하는 관람객 수를 제한함으로써 편안한 분위기를 유지한다.

어휘 maintain (관계, 상태, 수준 등을) 유지하다 relaxing 편안한, 느긋한 atmosphere 분위기

120. 형용사 어휘 innovative
해석 PowerVox는 폐기물 처리 비용 문제에 대해 새롭고 획기적인 해결책을 찾아냈다.

어휘 innovative 혁신적인, 획기적인 disposal 처분, 폐기 loyal 충실한 casual 편한, 격식을 차리지 않는 appointed 임명된

121. 한정사 자리
해설 빈칸에는 뒤에 있는 명사구 job applicant를 수식하는 말이 들어가야 한다. 선택지 중 명사를 수식할 수 있는 것은 의문한정사인 (D) which뿐이다. 빈칸에 (A) if나 (B) whenever와 같은 접속사가 들어가려면 job applicant 앞에 관사가 있어야 하기 때문에 오답이다. 참고로 이 문장은 빈칸 앞에 생략되어 있는 명사절 접속사 that이 '------- ~ role'을 이끄는 구조이고 they believe는 삽입절이다.

해석 위원회 위원들은 그들이 생각하기에 어느 후보가 그 자리에 가장 적합한지 우리에게 말해 줄 것이다.

어휘 be suitable for ~에 적합하다

122. 접속사 어휘 although
해석 Ericson Construction의 임금은 평균보다 높은데도 불구하고 직원 모집에 어려움을 겪고 있다.

어휘 although 비록 ~일지라도 wage 임금, 급료 have difficulty with ~에 어려움을 겪다 recruitment 모집, 채용 because ~ 때문에 as if 마치 ~인 것처럼 whether ~이든 (아니든)

123. 현재분사 vs. 과거분사
해설 빈칸 앞에 동사가 있고 뒤에는 명사가 이어지므로 빈칸에는 명사를 수식하는 말이 들어가야 한다. 선택지 중 명사를 수식할 수 있는 것은 과거분사 (B) rejected와 현재분사 (C) rejecting인데, 수식 대상인 manuscripts는 행위자에 의해 '거절당하는' 대상이기 때문에 빈칸과 수동 관계이므로 (B)가 정답이다.

해석 Garrison Publishing은 나중에 시장 상황이 긍정적으로 바뀔 경우에 대비해서 거절당한 원고를 5년간 파일로 보관한다.

어휘 manuscript (책의) 원고 in case ~한 경우에 대비하여 desirable 바람직한, 호감 가는

124. 부사 어휘 remotely
해석 재택근무를 하는 직원들은 원격으로 회사 문서에 접속하여 필요한 파일을 내려받을 수 있다.

어휘 work from home 재택근무를 하다 access 접속하다; 접근하다 remotely 원격으로, 멀리서 absolutely 절대적으로 seriously 심하게, 진지하게 predictably 예측한 대로

125. 전치사 자리 + 어휘
해설 빈칸에는 뒤에 있는 명사를 목적어로 취할 수 있는 말이 들어가야 한다. 선택지 중 전치사구인 (A) ahead of와 (C) along with가 정답 후보인데, 문맥상 오리엔테이션 며칠 전에 읽어 볼 수 있도록 취업 규칙을 발송했다는 내용이 되는 게 자연스러우므로 '~보다 전에'를 뜻하는 (A)가 정답이다.

해석 인사 담당자는 신입 사원들에게 취업 규칙을 발송하여 오리엔테이션 며칠 전에 읽어 볼 수 있도록 했다.

어휘 dispatch 보내다, 발송하다 new hire 신입 사원 along with ~와 함께

126. 전치사 어휘 rather than
해석 송장을 직접 디자인하는 대신에 많은 새로운 사업주는 디자인 서식 사용을 선호한다.

어휘 rather than ~라기보다는 prefer 선호하다 in light of ~을 고려하여 among (셋 이상) 사이에 into ~ 안으로

127. 부사 자리
해설 빈칸 앞에 전치사가 있고 뒤에는 형용사와 명사가 이어지므로 빈칸에는 형용사를 수식하는 말이 들어가야 한다. 따라서 선택지 중 부사인 (C) considerably가 정답이다.

해석 항공편 대신 배편으로 물품을 보낼 경우 고객들은 상당히 더 저렴한 요금으로 해외에 물품을 보낼 수 있다.

어휘 overseas 해외에, 해외로 considerably 상당히

128. 구동사 어휘 pour in
해석 할인 코드가 실수로 온라인에 유출되는 바람에 신형 태블릿 컴퓨터 주문이 쇄도했다.

어휘 accidentally 실수로; 우연히, 뜻하지 않게 leak 유출[누설]하다; 새다 pour in (많은 양이) 쇄도하다, 쏟아지다 get along 잘 지내다 carry out ~을 수행[실행]하다 settle up 정산하다

129. 접속사 어휘 now that
해설 빈칸 뒤에 완전한 절이 있으므로 빈칸은 접속사 자리이다. 따라서 전치사구인 (D) because of는 답이 될 수 없다.

해석 이제 관광 성수기가 끝나서 지역 주민들은 교통 정체를 덜 겪고 있다.

어휘 local resident 지역 주민 traffic delay 교통 정체 now that 이제 ~이므로 so that ~하기 위해서 as though 마치 ~인 것처럼 because of ~ 때문에

130. 수 일치 + 태
해설 주어 an incorrect password가 단수이므로 동사도 단수

형으로 수 일치해야 한다. (B) has been entered와 (C) was entering이 정답 후보인데, 빈칸 뒤에 목적어가 없고 주어 an incorrect password는 행위를 받는 대상이므로 빈칸에는 [be + 과거분사] 형태의 수동태가 적절하다. 따라서 (B)가 정답이다.

해석 잘못된 비밀번호를 세 번 입력하고 나면 사용자는 시스템에 접속할 수 없게 될 것이다.

어휘 lock A out of B 문을 잠가서 A가 B에 못 들어가게 하다 incorrect 부정확한 enter 입력하다; 입장하다, 들어가다

131-134. 광고

Romano Cinema 특별 할인!

Romano Cinema에서는 관람권을 파격 할인하여 여러분의 새해 출발을 돕고자 합니다. 1월 2일부터 1월 19일**131까지** 모든 상영 영화 관람권은 한 장 구입 시 한 장을 무료로 드립니다. 모든 **132지점**에서 이 특가 행사를 진행 중이며 원하는 만큼 몇 번이든 이 행사를 이용하실 수 있습니다. 모든 무료 관람권은 **133구입된** 관람권과 같은 영화용이라는 걸 유념해 주시기 바랍니다. 아울러 영화관에는 영화를 보면서 즐기실 수 있는 맛있는 스낵류가 다양하게 마련되어 있습니다. **134매점에 들러 구입하시기 바랍니다.**

어휘 admission 입장료; 입장 허가 screening (영화 등의) 상영; 심사, 검사 take advantage of ~을 이용하다 note 주목하다; 언급하다 a range of 다양한

131. 전치사 어휘 through
(A) onto ~로, ~의 위로
(B) toward ~을 향하여
(C) within ~ 내에
(D) through (~부터) ~까지

해설 through는 '(~부터) ~까지'를 뜻하여 A through B라고 쓰면 어떤 행위가 A부터 B의 끝까지 이어진다는 걸 강조하게 된다.

132. 명사 어휘 location
(A) statuses 신분, 자격; 지위
(B) locations 지점, 장소, 위치
(C) directors 감독; 임원; 책임자
(D) exhibits 전시회

133. 현재분사 vs. 과거분사
해설 빈칸 앞에 관사가 있고 뒤에는 명사가 이어지므로 빈칸에는 명사를 수식하는 말이 들어가야 한다. 선택지 중 명사를 수식할 수 있는 것은 과거분사 (B) purchased와 현재분사 (D) purchasing인데, 수식 대상인 tickets는 행위자에 의해 '구입되는' 대상이기 때문에 빈칸과 수동 관계이므로 (B)가 정답이다.

134. 문맥에 맞는 문장 고르기
(A) 수상 후보들은 곧 발표될 예정입니다.
(B) 이 자리에 지원하시려면 우리에게 연락해 주십시오.
(C) 매점에 들러 구입하시기 바랍니다.
(D) 영화 상영 시간은 변경될 수 있습니다.

어휘 award nomination 수상 후보 apply for ~에 지원하다 stop by ~에 들르다 concession stand 매점 running

time 상영 시간 vary 달라지다; 다양하다

135-138. 기사

Kenwyn Beach Resort가 다음 달로 개장일을 잡았다. 리조트에는 투숙객을 위한 널찍한 스위트룸과 구내 레스토랑 세 곳, 실내 및 실외 수영장 등이 **135포함될 예정이다.**

현재는 그 리조트가 들어선 해변 지역은 몇십 년 동안 공터인 상태였다. 이곳의 이전 소유주는 Capital Properties로 개발 자금을 구하기 위해 고전했다. **136결국 그 회사는 이곳을 매각하기로 결정했다.** V&G Investments가 이 부지를 확보해 리조트를 건설하고 Kenwyn Beach Resort라고 명명했다.

건축가인 Oscar Strope가 아름다운 환경과 **137풍광**을 활용하여 리조트 전체를 설계했다. 이 지역의 다른 리조트들을 미루어 보아 Kenwyn Beach Resort는 꽤 **138인기를 얻을** 것으로 보인다.

어휘 grand opening 개장, 개점 spacious 넓은, 널찍한 suite 스위트룸, 특실 on-site 현장의 previously 이전에, 앞서 struggle 고군분투하다 funding 자금 procure 구하다, 조달하다 property 부동산; 건물 architect 건축가 facility 시설 based on ~에 근거하여

135. 능동태
해설 빈칸 뒤에 목적어가 있으므로 빈칸에는 능동태가 들어가야 한다. 따라서 (A) will include가 정답이다.

136. 문맥에 맞는 문장 고르기
(A) 다른 부지들은 아직 매매가 가능하다.
(B) 결국 그 회사는 이곳을 매각하기로 결정했다.
(C) 관광철은 여름 내내 계속된다.
(D) 소유주는 이 분야에 경험이 많다.

어휘 run (특정 기간 동안) 계속되다 throughout ~ 내내; ~ 전역에

137. 명사 자리 + 어휘
해설 빈칸 앞에 등위 접속사 and가 있으므로 빈칸에는 앞에 있는 setting과 병렬 구조를 이루어 전치사 of의 목적어 역할을 할 수 있는 말이 들어가야 한다. 선택지 중 명사인 (A) scenery와 (D) scenario가 정답 후보인데, 문맥상 아름다운 환경과 풍광을 활용하여 리조트를 설계했다는 내용이 되는 게 자연스러우므로 '경치, 풍경'을 뜻하는 (A)가 정답이다.

어휘 scenario 시나리오, 각본

138. 형용사 어휘 popular
(A) definite 확실한, 분명한
(B) general 일반적인, 보통의
(C) heavy 무거운
(D) popular 유명한, 인기 있는

139-142. 이메일

수신인: 마케팅부 직원들
발신인: Richard Hayes
날짜: 6월 18일

제목: 웹사이트

첨부 파일: 새로운 색 배합

마케팅부 직원 여러분께,

우리 웹사이트에 쓸 새로운 색 배합 옵션들을 **139 간략히 소개한** 첨부 파일을 확인해 주시기 바랍니다. 업데이트된 **140 디자인**은 Camden Sales가 좀 더 현대적인 이미지로 보이게 할 것입니다. **141 또한 더 젊은 고객들을 많이 끌어들일 겁니다.**

옵션들을 신중하게 검토해 주실 것을 요청합니다. 목요일 퇴근 때까지 어떤 색 배합이 가장 좋을지에 대한 여러분의 생각을 제게 이메일로 보내 주세요. **142 그렇지 않을 경우 여러분의 의견은** 반영되지 않을 것입니다.

Richard Hayes

어휘 color scheme 색 배합   option 선택(권)   portray 묘사하다, 그리다   look over ~을 (대강) 살펴보다   take ~ into consideration ~을 고려하다

139. 수 일치 + 태

해설 빈칸 뒤에 목적어가 있으므로 빈칸에는 능동태가 들어가야 한다. (B) outline과 (C) outlines가 정답 후보인데, 주격 관계대명사절의 동사는 선행사에 수 일치하므로 단수 동사인 (C)가 정답이다.

어휘 outline (간략히) 설명하다

140. 명사 어휘 design

(A) schedule 일정
(B) label 상표, 라벨
(C) policy 정책, 방침
(D) design 디자인

141. 문맥에 맞는 문장 고르기

(A) 또한 더 젊은 고객들을 많이 끌어들일 겁니다.
(B) 사람들은 대부분 이 소프트웨어가 사용하기 쉽다고 생각합니다.
(C) 다행스럽게도 지난달 매출이 크게 올랐습니다.
(D) 여러분을 향후 비슷한 프로젝트에 추천하겠습니다.

어휘 attract 마음을 끌다, 끌어들이다, 유인하다   a great number of 많은   fortunately 다행스럽게도   significantly 상당히; 의미 있게, 중요하게

142. 접속부사 어휘 otherwise

(A) To that end 그러기 위해서
(B) Otherwise 그렇지 않으면; 그 외에는
(C) In contrast 반면에, 그에 반해서
(D) Similarly 마찬가지로, 유사하게

143-146. 기사

신발 제조업체인 League Footwear는 EG Sports를 **143 인수했다**는 걸 오늘 공식화했다. "트렌디한 운동화로 잘 알려진 EG Sports는 수년간 시장에서 **144 인상적인** 성공을 보여 주었기에 EG Sports를 League Footwear의 식구로 맞게 되어 자부심을 느낍니다." League Footwear의 대표인 Nathan Dale이 말했다.

"편안함과 기능 모두 확실하기에 고객들이 우리 회사의 고품질 제품 **145**을 신뢰한다는 걸 알고 있습니다." Mr. Dale이 설명했다. "우리 회사를 통해 판매될 EG Sports 제품은 모두 똑같이 높은 수준을 유지할 것입니다. **146 그러니 고객 여러분은 안심하고 구입하셔도 됩니다.**"

어휘 manufacturer 제조업체, 제조사   confirm 확정하다; 확인하다   athletic shoes 운동화   demonstrate 보여 주다; 입증하다   representative 대표자   ensure 보장하다, 확실히 하다   comfort 안락, 편안; 위안   performance (기계, 차량 등의) 성능; 성과; 공연

143. 동사 어휘 acquire

(A) advised 조언했다
(B) acquired 습득했다, 획득했다
(C) consented 동의했다
(D) sustained 지속했다

144. 형용사 자리 + 어휘

해설 빈칸 앞에 동사가 있고 뒤에는 명사구가 이어지므로 빈칸에는 명사를 수식하는 말이 들어가야 한다. 선택지 중 형용사 (C) impressive와 과거분사 (D) impressed가 정답 후보인데, 문맥상 인상적인 성공을 보여 줬다는 내용이 되는 게 자연스러우므로 '인상적인'을 뜻하는 (C)가 정답이다. impressed는 '깊은 인상을 받은, 감명을 받은'이라는 뜻으로 감명을 받은 주체가 사람이 되어야 하기 때문에 오답이다.

145. 구동사의 전치사

해설 빈칸 앞에 동사 rely가 있으므로 빈칸에는 rely와 어울려 쓰이는 전치사가 들어가야 한다. 따라서 (C) on이 정답이다. rely on은 '~을 믿다, ~을 신뢰하다'를 뜻한다.

146. 문맥에 맞는 문장 고르기

(A) 그러니 고객 여러분은 안심하고 구입하셔도 됩니다.
(B) 선택할 수 있는 다양한 사이즈가 있습니다.
(C) 대회에 관한 더 자세한 내용은 온라인에서 찾을 수 있습니다.
(D) 따라서 매장별로 영업시간이 다를 겁니다.

어휘 with confidence 자신 있게, 안심하고   a range of 다양한   competition 대회; 경쟁(자)   therefore 그러므로   retail store 소매점

147-148. 이메일

수신인: Simon Ethridge
발신인: Christy Lansing
날짜: 7월 28일
제목: 편지

Mr. Ethridge께,

147 귀하의 7월 26일자 편지를 받았음을 알려 드리고자 이메일을 보냅니다.

147 148 모든 팀에게 귀하의 마지막 근무일이 8월 11일이라는 것을 공지해 두었습니다. 귀하가 쓰던 회사 소유의 장비는 IT 부서에서 처리할 것이니 **148 귀하의 마지막 근무일 전까지는 내선 번호 25로 IT 부서에 전화하셔서** 필요한 준비를 해 주시기 바랍니다. Kessla Data를 위한 귀하의 노고에 감사드립니다.

어휘 **inform** 알리다, 통지하다　**handle** 다루다, 처리하다
equipment 도구, 장비　**extension** 내선 번호; 연장, 확대
make an arrangement 준비하다　**appreciate** 고마워하다;
인정하다; 감상하다　**contribution** 기여, 공헌; (신문, 잡지 등의) 기
고문

147. Ms. Lansing이 이메일을 보낸 이유는 무엇인가?
(A) 사업장 폐쇄를 확인하기 위해
(B) 은행 기록을 업데이트하기 위해
(C) 사직서를 수리하기 위해
(D) 승진을 제안하기 위해

해설　**주제/목적**
첫 문장에서 Ms. Lansing은 Mr. Ethridge가 보낸 편지에 대한
답장으로 이메일을 보낸다고 밝히고 있다. 이어서 Mr. Ethridge의
마지막 근무일을 언급하는 것으로 보아 Mr. Ethridge가 이미 사직
서를 제출했고 이를 받아들여 퇴직 절차를 알리기 위해 이메일을 보
낸 것임을 알 수 있으므로 (C)가 정답이다.

어휘 **closure** 폐쇄　**acknowledge** 인정하다; 감사를 표하다
resignation 사임, 사직　**promotion** 승진, 진급; 홍보, 판촉

148. Mr. Ethridge는 8월 11일까지 무엇을 해야 하는가?
(A) 서식 작성하기
(B) Ms. Lansing과 만나기
(C) IT 팀에 연락하기
(D) 개인 소지품 치우기

해설　**세부 사항**
8월 11일은 Mr. Ethridge의 마지막 근무일로 그날 전까지는 IT
부서에 전화하라고 했으므로 (C)가 정답이다.

어휘 **remove** 제거하다

149-150. 공지

8월 22일 화요일에 Despard Water Co.의 작업반이 이 지
역 하수관 교체 작업을 시작합니다. **150**작업이 진행되는 동안 플
로렌스 스트리트가 일시적으로 폐쇄되므로 그동안은 **149**이곳
Livonia Tower의 주차장 입구로 출입할 수 없게 됩니다.
1508월 22일 오전 8시부터 8월 23일 오후 4시 사이에 **149**차량
을 써야 하는 입주민들은 작업 시작 전에 근처 도로에 주차하시
기 바랍니다. 이번 일로 불편을 끼쳐 죄송합니다.

어휘 **crew** (특별한 기술을 가지고 공동으로 작업하는) 팀, 조
replace 대체하다, 교체하다　**sewer line** 하수관
temporarily 일시적으로, 임시로　**carry out** ~을 수행[실행]하다
entrance 입구　**parking lot** 주차장　**inaccessible** 접근할 수
없는　**resident** 주민　**inconvenience** 불편

149. 공지는 누구를 대상으로 하는가?
(A) 시 공무원들
(B) 건물 입주자들
(C) 공사 인부들
(D) 부동산 개발업자들

해설　**세부 사항**
하수관 교체 공사로 인한 건물 주차장 입구 폐쇄를 알리면서 차량을
써야 하는 입주민은 근처 도로에 주차하라고 한 것으로 보아 건물 입
주자들을 대상으로 한 공지이므로 (B)가 정답이다.

어휘 **tenant** 세입자

150. 공지에 따르면 8월 23일 오후 4시에 무슨 일이 있겠는가?
(A) 주차장 입구가 폐쇄될 것이다.
(B) 거리가 포장될 것이다.
(C) 도로 통행이 재개될 것이다.
(D) 작업반이 프로젝트를 평가할 것이다.

해설　**세부 사항**
플로렌스 스트리트가 일시적으로 폐쇄되는 기간이 8월 22일 오전
8시부터 8월 23일 오후 4시까지라고 했으므로 8월 23일 오후 4시
에는 이 도로 통행이 재개된다는 것을 알 수 있다. 따라서 (C)가 정
답이다.

어휘 **pave** (길을) 포장하다　**assess** 평가하다

151-152. 이메일

수신인: Rebekah Ingram
발신인: Montoya Fashions
날짜: 11월 18일
제목: 반품 요청

Ms. Ingram께,

아래와 같이 귀하의 반품을 접수하였습니다.

명세: Fieldcrest 캐시미어 스웨터, 진회색, 미디엄 사이즈
제품 번호: 748592
구입가: 125달러

환불을 처리하고 있으며 구입 시 사용하셨던 신용 카드로 영업
일 기준 5일 이내에 환불될 것입니다. **152Montoya
Fashions**의 포인트를 적립받았다면 30일 이내에 귀하의 계
정에서 차감될 것임을 알려 드립니다.

151아울러 현재 **49.99**달러에 판매하고 있는 연말연시용 신상
파티 드레스도 놓치지 마세요! 카탈로그를 보려면 여기를 클릭
하세요.

Montoya Fashions 고객 서비스 팀

어휘 **return** 반환, 반품　**request** 요구, 요청(서)　**process** (컴
퓨터로) 처리하다; 가공하다　**reward** 보상(금)　**deduct** 공제하다
just in time for ~에 시기를 딱 맞춰, ~에 알맞은 시기에　**browse**
둘러보다

151. 이메일의 목적 중 하나는 무엇인가?
(A) 신상품을 홍보하기 위해
(B) 결제가 되었음을 확인해 주기 위해
(C) 계정에 로그인하는 방법을 설명하기 위해
(D) 신용 카드 정보를 요청하기 위해

해설　**주제/목적**
이메일 앞부분에서는 반품 접수가 되었음을 알리며 환불 처리 과정
을 설명하고 있고, 뒷부분에서는 신상품을 홍보하고 있으므로 (A)가
정답이다.

어휘 promote 홍보하다; 승진시키다 confirm 확인하다; 확정하다 sign into an account 계정에 로그인하다

152. Montoya Fashions에 대해 암시된 것은 무엇인가?
(A) 반품 기한이 30일 이내이다.
(B) 포인트 제도를 시행한다.
(C) 반품 시 상품 교환권으로만 돌려준다.
(D) 인테리어 소품을 판매한다.

해설 **추론/암시**
포인트를 적립받았다면 30일 이내에 계정에서 차감될 거라고 한 것으로 보아 Montoya Fashions는 상품 구매 시 포인트를 적립해 준다는 걸 알 수 있으므로 (B)가 정답이다.

어휘 loyalty program 고객이 상품을 구매하거나 이용할 때마다 포인트 등의 보상을 주는 제도 give store credit (환불금 대신) 물건 가격만큼 상품권[포인트]을 주다

153-154. 문자 메시지

> Albert Cotter (오전 9시 52분) 안녕하세요, Ella. 오늘 급한 프로젝트 있어요?
>
> Ella Bohn (오전 9시 53분) 별로요. 왜 물어보시는 거예요?
>
> Albert Cotter (오전 9시 54분) ¹⁵³Betsy와 제가 곧 있을 인턴십 프로그램을 논의하기 위해 4시에 회의를 할 거예요. 후보들을 최종 확정했으니 1주차 오리엔테이션 워크숍을 개발해야 하거든요.
>
> Ella Bohn (오전 9시 55분) 그거라면 제가 도울 수 있어요. ¹⁵⁴5시까지는 끝나겠죠?
>
> Albert Cotter (오전 9시 56분) 그렇고말고요. 아무도 늦게까지 일하지 않을 거예요.

어휘 urgent 긴급한 upcoming 다가오는, 곧 있을 now (that) 이제 ~이므로 candidate 후보, 지원자 finalize 결론짓다 wrap up (~을) 마무리하다, (~을) 끝내다

153. Mr. Cotter가 오늘 회의에 참석하는 이유는 무엇인가?
(A) 인턴십 지원서를 검토하기 위해
(B) 교육 프로그램을 만들기 위해
(C) 그룹 인터뷰를 실시하기 위해
(D) 직무 기술서를 작성하기 위해

해설 **세부 사항**
오전 9시 54분에 Mr. Cotter가 Betsy와 4시에 인턴십 프로그램 관련 회의를 한다고 했다. 이어서 1주차 오리엔테이션 워크숍을 개발해야 한다고 한 것으로 보아 교육 프로그램을 만들기 위해 회의를 한다는 걸 알 수 있으므로 (B)가 정답이다.

패러프레이징 develop the orientation workshops → create a training program

어휘 application 지원(서), 신청(서); 적용 conduct (특정 활동을) 수행하다; 지휘하다 job description 직무 기술서

154. 오전 9시 56분에 Mr. Cotter가 '그렇고말고요'라고 쓴 의도는 무엇인가?
(A) 회의가 오후 5시까지는 끝날 것이다.
(B) 회의에는 5명이 참석할 것이다.

(C) 서류 다섯 부를 준비해야 한다.
(D) 일부 직원은 다섯 번 만나는 것이다.

해설 **의도 파악**
오전 9시 55분에 Ella Bohn이 5시까지 끝나는지 물은 말에 대한 대답으로 한 말이다. Precisely는 상대방의 말에 동의를 나타내는 표현으로 '그렇고말고'를 뜻하므로 Mr. Cotter가 Ella Bohn의 물음에 강하게 긍정하는 의미에서 한 말이라는 걸 알 수 있다. 따라서 (A)가 정답이다.

어휘 attendee 참석자

155-157. 기사

> **Carson's Bike Shop 여전히 운영하다**
>
> 필라델피아 (10월 30일)—자전거 수리점이자 자전거 부품 판매점이기도 한 Carson's Bike Shop이 개점 25주년을 맞는다. ¹⁵⁵**이 업체의 설립자인 Carson Reese**는 사이클링이 취미여서 자전거를 수리하는 법을 독학했다. 그는 ¹⁵⁵**회계 분야를 맡기기 위해** 형제인 **David Reese**를 영입했고 사업은 꾸준히 성장했다.
>
> ¹⁵⁵**이 업체는 저렴한 비용으로 수리 서비스를 제공하면서 자전거 부품 및 사이클링 부대 용품 판매를 통해 대부분 수익을 냈다.** 이러한 ¹⁵⁶방식 덕분에 이 업체는 ¹⁵⁵오랜 시간에 걸쳐 단골 고객층을 구축했다. 수요가 증가함에 따라 ¹⁵⁵자전거 수리공을 더 많이 채용하고 새로운 서비스들이 추가되었다. 5년 전에 윌로우 그로브에 2호점을 열었고 지난봄에는 트렌턴에 3호점을 열었다. ¹⁵⁷**Carson's Bike Shop**은 필라델피아에서 자전거 경주 대회를 주최하고 스포츠와 관련된 자선 단체에 기부하면서 ¹⁵⁵사이클링 커뮤니티에 지속적으로 이바지하고 있다.

어휘 part 부품 celebrate 기념하다 found 설립하다 accounting 회계 steadily 점차, 꾸준히 make money 돈을 벌다 approach 접근(법) build up ~을 쌓다 loyal customer base 단골 고객층 demand 수요, 요구 mechanic 정비공 branch 지점, 지사 contribute to ~에 기여하다 arrange 마련하다, 준비하다 make a donation 기부하다 charity 자선 (단체)

155. 기사의 주된 내용은 무엇인가?
(A) 새로운 발명품의 성공
(B) 사이클링 업계 동향
(C) 한 가게의 이전
(D) 한 업체의 역사

해설 **주제/목적**
Carson's Bike Shop이라는 업체의 설립자와 설립 배경 그리고 업체의 성장 및 현재의 사회 공헌 활동에 이르기까지 이 업체의 연혁에 대해서 설명하고 있으므로 (D)가 정답이다.

어휘 relocation 이전

156. 두 번째 단락 네 번째 줄의 'approach'와 의미상 가장 가까운 것은?
(A) 움직임, 이동
(B) 접근; 접속
(C) 도착

(D) 전략, 계획

해설 동의어 찾기

approach가 있는 This approach helped the shop build up a loyal customer base는 '이러한 방식 덕분에 이 업체는 단골 고객층을 구축했다'는 의미이며, 여기서 approach는 '접근 방식'이라는 뜻으로 쓰였다. 따라서 (D)가 정답이다. (B) access는 어떤 장소에 드나들기 위해 접근한다는 의미가 내포되어 있어 '접근 권한'의 뉘앙스가 강하기 때문에 답이 될 수 없다. have **access** to the company files(회사 파일에 접근권을 갖다)와 adopt a new **approach** to the problem(그 문제에 새로운 접근 방식을 채택하다)를 비교해 보면 이해가 쉽다.

157. Carson's Bike Shop에 대해 사실인 것은 무엇인가?
(A) 자전거 부대 용품을 디자인한다.
(B) 운동 경기 대회를 주최한다.
(C) 최근에 매각되었다.
(D) 윌로우 그로브에서 사업을 시작했다.

해설 NOT/True

마지막 문장에서 Carson's Bike Shop이 필라델피아에서 자전거 경주 대회를 주최한다고 했으므로 (B)가 정답이다.

패러프레이징 arranging bicycle races → organizes athletic competitions

어휘 organize 준비하다, 정리하다; 조직하다, 구성하다   athletic 운동의; (몸이) 탄탄한   competition 대회; 경쟁(자)

158-160. 이메일

> 수신인: Shirley Amundson
> 발신인: Romulus Cruise Lines
> 날짜: 7월 11일
> 제목: 나폴리 크루즈 여행
>
> Ms. Amundson께,
>
> 9월 20일에 이탈리아 나폴리를 출발하여 9월 27일에 돌아오는 Romulus Cruise Lines의 크루즈 여행을 예약해 주셔서 감사합니다.
>
> ¹⁵⁸고객님의 특실에는 다양한 영화를 갖춘 평면 TV와 책상, 킹 사이즈 침대, 그리고 전용 발코니가 있습니다. 유람선에는 몇 개의 식당과 음악을 감상할 수 있는 라운지와 대형 강당이 있습니다. 맨 위 갑판에는 수영장과 온수풀, 미니 골프 코스도 있습니다.
>
> 항구에 있는 주차장에 유료 주차할 수 있지만 이 주차장은 Romulus Cruise Lines와는 관계가 없다는 점을 알려 드립니다. ¹⁵⁹나폴리 국제공항과 항구를 오가는 저희의 무료 셔틀버스를 이용하실 수 있습니다. 고객님의 크루즈 여행 티켓 확인 이메일을 보여 주시기만 하면 됩니다.
>
> 여행 준비를 하실 때는 ¹⁶⁰가지고 승선할 수 없는 물품이 몇 가지 있다는 점을 유념해 주십시오. 이 물품 목록을 보려면 **www.romuluscruiselines.com/boarding**을 방문해 주시기 바랍니다.
>
> 즐거운 여행 하세요!
>
> Michael Silva
> Romulus Cruise Lines

어휘 book 예약하다   depart 출발하다   on-demand films 소비자가 원하는 걸 골라서 볼 수 있도록 다양한 영화나 미디어 콘텐츠를 제공하는 서비스[플랫폼]   feature 특징으로 하다, 특별히 선보이다   auditorium 강당   deck 갑판   hot tub 온수 욕조   for a fee 유료로   be affiliated with ~와 제휴하다   confirmation 확인 (서)   keep in mind 명심하다, 기억해 두다   on board 승선한

158. 이메일의 목적 중 하나는 무엇인가?
(A) 고객에게 피드백을 요청하기 위해
(B) 유람선의 편의 시설들을 설명하기 위해
(C) 출발일 변경을 알리기 위해
(D) 유람선 선실 업그레이드를 제공하기 위해

해설 주제/목적

두 번째 단락에서 특실에 마련된 시설과 유람선의 다양한 편의 시설들을 소개하고 있으므로 (B)가 정답이다.

어휘 amenities 편의 시설   departure 출발

159. Romulus Cruise Lines 승객들은 무엇을 이용할 수 있는가?
(A) 나폴리행 항공편 할인
(B) 항구에 무료 주차
(C) 무료 셔틀버스 서비스
(D) 현지 식당 이용권

해설 세부 사항

크루즈 티켓이 있으면 공항에서 항구까지 무료로 셔틀버스를 이용할 수 있다고 했으므로 (C)가 정답이다.

어휘 complimentary 무료의   voucher 상품권, 쿠폰   local 지역의, 현지의

160. Mr. Silva에 따르면 Ms. Amundson은 웹사이트에서 무엇을 찾을 수 있는가?
(A) 향후 예약 시 사용할 수 있는 쿠폰
(B) 제한 물품에 대한 정보
(C) 이전 여행의 사진들
(D) 승객들의 후기

해설 세부 사항

마지막 단락에서 가지고 승선할 수 없는 물품들이 있다는 점을 상기시키면서 웹사이트를 방문하여 이 물품들을 확인하라고 했으므로 (B)가 정답이다.

어휘 restricted 제한된   previous 이전의   testimonial 추천의 글, 추천서

161-163. 편지

> 5월 8일
>
> Wendy Sanford
> 660 로즈우드 코트
> 브록포트, 뉴욕주 14420
>
> Ms. Sanford께,
>
> ¹⁶¹고객님의 주택 보험이 곧 만료됨을 알려 드리고자 합니다. 아래 세부 사항을 확인하시기 바랍니다. ¹⁶³주택은 항상 보험에 가입해 두는 것이 중요합니다. 고객님의 현재 보험이 만료되기 전에 새 보험을 준비하셔야 합니다. 그렇지 않으면 고객님의 주택

과 재정에 위험이 발생할 수 있습니다.

162보험 유형: 주택 및 재산 보장 기본형

증권 번호: 374109

만료일: 6월 4일

주택 보장 기본형 보험료는 160달러, 주택 보장 고급형 보험료는 180달러, **162주택 및 재산 보장 기본형 보험료는 205달러**, 주택 및 재산 보장 고급형 보험료는 225달러입니다. **162이 보험료는 작년에 고객님이 현재 보험을 가입한 이후 변동이 없습니다.**

고객님의 보험을 갱신하려면 www.trustedinsuranceinc. com/renew에 접속하여 고객님의 증권 번호를 입력하고 화면에 나오는 지시 사항을 따르기만 하면 됩니다. 이 과정은 10분이 채 걸리지 않을 것입니다.

Manuel Shapiro

Trusted Insurance Inc. 고객 서비스 담당자

어휘 home insurance policy 주택 보험 expire 만료되다 property 부동산; 건물; 재산, 소유물 insure 보험에 들다 at all times 항상 policy 보험 증권 in place 준비가 되어 있는; 제자리에 있는 expiration 만료, 만기 current 현재의, 지금의 rate 요금; 이율; 비율 purchase 구매, 구입; 구매[구입]한 것 renew 갱신하다, 연장하다 instructions 지시; 설명서

161. 편지를 쓴 이유는 무엇인가?

(A) 고객의 연락처 정보를 확인하기 위해

(B) 주택의 가치를 확인하기 위해

(C) 연체 대금을 요청하기 위해

(D) 보험 상태를 설명하기 위해

해설 **주제/목적**

첫 문장에서 주택 보험이 곧 만료된다는 것을 알리며 만료일 전에 보험을 갱신할 것을 당부했으므로 (D)가 정답이다.

어휘 overdue (지불, 반납 등의) 기한이 지난 payment 지불

162. Ms. Sanford는 작년에 얼마를 지불했겠는가?

(A) 160달러

(B) 180달러

(C) 205달러

(D) 225달러

해설 **추론/암시**

Ms. Sanford가 가입한 보험은 주택 및 재산 보장 기본형으로 보험료가 205달러라고 했는데, 작년에 Ms. Sanford가 가입한 이후로 보험료에 변동이 없다고 했다. 따라서 Ms. Sanford는 작년에 현재 보험료와 동일하게 205달러를 지불했을 것임을 추론할 수 있으므로 (C)가 정답이다.

163. [1], [2], [3], [4]로 표시된 곳 중에서 다음 문장이 들어가기에 가장 적절한 곳은 어디인가?

"그렇지 않으면 고객님의 주택과 재정에 위험이 발생할 수 있습니다."

해설 **문장 삽입**

주어진 문장에서 그렇게 하지 않으면 주택과 재정에 위험이 발생할 수 있다고 한 것으로 보아 주택 보험의 중요성과 가입을 유도하는 내용이 선행되어야 함을 알 수 있다. [2] 앞에 주택 보험 가입의 중요

성을 강조하며 보험 만료 전에 새 보험을 준비하라고 당부하는 내용이 있으므로 주어진 문장은 [2]에 들어가는 게 가장 적절하다. 따라서 (B)가 정답이다.

어휘 finances 자금, 자본 at risk 위험에 처한

164-167. 온라인 채팅

Helen Snyder [오전 9시 24분] 안녕하세요, Lee, Aubrey. 연말 시상식 연회의 시상자가 정해졌나요? 계획이 제대로 진행되고 있는지 확실히 하고 싶어서요.

Lee Roth [오전 9시 25분] 네, **164Adele Ruiz와 Craig Jacobson**이 올해 시상을 맡을 거예요.

Helen Snyder [오전 9시 26분] 잘됐네요! 시상식 만찬 때 그들의 자리는 무대 가까이에 배치할까요?

Lee Roth [오전 9시 27분] 네, 시상자들은 앞쪽에 앉을 거예요. Glendale Hall을 또 이용할 가능성이 가장 높지만 Daubert Hotel의 Tina Vance가 보낼 견적을 한번 기다려 보는 중이에요.

Aubrey Lujan [오전 9시 29분] 실은 한 명 더 있어요. **165Bonnie Nelson**도 무대에 오를 거예요.

Lee Roth [오전 9시 30분] 아, 그렇죠. 그걸 깜빡했네요. 일이 너무 급하게 진행되고 있어서요.

Helen Snyder [오전 9시 31분] **166Bonnie Nelson**이요? 저는 임원들만 시상을 하는 걸로 알고 있었는데요.

Aubrey Lujan [오전 9시 32분] **166**올해는 이사진이 수상자 선정에 아주 긴밀하게 관여했기 때문에 그분들도 있어야 한다고 생각했어요.

Helen Snyder [오전 9시 33분] 그 말도 일리가 있네요. **167Lee**, 시상자 모두에게 연락해서 언제 전화 회의를 할 시간이 되는지 물어봐 주세요.

어휘 presenter 시상자; 발표자 awards banquet 시상식 연회 be on track 제대로 진행 중이다, 착착 진행되다 portion 부분, 일부 quote 견적가 take the stage 무대에 오르다 executive staff member 임원, 간부 give out ~을 나누어 주다 board member 이사진 be involved in ~에 관여하다 closely 밀접하게; 면밀히 represent 대표하다; 보여 주다, 나타내다 make sense 일리가 있다 conference call 전화 회의

164. 누가 시상을 할 것인가?

(A) Ms. Snyder

(B) Mr. Roth

(C) Mr. Jacobson

(D) Ms. Vance

해설 **세부 사항**

오전 9시 25분에 Mr. Roth가 Adele Ruiz와 Craig Jacobson이 올해 시상을 맡을 거라고 했으므로 (C)가 정답이다.

165. 오전 9시 29분에 Ms. Lujan이 '실은 한 명 더 있어요'라고 쓴 의도는 무엇인가?

(A) 새로운 수상 분야가 생겼다.

(B) 행사에 세 번째 시상자가 있을 것이다.

(C) 다른 장소도 아직 이용 가능하다.

(D) Mr. Roth에게 새 업무가 배정되었다.

해설 의도 파악

앞에서 시상자와 관련된 이야기를 하고 있는데 Ms. Lujan이 실은 한 명 더 있다고 덧붙였다. 이어서 Bonnie Nelson도 무대에 오를 거라고 한 것으로 보아 시상자가 두 명이 아니라 세 명이라는 것을 알리고자 한 것이므로 (B)가 정답이다.

어휘 venue 장소　assign 맡기다, 배정하다

166. Ms. Nelson은 누구이겠는가?

(A) 수상 후보자

(B) 회사 임원

(C) 이사

(D) 부서장

해설 추론/암시

오전 9시 29분에 Ms. Lujan이 Bonnie Nelson도 무대에 오른다고 하자 Ms. Snyder가 임원들만 시상을 하는 줄 알았다고 했다. 이에 Ms. Lujan이 이사진이 수상자 선정에 깊이 관여했기 때문에 이사진을 대표하는 시상자도 있어야 한다는 생각을 반영한 결과라고 했으므로 Bonnie Nelson은 이사들 중 한 명임을 알 수 있다. 따라서 (C)가 정답이다.

167. Ms. Snyder는 Mr. Roth에게 무엇을 하라고 요청하는가?

(A) 시상자들이 시간이 나는지 알아보기

(B) 행사 장소를 빨리 확정하기

(C) 수상자 목록 출력하기

(D) 초대장 보내기

해설 세부 사항

오전 9시 33분에 Ms. Snyder가 Lee, 즉 Mr. Roth에게 시상자 모두에게 연락해서 언제 전화 회의를 할 시간이 되는지 물어보라고 했으므로 (A)가 정답이다.

패러프레이징 ask when they are free → Find out the presenters' availability

어휘 availability 이용 가능성, 시간 가능 여부　finalize 결론짓다
forward 보내다

168-171. 채용 공고

지원하려면 hr@lynnenergyadvisors.com으로 자기소개서와 이력서를 보내 주십시오. ¹⁷¹가능한 한 빨리 근무를 시작할 수 있는 분을 선호합니다. 하지만 적합한 지원자라면 얼마든지 기다릴 용의가 있습니다. 전체적인 직무 소개를 보려면 www.lynnenergyadvisors.com을 방문하십시오.

어휘 consecutive 연속의　be familiar with ~에 익숙하다
procedure 절차　involve 포함하다, 관련시키다　daily 매일
complete 완료하다, 완성하다　demonstrate 보여 주다; 입증하다
다　cover letter 자기소개서　résumé 이력서　job
description 직무 기술서

168. Lynn Energy Advisors에 대해 암시된 것은 무엇인가?

(A) 평판이 좋다.

(B) 소유주가 바뀌었다.

(C) 휴스턴으로 이전할 것이다.

(D) 타사에 뒤지지 않는 급여를 제공한다.

해설 추론/암시

3년 연속 업계에서 가장 신뢰받는 컨설팅 업체로 선정되었다고 했으므로 (A)가 정답이다.

어휘 reputation 명성, 평판　ownership 소유(권)
relocate 이전하다　competitive 경쟁력 있는; 경쟁을 하는

169. 이 직책에 대해 명시된 것은 무엇인가?

(A) 신입 프로그래머들을 대상으로 한다.

(B) 승진 기회가 많다.

(C) 지원자들의 신원 조회를 요구한다.

(D) 에너지 생산을 관리하는 업무이다.

해설 NOT/True

경력은 필수 요건이 아니기에 최근 대학 졸업자들에게 이상적인 자리가 될 거라고 했으므로 (A)가 정답이다.

어휘 be intended for ~을 대상으로 하다　entry-level (회사,
조직 등에서) 말단의; 초보자용의　background check 신원 조회
applicant 지원자　maintain (관계, 상태, 수준 등을) 유지하다

170. 이 일의 필수 요건으로 언급된 것은 무엇인가?

(A) 소규모 팀 관리하기

(B) 세세한 것에 주의 기울이기

(C) 소프트웨어 관련 문의에 답변하기

(D) 동료들의 보고서 확인하기

해설 NOT/True

아주 사소한 부분까지도 신경 쓰면서 일을 마무리하는 능력은 필수라고 했으므로 (B)가 정답이다.

패러프레이징 demonstrating care for even the smallest detail → Paying attention to detail

어휘 respond 대답하다; 반응을 보이다

프로그래머 구함

Lynn Energy Advisors
휴스턴, 텍사스주

Lynn Energy Advisors는 에너지 사용을 추적하여 보고하는 스마트폰 앱을 개발할 프로그래머 몇 명을 구하고 있습니다.

¹⁶⁸Lynn Energy Advisors는 3년 연속 업계에서 가장 신뢰받는 컨설팅 업체로 선정되었습니다. ¹⁶⁹경력은 필수 요건이 아니므로 최근 대학 졸업자들에게 이상적인 자리가 될 것입니다. 지원자는 다양한 소프트웨어 개발 도구를 잘 다룰 줄 알아야 하고 데이터 보호 절차를 잘 알고 있어야 합니다. 매일 보고서를 작성하고 저장해야 하는 업무이므로 ¹⁷⁰아주 사소한 부분까지도 신경 쓰면서 일을 마무리하는 능력은 필수입니다. 다섯 명이 소규모 팀을 이루어 일하게 됩니다.

171. [1], [2], [3], [4]로 표시된 곳 중에서 다음 문장이 들어가기에 가장 적절한 곳은 어디인가?

"하지만 적합한 지원자라면 얼마든지 기다릴 용의가 있습니다."

해설 문장 삽입

주어진 문장에 However(하지만)가 있으므로 표시된 곳의 앞 문장

이 주어진 문장과 대조되는 내용이어야 한다. 주어진 문장은 적합한 지원자라면 얼마든지 기다릴 수 있다는 내용인데, [4] 앞에서 가능한 한 빨리 근무를 시작할 수 있는 분을 선호한다고 했으므로 주어진 문장은 [4]에 들어가는 게 가장 적절하다. 따라서 (D)가 정답이다.

어휘 be willing to do 기꺼이 ~하다   candidate 후보, 지원자

172-175. 공고

올랜드시 **172제안서 요청**

개요
172올랜드시에서는 도심 전역에서 사용될 디지털 주차 요금 징수기에 대한 제조사들의 제안서를 받습니다. 이는 8월 18일까지 공급되어야 합니다.

목적
우리 시의 구식 동전 투입식 주차 요금 징수기는 더 이상 우리 지역민들의 요구에 부응하지 못하고 있어서 디지털 주차 요금 징수기로 교체될 것입니다. **173B 다양한 신용 카드와 휴대 전화 기반 결제 앱들을 도입하여** 결제 과정이 더 편리해질 뿐만 아니라 **173C 디지털 주차 요금 징수기는 징수기를 확인하고 비우는 일을 해야 하는 시의 인력에 관한 비용도 줄여 줄 것입니다. 173D 디지털 주차 요금 징수기는 차량이 주차 장소를 비울 때를 인식하여 사용한 시간만 요금을 청구하기 때문에 운전자들의 비용도 줄어듭니다. 174 디지털 주차 요금 징수기를 설치한 시들은 타지에서 온 방문객들의 수많은 긍정적인 후기 덕을 보고 있습니다.** 간단하고 직관적인 인터페이스 덕분에 디지털 주차 요금 징수기가 사용하기에 더 쉽기 때문입니다.

세부 사항
제조사는 야외 사용에 적합한 디지털 주차 요금 징수기 1,800 대를 제공해야 합니다. 24시간 모니터링이 가능해야 하고 **175교통 정보 상황실에 실시간으로 데이터를 업로드할 수 있어야 합니다.** 주차 요금 징수기의 터치스크린 화면은 어떤 밝기에서도 글자를 확실하게 보여 주어야 합니다.

제안서를 제출하려면 j.bahr@orland.gov로 Jason Bahr에게 늦어도 2월 3일까지 입찰서를 보내 주십시오. 제출에 필요한 서류 목록을 찾아보려면 www.orland.gov/project0894를 방문하십시오.

어휘 proposal 제안(서), 제의   submission 제출, 접수 manufacturer 제조업체, 제조사   parking meter 주차 요금 징수기   throughout ~ 전역에   outdated 구식의, 예전의 meet one's needs ~의 요구를 충족시키다   in addition to ~ 외에도, ~뿐만 아니라   regarding ~에 관하여   personnel 인원, 직원들   vacate (건물, 자리 등을) 비우다   charge (요금 등을) 부과하다; 충전하다   benefit from ~로부터 이익을 얻다 intuitive (직관적이어서) 사용하기 쉬운; 직관적인   specifics 세부 사항   suitable for ~에 적합한   be capable of ~할 수 있다 round-the-clock 24시간 계속되는   transportation 교통; 운송, 수송   lighting 조명   bid 입찰   no later than 늦어도 ~까지

172. 공고의 목적은 무엇인가?
(A) 공영 주차장 벌금을 소개하기 위해
(B) 시에서 주차 공간이 필요함을 설명하기 위해
(C) 주차 요금 변경 사항을 설명하기 위해
(D) 업체들에게 입찰서 제출을 독려하기 위해

해설 **주제/목적**
공고의 제목이 '제안서 요청'이고 개요에서 올랜드시가 제조사들의 제안서를 받고 있다고 했으므로 (D)가 정답이다.

어휘 fine 벌금   encourage 권장하다, 장려하다

173. 이 주차 요금 징수기의 장점으로 명시되지 않은 것은 무엇인가?
(A) 운전자들이 주차 공간을 더 쉽게 찾을 수 있다.
(B) 다양한 결제 방식을 사용할 수 있다.
(C) 인건비가 줄어들 것이다.
(D) 주차 요금 징수기 사용자들은 초과 요금을 내지 않을 것이다.

해설 **NOT/True**
운전자들이 주차 공간을 더 쉽게 찾을 수 있다는 언급은 없으므로 (A)가 정답이다.

패러프레이징 (C) cut costs regarding city personnel → will be a reduction in staffing costs

어휘 parking spot 주차 공간   a variety of 다양한 reduction 축소, 삭감   staffing costs 인건비   overcharge 과다 청구하다

174. 디지털 주차 요금 징수기 사용을 시작한 다른 시들에서는 무슨 일이 있었는가?
(A) 관광객들로부터 더 호의적인 평가를 받았다.
(B) 도심의 교통 정체가 줄어들었다.
(C) 운송 사업으로 더 많은 돈을 벌었다.
(D) 해당 지역에 주요 제조사의 수가 늘었다.

해설 **세부 사항**
디지털 주차 요금 징수기를 설치한 시에 방문한 사람들이 긍정적인 후기를 많이 남겼다고 했으므로 (A)가 정답이다.

패러프레이징 have benefitted from a greater number of positive reviews from out-of-town visitors → received more favorable reviews from tourists

어휘 favorable 호의적인; 유리한   traffic congestion 교통 정체

175. 제안된 요금 징수기에 대해 언급된 것은 무엇인가?
(A) 현재의 요금 징수기와 같은 크기여야 한다.
(B) 예비 배터리 시스템이 있어야 한다.
(C) 특정 장소에 정보를 보내야 한다.
(D) 국내에서 생산되어야 한다.

해설 **NOT/True**
디지털 주차 요금 징수기는 교통 정보 상황실에 실시간으로 데이터를 업로드할 수 있어야 한다고 했으므로 (C)가 정답이다.

패러프레이징 uploading real-time data feeds to the transportation office → must send information to a certain location

어휘 backup 지원, 예비(품)   location 장소, 위치; 지점 domestically 국내에서

176-180. 웹페이지&이메일

Spark Rentals가 저렴한 대여료로 여러분의 돈을 절약해 드릴 수 있습니다. 구입하는 대신 적은 비용을 내고 대여하세요! 저희의 모든 대여 제품은 철저히 검수하여 최적의 성능을 보장합니다. **176 더 이상 배송 서비스는 제공하지 않는다는 점을 알려드립니다.** 따라서 여러분이 직접 제품을 가져가고 반납할 준비가 되어 있어야 합니다.

검색어:

카펫 청소 장비

2건의 검색 결과:

	24시간	**180 주말**
Viko Eco-wash 카펫 청소기 (1.6리터 탱크)	29.99파운드	65.99파운드
180 Viko Standard 카펫 청소기 (3.8리터 탱크)	39.99파운드	**180 85.99파운드**

어휘 affordable 가격이 알맞은 a fraction of the cost 적은 비용, 낮은 가격 thoroughly 완전히, 철저히 ensure 보장하다, 확실히 하다 optimum 최적의 performance (기계, 차량 등의) 성능 pick up ~을 찾아오다, ~을 수령하다 drop off ~을 갖다 놓다 in person 직접 search term 검색어

수신인: Lucas Soltis
발신인: Isabelle Guthrie
날짜: 3월 4일
제목: 카펫 청소기

안녕, Lucas,

전에 친척들의 방문에 대비해서 집을 대청소할 예정이라고 했잖아. 나도 청소를 좀 해야 해서 전문가급 카펫 청소기를 대여하기로 했거든. **179 대여해 주는 업체 중 가장 가까운 데가 Spark Rentals라고 앤캐스터에 있는데 약 30분 거리야. 180 나는 이번 주말 동안 청소기를 대여할 계획이라 179 금요일 아침에 가지러 가서 월요일 아침에 반납할 거야. 180 탱크 용량이 더 큰 기기를 가져올 건데** 그렇더라도 내 차에는 잘 들어갈 테니까 그걸 운반하기 위해 트럭이 필요하지는 않을 것 같아.

주말에 청소기를 사용할 생각이 있니? 나는 토요일 늦은 오전까지는 우리 집 청소를 다 끝낼 수 있을 거야. 그러고 나면 나머지 주말 동안은 네가 쓰면 되니까 **177 우리가 비용을 분담해서 지출을 줄일 수 있을 거야.** 갑작스런 이야기라는 걸 **178 잘 알고 있으니까** 네가 안 된다고 해도 괜찮아. 네 생각이 어떤지 알려 줘. 나는 내일까지는 온라인으로 예약하고 결제하고 싶어.

Isabelle

어휘 relative 친척 professional-grade 전문가급의 device 장비, 장치 fit in ~에 잘 맞다 transport 운송하다, 수송하다 short notice 갑작스런 통보 work for ~에게 잘 맞다

---

176. 웹페이지가 Spark Rentals에 대해 암시한 것은 무엇인가?
(A) 전에는 고객들에게 장비를 배송해 주었다.
(B) 사업체에는 할인을 해 준다.
(C) 특별 요청 시 새 장비를 입수할 수 있다.
(D) 일부 장비는 사용 후에 판매한다.

해설 **추론/암시**
더 이상 배송 서비스는 제공하지 않는다는 말에서 전에는 배송 서비스를 제공했다는 것을 알 수 있다. 따라서 (A)가 정답이다.

어휘 acquire 습득하다, 획득하다

177. Ms. Guthrie가 보낸 이메일의 목적은 무엇인가?
(A) 프로젝트 날짜를 변경하기 위해
(B) 청소용품을 추천하기 위해
(C) 돈을 아낄 수 있는 기회를 제안하기 위해
(D) Mr. Soltis를 초대하기 위해

해설 **주제/목적**
자신이 대여한 청소기를 주말 동안 같이 쓰고 비용을 분담하여 지출을 줄이자고 제안하고 있으므로 (C)가 정답이다.

178. 이메일에서 두 번째 단락 세 번째 줄의 'appreciate'와 의미상 가장 가까운 것은?
(A) 평가하다
(B) 이해하다, 알다
(C) 고마워하다
(D) 즐기다

해설 **동의어 찾기**
appreciate가 있는 I appreciate that this is short notice는 '갑작스런 이야기라는 걸 알고 있다'라는 의미이며, 여기서 appreciate는 '인정하다'라는 뜻으로 쓰였다. 따라서 (B)가 정답이다.

179. 이메일에서 Ms. Guthrie에 대해 암시된 것은 무엇인가?
(A) 주중에 앤캐스터에 갈 것이다.
(B) 매년 카펫을 청소한다.
(C) 트럭을 소유하고 있다.
(D) 전에 Spark Rentals를 이용한 적이 있다.

해설 **추론/암시**
Ms. Guthrie가 이용하려는 업체인 Spark Rentals는 앤캐스터에 위치해 있는데 금요일 아침에 청소기를 가지러 간다고 했으므로 (A)가 정답이다.

180. Ms. Guthrie는 Spark Rentals 웹사이트에서 얼마를 결제할 것 같은가?
(A) 29.99파운드
(B) 39.99파운드
(C) 65.99파운드
(D) 85.99파운드

해설 **두 지문 연계_추론/암시**
두 번째 지문에서 Ms. Guthrie는 주말 동안 청소기를 대여할 계획이며 탱크 용량이 더 큰 것을 가져올 거라고 했다. 이에 첫 번째 지문에서 용량이 큰 청소기의 주말 대여료를 확인하면 85.99파운드이므로 (D)가 정답이다.

181-185. 기사&채용 공고

Beamont Laboratories가 연구 개발 팀을 확충하다

브리즈번 (8월 3일)—세계적인 브랜드의 화장품 생산을 전문으로 하는 회사인 Beamont Laboratories가 헤어 관리 제품을 찾는 고객들의 요구에 부응하고자 R&D 인력을 확충할 예정이다. 브리즈번에 본사를 두고 **181 18년 전에 설립된 Beamont Laboratories**는 환경 책임뿐만 아니라 혁신성에서도 선두적인 역할을 해 오고 있다. 그 덕분에 꾸준한 성장을 이어 오고 있는데 지난 5년은 성장세가 특히 두드러졌다. **183 이번 확충이 예정된 곳은 캔버라에 기반을 두고 있는 연구소이다.** 멜버른과 뉴캐슬에도 더 작은 규모의 연구소들이 있다.

181 새로운 팀을 이끌 사람은 Gemma Gabriel로 회사 창립 때부터 함께하며 신입 연구원으로 시작해 차근차근 승진한 인물이다. 그녀는 인기 있는 제품인 Ordell의 개발 책임자였는데 **182 Ordell은 피부가 민감한 사람들을 위해 특별히 만들어진 샴푸이다.** Ms. Gabriel이 채용 과정을 처음부터 끝까지 감독할 예정이다.

어휘 expand 확대하다, 확장하다 specialize in ~을 전문적으로 하다 cater to ~을 만족시키다 headquartered (특정 장소에) 본사가 있는 found 설립하다 innovation 혁신 environmental 환경의 responsibility 책임 steady 꾸준한, 지속적인 expansion 확장 work one's way up ~가 승진하다 be in charge of ~을 담당하다 sensitive 민감한, 예민한 oversee 감독하다

Beamont Laboratories 채용 공고
183 직책: 수석 화장품 연구원
게시일: 8월 10일

지원 마감일: 9월 15일

인력을 확충하는 우리 R&D 팀에 꼭 필요한 인재가 되어 주세요.

주요 업무:
- 여러 프로젝트의 제품 개발 일정 세우기
- 견본품 개발, 분석, 테스트하기
- 발전하는 연구 기술들을 지속적으로 숙지하기
- **185 연구에 사용할 제반 장비 및 물품 조달하기**
- 향후 생산에 대비하여 정확한 비용 견적 산출하기

화학이나 관련 분야 학위가 있어야 합니다. (석사 학위 우대) **184 면접 기간은 10월 20일부터 11월 1일까지이고 근무 시작일은 11월 22일입니다.**

어휘 job opening 채용 공고 senior 고위급의 post 게시하다 integral 필수적인 analyze 분석하다 advancement 발전, 진보 source (특정한 곳에서) 얻다 relevant 관련된, 연관된 accurate 정확한, 정밀한 cost estimate 비용 견적

181. Ms. Gabriel에 대해 명시된 것은 무엇인가?
(A) 일 때문에 브리즈번으로 이사할 계획이다.
(B) 5년 전에 현재 직급으로 승진했다.
(C) Beamont Laboratories에서 일한 지 18년 되었다.
(D) 곧 Beamont Laboratories에서 은퇴할 것이다.

해설 **NOT/True**
첫 번째 지문에서 Gemma Gabriel은 회사 창립 때부터 함께했다고 했는데 앞에서 Beamont Laboratories는 18년 전에 설립되었다고 했으므로 (C)가 정답이다.

어휘 relocate 이전하다 promote 승진시키다; 홍보하다

182. Ordell에 대해 언급된 것은 무엇인가?
(A) 이 회사의 베스트셀러 제품이다.
(B) 천연 성분으로 만들어진다.
(C) 스킨로션으로 사용할 수 있다.
(D) 헤어 관리 제품의 일종이다.

해설 **NOT/True**
첫 번째 지문에서 Ordell은 피부가 민감한 사람들을 위해 특별히 만들어진 샴푸라고 했으므로 (D)가 정답이다. Ordell이 인기 있는 제품이라는 언급은 있으나 베스트셀러라고 하지는 않았으므로 (A)는 오답이다.

어휘 ingredient 재료, 성분

183. 새로운 수석 화장품 연구원은 어디에서 일하게 될 것 같은가?
(A) 브리즈번에서
(B) 캔버라에서
(C) 뉴캐슬에서
(D) 멜버른에서

해설 **두 지문 연계_추론/암시**
두 번째 지문에서 Beamont Laboratories가 수석 화장품 연구원을 채용한다는 걸 알 수 있다. 이어서 첫 번째 지문을 보면 이번 확충이 예정된 곳은 캔버라에 기반을 두고 있는 연구소라는 내용이 있으므로 (B)가 정답이다.

184. 최종 합격자는 언제 선정될 것 같은가?
(A) 8월에
(B) 9월에
(C) 10월에
(D) 11월에

해설 **추론/암시**
두 번째 지문에 면접이 11월 1일까지이고 근무 시작일은 11월 22일이라고 나와 있으므로 최종 합격자 선정은 11월에 이루어진다는 걸 추론할 수 있다. 따라서 (D)가 정답이다.

185. 이 직책의 한 가지 업무는 무엇인가?
(A) 필요한 물품 확보하기
(B) 팀원들에게 기술 교육하기
(C) 생산 시설 점검하기
(D) 예비 고객과 만나기

해설 **세부 사항**
두 번째 지문에 있는 주요 업무 중 연구에 사용할 제반 장비와 물품을 조달해야 한다는 내용이 있으므로 (A)가 정답이다.

패러프레이징 Sourcing all relevant equipment and materials → Procuring necessary supplies

어휘 procure 구하다, 조달하다 inspect 검사하다, 점검하다 prospective 장래의, 예비의; 기대되는, 가망 있는

186-190. 이메일&일정표&이메일

수신인: 지역 문화 센터 전 회원

발신인: 지역 문화 센터

제목: 여름 미술 강좌 시리즈

날짜: 6월 10일

첨부 파일: Summer_art_lecture_series

지역 문화 센터 회원 여러분께:

여름 미술 강좌 시리즈가 얼마 안 남았습니다! 첨부한 일정표를 확인해 주시기 바랍니다. 올해 우리 강사들은 모두 새로 오신 분들인데 **187 예외적으로 디지털 시대의 미술에 관한 강의를 했던 강사만 수요가 많아 다시 모시게 되었습니다.**

www.commartscenter.org에서 수강권을 주문해 주세요. 제일 큰 강의실에서 하는 강의는 단체 예약(5인 이상)만 받는다는 점을 알려 드립니다. 참고로 **186 Rivas Room은 150명이 들어갈 수 있는 공간이 있고** Mercier Room은 90명을 수용할 수 있습니다.

어휘 nearly 거의　attached 첨부된　except for ~라는 점만 제외하면　give a talk 강연하다　demand 수요, 요구　venue 장소　accommodate 수용하다

지역 문화 센터
여름 미술 강좌 시리즈

강의명	강사	날짜와 시간	장소
빛과 수채화	Annie Cho	6월 29일 오후 7~9시	Chester Room
친환경 물품	Samuel Delgado	7월 2일 오후 1~3시	Barron Room
187 디지털 시대의 미술	**187 Bianca Fallici**	7월 8일 오후 3~5시	Rivas Room
건축 속 미술	Hugo Beckham	7월 25일 오후 3~4시	Chester Room
189 알려지지 않은 미술사	**189 Hai Feng**	7월 31일 오후 6~8시	Mercier Room
혼합 매체 창작품	Yolanda Florez	8월 4일 오후 7~8시	Rivas Room

어휘 watercolor 수채화; 물감　eco-friendly 친환경적인 supplies 비품　undiscovered 발견되지 않은　mixed media 혼합 매체, 여러 시각 매체를 결합하여 예술품을 만드는 기법

수신인: Gerard McCray

189 190 발신인: Hai Feng

날짜: 8월 5일

제목: 감사합니다!

Mr. McCray께,

여름 미술 강좌 시리즈에서 강의하도록 초청해 주셔서 감사합니다. 정말 좋은 경험이었고 나중에 또 참여하고 싶네요. 강의 장소가 정말 인상적이었습니다. 강의실이 다소 비어 보이기는 했

지만 공간이 워낙 넓었기 때문이었겠지요. **190 실은 참석자 수가 제 예상보다 훨씬 많아서 그 점이 정말 좋았습니다.**

188 아울러 Tony Sheridan에게 특히 감사의 말을 전하고 싶습니다. 강의 시작 때 기술적 지원에 대한 제 요청에 즉각 대응하여 문제를 빨리 해결해 주셨거든요. 다행히도 그 덕분에 강의를 취소하는 대신 **189 15분만 늦게 시작하면 되었습니다.**

Hai Feng

어휘 participate 참여하다　attendee 참석자　in addition 게다가　grateful 감사하는　promptly 지체 없이; 정확히 제시간에　assistance 도움, 지원　resolve 해결하다　issue 문제, 사안　fortunately 다행스럽게도

---

186. 어떤 강의실이 100명 넘게 수용할 수 있는가?

(A) Barron Room

(B) Chester Room

(C) Mercier Room

(D) Rivas Room

해설 **세부 사항**

첫 번째 지문에서 Rivas Room은 150명이 들어갈 수 있다고 했으므로 (D)가 정답이다.

187. 누가 전에 그 강좌 시리즈에서 강의를 한 적이 있는가?

(A) Ms. Cho

(B) Mr. Delgado

(C) Ms. Fallici

(D) Mr. Beckham

해설 **두 지문 연계_세부 사항**

첫 번째 지문에 올해 강사진은 모두 새로운 사람들이지만 디지털 시대의 미술에 관한 강의를 했던 강사만 다시 불렀다는 언급이 있다. 이에 두 번째 지문에서 디지털 시대의 미술 수업을 한 강사를 확인하면 Bianca Fallici이므로 (C)가 정답이다.

188. Mr. Sheridan은 누구이겠는가?

(A) 기사

(B) 행사 기획자

(C) 연구원

(D) 행사장 소유주

해설 **추론/암시**

세 번째 지문에서 Tony Sheridan이 기술적 지원에 대한 요청에 즉각 대응하여 문제를 빨리 해결해 주었다고 했으므로 Mr. Sheridan은 기술 관련 업무를 하는 사람임을 알 수 있다. 따라서 (A)가 정답이다.

189. 어떤 강의가 시작 시간이 지연되었는가?

(A) 친환경 물품

(B) 건축 속 미술

(C) 알려지지 않은 미술사

(D) 혼합 매체 창작품

해설 **두 지문 연계_세부 사항**

세 번째 지문에서 이메일 발신인인 Hai Feng이 자신의 강의가 15분 늦게 시작되었다고 했다. 이어서 두 번째 지문을 보면 Hai Feng은 알려지지 않은 미술사 수업을 했으므로 (C)가 정답이다.

190. Mr. Feng에 대해 암시된 것은 무엇인가?
(A) 전에 Mr. McCray와 일했었다.
(B) 참가자 수에 만족했다.
(C) 강의실이 더 크기를 바랐다.
(D) 강의에 참석하기 위해 장거리 이동을 했다.

해설 **추론/암시**
Mr. Feng은 세 번째 지문인 이메일 발신인이다. 해당 이메일에서 Mr. Feng이 참석자 수가 예상보다 훨씬 많아서 좋았다고 했으므로 (B)가 정답이다.

패러프레이징 the number of attendees → the turnout

어휘 turnout (행사 등의) 참석자 수

191-195. 웹페이지&이메일&이메일

Tree Care Foundation(TCF)은 삼림 지대에 있는 나무들의 건강을 지키기 위해 전력을 다하고 있습니다. **191 우리 자원봉사자들은 수목병과 해충을 찾아내어 그것들이 영향을 미치는 지역에서 어떻게 그리고 어디로 확산되는지 알아내는 데 중요한 역할을 합니다.** 이는 우리가 수목병 발생을 통제하고 나무 손실을 줄이는 조치를 취하는 데 도움이 됩니다.

자원봉사 활동 소개:
- 온라인으로 신청서를 작성하여 지원 후 간단한 전화 면접을 실시합니다.
- 필요한 기술을 배우기 위해 연수에 참석합니다.
- **192 TCF에서 자원봉사 활동을 최소 12개월간 하면서 실태 조사를 한 달에 두세 번 실시합니다.**

어휘 be dedicated to ~에 헌신하다, ~에 전념하다 woodland 삼림 지대 volunteer 자원봉사자 essential 필수적인 identify 확인하다, 알아보다 pest 해충 determine (구체적 증거로) 판단하다, 알아내다 affect 영향을 미치다 take measures 조치를 취하다 outbreak 발생, 발발 complete (서식 등을) 빠짐없이 작성하다 brief 간단한; (시간이) 짧은 session (특정 활동을 위한) 시간 commit to (일, 활동 등에) 전념하다 survey (설문) 조사, 검사

수신인: Aida Ferreira, Kevin Murray, Sharad Dhibar, Ruth Bryson
발신인: Ashley Jackson
날짜: 3월 5일
제목: 연수

192 자원봉사자 여러분께,

Tree Care Foundation(TCF) 활동에 동참해 주셔서 감사합니다. 여러분과 같은 자원봉사자 덕분에 7년 전 **193 Curtis Baxter가 우리 자선 단체를 설립한 이후로** 괄목할 만한 성장을 할 수 있었습니다.

이 과정의 다음 단계는 집중 연수를 이수하는 것입니다. 이는 3월 20일 토요일 오전 9시부터 오후 4시까지 일정이 잡혀 있습니다. Aldredge Nature Center에서 열릴 예정이며 점심이 제공될 것입니다. **193 Mr. Baxter가 교육을 담당할 것입니다.**

첫 연수를 마치고 나면 그 다음 주에는 숙련된 멤버의 지도하에

아래와 같이 실태 조사를 하게 될 겁니다.

이름	담당 지역
Aida Ferreira	웨슬리 우드랜즈
Kevin Murray	반브룩 포레스트
Sharad Dhibar	말함 포레스트
194 Ruth Bryson	**194 덴턴 국립 자연 보호 구역**

궁금한 점이 있으면 연락 주세요.

Ashley Jackson

어휘 thanks to ~ 덕분에 considerably 상당히 complete 완료하다, 완성하다 intensive 집중적인 take place 열리다, 일어나다 be in charge of ~을 담당하다 initial 처음의, 초기의 supervise 감독하다 experienced 숙련된, 경험이 풍부한 assign 맡기다, 배정하다

194 수신인: Stanley Walton
194 발신인: Ruth Bryson
날짜: 3월 23일
제목: 실태 조사 지도 관련

Mr. Walton께,

194 이번 주 금요일에 있을 저의 실태 조사 지도 때 직접 만나 뵙게 되기를 고대하고 있습니다. 제 근무 일정에 맞춰 원래 시작 시간을 조정해 주셔서 감사합니다. 저는 현장까지 차를 가지고 갈 계획이라 오후 2시에 거기에서 뵙게 되겠네요.

195 저는 첫 연수에서 배부받은 장비를 다 가져가려고 해요. 그런데 그걸 보호하기 위해 어떤 식으로 포장해야 하는지 모르겠어요. 저는 그냥 일반적인 배낭을 사용하는데 **195 부서지기 쉬운 부품이 망가지지 않기를 바라거든요.** 제가 특별히 취해야 할 조치가 있다면 알려 주세요.

감사합니다.

Ruth Bryson

어휘 look forward to ~하는 것을 고대하다 in person 직접 appreciate 고마워하다; 인정하다; 감상하다 adjust 조정하다 original 원래[본래]의; 독창적인 accommodate 고려하다, 참작하다 gear (특정 활동에 필요한) 장비, 복장 distribute 나누어주다, 배부하다 wrap up ~을 싸다, ~을 포장하다 fragile 깨지기쉬운, 취약한 component 부품

191. TCF 자원봉사자들의 주요 업무는 무엇인가?
(A) 나무 프로젝트를 위한 기금 모금하기
(B) 삼림 지역에 나무 심기
(C) 수목병 확산 추적하기
(D) 나무 가지치기

해설 **세부 사항**
첫 번째 지문에서 자원봉사자들이 수목병과 해충을 찾아내어 그것들이 어떻게 그리고 어디로 확산되는지 알아내는 데 중요한 역할을 한다고 했으므로 (C)가 정답이다.

어휘 funds 자금, 기금 track 추적하다 spread 확산, 전파 clear away ~을 치우다, ~을 제거하다

192. 첫 번째 이메일의 수신인들에 대해 암시된 것은 무엇인가?

(A) 그룹 인터뷰에 참석했다.

(B) 최소 일 년 동안 TCF에서 활동할 것이다.

(C) 매주 두세 번의 실태 조사를 실시할 것이다.

(D) 자신들이 일할 장소를 선택할 수 있다.

해설 **두 지문 연계_추론/암시**

첫 번째 이메일의 수신인은 TCF의 자원봉사자들이다. 이어서 첫 번째 지문인 웹페이지를 보면 자원봉사자들은 TCF에서 자원봉사 활동을 최소 12개월간 한다는 내용이 있으므로 (B)가 정답이다.

어휘 at least 최소한

193. 3월 20일자 연수에 대해 명시된 것은 무엇인가?

(A) 이 자선 단체의 설립자가 진행했다.

(B) 약 3시간 동안 이어졌다.

(C) 여러 장소에서 시행되었다.

(D) 오후에 시작되었다.

해설 **NOT/True**

두 번째 지문에서 이 자선 단체를 Curtis Baxter가 설립했는데 그가 교육을 담당할 거라고 했으므로 (A)가 정답이다.

어휘 founder 설립자, 창업자 approximately 대략, 약 conduct (특정 활동을) 수행하다

194. Mr. Walton은 어디에서 실태 조사를 할 것 같은가?

(A) 웨슬리 우드랜즈에서

(B) 반브룩 포레스트에서

(C) 말함 포레스트에서

(D) 덴턴 국립 자연 보호 구역에서

해설 **두 지문 연계_추론/암시**

세 번째 지문인 두 번째 이메일의 수신인이 Mr. Walton이다. 이메일 발신인인 Ms. Bryson이 첫 문장에서 실태 조사 지도 때 직접 만나 뵙게 되기를 고대하고 있다고 한 것으로 보아 Mr. Walton은 Ms. Bryson과 함께 실태 조사를 한다는 걸 알 수 있다. 이에 두 번째 지문에서 Ms. Bryson의 실태 조사 담당 지역을 확인하면 덴턴 국립 자연 보호 구역이라고 나와 있으므로 (D)가 정답이다.

195. 두 번째 이메일에서 Ms. Bryson은 무엇에 대해 우려하는가?

(A) 장비가 파손되는 것

(B) 주차가 어려운 것

(C) 외딴 장소를 찾는 것

(D) 적절한 장비를 구입하는 것

해설 **세부 사항**

첫 연수에서 배부받은 장비를 다 가져가려고 하는데 부서지기 쉬운 부품이 망가지지 않기를 바란다고 했으므로 (A)가 정답이다.

어휘 damage 손상을 주다 remote 먼; 원격의

196-200. 이메일&이메일&웹페이지

수신인: Jeanette Patterson

196 발신인: Mason Emery

날짜: 4월 19일

제목: 스프링클러 시스템

Ms. Patterson께,

---

196 고객님의 호텔에 스프링클러 시스템과 설치 업체를 추천해 드리게 되어 매우 기쁩니다. 하지만 고객님의 요구를 최대한 맞추기 위해 다음 질문들에 답변해 주시기를 요청드립니다.

198A 1. 이 시스템은 잔디에만 사용하십니까 아니면 화단에도 사용하십니까?

198B 2. 해당 구역에는 보행자가 많습니까? 튀어 오르지 않는 고정식 스프링클러는 가격이 저렴하지만 보행자가 걸려 넘어질 위험이 있습니다.

3. 향후 몇 년 안에 고객님의 부지에 건설 공사가 예정되어 있습니까?

4. 이 시스템이 얼마나 빨리 필요하십니까? 197 땅이 얼면 시스템을 설치할 수 없기 때문에 1년 중 여름이 가장 바쁜 시기입니다.

198D 5. 고객님의 호텔이 문을 여는 동안은 업체가 주중에 작업할 수 있습니까? 일부 굴삭 장비는 방해가 될 수 있습니다. 하지만 주말 작업은 수요가 많습니다.

위의 추가 정보를 주시는 것에 대해 미리 감사드립니다.

Mason Emery

어휘 flower bed 화단 permanent 영구적인, 상시의 pop up 튀어 오르다 pose a hazard 위험을 초래하다 in place 준비가 되어 있는; 제자리에 있는 dig (땅을) 파다 disruptive 지장을 주는 in advance 사전에, 미리 additional 추가의

수신인: Mason Emery

발신인: Jeanette Patterson

날짜: 4월 20일

제목: RE: 스프링클러 시스템

Mr. Emery께,

Charter Hotel의 브리지뷰 지점 부지에는 사방에 담장이 둘러쳐져 있습니다. 높이 올린 화단이 몇 군데 있긴 하지만 198A 잔디가 있는 부분에 그 시스템이 필요합니다. 우리 호텔에는 바닥이 포장된 테라스가 있어서 투숙객 대부분이 그곳에서 야외 활동 시간을 가지거든요. 199 개들이 잔디에서 자주 뛰어놀지만 198B 투숙객은 거의 들어가지 않습니다.

호텔 문을 닫을 수는 없기 때문에 198D 작업 인부들은 주중 언제든 와도 됩니다. 고품질 시스템이라면 얼마든지 돈을 더 지불할 용의가 있다는 점을 알려 드리며 200 우리는 경력이 오래된 업체를 원합니다.

도움 주셔서 감사합니다.

Jeanette Patterson

어휘 fence in ~에 울타리를 치다 raised 주변보다 높은, 높이 올린 grassy 풀로 덮인 pave (길을) 포장하다 patio 테라스 shut down 문을 닫다 in business 사업을 하는 assistance 도움, 지원

우리 웹사이트 이용자들이 각 지역 최고의 스프링클러 시스템 설치업체를 뽑는 투표를 했습니다. 아래에서 브리지뷰의 결과를 보실 수 있습니다.

업체명	전문 분야	특이 사항
Irrigation Solutions	실외 스프링클러	최근 오픈, 빠른 결과물
Lawn Doctors	실외 스프링클러	작년 오픈, 최저 가격
200 Tyler Landscaping	200 모든 분야	200 20년 동안 이 지역에서 영업 중
Waterworks Sprinklers	실내 화재 안전	25년 경력, 합리적인 가격

어휘 region 지역 specialization 전문화 outdoor 야외의 locally 지역에서, 현지에서 indoor 실내의 reasonably priced 가격이 적정하게 매겨진

196. Mr. Emery는 어디에서 일할 것 같은가?
(A) 제조 회사에서
(B) 컨설팅 회사에서
(C) 부동산 개발 회사에서
(D) 마케팅 회사에서

해설 **추론/암시**
첫 번째 지문인 첫 번째 이메일의 발신인이 Mr. Emery다. 해당 이메일에서 스프링클러 시스템과 설치 업체를 추천하기 전에 몇 가지 질문으로 고객의 요구 조건을 확인하는 것으로 보아 Mr. Emery는 고객에게 컨설팅하는 일을 한다는 걸 알 수 있다. 따라서 (B)가 정답이다.

197. Mr. Emery가 스프링클러 시스템에 대해 암시한 것은 무엇인가?
(A) 전문가에게 정기적으로 점검을 받아야 한다.
(B) 땅이 어느 정도 따뜻할 때 설치해야 한다.
(C) 시의 상수도에 연결할 수 있다.
(D) 장기적으로는 사용자의 비용을 절감해 줄 것이다.

해설 **추론/암시**
첫 번째 지문에서 땅이 얼면 시스템을 설치할 수 없다고 했으므로 (B)가 정답이다.

어휘 inspect 검사하다, 점검하다 professional 전문가 regularly 정기적으로, 규칙적으로 hook A up to B A를 B에 걸다 in the long run 결국에는

198. Mr. Emery의 질문 중에서 Ms. Patterson이 답변하지 않은 것은 어느 것인가?
(A) 1번 질문
(B) 2번 질문
(C) 3번 질문
(D) 5번 질문

해설 **두 지문 연계_세부 사항**
두 번째 지문에서 Ms. Patterson은 1번과 2번 그리고 5번 질문에 차례로 잔디가 있는 부분에 그 시스템이 필요하다, 투숙객은 거의 들어가지 않는다, 작업 인부들은 주중 언제든 와도 된다는 답변을 했다. 하지만 향후 몇 년 안에 호텔 부지에 건설 공사가 예정되어 있는지 묻는 3번 질문에 대한 답변은 없으므로 (C)가 정답이다.

어휘 address 말하다, 언급하다; 연설하다; (문제 등을) 다루다

199. 두 번째 이메일에 따르면 Charter Hotel에 대해 사실일 것 같은 것은 무엇인가?
(A) 최근에 브리지뷰에 지점을 열었다.
(B) 일 년 중 일부 기간은 문을 닫는다.
(C) 호텔에 반려견 입장을 허용한다.
(D) 혼잡한 도로 근처에 위치해 있다.

해설 **추론/암시**
개들이 잔디에서 자주 뛰어논다고 한 것으로 보아 호텔에 반려견을 들여도 된다는 걸 추론할 수 있으므로 (C)가 정답이다.

200. Mr. Emery는 어느 회사를 추천할 것 같은가?
(A) Irrigation Solutions
(B) Lawn Doctors
(C) Tyler Landscaping
(D) Waterworks Sprinklers

해설 **두 지문 연계_추론/암시**
두 번째 지문에서 Ms. Patterson은 경력이 오래된 업체를 원한다고 밝혔다. 세 번째 지문에 있는 스프링클러 시스템 설치업체 목록에서 경력이 오래되었다고 할 수 있는 업체는 Tyler Landscaping과 Waterworks Sprinklers인데, Waterworks Sprinklers는 전문 분야가 실내 화재 안전이므로 잔디에 물을 주기 위한 용도와 맞지 않다. 따라서 (C)가 정답이다.

에듀윌 토익 단기완성 700+

정답 및 해설

고객의 꿈, 직원의 꿈, 지역사회의 꿈을 실현한다

펴낸곳 (주)에듀윌 **펴낸이** 김재환 **출판총괄** 오용철
개발책임 이순옥 **개발** 김상미, 천주영, Julie Tofflemire
주소 서울시 구로구 디지털로34길 55 코오롱싸이언스밸리 2차 3층
대표번호 1600-6700 **등록번호** 제25100-2002-000052호
협의 없는 무단 복제는 법으로 금지되어 있습니다.

에듀윌 도서몰 book.eduwill.net
· 부가학습자료 및 정오표: 에듀윌 도서몰 → 도서자료실
· 교재 문의: 에듀윌 도서몰 → 문의하기 → 교재(내용, 출간) / 주문 및 배송

공식만 알아도 정답까지 1초컷

쉬운 토익 공식

에듀윌 토익 AI앱

업계
최초

공식
추천

100%
무료

* 2022년 3월 30일 기준, 동종 업계 토익 관련 앱 비교 기준

업계 최초 대통령상 3관왕,
정부기관상 19관왕 달성!

2010 대통령상

2019 대통령상

2019 대통령상

대한민국 브랜드대상
국무총리상

국무총리상

문화체육관광부
장관상

농림축산식품부
장관상

과학기술정보통신부
장관상

여성가족부장관상

서울특별시장상

과학기술부장관상

정보통신부장관상

산업자원부장관상

고용노동부장관상

미래창조과학부장관상

법무부장관상

2004
서울특별시장상 우수벤처기업 대상

2006
부총리 겸 과학기술부장관 표창 국가 과학 기술 발전 유공

2007
정보통신부장관상 디지털콘텐츠 대상
산업자원부장관 표창 대한민국 e비즈니스대상

2010
대통령 표창 대한민국 IT 이노베이션 대상

2013
고용노동부장관 표창 일자리 창출 공로

2014
미래창조과학부장관 표창 ICT Innovation 대상

2015
법무부장관 표창 사회공헌 유공

2017
여성가족부장관상 사회공헌 유공
2016 합격자 수 최고 기록 KRI 한국기록원 공식 인증

2018
2017 합격자 수 최고 기록 KRI 한국기록원 공식 인증

2019
대통령 표창 범죄예방대상
대통령 표창 일자리 창출 유공
과학기술정보통신부장관상 대한민국 ICT 대상

2020
국무총리상 대한민국 브랜드대상
2019 합격자 수 최고 기록 KRI 한국기록원 공식 인증

2021
고용노동부장관상 일·생활 균형 우수 기업 공모전 대상
문화체육관광부장관 표창 근로자휴가지원사업 우수 참여 기업
농림축산식품부장관상 대한민국 사회공헌 대상
문화체육관광부장관 표창 여가친화기업 인증 우수 기업

2022
국무총리 표창 일자리 창출 유공
농림축산식품부장관상 대한민국 ESG 대상